MAINSTREAMS OF MODERN ART

Ingres: *The Bather of Valpinçon*

On the principle that anyone beginning a trip should have a general idea of the route he is to take, the following fifteen paintings are offered as an introduction to this book. They are waystops, and they reappear in the body of the text.

As the nineteenth century opened, painting was dominated by France (as it continued to be), and French painting was dominated by the classicists. As an adjunct to the political idealism of the French Revolution in its first days, classicism in painting was dedicated to a revival of the intellectual purity and the moral force of ancient Greece and Rome as they were currently imagined by philosophers and aestheticians. But before long, classicism degenerated into a fettering code of arbitrary rules and standards. By the middle of the century the demigod of the school was a pedantic tyrant and a great artist named Jean Auguste Dominique Ingres, who mercilessly dictated these sterile recipes, yet rose above them in his own art. His *The Bather of Valpinçon* observes the rules in its precision, its enamellike surface, its carefully controlled drawing, its limitation of color within sharply defined boundaries. But in spirit the picture is sensuous beneath its careful surface. Ingres was a classicist by habitual conviction, but by the evidence of his work he had more in common than he realized with the warmth and sentiment of the men who were in revolt against his dogma — the romantics. (Louvre, Paris. Reproduction courtesy Phaidon Press, Ltd.)

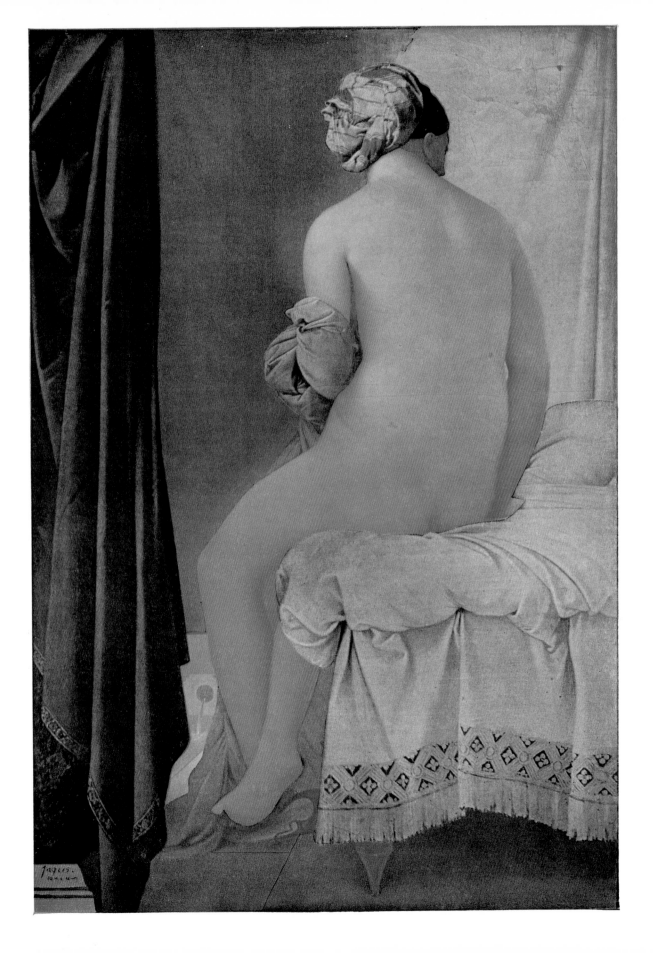

Delacroix: *The Abduction of Rebecca*

The romantics believed in the expression of emotion at whatever violation of convention, believed in originality rather than in rule, in complication rather than in purity, and preferred risk to safety. Romanticism was a way of life as well as a revolt in the arts, and its triumph was inevitable in times when the world's disorder gave little support to the classical ideal of ultimate order and serenity. Romanticism was international, with a strong early impulse in Germany, but found its leader and spokesman, as far as painting was concerned, in Eugène Delacroix, another Frenchman. His *Abduction of Rebecca* contrasts in every way with Ingres's *The Bather of Valpinçon;* it is a turbulent subject turbulently painted in rich colors that shatter and explode across swarming and fluttering masses, expressing everywhere the agony and excitement of the human spirit. Yet for all this emotionalized effect, Delacroix as much as Ingres, or even more than Ingres, achieved his ends by intellectualized use of his means. He regarded himself as a true classicist and the nominal classicists as false ones, since his goal was the total expression of human emotion on the grand scale, in images of universal significance. (Metropolitan Museum of Art, New York, Wolfe Fund.)

Eakins: *Miss Van Buren*

In spite of their differences, the classicists and the romantics shared a mutual characteristic: they were idealists who ignored the world around them to explore imagined ones. As the century began to coalesce into the great age of the common man, dominated not by theoretical ideals but by bourgeois practicality, a new school triumphed over the two earlier ones and put an end to their war with one another. The Ingres and the Delacroix of realism was Gustave Courbet, who said, "Show me an angel and I will paint one." In one form or another, realism dominated painting until near the end of the century, and in America it found a great man in Thomas Eakins, for whom Ingres's serene bathers and Delacroix's abducted maidens were less interesting than the people he saw going about their daily affairs in his native Philadelphia. Eakins's portrait of Miss Van Buren is one of the most impressive of his revelations of personality and his creations of poetic mood achieved through what seems to be nothing more than the objective recreation of the natural appearance of an everyday subject. (Phillips Collection, Washington, D. C.)

Manet: *Boating*

In France, realism found its most delightful expression in its variation, impressionism. The impressionists are the best loved painters today. Everyone knows Renoir, Degas, and Monet. But the early struggles of these men were without precedent. Some of them were frequently without money to buy paints while established hacks, now forgotten, sold pictures for high prices as fast as they could paint them.

The impressionists' first martyr was a man a little older than they, who paved the way for them — Édouard Manet. He fortunately had private means of support while he was attacked and vilified for the revolutionary character of an art that now seems conventional enough. Impressionism was an art of suggestion, an art of intimate charm, of commonplace subjects informally presented but elevated above the commonplace by unusual perceptions and a vibrant love of the good but simple things of life. Manet's *Boating* was painted late in his career when he adopted some of the impressionists' cursory technique and shared briefly their fascination with subjects in open air impregnated with shimmering light. This detail, at approximately the size of the original, may show why impressionism offended a public that had become accustomed to the idea of painting as the approximation of the appearance of objects in photographic detail. (Metropolitan Museum of Art, New York, H. O. Havemeyer Collection.)

Seurat: *The Bridge at Courbevoie*

By the time the century entered its last decade, the impressionists had won their battle, but impressionism had also revealed its limitations. The several men who departed from impressionism to open the way to what we call "modern" art are grouped under the not very descriptive title of post-impressionists, which means nothing more than that they found their individual solutions to problems with which impressionism was not concerned.

Georges Seurat based his art on impressionism's bright, broken color, but he disciplined it relentlessly into myriads and myriads of tiny dots applied with scientific calculation. Impressionism's limitation was a loss of form, a suggestion of transience and hence of triviality. Seurat returned to the classical ideal of rule and regulation, of precision and exquisitely adjusted balance. But he retained the impressionist love of sparkling light and communion with the world of everyday experience. He died just as he entered his thirties, but not before he had demonstrated that formal discipline need not imply sterile repetition. (Home House Society, Courtauld Institute of Art, London.)

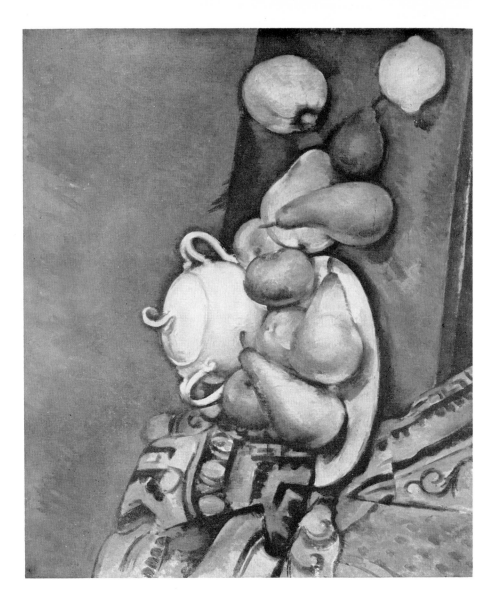

Cézanne: *The White Sugar Bowl*

The problem of reconciling impressionism and formal discipline was attacked in a different way, and a more revolutionary one, by the giant of modern painting — Paul Cézanne.

To try to say much about Cézanne's theories in a paragraph is utterly pointless. We can say that they were based on the conviction that impressionist intimacy and love of the visible world could be combined with the classical ideal of universal statement, that common objects and people could be as majestic as mountains and gods. Cézanne's overwhelming importance in modern painting is that in solving his problems he never hesitated to violate such conventions as perspective and "normal" appearance, to tilt or warp a form into balance with another, itself tilted or warped, until his picture was brought into a state of balance that represented the inherent order of the universe and the dignity of man within it. Cézanne's distortions are acceptable now even to the uninitiated, because in comparison with the much more violent distortions of contemporary art, of which they were a source, they seem mild. But through these distortions and through the theories that led to them, Cézanne changed the direction that art had been following for nearly seven hundred years. (Collection Henry P. McIlhenny, Philadelphia.)

Van Gogh: *Self-portrait*

Seurat and Cézanne reinterpreted and revitalized the classical ideal. Two other men, in the meanwhile, continued and extended the romantic tradition of revolt and personal emotionalism. They were Vincent van Gogh and Paul Gauguin, whose tragic and disastrous lives were interlocked.

Van Gogh, who was not mad, has become the symbol of the mad genius cherished by everyone who believes that emotionalized painting is a spontaneous gushing-out of the soul onto the canvas. Van Gogh's art seems to support such an idea, in its rush, its vehemence, even in the physical character of his pigment, which may twist and swirl or be thrust upon the canvas as if the artist were impelled to create by forces beyond his control. But everything that van Gogh wrote about his way of work, and all the studies he made for his paintings, show that his intensity is relayed to us through means that he developed painfully and studiously. Poverty, loneliness, and ill health drove him to suicide in his thirties. During his lifetime he had sold exactly one picture, unless we count those that he traded for paints and brushes. (Fogg Art Museum, Cambridge, Mass., Maurice Wertheim Collection.)

Gauguin: *The Vision after the Sermon – Jacob Wrestling with the Angel*

Gauguin also died in poverty, alone, and miserably, and his life was at least as disordered as van Gogh's. The difference is that Gauguin chose his way of life, while van Gogh's was imposed upon him. A successful businessman, Gauguin first painted as a hobby, then as a passion that bankrupted him, cost him his family, and led him finally to a life in the South Seas that was idyllic enough in theory but sordid and violent in fact.

Gauguin was led to the South Seas by an appetite for primitive and exotic subjects that had preoccupied him from his earliest days as an artist. He painted *The Vision after the Sermon*, showing Breton peasants witnessing their literal conception of the struggle between Jacob and the Angel, in much the same spirit in which, later, he painted the natives of the South Seas haunted by the spirits they believed in. In returning to forms of primitive inspiration and expressing his primitive subjects in nonnaturalistic color, Gauguin along with *Cézanne* and van Gogh gave impetus to the modern idea of painting as the invention of forms and colors rather than as the imitation of nature. (National Gallery of Scotland, Edinburgh.)

Nolde: *Life of Maria Aegyptiaca*, First Episode: "Early Sinful Life"

From these men and others who struck out in new directions, the complicated and contradictory revolutions, assaults, and forays of twentieth-century art developed. The most direct followers of van Gogh and Gauguin were the German expressionists, who painted vigorously from the first decade of the new century until the time of Hitler with his art "reforms." Religion, sex, and the compassionate observation of human misery were among the major obsessions of the expressionists, always with the most intense personal reference, in pictures dedicated as were van Gogh's to the release of some inner anguish. As all the new isms were to be, expressionism was greeted with furor, diatribes, and laughter by the general public but was supported by an increasing number of dealers, collectors, and advanced critics. Emil Nolde's *Life of Maria Aegyptiaca* with its intentional ugliness, its therapeutic coarseness, its exaggerated violence of color, was offensive to a public that had only recently come around to accepting as "modern" the gentle, lyrical world created by the impressionists. The expressionist movement spread beyond Germany but was basically northern in its brooding emotionalism, just as van Gogh, the Dutchman painting in France, was northern in his similar introspection. (Kunsthalle, Hamburg. Reproduction courtesy Frederick A. Praeger, Inc.)

Matisse: *Madame Matisse (The Green Line)*

The pathos, melancholy, and brutality of expressionism as it developed in Germany were foreign to the temperament and tradition of France. The parallel movement there was fauvism, also based on color, as German expressionism so largely was, but more closely related to the decorative color compositions of Gauguin than to the emotionalized color of van Gogh. The use of color for its own sake as much as for its expressive power marks Henri Matisse's fauvist portrait of his wife (usually called *The Green Line*) as an intellectual and theoretical exercise in spite of its undeniable expressive force. Balancing color against color, Matisse reduces his background to arbitrary areas, and in the face he introduces the unnaturalistic green line down the center for the reason that it is needed there as part of a scheme that falls to pieces without it.

Fauvism was a brief and loosely organized movement, the result of the largely coincidental appearance of a group of young Frenchmen experimenting with color as an abstract structural device. In a matter of a few years each member of the group had branched off into further experiments in different directions. More than any of them, Matisse remained first of all a colorist in a long lifetime during which, with Picasso, he became a most potent force in the transformation of the art of painting in the twentieth century. (*Statens Museum for Kunst*, Copenhagen, Rump Collection. Permission courtesy Mme. Marguerite Duthuit.)

Gris: *The Violin*

Even more than fauvism, cubism was an affront to a startled public and the majority of painters and critics. The two movements appeared at the same time; of the two, cubism was the more fertile one and the more disruptive.

Cézanne had established the idea that the form of natural objects might be subjected to whatever dislocations best served the painter in his effort to build pictorial structures. The cubists went further, extending this aspect of Cézanne's theories and combining them with others, until the visible world was only a point of departure for the creation of complicated geometrical structures in which objects finally became totally undecipherable. Juan Gris's *The Violin* was painted at a time when cubism had passed through its most extreme phase, and the objects that had been disintegrated in a theoretical demonstration had been partially reassembled. *The Violin* is a pattern in which discipline, harmony, and even poetic mood should be apparent to anyone willing to accept the legitimacy of other standards in painting than purely representational ones. But even today not everyone can do so, in spite of the fact that cubism as an independent movement has been absorbed by later ones, and the public has had half a century to absorb its shock. (*Kunstmuseum,* Basel.)

Picasso: *Girl before a Mirror*

Cubism released the genius of the most prolific, the most inventive, and the most eruptive painter of the century, the Spaniard Pablo Picasso. In spirit Picasso's work ranges from the tender melancholy of certain pre-cubist pictures to the titanic wrath of his *Guernica*, from sheer playful legerdemain to philosophical speculation to a kind of willful and grotesque brutality. Since cubism, of which of course he was an originator, Picasso has sallied away from and back to and around and about cubism's theories, adapting and transforming them in a hundred ways. Like so much of his work, his *Girl before a Mirror* is many things to many men — an analytical challenge to psychiatrists, a stunning pattern ready for filching to decorators, a landmark to historians of Picasso's development, a symbol of the twentieth century to sociologically minded aestheticians, and still, after so long a time, a gargantuan piece of charlatanry to people who refuse to accept its premises as honest ones. (The Museum of Modern Art, New York.)

Léger: *The City*

Cubism produced variants at every hand. Conspicuous among them was the mechanistic art of Fernand Léger, one of several painters and groups of painters who held the theory that since the twentieth century is the age of the machine, twentieth-century painting must "bear comparison with any manufactured object" in sleekness, and reflect at the same time the driving, pistonlike energies of the age, and the clamorous, dehumanized, strident rhythms of the modern metropolis. Léger attempted a synthesis of these ideas in *The City* with its clashing forms, its raucous color, but at the same time its painstaking pseudomechanical conventionalizations of such forms as telephone poles, billboards, girders, factories, robotlike human beings, and less readily identifiable elements suggesting parts of motors. But in the end, *The City* is an abstract painting rather than a subject picture – that is, pure form and pure color must be enjoyed more for themselves than for anything they "say." (Philadelphia Museum of Art, A. E. Gallatin Collection.)

Rivera: *Sugar Cane*

The most frequent and the most legitimate objection to abstract art is that the artist may sacrifice more through loss of meaning to a large audience than he gains in interest to a small one. The most forthright rejection of abstraction was made on the American continent, first in Mexico and then in the United States, by artists who had experimented with it and found it wanting. In Mexico the rejection was most dramatic when a group of painters undertook to decorate public buildings with frescoes directed not toward the intellectual pleasure of aesthetes but to the consciousness of the mass of the people, telling them the story of their national history and propagandizing for the government. In unabashedly propagandistic terms, Diego Rivera's *Sugar Cane* shows a foreign landlord prostituting the resources and the people of Mexico under a semifeudal system that the government intended to abolish.

In the United States the reaction against abstraction took a somewhat different form, glorifying the homely and provincial aspects of life in the part of the country least sympathetic to the cosmopolitanism of abstract art, or sometimes mildly satirizing the mores of the self-righteous. (Philadelphia Museum of Art, Gift of Mr. and Mrs. Herbert C. Morris.)

Chirico: *Melancholy and Mystery of a Street*

In Europe also there was a reaction against the often frigid and impersonally logical nature of abstraction. Surrealism, the cult of the mysterious, the irrational, and the bizarre, was an art of poetry and dream, distinguished from other painting of this general kind by its preoccupation with contemporary investigations of morbid psychology, and particularly with the theories of Sigmund Freud. In order to present their fantasies at maximum shock strength, the surrealists abandoned abstraction for the most acutely detailed representation of objects, although these objects were combined in irrational and usually nightmarish ways.

The great surrealist was Giorgio de Chirico, a man who had no formal connection with the movement but anticipated it in his vistas of deserted city squares illuminated by vivid but inexplicable light and spotted here and there with inexplicably sinister objects or figures. As a manifestation of the romantic spirit, surrealism, now dead as an organized movement, has been absorbed, with the other schools and movements we have seen here, into the mainstream of contemporary painting as it continues to flow, to meander, to divide, and to rejoin itself on its course into the future. (Collection Mr. and Mrs. Stanley Resor, New Canaan, Conn.)

John Canaday

MAINSTREAMS OF MODERN ART

SIMON AND SCHUSTER · NEW YORK

A BOOK OF THIS KIND INVOLVES SO MANY PEOPLE IN ITS PREPARATION THAT WHEN it is completed the author feels that it is only partly his own. The museums and the collectors who have made possible the illustrations are acknowledged in the captions, but there are so many other individuals who have been helpful to the author, or merely patient with him, that only a few of them can be thanked here.

The first must be Marshall B. Davidson of the Metropolitan Museum of Art; to him I owe the opportunity to write this book, which I hope will not disappoint him.

Among readers of the manuscript in various stages, Thomas M. Folds of Northwestern University managed to point out flaws and suggest corrections without damaging an old friendship. William C. Kortlander of the University of Texas offered numerous specific comments to the benefit of the text while it was in progress, and David M. Robb of the University of Pennsylvania read the final draft with infinite charity.

Without the assistance of Mrs. Alice H. Fincke of the Carl Schurz Memorial Foundation, in Philadelphia, there would have been no illustrations for many of the nineteenth-century German paintings discussed in one section of the book. Bruce St. John of the Wilmington Society of the Fine Arts supplied some interesting material on Burne-Jones, in connection with the Samuel and Mary R. Bancroft collection of Pre-Raphaelite painting under his care. Mrs. Henry W. Howell, Jr., of the Frick Art Reference Library, and members of her staff, ferreted out several bits of obscure information. Pearl L. Moeller of The Museum of Modern Art went out of her way to solve several problems that arose in connection with color plates. And everybody at the Philadelphia Museum of Art was considerate, with Marjorie E. Lyons, the Museum's librarian, and Alfred H. Wyatt, its photographer, doing more than their share in responding to daily cries for assistance.

To all these people I am grateful. But to one other I am more than grateful and more than indebted for practical help, for encouragement, and for a sharing of ideas about painting. The best parts of this book belong

To Katherine

J. C.
Philadelphia Museum of Art
April 29, 1959

CONTENTS

ILLUSTRATIONS

PART I

The Nineteenth Century in France

CHAPTER 1

Revolution

Modern Art, Tradition, and David

Where does modern art begin? And why does this version of its story begin with a man named Jacques Louis David, born more than 200 years ago?

Modern art begins nowhere because it begins everywhere. It is fed by a thousand roots, from cave paintings 30,000 years old to the spectacular novelties in last week's exhibitions. We are pressed upon by bewildering accumulations of every art from every period; a painter may live in South Dakota and find his major stimulation in the sculpture of ancient China. His art may be a compound of his reactions to objects and ideas as diverse as the structure of the internal combustion engine, the theories of Sigmund Freud, and the painting of Rembrandt. The public museum is something new; we think of it as having always existed, but it is a modern institution, and what the old masters knew of the art of the past was only a fraction of what any casual student can see today in museums—and cannot avoid seeing in floods of reproductions that have added their special complication by taking the Sistine Ceiling, for instance, and transforming it into a miniature painting the size of an ordinary envelope.

For the artist, the past used to be a stream; now it is an ocean. It used to be a road, now it is a forest. Tradition in art used to mean a steady sequence of change within boundaries. Today the boundaries are vague, if they exist at all. Horizons are infinite; the artist is tempted to explore in a hundred directions at once.

As an example more obvious than most, the art of the modern Italian painter Amedeo Modigliani (1884–1920) reflects in

3

1. BELGIAN CONGO: *Head*. Wood, 13¾" high. University Museum, Philadelphia.

2. BOTTICELLI: Detail from *Birth of Venus, c.* 1485. Uffizi, Florence. (Photo Anderson.)

about equal parts the wonderful linear contours of his compatriot of nearly 500 years before, Botticelli, and the stylizations of African tribal sculpture. African sculpture [1] is part of the savage ritual of magic and incantation. Botticelli's Venus [2] is a Renaissance intellectual's revery upon classical antiquity. Yet these two arts, so wildly separated, are harmoniously unified in another that is concerned with the Parisian bohemia of the early twentieth century [3]. Half a dozen other influences contributed to Modigliani's painting, quite aside from the infinite number that are bound into it in secondary ways. They would include the French classical master, Ingres; Modigliani's contemporaries, the expressionists; probably the late medieval religious paint-

ings of the Sienese school; the revolutionary art of Cézanne; the *fin-de-siècle* art of Toulouse-Lautrec. But the most important factor in the compound of Modigliani's art is not Botticelli or African sculpture. Nor is it Ingres or the expressionists or the Sienese or Cézanne or Toulouse-Lautrec. It is Modigliani, an artist of creative talent, sensitive intelligence, and aesthetic discretion, who imitates none of these men or schools but fuses whatever he takes from them with his own perception of the world into an expressive art of great individuality.

We talk about "traditional" painting today, meaning the opposite of "modern" painting. Yet if tradition means the transmission of ideas or ways of doing things from ancestors to posterity—as the diction-

3. MODIGLIANI: *Female Portrait*, 1918. 39½ x 25½″. Collection Louis E. Stern, New York.

ary says it does—then Modigliani must be one of the most traditional painters who ever lived. But, like other modern artists, he has found his ancestors in the most diverse and unexpected combinations. The orderly sequence from one generation of painters to the next has given way to a series of abrupt dislocations to such an extent that, if we have a tradition, it is the contradictory one that each new generation is under some kind of obligation to refute and violate the ideas of the preceding one.

For this reason Jacques Louis David offers a starting point for this story of modern art. He cut off from a long tradition to begin a new one, and he cut off so suddenly, with such violence even, that the course of painting ever since has been a history of revolutions and counterrevolutions, developing so rapidly that one is hardly established before it is being shouldered aside by the next. As successive groups of painters seek to establish a norm within this infinitely rich chaos, other groups arise, determined to upset whatever norm is temporarily achieved. The history of modern painting begins with David's break from tradition just as the history of modern Europe begins with the French Revolution, in which David was a conspicuous figure.

David's Life

As often as not, a knowledge of the events of a painter's life is unnecessary to understanding his art, but David's is one of those cases where some acquaintance is imperative. Early disappointments, an attempted suicide, a Roman experience, and thereafter his participation in the turbulent political events of his time not only determined the character of his own art but redirected the course of European painting. During twenty years of roaring success, David painted a series of sensational pictures that annihilated not only every living competitor of the old school but the tradition of the most eminent painters for several generations back as well. He established himself as art dictator of France, where his paintings influenced everything from philo-

sophical morality to interior decoration. Political theorists used his paintings to support their arguments, and every woman in Europe with any pretensions to chic discarded her wardrobe and changed her hair-do to make herself over in the pattern of the female type he invented to enact his pictorial dramas. It was the most drastic "new look" in the history of fashion, but it was only a footnote to David's career.

As a student David was a protegé of the Royal Academy of Painting and Sculpture, an institution that he would later cut down, then make over in his own image. He attempted suicide after four consecutive failures to win its *Prix de Rome*. This "Rome Prize" was (and still is) the most coveted official student award in France. It took the winner to the Academy's branch in Rome for three years; during this time his only obligation was to produce one work annually to send back to Paris. A *Prix de Rome* man was also assured of very considerable advantages upon his return to France, since his career was sponsored by established academicians in a position to throw commissions and attention his way. The whole situation, of course, was based on the premise that a *Prix de Rome* winner was dedicated to the perpetuation of the academic tradition.

David failed in his suicide when fellow students broke into his studio in the Louvre, suspicious because it had been locked for days. (The Louvre was not then a museum; the buildings included, among many other things, quarters for the talented young men who, like David, received stipends from the king to follow their studies.) He had intended to starve himself to death and probably would have done so. The choice of method says a great deal about David's temperament, at once intense and dogged, sensitive yet Spartan. These characteristics appear in his art, where emotion is held in check by icy control.

In 1774 David competed once again for the *Prix de Rome* and won it. He was twenty-six years old, unusually mature for a *Prix de Rome* winner and—which was even more unusual—full of hidden resentment against the Academy and suspicious of its standards.

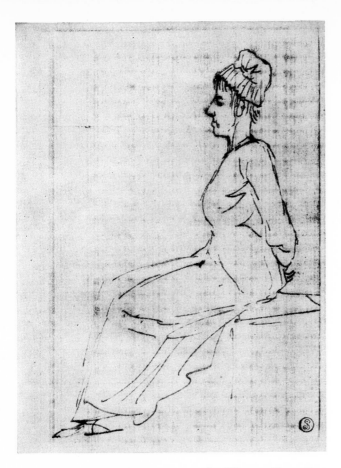

4. DAVID: *Marie Antoinette on the Way to Execution,*
1793. Pen and ink, 5¾ x 4″. Louvre, Paris.

By a unique extension of artistic success
into the field of government, possible only
in the one country in the world where art
is debated as fervently as politics, the pictures David painted during the next fifteen
years lifted him from the position of a near-
failure to the eminence of the Revolution's
prophet and then made him one of its leading participants. (Just how this happened
we will see when we look at the pictures
themselves.) He served among other capacities as a member of the legislative body
voting life or death for his former patron,
Louis XVI. David's vote was among those
that sent this ineffectual, confused, and
incompetent young man to the guillotine.
David also guillotined the Royal Academy
in which he had been nurtured, crying out
for its abolition "in the name of humanity,

in the name of justice, for the love of art,
and above all for the love of youth." He
called the Academy's schools *funeste,* an
adjective that pales in translation as *fatal*
or *deadly.* Fatal or deadly they may have
been, but a few years after David abolished
them they rose from their own ashes, more
funeste than ever, dominated this time by
the theories of David himself.

The Revolution was followed by the period of violence and confusion so appropriately called the Terror, when no man's
neck was safe from the knife. During these
days David, still among the powerful, abandoned personal friends to the executioner
with an expedient callousness for which he
has never been forgiven. Some of his actions at this time make it difficult not to
see him as a fanatic. Mrs. Siddons, the English actress, reported to a friend that she
was present when David, told that eighty
people had been beheaded that morning,
answered, "Not more?" He used to sit outside the *Café de la Régence* sketching the
prisoners on their way to the scaffold. When
Marie Antoinette was beheaded, he did a
heartrending sketch of her [4], bound hand
and foot as he saw her from a window on
the way to execution, bedraggled, emaci-
ated, prematurely aged by her frightful imprisonment, with no suggestion of beauty
left, yet with a dignity she had never managed to achieve as queen of France.

This man David was a curious personality, given to passionate loyalties and passionate grudges, a man of fervent temperament who imposed upon himself a frigid
manner, of sensitive perceptions which he
rejected as unworthy. Because his career
and his art are full of contradictions, his
biographers have taken sides according to
their own convictions. Some see in him a
bloodthirsty despot never forgiving the men
who for so long had denied him the *Prix
de Rome,* using his power vengefully to destroy the tradition they represented. Others
find him devoted to high principles, even
if a little prone to inflict them on others as
severely as he imposed them upon himself.
Frequently the same facts support either
judgment, since they must be evaluated in
the unnatural lights of the Revolution and
the Terror.

Despot or idealist, David himself narrowly escaped the guillotine. He fell from power with his Jacobin partner Robespierre, whose terrorist excesses had become intolerable. Robespierre was beheaded. But there was a delay before David came to trial; when he did, his defense was that he had never been sympathetic to Robespierre's policies, that he had strung along with him only to give what service and protection he could to the arts of France. It is recorded that he "sweated enormously" on the witness stand, that he was pale and trembling, mumbling and stammering pitifully in his own defense against the murderous oratory of the prosecutor, one of the finest speakers of the day. It is not surprising that a man in danger of his life, with no reason to expect clemency, should sweat, nor is it damning that, in the circumstances, one should mumble whose upper lip was disfigured, as David's was, with a tumor that impeded his speech even in the happiest situations. In any case, David escaped execution. Instead, he was imprisoned.

But for this extraordinary man even the circumstances of prison were exceptional and rebounded ultimately to his advantage. His cell was a room in the Luxembourg Palace overlooking a corner of some of the loveliest gardens in the world. The family governess made daily trips to the palace gardens where David's children played as he watched from his window. Former students kept him supplied with painting materials, and he began work on sketches for one of his most ambitious pictures, *The Battle of the Romans and Sabines* [11], a work that was to re-establish him more firmly than ever in a career which seemed lost. When he was released in a general amnesty, he had been in prison only a few months.

David completed *The Sabines* in a studio where women of fashion begged to pose for him as if they already knew the picture was to be one of the most famous in the world. In the meanwhile France had come under the leadership of the young general Napoleon Bonaparte. He visited David's studio to see *The Sabines* and recognized the potential of this man's art as propaganda that could be as effective for the empire he

planned as it had been for the Revolution. Napoleon conceived an image of himself as a modern version of a conquering Roman emperor, partly because of his personal conviction that he was just that and partly as a matter of what would now be called public relations. Official architecture had been a recombination of classical elements under the dictates of the Royal Academy, but now Napoleon demanded an architecture that would be true archaeologically. Paris was to become a second Rome—but larger—as a setting for the new conqueror. For his church, La Madeleine, Napoleon demanded of his architects the most perfect classical temple since antiquity. The Arc de Triomphe is a handsomely inflated version of ancient Roman models, so large that the originals would look like guard stalls alongside it. David's painting was the perfect accessory to these conceptions, and Napoleon took the artist under his wing.

Thus the young man who had begun his career under the patronage of the king of France, who had continued it as spokesman for the Revolution and the Terror, finally became First Painter to the Emperor and art dictator of the country that has set the course of Western painting ever since.

Napoleon once said, "David, I salute you." He was commenting on a painting, recognizing its success without risking a critical judgment. But the same comment, with the same reservation, could refer in all appropriateness to David's life.

David's Painting

David won his *Prix de Rome* with a respectful exercise giving no indication—except by hindsight—of the Davidian revolution to come. *Antiochus and Stratonice* [5] is full of derivative references flattering to the leading academicians of the day. Like any other student involved in a school competition, David produced a demonstration of how well he had learned his lessons. The picture includes a nude torso to prove that he knew muscular anatomy and could draw and paint the human body accurately with conventional heroic modifications; his skill with drapery is demonstrated to the point

5. DAVID: *Antiochus and Stratonice*, 1774 (*Prix de Rome*). 47¼ x 61". *École des Beaux Arts*, Paris. (Photo Giraudon.)

of excess in great billowing areas wherever he needs filler; the male figure leaning forward just to the right of the picture's center, reduced almost to silhouette in the head and shoulders and emerging into brilliant illumination in the hand and the spread of cloak just below, is a sort of final examination passed with honors in chiaroscuro, which means the revelation of forms in strong light and dark shadow. The elaborated architectural background shows that the candidate had mastered perspective, and also supplies the air of pomp and circumstance necessary to a picture obliged to take itself so seriously. Compositionally—that is, in the way the objects and figures are arranged in the picture space—these various exercises are nicely, if conventionally, pieced together.

The story, for whatever bearing it has, tells of the young prince Antiochus (supine upon the couch) who languished to the point of death from an unidentifiable malady until the doctor Erasistratus (seated beside him, at the left) diagnosed it for what it was: Antiochus was lovesick for his father's wife, the beautiful Stratonice (standing at the right). Such a tale of repressed passion offers material for tense and personal expression—and received it, later on, in a painting by one of David's own pupils [67]—but David uses it only as a framework for a charade posed by models in appropriate attitudes. But hindsight shows us that, if most of the picture is blowzy and pointlessly complicated, the figure of Erasistratus has an aggressive force in which we can imagine the germ of the style of the picture that redirected the course of French painting and began the history of modern art—David's *The Oath of the Horatii*.

"The Oath of the Horatii"

With *The Oath of the Horatii* [6], which he completed in 1785, David came fully into his own as an original creative painter. It is a superb picture. It is called stiff and cold; such adjectives as *harsh* and *wiry* are habitually applied to its color and drawing, with only partial justice, as if they were entirely derogatory. Actually these qualities are in themselves remarkable, and they have an expressive reason for being.

The Oath of the Horatii contrasts on every hand with *Antiochus and Stratonice*. Its surface is as hard as enamel, the edges of its forms are mercilessly uncompromising, revealed in a flat, uniform illumination instead of theatrical spotlights. In drapery passages the windy profligacy of the earlier picture has been chastened into order and definition. Everywhere the antithesis continues. Compositionally, *Antiochus and Stratonice* is extravagant; *The Oath of the Horatii* is spare, organized almost mathematically into unit variations of the number 3. Against three simple arches the participants are divided into three groups of generally triangular shapes—the three sons, the father holding their three swords, and the group of women. In this last group the triangular severity is appropriately relaxed (but not abandoned), and the linear patterns are appropriately more graceful. The three groups, considered as a unit, are united in a final triangle binding the picture into a decisive whole. The subterfuge of the "academic machine," which means a picture organized on standard formulas with all their complicated trappings, has been rejected for a rigid structure where economy, precision, and force must reveal any weak or extraneous element. *The Oath of the Horatii* offers the artist no refuge behind the facile piling-up of incidentals; he must be revealed as the master of his expression or be exposed as inadequate to its demands.

That David invented a new style of painting need not have had any importance in itself; the important thing is that he had to invent it in order to express what amounted to a moral and philosophical revolution in art, which also explains his choice of subject. The three stalwart young Romans are vowing to their father that they will return victorious or give their lives in a duel with three warrior brothers of the city of Alba, a duel to be fought in the presence of the armies of both cities to determine which city will rule the other. The special complication in this situation is that one of the grieving women to the right is not only the wife of one of the Roman warriors but the sister of one of the Albans as well. In addition, the youngest of the women is a sister of the Romans but the fiancée of one of the Albans.

Thus the subject of *The Oath of the Horatii* is dedication and sacrifice. Instead of the lovesick Antiochus we have vigorous young males pledging their lives to the defense of their honor, their family, and their country. The chaste matron and the swooning girl express their grief with admirable reserve, submissive to the will of the dominant men. Their dignity is a rebuke to Stratonice's simpering grace, just as the virility of the young Horatii is contemptuous of Antiochus's amorous languor. Service to a moral and social ideal is glorified as a virtue opposed to its parallel vice, the indulgence of personal yearnings. Just so, severity and masculine force replace elegance and feminine sensitivity in David's new style. Rich complications have given way to austerity; fashionable invention has been rejected for philosophical order.

Composition of this kind is not achieved in a single step; the rule in picture-making is that simplicity is reached by reduction from complexity. When he first began work, David chose another incident from the story of the Horatii as dramatized by Corneille, the god of French classical drama. In this tragedy the three Albans and two of the Roman brothers are killed; the remaining son returns covered with the blood of his sister's fiancé, and she denounces him and Rome. As a patriot, he runs his sister through with his sword.

An early sketch for the picture represents this final scene, where the elder Horatius pleads for his son while the body of his daughter lies on the steps of the platform where they stand. The composition was to have been even more elaborate than

6. DAVID: *The Oath of the Horatii,* small version, after 1784. 50 x 65″. Toledo Museum of Art, Gift of Edward Drummond Libbey.

Antiochus and Stratonice. The old father, swathed in a toga, gestures grandiloquently in one direction while two male figures rush past him in another. The son stands in elaborate theatrical battle gear, including a voluminous cape. The background was to have been a palatial architectural invention on several levels, rising above masses of incidental figures in the foreground and supporting other agitated groups on a balcony. For good measure, there was to have been a full landscape in the distance, including a large temple.

Such a fulsome arrangement was out of key with the ideal of sincerity and moral strength, and David abandoned it (perhaps upon the advice of friends) for the scene showing the sons taking their oath before departure. The palace in the background was reduced to a stark enclosure; the landscape was eliminated as having nothing to do with the action; costumes were simplified. The new composition was less obviously dramatic but more forceful, and with the narrative reduced to a minimum its symbolism was emphasized.

The Oath of the Horatii was a sensation when David exhibited it in his studio in Rome. He completed it there during a second sojourn made possible by his father-in-law, who supplied him with funds to support himself, his wife and family, and an

7. DAVID: *The Death of Socrates,* 1787. 51 x 77¼". Metropolitan Museum of Art, New York, Wolfe Fund.

entourage of servants and assistants. The investment was a good one. The picture was brought back to Paris for the Salon (the annual official exhibition dominated by the Academy) and although badly placed, it caused such riotous excitement that it was rehung in a better position. A few pedants criticized the composition as oversimplified and on a single plane—that is, stretching across the picture surface rather than, so to speak, "puncturing" the canvas and going back into space. But these objections were lost in the general enthusiasm, which was increased by a factor that was to affect the reception of David's work from this time on: *The Oath of the Horatii* was interpreted as an allegory of contemporary events.

To adherents of the burgeoning Revolution, the picture seemed to proclaim the virility of new republican ideals in opposition to the degeneracy of the old regime. It is impossible to know how specifically David meant to reflect political convictions or theories, but it is certain enough that his own temperament was sympathetic to the new ideas—or at least unsympathetic to the

established order, of which the Academy was a manifestation. With the explosive success of *The Horatii* David became identified with antiroyalist thought. Ironically, the picture had been commissioned by the king. And it was so admired by one high-living member of the court, the Comte de Vaudreuil, an intimate of Marie Antoinette, that he commissioned David to do a copy in a smaller size. (He had to sell it later to pay gambling debts.) The smaller version is illustrated here. It differs from the larger one in the Louvre by the addition of the spindle lying on the floor by the grieving women.

David followed *The Horatii* with an even icier painting reflecting again the theme of self-sacrifice with moral and philosophical associations translatable into terms of revolutionary political ideas, *The Death of Socrates* [7]. The philosopher whose thought was based on the idea of studying man instead of inventing systems of false rhetoric, who sought the moral bases for human conduct, who did his teaching where crowds of the people gathered instead of within a

8. David: *Lictors Bringing Back to Brutus the Bodies of His Sons*, 1789. 128 x 166½".
Louvre, Paris.

closed circle of sophisticates, and who died for the defense of his ideas, was even more directly identifiable with the principles of the Revolution than *The Horatii* had been. David shows Socrates about to carry out the sentence of death by drinking hemlock, while his disciples do their best to conceal the weakness of emotionalism.

These "stoic" pictures with political overtones reached their climax—not aesthetically, but politically—in a picture of Brutus, First Consul of Rome, sternly repressing his grief as the bodies of his two sons, whom he had condemned to death for conspiring against Roman liberty, are carried home for burial. *Lictors Bringing Back to Brutus the Bodies of His Sons* [8] was completed and exhibited the very year of the Revolution. Even more than *The Horatii* it was a sensation as a political allegory. Just as Brutus had sacrificed his own sons to the cause of Roman liberty, so must the French people

purify their country at no matter what costs. Brutus's strength was openly compared with the weakness of Louis XVI, who had allowed members of his family to emigrate and take up arms for other countries against France. Again the pedants objected, this time because the figure of Brutus, the main character, was thrown into deep shadow. The dramatic and psychological effectiveness of this device is obvious, of course, but it went against the rules. No one else cared; the picture was a fantastic success, talked of everywhere, and in the theater where Voltaire's drama on the same subject was being performed, the actors assumed the attitudes painted by David. *Brutus*, too, was purchased by Louis XVI. David's apologists point out that later on, when he voted for the death of the King, David could not have done otherwise without giving the lie to the moral themes of *The Horatii* and *Brutus*.

David and the Revolution

With the Revolution achieved, David found himself its spokesman and propagandist, the pictorial historian of its great events. One of the most important of these events was the Oath of the Tennis Court, when on the 28th of June, 1789, the deputies of the Third Estate swore not to disband until they had given France a constitution. Louis had refused them their usual room for assembly and they had met instead in the indoor tennis court from which the event, and David's picture of it, are named. But the picture was never finished. Before it was nearly done too many of the men represented in it had become suspect.

For a few years after the Revolution David turned his hand to any professional chore for the new government. He was the official supervisor of state ceremonies and designed celebrations on such a scale that virtually the entire population of Paris was directed to take part in them. The citizens grumbled somewhat at this; it seemed a little out of line with the new freedom. David designed playing cards eliminating the king, queen, and knave, now too suggestive of royalty. He designed a new costume for the citizens' everyday dress; it failed to catch on. He was involved with the seizure of the royal collections and others, which were declared the property of the people and have been so ever since as the core of the Louvre Museum. And he produced a painting that may be his masterpiece: *Marat* [9].

David is always a contradictory figure. No sooner is he identified in one character than he reveals himself in another. In *Marat,* painted four years after the *Brutus,* he abandons the harshness of his stoic conceptions for a compassionate nobility all the more surprising in a subject that in essence was both violent and grotesque.

Marat, a leading figure in the Reign of Terror and a close friend of David's, was assassinated in his bathtub by a woman named Charlotte Corday. Although she was a Revolutionary sympathizer, Corday was outraged by the excesses of the Terror and appointed herself judge and executioner of at least one of the guilty, Marat, and was

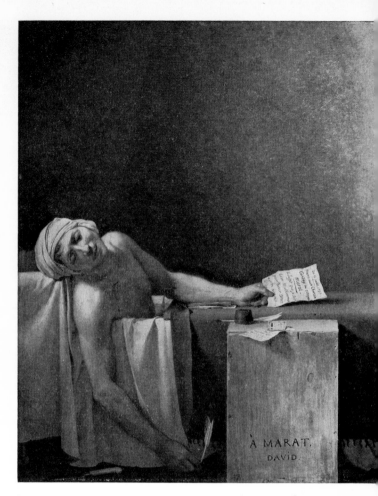

9. DAVID: *Marat,* 1793. 65 x 50⅜". *Musée Royal des Beaux Arts,* Brussels.

herself guillotined for his assassination. All this occurred, and David's picture was painted, in 1793.

The idea of a dedicated lady in full visiting regalia attacking a naked man in his tub has inevitable associations with the ludicrous along with the terrible, even after we know that the bath was a medicinal one in which Marat spent his days because he was afflicted with an eczema. Lining the tub with sheets and wrapping his head in a turban, no doubt also medicated, he received callers and carried on business as usual—or as best he could in the circumstances. Corday gained an audience by sending a note saying she had information of vital importance to France. Marat's tub was rigged with a cover to serve as a desk;

10. BERTHAULT, engraved after SWEBACH: *Assassination of Marat*, from *Collection Complète des Tableaux Historiques de la Révolution Française*, Paris, 1802. Philadelphia Museum of Art, Gift of Mr. and Mrs. Adrian Siegel.

only his head and shoulders emerged above it and thus imprisoned he had no defense against Corday's dagger.

From this situation, which would seem impossibly guignolesque, David extracted a great picture. How he went about it may be revealed by a feeble treatment of the same subject [10] included in a pictorial history of the Revolution published in Paris in 1802. Here various people, attracted by the victim's cries, have rushed into the room and seized Corday (hat either knocked askew or set at a modish angle; it is impossible to tell which). But in spite of all that is supposed to be going on, no feeling of excitement is relayed to the observer. The story is not even clearly told, although presumably it is faithful to factual circumstance. Included in the general clutter of incidental figures is each detail selected by

David: the tub, the cloth hanging over its side, Marat in his turban, some writing materials on a stand by the tub's side, Corday's letter requesting an audience. But where one picture remains an ill-told anecdote at best, the other, by selection, modification, and arrangement of a few meager elements, distills from the event its essence as David felt it.

Bathed in a gentle fall of light with quiet modulations of shadow, each ugly, ordinary, or utilitarian object is invested with dignity, and all are unified with one another in quiet harmony. From a particularized subject full of sordid and commonplace details, David developed a generalized statement in noble and ideal terms. Here he approaches a classicism truer than that of his classical subjects with their trappings imitated from ancient Rome.

11. David: *The Battle of the Romans and Sabines*, 1799. 152 x 204¾″. Louvre, Paris.

David: The Triumph of Classicism

David's preoccupation with the ancient classical world, while not specifically mentioned, has been implied in the early series of "stoic" pictures: *The Horatii, Socrates,* and *Brutus.* Classicism in one form or another is a constant in French art, and David's art was the climax of a vogue for classical decoration that had already been stimulated by the first excavations of the buried Roman cities of Pompeii and Herculaneum. One of David's masters was Joseph Marie Vien (1716–1809), who made considerable but quite superficial use of classical motifs in his painting and who was appointed director of the Academy's school in Rome the same year David won the *Prix.*

Student and master left Paris together, with David declaring that he would not be "seduced by the antique" because it lacked vivacity and life—which it certainly did in Vien's hands. But when David saw the remains of Pompeii he said it was as if "cataracts had been removed from his eyes."

Neo-classicism* usually manifested itself in superficial borrowing from the forms of ancient art, capitalizing on their grace and novelty with no concern for their corresponding philosophical ideas. But David's

---

* *Neo-classicism,* strictly speaking, should be used to distinguish nineteenth-century revived classicism from the genuine classicism of antiquity. But this is a nuisance, and the differentiation is usually clear in context, so *classicism* will usually be used for both in this book.

12. DAVID: Preliminary drawing for Figure 11, 1795. Louvre, Paris.

classical reference is a double one. Like the other classicists, he used classical forms parasitically, copying them outright from fragments of painting and sculpture.* But unlike the others, David wanted through these borrowed forms to revive the supposed moral virtues of ancient Rome.

Even so, David was under one misconception as to the nature of classical art which was common to his century and to a great extent remains common to this one. A German, Johann Joachim Winckelmann (1717–1768), the first archaeologist to study the monuments of antiquity with

scientific method, had written a celebrated history of ancient art in which he defined beauty as synonymous with perfection. He codified the characteristics of classical art and insisted that all great art must be static because movement is an "accident." What Winckelmann did not understand was that classical art was warm, even sensuous. He confused its repose, its reserve, its calm, with a kind of frigidity, and his followers confused its idealization with prettification. A sculptor friend of David's in Rome, Quatremère de Quincy, introduced David to the theories of Winckelmann as a law permitting of no exception and no variation, and David retained all his life this limited and inaccurate concept of the classical spirit.

* In *The Oath of the Horatii* the head of the father is copied from the Roman equestrian statue of Marcus Aurelius, to name one example in a long list of specific borrowings.

David's archaeological neo-classicism reached its climax in *The Sabines* [11], which he completed in 1799 nearly five years after his trial and the brief imprisonment during which he made the first sketches for it. According to the legend, the Sabine women were abducted by the Romans, who took them to wife. Later when the fathers marched against the ravishers, the women threw themselves and their children between their Sabine fathers and their Roman husbands to stop the carnage. In David's picture the Sabine woman in the center is Hercelia; her husband Romulus is about to throw his javelin at Tatius, who bends to parry the blow. According to one story, David selected the subject because he was moved by the devotion of his wife, who returned to him when he was sent to prison. (She had left him when he voted for the death of the king.) According to another, Hercelia symbolizes France throwing herself between the warring parties in the civil conflict that tore the country after the Revolution. By the time David finished the picture, France had finally reached unity under Napoleon, and David is supposed to have agreed when the latter explanation was suggested, saying that was exactly what he had in mind. In that case, he had been extraordinarily prophetic in the first sketches five years earlier. A likely explanation is simply that the subject attracted him as a subject, all symbolism aside. It recalls his first success, *The Horatii*, in the conflicting loyalties of wives to their husbands at war with their families; also it must have given David pleasure to return to a purely classical subject after devoting himself for several years to pictures of the Revolution. Whatever his reasons for painting *The Sabines*, the uncanny dovetailing of his pictures with current political events, which had worked with *The Horatii* and *Brutus*, worked again. When Napoleon saw *The Sabines* in David's studio, he knew that he had found the man to direct French painting in his, Napoleon's, course toward empire.

In *The Sabines* David sought an extreme accuracy of archaeological truth. In addition, he modified the severity of his "Roman" classicism for a more "Greek" refine- ment. The words have to be put in quotes because the archaeology is as faulty as the idea that Roman art was as severe as the ideals of the early Republic. Actually, all such inaccuracies or misconceptions are quite beside the point, since the neo-classical style is important only as itself, not as a re-creation of the past.

The Sabines is a fascinating picture with many faults. Even its admirers admit that it is rather chilly. For all the violence of the subject, the figures are of an extreme and even disturbing rigidity. Inspired by classical sculpture, they are not so much sculpturesque as stony. The vivacity, the sense of life, that David had once found lacking in classical art is certainly lacking here. Also, the architectural background is divorced from the friezelike grouping of women and warriors; it hangs behind them like a rented backdrop. Seen at full scale (it is a large picture, seventeen feet wide), *The Sabines* tends to break into beautifully designed studies competing with one another, although individually the passages are of great attraction. The theatrical elegance of the central standing female figure and the nude warrior to the right—Hercelia and Romulus—cannot be denied, and if a single pair of figures had to be selected to represent neo-classical types at their typically most ornamental, these might well be the ones. But the words used here are *theatrical* and *elegance*, and neither is particularly associated with the high moral disciplines that can be read into David's earlier work. He has changed. In *The Sabines* these disciplines are patently specious, although the technical disciplines of concise drawing and calculated balance are exaggerated. Classicism is again decorative style, as it was in the work of David's precursors and as it continued to be in the work of his followers, though upon its technical disciplines David insisted to the end.

Academic drawing had always been based on a study of the nude; it was standard practice to make preliminary drawings from the nude even for draped figures. In a study for the figure of Tatius in *The Sabines* David begins with the skeleton, builds the muscles on it, and finally indicates the helmet sketchily [13]. From

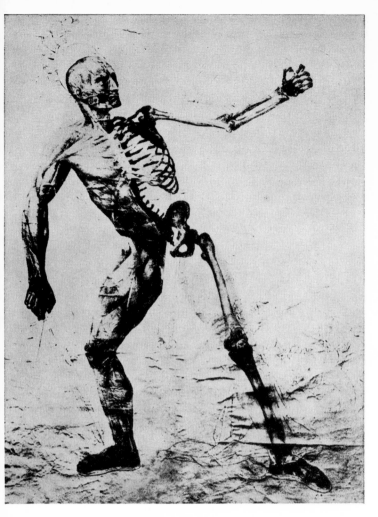

13. DAVID: Study for Tatius in *The Sabines*. Location unknown.

studies like this one David went ahead to refine or idealize nature to one degree or another. In *The Horatii* the anatomy is realistic, but in *The Sabines* David's stated purpose was to go beyond realism to an ideal beauty. He had wanted to leave the figures of the Horatii nude, in accordance with the forms of classical sculpture, but had dared not. Compositional studies for *The Sabines* [12] show that David still felt under this restraint when he began the picture. (They also show that the rigidity of the final scheme was imposed by degrees upon a much freer one.) But by the time he was ready to complete it, modes and manners had relaxed to such an extent that he

not only stripped the male figures but clothed the female ones in diaphanous garments that would have been altogether inappropriate to the severe conceptions of his early work.

David violated precedent by setting up *The Sabines* in his studio and charging admission to see it, a practice that had been forbidden by the Royal Academy. But there was no more Royal Academy and people flocked to see the picture as they had flocked to the Salons to see *The Horatii* and *Brutus*. As they paid their entrance fee, visitors were given a printed statement defending the admission charge. David made enough money to buy himself a comfortable country place outside Paris.

David and Napoleon

Now, under Napoleon, social Paris became a carnival. Freed from the moralistic restrictions of the Revolution and confident once more that the ground was not going to open beneath their feet or the guillotine descend on their necks, people with money indulged in pleasures as vain and often as licentious as the former excesses of the vanished world of the French court. David's influence on the mode reached a point without parallel in the history of the arts. A fashionable ball was a phantasmagoria of classical goddesses; a well-appointed room was as Greek or Roman as a working compromise with contemporary living would allow. The styles of decoration and costume called Directoire and Empire after the divisions of Napoleon's reign owe everything to David. The classical furniture he had designed and built for studio use was imitated in tens of thousands of pieces not only in Paris but everywhere in Europe and even in America. He now occupied himself with official paintings for Napoleon, plus whatever other commissions it interested him to accept. After the wild success of *The Sabines*, Madame Récamier, an ambitious charmer who put the highest premium on her position as a leader of social and intellectual Paris, was not too proud to write him, "I have arranged things so that I can sit for my portrait under the conditions you

14. DAVID: *Madame Récamier*, 1800. 68 x 85¾". Louvre, Paris.

explain. I hope that you understand the great value I attach to a work by you. I will be at your orders for the sittings; let me know when it is convenient for you to begin."

The portrait [14] is one of the most delicate of David's works, an exquisite summary of the spirit of the Directoire style at its purest. It is also one of the most painterly; because it was never finished, it never received the final polish to which David reduced the surface of his other work. Madame Récamier is not posed in costume for an archaeological costume ball but is in fashionable toilette with the exception of the bare feet, a detail David insisted on although it pushed the vogue for classical imitation beyond the point acceptable even to Madame Récamier. A more serious disagreement arose when David insisted on another point: he painted the hair light brown in harmony with the color scheme of the rest of the picture and in line with the formula for classical beauty. Madame Récamier's hair was coal black and she was

proud of it. Without telling David, she went to his most successful pupil, Gérard, who could be depended on to do the kind of portrait she wanted. Gérard reported to David, who told him to go ahead but refused to finish the first commission. Left thus, the portrait reveals the touch of David's brush as so deft, so sensitive, yet without any sacrifice of precision and assurance, that we realize how much was polished out of the rest of his work. With the exception of *Marat*, this is the only painting David regarded as a major one where his personal sensitivity as an artist is not impinged upon by the cruelly self-disciplined exaggerations of craftsmanship.

When Napoleon assumed the title of Emperor in 1804, David was given the title of First Painter. He had long since relinquished all political activity, and he painted now to commemorate the events of Napoleon's reign but not to comment on them beyond a general presentation of the Emperor in dignified and glorified terms. The spirit of the Napoleonic commissions is best

15. DAVID: *Le Sacre*, 1805. 204 x 366″. Louvre, Paris.

summarized in *Le Sacre* [15], a vast canvas of some 500 square feet that was to have been one of a series of four (two were completed) apotheosizing the Emperor after his coronation. *Le Sacre* is the coronation scene itself, a mass portrait of superhuman dimensions. A church was commandeered to serve as a studio—similarly, in 1792, a church had been commandeered for work on *The Oath of the Tennis Court*. This was in 1805 and David was nearly sixty; he had a corps of assistants. There was a specialist in perspective, named Degotti, for the backgrounds; a pupil, Georges Rouget, was the chief of several other lieutenant painters. Even so, David did a portrait drawing for each of the heads. The assistants transferred these to the canvas and roughed them in; David finished each one himself.

Le Sacre shows Napoleon, already crowned, in turn crowning his Empress in the presence of the Pope, a host of dignitaries, and the distressingly unimpressive members of the family. Napoleon preferred to be represented at this moment rather than the one in which he knelt to be crowned by the Pope, since thus he was not put on record at any man's feet. It has been objected that the attendant figures of the court have the air of parvenus in their Sunday best. That, of course, is exactly what they were.

For this as for the other pictures David painted of him Napoleon refused to pose. "Why do you need a model?" he asked. "Do you think the great men of antiquity posed for their portraits? Who cares whether the busts of Alexander the Great look like him? It is enough that we have an image of him that conforms to his genius. That is the way great men should be painted." In *Le Sacre* the great man is painted as a handsome, almost boyish fellow, and he places the crown upon the head of an outrageously rejuvenated Josephine, for whose figure one of David's daughters posed. When an acquaintance objected to this flattering transformation of a woman who was a badly preserved forty-one, and six years older than her husband, David

16. DAVID: *Madame Sériziat*, 1795. Panel, 51½ x 37¾". Louvre, Paris.

17. DAVID: *Monsieur Sériziat*, 1795. Panel, 50¾ x 37¾". Louvre, Paris.

quashed the objection by suggesting that it be made directly to the Empress herself.

In *Le Sacre* David had a next-to-impossible assignment. It was not only that the picture had to be so large. Mythological or ancient historical references were ruled out by Napoleon's demand for a straightforward record of the event, and without them David was forced into a rather pedestrian realism, saved from dullness only by the magnificence of the staging of the actual ceremony. On the whole, *Le Sacre* is a ponderous and wearisome picture in spite of everything David could do. But it is probably the most familiar of all pictures to French school children and remains for Frenchmen the symbol of the glorious days of Napoleon's zenith.

Given the initial handicaps, David's solution was more than adequate. He solved the problem of organizing so many figures partly by grouping, but even more by a less apparent device, a consistent illumination that binds each participant into convincing relationship to the others. There is nothing subtle about this light; it unifies the picture only because it falls so logically everywhere. As a help, David studied a scaled mock-up of the scene, built for him complete with costumed miniature figures. Yet in the end *Le Sacre* is not a stirring picture except by association of ideas. In it David is the soundest of craftsmen, but he is not an artist of emotional or intellectual force.

David: The Artist

What about David as an artist of personal sensitivity, an artist who can respond to human joy and sorrow, gaiety and confusion, hope and disappointment, revery and

18. DAVID: *Antoine Mongez and His Wife Angelica*, 1812. Panel, 37¾ x 54". *Musée de Lille*.

excitement, and communicate with us as other human beings?

In this respect David often denies himself, on the stoic principle that the expression of emotions of either pleasure or pain is a weakness. Even in a picture of the stature of *The Oath of the Horatii*, the observer is likely to feel that he is not so much sharing an experience or an idea as being taught a lesson—which happens to be exactly what the encyclopedist Diderot, just before the Revolution, stated as the function of painting.

But in his portraits David frequently relents, especially when the sitters are close friends and the pictures were not intended for formal public exhibition. After his release from prison he stayed for a while with his wife's sister, Émélie Sériziat, and her husband. David was a man who had been bitterly chastised, who had narrowly escaped execution, whose career seemed to be in ruins. He had always been a man with a reputation for severity, yet during his imprisonment his friends and his family had shown him loyalty and affection. During the two months he spent with the Sériziats he must have been conscious of his good

fortune, grateful for the kindness of people, perhaps even aware of and regretful for his own iciness. There was a particularly affectionate bond between David and Émélie; the portrait he now painted of her [16] is a delight and a revelation of gentle sensitivities rarely suggested in his work up until this time. The informality of the pose, the freshness of the color, the loving attention to engaging details of costume and the sweetness of the little bouquet of flowers— all these are specific attractions but they only partially account for something more elusive, a tenderness and human warmth, an intimacy of personal response between painter and subject.

The air of intimacy and informality is not accidental, for the picture is carefully composed. The placement of the child is masterly. In a more conspicuous position he would have detracted from the picture as David conceived it, since this is a portrait of Émélie Sériziat, not a picture of a mother and child. As it is, the child is very nearly crowded out of the picture, which would have been unpleasant if David had not turned the head so that we are regarded with open curiosity. The child seems almost to have slipped into the range of the picture by accident, without knowledge that he would be painted; he is held in perfect balance, neither detracting from the main subject nor altogether subjugated to it. The companion portrait of Monsieur Sériziat [17] is closer to Davidian formula, but not close enough for its precision to turn frigid.

The Sériziats were painted in 1795. Seventeen years later David painted a double portrait of his friend Antoine Mongez and his wife [18]. Like the Sériziat portraits, this one was a labor of love. It is inscribed "Amicos Antonium Mongez et Angelicam uxorem amicus Ludovicus David. Anno MDCCCXII."

The Latin is not an affectation but appropriate in a portrait of Mongez, the author of a scholarly dictionary of antiquities. His hand rests on this volume and also holds a coin, symbol of his function as an administrator in the government's department of finance. His wife Angelica had been a student of David's; she costumed the figures for his mock-up of *Le Sacre* and executed minor passages in that gigantic picture. The Mongez portrait is more formal than those of the Sériziats but no less warm, and as a presentation of two rich personalities it even surpasses them. It is as if we met the young Sériziats after a passage of years and a happy transition into middle age.

When Napoleon fell, David was exiled. He finished his life in Brussels, painting away at whatever assignments it pleased him to set himself, venerated by followers of the tradition he had established, the grand old man of French painting. In his youth, still competing for the *Prix de Rome,* he had painted a picture of *Mars Vanquished by Minerva* [19]—the forces of violence and confusion conquered by the intellect. It is a windy picture, full of the artificialities and mannerisms of eighteenth-century painting that David later annihilated with his classical style. His last work, completed in exile fifty-three years later, in 1824, the year before his death, is another version of the defeat of Mars [20]. In the early picture Venus floats near by in support of Minerva, but in the later one she replaces her. In *Mars Disarmed by Venus and the Graces* violence and confusion are conquered not by the intellect but by the heart. Cupid unbinds the sandals of the god of war, who relinquishes his sword and shield to the Graces. Venus places a wreath of blossoms on his head; a pair of doves bill and coo on his muscular thigh. The picture is a little cloying, a little overgraceful. It may be an old man's revery, but if it is, it may be also his apology for the fanatic severity of his earlier convictions.

Sculptors and Other Painters

Neo-classical sculpture has little place in a story of modern art, for sculpture found no David and followed a speciously classical formula of prettiness and high polish which, as we will see in a moment, also infected the second generation of neo-classical painters. For the record, however, the names of the Italian sculptor Antonio Canova (1757–1822), the Frenchman Antoine Denis Chaudet (1763–1810), and the pedantic

19. DAVID: *Mars Vanquished by Minerva,* 1771. 45 x 55". Louvre, Paris.

20. DAVID: *Mars Disarmed by Venus and the Graces,* 1824. 118 x 103". *Musée Royal des Beaux Arts,* Brussels.

21. CHINARD: *Madame Récamier*, 1802–05. Marble, life size. *Musée des Beaux Arts*, Lyon.

22. J. B. REGNAULT: *Three Graces*, Salon of 1799. 78¾ x 60¼", octagonal. Louvre, Paris.

Dane, Bertel Thorwaldsen (1770–1844), must be mentioned. Some of the most rewarding bits of neo-classical sculpture are found spotted among the works of more obscure men. An example [21] is a bust of Madame Récamier (who never tired of commissioning images of herself) by Joseph Chinard (1756–1813), where sensitive realism brings unusual life to classically derived forms of the kind that were worked to death in the majority of cases.

Among painters, David's contemporary rival was a man seldom thought of today, Jean-Baptiste Regnault (1745–1829), who won the *Prix de Rome* in 1776 two years after David. Unlike David, who was suspicious of antiquity before the "cataracts were removed from his eyes," Regnault was dedicated to classicism from the beginning, but only in its superficial aspect as a store-house of graceful forms. He remained a painter of the eighteenth-century court with all its caprice, seductive posturings, and artifice. In his *Three Graces* [22], as a single example, he borrows an arrangement directly from a popular and often-repeated piece of classical sculpture, but the luscious girls he paints are classical in pose only; otherwise they remain the little courtesans and coquettes popularized by the eighteenth-century court painter Boucher.

As early as 1808 David was saying, "The direction I have set for the fine arts is too severe to please for very long in France." This was true, and had already become apparent before David became aware of it. We have just seen that even in his own work he did not maintain the severity of his earliest successes. The second generation of classicists paid brush-service to the

23. GÉRARD: *Psyche Receiving the First Kiss from Cupid*, 1798. 42½ x 52″. Louvre, Paris.

24. GUÉRIN: *Aurora and Cephalus*, 1810. 99¼ x 72″. Louvre, Paris.

master, imitating his technical polish without understanding the philosophical intention behind it. Their spirit is closer to Regnault's. This was true even of David's favorite pupil, François Gérard (1770–1837). At sixteen Gérard was studying in David's studio, and David remained his sponsor from then on. For a while he gave up painting when David succeeded in getting him named a member of the Revolutionary Tribunal; it is difficult to think of Gérard in this capacity after acquaintance with his sugary *Psyche Receiving the First Kiss from Cupid* [23] or for that matter any of his other pictures. It is customary to deny virtues of any kind to Gérard, as if his art were entirely detestable, and it is true that in comparison with David's strength Gérard's affectations are appalling. But if the standard of judgment is lowered to that of the fashionable exercise, which is Gérard's proper level, he doesn't come off too badly. Some of his portraits are charming.

Gérard's reputation during his own time was so inflated that critics ever since seem to have been trying to cut him down to size. He had a series of brilliant Salon successes, of which *Psyche Receiving the First Kiss from Cupid* was the climax. He painted Napoleon's family and leading dignitaries. After Napoleon fell and David was exiled, Gérard continued his dazzling career. The statesman Talleyrand presented him to Louis XVIII, the restored Bourbon, and he became the favorite painter of the court and the world surrounding it. In 1819 he was created a baron. His father, a Frenchman, and his mother, an Italian, had been servants before the Revolution.

25. GUÉRIN: *Phaedra and Hippolytus*, 1802. 101¼ x 139¾". Louvre, Paris.

Whatever his shortcomings as a philosophical moralist or an intellectual classicist, Gérard is a tower of strength in comparison with his immediate contemporary Pierre-Narcisse Guérin (1774–1833), a pupil not of David's but of Regnault's. Another *Prix de Rome* winner, Guérin made an exaggerated success in the Salon of 1799. The Royalist party interpreted his picture of *Marcus Sextus Returned from Exile* as a symbol of the return to France of the emigrés who had left during the Revolution, a stroke of luck. Among biographies of successful men, Guérin's is refreshing, because he was a lazy student who had not been interested in becoming a painter in the first place. Whether he ever became much of one is open to question, but everything fell into his lap, including finally the directorship of the Academy's school in Rome. Two of his paintings, *Aurora and Cephalus* [24] imitating Regnault's sensuous prettiness and *Phaedra and Hippolytus* [25] imitating David's

spareness and precision, show how well he learned to go through the classical motions and how little connection he had with the classical spirit in either direction. *Aurora and Cephalus* is incredible in its candified suggestiveness; *Phaedra and Hippolytus* is not so much a painting as it is a scene from a drama performed by some of the most incompetent actors ever to have become involved in a classical tragedy. Yet from Guérin's studio came two of the most important painters of the century, Géricault and Delacroix, with whom the next chapter of this book is concerned, as well as many competent painters of less importance who are secure enough in their small niches.

Two other students of David's must be mentioned parenthetically: Étienne-Jean Delécluze (1781–1863), because his name frequently appears as the defender of classicism when it came under attack—he stopped painting early, after a good start, to devote himself to writing—and Jean August Dominique Ingres, because he is

26. Prud'hon: *Justice and Divine Vengeance Pursuing Crime*, 1808. 95¾ x 115″. Louvre.

one of the greatest of all French painters. Ingres quarreled with David after a close early association; he will be given a chapter in this book later on.

Finally, one man, Pierre Paul Prud'hon (1758–1823), in nineteenth-century classicism is that anomaly which turns up in every school: the painter of talent and originality who was accepted by the school yet seems to bear no relationship to it. While the other classicists were sharpening their lines to razor-edge precision and polishing their forms to tinny brilliance, Prud'hon developed a style based on soft, yielding volumes emerging from and melting into smoky shadows, a style derived from Leonardo da Vinci and, even more, from Correggio, although these late fifteenth- and early sixteenth-century Italians were not much in classical favor. Prud'hon was an enthusiastic user of the new bitumen pigments, which gave wonderful velvety depths to shadows. As it turned out, these

pigments blistered, cracked, darkened, and peeled with age, so most of Prud'hon's canvases are in ruinous condition. His best-known painting, *Justice and Divine Vengeance Pursuing Crime* [26], is a ghost of itself, but still suggests the moody poetry, a little forced sometimes, that marked Prud'hon at his best. Slightly younger than David, but within his generation, Prud'hon was befriended by David during a difficult, unsavory, and emotionally disturbed life.

Prud'hon's drawings are often more satisfying than his paintings. As an example, a nude study in black and white chalk on gray-blue paper [27] combines sound formal description with the effect of soft, spreading illumination he cultivated. Perhaps his paintings had more of this quality before they deteriorated; or perhaps the drawing is more successful than the paintings ever were simply because Prud'hon's talent was not strong enough to encompass more ambitious conceptions.

27. PRUD'HON: *Nude,* date unknown. 15 x 13″. Collection Henry P. McIlhenny, Philadelphia.

The Break with Classicism

To call these men minor classicists reduces the list of major ones to a single name, David, always excepting Ingres, who was disinherited. And whatever their differences, all these men share one similarity that cuts them off from David: they all hint at connections with lyricism or personal emotionalism. This spirit was in the air. More than David's disciplined classicism, it was the spirit of the new century. It was romanticism. It was a force too strong to be held in check by the classically minded Academy, and it breaks through openly in the painting of two nominally classical artists, Girodet and Gros, whom it is now time to consider.

CHAPTER 2

Romanticism

The Romantic Spirit

David declared that "Art should have no other guide than the torch of Reason," but this dictum is opposed by a sentiment held dear by the French: "The heart has its reasons which Reason does not know." The romantic movement was a revolt of the heart against Reason, of emotion against intellect, of the mysterious against the rational, of the individual against formula—in short, of the senses and the imagination against everything else.

No art of much consequence is created without some fusion of emotional and intellectual values, and this truth the romantic artists did not deny. But they trusted their hearts before their heads, put their intellect at the service of their instincts. If a conflict between emotional and intellectual values forced them to a choice, they dropped the torch of Reason to follow their unreasonable impulse, even when they were not certain where it might lead them. They would abandon moderation for excess, when necessary, accept confusion rather than run the risk of sacrificing spontaneity to lucidity, were willing to be utterly illogical if within their hearts they felt that they might stifle emotional truth by subjecting it to analysis. The classicists had spoken rationally of "Beauty, sublime and severe, which can be defined only by theory and understood only by Reason."* But the romantics worshiped a beauty sublime and passionate, which could not be defined and could be appreciated only by the heart.

* Quatremère de Quincy.

For all these reasons, romanticism out of control was often turgid, bizarre, formless, hysterical—just as classicism misunderstood had grown sterile, repetitious, and frigid. Classicists and romantics accused one another of these faults in the conflict that put them at one another's throats shortly after David's death, in a struggle that took surface form as a romantic rebellion against the platitude and monotony and hampering restrictions of the classical dogma as observed by the second-rate painters in control of the Academy. But romanticism went deeper than professional antagonisms and theories of art. It was a way of life, a way of life demanding spiritual nourishment of a special kind that classicism did not offer.

Classicism assumes the existence of a perfect order, hidden but discoverable beneath the chaos of human experience. But the assumption is not often justified by the world around us, and certainly was not justified by the succession of events in France for several decades after 1789—the tumult of the Revolution, the hysteria of the Terror, the bloody grandeur of Napoleon's triumphs, the shattering disillusion after his fall, and all the subsequent corruption and dissension. Yet classical artists continued to put a premium on balance, precision, and rule in a world that was lopsided, confused, and unpredictable. The romantics would have none of their outworn formulas.

David's art had been an expression of eighteenth-century philosophy that deified Reason, but the century had also produced a philosopher who gave the romantics a different point of departure. He was Jean Jacques Rousseau (1712-1778), who preached a return to nature, the essential goodness of man, the rights of the individual. It is only a step from Rousseau's idea that man is naturally noble to the idea that his untrammeled emotions, his instincts "in the raw," are merely sterilized, not refined, by the classical process of intellectualizing. The romantics took this step. The classical artists and philosophers had stood aside from mankind's experience to see it in breadth and to create a man-made harmony from its confusions. The romantics refused to stand aside; they plunged into the midst of experience to savor its contradictions, and when the world was too much for them, when their battered souls demanded surcease, they found it not in the contemplation of synthetic order but in imagined worlds of curious and exotic invention. Like the classicists, the romantics haunted Rome, but for different reasons. To the romantic eye, the ruins of the ancient world were not reminders of Reason. They were reminders of man's mortality. Choked by vines and grasses among the crumbling stones, the broken monuments of antiquity evoked lost battles, dead loves, and mysteries. They were settings for melancholy revery, for trysts, for episodes of sweetness or of violence. For the romantic, even the classical world was fodder for emotional yearnings.

Romantic Classicism: "Atala"

In painting, the romantic spirit appeared first in classical disguise. It is hinted at in the sugar-syrup sentiment of some of David's followers, as we have already seen, and is strong in the work of Anne-Louis Girodet-Trioson (1767–1824). Girodet was a student of David's as well as a *Prix de Rome* winner (in 1789, with Gérard second). He was busy with *The Entombment of Atala* [28] while David was putting the finishing touches on *Le Sacre*. Technically *The Entombment of Atala* is a fine classical showpiece. But conceptually it belongs to the opposing camp.

This camp had hardly begun to gather its forces. The first indications of what was about to happen were literary ones, and *The Entombment of Atala* was the result of one of them. In 1801 a young aristocrat, adventurer, and romantic spirit named René de Chateaubriand published a brief novel, *Atala*, a curious compound of the fantastic, the irrational, the beautiful, and the absurd, except that in romantic conception nothing is absurd simply because it appeals to the heart at the expense of all logic. *Atala* was a great success; it was sensational on several scores. The scene was laid in the mysterious and fascinating American wilderness; the characters were

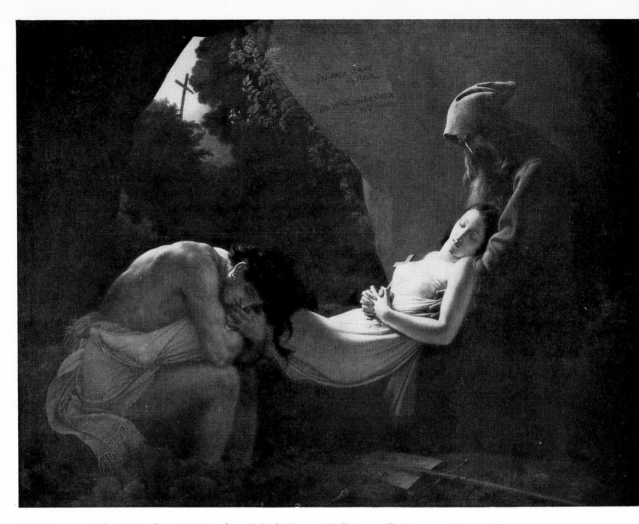

28. GIRODET: *The Entombment of Atala*, 1808. 82¾ x 105″. Louvre, Paris.

American Indians (Atala, the heroine, was a half-breed girl); and the plot had a strong, if artificial, flavoring of religious sentiment. (Christianity had become fashionable with Napoleon's re-establishment of the Church after the Revolution.)

Girodet's picture was painted seven years after the appearance of the novel and illustrates its final episode. The maiden Atala has died rather than yield her virginity in marriage to her lover, in observance of a vow made not by Atala but by her mother many years before. (This is only a minor complexity in a plot that would sound ludicrous in summary.) The other characters in the picture are her lover

Choctas and a priest attached to a never-never mission in the Florida jungles. The several romantic elements here had better be examined one at a time:

First, the story of Atala is romantic because it is preoccupied with personal emotionalism. The problems faced by the Horatii, by Socrates, by Brutus, and by the Sabines may have involved personal distress, but this was incidental to the importance of a general social moral ideal. The reverse is true in Atala's case. Although she has sacrificed herself, it is not for the State or a political theory. Her difficulties were entirely personal and hence puny by Davidian standards.

29. GIRODET: *Ossian Receiving the Generals of Napoleon*, 1802. 75½ x 71½″. Malmaison.

30. GIRODET: Preliminary study for Figure 29. 13 x 11¼″. Louvre.

Second, the picture violates the ideal of reserve nominally demanded by classicism. Everything in it seeks to stir the observer's emotions—the exaggerated light dramatizing a moody setting, the pathetic beauty of the dead girl, the anguish of her lover.

The Christian element, being nonrational, is unclassical; and finally, the Atala story is romantic in its exoticism. A yearning for the far away and the long ago, for the high colors and fantastic peoples and curiosities of the Orient or the wilderness or of any place offering escape into the vivid and the mysterious—this yearning was a trait of the romantics in their search for release, stimulation, and fulfillment.

These romantic heresies announce themselves rather hesitantly in Girodet's picture, however, and are all but concealed beneath its classical veneer. Atala might be a beautiful Greek maiden, and her gauzy robe is inexplicable in any but classical terms. The nudity of her mourning lover is the idealized nudity of classical sculpture, not the rough nudity of a savage; Choctas might be a gladiator. And technically the painting is tight and smooth enough to satisfy any classical pedant. The dramatic light and shade is something of a departure from standard procedure, but otherwise Girodet hints at none of the technical innovations that in full-blown romantic painting were to shock the Academy more than the romantic spirit did.

The traditional recognition of *The Entombment of Atala* as a tentative romantic expression has obscured the importance of an earlier painting by Girodet, an extremely curious hybrid which, with a slightly different history, might have become the manifesto of romantic painting. *Ossian Receiving the Generals of Napoleon* [29] is a fantastic and complicated allegory celebrating the Continental Peace of 1801; it shows the ghosts of Napoleon's generals being received into a light-shot otherworld by the ghost of Ossian, a Gaelic bard of the third century. This extraordinary juxtaposition of characters is an offshoot of an audacious literary forgery. In 1760–1763 the Scotch writer James Macpherson published some grandiose and somber poems of his own invention, presenting them as translations of Ossian. The poems were received with enthusiasm, and Ossianism reached the proportions of a cult in France, an early indication that the romantic yearning for the exotic and the grandiloquent was already stirring. Girodet's Napoleonic allegory forced current events into parallel with Macpherson's forged Gaelic legends—an obvious violation of classical doctrine, which demanded parallels with ancient Rome or Greece. The picture further violates every classical regulation in its swirling, visionary composition, especially as Girodet first conceived it in a preliminary study [30]. In the final version he compromised to some extent, polishing his romantic fantasy into superficial accord with classical disciplines as far as the individual forms are concerned. Yet even this compromise is interesting as a final contradiction, between reason and fantasy, in a conception paradoxical from the beginning. Fantastical invention seems to have been natural to Girodet's talent, but *Ossian Receiving the Generals of Napoleon* was badly received at the Salon, and Girodet never attempted anything like it again. What could have been a romantic manifesto ended as the most curiously isolated and artificial concoction of the neo-classical school.

Napoleonic Romanticism: Gros

In its precision and balance, *The Entombment of Atala* implies that life is harmonious and orderly even when mildly compromised with sentiment. True romanticism could not allow such a compromise, and Napoleonic France produced a generation unwilling to accept it, a generation accustomed to violence, thirsty for strong experiences, goaded by an acute awareness of the transience of life. Anguish this generation could understand, and exaltation and despair, but not serenity nor repose. To the young officers back from the Napoleonic battlefields, the classical tragedies in the Parisian theaters and the classical paintings in the Salons seemed, somehow, not so stirring as they had remembered.

31. GROS: *Colonel Fournier-Sarlovèze*, 1812. 96¾ x 68″. Louvre.

Much more than in the tepid, graceful *Entombment of Atala*, the new ferment is at work in the painting of Antoine Jean Gros (1771–1835), a member of Napoleon's staff and a pupil of David's, by temperament a romantic of an extreme type—melancholy; brooding; impressed with the prescience of death, the suffering of man in the world, and the tragedy that not even greatness (as exemplified for Gros in Napoleon, whom he idolized) is immune to error, confusion, and malevolence. Romantic sensibility could find exaltation in suffering; melancholy was often cultivated as a pose; the voluptuousness of spiritual torment became one of the romantic pleas-

32. GROS: *Christine Boyer*, c. 1800. 84¼ x 52″. Louvre, Paris.

committed suicide in three feet of water, at the age of sixty-four. It may seem absurd to suggest that his inability to reconcile the classical ideal he yearned to believe in with the romantic one he could not help believing in was a contributing factor to his suicide. But it seems absurd only because it is difficult to imagine today the furore of the romantic–classic conflict at a time when the arts were so much a part of national life. In a France still trying to come to balance after the Revolution and the Napoleonic disaster, the exhibition of a picture or the publication of a work of fiction or the staging of a play could become a national issue.

In Italy, where his Napoleonic service took him, Gros saw works of Michelangelo, Rubens, and Van Dyck. The first two especially were the antithesis of the neo-classical ideal in their swirling movement, emotional intensity, twisting forms and, in the case of Rubens, the opulent color applied with dash and freedom. These were the men with whom the repressed romantic Gros had a natural temperamental affinity, and in spite of everything he could do to maintain his allegiance to the dogmas of classicism, their influence kept breaking through. Gros was a fine painter with a superb feeling for dramatic composition, a painterly painter with a natural painter's love for the manipulation of pigment, which he sought to repress in accord with David's dictum, "pas d'emportement du pinceau." But his brush very nearly carried him away—by Davidian standards—in some passages of his portrait of *Colonel Fournier-Sarlovèze* [31]. The romantic pose— hand on hip; head thrown back while he scans the distance; sword drawn from scabbard as he stands debonair, dashing, confident, handsome, and elegant against the dramatic background—cries aloud for equally dramatic brushwork. In the lining of the cape, the crumpled papers tossed on the ground, and especially the ornamentation of gold braid and tassels, Gros yields to temptation; the paint is thick and rich and freely applied in character with the subject's romantic flair.

The portrait of *Christine Boyer* [32] is an even greater departure from classicism, because its romantic mood is more arbi-

ures, especially when this torment could be displayed in attitudes becoming to the tormented.

But the suffering could be real, and with Gros it was. Five years after the date generally accepted as the victory year of romanticism, 1830 (when Victor Hugo's romantic drama, *Hernani*, was tempestuously presented in declared opposition to the standards of the classical theater), Gros

33. GROS: *Napoleon Visiting the Pesthouse at Jaffa*, 1804. 209 x 283". Louvre, Paris. Detail on opposite page.

trarily selected and the means of creating it are more artificial. To paint a general's portrait reflecting the color and excitement of battle is only to capitalize upon circumstantial material. But the *Christine Boyer* is deliberately romanticized. A lovely woman in elegant indoor attire is moodily and inexplicably posed by the side of a stream in a shady woods. Her crimson shawl falls on a mossy rock; a waterfall behind her tumbles into a rocky bed; the stream flows toward us through the darkening woods from a little cave of light in the distance. The trees are dense and dark along the banks and behind the beautiful quiet face. This face is turned slightly away from us to gaze upon a single rose floating on the current (at the extreme lower right corner of the picture), which

in a moment will be carried beyond our vision, and beyond hers.

The picture's exceptional quality is a poetic mood created by romantic emphasis on details like these to stir our sensibilities. Romanticism is first of all a state of sensibility; the romantic temperament feels an obligation to develop sensibilities to their utmost rather than to discipline them. The braggadocio and display of the *Fournier-Sarlovèze* portrait are one manifestation of these ideas; the feminine languor and sentimental melancholy of *Christine Boyer* are another.

But these are portraits, where a painter is less vulnerable to rule and regulation than he is in official pictures. In official subjects intended for public display the contradiction between Gros's temperament

34. GROS: Detail from Figure 33.

35. REMBRANDT: *Christ Healing the Sick, c.* 1649. Etching, 10⅞ x 15⅜". National Gallery, Washington, Rosenwald Collection.

and the classical style is more apparent and his struggle more painful. In 1804 he was commissioned to commemorate an incident when Napoleon, during his Near Eastern campaign of 1798–1799, visited the pesthouse in Jaffa where members of his troops were dying of the plague [33]. Actually the pesthouse was an ordinary hospital, but in the interest of dramatization Gros shifted the scene to a mosque. In doing so he reversed the approach used by David in, for instance, his *Marat:* instead of eliminating details to reduce the episode to its essentials, as David had done, and then reducing those essentials to an ultimate purity and simplicity almost abstract, Gros romantically added details and then used every possible means to increase their emotional impact. Colors are heightened, intensified, and contrasted. Whole passages are thrown into obscurity while others are pulled into strong light, reviving and going beyond David's theatrical lapse in his *Brutus* with its shadowed foreground figure. Hardly a detail has not been romanticized, but at the same time the picture clings to a token observance of the official tradition. For all their Orientalism, the arches of the mosque arranged across the background suggest the architectural flats of *The Horatii.* The nude figure lying face down in the foreground tearing at itself in agony may be romantic in its violence, but it is also a meticulous anatomical study in David's studio tradition. But the romantic focus of the picture is the nude bearded man who, dying, turns his head worshipfully toward the General [34]. The flexibility and the individualization of this figure make it the reverse of the conventionally proportioned, idealized, sculpturally modeled Davidian figure. And Gros's emotional conception of the subject, where Napoleon appears as a sort of Christ, touching the plague sores as if his bare hands would heal them miraculously, relates *Napoleon Visiting the Pesthouse at Jaffa* less closely to David than to a great romantic etching of the seventeenth century, Rembrandt's "Hundred Guilder Print," *Christ Healing the Sick* [35].

With the *Pesthouse* Gros came as close as he was ever to come to realizing his

36. GROS: *Hercules and Diomede,* Salon of 1835. 167½ x 127¼". *Musée des Beaux Arts,* Toulouse.

potential as a romantic painter on the grand scale. (His *Battle of Eylau* is a second, but not a very close second.) After the fall of Napoleon, he attempted to find in idolization of the restored Bourbons the same spiritual support he had found in idolizing Napoleon I, but if his painting from that time on is any indication of his emotional life, this life was remarkably sterile. By 1820 the romantic movement was flourishing, but Gros, still obdurate, tried to go back to the sources of the classical style in order to recultivate it in noble purity. The experiment was a debilitating one. His work became mannered instead of noble, empty instead of pure, and his last picture, *Hercules and Diomede* [36], was laughed at in the Salon of 1835, the year of his suicide.

The romantic banner Gros might have carried had been picked up in the meanwhile by the young Théodore Géricault (1791–1824), and upon Géricault's early death at thirty-three, had passed to Eugène Delacroix (1798–1863), an even younger painter whose work Gros had first admired and then, with his typical recoil from his spontaneous sympathies, disparaged.

The Romantic Declaration: *Géricault and the "Raft of the Medusa"*

On the 2d of July, 1816, the French frigate *Medusa* was wrecked in a storm off the west coast of Africa. When it became obvious that the vessel was lost, a raft was improvised from parts of it as it sank. Onto this makeshift were crowded 149 passengers and members of the crew. By the time they were sighted, only fifteen men had survived thirst, madness, and cannibalism. Géricault's picture of this horror [37] became for romanticism what *The Oath of the Horatii* had been for classicism a generation earlier, a public declaration of new principles and a standard around which a new school rallied in revolt.

Like David's earliest successes, the *Raft of the Medusa* attracted general attention because of its connection with exciting current events. Unlike David's, Géricault's picture actually represented the contemporary event in a contemporary way instead of allegorizing or symbolizing it in images of the past. The classicists fumed that the picture was vulgar and sensational, but this did not disturb a vulgar public interested in sensationalism. Nor was the public much impressed by the academic objection that here ordinary seamen were represented with the seriousness and on the grand scale appropriate only to the gods, heroes, and events of the ancient world. The *Medusa* had sunk in circumstances that were seized upon by the liberal party to attack the corruption of the administration (officers towing the raft from a lifeboat were accused of having cut it loose and left it adrift).

Géricault exhibited the picture in the Salon of 1819 (the official catalogue naïvely listed it only as *A Shipwreck,* to no one's confusion), and it was such an attraction that thereafter he traveled with it to England and made a considerable sum in gate receipts. The public that flocked to see the *Raft of the Medusa* came to see a sideshow novelty as much as it came to see a work of art. Certainly not one person in a hundred came to see a romantic manifesto, but this backdoor introduction of

37. GÉRICAULT: *Raft of the Medusa*, 1818. 193 x 282″. Louvre, Paris.

large numbers of people to romantic painting was valuable to the movement, whether or not people were conscious of the picture's revolutionary character or its merits.

These merits were considerable, but their revolutionary character was only relative. To abandon David for new gods, Rubens and Michelangelo; to use color as an emotive element instead of as a decorative tint applied to sculpturesque forms; to subject the composition of a picture to its expressive character rather than to force expression into a standard composition—all this was counterrevolution against the Davidian revolution that had congealed into a formula, but none of it was innovational by historical precedent.

The composition of the *Raft of the Medusa* skips backward more than a cen-

tury to recall the pictorial arrangements of seventeenth-century Italian painters, for example, Caravaggio, who made a similar revolution against the classical compositions of his own time. The survivors are shown in every attitude of anguish and despair. Sighting the rescue ship in the far distance, they have raised one of their number aloft on their shoulders.* He waves a shirt in a pitiable effort to attract attention. Straining, gesticulating, swooning, the *Medusa's* survivors are intertwined in a turbulent mass of forms recalling the cascades of damned souls in Last Judgments by Michelangelo and Rubens. The

---

* This particular survivor is a Negro; his presence is justified by historical fact, but his introduction into Géricault's picture is often pointed out as evidence of the romantic interest in exotic types.

38. Géricault: Detail from *Raft of the Medusa*, Figure 37.

forms rush upward across the canvas from left to right, culminating off balance in a jagged peak like a wave about to break and topple. Such grouping is obviously more expressive of movement and excitement and confusion than David's neat seesaw in *The Sabines*, frozen forever into the classical demand for symmetrical balance—although *The Sabines* is as much a subject of movement and excitement and confusion as is the *Raft*. Géricault's departure from seesaw balance seemed outrageous to the academicians, although he quite adequately brought his composition into equilibrium, countering the strong upward left-to-right movement by reversing it in the lines of the mast and ropes, lines that are continued and echoed in various of the figures on the raft itself.

What means does Géricault use to convey emotions of pity, terror, and horror? These emotions are not merely the result of the subject. Where David would have "purified," Géricault has intensified [38]. Irregular broken forms are more suggestive of excitement than smooth, even ones. Hence Géricault exaggerates all the natural irregularities, the hollows and protrusions, of heads and bodies that David would have smoothed out in submission to a preconceived ideal. Above all, Géricault dramatizes his forms by revealing them at maximum intensity in brilliant light and dense shadow. And where David's color—rather flat, very ornamental, "tasteful"—is simply color, the turgid darks and ominous greens

39. GÉRICAULT: After Death (study), *c.* 1818. 17¾ x 22″. Art Institute of Chicago, Munger Collection (McKay Fund).

of the *Raft of the Medusa* are correlated to its subject. The picture is not a masterpiece of color, and it has darkened so much that we cannot be certain of its original scheme, but the conception of color as an expressive element is unquestionably present.

For his models David used the best-muscled and most perfectly proportioned human beings available to the studio, made precise imitative studies from them, and then modified his studies to bring them into correspondence with his recipe for the ideal type. Géricault abandons this idea that beauty is synonymous with perfection. A romantic, he finds beauty even in ugliness if ugliness reveals a state of soul. Instead of the athletes who posed for David, Géricault sought out the survivors of the *Medusa* and made sketches of them. One survivor was the ship's carpenter; he constructed for the artist a model of the raft.

But all this was only documentation of literal fact. Valuable as it was, it did not necessarily correspond with expressive truth. So Géricault visited hospitals and sketched men as they were dying. He sketched in morgues [39] and madhouses. According to one story, he kept corpses in his room to make studies from them—until the neighbors complained.

For all its merits the *Raft of the Medusa* has some conspicuous disharmonies. The old man with his head supported on his fist [38] near the left edge of the raft is altogether out of key; he suggests a classical philosopher strayed from David's studio into this improbable situation. The body of the nude youth he partially supports, and that of the one to the lower right, head trailing in the water, are magnificent studies in themselves and give the impression of being the parts of the picture that most interested the painter, but they are a little overconspicuous, becoming demonstration pieces. The whole picture, for that matter, may be only a first-rate studio exercise, admirable for the originality and courage of the devices it employs. But this is picking flaws in the work of a very young man whose achievement was to crystallize a new direction for painting. It is difficult to remember that Géricault was a student of Guérin, that candy-box classicist.

Géricault's reputation as a painter could rest on the *Raft of the Medusa* alone, and for that matter it very nearly does. The *Raft* was the only large or complicated composition he ever completed, although he left numerous sketches and some small versions for a similarly ambitious project, *Riderless Races at Rome* [40], races in which riderless horses were goaded into frenzies. He is an uneven painter. Sometimes his pigment has a coarse and heavy-handed quality, and his drawing may be so careless that legs and arms dangle as if shrunken or unattached within trousers or sleeves. At other times his draughtsmanship is masterful, his painting as strong and sure as it is sensitive, as in a *Portrait of a Young Man* [41].

Subjects of cruelty and morbidity occur so frequently in Géricault's work that his detractors hint at unhealthy preoccupations. But an interest in acute sensitivities even to the point of abnormal states of mind was inherent in romantic emotionalism. For the greatest romantics, suffering and violence may be transmuted into expressions of the human spirit struggling for release; and in exploring the dark areas of life the romantic finds beauty in unexpected places. Rembrandt was a romantic in the seventeenth century when he used derelicts and outcasts as models for tragic kings; in faces eroded by suffering he found inner beauties more expressive than the beauty of conventionally handsome sets of features or classically idealized ones. If Géricault is asked to meet such a standard, then it is true that he often seems merely a fascinated observer of madness and physical anguish for their own sakes. But his accurate studies of the insane have a special significance, because they were made

40. Géricault: *Riderless Races at Rome*, 1817. 17 x 23″. Walters Art Gallery, Baltimore.

41. Géricault: *Portrait of a Young Man*, 1825. 23¼ x 18¾″. Fogg Art Museum, Cambridge, Mass., Grenville L. Winthrop Bequest.

42. DELACROIX: *Self-portrait*, 1837 or 1838. 25¼ x 20″. Louvre, Paris.

at a time when different kinds of insanity were first being recognized by a few doctors, among them Géricault's friend, Doctor Georget, for whom he did a series of paintings.

When Géricault died at thirty-three,* his friend Delacroix was twenty-five. In a lifetime of battle against pedantry, Delacroix was to bring romantic painting to fruition.

Delacroix

As a student and young painter Delacroix was closely attached to Géricault. Géricault was eight years older, wealthy, adventurous, fond of high living, and knowledgeable about the world—about several worlds, in fact. Bohemianism was a natural

---

* This was in 1824; David died the following year. Géricault, who had once had ambitions to be a jockey, died of complications following a fall from a horse.

by-product of the romantic premise that the artist's innate sensitivities are a gift so special that he is under a kind of moral obligation to develop them by indulging them to the fullest. Since these indulgences involve forays outside the bounds of the bourgeois conventions that dominated the nineteenth century, the early romantics confirmed the idea of the artist as a loose-living renegade from society—which still persists. Géricault was Delacroix's mentor as a youthful bohemian in Paris, although both men by birth were wealthy and of high social position.

But after his companion's death, Delacroix abandoned this experimental slumming for his natural habitat, the brilliant world where the upper bohemia of successful actors, writers, and painters overlapped the established order of social position and political intrigue. Here he was admired and sought after, but even while he was still a young man he began to withdraw into his work, seeing only the few people who continued to interest him as his own ideas began to crystallize. That the names of these people were great names (Chopin was his most intimate friend) was only coincidental.

Toward the end of his life Delacroix saw almost no one, remaining at work in his studio as a recluse, but still so glamorous a figure that when he did go out he was followed in the streets as a demigod by the young artists for whom he had become the symbol of revolution, independence, and integrity.

Nothing in Delacroix's life was so important to him as the theories he was developing through experiment and research. He never married, and although he had several liaisons and any number of what he described as "charming encounters," his grand passion was painting. But he was never one of those painters who could dash off a picture. He worked continually and hard; his total works are estimated at more than 12,000, although he was handicapped by various physical ailments, including a recurrent debilitating fever. The man Delacroix is well summed up in his own self-portrait [42] with its attraction, its suggestion of romantic fire, but in the end its

43. DELACROIX: *The Lion Hunt,* 1861. 30 x 38⅝″. Art Institute of Chicago, Potter Palmer Collection.

hauteur. He was handsome, febrile, yet somehow unapproachable. Above all he disdained the emotional profligacy and the lack of discipline thought of as typically romantic, which was why he resented classification with such other romantic rebels as the writer Hugo, the musician Berlioz, and, above all, the painter Boulanger, who was Hugo's choice as the official leader of the romantic school. As for Aurore Dupin, the woman who called herself George Sand and led her own life with the romantic lack of discipline of the heroines of her novels, Delacroix knew her long and intimately but referred to her commiseratingly as "Poor Aurore."

Delacroix: His "Classicism"

By the standard of swooning emotionalism and self-indulgence, Delacroix was not a romantic spirit at all. By any standard he was one of the most acutely, objectively analytical men who ever painted a picture. And to understand his art in such typical pictures as *The Lion Hunt* [43] and *The Abduction of Rebecca* [44], we must recognize certain qualities that seem contradictory to romanticism. Delacroix's romanticism is theoretical rather than felt, calculated rather than inborn. He regarded himself as a true classicist, as opposed to the false classicists who merely imitated

44. DELACROIX: *The Abduction of Rebecca*, 1846. 39½ x 32¼". Metropolitan Museum of Art, New York, Wolfe Fund.

classical precedents without understanding the classical spirit. True classicism is concerned with generalizing human experience into universal symbols. Venus is not a beautiful woman, but all beauty; Minerva is not a local bluestocking, but a symbol of the majesty and power of the intellect. The kings in classical tragedy are not certain men who had certain experiences as rulers of kingdoms, but symbols of mankind in its nobility and its frailty. Romanticism, on the other hand, is concerned with the individual and his search not so much for the meaning of life as for the meaning of his own individual life. But the art of Delacroix shows us that creative genius transcends the limits of a category. Categorized as romantic, his Arabs, lions, pashas, warriors, and all the rest do not end as specific individuals represented in one dramatic moment of their lives. They are images of the total emotional life of humanity. The poet and critic Baudelaire called Delacroix's work "a kind of remembrance of the greatness and native passion of the universal man."

Delacroix's effect of romantic vehemence was achieved painstakingly; he invented ways and means to achieve it; his turbulent forms in all their complexity are as carefully patterned as are David's static, stylized ones. The famous "drunken broom" with which the classicists accused him of painting was not drunken at all. The breadth, irregularity, and apparent spontaneity of his brush stroke was produced with as much care as any classical painter took in smoothing out his surface to an impeccable polish. The colors that appear to swarm across Delacroix's canvases, as if jostling and interrupting one another, are selected and juxtaposed by no chance but in accord with theories so highly developed that alongside them the classicist's use of color as a decorative accessory is elementary. Romanticism is emotional, but Delacroix's emotionalism is achieved intellectually. This paradox must be accepted if his work is to be understood.

Delacroix: Early Works and Scandals

Delacroix's career opened with an early success, *Dante and Vergil in Hell* [45] showing the poets crossing the Styx; it was exhibited in the Salon of 1822 when Delacroix was twenty-five years old. (Géricault had just died.) Géricault's true masters, Rubens and Michelangelo, had become Delacroix's also, and they inspired the agitated and tormented forms of the picture. The nude male in the water alongside the boat is especially Michelangelesque; he might be the Adam from the creation scene on the Sistine ceiling in a variation of pose. Delacroix's teacher Guérin was horrified by *Dante and Vergil* and advised him not to exhibit it, but Gros, who was a member of the Salon jury that year, admired it so much that he had it framed at his own expense. Delacroix could not afford a frame; he had lost the fortune he would have inherited from his parents, now dead, in a disastrous lawsuit with another family.

It was at this time that Adolphe Thiers, a shrewd statesman but a man of little taste in the arts, came to Delacroix's rescue with the "mysterious" official patronage that continued, with only occasional interruptions, throughout the artist's life. Although he was the putative son of the French minister to the Netherlands, a man well established in influential circles, Delacroix was prob-

45. DELACROIX: *Dante and Vergil in Hell*, 1821–22. 73½ x 94½". Louvre, Paris.

ably the actual son of a much more influential man, the statesman Talleyrand. Various coincidences support conclusions that could be drawn from his strong resemblance to Talleyrand, and nothing but the presence of an influential behind-the-scenes sponsor explains why Delacroix was virtually a ward of the State after his parents' deaths. His pictures were loathed and feared by Salon juries and vituperated by official critics, but again and again they appeared in the official exhibitions and were purchased by the government. Delacroix was awarded important commissions for murals in public buildings (the Palais Royal, the Palais Bourbon, the Luxembourg, and the Louvre among them) over the heads of the established hacks who would ordinarily have received these lucrative plums, as well as other semiofficial and private commissions where influence was usually more important than talent. Thus the government unwittingly acquired masterpiece after masterpiece and became, in effect, the medium for discrediting the classical hangers-on who were entrenched in its official schools. The dismay of the academicians can be imagined when Thiers manipulated the purchase of *Dante and Vergil* by the State. Delacroix was regarded as an irreverent upstart from this time forward.

46. DELACROIX: *Scenes of the Massacres of Scio*, 1824. 166 x 138½" Louvre, Paris.

47. DELACROIX: Detail from Figure 46 (extreme left of picture).

Two years later, in 1824, Delacroix came into greater prominence with his *Scenes of the Massacres of Scio* [46, 47], of which the Academy made a scandal. Even Gros, who had defended *Dante and Vergil*, reversed his opinion of Delacroix and called *Massacres of Scio* the massacre of painting.

There were routine objections to Delacroix's choice of a contemporary subject,*

* As an episode in the Greek-Turkish War, the population of the island of Scio, where 100,000 Greeks had lived, had just been reduced to 9,000 in one of the most terrible massacres in the history of human cruelty. *Scenes of the Massacres of Scio* was in part inspired by Delacroix's admiration of the arch-romantic spirit and romantic poet Lord Byron, whose chivalrous participation in the Greek war cost him his life at Missolonghi in the same year. Delacroix also painted a *Greece Expiring on the Ruins of Missolonghi* as a tribute to Byron and a lament for him as well as a memorial to the Greek insurrectionists.

but what really appalled Gros and the other academicians was Delacroix's use of color. *Massacres of Scio* had come to the jury as a fine example of sound, adequately conventional painting and had been accepted for exhibition. But in the interval between acceptance and the opening of the Salon, Delacroix repainted it. Painters were customarily allowed to retouch or varnish their work after acceptance, but it happened that Delacroix experienced one of the transforming revelations of his artistic life, and was impelled to transform *Massacres of Scio* as a result: he had seen a picture called *The Hay Wain* [313] sent to the Paris Salon that year by the English landscapist Constable.

Constable painted by juxtaposing spots of color rather than blending them. By French academic technique of the time, a passage changing from one tint to another would be meticulously smoothed out or "blended" (there were special brushes for this), but Constable applied his colors in strokes of graduated shades, so that the transition was made in a series of easily perceived jumps, juxtaposed rather than mushed together. The result was a greater freshness, vividness, and life to the color, as well as a sense of more immediate contact between painter and observer. The painter's presence is suggested when we can follow each stroke of his brush; whether we are aware of it or not, our participation in such a painting is greater than it is before a highly polished work where the technique is, so to speak, invisible. Delacroix once said that painting is a bridge between the thought of the painter and the thought of the observer, and Constable's bridge must have seemed to him a more direct and effective one than he had known before. In re-painting *Massacres of Scio* Delacroix began the experiments with color that were to occupy him for the rest of his life and were to be enlarged upon by several generations of painters into our own century.° He freed color from the restrictions David had put on it; he revived some of its uses as he observed them in the eighteenth-century painters David had rejected, and he added new ones of his own.

By Davidian formula color is, in effect, nothing more than a decorative dye applied to carefully drawn and modeled forms, as though each object had been completely modeled without color, as though it had been carved in white stone, and the color then washed over it as a photograph might be tinted. The color of each form—blue drapery, green leaf, gray wall—is held concisely within neat, unyielding contours. But with Delacroix the color explodes, shattering boundaries and unifying all forms with flecks and bits of pigment related to other areas. "Color is a merging of reflections," Delacroix said. An area of blue may be shot through with purples and greens and oranges; a passage of flesh (to which David would have given a smooth, uniform, pinkish tint) will be enriched with green in the shadow, blue in the highlights.

Obviously this aspect of painting is difficult to cope with in verbal description and black and white illustration. Even color illustration is not too much help with the reduction in size and loss of texture involved. But even in black and white it may be sensed that David's color exists only as an overlay. It may be bright and clear, but in Delacroix it is vivid and rich because variations are bound into variations of form; form and color enhance one another. A shift from one color to another as a form projects or recedes in painted space may either emphasize or minimize the projection or recession. Impossible as it is to demonstrate these simple points except in the presence of the paintings themselves, it is important nevertheless to remember that for Delacroix color *was* painting, it was the structure of painting as well as the basis of painting's expressive nature. All this will be more clear in retrospect as we see the painting of the century following Delacroix, because his color is the foundation of theories that build on one another in regular sequence, and are still developing.

Delacroix: His Orientalism

In 1827 Delacroix painted his largest and most ambitious demonstration picture, and the only one that was a failure with both classicists and romantics, *The Death of Sardanapalus*. The subject reflects the vogue for Orientalism that was a strong element in romantic painting and literature, offering as it did all the exotic color and savage passion denied by classical modera-

---

° *The Hay Wain* is a large picture, and loses pertinence as a technical example when reduced to the size of a page. But some of Constable's freshness and freedom as a manipulator of paint may be seen in other illustrations of his work [312, 314]. The question may be asked why Constable's picture was acceptable to the Salon jury if Delacroix's adoption of its technique was found so shocking. One answer is that *The Hay Wain* is a picturesque landscape and hence, by academic category, not a picture of first importance. A formal and pretentious subject had to observe the rules more closely. Also, *The Hay Wain* was painted by an Englishman. Frenchmen have never been able to take English painting very seriously. They find it charming but are unable to think of it as important, and in painting of little importance some eccentricity is not objectionable.

48. DELACROIX: Detail, figures about life size, from *The Death of Sardanapalus*, 1827 version. Louvre, Paris.

jects are spread around in opulent confusion. The confusion was objected to, also the "vulgarity," a favorite word with the critics, who were to continue to apply it over a period of some seventy-five years to the quality of life in any painting not classically stillborn. Oddly enough, if any shortcomings are apparent in *Sardanapalus* today, they do not lie in its confusion, which is calculated, but in the excess of this calculation, which reduces the vitality of the frenzied subject. *Sardanapalus* has passages of superb painting; the flesh of the central female figure [48], the jewels, the stuffs, are as rich as even Rubens could have made them. But the total effect, while gorgeous, is more gorgeous than passionate. Delacroix himself was dissatisfied, and seventeen years later, in 1844, he repeated the picture in much smaller dimensions [49]. In the years between the two versions he had brought his theories to maturity.

The remarkable thing about the late version is that while it was virtually seventeen years in the painting, it has all the effect of spontaneous emotional fervor. When Delacroix said, "All precautions have to be taken to make execution swift and decisive" in order not to lose "the extraordinary impression accompanying the conception" of a picture, he was denying the laborious methods of classicism. But he was denying as well, by the words *precautions* and *decisive*, the hit-or-miss improvisation by which an artist may try to capture the "extraordinary impression accompanying the conception" in the heat of the moment. Delacroix's sketches frequently have this quality of improvisation; there is a sketch in the Louvre for *Sardanapalus* that has it, but the sketch also has the formless, ambiguous passages that are inevitable at the same time. Delacroix's problem was the problem of the romantic creator in any of the arts—to give form to emotional experience without sacrificing its quality of immediacy.

In a subject of violent action the quality of immediacy cannot be retained within the seesaw balance of Davidian composition, as has already been pointed out in the *Raft of the Medusa*, where the composition was built on a strong diagonal movement. But

tion. But among the romantics only Victor Hugo liked *Sardanapalus*, which was at least consistent since, having shown little perception of Delacroix's virtues, he now found virtues in a painting where everyone else found defects.

The potentate Sardanapalus, preparing to immolate himself, is shown on his funeral pyre, which is concealed beneath cushions and a glorious rose-colored fabric, while slaves bring in his favorite wives, horses, and dogs and cut their throats in order that nothing Sardanapalus has enjoyed in life may be enjoyed by anyone else after his death. Jewels and great heaps of other ob-

49. DELACROIX: *The Death of Sardanapalus,* 1844 version. 29¾ x 37″. Collection
Henry P. McIlhenny, Philadelphia.

the upward rush of Géricault's shipwrecked
figures is still essentially an upward rush
across the surface of the picture. In *Sardanapalus* we are led *back into* "space" created by the painter, something like the
space of a large stage. The Sabines and the
Horatii enact their dramas on the shallow
area between footlights and curtain. In the
Raft of the Medusa the space is hardly
deeper, although theoretically the ocean
background stretches to the horizon. But in
The Death of Sardanapalus the curtain has
gone up and the stage is filled with figures
and trappings surging into its depths, backward and across to the climactic figure of
the dying potentate. It is fine theater, and
very romantic theater. It is also composition
into the picture depth on a diagonal. The
advantages of this kind of composition
should be apparent if the effect of turbulence in Delacroix's picture is contrasted
with the rigidity of David's. Each type of
composition, of course, achieves its own
end. By Delacroix's aesthetic, David's composition was obvious and limited. By David's, Delacroix's would have seemed over-
complicated, overdramatic. These contrasting uses of space—shallow and defined, or
deep and free—characterize, respectively,
neo-classical and romantic composition.

50. DELACROIX: Page from his Moroccan journal, April 11, 1832. Ink and watercolor. *Bibliothèque d'Art et d'Archéologie*, Paris.

in 1832 he made a trip to Morocco.* From the silvery light of Paris and the civilized emotional climate of that city with its pale and cultivated inhabitants, he was plunged into a world where he was surrounded by half-barbaric figures, golden skinned or black, robed, turbaned, or naked, moving among strange vegetation and strange architecture or against the even stranger blankness of desert sand and desert sky. Everything was revealed in a blazing light where colors were vivified and contrasts were exaggerated beyond anything Delacroix had imagined at second hand.

The first entries about this trip, in the journal where for years he had kept an orderly record of his activities and theories, are the fragmentary and disconnected scribblings of a man clutching at new images so exciting that he is in terror of being unable to absorb them:

". . . the sea a dark greenish blue like a fig, the hedges yellow at the top because of the bamboo, green at the base on account of the aloes . . . the sons of the caid. The oldest one, his dark blue burnous; caftan of a canary yellow . . . a Jewess, red skullcap, white drapery, black dress. Heads of Moors like those of Rubens, nostrils and lips rather coarse, bold eyes. Rusty cannon. Graves amid the aloes and the iris. The almond trees in flower. The Persian lilacs. The little white house in the shadow amidst the dark orange trees. The horse through the trees. The red veil. The beautiful eyes. Wax torches. Tumult."

Everywhere these notes are interspersed with sketches, quick, vivid, spotted with bright notes of watercolor [50]. Delacroix saw everything he had ever imagined, and more—fantastic banquets and entertain-

Between the two versions of *Sardanapalus* Delacroix absorbed the second determining experience of his life—second only to his discovery of color in *Massacres of Scio*. He had tried to develop his theories of color in various Oriental subjects, as offering the most appropriate raw material, but his Orientalism, as in *Sardanapalus*, was of a storybook kind, concocted from hearsay, legend, and the accumulated fantasies of other writers and painters. Then

* Delacroix was attached to a mission organized under a young aristocrat, the Count de Mornay. The year before, France had made its conquest of Algeria, and the sultan of Morocco was a touchy neighbor. De Mornay's mission was to conclude a treaty of good will. He had met Delacroix in the upper bohemia of the arts that they both frequented, and attached the artist to his mission at the urging of a sprightly creature named Mlle. Mars, a comédienne and an enthusiastic collector of scalps among the infatuated gallants and intellectuals of her day.

ments in the sultan's palace, local ceremonies among the people, weddings and funerals, and from a window in Tangiers the hysteria of a fanatic religious sect. Everywhere the world was strange, wild, and wonderful.

His notebooks and his recollections were his storehouse after his return. Other painters might have been content to use the exotic material for its inherent color and novelty. But Delacroix was not interested in painted travelogues. The value of the material to him was that he found through it, at last, his synthesis of human emotion and the intellectual devices for its interpretation; the picturesqueness of the material is incidental; the depth of the Moroccan experience is apparent not only in pictures directly connected with it, such as *The Lion Hunt* [43], but also in *The Abduction of Rebecca* [44], which is an incident from Scott's *Ivanhoe*, and the Biblical *Good Samaritan* [51], and in all Delacroix's other work where he realizes Baudelaire's "remembrance of the greatness and native passion of the universal man."

Delacroix: Recognition and Followers

French artists may revile the Academy and may be reviled by it, may abhor the practices of the men who control it, may oppose everything it stands for at the moment—but they continue to venerate it as an institution and as an abstract idea, a symbol of the prestige of the arts in the national life of their country. No matter what their experience of academic abuses, all Frenchmen eligible for election to the Institute of France* covet one of its chairs, and Dela-

* The Institute of France is composed of five Academies, as follows: (1) the French language, (2) literature, (3) social sciences and history, (4) mathematics and physical sciences, (5) fine arts. Each Academy is self-perpetuating; upon the death of a member a new one is elected for life from aspirants who have presented applications. Intrigue and favoritism are inevitable in the elections, and Academy membership has included some of the most trifling talents, but it has also included eventually most of the great ones who have lived long enough.

croix was no exception. He made eight applications, which were rejected, and a ninth which was accepted in 1857, six years before his death.

Even so, the official world continued to snub him on most occasions. In 1861 he completed a set of three murals in the Church of St. Sulpice, after twelve years of work filled with interruptions. The Superintendent of Fine Arts, who was the philistine Count de Nieuwerkerke, refused to look at them; the court and the world of official painting also stayed away from the opening exhibition. Such men as Théophile Gautier and Baudelaire came and admired the pictures tremendously, but whether they were admiring them as mural paintings or as a manifestation of Delacroix's perseverance and integrity in the solution of a difficult problem is a real question. Today, similarly, the St. Sulpice murals are likely to be most praised by those admirers of Delacroix who like to see, in his mural of *Jacob Wrestling with the Angel*, a symbol of the painter's struggle for the fulfillment of his admirable theories. The other subjects were *Heliodorus Driven from the Temple* and, on the ceiling vault, so small and so ill lit that it is seldom noticed, *St. Michael Killing the Dragon*. Compared with his great easel pictures, these are curiously static, dry, overstudied compositions.

Even while Delacroix was being snubbed, the romantic ideal had been vulgarized by his imitators in ways sufficiently emasculated to establish a pseudoromantic product as a standard Salon item. Thus on the coattails of second-raters he was finally accepted as the leader of a recognized school. In the important Salon of 1855, which will be described in some detail later in this book, a room was set aside for some forty of his paintings, amounting to a retrospective of his career. He was elected to the Institute two years later, and he exhibited in the Salon for the last time two years after that, in 1859, with eight pictures. The year of his death, 1863, coincides with the date of the *Salon des Refusés*, also to be treated in detail later, an event that divides the art of the nineteenth century with a boundary as sharp as the one established

51. DELACROIX: *The Good Samaritan*, 1850. 13¾ x 11″. Philadelphia Museum of Art. Anonymous loan.

52. DELAROCHE: *The Children of Edward*, 1830. 71 x 84″. Louvre, Paris.

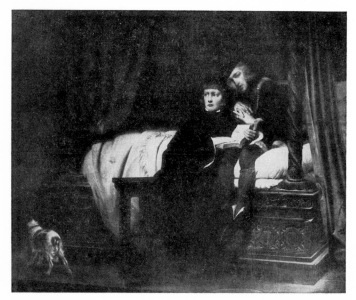

between the eighteenth and nineteenth centuries by the Revolution and David.

Like David among classical painters, Delacroix is unapproached by any of his romantic contemporaries. This is less surprising than in the case of David, since Delacroix did not teach. But he was imitated. His most superficial imitator was a tremendous success: while Delacroix struggled to achieve his synthesis of human emotions, Paul Delaroche (1797–1856) capitalized on the romantic sentiment of the period by plagiarizing whatever elements of Delacroix's art had become generally palatable. Delaroche was not a true romantic. He was an unimaginative illustrator of historical anecdotes possessed of romantic interest. Historical novels were in great vogue, and Delaroche offered their pictorial counterparts. His pictures are quite objective reproductions of models posed in medieval and Renaissance trappings against period backgrounds. The best known are *The Children of Edward* [52], showing the two little sons of Edward IV in the Tower awaiting execution, and *The Death of Queen Elizabeth*. Both pictures are still seen now and then, and until recently they were used as illustrations in every other schoolbook on English history and literature. Delaroche, only a few months older than Delacroix, was elected to the Institute on the strength of such tepid narratives. Upon Delaroche's death Delacroix, finally elected, assumed his imitator's chair, an irony that comes to mind first when Delaroche's name is mentioned nowadays, because it is the only circumstance lending any interest to his career. He was a student of Gros.

Some other mentionable French romantic painters are listed here, in order of birth:

Alexandre Gabriel Decamps (1803–1860), a respectable painter, was trained as a classicist but revolted early against the tradition. He is discussed later in connection with the Salon of 1855, where he shared honors with Delacroix.

Eugène Devéria (1805–1865), a pupil of Girodet, for a while seemed on the point of major romantic achievement. After a great success in his Salon debut of 1827 with *The Birth of Henry IV* [53], he failed his promise and became a dry and unoriginal painter of history pictures, ending as a second-rate Delaroche. *The Birth of Henry IV* has recently been cleaned up and rehung in the Louvre. For such a huge painting, it is rather easy to pass by; perhaps the competition of *The Death of Sardanapalus* facing it on the opposite wall is too much. But upon examination it is seen to contain many passages of good solid craftsmanship. To find much more is difficult.

Prosper Georges Antoine Marilhat (1811–1847) first appeared in the Salon of 1831. Thereafter he traveled widely in Syria, Egypt, and Palestine, his special version of the Oriental vogue having to do with desert landscapes, caravans, and Oriental cities [54]. He painted with an agreeable illustrative honesty and a nice feeling for pigment.

Eugène Fromentin (1820–1876) was a painter and writer whose Orientalism was derived first from Marilhat, later from Delacroix. As a painter he had considerable facility, but as time goes on his pictures look more and more like attractive exercises in the manner of other men. His writing has retained the freshness that has begun to stale in his painting. Much of his criticism is unusually perceptive.

Alfred Dehodencq (1843–1882) had a satisfactory Salon career; his work is being revived today on a small scale.

Henri Regnault (1843–1871), as his dates show, was a long generation younger than Delacroix. In 1866, at which time Delacroix had been dead for three years, Regnault won the *Prix de Rome* with a classical subject. In Italy he painted his well-known *Automédon and the Horses of Achilles* [55], a stirring picture that might have struck Delacroix himself as promising in its romantic excitement, although it still smacks a bit of brilliant student work. With a first medal in the Salon, a brilliant colorist, intelligent and industrious, he seemed set not only to make a conventional success but, at the same time, to continue and build

53. DEVÉRIA: *The Birth of Henry IV*, 1827. 190 x 154″. Louvre.

54. MARILHAT: *Oriental Caravanserai*, date unknown. 10¾ x 17″. Philadelphia Museum of Art, John G. Johnson Collection.

55. H. REGNAULT: *Automédon and the Horses of Achilles*, 1868. 124 x 129½″. Museum of Fine Arts, Boston.

56. MICHEL: *The Old Chateau*, date unknown. 20½ x 27⅞″. Philadelphia Museum of Art, John G. Johnson Collection.

upon the art of Delacroix. But Regnault was killed at the age of twenty-eight in the Franco-Prussian War.

One other name should be remembered, this time a man who was even earlier than Géricault, Georges Michel (1783–1848). He is a rather isolated painter who is frequently grouped with Géricault among the first romantics. He painted picturesque squalor, bent trees, lonely ruined towers in dramatic silhouette against golden skies [56], referring to Rembrandt for some of his strong effects of chiaroscuro. As a forerunner of romanticism, Michel is still much respected in France but is almost forgotten elsewhere.

CHAPTER 3

Ingres

The Pedant

In 1824, the year of Delacroix's romantic blast with *Massacres of Scio*, the classical school was without a leader. David was not only a very old man but in exile; Gros was floundering and compromising. Both Gérard and Guérin were alive, but neither had the qualifications for leadership. But that year a self-exiled student of David's returned from Italy. He had been working on a large religious picture, *The Vow of Louis XIII* [63], a commission for the cathedral in his provincial home city of Montauban. He brought *The Vow of Louis XIII* with him for exhibition in the Salon, much concerned as to its reception, since he had been in and out of academic favor for a long time and had no idea whether he would be attacked again or received as the prodigal son. There had been a hint that he might be in the Academy's good graces; to his surprise he had been elected its corresponding member in Florence a few months earlier.

The Vow of Louis XIII was a success. The Salon that year centered around it and the scandalous *Massacres of Scio*. Jean August Dominique Ingres (1780–1867) became the new leader of classicism, and for the rest of their lives he and Delacroix were identified as opposing generals in the classic-romantic imbroglio. At times the conflict came down to personal terms—at least on Ingres's part. Eighteen years older than Delacroix, he was an old man before he ever offered his hand to his romantic adversary. Delacroix recognized Ingres's virtues; Ingres never conceded any to Delacroix, perhaps because in his heart he felt ill equipped for the struggle he had en-

57. INGRES: *The Envoys of Agamemnon, 1801, Prix de Rome. 43¼ x 61". École des Beaux Arts,* Paris. (Photo Giraudon.)

tered into and was jealous of the ease and flourish with which Delacroix seemed to lead his life. Ingres was a pedestrian personality, stubborn and plodding, while Delacroix was spectacular and aristocratic in contrast to Ingres's humble origin and bourgeois ambition. Delacroix painted brilliantly and theorized even more brilliantly. Ingres's pronouncements were stuffy. From all he wrote and said, it is possible to cull only here and there a phrase not embarrassing in obviousness, obtuseness, and pedantry. He was a poor talker.

But he was a great painter. His own art did not prove the validity of the dogmas he defended; it showed only that no dogma, not even one self-imposed, could stifle a creative spirit so powerful that it demanded expression on any terms. As the official leader of classical painting Ingres had to fight not only Delacroix but a second and even more formidable adversary—the romantic painter who existed within himself.

Unlike Gros, who recognized a similar conflict and subjugated his personal expression to classical doctrine, Ingres seems never to have realized where the problem lay. He was shocked and puzzled when classical painters found his work unclassical. He failed to see that romanticism goes deeper than the surface of strong light and shade, swirling action, broken color, and asymetrical composition, none of which he used. He also failed to see that classicism goes deeper than controlled outline, flat color, tight surface, and symmetrical balance, all of which he continued to use obediently. His attitude toward the Academy remained that of the brilliant student intent upon making good marks to win first prize, even when he was the Academy's leader and spokesman.

Ingres was a great painter in spite of himself. Just how this happened is best explained by examining a group of typical pictures in chronological order.

57

The Student

At seventeen Ingres came to Paris and entered David's studio. His grandfathers had been a tailor and a wig-maker; his father was a carver of sculptural ornaments. At fourteen the boy was playing the violin in an orchestra to make a little money.[*] Later he won prizes in drawing, and in Paris under David he continued to win them. He became David's favorite student—for a while. David painted his portrait, as affectionate, engaging, and informal a little picture as the great disciplinarian ever allowed himself to do. By 1800 Ingres was assisting David in important work. He painted, for instance, the classical standing lamp that is a conspicuous part of the portrait of *Madame Récamier* [14]. But about this time an unexplained but serious rift developed between Ingres and David. It was never mended.

Ingres had done well in preliminary competitions for the *Prix de Rome* and now, in 1801, he won it. The full subject of his competition picture was *The Envoys of Agamemnon, Sent to Achilles to Urge Him to Fight, Find Him in His Tent with Patroclus Singing of the Feats of Heroes* [57]. As an exercise in the design of male nudes, ranging from the too-muscular giant at the right to the too-lissome youths at the left,[†] the picture has all the artificiality, the precision, and the respect for recipe of a typical *Prix* winner. It also holds some prophecy of Ingres's future work, the germs of his originality. This originality began to appear during the next few years, to the distress of his sponsors.

The state of France's finances in 1801 was so precarious that, although Ingres had won the *Prix*, no money could be found to send him to Rome. In the five years before the money was available, the State gave him a studio and an allowance-in-disguise in the form of occasional commissions. Ingres also did a number of portraits on his own and exhibited in the Salon. But bizarre elements began to appear in his work—bizarre, that is, by the standard of conformity expected of a *Prix de Rome* man—and they culminated in his portrait of *Madame Rivière* [58], exhibited with several others in the Salon of 1806.

Madame Rivière is a masterpiece of linear design. Present everywhere, its pattern is most apparent in the folds of the gauzy scarf and the large shawl flowing through the lower half of the picture. Here sinuous, there suddenly straightening, here moving slowly, next breaking into swirls or ripples, the lines defining folds and hems have their own beauty as abstract rhythmic patterns more important than their function as description. For the first time Ingres was called "Gothic," an epithet that was to haunt him for life.

Gothic was a term of opprobrium in the classical vocabulary because it summarized the qualities antithetical to *classic*, and the classicists had never admitted the possibility of more than one standard of beauty. In late Gothic sculpture and painting, drapery was represented in exaggerated bunchings and knottings, the opposite of classical simplicity, in patterns of nervous intensity the opposite of classical repose. The intensity is not reflected in Ingres's particular and very personal use of line in the *Madame Rivière*, a graceful and seductive picture. It shares with Gothic art an interest in the edges and contours of bunched forms, but these are organized into a different, more flowing kind of pattern as a way of drawing form and composing a picture. Each line is a delight to follow individually, full of its own sensitivity, invention, and variety, yet no line exists independently. Each one mutually supports and is supported by every other one. The over-all pictorial structure is an integration of broad general movements within which the individual lines are intertwined. A major current flows in a long curve from the bottom of the picture along the hand and up the arm, then along the shoulders where it merges with a quieter, horizontal, stabilizing pattern running from one side of the frame to the other. Such "currents" may be picked up

---

[*] He continued to play the violin all his life, as a diversion and a solace; hence the phrase *"violon d'Ingres"* by which the French mean any cherished and sustaining hobby.

[†] —all identifiable according to the story in the *Iliad,* which Ingres studied carefully.

58. INGRES: *Madame Rivière*, Salon 1806. Oval 45⅝ x 35½". Louvre. (Photo Giraudon.)

anywhere in the picture; each one merges or divides along its course to flow into or serve as origin for others.

Consciously or not, Ingres violated the classical dogma of accurate or idealized proportion to create this rhythmic structure. It is true that if the lady should stand up, her arms hanging at her sides would be of grotesquely different lengths. The right one is elongated and the left one, resting on the pillow, is shortened. These distortions were dictated while the abstract pattern was being evolved from a series of natural forms. The long even curve of the right arm establishes the main direction of the linear currents eddying around it; the left one reverses these currents, checks them and brings us into quieter areas (the pillow and the bodice) that serve to relieve and accentuate the more active areas surrounding them. Except to a dogmatist the distortion would be neither noticeable nor disturbing. It is even less noticeable that the figure of Madame Rivière exists ambiguously from the waist down. The linear currents are so fascinating in themselves that it makes no difference that the disposition of the clothing describes only a token relationship between the forms of the body and the couch upon which they lie. But the academicians were outraged, especially because these heresies against academic convention were made by a young man to whom they had already awarded the *Prix de Rome*—for which funds had at last been found.

The Expatriate

With *Madame Rivière* and his other Salon pictures of 1806 labeled "Gothic," "bizarre," and "revolutionary," Ingres left for Rome hurt and confused. He was twenty-six years old; Girodet had not yet painted *The Entombment of Atala*, David was working on *Le Sacre*, Géricault was only fifteen, and Delacroix was a child of eight.

For the next fourteen years Ingres stayed in Rome, and then spent four years in Florence, with a brief excursion to Paris in between. He was thus an expatriate while romanticism announced itself tentatively in *Atala*, made its first sensation with the *Raft of the Medusa*, and found its great man with the exhibition of *Dante and Vergil* in 1822.

Ingres was more than content to stay away. He was as enchanted with Rome as he was disenchanted with Paris. Rather than return, he broke his engagement to a young woman named Anne Marie Julie Forestier, and after another abortive engagement to the daughter of a Danish archeologist he proposed by letter to Madeleine Chappell, a milliner several years older than he and a cousin of one of his

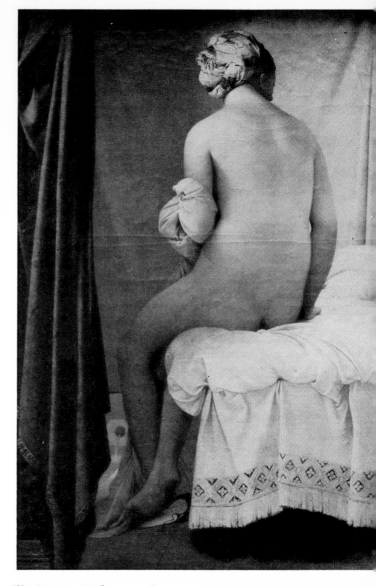

59. INGRES: *Bather of Valpinçon*, 1808. 56⅝ x 38¼". Louvre, Paris. (Photo Giraudon.)

friends in Rome. He had never seen Madeleine, who was in her thirties. She came to Rome and they met, romantically, at the tomb of Nero. The marriage was a success.

During the years in Rome between his arrival and his marriage, the "eccentricities" of Ingres's style had become more and more pronounced, which means that he had continued to develop as an original painter in spite of what he regarded as his loyal adherence to conventional classical disciplines. His *Bather of Valpinçon* [59], painted in 1808, could be Ingres's masterpiece if one picture had to be chosen from many eligible ones. It presents the typical Ingres paradox of classical derivations combined with extremely personal and, now, even sensuous responses. Nominally the *Bather of Valpinçon* has the closest classical associations, since the pose of the figure, with the cloth twisted about one arm, is borrowed from the figure of a Nereid on a Roman sarcophagus. But there all resemblance to classical sculpture ends, and although the picture is smoothly painted, with precisely defined contours, these neoclassical elements are superficial. Again, line is the picture, this time not in the complicated patterns of the *Madame Rivière* but in a reduction of the drawing of the nude body to a few subtle, almost eventless contours, suddenly contrasted with the bunched convolutions of the cloth and the turban, all played against the long straight folds of the curtain at the left, briefly echoed at the upper right. Like the contours, the modeling of the body is reduced to an ultimate simplicity and is correspondingly subtle. And a new—and thoroughly un-Davidian—element appears in the painter's sensuous response to the warmth and softness of the naked flesh.

The first series of Roman paintings reaches its climax three years later (1811) in *Jupiter and Thetis* [60, 61]. Ingres's *Prix de Rome* picture had shown Achilles and his loved friend Patroclus being called into Agamemnon's support by his ambassadors. *Jupiter and Thetis* illustrates a climactic episode later in the same story. It is certainly the most bizarre of all Ingres's paintings. The curious distortion of the woman's throat, the indescribable quality of her arms, flowering into tiny hands, the fantastic complications of the drapery falling from her body and disposed in utterly illogical folds and rills, the figure of Jupiter with its gigantic, soft torso and its diminutive face encircled by a black wreath of hair and beard—all these, with all the other curious and meticulous details, pushed just to the point of the grotesque, even to the edge of the repellent, are saved in the end by the assurance of their design and, above all,

by the sensation they convey that they are distilled from secret inner experience.

Actually, the picture follows explicitly Homer's account of how Thetis, a sea nymph, begged Jupiter to grant victory to the Trojans, to avenge an insult to her son Achilles. The request is granted in spite of the fact that in granting it, Jupiter must incur the wrath of Juno. The god had once renounced his secret love for Thetis and yielded her to Achilles' father.

In his copy of a French version of the *Iliad*, Ingres marked a passage that especially interested him; a paraphrase may give some idea of how closely he captured the essence of the episode:

"Thetis arose from the waves of the sea, and at the break of day rose through the immensity of the sky to Olympus. There she found him whose eye sees all the universe, the son of Saturn, seated far from the other gods on the highest summit of the mountain. She appeared before him and, with one hand upon his knees and lifting the other to his chin, she implored the monarch. But the god who commands the clouds answered nothing; he remained long in silence. Then this god of thunder let escape from his breast a profound sigh, and said, 'I promise you the satisfaction of your desires, and in pledge I accord you the sign of my sacred head.' Thus he spoke, and knit his black brows; the divine hair stirred upon the immortal head, and vast Olympus trembled, and Thetis, from the height of dazzling Olympus, threw herself again into the depths of the sea."

Yet, in spite of Ingres's close adherence to the text, *Jupiter and Thetis* is not a literary picture, not a mere illustration. It is complete in itself, legitimately and independently a pictorial expression. Even with no literary reference as a guide, the observer cannot but understand the drama of the moment, the nymph's hesitant temerity as she touches the face of the god, the power of the god himself, and the tension as he weighs whatever secrets must determine his response.

Jupiter and Thetis was the last of the paintings Ingres sent back to Paris under the regulation requiring an annual work

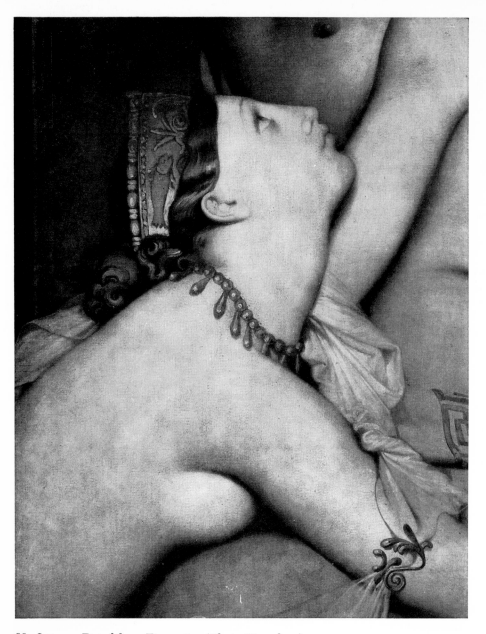

60. INGRES: Detail from Figure 61. (Photo Giraudon.)

from a *Prix de Rome* winner, and he kept a special affection for it all his life. It is the most personal of his major works, impregnated as it is with the element that most intimately characterizes Ingres's art, an element regarded dubiously by many people attempting to evaluate him: an obsessive sexuality that defies the mask of classical idealization. Basic to Ingres's conception of his subjects (in all likelihood unconsciously so on Ingres's part), sexuality is present as if by subterfuge. Where an open and virile masculine sensuousness would not be questionable, there is a suggestion of secret sensual revery. A psychiatrist might find it natural that *Jupiter and Thetis* and others of Ingres's early Roman pictures with the same quality were painted while the ar-

61. INGRES: *Jupiter and Thetis*, 1811. 130 x 101". *Musée Granet*, Aix-en-Provence.

tist's personal life was disturbed by his two abortive engagements and the curious circumstances of his courtship of Madeleine Chappell, and equally natural that after his happy marriage in 1813 his painting took a "healthier" direction. But these same pictures can be defended as Ingres's finest work. According to one theory, all creative art is a kind of purification for the artist, and if *Jupiter and Thetis* was abstracted from Ingres's personal emotional confusions then it is a very "modern" picture of a kind frequent in the twentieth century, where the creative act becomes a kind of release and a private confessional for the artist, and the resulting work of art is only incidentally intended for the public, who is free to make of it what it will.

THE EXPATRIATE · 63

The Troubadour

In Rome Ingres found in Raphael a new idol among the old masters, and for him the fifteenth-century Italian replaced all other official academic deities. Ingres's nature inclined toward gentle grace, which Raphael offered; at the same time Raphael was acceptable to an avowed classicist because his derivations from classical antiquity were quite direct. But Raphael's influence on Ingres was not altogether for the best and is an element in a not very happy footnote to his total work: his troubadour pictures.

Troubadour painting was a school within a school, and although it flourished under painters who had been trained by David, classical subjects were abandoned for historical anecdotes of the middle ages and the Renaissance. Ingres, their contemporary, painted troubadour subjects when these men were having their first success, combining this kind of picture with the ones we have just seen. His troubadour subjects included a *Betrothal of Raphael*, painted in 1812, no doubt more than coincidentally the year of his own second betrothal, and *Raphael and La Fornarina*. These were the only two pictures Ingres completed in a projected series covering the life of his new idol. He repeated the second subject many times, finally with a variation as late as 1860, of which he wrote, "I hope it will cause all the others to be forgotten." He also made repeated versions of *Paolo Malatesta and Francesca da Rimini* [62]. Other subjects were *Henry IV Playing with His Children While the Spanish Ambassador Is Being Admitted*, *King Philip of Spain Investing the Marshal of Berwick with the Golden Fleece*, *The Death of Leonardo da Vinci in the Arms of Francis I*, and *Aretino in the Studio of Tintoretto*. These labored storytelling pictures seem a waste of Ingres's meticulous technique. Except for the two Raphael subjects and the *Paolo and Francesca* they hardly suggest his linear beauties.

It was specifically the vogue for troubadour painting that inspired David's complaint in 1808 that the direction he had set for the fine arts was too severe to please for very long in France. "In ten years the study

62. INGRES: *Paolo Malatesta and Francesca da Rimini, c.* 1814. Panel, 13¾ x 11". *Musée Condé,* Chantilly.

of the antique will be abandoned," he said. "I hear the antique praised on every side but when I try to find it applied, I discover that it never is. All these gods, all the heroes, will be replaced by chevaliers, by troubadours singing beneath the windows of their lady-loves, at the foot of medieval towers." The invasion of Olympus by troubadours was another of the many indications that the romantic spirit was inherent in the thought and feeling of the early nineteenth century. The troubadour subject was natural to romanticism and was much used in romantic treatments by romantic painters and dramatists, and troubadour pictures were also among the ancestors of the acres of history pictures covering Salon walls later on. As far as Ingres was concerned, the subjects offered him nothing, nor did he have anything to bring them. And there is much of their dryness in the important but essentially dull *Vow of Louis XIII.*

63. INGRES: *The Vow of Louis XIII*, 1824. (Upper portion, width 103″.) Cathedral, Montauban.

64. INGRES: *Apotheosis of Homer*, 1827. 152 x 203″. Louvre, Paris.

The Prodigal

But whatever its faults, *The Vow of Louis XIII* [63] was a success with everyone. After its triumphant exhibition in the Salon of 1824, the classicists, relieved to have found a new leader, welcomed the *Vow* as his inaugural address, and the romantics, including Delacroix, were glad to see the end of the Davidian formula. The classicists' approval was an about-face; they had consistently attacked Ingres's Salon pictures. Cries of "Gothic" had resounded again in 1819. By some extraordinary feats of critical gymnastics invoking as a bad example the Italian primitive master Cimabue, the academicians had managed to make the same objections to the simplicity of Ingres's Roman painting* that they had made to the complications of *Madame Rivière*.

The Vow of Louis XIII was acceptable to the academicians because it was a thoroughly derivative picture. Ingres received the commission for it in the first place on the strength of a painting of *Christ Delivering the Keys to St. Peter*, which he had completed in 1820 for the Church of San Trinità dei Monti in Rome, a lamentable picture, a pasting together, to the point of plagiarism, of elements from Raphael. *The Vow of Louis XIII*, while it remains a greatly respected work today, is really not much better on that score, although the pasted-together ensemble is more agreeable. But for the academicians this fault was a virtue. They were willing to accept the renegade who had returned to the fold with a large imitation of a certified old master. They forgave the original excesses of his youth.

Delighted to return, Ingres remained in Pairs for ten years. He received one official award after another and was named President of the *École des Beaux Arts*, the official school. He taught the academic recipes to as many as a hundred students at a time, enforcing classical dogma relentlessly (teaching beauty as one teaches arithmetic, Delacroix said), and he was even success-

* Specifically, the objections centered on a reclining nude, the *Grande Odalisque*, now in the Louvre. See [89].

ful now and then in reducing his own art to dry conformity. His major commission of the period, the *Apotheosis of Homer* [64], is an exquisitely studied demonstration of the classical rules, the picture every *Prix de Rome* contestant would have painted if he could have.

But the accord between Ingres and the world of academic success was not quite as warm as it appeared to be. He had grown increasingly irascible, and when another large religious picture, *The Martyrdom of St. Symphorien* [65], received a bad reception in the Salon of 1834, Ingres asked to be transferred back to Rome as Director of the Academy there. He was given the appointment and left again for Italy in much the same frame of mind as before. He refused all commissions, forbade henceforth the showing of any of his pictures in the Salon, and painted, among others, two pictures in which the spirit of his early Roman work is recalled with renewed and extraordinary intensity.

In both of these a languorous sexuality is expressed in forms of brilliant precision, a contrast that comes close to being jolting in one of them, the vividly tinted *Odalisque with the Slave* [66]. The other, *Stratonice* [67] repeats the subject with which David had won the *Prix de Rome* long before [5] and in spirit recalls Ingres's own *Jupiter and Thetis*. Within an elaborate Greek interior, where every mosaic, every vein of marble, every smallest detail of carved ornament, every implausible fold of drapery, is rendered with the microscopic intensity of a revelation, a dream, or a vision, the figures in the drama of repressed passion are transfixed in attitudes of extreme artificiality. Like *Jupiter and Thetis*, *Stratonice* is saved from mawkishness or absurdity by qualities that may be sensed but are not easy to explain. They have to do with the consistency of the vision, where each of a multitude of details is conceived in harmony with all the others, and conception is totally integrated with execution. It is possible to be puzzled by this conception or to be unsympathetic to it, but it is impossible not to feel that every form, every line, and every relationship of the painted images are expressions of emotional con-

65. INGRES: *The Martyrdom of St. Symphorien*, 1865. 14⅛ x 12¼″. Reduced replica with minor variations from the picture for the Cathedral of Autun, 1834. Philadelphia Museum of Art, John G. Johnson Collection.

victions passionately held by the artist who created them.

Ingres completed these two pictures, after interruptions, in 1840. He was sixty years old. The following year, in bad health, he returned to Paris. The prodigal's second homecoming was triumphant with official receptions and awards. He began work on two mural commissions, *The Golden Age* and *The Age of Iron*. The first was never finished and the second was only sketched in. The fragments are not impressive. Possibly Ingres might have reached some conclusion to the struggle between sensuous forms, academic doctrine, and elaborated allegory that tears them apart, but in their present state they are like battlegrounds abandoned in fatigue.

66. INGRES: *Odalisque with the Slave*, 1842. 28 x 39⅜".
Walters Art Gallery, Baltimore.

67. INGRES: *Stratonice*, 1866. 24 x 36¼". *Musée Fabre*, Montpellier. Variation on version of 1840. *Musée Condé*, Chantilly. (Photo Giraudon.)

In 1849 Madeleine Chappell died. The marriage that had begun with such an extraordinary courtship had been an ideal one, and Ingres was inconsolable until three years later when he yielded to the urging of friends and remarried, at seventy-one. In 1855 he was induced to relent in his determination never to exhibit again in the Salon, and like Delacroix in that year he had a gallery to himself for a retrospective collection. There were further honors at home—he was even named a senator in 1862—and his renown became international with honorary membership in the academies of other countries. When he died in 1867 he was eighty-six years old. He had outlived Delacroix, although classicism had not.

Two pictures from these last years enjoy somewhat inflated reputations. In 1820 Ingres had begun work on a standing female nude, *La Source* [68]. Now, thirty-six years later, he completed it with the help of pupils. The figure with its softened contours and cottony flesh is a superior academic studio piece, but it is a very poor second to the two great Roman nudes, the *Bather of Valpinçon* and the *Grande Odalisque*. The face, a symmetrical mask on the classical formula, has grown vapid. By most standards *La Source* is a fine picture, but not by the standard of Ingres at his greatest.

In 1862 (according to the date on the picture) or 1863 (according to a letter in which he mentions it) Ingres completed *The Turkish Bath* [69], a recombination of figures from several pictures painted in different periods. The Bather of Valpinçon, now playing a mandolin, dominates a confused arrangement of some twenty-five naked and ill-assorted harem women, ranging downward from the Bather's undiminished loveliness to the almost comical vulgarity of the squirming masses of flesh in the background. One conspicuous head, just behind the upraised arm of the reclining figure in the right foreground, with its cheek against the ear of the adjoining figure, is wedged into the composition in such a way that it would be physically impossible for a body to exist normally attached to it. *The Turkish Bath* had a difficult history, explaining some of its defects.

68. INGRES: *La Source*, 1820–56. 64½ x 32¼". Louvre, Paris. (Photo Giraudon.)

Ingres completed it about 1852 as a rectangular composition, then reworked it several times, once after it had been returned by a purchaser, and finally changed its shape to the present circular one, with necessary additions and subtractions. He was eighty-three by the time he made this final revision.

69. INGRES: *The Turkish Bath, c.* 1852–63. Diameter 42½″. Louvre, Paris.

Portraits and Drawings

As a portraitist Ingres was so prolific and worked so frequently at his highest level that it is difficult to eliminate dozens of superb pictures in order to select a representative few. The early "Gothic" portrait of *Madame Rivière* has already been considered. In comparison with it, the portrait of his friend the painter *François Marius Granet* [70] is more restrained, not only because the subject is a man but because Ingres has come under new influences. He never repeated the complexity of linear flow that marked *Madame Rivière*, either because of the criticisms of it or because in

Italy he discovered the portraits of the Italian Renaissance and was attracted by their greater simplicity—or, of course, because of both. In the portrait of Granet, the head surmounts a generally pyramidal mass and is lifted above the distant horizon in order to play its lines and shapes against an eventless passage of sky. The strongest value contrasts, the white collar and the dark hair, frame the face as a further assurance that it will remain the undisputed focal point of the composition. The architectural landscape background is full of interest, but since it is reduced to small scale in the distance it emphasizes the largeness of the figure to lend it additional importance.

70. INGRES: *François Marius Granet*. Date unknown. 28¾ x 24″. Museum, Aix-en-Provence.

71. INGRES: *Comtesse d'Haussonville*, 1845. 53½ x 36¼″. Copyright The Frick Collection, N.Y.

These are all standard Renaissance devices worn threadbare in the work of any number of painters who used them in very much the way Ingres did; they are not difficult to employ skillfully. Ingres's *Granet* is a masterpiece because over this conventional framework he builds his own linear pattern, combining the sinuosities of the edges of the open cape and its thrown-back collar with the contrasting solidity of its general silhouette; contrasting equally the unqualified rectangularities of the book, the bit of wall, and the buildings in the background, with the irregular shapes of the white collar, the head, and the locks of hair patterned against the forehead. All the forms have more mass, more solidity, and are more naturalistic than those of the *Madame Rivière*, but they are still drawn in linear arabesques that have their own abstract beauty. And in both portraits the sen-

suousness of Ingres's response to human beauty warms and illuminates these images presented with such precision and control.

The background of the *Granet* is a specific reference to place. It shows the Villa Medici, the Renaissance palace acquired by the French Academy as its Roman base. With its gardens, its fantasy of a façade, its sculpture, its great halls, its towering position on the most beautiful of the Roman hills, looking across the most spectacular panorama of the city, the Villa Medici was a paradise for the *Prix de Rome* winners, who lived and painted there (and still do). Like Ingres, Granet was a *Prix de Rome* man. (For a while he enjoyed a success in Paris, although his work is forgotten today—which is a mercy.) Ingres's portrait of him hangs in the municipal museum in his home city of Aix-en-Provence. A few feet away *Jupiter and Thetis* covers the end

72. INGRES: *Comtesse de Tournon*, 1814. 36⅝ x 28¾". Collection Henry P. McIlhenny, Philadelphia.

wall of the gallery, a combination evoking Ingres's young manhood in Rome.

The general formula of the *Granet* served Ingres for many of his finest early portraits. In later ones, such as that of the young *Comtesse d'Haussonville* [71], done in 1845, he shows greater dependence on accessory details for their inherent interest as objects, more complication for the sake of stunning naturalistic rendering (in the stuff of the dress, for instance) at the expense of linear invention. Toward the end this tendency dominated the painter to the point where a portrait is in danger of hold-

ing more interest as a contemporary record of an interior and a lady's toilette than as a transmutation of fact into art. But Ingres never entirely succeeded in his effort to be anything but himself. Ingres the academician never quite managed to stifle Ingres the original artist.

Ingres had one great limitation as a portrait painter, if one demands that a portrait be not only a fine painting but an interpretation of character. In his average portrait whatever we learn of the sitter's character we must infer by association. Sometimes these associations are strong. The early

(1812) portrait of the *Comtesse de Tournon* [72] presents one vivid individual among Ingres's gallery of somewhat repetitious and superficially explored personalities. Yet even in this case we may feel that the old Countess was a person of such sprightly character and such characterizing features that some reflection of her individuality was inevitable in anything like an accurate reproduction of her appearance. Here the sitter seems to have imposed her personality upon the painter, where ordinarily when Ingres painted a portrait it was the other way around.

The great exception among all Ingres portraits is the one of *Monsieur Bertin* [73], the founder and director of *Le Journal des Débats*. Here it is obvious that Ingres was seeking something beyond a satisfactory "likeness" or an elegant effigy. The selection of pose, the tension in the position of the hands on the knees as the man leans forward slightly, the elimination of accessory detail, the sharp, decisive patterning of the hair—which in a preliminary drawing is shown to have been, actually, rather limp and characterless—all contribute to the impression of shrewdness and energy that would not have been present in a simple transcription of the subject's appearance as he sat patiently for the artist.

A drawing by Ingres is of such delicacy that it is brutalized in even the best reproduction. He drew constantly and made innumerable preliminary studies for his paintings. The *Musée Ingres* in his native city of Montauban is the great treasure house of these studies, but hundreds of Ingres drawings are in museums and collections elsewhere. These include especially the small portrait sketches in pencil made sometimes as preliminary studies, or often as a souvenir given in affection or in an effort at ingratiation to the aristocrats who came through Rome in steady streams. One of these is the *Comte Turpin de Crissé* [74], with the head typically modeled in more detail than the figure, which is sketched in with absolute assurance but with only an occasional light indication of shadow to enhance the form, which is otherwise revealed entirely by line. Ingres frequently catches a stronger suggestion of personality in these

73. INGRES: *Monsieur Bertin*, 1832. 45¾ x 37⅜". Louvre, Paris.

drawings than he tries for in more carefully studied paintings. Jaunty elegance, alert, sophisticated intelligence, social aplomb, and even a hint of amused cynicism are presented in the features and the pose as Ingres has transcribed them quickly here with the model before him. If Ingres seldom reflects his sitter's individuality with equal brilliance in his paintings, it is because his immediate response to a subject, which was instinctively perceptive, was not ordinarily increased and deepened by further reflection; rather it was lessened by further study of the portrait as a problem in design. If this is a limitation it must be accepted as one playing its own part, not necessarily negative, in Ingres's creation of some of the most extraordinarily effective portraits in the European tradition.

In his portraits Ingres is a great stylist; so is he, of course, in his subject pictures. But he must remain only a stylist, nothing more,

74. INGRES: *Comte Turpin de Crissé*, probably 1818. Pencil on white paper. 11⅝ x 8⅞". Collection Walter C. Baker, New York.

even in such pictures as *Jupiter and Thetis*, unless his characterizing element of hidden and even unconscious personal emotional expression is recognized. Baudelaire, who was so perceptive of the universal significance of the conceptions released through Delacroix's romantic forms, searched uneasily in the art of Ingres for meanings he seems to have suspected were concealed beneath the polished surface and fettered within the implacable contours of Ingres's style. He never convinced himself that these meanings were there. But the twentieth century, with its exploration of the hidden impulses of the creative act, has revealed Ingres as an intense, intimate, and even secret artist of the most personal kind beneath his stylizations and pedantry.

CHAPTER 4

Realism

Idealism and Disillusion

For all their differences, the classicists and the romantics held one conviction in common, and it was a basic one: they thought of life and the world as a mystery that could be explored to discover the reason for man's existence. Neither doubted the assumption that we are here for a reason and that our being is justified and meaningful. For both, nature—all the different facets of life, of the world—was what Delacroix called "a vocabulary" that could be used to study the mystery's solution. Classic or romantic, the idealist assumes that within all the conflicts and contradictions, all the ambiguities and confusions of life, somewhere there is a harmony, a discoverable truth, by which man can understand the fact that he exists. The forces around him and within him, all apparently working at odds against one another, must certainly be not accidental, as they appear to be, but animated toward meaningful order; must certainly be some part of a universal plan within which we move for some purpose toward some reward, some profound satisfaction of the human yearning to be more than an organism that is born, suffers, and dies.

The classicist sought to clarify the mystery by intellectualizing man's experience. The romantic sought its heart in the more ambiguous area of the "soul" and was willing to cultivate even life's suffering in the conviction that emotional experience holds the answer everyone seeks. But in the end—and this is the important point—both classicist and romantic were idealists, refusing to accept the world at face value, rejecting it in the end, forcing the experience of life into their respective and equally arbitrary molds in spite of repeated evidence

El sueño de la razon produce monstruos.

75. GOYA: *The Sleep of Reason Produces Monsters*, 1797–98.
Etching and aquatint, 8⅜ x 5⅞″. From the *Caprichos*. Philadelphia
Museum of Art, gift of Smith, Kline and French Laboratories.

Goya: His World

Goya was a contemporary of David almost to the exact years, having been born two years earlier than the master of classicism and dying three years after him. Yet as a young man he discarded the classicism of his teachers, and he was never affected by the type of romanticism that developed in France. In his very old age Goya visited Paris and is said to have admired the work of the young Delacroix. But he could have told himself that the vehemence of his own work—its emotional color and its dramatic force—not only exceeded that of this Frenchman who was fifty-three years younger but that his, Goya's, art was born from a fervent experience of life that gave it a vitality alongside which Delacroix's romanticism was a theoretical demonstration.

Because of his fire and his dramatic vigor, Goya is often called a romantic painter. Because he deals so frequently with horrors and with the fantastic, he may appear to be a painter of the world of imaginative emotionalism inhabited by one type of romantic. But Goya was a realist because he saw the world without illusion. No other painter has seen it more naked of saving grace, either of reason or of sentiment, of intellect or of soul. Even when his visions are most monstrous, even when he is most outraged by what he sees and records it most violently, Goya is a realist in the basic sense: he sees the world around him for what it is and he accepts its existence as unalterable fact. The world Goya saw was not a world he could condone; but neither did he hope to change it or to discover hidden within it the classicist's order or the romantic's yearning conviction of some ultimate, if undecipherable, meaning.

The circumstances surrounding Goya in his daily life as a Spaniard offered no nourishment for idealism of any kind. While David was synthesizing an art in praise of Reason, stimulated by the French philosophers who had deified it, Goya was working at the court of Spain, surrounded by a group of human monsters who have never been surpassed for stupidity, viciousness, ignorance, greed, and corruption, in a coun-

that they could never get more than a part of it to fit.

By the middle of the nineteenth century, twenty-five years after David's death and a decade before Delacroix's and Ingres's, painters were becoming disillusioned with idealism in either form and were turning to realism, which in several forms was to dominate painting until near the end of the century. Meanwhile, the movement had been anticipated by one of the most unillusioned painters who ever lived, the Spaniard Francisco Goya (1746–1828).

try intellectually all but inert, with a populace brutalized by poverty, bigotry, and oppression. The national characteristics of Spain included a catalogue of all evil and misery, and Goya's observation of the world gave him no reason to believe that the eighteenth-century philosophers' dream of Reason had produced anything more than monsters. He said as much in a print showing a student asleep over his books while the air around him is filled with screech owls and bats [75]. The print has been given various interpretations, but any interpretation must accept its premise of the triumph of nightmare. Man's incapacity to think his way toward reasonable and humane existence is parabled in another print [76] in which a philosopher or teacher mouths by rote the phrases of learning to an audience deaf, dumb, and blind to thought of any kind, the whole scene taking place upon a branch so rotten that it will presently drop everyone into an abyss of which they are not even aware.

The wonder is that from such a world a man like Goya managed to emerge at all. To his common origin he owed his physical vigor and, for that matter, his intellectual vigor, which would have been stultified and corrupted if he had grown up in the world he entered later. To this world, the world of his patrons, the court and the circles surrounding it, he owed his living, the opportunity to paint, and thus eventually his fame, but he never conceded a point in his contempt for it. Goya was incapable of the kind of flattery exercised by David when he painted Napoleon's disintegrating empress as a mere slip of a girl in *Le Sacre*. Fortunately, flattery was never required of him. His portraits of the royal family are explicitly of abominable, contemptible, mediocre, or at best pathetic characters. That these portraits were accepted and that he was commissioned to repeat them is proof enough that the sitters were as stupid as he painted them to be, so satisfied with themselves that they admired their own images without seeing the ghastly revelation beneath the painted reflections.

The Family of Charles IV [77] shows a group of pompous freaks, swathed in velvets and silks and dripping with jewels. It

76. GOYA: *Ridiculous Folly*, 1813–20. Etching and aquatint. 9½ x 13¾". From the *Disparates*. Philadelphia Museum of Art, gift of Mrs. R. Sturgis Ingersoll.

has been nicknamed once and for all "the grocer and his family who have just won the Grand Lottery," a witticism hard on grocers and their families but charitable to the King of Spain and his. The monarch stands in the foreground on the right, his chest and belly ablaze with decorations. A glance is enough to substantiate the story that during the day he would ask his minister, a villain named Manuel Godoy, "how things were going" and without waiting for an answer would consider his obligations as ruler of a nation completed for another twenty-four hours. His grotesque queen stands in the center, embracing her daughter and holding the hand of her son awkwardly enough to suggest that these maternal gestures were unfamiliar ones for her. These children are presumed to have been fathered by the same Manuel Godoy, whose duties at court extended beyond the usual ministerial ones. This queen, Maria Luisa of Parma, also granted her favors to an occasional servant. There have been more vicious women in history, but they were women of greater intelligence and hence capable of greater inventiveness than this one. To the left foreground is Ferdinand, heir to the throne, who is a blank. Behind him is the face of a witch, the King's sister. Only the young couple at the

77. GOYA: *The Family of Charles IV*, 1800. 110 x 132″. Prado, Madrid. (Photo Anderson.)

extreme right seem normal. Goya has sympathetically concealed the spinal deformity with which this one of the King's children was born, translating it into a posture twisted because she carries her child in her arms. Her young husband is also a human being. But the children on each side of the Queen are devoid of innocence. The hard-faced little boy is like his father—not the King—and the girl is already an echo of her mother. Behind this collection, almost obscured in deep shadow, at the far left, Goya is at work on the picture.

In Goya's art his contempt for the men around him widens to become a horror of mankind. In his portraits of children he comes closest to relenting, yet even here, as in the *Don Manuel Osorio de Zuñiga* [78], he may see purity and innocence as nothing but fodder for corruption. From the shadows behind the utterly charming image of the little boy gleam the eyes of cats in wait to devour the fragile bird. Goya's young women are creatures of fire and beauty, but without tenderness, and he is fond of playing them in front of figures of frightful old hags. On the surface this contrast reminds us that youth and beauty are transient, but it is even more emphatically a statement that the human spirit is not only subject to

78. GOYA: *Don Manuel Osorio de Zuñiga, c. 1787. 50 x 40".* Metropolitan Museum of Art, New York, Jules S. Bache Collection.

79. GOYA: *Que Tal?, c. 1801. 71¼ x 48½". Palais des Beaux Arts,* Lille.

corruption but apparently, to Goya's way of thinking, impotent to withstand it. *Que Tal?* [79] tells us that time does not ripen humanity into wisdom, but rots and withers it into foolishness and evil.

For Goya, evil is the ultimate reality, violation and degradation are man's fate. He never condones these truths, holding them to be self-evident, but he hardly protests against them. He states vehemently that they are abominable, but he never suggests the possibility of amelioration or correction. *And Nothing Can Be Done about It* is the title of another of his prints [80], one from a series making up as horrifying a record of cruelty as has ever been set down in any medium: Goya's *Disasters of War*.

Between 1808 and 1814 Goya witnessed the Napoleonic invasions of Spain, the

guerrilla warfare that followed them, the famine of 1812 that was one result of them, and the return of the Inquisition under Ferdinand VII. Even granting the different viewpoints of a Frenchman and a Spaniard on the subject of Napoleon, we must recognize that the contrast between the treatment of the Napoleonic legend in French painting and Goya's observation of terrible fact is a legitimate, if extreme, example of the difference between romantic or classical idealism and realism. There is no glory in Goya's war, no grandeur in victory or grand emotion in defeat; there are only rape, slaughter, and mutilation. His subject is human bestiality. The victims get second billing to the rapists, butchers, and mutilators; we are appalled by the perpetrators but not led to great compassion for the vic-

80. GOYA: *And Nothing Can Be Done about It* (*Y no hai remedio*), 1810–20. Etching and aquatint, 15½ x 16⅜″. Philadelphia Museum of Art, gift of Smith, Kline and French Laboratories.

tims, whose agony, no matter how frightful, we must accept as a human condition beyond correction. Gros's *Pesthouse at Jaffa* [33] is by comparison an Elysium.

In such a world reality is close to nightmare, and if we have called Goya a realist we must also say that he created some of the most fantastic visions in the history of art. *The Disasters of War* are realistic in fact and in representation, lamentable as it may be that the world offers material for this realism. The set of prints called the *Caprichos* are fantasies, yet their comments on greed, superstition, stupidity, bigotry, avarice, and indifference are comments on man as a social being with responsibilities for which he is accountable, a concept that is fundamental in realistic art. The *Caprichos* are social comment made in terms of the grotesque, the monstrous, and the hallucinatory. In some of Goya's work, the hallucination passes beyond such comment and becomes a symbolical damnation of hu-

manity, as in the ghastly *Saturn Devouring His Sons* [81]. These morbidities are Goya's answer to the romantic dream of noble passions, and instead of the classicists' Olympians he shows a terrifying *Colossus* [82] dwarfing the world, a magnificent and brutish figure who dominates the universe yet looks upon it without comprehension.

Goya: His Isolation

Some of the most trenchant observations of human vanity and corruption have been made by painters or writers who have moved freely within a specific world, and have been accepted as part of it by its denizens, while within themselves they have remained separated from it by some isolating circumstance. These men remain free to observe with the objectivity of an outsider, yet with intimate access to their material. Goya was such a man. As the

81. GOYA: *Saturn Devouring His Sons*, date unknown. 57½ x 32½". Prado, Madrid. (Photo Anderson.)

82. GOYA: *Colossus*, c. 1818. Etching and aquatint, scraped, 11⅜ x 8¼". Metropolitan Museum of Art, New York.

official painter of the court he was intimately associated with the aristocratic world. His mistress was the Duchess of Alba, supposed to be the most beautiful woman in Spain and by all accounts so entrancing that she is forgiven much that would be held against a plainer woman. This was a real love affair, and in spite of the Duchess's high station, it was not so much a part of Goya's participation in the world of wealth and position as it was a continuation of his youth as a hard-working and hard-living painter in Madrid's world of brawls and the bull ring. Goya himself was an amateur bullfighter and, by legend, a good one. Later he did a series of etchings, the *Tauromachia*, on this sport or art. Here, as in his paintings of the life of the city, its strollers, its beggars, its people of the streets, he is established historically as a realist finding material in the life around him and commenting on it in contemporary terms, without reference to ancient gods and heroes or exotic or picturesque places or customs. (If the city life he painted has an exotic flavor for us, it did not for him.)

Goya's withdrawal from this life—from life in general, for that matter—a spiritual withdrawal that left him a figure moving actively among people yet observing them from seclusion, was the result of a desperate

83. GOYA: *Portrait of His Wife, Josefa Bayeu, c.* 1798. 32 x 22". Prado, Madrid. (Photo Anderson.)

illness that left him totally deaf upon his recovery in 1793, at the age of forty-six. Whatever elements in his temperament that had predisposed him to the contemplation of human folly were now exaggerated; the isolation of deafness also coincided with his rise in official favor and his increasing contact with the world of the court.*

* Goya had become a court painter under Charles III in 1786 and was raised to *pintor de cámara* in 1789 by Charles IV, at about which time he seems to have studied the liberal ideas of the French encyclopedists, who were popular with Spanish intellectuals. This period of relative optimism was terminated by his illness in 1792 with convalescence and deafness in 1793. He became president of Spain's Royal Academy in 1795 and First Painter to the King in 1799.

The first years of deafness and isolation produced the *Caprichos,* a set of eighty aquatints† first announced to the public in 1797 and published two years later. *The Sleep of Reason Produces Monsters* [75] was its first plate and its theme. In the *Caprichos* unreasonable man defeats himself and tortures his fellows with every cruelty, indignity, and foolishness; the pattern of Goya's pessimism is set, and from this time on, circumstances continue to increase his paradoxical combination of vehemence and detachment. In 1802 the Duchess of Alba died. Goya was fifty-six years old. He witnessed the Napoleonic invasions and the uprisings in Madrid before the death of his wife ten years after that of his duchess. He had been married for thirty-six years to Josefa Bayeu, the sister of a painter with whom he had an early association. She was a devoted and loyal woman who bore him twenty children, some of whom lived; he painted a very sympathetic portrait of her [83].

Goya was now so cut off from human contact and so embittered that he left Madrid to go into seclusion in his country house, *La Quinta del Sordo* (Deaf Man's Villa). This was about 1814; he was sixty-eight but a man of astounding vigor. He etched the *Tauromachia,* a set of forty large plates telling the history of the bullfight and its heroes, and by 1819, at seventy-three, he had produced another set of twenty-two etchings and aquatints, the *Disparates,* and completed *The Disasters of War,* although for political reasons these latter were not published until 1863, long after his death.

The *Disparates* are the most fantastic of Goya's prints and in many ways the most

† Aquatint is a method of acid-biting a metal plate in such a way that the effect of a graded wash is approximated, thus allowing nuances of light and shade not possible in ordinary etching. It is usually combined with etching, as in Goya's work. The process was developed as a secret one by Jean Baptiste Le Prince (1734–1781) and had become public property only shortly before Goya used it, having been revealed in a technical manual, *Encyclopédie Méthodique,* in 1791. Aquatint was particularly valuable to Goya since its wide range from deep shadow to brilliant light was so adaptable to the nightmarish illumination of the spectral regions he was creating.

84. GOYA: *El Famoso Americano, Mariano Ceballos*, 1825. Lithograph, 12¼ x 15¾".
Philadelphia Museum of Art, McIlhenny Fund.

philosophical; they are grotesque allegories whose interpretation Goya leaves up to the observer. Interpretation is not always possible in precise terms, but as the summation of all Goya's previous work the meaning of the *Disparates* is clear enough, and horrifying; Goya's deepest and bitterest experience is translated into fantasies of horror, outrage, and despair. On first publication they were given the title *Proverbios* (*Proverbs*) by the puzzled and no doubt frightened Academy. The title is apt, in that a proverb expresses some fundamental and enduring idea concerning man's life, disguised as humor or grotesquerie, but not apt in that proverbs grow out of the experience of a people, and the *Disparates* are Goya's own. The word means, approximately, *Fantastic Blunders*. Goya repeated the subjects in fresco on the walls of *La Quinta del Sordo;* the country villa became a compartment of hell transplanted into the Spanish countryside.

In 1824 Goya went into voluntary exile in France. Settled in Bordeaux, his eyesight failing and his vigor at last waning, he began working in the new medium of lithography* and produced four large stones continuing the *Tauromachia*, of an almost orgiastic vitality [84]. He died in Bordeaux in 1828, at eighty-two.

---

* Lithography, a process of drawing on prepared stone and then printing from it, was invented by Aloys Senefelder. It is the most direct of all the art printing processes, imposing a minimum of technical barrier between the artist's hand and the completed print. The artist draws on smooth stone just as he would do on paper; the drawing may be transferred repeatedly to paper with very little change in character. Lithographic darks are even richer than those of aquatint, and every nuance between black and white is possible. The fine-grained texture of the stone gives lithograph its particular individuality, although in modern variations of the technique other surfaces than stone are often used.

85. GOYA: *El Pelele* (*The Manikin*), 1791. 105 x 63″. Prado, Madrid.

86. GOYA: *Marquesa de San Andrès*, 1785–90. 33 x 22″. Private collection.

Goya: His Innovations

The first influences on Goya as a painter were at odds with one another, and he was at odds with both of them. For a century Spain had been dependent on imported artists, and Goya was first subjected to the borrowed rococo forms of various Italian masters, the kind of painting that inspired David's revolt, and then to the art of Raphael Mengs, a neo-classicist of exceptional dryness, with whom he worked for a while. Goya rejected classicism on sight, but when Mengs and Francisco Bayeu used their influence to get him a place with the Royal Tapestry Works in Madrid in 1776, he produced a series of vivacious decorative paintings that easily hold their own alongside those of the eighteenth-cen-

tury Italians whose tradition they follow. But even while Goya is painting within the rococo tradition of lightness and charm, sinister implications are at play beneath the artificial gaiety. The jolly girls who toss the puppet in a blanket in *El Pelele* [85] are young witches. If their victim is only a puppet, it is because they are still novices. Later they will substitute human carrion for the rag doll; this holiday in a park is only a rehearsal for a witches' sabbath.

Portrait commissions came Goya's way readily. His earliest portraits are rich technical displays with the models posed rather stiffly, a bit overweighted sometimes with incidental elaborations of costume, partly of course because the dress of the period so dictated, as in the portrait of the *Marquesa de San Andrès* [86]. The subject is not deeply explored as a personality; we make our own deductions from the lively objectivity of Goya's re-creation of the lady's features, but we are not told much about her. She regards us with an alert and vigorous glance, yet as far as Goya's characterization of her as an individual is concerned, she might be any one of hundreds like her. But a few years later Goya stands the *Marquesa de La Solana* [87] before us as a complete individual. Her homely features are presented without idealization, but never for a moment does Goya regard any detail of them, or of her costume, as incidental portions of a still-life that happens to be composed of a human being dressed in a certain way. Every element in the portrait of the *Marquesa de La Solana* contributes to the creation of a total personality, subtly projected. The earlier *Marquesa de San Andrès* is a catalogue of accessories, and the fact that styles in dress had changed between the two portraits is only a superficial explanation of their difference. In the later one the lace of the skirt and the shawl could have been played up as accessory details; instead they are all but eliminated in the reduction of the composition to large simplified areas of blacks and grays, within which the pinkish tones of the face and the bow of ribbon perched above it take on an extraordinary life. The portrait is a play between the face and the ribbon bow; the reality of the face, its rather stubborn strength, is emphasized by its existence within the disharmoniously dainty and feminine frame of the shawl and the climax of the fashionable absurdity of the bow. Larger than the face and brighter in color, elegant and dainty where the face is plain and coarse-featured, the bow is the first thing one sees in the picture. But it immediately loses its battle for attention to the face beneath it, a face that appears to tolerate the incompatible accessories surrounding it as a concession to the necessities of mode but goes on about its own more important business without giving them further thought.

This superb portrait was painted just before Goya's climactic illness. As a piece of pure painting, it reflects his discovery of Velásquez in the royal collections, now ac-

87. GOYA: *Marquesa de La Solana,* 1791–95. 71¼ x 48". Louvre, Paris.

cessible to him. It is also a prelude to his experiments in the use of color and the representation of form that were in full stride by 1800, the year of the portrait of the royal family. Historically these experiments are as important as Delacroix's later ones.

Goya was dissatisfied with the light, fresh touch of his early paintings and their clear, fresh, attractive but rather obvious decorative colors. As Delacroix was to do, he fumed against the painting methods that

84 · REALISM

made a painting only a kind of tinted drawing. His experiments were not in the same direction as Delacroix's were to be, but he was working away from the same dissatisfactions when he complained, "Always lines, never bodies! Where does one see lines in nature? I see only forms, forms that are lighted and forms that are not, planes that are near and planes that are far, projections, and hollows. I see no lines or details, I don't count each hair on the head of a passerby, or the buttons on his coat. There is no reason why my brush should see more than I do."

What this means is that Goya was hunting a way of painting that would present an image with the immediacy of instant vision. This, of course, is visual realism—not the search for an ideal and not the imitation of nature in detail, but the capturing in paint of the impact of life as we meet it head on. We see first in breadth, in masses; we receive a total impression that carries with it a certain emotional impact. Later we may examine things more closely, may relish the beauty of a line, the complexity of a part within the whole, may perceive individual hairs on a head or buttons on a coat down to the way they are sewed on. Such details may offer a great deal of interest or aesthetic pleasure, but to Goya's way of thinking they obscured the point, which was to capture the quality of the whole, to record it in such a way that its immediate vividness, as it impressed him, was expressed with truth at maximum intensity. Since a picture cannot be painted in the space of a glance, his problem was to discover a way of painting an image that would retain this immediate intensity. Of course this can always be done to some extent in a quick sketch. But that, again, was beside the point, since a sketch is only suggestive, and dependent for its effect on its very incompleteness. Along with immediacy and intensity Goya wanted the decision and the completeness that distinguish a work of art from a fragment of nature.

To work out some of the problems involved in training his brush not to "see more" than he did, Goya set himself an exercise that produced two of his most celebrated paintings, the paired *Nude Maja*

[88] and *Clothed Maja*° [90]. It was inevitable that legends should accumulate around such a startling pair of pictures, which look like anything but analytical studies in technique, and inevitable too that these legends should attach themselves to the Duchess of Alba. The most popular story is that the Duchess posed for the *Nude Maja* during the Duke's absence and that the *Clothed Maja* was dashed off quickly when the lovers received word of the Duke's imminent return, an anecdote false in every factual and psychological detail except that the features of the girl in the *Majas* are close to those of the Duchess in Goya's several portraits of her. But since Goya used these features as a type for the spirited, vixenish young beauties who populate his work, the resemblance means nothing.

The *Majas* were painted about 1800, the year David painted *Madame Récamier* [14], a perfect contrast to the *Clothed Maja*, opposing the fashionable grace and artificiality of the neo-classical portrait with the bold vitality of Goya's realism. The *Nude Maja* and Ingres's *Grande Odalisque* [89]—the comparison is legitimate in spite of the disparity of dates—are in even more extreme and enlightening contrast. With Delacroix's *Odalisque with Parrot* [91] the classical-romantic-realistic comparison is complete. In their different ways, the Frenchmen poeticized a nude model to accord with an arbitrary standard. Goya painted—magnificently—simply a naked girl, audacious, almost insolently matter-of-fact in her nakedness. If the figure is unidealized, if the nakedness is piquant be-

---

° *Maja* and its masculine equivalent *majo* are untranslatable. Dictionaries give *fop* or *dandy* for *majo*. *Gallant* is close. *Coquette* might do for *maja* but not very well. The words carry associations of youth, good looks or prettiness, city pleasures, flirtatious display, fancy dress without high fashion, and common rather than aristocratic origin, with probabilities of flexible morality. As part of an international movement of dandyism at the end of the eighteenth century, these Spaniards had their counterparts in England in the macaronis, and in France in the *merveilleuses*, who adopted eccentric modes of dress. The clothing worn by *majos* and *majas* eventually became the national dress of Spain.

88. GOYA: *Nude Maja, c.* 1797–98. 37⅜ x 74¾″. Prado, Madrid. (Photo Anderson.)

89. INGRES: *Odalisque en Grisaille, c.* 1813, study for *Grande Odalisque.* 32¾ x 43″. Metropolitan Museum of Art, New York, Wolfe Fund.

cause the image seems so literal, this same literalness saves it from lasciviousness. It is too frank to be suggestive. As is always pointed out, its clothed companion piece with its gauzy, clinging, half-concealing half-revealing gown comes closer to being the suggestive one of the pair.

Technically the innovation in the *Majas* has to do with reducing the image to its essential planes, which are painted in bold, flat areas instead of being fused in subtle modulations from one to another. This does not mean a simpler, easier way of painting. Goya's boldness takes as much calculation as Ingres's subtlety; the forms and colors that seem so direct and uncomplicated are disposed in relationships as firmly integrated with one another as in any other form of picture-making. Delacroix's problem—"All precautions have to be taken to make the execution swift and decisive" in order not to lose "the extraordinary impression accompanying the conception"—is also Goya's, with the difference (in the case of the *Majas*) that where Delacroix is concerned with recording inner, emotional, impressions through exotic images, Goya pre-

sents us with what appears to be an image of brilliant external reality. The important words here are *what appears to be*, because Goya is not merely reproducing the object he sees, camera fashion. He is preserving his own vision of reality in such a way that we see it and respond to it as he did, not as

86 · REALISM

90. GOYA: *Clothed Maja, c.* 1797–98. 37⅜ x 74¾". Prado, Madrid. (Photo Anderson.)

91. DELACROIX: *Odalisque with Parrot,* 1827. 9½ x 12½". *Musée des Beaux Arts,* Lyon.

we might respond to the actual object if we saw it ourselves. If Goya had sought out new means of representation only in order to reproduce visual fact, the search would have been pointless. The point was to discover a new way of representation which, by preserving his own vision of the world,

would be for him the best possible vehicle of expression.

The *Majas* occupy a special place in Goya's work as demonstrations, in addition to being arresting paintings in themselves. Expressively, however, they are excelled by other paintings where Goya's realism is an interpretative vehicle more than a technical process. One example is the portrait of *The Toreador José Romero* [92]. As pure painting the picture is opulent in texture and color, with the rich red lining of the cape curving up to the shoulder, the blue-green of the wide sash, the ruddy flesh tints, the blacks of the hair and the vest, and the pulsating lights everywhere on silks, velvets, and gilt embroidery. Against this brilliance Goya plays the reserved, even pensive, face of the young man. The hands, held so quietly, have an almost feminine delicacy, remindful of the precision, the refinements, the nuances, that differentiate a toreador from a butcher.

The difference between the *Majas* and a portrait like this one is the difference between an exercise in which the interest of the subject is incidental to its presentation, and an interpretation in which presentation serves expression. Goya's genius here and in other portraits lies in his revelation of the character of the sitter in what appears to be an altogether objective statement of the features. Like many other painters, Goya achieves this revelation by controlling the objective reality through selection and modification of pose and details. Where an unimaginative portraitist would have posed his bullfighter in an attitude of theatrical braggadocio suggestive of the usual connotations of the bullring, Goya cut through this overlay of convention and habit and produced, instead, a painting that not only characterizes the sitter but extends its comment into the area of philosophical speculation. Yet all this is achieved through the devices of surface realism, without symbolical clues or idealistic references. It was to this end that Goya found it necessary to discover his way of painting in which "his brush should not see more than he did." And, once discovered, this way of painting served him not only as a painter of the familiar world but also as a painter of scenes of horror, fantasy, and violence, to which the quality of "immediate vision" brings an appalling reality.

On May 2, 1808, citizens of Madrid rioted against French soldiery, and on the following day the captured rioters were taken into the countryside near the city and shot. Goya recorded both events in a pair of pictures in 1814, six years after the events. If the picture of the executions of May 3 [93] had no other virtues, it would still demonstrate that Goya's way of seeing and painting "only forms, forms that are lighted and forms that are not, planes that are near and planes that are far, projections, and hollows" gives to the subject, painted long after the event, the quality of an event that happens as we look at it. The victims, and the barren mound behind them, stand out against a dark sky in an explosion of light and blood. One man spreads his raised arms in defiance against the executioners. Another, a priest, prays; another seems only half comprehending; others clutch at themselves in terror or hide their faces in despair. Ranged in front of them, the uniformed soldiers, rifles firing, are like

92. GOYA: *The Toreador José Romero*, date unknown. 36 x 29½".
Collection Mrs. Carroll S. Tyson, Chestnut Hill, Pa.

automatons. Their faces are not shown, their stances are identical, they are painted in dull grays and browns. This depersonalization accentuates the humanity of the victims, and especially it makes the central defiant figure a symbol of the individual's revolt against the forces of organized oppression, even though, in Goya's world, he is impotent before them.

Not much later, Delacroix was to commemorate a similar popular uprising in Paris, which took place in 1830, with his *Liberty Leading the People* [94]. As a romantic idealist he gives us a flurry and surge of drapery around an allegorical female figure leading other figures who thus, inevitably, lose their human identity and become allegorical symbols also. Or, if we try to regard them as human beings, they

93. GOYA: *The Executions of May 3, 1808,* 1814. 104¾ x 135⅞". Prado, Madrid. (Photo Anderson.)

94. DELACROIX: *Liberty Leading the People,* 1830. 102½ x 128". Louvre, Paris.

are at best actors in a costumed pageant. Goya's central figure of the man with arms spread wide may be, as we have just said, something like a "symbol" of the spirit of liberty unquenchable in mankind, but if Goya had such an idea in mind he delivered it in terms of the facts of this world, not in a vision of an artificial one. Both pictures can be compared with *The Oath of the Horatii* [6] as a third treatment of the same general theme: the individual's sacrifice of self to an ideal of freedom and justice. Of the three, Goya's alone meets the world on its own terms. David's by this standard (which, of course, is not the standard to which David aspires) is chilly and abstract; Delacroix's is a bit high-flown. In both of them life serves as material for art, which then becomes important for its own sake,

95. DAUMIER: *The Battle of Schools,* from *Le Charivari,* 1855. Lithograph.

relegating life to second place. In Goya the raw material of life is ordered and intensified by an art that reveals, but never takes precedence over, the world in which man lives. This is why Goya is first a realist, although he is as dramatic as any romantic, as fantastic as any visionary. His art became a mine for later movements whose aims might even be at loggerheads with one another—impressionism, expressionism, even surrealism, all of which we will see. Goya demonstrates again that the arbitrary boundaries of one ism or another are never wide enough to encompass the total of a great artist's work.

This is especially true of another artist who by classification must be called a realist, a man who knew the world as well as Goya did, who painted it as literally yet more intimately, who was as aware of man's foibles and vanities as Goya was, and suffered more from them—yet who found man good where Goya found him ultimately base: the Frenchman Honoré Daumier.

Daumier: Realism and Bourgeois Culture

Daumier (1808–1879) was born in Marseille the year of the riots in Madrid and the executions of May 3. By 1830, the year of the uprisings celebrated in Delacroix's *Liberty Leading the People,* he was working at his first job in Paris as cartoonist for a publication called *La Caricature.* During the next forty years he produced some 4,000 popular cartoons by which he made his living as well as innumerable drawings and sketches and hundreds of paintings. Daumier was the noblest realist of them all; he was one of the finest painters of any school in nineteenth-century France; and he was buried in a pauper's grave at the age of seventy-one.

Just as romanticism had been the natural expression of the turbulence of the first half of the nineteenth century in France, so realism replaced it just as naturally as an expression of the second half. Daumier

96. DAUMIER: *Boy Running*, date unknown. Crayon and Wash, 6 x 9″. National Gallery of Art, Washington, D.C., Rosenwald Collection.

lived in the era of the *Bourgeoisie Triumphant*, the practical, matter-of-fact, cautious, comfort-loving man, scornful of theory if it did not serve a tangible, profitable end (hence he was no classicist) and suspicious of passion if it threatened his security (and hence he was not a romantic). He was the realistic man, the little man of great common sense.

If his world sounds like an infertile one for the artist, that is only because we forget what an artist is: if he is truly creative, an artist absorbs the gross experience of his time and distills from it its essential meaning. In France, around the middle years of the century, creative men in all the arts ceased to yearn toward ancient Greece and Rome, returned from the long jaunt to the Orient and began to examine things as they found them at home. They discovered in the prosaic world infinite material and, above all, infinite variety. They discovered that a peasant woman was a better subject for them than Ceres, that a respectable

bourgeoise housewife offered possibilities not even hinted at by Venus, and even that a common prostitute could be painted or written about more rewardingly than a harem full of odalisques. A street in Paris was discovered to be more dramatic than an Arabian lion hunt. And if a woman choosing a hat in a millinery shop was involved in making a decision less strenuous than the ones made by the Horatii or the Sabines, nevertheless her dilemma had its own legitimacy and could be the subject of a work of art commenting on human life.

Nor need such a comment be trivial. It had, among other advantages, the great one of being a comment made at first hand, as if made on the spot instead of being trumped up in the studio. To make such comments at full force, painters invented new techniques that horrified the Academy and eventually destroyed it as a potent force in French art. Artists discovered in realism the most flexible of all approaches to expression. Freed from the restrictions and recipes of classicism, no longer goaded by the romantic obligation to theatricalize, they discovered that the world around them offered everything, that at last the individual was freed to speak as he chose about what interested him most, to interpret the world according to his own convictions instead of echoing another man's formula. Classicism had shrunk like a dried pea; romanticism had swollen until it burst; realism offered the world of everyday as the painter's lodestone.

Realism served painters of all temperaments. Within the world at hand the man of classical temperament could find images of universal truths. The romantically inclined could find the passion he yearned for. The cynic, the sentimentalist, the social theorist, the objectivist, the wit—each might create his own image from the raw material of a single subject that in itself might be the most commonplace fragment of the world, familiar to everybody. Thus in its very flexibility, realism became more demanding than either classicism or romanticism had been: without the established devices of a David or a Delacroix to follow, the realist was exposed as whatever kind of man he was, big or little of spirit, imaginative or pedestrian in his perception of the world.

Daumier is the French counterpart of Goya in his contempt for hypocrisy, falsehood, and injustice. If he is a lesser master, it is because he was never allowed to reach full stature as a painter. Goya's *Caprichos* were withdrawn a few days after they were published, and he escaped punishment by the tribunal of the Inquisition for the temerity of his subjects only because he had had the greater temerity to dedicate them to Charles IV (who could have found everything he stood for attacked in them) and to seek, successfully, the King's protection. But Daumier, on the other hand, was imprisoned for a published caricature of his king, and his serious work was curtailed in 1835 under severe restrictions of the freedom of the press. Hobbled by poverty, without a market for his kind of painting, he was unable to paint at all until he was forty, and then he painted in complete obscurity with neither the time nor the

97. DAUMIER: *Grandes Eaux à Versailles*, from *Le Charivari*, July 28, 1844. Lithograph, 9 1/16 x 7 1/4″. The title is a pun, *Grandes Eaux* being literally *Great Waters* but referring to Versailles's famous fountains. Collection Carl Zigrosser, Philadelphia.

money—and, for that matter, not the reason—to do the ambitious pictures that force an artist's growth and prove his mettle. But Daumier was a great painter, and certainly one of the two or three finest draughtsmen of his century. And if compassionate observation of man in his frailty and his nobility is a standard of comparison, then Daumier surpasses Goya, and only Rembrandt, in the seventeenth century, can keep him company.

Because he was a man of the nineteenth century, Daumier, unlike Rembrandt, made his most profound statements by means of the most commonplace subjects, usually the city streets and the ordinary people in them. Instead of inventing allegories, fan-

98. DAUMIER: *Saprelotte!—Full!*, from *Le Charivari*, 1848. Lithograph, 10¼ x 8⅝″. Collection Carl Zigrosser, Philadelphia.

99. DAUMIER: *Before Moreau's Picture at the Salon*, from *Le Charivari*, 1864. Lithograph, 9½ x 8¼″. Collection Carl Zigrosser, Philadelphia.

tasies, and nightmares as Goya did to reveal man's nature, Daumier observed the attitudes men assumed and the expressions on their faces and reproduced their essence, while seeming only to sketch them casually, candid-camera fashion, as they went about the routine of their daily affairs.

Daumier: Social and Political Comment

Daumier was an untrained artist. He learned to draw by observation; he never dissected a body, but he knew more about the way a body moves, the way muscles and fat are disposed upon the skeleton, than any painter who made a fetish of classical anatomy. *The Battle of Schools* [95] is a caricature comment on the revolt of the realistic painter against academic idealism. A dirty little fellow in peasant clothes, armed with a thick heavy brush, faces a skinny academician, posed in the attitude of David's Romulus from *The Sa-*

bines and armed with a palette and a mahl stick (which was an accessory to the creation of the slick finish of academic painting). The reason this burlesque of the beautiful body of David's classical athlete is so funny is that its comic exaggerations of a skinny naked man are so true, so logical. These shrunken hams and knobby joints and pipestem legs are at least as brilliant a variation on the human form as are the Davidian forms they caricature, and they are based on a more supple familiarity with anatomical fact.

Daumier learned to draw as a caricaturist, and in his transition from caricature to serious painting he held to the strict economy of statement which is caricature's essence. In a few bent lines and an area or two of wash he could capture the physical mass, the action, and the inner nature of his subject, whether a group of people waiting at a station or a frightened boy running [96]. In this way, too, he resembles Rembrandt, who was Daumier's drawing master as nearly as he ever had one.

100. DAUMIER: *Behind in the Rent,* from *Le Charivari,* 1847. Lithograph, 10⅛ x 7½".

101. DAUMIER: *Turtledoves—Just the Way We Were,* from the series *Tout ce qu'on voudra,* 1848. Lithograph, 10½ x 9". Both Collection Carl Zigrosser, Philadelphia.

Daumier is the only important painter of the nineteenth century in France whose development was entirely independent of the Academy and the Salon: he neither received their favors nor needed to battle their opposition. This was because he did not regard himself as a painter with a career to make and a reputation to establish. He was a professional artist with a living to earn, and he earned it by working against deadlines for periodicals.

Such work could have been a prostitution of his genius if he had curried favor by yielding to popular standards. Instead, Daumier created a new standard that lifted the cartoon of social and political comment to the level of serious art. Even when his cartoons are most humorous they are never entirely trivial. When he draws a funny face, it is also the face of a specific character, produced by a way of life acting upon a temperament. In it we recognize an individual of a social type within a complicated social system.

The favorite target of Daumier's benign exposures was the lower middle class, uncomfortable in its dutiful pretensions to gentility [97–101]. He shows its members exhausted and puzzled at Salon exhibitions, drenched in their Sunday best by sudden downpours on an excursion to Versailles, harassed by squawling brats who nullify the order and comfort of their flats, reduced to a thousand indignities by the frictions and irritations of living with their fellows who never quite recognize in them the superiorities they aspire to within themselves. Behind in their rent, they have humiliating encounters with the landlord on the stairs. The bus doesn't wait for them. Friends yawn at their funny stories; their collars are always too tight or too loose; and they realize one day that they and their mates look terrible in their bathing suits. But their lives are also full of sudden small domestic felicities. A middle-aged couple resting under a tree remember their youth as they watch birds nesting. Young parents glow

102. Guys: The King and Queen of Greece and their suite passing the base of the Acropolis, 1854. Pencil and watercolor, 10¾ x 16. Collection T. Edward Hanley, Bradford, Pa.

with pride at their little boy, although he is an absurd replica of his pompous father. Friends exchange intellectual platitudes about the Salon success of the year, impressed with one another's acumen.

The quality that raises these typical Daumier cartoons above the level of humorous journalism should be apparent when they are compared with the pictorial reporting of Daumier's contemporary, Constantin Guys (1805–1892), who is now recognized as a minor master although, like Daumier, he was seldom thought of as an artist during his lifetime. Guys seems to have been in accord with this opinion; today he would probably have been a news photographer.

Guys avoided attention and his life is not well documented, but what we know of it is fascinating enough. At eighteen he was a soldier with Byron in the Greek war, and four years later he was a dragoon in the French army. He traveled everywhere in Europe and went to the Orient. For a

while he lived in London, giving lessons in French and in drawing and selling sketches to magazines. At the middle of the century (which his life nearly spanned) he was a war correspondent for the *Illustrated London News*, one of the few journals of the time carrying pictures of current events; he covered the Revolution of 1848 and the Crimean War. Between wars he covered the ballet, opera, and the like.

His wonderful sketches, done on the spot, would be sent to the journal for wood engraving, the means of reproduction then most in use. They would lose much of their own character in this translation, but many of the originals still exist. The one illustrated here [102] shows the King in the streets of Athens, and some of the notes scribbled across the lower part of the drawing read: "For details of costumes of the parties in the Royal Cortège, the gendarmes, the people crowding the gardens, lining the street, etc. etc., see the annexed sketches. Acropolis on the right—further up in the background the new observatory—built on top of the hill. Carriages in the garden crowded with ladies with national and French fashionable costume indifferently." From notes like these the wood engravers filled in details. Sometimes a drawing would bear a note such as, "Observe all details of costume, they are entirely accurate, change background at will—make it snow if you wish."

But only a fraction of the drawings and watercolors of modes and manners for which Guys is best known [103] were done for reproduction; he seems to have drawn all the time, year after year, thousands of drawings. Pen or pencil with wash, sometimes monochrome, sometimes with a touch or two of additional color, sometimes watercolor in a few fresh clear tints, were his medium. He evokes the epoch of the Second Empire with its crinolines, its courtesans, its display, its high style flavored with a dash of vulgarity—the epoch's, not Guys's. One of his favorite subjects was the promenade in the Bois de Boulogne, with its prancing horses and its carriages filled with women in great masses of finery—hats, ruffles, ribbons, shawls, with lace-trimmed umbrellas rising above them like the smallest flowers springing out of great bouquets.

Among his contemporaries, Guys, like Daumier, had a few admirers among knowledgeable painters and critics. The great Manet (soon to be seen) was one of them, and Baudelaire published a famous article on him in the journal *Figaro* in 1863 (but written in 1859) called "A Painter of Modern Life." (Guys refused to let his name be printed, but permitted the use of his initial, which occasionally appears on a drawing.) Baudelaire recognized the elegance of Guys's style, and the deft economy with which the artist caught the visual essence of his subjects. But compared with Daumier, Guys is a reporter with exceptional vivacity and charm but not much depth. This is comparison with a giant, and does not affect the truth that Guys is an artist of stature as well as a recorder of the modes and manners of a particular society. His drawings are works of art marked by finesse and flair and infallible sensitivity to the most telling details of fashionable trap-

103. GUYS: *Une Elegante*, 1850–60. Watercolor, 15¼ x 10½". Fogg Art Museum, Cambridge, Mass., Maurice Wertheim Collection.

pings. But Daumier's cartoons are works of art rooted in the same humanitarian spirit that inspired his greatest painting.

Daumier's cartoons are based upon the assumption, never questioned, that man is good, whatever indignities, absurdities, and brutalizations life may inflict upon him. This was also Rembrandt's assumption, except that Rembrandt could not go so far as to admit the absurdities. That Daumier admits them, even cherishes them, explains the attraction held for him by a favorite subject, Don Quixote [104]. The addle-pated old man, mounted on his bony nag of a charger, his own bony silhouette topped off by the tin basin he imagines to be a knightly helmet, rides forth toward one imagined chivalric adventure after another, followed by his fat, stolid, uncomprehending and loyal lackey, Sancho Panza, who pulls his master out of one mud puddle or dung heap after another, where the old man's adventures always end. The story of Don Quixote is nominally a satire on the

104. DAUMIER: *Don Quixote and Sancho Panza*, date unknown. 22¼ x 33¼″. Collection Mr. and Mrs. Charles S. Payson, New York.

105. DAUMIER: *The Witnesses*, 1872. Lithograph, 10 x 8¾″. Metropolitan Museum of Art.

romantic foolishness of chivalric fiction, but it is also an undercover affirmation of the invincibility of the spirit: after each humiliating fall the old man pulls himself together and dodders forth toward a new one, his illusions intact. The paunchy bourgeois who gets caught in the rain, who misses his bus, who goes through a terrible world sustained by a blind, unreasoning conviction of his own importance—to Daumier, this paunchy bourgeois is noble in his absurdity if he remains an honest man.

But when Daumier is confronted with corruption, stupidity, hypocrisy, or chicanery in high places, his tolerance vanishes. *The Witnesses* [105] could serve as well today as an indictment of warmongers as it did in 1872. In fact it has done so, in hundreds of descendants, ever since. The politicians ranged in tiers in *Le Ventre Législatif* (*The Legislative Belly* [106]— usually more politely translated as *The Legislative Body*, at the expense of Daumier's point) are individually identifiable

106. DAUMIER: *Le Ventre Législatif,* 1834. Lithograph 11 x 17″. Collection Carl Zigrosser, Philadelphia.

as Louis Philippe's henchmen, but even without this reference the caricatures stand as murderous revelations of the mentality of corrupt political opportunists anywhere, any time.

In the same year as *Le Ventre Législatif,* 1834, Daumier published the great lithograph, *Rue Transnonain* [107]. At the time of its publication the title was enough to explain the scene where a family lies murdered in the disorder of a bedroom—a father in nightshirt and nightcap, lying on the body of his child, with the body of a woman in the shadows at the left, and the head of an older man projecting into the picture at the right. The Rue Transnonain was a street in Paris inhabited by workers who were suspected of participation in the disorders of the Republican Revolt of 1834. When it was fired on from an apartment house, the civil guard broke in and shot the inhabitants, innocent or guilty.

David, as he did in *Marat* [9] would have idealized the figures in the scene as far as possible, certainly substituting a beautiful body for that of the stocky, paunchy father. The rumpled nightshirt

would have fallen into folds of classical purity. Delacroix would have chosen a different moment, perhaps the tumultuous entrance of the guard into the room, a swirl of figures, a sort of *Sardanapalus* [49] or a *Scio* [46] in a new locale. Either artist, on the evidence of similar achievements, might have produced a fine picture. But Daumier rejects these dramas to bring us into the room, in all its commonplaceness. He shows us the grossness of the father, the intimate disorder of the bed, and the woman's body sprawled and ugly, the more pathetic because it is mercilessly real.

Daumier: His Faith

Daumier turned out his lithographic cartoons for popular consumption in journals on the average of three a week, with occasional individual stones, such as *Rue Transnonain,* for general sale. In the humorous cartoons having to do with the daily scene, the faith Daumier lived by is only implied in the affectionate quality of his raillery. More searching comments would have been

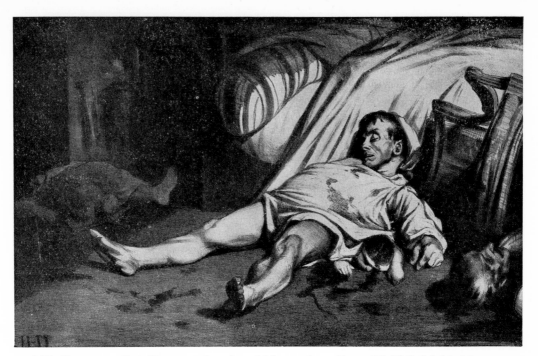

107. DAUMIER: *Rue Transnonain*, 1834. Lithograph, 11¼ x 17⅜". Philadelphia Museum of Art, Bequest of Fiske Kimball.

108. DAUMIER: *After the Trial,* date unknown. Watercolor, 11 x 14¼". Philadelphia Museum of Art, Anonymous Loan.

inappropriate, wasted, and for that matter impossible, since no man can produce three major works every seven days.

But in his paintings, which were known to only a few people during his lifetime, he speaks at full strength to say that, in spite of Rue Transnonains, Legislative Bellies, and the skeletons of men killed by war and starvation, mankind is good. This is Daumier's faith. The mere fact that he held it does not make him a greater or a lesser artist than a pessimist like Goya. Optimism and pessimism are not aesthetic qualities. Nor, of course, is it "good" or virtuous to believe that mankind is "good." Pollyannaism is likely to be more dangerous than skepticism, sentimentalism more vicious than cynicism. But Daumier is neither a Pollyanna nor a sentimentalist, and his conviction that mankind is ultimately good must be recognized if his painting is to be understood as anything more than a representation of people going about the routine of their daily affairs.

In his paintings Daumier seldom accuses, preferring to affirm the triumph of good rather than to expose the evils standing in its way. True, there are the numerous savage representations of lawyers [108], who for Daumier, familiar with the venal courts of the period, were a compound of arrogance, pomposity, and corruption, feeding on the ills and confusions of other men. But for all their trenchancy, these pictures are exceptions. We need only compare the *Third Class Carriage* [109], with its young peasant mother and children accompanied by the old grandmother, with any young beauty and old hag of Goya's to understand that, where Goya believes that life is a process of physical and moral corruption, Daumier finds life ultimately incorruptible —by its very force of growth and continuation, if by nothing else.

Daumier states this conclusion even more universally in *Soup* [110], where the peasant mother feeds voraciously on the food she has torn from the earth while her child suckles at her breast. The two figures are bound together in a circular pattern of lines suggesting in their inevitable continuity not only the endless cycle of life but, by their fierce vitality, the triumphant force of man's constant self-regeneration.

Yet, magnificent as they are, Daumier's pictures of peasants, of people close to the soil, are not his most individual or his most subtle achievements. His peasants are still related to "nature's noblemen," not too much changed from the "noble savage" conceived in the eighteenth century. And while Daumier was working, the painter Millet (to be seen shortly) was also discovering the peasant in similar interpretations. Daumier's individual achievement rests, finally, in his discovery of human nobility in a more obscure quarter: that vast middle ground between the man of the soil at one end and the man of worldly position or intellectual achievement at the other, within the dreary reaches of undistinguished city streets where ordinary people live out their lives in rented cells. Daumier's man is the little man of good will whom he first discovered by satirizing him, the good bourgeois who for all his confusions is neither vicious nor a fool in the long run. In *The Print Collector* [111], Daumier declares his faith in this man as a rational creature.

The Print Collector is painted in a few scrubs of color dominated by grays and browns. It shows a man of no particular

109. DAUMIER: *Third Class Carriage*, c. 1862. 25¾ x 35½". Metropolitan Museum of Art, New York, H. O. Havemeyer Collection

110. DAUMIER: *Soup*, date unknown. Wash drawing, 11 x 15¾" Louvre, Paris.

distinction or individuality, although he exists vividly, looking through a portfolio of prints in a small shop. His figure is reduced nearly to silhouette; the simplification is extreme, but an additional line of detail would be superfluous. The man is all there —the body beneath the clothes, the spirit within the body. The clothes tell us of a position in the world—not a position of any consequence; the body tells us other facts—

111. DAUMIER: *The Print Collector*, date unknown. 13⅜ x 10¼".
Philadelphia Museum of Art, Wilstach Fund.

112. DAUMIER: *First Class Carriage*, 1864. Wash drawing, 8 x
11¾". Walters Art Gallery, Baltimore.

age, and that this is a city man, for instance. We do not need to deduce these various facts. We are presented with them complete, in the total impression of the man's reality, as we might understand them at a glance, without deduction or specification, if he passed us on the street. We can say flatly that this is a middle-class man who collects prints as a hobby; beyond that, we may ponder the idea that print-collecting is not a necessary animal function, such as feeding and sleeping; and that, hence, it is proof that this is a human being possessed like other human beings of the thing that separates him from the animals, called intellect, soul, consciousness, ego, or any of dozens of other names. We may even point to various means Daumier has used to say this. We can make a symbol, for instance, of the way the figure emerges from mysterious shadows into even more mysterious lights. But in the end we cannot altogether explain how Daumier says that man is part of a miracle so good that none of his frailties is of any importance when balanced against the fact of his existence.

Daumier's basic premise of goodness alleviates the melancholy of his second one: that within the crowds and conformity of the city the individual is psychologically isolated. Daumier is the first painter to express this phenomenon of modern life. He represents his print collector alone—literally alone in the picture, although the crowds passing on the street, the proprietor of the shop, and other customers are certainly near by. And each of the people in the *First Class Carriage* [112] is alone in his own world, even while crowded side by side with the other passengers. In some of Daumier's pictures men establish a tenuous bridge between themselves. An artist shows his prints to a collector; two men ponder a game of chess, warmed by an illusion of intimacy through recognition of the identity of their mutual isolation; prisoners sing together [113]; old friends share a drink at a table in a garden [114]. These moments of intimacy are poignant because they are rare. In *The Drama* [115] Daumier shows us an audience carried away by a performance on the stage, each man unconscious of the shouldering and pressing of the other people around him, absorbed in an illusion created by shoddy scenery and wild posturings, an illusion more real than his contact with his fellow men will be when the performance is over and he leaves the theater with the crowd.

Daumier: His Life

A few facts of Daumier's life are pertinent here. Daumier showed precocious talent as a child, but his family, which had moved from his birthplace of Marseilles to Paris, refused to let him study art. He entered painting by the back door of journalism. At twenty-two he was doing political cartoons on *La Caricature*, and it was for one of these that he was imprisoned for six months, when he was twenty-four. This was in 1832, and the cartoon was *Gargantua*, showing Louis Philippe swallowing bags of gold extracted from the people.

Daumier's drawing at this period was rather solidly modeled within closed outlines, as can still be seen in *Le Ventre Législatif* and *Rue Transnonain*. His history as a draughtsman is one of steady change toward a more broken, open, nervous, expressive line, with greater and greater economy of modeling, as evident in the other drawings just illustrated. A pen and ink drawing of a horse and rider [116] shows how far he carried this technique.

In 1835 *La Caricature* was replaced by *Le Charivari** on which Daumier worked for the rest of his professional life. The realistic novelist Balzac was also a member of its staff and commented that "this boy has some Michelangelo under his skin." Baudelaire was one of the very few others who recognized in Daumier something more than a skillful commercial cartoonist.

In 1877 Daumier's eyes failed after forty years of overwork. Corot, a saint among painters, had given him a small country cottage some years before, and Daumier retired there on a state pension awarded

---

* A *charivari* is a mock serenade of discordant noises, made by beating on pots and pans, howling, and yelling, beneath the windows of someone who has given displeasure—a good name for a critical journal.

113. DAUMIER: *Prison Choir*, date unknown. 19¾ x 24″. Walters Art Gallery, Baltimore.

114. DAUMIER: *The Good Friends*, date unknown. Wash drawing, 9¼ x 11⅞″. Baltimore Museum of Art.

him by the Third Republic. The pension was more than deserved. Under the various regimes since 1830 Daumier had been unyieldingly and courageously a republican propagandist.

When Daumier died two years after his retirement the hundreds of paintings in his

115. DAUMIER: *The Drama*, date unknown. 38 x 35″. *Neue Stadt-galerie*, Munich.

116. DAUMIER: *Rider*, date unknown. Pen drawing, 8¼ x 10½″. Private collection.

little house were purchased by a syndicate from his widow for almost nothing. When they were put on the market years later, plus numerous forgeries that still cause confusion, they were worth a fortune. The paintings date from 1848, when Daumier presented an allegorical figure of the Republic in a competition for mural decorations in the Hôtel de Ville—which, of course, he did not win. His first exhibition was arranged in 1878 just before his retirement, when he was seventy years old. Thus it happened that the school of realism, where in retrospect Daumier is a major figure, had been born, had fought its battles, and had given way to a new variant called impressionism before these realistic masterpieces were known.

In the meanwhile realism's battles had been fought, not expertly but with the greatest of pleasure, under the leadership of a painter who fell half by accident into that position, a man a decade younger than Daumier who died the year before Daumier's tardy exhibition, and who had left France some years before that—Gustave Courbet.

Courbet: His Theories versus His Practice

The theories of realism as advanced by Courbet (1819–1877) were not very complicated. Neither were they always very clear, since Courbet was not much of an analytical thinker. When it was necessary for him to formulate a written statement, he did so with the help of friends who were better at words than he was. Perhaps this explains why what Courbet said about painting and what he did in painting never quite agree. With the best intentions in the world his friends were likely to clarify his half-formed theories in directions expedient to purposes immediately at hand, with less regard for Courbet's painting than for their own convictions.

"Show me an angel and I will paint one" is the bluntest of Courbet's pronouncements. He held that "painting is an essentially concrete art, and can consist only of the representation of things both real and existing"—a limitation that would have ruled out all classical painting except portraits, all romantic invention, and most of the work of the old masters most admired by Courbet himself.

Nor is Courbet's own painting so objective as such pronouncements imply it should be. Although he stated that he wanted to "translate the customs, the ideas, and the look" of his own time into pictures, he added that he wanted to do so "according to his own understanding" of them. This means that while he referred directly to the world around him for his material, instead of to an imagined antiquity or a romantic Orient, he interpreted what he saw rather than merely transcribing it. And if he did not paint angels, if he painted only what he could see, what Courbet chose to see was unusually dramatic rather than prosaic. Even when a subject was nominally prosaic, he observed it more romantically than would be expected from a painter tagged "realist" and dedicated to the annihilation of the romantic ideal. His realism was conscious, but his romanticism was inborn.

It must be remembered, too, that we see Courbet's innovations in reverse perspective. We look at them from this side, across an intervening century during which realism went far beyond Courbet in the direction he set. From this distance he seems as romantic as he does realistic, but in the Salons of his own time his realism was extreme.

But all these considerations are historical. Historically it is important that Courbet was called a realist, an anti-idealist. But beyond that, beyond realism or idealism or any other ism, Courbet is a painter, in the purest sense of the word *painter*. His paint simply as paint, as a rich oily substance applied to canvas, is magnificent.

His *Young Bather* [117] is typical of many Courbets that are likely today to strike us first with the mincing artificiality of the pose. The fact that in combination with this artificiality the model is painted with a high degree of realism may even make the picture a bit ludicrous; standards in feminine beauty have changed, and we see only an overweight young woman affecting an unconvincing daintiness. The es-

117. COURBET: *Young Bather,* 1866. 51¼ x 38¼". Metropolitan Museum of Art, New York, H. O. Havemeyer Collection.

118. COURBET: *Woman with a Parrot,* 1866. 51 x 77". Metropolitan Museum of Art, New York, H. O. Havemeyer Collection.

119. COURBET: *Two Girls on the Banks of the Seine*, 1856. 66½ x 81⅛". *Petit Palais*, Paris.

sential realism of the picture is further compromised by the landscape background that has been trumped up behind the figure. The branch the model holds in her left hand is retouched with a few leaves, but it is still a studio prop not very convincingly related to the tree it is supposed to grow from. Such inconsistencies conceal the revolutionary character of the *Young Bather*, although nothing can conceal the magnificence of its painting.

In the *Woman with a Parrot* [118], painted late in Courbet's career at a time when he was having a period of fashionable success and his disciples were accusing him of compromising with conventional standards of prettiness, his innate romanticism is given full play. As an avowed realist Courbet may have painted the model very much as she looked, posed in the studio. Nevertheless, the pose is theatrical and the whole

affair several steps removed from what one would expect to encounter in the course of daily events, even if it is less so than an angel with wings. The picture is full of artificialities that contradict its realism, but all contradictions are meaningless in the face of the sumptuousness of the paint, applied with such richness and vigor as to make the flesh and the gleaming torrent of chestnut hair almost tangible.

Ultimately it is in this tangibility of the image that Courbet's realism lies. In *Two Girls on the Banks of the Seine* [119], one of the most luscious paintings of the century, the weight of languid flesh is all but palpable against the cool moisture of grass and leaves; the heavy cloth and airy lace have their own existence. In the portrait of *A Spanish Woman* [120] the hand concealed in the heavy hair exists as certainly as the visible portions of the figure, because the tangibility of the whole carries with it the feel of the palm pressed into the dark locks. This is Courbet's realism. But the mood of both pictures is romantically evocative. The dark shadows, the rich lights, the color that swells and recedes from black to brilliance, are moody and dramatic. It is a mood Courbet repeats again and again with complete independence of his subject. *Lady in a Riding Habit* (*L'Amazon*) [121] is a portrait of Louise Colet, a poetess of sorts with a spectacularly original and irritating personality. Courbet is not realist enough to present her features with objective accuracy or to explore her character; she serves him only as a figure emerging romantically from lushly romantic shadows. In his landscapes [122] Courbet goes to nature instead of fabricating a vision, but if he begins with real rocks, real streams, real trees, and real deer with their russet pelts, he ends by investing nature with an almost supernatural richness, where grottoes of foliage sink into greenish-black shadows and come forward into vitreous lights, where slabs of rock disappear from the warm sun into cool, heavy water, a nature as sensuous as flesh.

And always there is the paint, its own fat oiliness a part of the expressiveness of the painted objects. Courbet frequently applied paint with his palette knife, the thin flexible blade that is ordinarily used to mix colors on the palette. He would strike in the side of a rock with the flat of the knife, or with its tip he would flick in a sparkle of light. He painted whole pictures in this way, a technique familiar enough today, but with him an innovation.

Courbet was a natural painter. His only instruction was brief and under poor masters. He was the son of a farmer—a wealthy one—near the provincial city of Ornans, not a locality offering much opportunity for the discovery and development of a painter's talent. When he went to Paris, Courbet found his teachers on the walls of the Louvre, especially in the paintings of such seventeenth-century masters as Zurbarán, with their heavy shadows and full, rounded forms.

In effect self-trained, Courbet nevertheless had a picture accepted in the Salon of

120. COURBET: *A Spanish Woman*, 1855. 32 x 25¾". Philadelphi Museum of Art, John G. Johnson Collection.

1844, one that he had painted two years earlier when he was only twenty-three. The picture, a self-portrait with a black dog, was not much noticed. He exhibited six canvases in 1848, an exceptional year, a year of revolution, when, without a jury, the Salon was thrown open to all comers.

The following year this excessive democracy was corrected; but in one of the efforts to liberalize the Salon that occurred sporadically during the century, the new government ruled that the jury be composed of painters chosen by election rather than appointed from the academic clique. This liberal jury awarded Courbet a medal for a painting called *After Dinner at Ornans*, a picture of ordinary people sitting around a table in a simple interior. Courbet also had

121. COURBET: *Lady in a Riding Habit*, c. 1856. 45½ x 35⅛".
Metropolitan Museum of Art, New York, H. O. Havemeyer
Collection.

another self-portrait in this Salon, a romantically conceived painting in heavy chiaroscuro, called *The Man with the Leather
Belt* [123]. Courbet was a handsome fellow,
and until he became grossly fat he never
tired of painting himself, always in the most
admiring way. This self-adulation would be
more bothersome if it were less naïve.

His early success did not last long in
official circles. The Salon juries subsequent
to the unusually liberal one of 1849 bitterly
resented the fluke that had given a medal
to this offensive intruder, and from that
time on Courbet was mercilessly attacked
by the Salon and reviled by conventional
critics. One wonders what they might have
said about Daumier (who was ten times the
realist Courbet was), if he had offered the

irritations to the aestheticians and the competition to the established painters that
Courbet did. For Courbet became a real
threat. While Daumier was painting in obscurity, Courbet was seeking recognition
through a declaration of war just as the romantics had done before him, choosing the
usual battlefield, the Salon, for his conquest.
He was a threat to the intellectual lethargy
of the average critic, who had no intention
of examining new ideas when the old ones
were so easy to repeat year after year, and
he was a potential competitor to the conventional painters who had staked out a
market in the gigantic salesroom that the
Salon had become.

Courbet: His "Socialism"

When Courbet won his medal he had no
theories about realism. He was painting
only what it appealed to him to paint. Both
After Dinner at Ornans and *The Man with
the Leather Belt* deny Courbet's later contention that the artist "does not have the
right to enlarge upon" nature, that he
"trifles with it at the risk of denaturing the
beautiful which exists in the most diverse
forms of reality." He claimed that "Beauty
as given by nature is superior to all the
conventions of the artist." But of course it
isn't, and in these early paintings as well
as in most of his later ones the conventions
of the artist serve Courbet well, not so
much in the direction of his "visible and
tangible world" as in the expression of
some poetic mystery existing beneath it.
Even *Two Girls on the Banks of the Seine*,
which takes art out of the studio and puts
it on a familiar river bank—reflecting the
kind of life enjoyed by the new middle
class with its gardens, its walks in the country, and its Sunday excursions—ends not as
a representation of two young bourgeois
women on the banks of the Seine but as a
sensuous evocation.

However, in certain pictures Courbet's
departure from conventional subject matter
and his relatively realistic treatment of it—
relative in comparison with the derivative
idealism making up the work of the rank
and file of his contemporaries—offered some

122. COURBET: *The Grotto*, c. 1860. 25¼ x 31⅛″. Baltimore Museum of Art, Cone Collection.

123. COURBET: *The Man with the Leather Belt*, c. 1844. 39½ x 32½″. Louvre, Paris.

basis for the attacks that were made upon him. His trouble with the Salon began the year following his medal. Under Salon regulations any painter who had won a medal could exhibit thereafter without submitting his work to the jury. The jury of 1850, back to normal abuses, suffered from its immediate predecessor's liberality. Courbet took advantage of his position as a previous medal winner to exhibit nine pictures, including a large demonstration piece called *A Burial at Ornans* [124], showing a group of peasants and *bourgeoisie* around an open grave in the harsh countryside near his native city.

A Burial at Ornans is an impressive picture, huge, sober, richly and conscientiously painted, a prodigious technical demonstration without fireworks. It is irreproachable as a demonstration of the academic virtues of sound draughtsmanship, and it is more

124. COURBET: *A Burial at Ornans*, 1849. 123 x 261". Louvre, Paris.

than adequate as a composition. But the attacks on it were virulent. Without much question the objections were quite arbitrary, being inspired more by Courbet's personal presumptuousness than by the inherent nature of the painting. Courbet had observed the simple people around the grave most sympathetically, but for the picture to have been labeled "socialistic" for this reason seems fantastic. Nevertheless this happened, and *Stonebreakers* in the same Salon, showing a laborer and a ragged boy at this work, was given the same tag. Both subjects were unusual, and in both pictures common people were represented without the sentimentality or condescension that would have made them acceptable to Salon taste. Compared with the prettified subjects alongside them on the walls of the exhibition, Courbet's peasants seemed like brutes, and the painter's normally sympathetic attitude toward them was found to be socially and politically offensive.

Courbet enjoyed the furore, especially since he soon found admirers outside the Salon. Because the aestheticians attacked his paintings as socialism, the socialists countered by defending them as art. This confusion of values was unfortunate for Courbet. Under the influence of the so-

cialist philosopher Pierre Joseph Proudhon, with whom he formed a friendship, Courbet began to take himself seriously as a political thinker. Labeled a socialist, he said that he was "not only socialist, but furthermore democratic and republican, in a word a partisan of all revolution and above all a realist, a sincere friend of the true truth." Such a statement sounds good at first, but it begins to fall apart when examined. Émile Zola, the realistic novelist and one of the great liberal spirits of the century, recognized Courbet's inadequacy as a social philosopher and said, "Oh, poor dear Master, Proudhon's book has left you with a case of democratic indigestion." Proudhon's book was the formulation of a theory of the social function of art that he set down in 1865, his *Du principe de l'art et de sa destination sociale.* Courbet boasted that *A Burial at Ornans* was the burial of romanticism, echoing Gros's remark that *Massacres of Scio* was the massacre of painting. He made an effort to bind his art to political theory, but the truth is that he was too much of a painter and not enough of a theorist to conceive a painting in anything but the shallowest of theoretical terms. In celebration of the appearance of his friend's book, Courbet painted a portrait of Proud-

125. Courbet: *Proudhon and His Daughters*, 1865. 66 x 78″. *Petit Palais*, Paris.

hon with his two little daughters [125]. The socialist philosopher sits in a very pose-y pose, with books and manuscript near by, painted with acutely naturalistic precision. Courbet's "democratic indigestion" is paralleled in the images of this picture, where he forces his realistic theory into a literal application and produces the most artificial painting of his career.

Courbet enjoyed being in the public eye, where he remained dramatically as he continued to exhibit scot-free of the jury in successive Salons. At the 1853 Salon, Napoleon III did him the service of threatening to slash one of his paintings with a whip. Fortunately Courbet was wealthy enough not to have to depend upon selling his pictures to the Salon public, and when he did sell he sold for good prices to collectors with special tastes. His chief patron was Alfred Bruyas of Montpellier, but the Comte de Morny, a powerful dignitary of the Second Empire, was also his patron in secret. Courbet used to visit Bruyas in

Montpellier, and has recorded one visit in a picture of staggering arrogance, *The Encounter*, which came to be called *Bonjour Monsieur Courbet* [126], showing the painter setting out for a day's work, posed to display his handsome bearded profile at its best, while Bruyas and a manservant address him with the subservient humility appropriate to vassals before their lord. Bruyas was not the kind of man shown here —but Courbet was.

Courbet: "The Painter's Studio"

At this time the Paris cafés were becoming more and more the meeting places for discussion and exchange of ideas between artists, as the younger ones began more and more to abandon the studios of official painters to seek out the men who were in revolt against the academic system. Courbet's special cafés were the *Brasserie des Martyrs* and the *Andler Keller,* where he

126. COURBET: *The Encounter*, 1854. 50¾ x 58½″. *Musée Fabre*, Montpellier.

was surrounded by admiring students. In spite of his egotism Courbet was interested in helping young painters. He visited their studios, was patient with their requests for aid, and seems generally to have given them the stimulus that they could not find in the hidebound instruction of the official schools.

Finally in 1861 there was a minor revolt within the sacred walls, and a group of students from the Academy petitioned Courbet to teach them. In a public letter, written with the help of his literary friend Castagnary, Courbet told them that he could not consent to enter into a student–teacher relationship because each man's art was necessarily his own if it was to be of any significance. But he took advantage of the opportunity to make a statement of faith, and he did consent to the setting up of a studio to give informal criticism to the students, who would be working largely on their own. The studio was not a great success, but it produced one noteworthy sketch

showing the class at work with a bull on the model stand instead of the usual nude. (The bull actually had been brought into the studio.) This was in line with the idea that realism should abandon all artificialities and deal with the coarse reality of simple things, but there is also something artificial about a bull on a model stand.

Courbet's pre-eminence as a rebel and martyr had been established a few years before this student petition. As the informally proclaimed leader of the realists, he had set about the production of a painting that would be his manifesto, standing in a corresponding position to *The Horatii* and *The Sabines* for classicism, and to *Raft of the Medusa* and *Massacres of Scio* for romanticism. The full title of the tremendous picture was *The Painter's Studio, a Real Allegory, Summarizing a Seven-year Phase of My Artistic Life* [127]. The title, and the conception of the picture, were presumptuous; Courbet never questioned for a moment that the general public would be as interested in the man Courbet as in the theory of realism, and this egocentricity is carried out literally in the composition. The artist is seated dramatically in the middle of his picture at work on a landscape. On one side of the studio are grouped the proletarian types who had served him as subjects, while on the other are various friends and well-wishers. In detail, the allegory runs something like this:

At left: a poacher and his dog (the Hunt, a frequent subject of Courbet's) seem to look with some suspicion at a sombrero, a guitar, and a dagger (Romantic Poetry—also, elements in certain very early paintings by Courbet). A death's head lies upon a copy of the periodical *Le Journal des Débats* (the Press, and perhaps a comment on censorship, or the sterility of critical journalism). A lay figure, or artist's manikin, hangs attached to a stake (either a symbol of academic art, or a reference to paintings of the Crucifixion, or both). A vine-grower (Labor) is surrounded by figures representing types who, in Courbet's half-jelled social philosophy, prey upon the people, namely, a Jewish secondhand dealer (Commerce), a buffoon (the Theater), a priest, and a prostitute.

So much for the left. At right: in the foreground, a man and woman who represent knowledgeable art lovers; a couple embracing near the window (Love? Possibly the free love of socialist liberation); the poet and friendly critic Baudelaire, reading a book and representing the Art of Poetry.* The critic Champfleury represents Prose; Proudhon himself, who probably suggested this allegorical mish-mash, represents Social Philosophy; one Promayet, Music, and one Max Buchon, Realistic Poetry. Finally, the enlightened collector and friend Bruyas symbolizes the Maecenas upon whose patronage the arts have always depended.

As for the nude model standing behind the painter, she may represent Courbet's realistic muse, but she also fulfills the unwritten law that every demonstration piece

---

* Baudelaire's friendly connection with Courbet did not last long. Later he referred to "the mob of vulgar artists and literary men whose shortsighted intelligence takes shelter behind the vague and obscure word Realism."

of this kind intended for Salon exhibition must include a nude, to show the painter's mastery, and some still life, here the magnificently painted yards of cloth she holds and the objects upon it where it tumbles onto the floor. As for the admiring small boy and the cat, their allegorical function is tenuous if it exists at all.

The absurdities of this rigmarole are so extreme that it would be unfair to enumerate them if Courbet's painting, as usual, did not make up for everything else. As a manifesto of realism the picture is as curious as it is as an allegory. Separate passages are only as realistic as Courbet usually was, which means that they are romantically presented. And when we add to this the unrealism of the arrangement, *The Painter's Studio* becomes a manifesto indeed—but not the one Courbet had in mind, proclaiming as it does the victory of his persistently romantic vision over his professed goal.

Courbet: The Pavilion of Realism

Courbet planned to exhibit *The Painter's Studio* along with a second showing of his first sensation, *A Burial at Ornans*, at the Exposition Universelle of 1855, one of the series of world's fairs staged in France at intervals during the century. For this Exposition the conditions of the Salon were modified. It was made international for the first time, with an international jury. The French entries were to summarize the preeminence of France in the arts, and in these special circumstances the *hors concours* ruling permitting medalists to exhibit without submitting to the jury was abrogated. Several of Courbet's entries were accepted, but *The Painter's Studio* and *A Burial at Ornans* were rejected by a jury that must have felt great elation in returning the *Burial* this time, in retaliation for Courbet's having inflicted it on an impotent jury in 1850.

The rejection of *The Painter's Studio* was especially disconcerting to Courbet, since Ingres, who had not entered a picture in the Salon for twenty years, had been induced to carry the banner for classicism with forty canvases, a retrospective of his career, while "modern" art was represented

127. COURBET: *The Painter's Studio,* 1855. 141 x 234". Louvre, Paris.

by Delacroix with about the same number. Romanticism, a quarter of a century after its youthful excesses, was becoming acceptable to the general public, although again Delacroix's mysterious political affiliations may have carried some weight.

To compete with these impressive displays of idealism, Courbet decided to exhibit his rejected paintings, with others, in a special building constructed at his own expense, which he called the Pavilion of Realism. David had made a small fortune through private exhibition of *The Sabines,* and so had Géricault with the *Raft of the Medusa,* but Courbet's Pavilion of Realism was a fiasco. It attracted so few visitors that he did not even recover its costs, a hard blow in itself but not nearly so hard as the humiliating implication of public indifference. The Pavilion of Realism was deserted during most of the Exposition, but its unhappy entrepreneur might have taken some comfort if he could have read an entry in the journal of one distinguished visitor. "I

went to see Courbet's exhibition," Delacroix wrote. "There alone for nearly an hour. I discovered a masterpiece in his rejected picture. I couldn't tear myself away from it. They have refused, there, one of the most extraordinary works of our time."

And of course Delacroix was right. *The Painter's Studio* is an extraordinary picture and a fine one. Its pretentious allegorical nonsense is not important. When all is said and done, Courbet remains here, as in all his work, a pure painter in spite of his theorizing and his politicking. The art of David is richer after we know it as a demonstration of a theory of art and a statement of social dedication. The more we know about Delacroix's aesthetics and his technical processes the more we find in his pictures. But with Courbet it is the reverse. His professed realism and his professed socialism are worse than no help at all in enjoying his art; they would actually stand in the way if we had to consider them, but fortunately we do not.

128. Poussin: *The Funeral of Phocion*, 1648. 46¾ x 70½″. Louvre, Paris.

Courbet was a painter-born, with neither Delacroix's intellect nor David's shrewdness. But beyond either of these men he had a capacity for responding to the everyday world, a talent of such strength that when his brush was in his hand his theories about art and society dropped away and left him purely and simply in the only capacity in which he was without question great and sure of his ground: great and sure of his ground as a man with a full-blooded love of sensuous experience and a painter who translated his world into corresponding images.

Courbet's world was a place where the literal reality of things—peasants at a funeral, deer in the green depths of a woods, a snow field, the sea, baskets of flowers, two girls lying on the grassy banks of a river—is identical with his unanalytical response to them. This response is not a complicated one but it is always present. He responds to the human warmth of simple people, to the cool secrecy of the woods and the rich waxy pelts of the deer, to the breadth of the sea or a river and the heavy sheen of its water or the tumbling foam of waves, to the opulence of healthy flesh and the heaviness of a coil of hair, to cloths and laces. In front of his paintings we need no theory, aesthetic or political, to derive the fullest satisfactions they have to offer. We are reminded of the wisest thing Courbet ever said: "There can be no schools; there are only painters."

Courbet's career, and his life, ended in a footnote beginning with the promise of glory and ending in exile. His Salon medal had coincided almost exactly with the election of Louis Napoleon as first president of the Second Republic, and the twenty years of his reign (as Napoleon III after 1852) were the great years of Courbet's life as a painter. In March, 1871, after the humiliating defeat of the Franco-Prussian War, the population of Paris rose against the government, and for a while it appeared that in the ensuing Commune Courbet was to be what David had been just after the Revolution. Suddenly his overpublicized socialism was not a liability but a recommendation, and he was elected to the body of representatives of the people, made president of an assembly of artists, and put at the head of a commission to safeguard the Louvre and other national art treasures. As David had done almost a hundred years before, Courbet now abolished the school of the Academy, as well as the Academy in Rome, and did away with Salon medals.

But these "reforms" lasted no time at all. The Commune ended in May, and reprisals began. Courbet was sentenced to prison, and after several months there he was removed to a nursing home. He was an aging man now, ill and, for the first time, defeated. During the rioting of the Commune a national monument, the Colonne Vendôme, had been wrecked. It was—and is—a giant column designed after the model of ancient Roman commemorative columns, a neo-classical tribute to Napoleon. Courbet, the anticlassicist, had once said that it should be torn down. Whether or not he had anything to do with its destruction is not certain, but he was ordered to pay the costs of its repair and re-erection. Even for Courbet, who was still a wealthy man, this was impossible. He managed to escape to Switzerland, where he died six years later.

The State of Landscape

While the partisans of Ingres, Delacroix, and Courbet were carrying on their three-cornered debate in the studios in Paris, something new was happening in the countryside near the capital. Easels were beginning to sprout among the woods, in the fields, and along the banks of rivers. For the first time, French painters were taking natural landscape seriously.

Landscape painting as the more-or-less accurate reflection of a specific scene from nature hardly existed (in France) before the second quarter of the nineteenth century. There were souvenir paintings of famous views, and occasional exceptions, such as David's view of the Luxembourg

Gardens painted from the window of the room where he was imprisoned, but there was not a landscape tradition as landscape is generally thought of today, having to do with trees, streams, hills, clouds, and other components of nature in their natural combinations. A literary gentleman-collector named Deperthes, in the eighteenth century, summed up the attitude toward landscape pretty well when he defined it as "the art of composing sites after choosing the most beautiful and the most noble elements offered by nature." Deperthes warned that "If the study of nature is indispensable, it should be considered nothing more than a secondary means in a type of painting which, if it is to be properly accomplished, demands above all the inventive skill and the purity of taste which alone can give order to the inspirations of genius."

The countryside in its uncorrected state was not very highly thought of. It was accidental, unorganized, and impure. Gardens were formal; the obvious thing to do with a tree was to line it up with other trees and trim the whole row into a common shape. In his studio the painter worked in much the same way, without the uniformity but with just as much artificiality in the creation of ideal shapes from natural ones. Landscape was synthesized from harmonized trees, perfected hills, well-disciplined streams, and generic clouds. The landscape painter's job was to organize these elements into compositions of purity, nobility, serenity, and perfect proportion. This is classicism, of course. Classical landscape was idealized; it was structural; it was heroic—a fitting counterpart to the figures of gods and heroes created in much the same way.

Such landscape may fall easily into the familiar traps of the classical style: monotony, sterility, and decorative formula. But it need not do so. The finest classical landscape ever painted is probably *The Funeral of Phocion* [128] by the Academy's seventeenth-century god Nicolas Poussin (1594–1665). (If it is not the finest, then some other one of Poussin's is.) It is an extremely complicated picture, but from its complication all confusion, agitation, and uncertainty have been removed. Each of its elements—and there must be hundreds of them—is conceived less as a tree, or a branch, or a wall, or a figure, or a building or a piece of cloth or a cart, than as an abstract form that must be adjusted to take its place in balance with all the other forms in the composition.

The satisfactions to be found in *The Funeral of Phocion* have nothing to do with the pleasures to be found in nature. Neither may much interest be looked for in its nominal subject. Phocion was an Athenian general who was unjustly convicted and executed for treason, and the picture shows his sheeted body being carried beyond the city walls to unsanctified ground. But the painter is not interested in telling the story or making a parable. The subject is of incidental, less than incidental, importance. The picture's title may be *The Funeral of Phocion* but its real subject is Order. The satisfaction to be derived from it comes from the contemplation of this order in its perfection, its serenity, its abstract clarity from which all confusion, accident, and impurity has been distilled.

But we have already seen that for the romantic soul perfect order was not enough. Or, rather, it was the wrong thing. The romantic responded to nature in its untrammeled aspects, seeing trees, streams, flowers, birds, clouds, the wind, the rain, and the simple people living close to these things, as manifestations of the vague, universal mystery toward which the romantic spirit yearns for emotional fulfillment. When this yearning was most intense it demanded turbulent aspects of nature to satisfy it, even menacing ones. "Arise, ye desired storms!" was a familiar romantic cry. Nothing could be too big or too disorderly—crags in disarray, wild valleys, tempests, cataclysms—or too exotic.

This emotionalized landscape, too, was conjured up in the studio, and it too had a tradition as old as that of classical landscape. As a single example, *The Cemetery* [129] by Jacob van Ruisdael (1628–1682) is filled with storm clouds, a rainbow, shattered trees, unruly water, a ruined abbey, with mysterious dark recesses and sudden spectral lights. And it is, of course, as care-

fully and as artificially a concocted landscape as is *The Funeral of Phocion.*

The new landscapists who fled the studios for the countryside were thoroughly sympathetic to the classical idea that landscape painting involved problems of composition, a balanced disposition of the forms within the picture space. They were even more sympathetic to the idea that nature was full of emotional connotations which it was the painter's privilege to reveal. But they subjugated both these ideas to a third: they believed that any fragment of nature as it existed, even the most familiar and commonplace bit of field, river bank, or forest, was a legitimate subject for a work of art that could be intellectually satisfying without classical artificialities, and emotionally expressive without recourse to the usual romantic stimulants.

There was some precedent for this way of feeling also, in England. English painters were already at work from something like the same point of view, and in seventeenth-century Holland there had been similar development along with romantic examples, such as the one we have just seen.[*] The Frenchmen drew freely from both sources without imitating either. The important point historically is that these were Frenchmen introducing a concept of nature altogether radical to the tradition of French landscape, a concept that was to become the dominant one during the next seventy years when French painters were setting new directions for the art of all the Western world.

---

[*] The English painters receive their due later on in this book. One of them, Constable, with *The Hay Wain* [313] of the 1824 Salon, has already been mentioned in connection with Delacroix. As for the Hollanders, it is conventional to point out that the bourgeois origin of their seventeenth-century school of realistic landscape corresponds to the bourgeois origin of the French painting about to be discussed here. This is true, with the difference that the Dutch landscapes were part of a movement in painting stimulated by the Dutch love of things the good burghers proudly treasured—their houses full of possessions, their countryside, and themselves. This was less true in nineteenth-century France. As a broad statement of the difference: the Dutch landscapes are records of fact, while the French ones are records of responses to fact.

129. RUISDAEL: *The Cemetery, c.* 1660. 56 x 74¼". Detroit Institute of Arts.

Barbizon: Rousseau, Dupré, Diaz

One of the centers for the painters who began to flee Paris to discover nature was Barbizon, a picturesque village on the edge of the Forest of Fontainebleau not far from Paris. The Forest of Fontainebleau is one of those neat, gracious woods never for a moment to be confused with a wilderness and seldom suggesting anything more savage than the upper reaches of Central Park. But it afforded vistas where the hand of rational man was as inconspicuous as it is allowed to be anywhere in France. And near the forest there were fields, peasants, and peasant cottages, which interested some of the painters, as well as chickens, ducks, and cattle, which held an unreasonable fascination for others of them. The Barbizon painters were not formally organized into a "movement," but the name of the village has attached itself to a dozen or so landscapists and painters of peasants or animals, of whom several spent a great

deal of time there. Others made occasional visits and still others worked elsewhere but in the same spirit.

The spirit is best classified as romantic-realistic. As realists the Barbizon painters made direct reference to nature and even worked directly in its presence with respectful attention to the actual disposition of its forms. It is difficult to make this sound like much of an innovation, today when everyone's idea of a landscape painter is an artist at an easel set out in the open air, but an innovation it was. Even Courbet ordinarily fabricated his landscapes indoors (as he shows himself doing in *The Painter's Studio*), although he made sketches for them out of doors (as he shows himself setting out to do in *Bonjour Monsieur Courbet*). His advice to young painters was to work from nature "even if from a dunghill." The Barbizon painters had been working from nature for years, being somewhat older than Courbet. And being much more temperate they were not interested in

130. T. Rousseau: *Under the Birches*, 1842. 16⅝ x 25⅜". Toledo Museum of Art, Gift of Arthur J. Secor.

dunghills. As romantic-realists they were interested not only in the look of nature but in discovering its "moods," the "spirit" of trees and fields and skies, "the oak wrestling with the rock," one of them said. But the mood was always discovered within the subject; the subject was never violated to serve the mood. Even when the final picture was to be painted in the studio, as it usually was, the painter subjected himself to the discipline of preliminary study out of doors, working closely within the bounds of the subject's physical identity.

These Barbizon painters were hard at work between 1830 and 1840. At first the going was difficult, upstream against the opposition of the Academy. For a while they were castigated as vulgar, but eventually most of them were accepted in the Salons and even won medals. On the whole they were quiet, unobtrusive men, and since landscape was a secondary art their deviations from the academic norm were less offensive than they would have been in the usual demonstration paintings. By the 1850's these artists were beginning to

have successes they continued to enjoy during the rest of their lifetimes while the Academy found its whipping boy in Courbet. By the end of the century, after their deaths, their vogue was tremendous, and they became stars of the international salesrooms, being collected with particular avidity in America. Their success—and while they were alive—was speeded by the aesthetic perception and the business perspicacity of a remarkable dealer named Georges Durand-Ruel (1864–1931).

In retrospect we see that it was the misfortune of the Barbizon painters to have laid so excellent a foundation for so exceptional a generation of painters—the impressionists who followed them—that their own work has suffered by comparison. By the 1920's their paintings were being pushed to less conspicuous places on museum walls, and today they have become more than anything else a storage problem. A few examples are given exhibition space as historical fillers; certain atypical paintings, on the contrary, are much sought after, for reasons that will become apparent shortly.

131. Dupré: *The Hay Wagon*, date unknown. 14¼ x 18⅛". Metropolitan Museum of Art, New York, Wolfe Bequest.

132. Diaz: *Forest Path*, date unknown. 28 x 23¾". Philadelphia Museum of Art, John G. Johnson Collection.

In the meanwhile, three typical Barbizon painters will do very well to represent the school: Théodore Rousseau (1812–1867), Jules Dupré (1811–1889), and Narcisse Virgile Diaz de la Peña (1807–1876). A fourth, Constant Troyon (1810–1865) made such a success in the Salon that he is taken up in the next chapter which discusses the state of that institution at mid-century.

Of the three, Rousseau is the most rewarding after continued acquaintance. He combines a sense of the monumentality of landscape with a passion for its individual forms amounting to nature worship. He is so impressed with nature as a force that every irregularity in the growth of a tree, every blade of green that springs from the earth, every cloud that scuds busily across the sky, has for him its own vigorous life as part of a purposeful scheme full of growth and activity. He sees no need to inject romantic folderol into nature because to conceal or change any part of the natural miracle would be only to weaken it. He sees no need to put it into classical order because he feels a more powerful order behind the growth of things, the turn of the seasons, the rising or setting of the sun [130]. He painted images of this cycle of omnipotent force as men have always painted images of their gods, but he did not have to fabricate an image because it was everywhere for him to see. Mystery, revery, and philosophical explanation are only incidental to his perception of the miracle around him. The miracle was tangible, self-explanatory. He accepted it at face value and gloried in it. He was a great bearded fellow—untrimmed beards were cultivated by the Barbizon painters along with other aspects of nature in its pure state—and the suave academicians enjoyed regarding him as an oaf. But during the 1850's he attained the general popularity of the school, and Salon success as well. He was not a commuting landscapist; he spent most of his life at Barbizon, and died there.

Rousseau's pantheism, for that is what it amounted to, was a kind of poetry, but it is doubtful whether the public who admired his landscapes were aware of this quality beneath the literal "picture of

133. DAUBIGNY: *River and Bridge,* date unknown. 10½ x 17⅜". Philadelphia Museum of Art, John G. Johnson Collection.

something" painted with a high degree of objective accuracy which they spontaneously respected. Poetry of a more obvious kind was cultivated by Jules Dupré [131]. He was closer to the romantic tradition than Rousseau was. (Delacroix spoke kindly of him.) He had a great enthusiasm for the English landscapists, who were also romantics who found poetry in simple aspects of the countryside. Dupré's mood, however, is more introspective than the cheerful English one. Individually his paintings are often effective in their hint of romantic pathos within the heart of nature, but he is repetitious, and after a while one suspects that his mood was continued as his trademark after it became a good thing on the market.

Narcisse Diaz is even more conventionally romantic. In fact he falls outside the realistic half of the romantic-realist classification suitable to the school as a whole. His pictures are frankly concoctions, his most typical ones being of small, secluded clearings in the forest from which the observer looks through the broken silhouettes of leaves and branches as if from a shadowed room or a grotto, at patches of light sky or open fields beyond [132]. Occasionally

these leafy cubicles are inhabited by human beings, by ideal figures such as nymphs in white robes, or even by mythological characters. It is a pleasant formula although Diaz forced it a little.

Daubigny

The truest poet of the group was neither Dupré nor Diaz, but Charles-François Daubigny (1817–1878), who discovered poetry within his subjects instead of grafting it onto them. It is a simple poetry, as direct as it is sensitive; there is never anything dramatic or high-flown about it. Daubigny's love of nature is at the opposite pole from Rousseau's fervent adoration of it. He contemplates quiet skies, gentle rivers, level, eventless fields, in calm light. Rousseau clutched with obsessed intensity upon every natural detail: the leaf was as important as the tree; he was reluctant to forego the joy of representing each blade of grass in a field. His problem was to capture the monumentality of the whole through the enumeration of an infinite number of parts.

134. MILLET: *The Sower*, 1850. 41¼ x 33″. Provident Tradesmen's Bank and Trust Company, Philadelphia.

135. MILLET: *The Gleaners*, 1857. 33 x 44″. Louvre, Paris.

Daubigny, instead, begins with the acceptance of wholeness. There is a kind of wisdom in the breadth of his vision, its calmness, its perception of the unity of natural objects which rises above their complication. His landscape is intimate and domesticated. Farm cottages rest in his countryside as naturally and as peacefully as the shrubs and trees that have grown there; so do the small stone bridges of France and the boats on the full, quiet streams [133]. Alone among the Barbizon painters Daubigny worked entirely out of doors, even adopting a little canopied rowboat as a floating studio in order to paint the banks of the river across a placid stretch of water. He loved the cool river light impregnating fresh moist air, the gentle sobriety of small farms and quiet fields in early morning or evening light. These observations, made and recorded in the open air, place Daubigny historically as the most important of the Barbizon painters; of them all, he made the most valuable contribution to the next generation, to an extent that is only beginning to be fully recognized.

As a mine for imitators, the landscape tradition of the Barbizon painters has yielded some of the most inane pictures ever turned out by commercial hacks. Their work has been deformed into countless pretty picturesque scenes of the kind used on scenic calendars, pasted on wastebaskets, and cut up for jigsaw puzzles. The resemblances of these superficial imitations are close enough to the originals to have clouded our perception of the unobtrusive virtues of the Barbizon school.

Millet

The history of art is full of drastic re-evaluations, especially in our time which is so full of shifts and upheavals and variety in points of view. Painters are especially vulnerable during the century after their death, and the reputation of Jean-François Millet (1814–1875) has tobogganed in recent years from a point high enough to make his descent very swift. A short generation ago sepia reproductions of three of his pictures, *The Sower* [134], *The Gleaners* [135], and *The Angelus* [136] hung in every classroom and Sunday school. They are typical of Millet's most ambitious work with their peasant figures generalized into large, semisculpturesque forms dominating the foreground of a deep landscape, thrown into grander-than-life eminence against the sky, meant to be symbolical of man's union with the earth. But Millet's noble poor seem a little self-conscious of their symbolical importance, a little too cleaned up to smack convincingly of the soil of which they are supposed to be an emanation. That this should be so today is striking evidence of how taste can reverse itself, since the objections to Millet during his lifetime, objections that were violent, were on the opposite score. "This is the painting of men who don't change their linen, who want to intrude themselves upon gentlemen; this art offends me and disgusts me." The speaker was a snob,° but it is still rather sad that Millet should have suffered so during his life on one score and should be discarded later on for the opposite reason.

The generations between Millet's death and his current fall from favor admired him as a painter who had achieved the ultimate statement of the nobility of the simple man, that idea begun so long ago and adapted to such a variety of expressions. The most successful example of Millet's variety was *The Sower*, which he repeated many times. The peasant is recognizable as one of Michelangelo's naked titans, descended from the Sistine ceiling, put into rough clothes, and given a bag of grain—a disconcerting blunder of miscasting. But if this initial hurdle is cleared, we see that the figure has considerable power, its gesture is a wide, generous one, harmonious with its amplitude and its symbolism.

The Sower symbolizes the turn of the seasons, the cycle of growth, fruition, and return to the soil. It may suffer in comparison with Daumier's *Soup*, but we condescend too easily to Millet. There are dozens of virtually unknown Millets, such as *The Bleaching Tub* [137], to rebuke us.

° The same Count de Nieuwerkerke, Director of Fine Arts, who refused to look at Delacroix's St. Sulpice murals.

136. MILLET: *The Angelus*, 1857–59. 21¾ x 26". Louvre, Paris.

137. MILLET: *The Bleaching Tub, c.* 1861. 17¼ x 13". Louvre, Paris.

138. MILLET: *The Quarriers*, date unknown. 29 x 23½". Toledo Museum of Art, Gift of Arthur J. Secor.

Here the breadth and solidity of the forms, without derivative reference, and the drama of the light are uncloyed by sentimental values. The abstract values of painting—formal relationships for their own sake —are at least as important here as are representational ones, and the representation is uncluttered by the pretentious anecdotal overlay that mars so much of Millet's work. And in an occasional atypical picture, *The Quarriers* [138] for example, Millet is suddenly released from the efforted and naïve solemnity he so often imposed upon himself and paints instead with assurance and fervor in forms of dramatic strength remindful of Daumier at his best.

Millet's failures came when he overreached himself and were inherent in his personality. He was the son of a farmer—

but not, like Courbet, of a prosperous one —and was only well enough educated to envy the condition of being a gentleman without having the means to turn himself into one. Nor had he the perception to recognize that it was not important for him to be one. He became stiff and forbidding, belonging nowhere. Young painters found him difficult to approach, although certainly he must have been hungry for the appreciation they were ready to offer. Although his pictures were accepted by the Salon, after his debut in 1847 with a classical subject, his tepid successes did not counteract the sting of harsh criticisms. He avoided Paris (no doubt because he could not afford to live there in the manner he thought he should), and he and Rousseau were the only two of the Barbizon group to settle in the village permanently. Altogether he had a difficult life. He was an honest man whose art was essentially traditional, was called radical, and now seems sentimental because he is best known by his second-best pictures.

Corot: His Popular Success

The best of the Barbizon painters are excellent men who would be difficult to include in a list of the great masters of painting. Their associate Jean-Baptiste Camille Corot (1796–1875) would be difficult to omit. Since he is not a classifiable painter, Corot is always grouped with the Barbizon school because he did some work out of doors, had certain affinities with the Barbizon spirit in some of his work, and knew and was sympathetic to the Barbizon men. He belonged to an older generation, having been born in the eighteenth century, three years before Delacroix and only seven years after the Revolution. He painted just as he pleased, propounding no set of theories in opposition to others, making no belligerent pronouncements, living the eighty years of his life so quietly and painting so modestly that it is always a surprise to discover how much influence he exerted. As an isolated instance, he was on the liberal Salon jury of 1849, the one that awarded the medal to the unknown Courbet for his *After*

139. Corot: *Souvenir de Mortefontaine*, 1864. 25¼ x 34½". Louvre, Paris.

140. Daumier: *Corot Sketching at Ville d'Avray, c.* 1854–56. Wash drawing, 12½ x 9½". Metropolitan Museum of Art, New York, H. O. Havemeyer Collection.

Dinner at Ornans to the embarrassment of subsequent juries. He was fifty years old before his own father, a prosperous merchant, realized that there was a serious painter in the family. In that year Corot was awarded the Legion of Honor, and for the first time his father stopped saying apologetically that "Camille amuses himself with painting" and said, "Well, since they have decorated Camille, he must have talent," as neat a statement as could be invented to summarize the bourgeois attitude toward aesthetic achievement.

At nineteen Corot was working in the family's business, his father having refused to give him the money to study art. Later he was given the allowance that had been allotted to a poor relation who had died, and he lived thus until his pictures began to sell, which they did when he was well along in middle age. There seems to have been no serious conflict within the family. If there were conflicts or upheavals of any kind in Corot's life, they left no mark on

141. COROT: *View at Narni*, 1826–27. 28 x 38″. National Gallery of Canada, Ottawa.

his work. He never married and seems never even to have been in love.

The pictures that began to sell so tardily were not his best ones. But they are still the ones best known and much loved by a wide public; they are also the ones connecting him most closely with the Barbizon school. Bad prints of his *Souvenir de Mortefontaine* [139], typical of the manner that brought him into popularity and kept him there for decades, used to hang on every other living-room wall. Fluffy trees, some grasses and shrubs flecked here and there with bits of light, a sweet body of quiet water, a mild sky, and a few small, graceful figures are combined and recombined in these pictures, painted as if seen through a cool haze. They are minor lyrics of great sweetness and tenderness, overfamiliar, and weak and obvious in comparison with Corot's best work. But they are lovely pictures and need not be rejected just because they give pleasure to so many people.

Popular success came to Corot during the 1850's. The Emperor purchased one of his poetic landscapes, *Souvenir de Marcoussis*, from the banner Salon of 1855, not as official patronage but because he liked it.

Dealers were quick to add snob value to a product that had already begun to find purchasers on the strength of its popular attraction. For the rest of his life Corot could sell as many of these pictures as he was willing to paint—more, in fact, and his pictures were forged by the hundreds. There is a story that when one poverty-stricken forger was suspected and forced to go to Corot with the picture he was offering as an original, Corot signed the forgery for him. This should not be true, but it is not out of character. Corot gave money to many artists, good or bad, who needed it. It has already been mentioned that he deeded over a country cottage to the aging and destitute Daumier, who left an affectionate record of Corot sketching at Ville d'Avray [140], a locality near Paris where Corot found many of his most intimate subjects.

Corot could have made a fortune if he had wanted to. He did make a great deal of money, which he did not need. His tastes were simple and he had been perfectly happy on his allowance. In the meanwhile, along with the pictures that were clamored for, he continued to paint the kind of pictures he liked best himself.

142. COROT: *Bridge and Castle of St. Angelo with Cupola of St. Peter's*, 1826–27. 10½ x 17″. California Palace of the Legion of Honor, San Francisco.

Corot and the Tradition of Landscape

Long before he hit upon his popular style, Corot was painting landscapes of an opposite solidity and definition. They are the first entirely legitimate descendants of Poussin's classical tradition after two centuries of great admiration and partial understanding. They are also among the forerunners of the modern movement, making Corot a bridge between tradition and revolution.

Corot's connection with Poussin [128] is most apparent in early pictures, such as *View at Narni* [141], where he takes an actual scene but idealizes it along Poussinesque lines. The connection is less apparent but goes deeper in pictures where he holds himself more closely to the actual appearance of the subject yet invests it with Poussin's monumental calm. As examples, his views of Rome (Rome especially, although he did similar cityscapes elsewhere)

respect objective fact with deceptive literalness. Buildings and hills are disposed approximately as they actually existed [142, 143], not juggled about at will, yet their formal relationships are as satisfying as those in a Poussin where all the forms are invented and arbitrarily combined.*

How did Corot manage to impose this perfect order on forms that in reality were combined by chance? Rome is a magnificent welter of structures and gardens, punctuated at random with some superbly organized vistas, but Corot did not choose these readymade compositions as subjects. Over-all, Rome is a hodgepodge of streets and buildings that have grown partly with-

* For purposes of completeness it has to be pointed out that Poussin's tradition as observed by Corot includes reference to the art of Poussin's contemporary, Claude Lorrain. But this is an unnecessary detour for getting to the main point. Lorrain's poetic devices may be echoed in *View at Narni* and are obvious in Corot's late, soft style. But Lorrain would never have painted as Corot does in the views of Rome. It is possible to imagine Poussin doing so.

126 · REALISM

143. Corot: *View of the Farnese Gardens*, 1826. 9½ x 15¾″. Phillips Collection, Washington, D.C.

out plan and partly according to a series of plans that interrupt and compete with one another. Corot takes views of this welter and brings them into classical order without appearing to depart from an approximation of photographic reality.

As an explanation of how he went about doing this, his own statement "Form and value—there are the essentials" tells everything and nothing. Form and value are part of the jargon of any tenth-rate painter. Corot's words tell us nothing we cannot see for ourselves, that like every painter working from nature he begins with the raw material presented by the forms and values as they exist, and makes his own adjustments of their relationships to achieve his own variation on the theme of the visible world. Thousands of painters do this, with varying degrees of technical skill. Some of the worst are more highly developed technicians than Corot was. But very few of them enlarge or clarify our experience. Certain of Corot's

adjustments are apparent to anyone. He avoids strong value contrasts, sticking to the middle range of half tones. He mutes color similarly. If it were possible to superimpose a photograph of the scene over one of his paintings, his variations from actual proportions and dispositions would not be extreme. But slight or great, they put the subject into order.

In this respect it may be illuminating to compare Corot's transmutation of a specific scene, a view of the Church of Santa Maria della Salute seen from across the Grand Canal in Venice [144] with the same subject as treated by one of the most commonplace spirits among nineteenth-century painters, the academician J. L. E. Meissonier [145]. One of the most successful painters of the day, Meissonier is the subject of more detailed comments later on in this book. He was a painter without technical limitations and equally without depth or sensitivity. The painting under consid-

144. COROT: *View of the Quay of the Schiavoni, Venice*, 1834. 12¼ x 11⅜". National Gallery of Victoria, Melbourne, Australia, Felton Bequest.

145. MEISSONIER: *View of Venice*, 1888. Louvre, Paris.

eration here is a muddle of gondolas, mooring masts, lanterns, water, and architecture, all painted with bright facility and a high degree of representational accuracy. From detail to detail Meissonier's collection of factual statements may be read with considerable interest by anyone with an affection for Venice, as a kind of snapshot reminder of that enchanted city, but beyond this limited function the picture does not exist. It is a parasite on its subject: it neither intensifies nor clarifies our sentiment or our understanding. At best it merely stirs up some pleasant associations and engages our attention momentarily because the representational trickery of brush and paint is so deft. It is an immediately attractive and then almost as immediately a wearisome picture. It badgers us with irrelevant details; it nags at us to admire the flashy skill with which they are represented. Oddly enough, for all its detailed accuracy it is only superficially a true picture of the scene. Looking across the Canal toward Santa Maria della Salute one is conscious of the openness of sky, the flatness of water, the isolation of beautiful monuments within these expanses. The

146. COROT: *The House and Factory of M. Henry*, 1833. 33 x 41″. Philadelphia Museum of Art, Wilstach Collection.

haphazard and accidental minutiae of the city are lost within this bigger scheme.

It is the big scheme with which Corot has concerned himself, not only by the selection of a more distant point of view but also by the arbitrary selection and placement of such elements as packing cases, barrels, and human figures, as well as moored boats, to balance and harmonize the architectural elements whose placement is predetermined. The resultant composition is more nostalgically a reminder of Venice than Meissonier's snapshot can ever be, even though it contains conspicuous elements, such as Oriental figures and sailing vessels, that none of us has ever seen there. But this evocative power is the least important aspect of Corot's achievement. Because he is an original spirit where Meissonier was a commonplace one, Corot sees Venice through a personality that invests it with the serenity and harmony of his own vision and thus enlarges our own vision of it. And quite aside from the fact that this is a picture of a certain city, it is a painting in which the disposition of forms would be deeply satisfying even if the subject were as completely an invented one as *The Funeral of Phocion*.

It is possible to discover in a general way how Corot's apparent objectivity has transcended itself, although his own comments on the quality of his objectivity are of no help at all. "I paint a woman's breast exactly as I would paint an ordinary bottle of milk," he said. No description could be more inaccurate than this one with its crassness and its implied denial of any selective response to visible reality. He could better have said, "I paint an ordinary bottle of milk as if it were a woman's breast," for every object he paints is part of a world elevated by the contemplation of this one with sentiment and dignity.

Like Poussin's, Corot's world is a quiet one where contemplation offers greater pleasures than action. Like Poussin's it is a world regarded from a distance, yet from this distance it is a world of extraordinary clarity. This clarity may be close to magical, as it is in the transformation of *The House and Factory of M. Henry* [146] and *Village Church, Rosny* [147] from commonplace-

147. COROT: *Village Church, Rosny*, 1884. 21½ x 31½″. Collection Mr. and Mrs. Lloyd Bruce Wescott, Clinton, N.J.

ness or pretty picturesqueness into enchantment. The eye is freed from its limitations and sees the smallest details in faraway objects. But these details are never prolix. Like everything else they are selected and adjusted into harmony and balance. Corot's world is simpler than Poussin's, more intimate because it is less complex. And where Poussin's world is created serene within a kind of crystal vacuum, Corot's has become serene surrounded by the breath of life. And in the two pictures just mentioned, the peaceful innocence so characteristic of Corot's world is emphasized by the suggestion of naïveté, almost of awkwardness, in the draughtsmanship of certain details, notably the human figures. This occurs frequently in Corot's paintings and is a larger factor in setting the character of his world than is generally recognized.

Apparently Corot never formulated a specific problem for himself, never worked toward the crystallization of any aesthetic theory. To say that he "felt his way" toward expression is misleading if it suggests fumbling. But it will do very well to describe his way of creating pictures, if by

"feeling his way" we mean the development of acute sensitivities to form and value and color relationships that must be brought into balance by a sense of their rightness without dependence on rule. When the composition of a picture is systematic (*The Oath of the Horatii*, or *Raft of the Medusa*), it is possible to define the relationship of each part to the whole without fear of misreading the painter's scheme. But when the composition is "felt," there is always the danger that an effort to analyze it by hindsight may yield conclusions that would surprise the painter who organized it in the first place.

Nevertheless, what can we find in a small Corot called *Mur, Côtes du Nord* [148], where he was free to dispose the forms compositionally in any way he chose, not being bound by the predisposition of forms existing as the buildings of a city? We might say that of the five little figures, the one to the left in the background group echoes the attitude of the corresponding one in the foreground pair, thus tying the groups together. Or reading the figures as a foreground group of two and a back-

148. Corot: *Mur, Côtes du Nord*, 1850–55. 13 x 21⅞". Philadelphia Museum of Art, John G. Johnson Collection.

ground group of three, we may enjoy the variety of this balance. On the other hand, the standing figure may be separated from the rest and we may find that the picture is composed as a kind of double seesaw with the mound of earth, center, as a pivot. One plank of the seesaw would stretch diagonally into the depth of the picture from foreground left to middleground right, balanced at either end by paired figures. The second plank on the same pivot would cross the first at right angles, balanced at either end by the standing figure and the pyramidal block centered above and behind the heads of the foreground figures.

Whether the picture is analyzed from any of these beginnings or from any one of a half a dozen other possible ones, everything in it falls reasonably into place. Yet the composition was probably not schematic in Corot's mind. *The Oath of the Horatii* and *Raft of the Medusa* are both variations on accepted schemes, the *Horatii* with icy brilliance, the *Raft* with respectable competence. But Corot could not bring himself to borrow even the elementary skeleton of an established compositional formula. "It is better to be nothing than to be the echo of other paintings," he wrote in his notebook. His quietness makes his originality inconspicuous, yet Corot was as original as any of the noisier revolutionaries who made great stirs in his lifetime.

Corot: Portraits and Figure Studies

During his lifetime Corot's portraits and figure studies were all but ignored; today they have become the most sought after of all his work. Usually these are of young women, only now and then of men or children. There are well above 300 of them, of which Corot exhibited only two, and they are the most personal work of an unusually personal artist. Like his landscapes, they are a firm bridge between tradition and contemporary painting. This is a general statement and is most important as a general one, but it may be brought down to specific terms by comparisons of Corot's *Woman with the Pearl* [150] with Leonardo da Vinci's *Mona Lisa* [149] and of

149. LEONARDO DA VINCI: *Mona Lisa, c.* 1505. 30½ x 20⅞". Louvre, Paris.

150. COROT: *Woman with the Pearl, c.* 1868–70. 27½ x 21¼". Louvre, Paris.

his *Interrupted Reading* [151] with Picasso's *Lady with a Fan* [152].

The similarity between *Woman with the Pearl* and *Mona Lisa* is too close to be accidental and, of course, Corot was familiar with the Renaissance masterpiece in the Louvre. Originally he followed it even more closely; he first painted the hair in an arrangement like Mona Lisa's and then modified it. The strands can still be seen as raised pigment in *Woman with the Pearl* although Corot has painted them out in giving his model a different coiffure. But for all its frank use of the earlier picture as a prototype, *Woman with the Pearl* is not an Italianate imitation but an original work of art. While French academic painters were imitating the surfaces of Renaissance painting, mistaking stylistic plagiarism for philosophical union with the masters (even Ingres was guilty sometimes), Corot brushed superficialities to one side and understood the formal construction upon which the Renaissance statement was based. Like *Mona Lisa, Woman with the Pearl* is a massing of volumes building from the hands, placed parallel to the picture plane, into the masses of the torso, turned slightly away into the picture space, and returning as the head returns toward a full frontal view. These major volumes and the movement from one to another are enriched by the minor ones that compose them. Corot understands this formal structure but

151. Corot: *Interrupted Reading*, 1865–70. 36½ x 25¾". Art Institute of Chicago, Potter Palmer Collection.

152. Picasso: *Lady with a Fan*, 1905. 39¾ x 32". Collection Mr. and Mrs. Averell Harriman, New York.

utilizes it for individual expression, just as an architect might understand the construction of Renaissance buildings with their arches and vaults and the nobility of their volumes but would make contemporary use of the concept without rebuilding a Renaissance palace. *Woman with the Pearl* has the tenderness and the intimacy of Corot's finest landscapes; it has also their structural subtlety of form and color which invests an apparently casual subject with a truly classical repose. Such trivial and apparently realistic details as the folds of a sleeve, a loosely fastened bodice, a fall of hair, are parts of an image so firmly integrated that trivialities are transmuted into ideal monumentality. Corot's achievement in paintings like this one was to bring into absolute harmony the apparently incompatible elements of intimacy and nobility, of sensitive vision and formal abstraction.

It is this formal abstraction that allies him to modern painting. Even more than *Woman with the Pearl, Interrupted Reading* seems casual in its pose. The pose, also, is more original and more complicated in its building up of mutually supporting and balancing volumes. The similarity to Picasso's *Lady with a Fan* is probably coincidental, but it is not very important whether the composition of the modern picture, consciously or not, stems from Corot's. What is important is that the masterful abstract construction, which in Corot is concealed beneath a deceptive appearance of inconsequential ease, is emphasized in Picasso where the pose is frankly an artificial one. In Picasso's design the abstractions of pictorial composition are exposed for their own interest, demanding at least equal attention with whatever emotional or evocative character the painting may also have. In other words, Corot's painting is traditional in that its abstractions are concealed from the lay observer even though they account for much of the painting's appeal to him; Picasso's is "modern" because these abstractions are brought to the surface and attention is called to them in order to make the most of the intellectual pleasure such abstractions afford.

This is the fundamental revolution in modern painting, and as this story goes on we will see that eventually the result is a reversal of values: in traditional painting, abstract values must be sought beneath the immediate representational and emotional or evocative ones. In modern painting, emotional and philosophical values may be deciphered within abstractions that seem at first not to offer them. But this is a parenthetical jump into the twentieth century, which the reader may feel free to forget for the moment. In the meanwhile, it is enough to remember that Corot is a formal painter as well as an artist of tender sensibility.

His *Mother and Child on Beach* [153] demonstrates both aspects with particular emphasis. The protective gesture of the young mother, which could easily have turned mawkish, is as dignified as it is gentle. The figure is designed in unusually large and simple volumes, with a broad and powerful movement initiated by the arclike fold at the bottom of the skirt, continuing in the emphatic one running along the right side up to the waist, then continuing along the back to terminate in the oval of the head. The broad sweep of this circling movement dips suddenly and flows along the long arms to terminate when it finds its goal, the figure of the child, which is painted as a solid, static pyramid, an effective brake on a movement so strong that it demands this decisive termination if it is not to carry us outside the picture. This strong static element on the left is reflected on the right by the two parallel horizontal bands of light cloth at the bottom of the picture and the triangular fold of cloth of the skirt just above them; this in turn is incorporated within the general movement of the forms first described.

It is difficult to avoid enumerating dozens of Corot's figure pictures in discussing

153. COROT: *Mother and Child on Beach,* 1868–70. 14⅞ x 18⅛". Philadelphia Museum of Art, John G. Johnson Collection.

them, since each one offers new delights and new variations on his theme. Yet this theme should seem limited, since again and again he presents us with a picture where the mood is one of gentle, inconsequential revery, touched by the faintest melancholy and a hint of languor, a mood that would pall and would certainly degenerate into trifling affectation if it were not stated in forms of such logical decision, revealed in steady, moderate light, constructed in colors dominated by the subtlest grays, grayed blues, creamy yellows, and occasional accents of rich reds. It is an art of nuances—nuances of form, of color, of mood. If the pictures have a quality of simplicity it is because these nuances are perfectly controlled to fuse form, color, and mood into a harmony so unified that it appears to have been arrived at all of a piece. One of the masterpieces is *Young Greek Girl* [155], a portrait of Emma Dobigny, a favorite model of Corot's. The Greek costume is only an accessory. Corot's "Albanian Girls," "Jewesses of Algiers," "Oriental Women," "Judiths," and "Gypsies" have nothing to do with the passionate drama of romanticism, nor do his occasional

154. Corot: *The Artist's Studio*, 1865–70. 16 x 13". Baltimore Museum of Art, Cone Collection.

155. Corot: *Young Greek Girl*, 1868–70. 32⅝ x 21¼". Collection Mr. and Mrs. J. Watson Webb, New York.

nude bacchantes have anything to do with revelries of the flesh.

Corot's figures are most at home costumed, and indoors. Although he frequently fabricates a landscape behind them, they remain surrounded by the quiet air, the peaceful seclusion, the intimate protection, of a simple and familiar interior. In one series of figure studies he represents models in his studio, showing a corner of the room, and his easel [154]. Corot's natural habitat is the secluded room, the quiet landscape, or the city in moments when its monuments and rivers and the spaces of its streets and squares are at rest. Yet Corot was an active man. He served on Salon juries; he traveled; he had a great success; he knew and was admired by the most conspicuous of his contemporary painters. But by the evidence of his art, which surely may be trusted, the world of activity did not impinge upon the world of contemplation in which he lived. Corot's world is exceptional in its privacy, more exceptional in that this privacy is untouched by the morbidity or bitterness of so many worlds where people live alone.

Corot once compared Delacroix to an eagle and himself to a lark. He was satisfied, he said, with his "own little music." From anyone else the comparison would be patronizing, and even from Corot it is misleading. His art is more robust and more profound than the comparison implies. It is an art of solidity, of modesty, of dignity, of contemplation, of serenity. It is an art where reverence for simplicity is combined with mastery of civilized nuance. These are not the virtues of "little music" or of little painting.

CHAPTER 5

The Salon at Mid-century

The Academy and the Salon

By every implication in this story so far, the Academy has been cast in the role of villain. This is type-casting, and like all type-casting it is the result of one magnificent performance. In the decades just after the middle of the century, following the relatively mild persecution of Courbet, the Academy seemed determined to annihilate all French painters of genius, offering its awards, both honorary and financial, to a clique that included some of the most desperately mediocre talents ever to have made their mark in the history of art.

The Academy's motives, like the motives of other villains, seemed to itself virtuous and high-minded. Its position seemed impregnable. But its defeat, after some spectacular battles, was sufficiently ignoble to satisfy its bitterest enemies. The very word *academic* has come to mean stuffy, trite, reactionary. An introduction to this chastened institution and the painters who received its favors is in order if we are to understand why it is still so beleaguered by historians of modern art, and why it rejected and reviled the men who have become recognized as the great painters of the time.

The Academy was founded in 1648 under the patronage of Louis XIV as the Royal Academy of Painting and Sculpture. It was soon dominated by a painter named Charles Lebrun (1619–1690), whose skillful and flatulent *Louis XIV Offering Thanks* [156] is a good example of the style to which he was addicted. Lebrun was an excellent painter, in the sense that he could be depended upon to turn out a good, workmanlike job on any assignment that

it can stand very well as a typical example of the kind of picture known unflatteringly as an "academic machine."

An academic machine is a technical exercise demonstrating the painter's degree of skill in manipulating the standard techniques of drawing, painting, and arranging a picture according to established formulas. And it should be said now that an academic machine is an academic machine whether the industrious hack is following Lebrun's formula or one of Picasso's. Contemporary exhibitions are full of pictures not only as meretricious as the worst of Lebrun's but fabricated on much less demanding patterns.

Because he was a pedant rather than a creative artist, Lebrun set the French Academy off in the wrong direction from the beginning. This could have doomed it to wither away into impotence, except that the Academy was maintained in a position of great power by circumstances having nothing to do with the creative genius or the creative shortcomings of the men who controlled it. The head of the Academy, in the service of the king, with fat commissions to dole out to the faithful, could dictate his own recipe as the credo of art—and those painters who were not willing to conform to his recipe could go elsewhere and do as best they could at keeping body and soul together.

The moving spirit behind the formation of the Academy was neither Louis XIV nor Lebrun, but the king's minister of finance, Colbert, who recognized Lebrun's special fitness for the job at hand and selected him for it. Colbert was one of those statesmen, appearing here and there in history, who have recognized the value of art as an instrument of national propaganda and have so employed it. Believing that a government is measured by the yardstick of the monuments created under it, Colbert conceived of the Academy as a caucus of architects, painters, and sculptors with authority to determine an appropriate national character for the arts.

The great French painter of the century was a man twenty-five years older than Lebrun, Nicolas Poussin, whose *Funeral of Phocion* [128] we have already seen.

156. LEBRUN: *Louis XIV Offering Thanks,* date unknown. 190 x 104". *Musée des Beaux Arts,* Lyon.

could be executed according to the rules. But when we have said that, we have come close to defining an industrious hack. And indeed Lebrun was frequently nothing more than that. *Louis XIV Offering Thanks* is far from his best or his worst picture, and

137

157. FELICIEN MYRBACH-RHEINFELD: *Candidates for Admission to the Paris Salon (Basement of Palais d'Industrie)*. Date unknown. Drawing, probably for an illustrated journal. Metropolitan Museum of Art, New York.

Poussin was fifty-four years old when the Academy was founded and had left France for the second time because he could not tolerate the intrigues of the established artists and could not prostitute himself to the grandiose projects for which Lebrun was soon to become the ideal director. Poussin spent most of his life in Italy where he was free to paint as he pleased, nourished by the monuments of classical antiquity in his creation of an art of serenity, of contemplation, of order and balance and depth.

Poussin would have been the natural leader of the Academy if its second and more admirable function had not gone begging. For in addition to regulating the character of the arts, the Academy was supposed to perpetuate all that was best in their great tradition. In truth, Colbert and Lebrun probably thought of these two functions as identical. But they could not be, because they were based on the premise that great art can be produced by formula, and it cannot. No formula can make a great artist out of a mediocre one, and any formula will restrict the expression of certain

painters, usually those with something new to say. The Academy patronized men of talent who were content to work within the formula it approved. This is all very well as far as it goes, since there was plenty of work to be done by men of conscience and discretion well-trained in their craft. This training the Academy could supply. But as a corollary, it is also true that the Academy often starved out men of genius, since by definition genius transcends formula by extraordinary powers of invention.

The artist without official standing could of course subsist on private patronage, as Poussin largely did, and during the eighteenth century the Academy's stranglehold was weakened by a class made up of individuals of wealth and cultivation in the arts, capable of recognizing original talents, who supported whatever painters pleased them, in or out of academic favor. But academic strictures remained effective in the official schools, where arbitrary standards were perpetuated and talent was disciplined into conventional channels by the prospect of material rewards for the docile student.

158. HEIM: *Charles X Distributing Awards, Salon of 1824, in the Grand Salon of the Louvre.* Exhibited Salon of 1827, re-exhibited 1855. 68 x 101″. Louvre, Paris.

These were the schools David cried out against, in the name of art, justice, and youth, when he annihilated the Royal Academy at the time of the Revolution.

But the new Academy under David's influence (not directly under him, for he consistently refused to accept official directorship of the school) was more vicious than it had been before. The worst aspect of the situation was that the Revolution shifted the market for paintings from a small, aristocratic, knowledgeable group of patrons to a large, common, aesthetically ignorant public. The Salon became a gigantic sales room to serve the *bourgeoisie,* who in their eagerness for the acquisition of "culture" accepted the academic stamp of approval as a guarantee of art.

The Salon was a cruel weapon. Its jury of admission held the power of professional life or death for the painter still in search of his public. The beginner who tried to bring his work to attention elsewhere was in the position of a merchant opening a store with merchandise stamped "defective" by government officials. Pictures poured in for submission to the Salon in such quantities [157] that as many as 4,000 might be rejected from a single exhibition, in spite of the fact that in the largest Salons as many as 5,000 might be hung, crowded on vast walls, frame to frame, from eye level to ceiling. The pictures in poor locations might be next to invisible but at least they had received the stamp of approval— literally the Salon stamp on the back— while rejected pictures might be returned to the artist indelibly stamped with the "R" for *refusé,* thus rendered unsaleable. A purchaser might take an option on a picture, subject to its passing the jury, or might refuse to accept one already purchased because it failed to do so. The presentation of awards at the end of the Salons were state events of solemnity and importance [158].

Although the system originated in France, it flourished vigorously, if less tempestuously, throughout Europe. England's Royal Academy was, and is, particularly respectable and its private receptions [352] were, and are, particularly fashionable. But in France the Salon became also a public battleground, with the academicians entrenched in fortified positions assaulted by rebel forces. Once they had battled their way in (as the romantic painters did) the rebels had a way of turning respectable themselves, joining ranks with the traditional painters to oppose the next wave of dissenters. During the nineteenth century, revolts followed one another so rapidly that a group of painters would hardly be established in a strategic position before it was attacked from the rear by another. The French public enjoyed the battles and took sides, mostly for the conservatives. Throngs of people crowded the exhibitions, and the Salon prize winners became the subject of vehement discussions.

Every fledgling painter hoped that from the colossal grab bag his entry would somehow emerge as the season's success, or, lacking that, even as the season's scandal— as the *Raft of the Medusa, Massacres of Scio,* and *A Burial at Ornans* had done. But these pictures were exceptions. Most of the entries fell obediently within conventional categories or failed to pass the jury. There would be the moralistic allegories; there would be the hundreds of history pictures celebrating great events in pompous terms; there would be the cute children, the sentimental anecdotes, the picturesque landscapes; and always there would be the armies of nudes—nymphs, Venuses, and bathers caught by surprise. There would be the imitations of every picture that had ever made a Salon success, warmed over and hopefully served up again. There would be the sound, craftsmanlike, first-rate work of second-rate men, and, here and there within the interminable stretches of bad, mediocre, and respectable painting would be a work of art. Almost a quarter of a million pictures were exhibited in Salons during the nineteenth century in France alone.

The painter's problem was how to compete for attention in such a field. Startling originality, by which painters may strain for attention today, was ruled out in the first place, if not by the painter's lack of imagination, then by the fact that the jury was unlikely to accept a startlingly original work. Sheer technical excellence was not much help either, since the over-all technical level of Salon pictures was very high. It is appalling to look over old Salon catalogues and see the hundreds of painters whose technical mastery seems equalled only by their aesthetic and spiritual idiocy. (Where are all these paintings now? Those in museums have sunk by degrees to the basements; the rest are in those even more mysterious limbos where unwanted paintings await an improbable resurrection.)

Subject—what the picture was "about," the story it told—took on exaggerated importance as one way of differentiating between pictures all cast in the same technical mold. Or a painter with the time, energy, and means to devote himself to the production of an unsaleable picture might stand out by means of another device: size. The Salon system produced the phenomenon of the demonstration piece painted for exhibition only, so large that it could not be lost in the crowd. But unless it was purchased by the State, a painter could do nothing with a demonstration picture after the Salon closed except roll it up and store it away in the hope that the State would eventually acquire it. This is what actually happened when the pictures were manifestos of new movements and were preserved, either by the painter or by perceptive collectors, until time had proven the importance of the movement. Courbet's mammoth *The Painter's Studio,* for instance, remained in his possession until his death, and was sold as part of the contents of his studio in 1881. After resale to another private collector, it was finally purchased for the Louvre in 1920, sixty-five years after Courbet painted it, with funds collected by public subscription.

The idea upon which the Salon system was supposed to be based was sound: the Salon was supposed to offer an annual exhibition of the best work by established painters and a proving ground for new talent. Jurors would have had to be superhuman to perform their task with complete effectiveness, but they were much less than that. If a generality is ever safe, it is safe to say that for several decades beginning around 1850 the men controlling the Academy and the Salon were all but blind aes-

159. LANDSEER: *A Distinguished Member of the Humane Society*, *c.* 1838. 42½ x 55″. Tate Gallery, London.

thetically, and all but sadistic in their persecution of any painter who fell out of line with their goosestep. This was bad enough, but their unpardonable crime was that they debauched public taste under the pretense —or, more generously, under the illusion— that they were elevating it in their systematic program to reduce the art of painting to sterile repetitions of exhausted formulas. Yet in spite of everything, these decades were one of the most vigorous, original, and productive periods in the history of painting. This fact is a tribute to the vitality of French creative genius, which to date has always emerged victorious in its constant struggle with equally French suspicion of change.

The Salon of 1855

The Salon of 1855 was a climactic one and has already been mentioned in connection with Delacroix, who was given a large retrospective as one section of it, with Ingres, who relented after twenty years of abstention from Salon exhibition to accept a similar honor, and with Courbet, who was rejected and built his Pavilion of Realism to get a showing for *The Painter's Studio*. It

was the biggest Salon ever held and was made international as part of the great Exposition Universelle of that year. We will use it here to examine the nature of Salon art, since its awards went to painters whose work is a summary of Salon standards at the time and for the rest of the century.

Ingres was induced to exhibit by hints that the government had him in mind for special honors when the awards were announced, but these honors did not materialize. He received the Salon's highest award, a Grand Medal of Honor, but so did nine other painters, including his enemy Delacroix. The report of the jury to Emperor Napoleon III carefully listed the winners alphabetically with no comment, although in classifications other than the fine arts the various juries gave reasons for their decisions. Apparently the competition among manufacturers or engineers, who sent in tens of thousands of exhibits, was less touchy and personal than the rivalry among painters and sculptors.

Of the ten Grand Medals of Honor in painting, three went to eminent foreigners: Peter von Cornelius (Prussia), Sir Edwin Landseer (United Kingdom), and Hendrik Leys (Belgium).

Von Cornelius (1783–1867) was an inevitable choice. He was Director of the Academy of Munich, a corresponding member for his country to the Institute of France, and he was also a conventional and skilled painter of portraits and scenes from religious history. The medal was a bow to France's neighbor to the east.

Landseer (1802–1873) received a medal as a similar gesture across the English Channel. A comparative youngster of fifty-three (Cornelius was seventy-two at this time, Ingres seventy-five), he was already the dean of English painters because no other man in the history of art managed to paint animals so much as if they were human beings. With its coy title, *A Distinguished Member of the Humane Society* [159] is typical of Landseer's pictorial manipulation of the pathetic fallacy. A generation now in its fifties and sixties must still remember the picture from their primers or framed on the nursery walls, for it became universally popular. Landseer

160. LANDSEER: *Blackcock, c.* 1874. 19¾ x 26″. Collection Henry P. McIlhenny, Castle Glenveagh, County Donegal, Ireland.

could paint a stag and invest it with all the dignity of an eminent conservative clubman. He also painted pictures that, like *Blackcock* [160], keep appearing as a rebuke to his wasted talent. *Blackcock* is a harmony in grays, tans, and whites, with a dash of bright blood on the snow. It is as richly painted as a Courbet, and it treats birds as birds, not as simpering human beings. Landseer was an expert draughtsman, and his drawings are beginning to interest collectors again. From the great mass of his work it would be possible to cull a small group of fine paintings.

Leys (1815–1869) was even younger but even better connected; he was a painter of history pictures, genre subjects [161], portraits, and official decorative pictures of the usual kind. There is nothing wrong with his work except that it is routine.

These three awards, however, were more concerned with international courtesy than with the art of painting. The awards made to Frenchmen give a more accurate idea of Salon taste.

Grand Medals of Honor, 1855

Although some of the award winners in 1855 now seem too bad to have been true, we can fairly use this year as an example because the awards were made with particular care to summarize France's preeminence in the arts. The sprinkling of good pictures among them shows that the jury was more perceptive than in many other years, and the inclusion of a few former heretics shows an effort toward open-mindedness. Even Courbet had some paintings accepted; it was the rejection of *The Painter's Studio* and, for exhibition a second time, *A Burial at Ornans,* that caused the excitement and in retrospect leaves the jury open to charges of bias. The 1855 jury was a good one as juries went.

Among the seven Frenchmen receiving the Grand Medal of Honor, the star was neither Ingres nor Delacroix, but a terrible little man named Jean Louis Ernest Meissonier (1815–1891), whose view of Venice [145] has already been compared with one

by Corot. At twenty-five Meissonier won his first Salon medal in the lower brackets, and a year later (1841) he was awarded a higher one. After two years he went up another notch, and he repeated this success five years later. Then in the 1855 exhibition came his Grand Medal of Honor for a picture called *La Rixe* (*The Brawl*) [162], which was such a success that Napoleon III selected it from all others for purchase and presentation to Queen Victoria as a souvenir of the English sovereign's visit to the Exposition. By now Meissonier was forty years old; he lived to be seventy-six and continued to accumulate honors until new ones had to be invented for him. He was the first French painter to receive the Grand Cross of the Legion of Honor, among other things. There was no question in his mind, and there seemed to be little in the minds of many rational people, that he was

161. LEYS: *Interior of an Inn*, 1849. 28⅞ x 35¼″. Philadelphia Museum of Art, John G. Johnson Collection.

162. MEISSONIER: *La Rixe* (*The Brawl*), 1855. 17¼ x 22″. Collection H.M. Queen Elizabeth II.

163. MEISSONIER: *1814*, 1864. 19¼ x 29½". Louvre, Paris.

the Leonardo da Vinci, the Michelangelo, of modern times. In his later years he cultivated a tremendous white beard that dropped to his waist. He was fond of patterning it carefully in a series of points and posing in a black velvet robe with a jeweled belt. In this costume and with his prize beard cascading down the velvet he would assume an expression of fiercely profound and melancholy thought, as one who has transcended the intellectual limitations of mortal man, and thus he would have himself photographed or painted.

It is maddening to remember that while this mean-spirited, cantankerous, and vindictive little man was adulated, great painters were without money for paints and brushes. The typical Meissonier is a dry, pinched, painstaking illustration of some event from military history, usually Napoleonic, or a semihumorous anecdote enacted by models in costume, frequently the costume of seventeenth-century musketeers. *La Rixe* is a variation, not humorous, on this formula, and it is one of his best works, probably his best in this genre category.

Meissonier offered the new picture-buying public exactly what it wanted. In the first place, his pictures told little stories; they were easy to "understand." And the little figures enacting these stories were laboriously and accurately detailed. The public demanded that a painting be something which had quite obviously been difficult to do, like a cathedral built from toothpicks. Not only did Meissonier put every tiniest highlight on every button, but it was even possible to identify a soldier's regiment from some of these buttons. What Meissonier lacked in imagination (which is to say, everything) he would have made up in meticulous execution, if such a void could have been filled by a device so meaningless.

It was not until after 1855, about 1859, that Meissonier began his series of Napoleonic subjects. His *1814* [163], showing Napoleon in the final days of the debacle of empire, is a good example and today the best known of his many pictures of Napoleonic victories and defeats. It is an achievement of a kind to do what Meissonier did:

164. DECAMPS: *Oriental Night Scene, c.* 1840. 20¾ x 20¼". Philadelphia Museum of Art, Johnson Collection.

to take the history of military campaigns where men died in blood, or of starvation and exposure, to take events that were flung across a continent, that marked the rise and the collapse of an empire and changed the direction of history in the Western world, to take triumphs and cataclysms full of glory, terror, and anguish, to take all this and reduce it to nothing more than a well organized collection of lead soldiers accurately uniformed. Meissonier has left accounts of his efforts to create the effect of snow by spraying miniature models with borax or sugar, accounts so naïve in their enthusiasm for imitation that they would be touching if this man had not been mistaken for a great painter. Nothing he ever did suggests for a moment that he conceived of painting as anything beyond a display of manual skill, or of his subjects as anything more than pegs upon which to hang this display. In his *1814*, it might be granted that the infinite details have been neatly packed into their container, and that the picture suggests, however faintly, some

mood of sadness and regret. But these are inadequate virtues in the circumstances. The defeated Emperor's air of dejection might just as well be that of a man who has committed an embarrassing *faux pas* at an important social gathering and has been sent home in bad weather with an unusually large escort. Whatever else we can read into *1814*, whatever it says of grandeur and collapse, we must read into it for ourselves by our knowledge and associations with the pictured event. The painting is, in short, completely a parasite on what it is about. In that capacity, of course, it is perfect.

For this very reason this kind of painting pleased—and on the same terms much of it still does, for that matter. But it has nothing to do with art for all that it has to do with craftsmanship, nothing to do with expression for all its detailed illustration, nothing to do with the human spirit or with the enlargement or intensification or clarification of human experience. Even as a technical exercise it is unoriginal; its superiority to the rank and file of Salon pictures is only one of degree, not of kind. Meissonier says nothing. Behind his preoccupation with representing scenes from Napoleonic history lies the confused thinking that can attribute greatness to a painting on the strength of the greatness of the pictured event. But greatness does not rub off in this way. Meissonier manages to reduce some of the most important, dramatic, and harrowing events in history to the expressive level of a well-shined shoe. The polish is admirable, but in the long run not very important.*

After Meissonier, whose art was so spectacularly pointless, the remaining Grand Medal winners, now forgotten, are a little dull. This is too bad in the case of Alexandre Gabriel Decamps (1803–1860), a

---

* Like all painters of skill without imagination, Meissonier was at his best when he was at his least pretentious. He did some very pleasant exercises where his photographic eye and his well-trained hand combined to reproduce nicely selected bits of typical French countryside. As literal objective mementos of a scene, these can be most attractive, and if Meissonier had painted nothing else he might have been remembered as a sound landscape painter of the second rank, limited but never bothersome.

165. DECAMPS: *The Experts*, 1837. 18¼ x 25¼″. Metropolitan Museum of Art, New York,
H. O. Havemeyer Collection.

painter for whom one would like to find a generous word. His work retains a certain vigor and some force of color. In *Oriental Night Scene* [164], as a typical example, reds and yellows are bright and rich against a ground of browns and blacks. Although a younger man than either Ingres or Delacroix, like them Decamps was given a room to himself for the exhibition of fifty pictures, and his work was discussed by the critics as if he were of their caliber.

Decamps tried his hand at a variety of pictorial work, including some political cartoons that might look better if they did not have to stand comparison with Daumier's, which were appearing at the same time. One painting, *The Experts* [165], showing some monkeys at work judging a picture, indicates that Decamps was not entirely fooled by the Salon system. But although one would like to do so, it is difficult to find Decamps very interesting today. He is a respectable painter but not a very stimulating one. Meissonier has a morbid fascination, but Decamps is too good to be

interesting as a bad painter. As a matter of fact he was one of the earliest Orientalists. He traveled in Asia Minor before Delacroix went to Morocco. But he was content to illustrate rather than to interpret, and as an Orientalist he remains a genre painter whose subjects are taken from Turkish and Arabian locales. This is why the majority of the critics in 1855 preferred him to Delacroix. He was easier.

The other Grand Medal winners may be considered briefly:

Émile Jean Horace Vernet (1789–1863), was the son and grandson of two other Vernets, painters of some distinction. The talent was running thin by the third generation but was still adequate for the manufacture of history and military subjects by the standard recipes. Vernet was a happy, popular, successful man whose family tradition certainly helped bring him his medal.

François Joseph Heim (1787–1865), was a classical painter of the most academic kind. From his *Prix de Rome* in 1807 to his Grand Medal of Honor in 1855 his career

166. Heim: *Scene from Jewish History,* Salon of 1824, re-exhibited 1855. 154¼ x 181⅛". Louvre, Paris.

could be used as an example to prove that slow, steady, and conventional wins the race. His *Scene from Jewish History* [166] is an exercise in Davidian style consistent enough to look for a moment like something more. Then one sees that it is nothing but an assemblage of polished but meaningless parts, an exercise indeed. It is the kind of picture that, if torn to pieces, might yield many fragments suggesting that the total might have been a neo-classical painting of the best kind, for in the fragments the Davidian disciplines are apparent, and one is free to believe that surely so much sound craftsmanship must have served some expressive purpose. Heim also painted the interior panorama of *Charles X Distributing Awards to Artists at the End of the Exhibition of 1824* illustrated in the early pages of this chapter [158]. Here he comes off better in a picture adapted to his talents, the detailed representation of an event where factual record is an end in itself.

Finally, Louis Pierre Henriquel-Dupont (1797–1892), was an engraver. He has some genuine historical importance since, after studying with Guérin as a very young man and then with an equally classical en-

graver, Bervic, he revolted against classical technique to develop a freer, more vigorous one. Thus in his small way he is a counterpart of Delacroix, the difference being that Delacroix was a creative artist as well as a technical innovator.

If we omit Ingres and Delacroix as great painters and Meissonier as an offensive one, this is a good sound list of accomplished wielders of the brush, boring rather than vicious. Its main fault is not its inclusions but its omissions. As a list of the living Frenchmen supreme among painters in 1855 it will not do. The most conspicuous absentees are Courbet, Daumier, and Corot. No jury can be held accountable for the re-evaluations of time, and a century has elapsed since 1855. But it should not have taken a crystal ball to see that Courbet was a better painter than, say, the genial and suave Vernet. And if Daumier was painting virtually in secret, it was because the Salon standard was so inimical to his genius that he did not find a public.

Salon awards were graduated downward from the Grand Medal of Honor through Medals First, Second, and Third Class, with the usual sop of Honorable Mentions at the bottom. In the long list of winners in these lower classes more names have endured and some became even more conspicuous in the Salon than the Grand Medallists above. Yet all the winners of the Grand Medal of Honor are at least hazily familiar names to anyone who has spent much time with the history of painting, while among the other awards, even the Medals First Class, there are utter strangers even to the specialist. Occasionally some one investigates these men, hoping to discover and revive a neglected painter of merit. So far no one has struck gold.

Medals First Class, 1855

Corot was recognized in the second rank of awards with a Medal First Class, and one went to Théodore Rousseau (who in 1867 was even to win a Medal of Honor). The jury's report lists forty-eight Medals First Class, thirty-two of them to French painters, seven to painters of the United

167. BONHEUR: *The Horse Fair*, 1853–55. 96 x 200″. Metropolitan Museum of Art, New York, Gift of Cornelius Vanderbilt.

Kingdom, and the rest scattered around other European countries. Among the other First Medalists, several are still familiar names:

Rosa Bonheur (1822–1899), who was an unusual woman, still has a following, especially in America where her *Horse Fair* [167] is perpetually admired. She was a child prodigy and exhibited in the Salon when only nineteen years old. By 1848, when she was twenty-six, she had already won a Medal First Class. In 1853 she came conspicuously into public favor with *The Horse Fair*, which was very large to have been painted by a woman and might have attracted attention even if it had been painted by a man. There was nothing feminine about Rosa Bonheur's painting, and there were many unfeminine aspects to her deportment. Like the lady romantic writer who adopted a man's name, George Sand, Rosa Bonheur affected men's clothes upon occasion. She was an admirer of Sand, and lived her own life freely with some of the same romantic flair. She knew everyone. She painted animals with great knowledge and sympathy. In many ways her work is arresting, but in the end she is a veteri-

168. BONHEUR: *Barbaro after the Hunt*, date unknown. 38 x 51¼″. Philadelphia Museum of Art, Wilstach Collection.

narian, not an artist. She never made Landseer's mistake of trying to turn her animals into noble human beings, but now and then she showed them involved in their own emotional difficulties, as in *Barbaro after the Hunt* [168]. She painted with a heavy, rich pigment and might have found a

169. FLANDRIN: *Study of Male Nude*, exhibited 1855. 38½ x 48¾".
Louvre, Paris.

source for this in Géricault. Toward the end
of her life, which coincided with the end of
the century, she tried to bring her work into
line with that of the impressionists, who
were the modern painters of her old age.
She did not succeed, but her attempt indicates an admirable open-mindedness and
a continuation of the determinedly unfeminine vigor that was her most individual
characteristic among women painters.

Alexandre Cabanel (1823–1889), was
another *Prix de Rome* winner whose life
was a succession of triumphs. Later he
twice won the Grand Medal of Honor, in
1865 and 1867. He was an extremely fashionable painter. Since one of his paintings
[191] is considered later in some detail,
this is enough about him here.

Léon Cogniet (1794–1880), was also a
Prix de Rome man, five years older than
Delacroix and like Delacroix a student of
Guérin's. Unlike Delacroix he remained a
loyal follower in Guérin's classical manner.
Since this manner was already watered
down in Guérin's work, its further dilution
in Cogniet's leaves very little substance.
Cogniet was a weak colorist and a routine
composer. He was one of those painters

who never advance beyond the stage of
favorite pupil. Like others of this type he
spent his life as a teacher of rules just as
he had learned them. Meissonier studied
under him; so did Rosa Bonheur.

Hippolyte Jean Flandrin (1809–1864),
was a disciple of Ingres. Ingres once threatened to resign from the Academy when the
Salon jury refused one of Flandrin's paintings. Occasionally Flandrin approximated
Ingres's quality, and he left one study of a
male nude [169] of an arresting sensuousness that has made it a great favorite in the
Louvre. But in searching for a style of his
own by following a series of enthusiasms
Flandrin failed to develop very far in any
of them. And the one in which he developed farthest, a modified troubadourism,
was not the most fortunate choice he could
have made.

Federigo de Madrazo (1815–1894), a
Spaniard, dominated Spanish official art as
a history and portrait painter. He was a
brilliant success as a painter of the Spanish
aristocrats, was much honored officially in
France also, and painted in a bright, flashy
manner.

Karl Ernest Rodolphe Heinrich Salem
Lehmann (1814–1882) is less impressive
than his name. Born in Kiel, a naturalized
Frenchman, a pupil first of his father and
then of Ingres, he followed the classical
formulas with such dryness and so obses-
sively that even his contemporaries found
him limited in this way. Nevertheless he
won Medals First Class in 1840 and 1848
as well as in 1855. He founded a prize to
encourage the defense of the academic
tradition. Possibly it is still awarded.

Joseph Nicolas Robert-Fleury (1797–
1890), was a student of Girodet and Gros.
Following at a safe distance behind the romantic vanguard, he capitalized on its successes whenever they could be made palatable to bourgeois taste. His career was a
succession of official honors and sinecures
culminating in the directorship of the
Academy's School of Fine Arts and then the
directorship of the Academy in Rome.

With Constant Troyon (1810–1865) we
come to a curious phenomenon: the cow in
nineteenth-century French painting. Before
his discovery of this animal's potential as

170. TROYON: *Cows Grazing*, 1856. 24 x 32¼". Philadelphia Museum of Art, John G. Johnson Collection.

an art subject, Troyon had already put behind him a successful career as a painter of landscape in the Barbizon spirit, and as was mentioned earlier he is ordinarily grouped with that school. At twenty-three Troyon made his debut in the Salon; at twenty-nine he was awarded a Medal Third Class and at thirty a Medal Second Class. At thirty-one he had a real Salon success with a picture of Tobias and the Angel in a landscape, which was praised by the perceptive and sophisticated critic Théophile Gautier and at the same time admired by the public. In 1846 Troyon reached the award of Medal First Class. The following year he visited Belgium, where he discovered the works of two seventeenth-century painters, Albert Cuyp and Paul Potter, whose landscapes were backgrounds for various domestic animals, especially cows. From that time on, cows and, to a lesser degree, sheep preoccupied Troyon. He painted them standing in pools, grazing in meadows, entering the fold, leaving the fold, and sometimes

just doing nothing at all. He was the best—for he was an excellent painter—of a considerable group of artists dedicated to the cow. They found a ready market for their work. The cow in the living room became a familiar item. The success of these pictures may have been a result of increasing urbanization, a bourgeois nostalgia for the countryside as cities became more crowded, more complicated, more mechanized. Critics praised Troyon's mastery of the anatomy of the cow with as much seriousness as they praised other painters' mastery of the nude. Whatever the explanation for his fascination with the cow, and if we forgive him some inevitable repetitiousness, Troyon was skillful in disposing these creatures pleasantly in landscapes of grassy charm under skies of agreeable tints [170]. His Medal First Class of 1855 was his third; he won a fourth in 1859. He seems to have been a generous and agreeable man, with much of the placidity characteristic of his favorite subject.

171. WINTERHALTER: *Prince Albert of Saxe-Coburg-Gotha, c. 1846. 94 x 61". National Portrait Gallery, London.

Finally, among the First Medallists whose names are still familiar, there was Franz Xaver Winterhalter (1806–1873), a German by birth but a cosmopolitan by nature and experience. A portraitist, he traveled from court to court all over Europe. There was hardly a king or queen or person of great title whom he did not paint at one time or another [171]. It is easy to see why he was so sought after. His women have a melting loveliness and his men an

aristocratic male elegance leading to the conclusion that European nobility of the mid-nineteenth century were a special race of unparalleled physical beauty. Winterhalter was one of those portraitists, most frequent in England, with a knack for retaining a likeness while beautifying the subject. His portraits still have great appeal in their decorative and triumphantly superficial way. Like many other painters who do not have much to say but do not pretend to be saying more than they can, Winterhalter is an enjoyable painter when accepted on his own premises.

One eminent painter, Thomas Couture (1815–1879), was awarded a Medal First Class but refused it, indignant because it was not a Grand Medal of Honor. A pupil of Gros, then of Delaroche, Couture was a *Prix de Rome* winner and made a successful Salon debut at twenty-three with a picture entitled *Young Venetian after an Orgy*. He was only thirty-two in 1847 when he won a Medal First Class with his *Romans of the Decadence* [178], another post-orgy scene that is such a perfect example of the academic concoction at its typical best that it is generally used today as an illustration when a single specimen must stand alone to typify the breed. Couture was a painter of great talent, little imagination, and a vast intolerance. We will see more of him and his *Romans of the Decadence* shortly.

Medals Second Class, 1855

In the longer list of Medals Second Class there are fewer names of importance. Two are somewhat younger men. Jean Léon Gérôme (1824–1904) lived into the twentieth century, as did Adolphe William Bouguereau (1825–1905). Just now the reputations of both these painters are at lowest ebb. With Meissonier they have become synonymous with the vicious tyranny of the academic formula in the latter half of the century, with its sterility, dogma, hypocrisy, and above all its selfishness and its blindness in the face of new developments. All this is true, so true that even the moderate virtues these men possess are usually denied them. But occasionally, and

172. Gérôme: *Pygmalion and Galatea*, date unknown. 35 x 27″. Metropolitan Museum of Art, New York, Gift of Louis C. Raegner.

173. Daumier: *Pygmalion*, 1842. From the series *Histoire Ancienne*. Lithograph, 9 x 7½″. Collection Carl Zigrosser, Philadelphia.

most tentatively, they are given a small kind word in recent criticism. This is especially true of Gérôme.

Gérôme was a painter who pushed the slick painting surface to its limit, and he was as handy as Meissonier with highlights on buttons. According to some accounts he was also nearly as odious a personality. But he was more of an artist. He was just as fascinated with technical display in details but he was more selective in their use. He had a sense of color—for Meissonier, one color was just about as good as another— and among the multitude of his paintings (for like other successful Salon painters he was extremely productive for an insatiable market) from time to time a work of surprising attraction occurs.

The slick, tight, surface typical of so much academic painting harks back to David's, as in *The Horatii*. Gérôme, in his *Pygmalion and Galatea* [172], a wonderful

and terrible picture, is painting a classical subject with a high polish, but we are a long way from the master of the Revolution and even further from Ingres. Neither the vigorous anatomical naturalism of *The Horatii* nor the sensuous idealization of a nude by Ingres has left a mark on this descendant, although the figures have been drawn with acute naturalism and then prettified. *Pygmalion* is a consummately obvious and vulgar picture.

The story is that of the young sculptor Pygmalion. Having done a marble statue of Galatea, he falls in love with his own work, which is brought to life by Venus, who has observed the young man's plight. Gérôme's statue-woman is painted in rosy flesh pinks in the upper parts where life has suffused it, and fades out gradually to pure marble white in the feet, where the process of vivification has hardly begun. Salon audiences found this tour de force ravish-

174. Gérôme: *Prayer in the Mosque of 'Amr, Old Cairo*, perhaps 1860. 35 x 29½". Metropolitan Museum of Art, Wolfe Bequest.

jewels, and other rich stuffs and objects of the Near East. Usually he used them as knickknacks to trick out some foolish anecdote, some trivial little story for the Salon public to read, but occasionally, as in *Prayer in the Mosque* [174] he seems to become another painter and his trivia coalesce into a picture that rises above them.

Prayer in the Mosque is more than a straight reproduction of an inherently interesting subject. The colors are beautifully modulated, juxtaposed in combinations of unexpected distinction; the figures are skillfully disposed within the space, the monotony of their long stretch back into deep perspective being broken here and there most judiciously; the airy columns of the mosque have an abstract interest beyond their interest as exotic architecture. Even when we admit that these volumes are inherent in the structure and not an invention of the artist, it is still true that Gérôme has made the most of them.

Like Gérôme, Bouguereau went on from his Medal Second Class in 1855 to the Grand Medal of Honor and the whole category of official awards. The birth and death dates of these two academicians coincided within a year, and each was a resounding commercial success on both sides of the Atlantic. Even more than Gérôme's, Bouguereau's name has become synonymous with the prostitution of technical prowess to any saleable subject. Whether he was painting high-class barroom nudes or holy pictures, Bouguereau was breathtakingly adept at assuming appropriate masks to conceal the meretriciousness of his conception. Whether painting nymphs and satyrs or *Youth and Cupid* [175] to titillate bourgeois sexuality or madonnas appealing to associative religious ideas in much the same way, Bouguereau was such a skillful performer that the buying public saw no inconsistency in the work of a man who alternated between the roles of lecher and mystic. And indeed there is no inconsistency here, since in neither role was Bouguereau an expressive artist: he was a salesman with an infallible eye for the market. But he was a technician of such prowess, in a style soft and slick at the same time,

ing, but time has not been gentle with the picture. Its pretensions and affectations are mercilessly revealed and even the nude girl, once captivating, looks a little comical since fashions in feminine loveliness have changed. It is extraordinary that a public with access to Daumier's hilarious burlesque of the same subject [173] could ever take Gérôme seriously again, but they continued to do so.

Salon painters were sometimes pseudo-classical, sometimes pseudo-romantic, but always genuinely opportunistic. Orientalism had long ceased to be a scandal and was popular in all kinds of treatments. Gérôme painted Oriental subjects without any expression of their mystery, their turbulence, or even essentially of their exoticism, in paradoxical combination with his tight pseudo-neo-Davidian style. He was a master at the rendition of the silks, brasses,

that anyone who is at all interested in paintings can hardly fail to respond to one by Bouguereau as a performance, no matter what he may think of it as a work of art. No matter how clearly one sees that *The Thank Offering* [176] is sentimentalized to the point of nausea, its technical aplomb remains staggering.

The wonder of a painting by Bouguereau is that it is so completely, so absolutely, all of a piece. Not a single element is out of harmony with the whole; there is not a flaw in the totality of the union between conception and execution. This, of course, is a requirement for any great work of art. The trouble with Bouguereau's perfection is that the conception and the execution are perfectly false. Yet this is perfection of a kind, even if it is a perverse kind, and Bouguereau is proof that the art of painting is so various and so complex that even "bad" pictures can be fascinating when considered as part of the whole of man's record of his own nature.

A Medal Third Class also went to Théodore Chassériau (1819–1856), who had begun as a student of Ingres and then had been attracted by the colorism and exoticism of Delacroix. He managed to fuse some of the sinuous grace of his first master with the warmth and light of romanticism; before his relatively early death he had developed a hybrid style of decorative attraction, which he displayed especially in murals.

The Salon Public

What, in summary, do all these pictures reveal as to the taste of the *bourgeoisie*, the new public of picture buyers? First of all, that a painting must in some way be ostentatious. It must pretend to a kind of profundity or sensibility, and it must do so without violating the veneer of shallow proprieties that passed for morality. If a specific moral lesson can be incorporated or implied, so much the better, but it must be a moral lesson flattering to bourgeois convenience. These components of a picture must be immediately apparent on the picture's surface; they must not be reached

175. BOUGUEREAU: *Youth and Cupid*, 1877. 75½ x 35″. Louvre, Paris.

via some philosophical bridge. This ordinarily means that the picture must tell a story of some kind. It must not exist simply as a painting; it must be a picture *of* something. That is why the Salon painter was a narrator first and a painter second. The public wanted pictures they could read as they would read stories or tracts.

176. Bouguereau: *The Thank Offering*, 1867. 58 x 42¼". Philadelphia Museum of Art, Wilstach Collection.

Whether or not he was conscious that he was doing so, the Salon painter sought to flatter the public. Continually, by implication, he assured them of their sensitivity, their cultivation, their intellect, their nobility of soul, their moral probity. The more this flattery was rewarded—by purchases—the more intense it became, and the more intense it became, the more it was re-warded by further purchases, in a vicious downward spiral. It must be remembered too that as the Salons became bigger and bigger the public was educated to lower and lower standards. Thousands of pictures were exhibited in each Salon, and there simply never are thousands of great painters alive at any one time, especially in any one country, even when the country is France. But all these thousands of pictures received the official stamp as great art. In these circumstances it is not surprising that by the 1860's, when the impressionists appeared, the public was offended by pictures painted in a revolutionary technique, pictures whose virtues ran counter to all the Salon vices that for so long had been mistaken for virtues of an elevated kind.

But to this summary of a depressing situation the reminder should be added that Delacroix, Ingres, and Corot were also alive and successful (Courbet, as well, was successful in his special way) and a generation of painters just then clearing their 'teens was assimilating the various contributions made by these giants of the first half of the century. Ingres's exquisite control and his respect for tradition; Delacroix's revolution of color and his insistence that the painter is independent of formula; Courbet's rejection of the ideal and the faraway in favor of the everyday world around us; and Corot's demonstration that the painter's private world could be explored to yield images of universal meaning —the young men who were to be known eventually as the impressionists were ready to build from these contributions, assimilating them without imitating the forms they had taken in the art of the great men of the first half of the century. The battle against academic dogma was a bitter one, and literally it very nearly cost some of the young impressionists their lives. But before the end of the century their victory was decisive.

Manet

The "Salon des Refusés"

The year 1863 is the sharpest dividing line in the history of painting since the French Revolution. It is the year of the *Salon des Refusés*—the Salon of the Rejected Painters. It centered around a painter named Édouard Manet (1832–1883).

It had been almost exactly a century since David had been admitted as a student of the Royal Academy. Now, within a decade, the leaders of classicism, romanticism, and realism disappeared, as if the decks were being cleared for a new generation of painters ready to make use of everything that had been discovered during a hundred years of revolutions and counter-revolutions. Ingres and Delacroix died; so did Rousseau; Courbet was in exile. The conflicts between one ism and another no longer seemed important to a group of young men who admired Ingres for certain virtues, Delacroix for others, Courbet for yet others, without feeling that the theories these men had defended were mutually exclusive. All three were admired and followed; so was Goya; so were the eighteenth-century court painters whose artificiality Goya and David had rejected. The art of the Venetian Renaissance was studied with new excitement. The young painters were learning from everything and imitating nobody.

But the academicians had learned nothing, and were still imitating themselves. In 1863 the Salon jury finally overstepped all bounds in its spite and favoritism; the trading of votes, the reactionary prejudices, were this time too flagrant to be tolerated. More than 4,000 paintings were rejected by a jury that seems to have been dominated by a forgotten pedant named Signol, a teacher at the *École des Beaux Arts*. The rejected painters and their supporters stirred up so much agitation that the Emperor stepped into the fracas. To judge from the kind of picture he was accustomed to buying for himself and as gifts for distinguished visitors, his taste in painting was in accord with the jury's. But as a politician in a country where art was a part of national life, Napoleon III could not ignore a group of artists and intellectuals that was growing as large as the Academy and its hangers-on—and making more noise. The revolt of the students who had petitioned Courbet to open a studio had occurred only two years before, in 1861. And in 1862 a commission had been appointed to look into the organization and policies of the Academy's school in Paris, its branch in Rome, and its Salon regulations. Ignoring these straws in the wind, the jury of 1863 kept on course and now found itself in rough weather. The Count de Nieuwerkerke, who seemed triply invulnerable as Director General of Museums, Superintendent of Fine Arts, and titular president of the jury, was summoned by the Emperor and ordered to give the rejected pictures a showing.

The official announcement of this unpleasantness was mild, stated not as a rebuke to the jury but only as a decision of the Emperor's to authorize a second Salon made up of paintings rejected from the regular one, in order to give the public a chance to judge for itself the legitimacy of the complaints that had reached him. This was sensational enough. By implication it was an official admission that academic judgment was not infallible. By implication-once-removed it was even more heretical: it made way for the premise that there is no single standard of excellence, no single formula by which the excellence of a painting may be calculated.

Having thus laid themselves open to public trial, the academicians set about gathering their forces to insure the failure of the *Salon des Refusés*. Meanwhile the rejected painters were in a quandary. Under the terms of the Emperor's order, they had two weeks in which to withdraw their pictures if they wanted to. At the end of that time the remaining pictures would be hung in other rooms near the Salon proper in the Palace of Industry, a vast structure built for the 1855 Exposition where the Salons were now being held. A few years before, a painter named Bonvin had arranged in his studio a small show of rejected works by various painters. This miniature preliminary *Salon des Refusés* had met with a scandalous reception, although some painters, including Courbet (whose own exhibition of rejected pictures in the Pavilion of Realism had been a failure), had spoken up for it. With this precedent the painters' dilemma was whether to risk a similar reception, whether to lay themselves open to the vindictiveness of future Salon juries, whether to exhibit in the humiliating role of a rejected painter against the odds that the exhibition would be a popular success, or whether to play safe by withdrawing. In the end most of the painters decided to risk it and only about 600 paintings were withdrawn, not a large proportion of those that had been refused.

The exhibition was both a success and a failure. Throngs crowded into it but not many people came to "judge for themselves the legitimacy of the complaints." Eager for the relaxation of a good laugh after the annual cultural exercise of the Salon proper, the public made the most of a double opportunity to demonstrate artistic perception, first by the usual appreciation of the accepted works, then by the derision—always so easy and so reassuring to the derider—of the rejected ones. The popular critics had a field day at the expense of the rejected painters, although an occasional picture was singled out for sympathetic comment even in the conventional press. The minority support was fervent; a painter and writer named Zacharie Astruc even founded a paper, issued every day during the run of the Salon, to defend the good pictures among the rejected ones, especially Manet's.

All in all, in terms of the moment, the *Salon des Refusés* was not a great success. It did not immediately impair academic prestige with the general public. But the public's easy scorn, the critical diatribes in the press, even the persecutions that the Academy continued to inflict on painters of originality, are not of importance in comparison with the fact that after 1863 the mortal illness of the academic organization was apparent to any good diagnostician. No matter that it took a long time to die, no matter that it grew increasingly vicious during its invalidism, its ultimate death as the dominant force in French painting was certain and the nature of its malady was recognized.

The *Salon des Refusés* established roots for the idea that every painter has the right to paint as he pleases and to be judged as an individual by other individuals, instead of painting according to the rules of a school whose officials have the power to grant or deny him the right to be seen. Delacroix and Courbet had fought for this idea, but they had been immune to the Salon's weapon of rejection, Delacroix by his mysterious influential connections and Courbet through the fluke of his early medal. The *Salon des Refusés* was a mass exhibition of painters who would ordinarily have been helpless against the esthetic censorship of the Salon system. Painters were achieving their own equivalent of freedom of speech.

The *Salon des Refusés* was no collection of masterpieces, and it must have included some really appalling pictures among the hundreds that legitimately had been turned down by the jury as inadequate attempts to meet academic standards. If the two exhibitions could be reassembled side by side today, they would probably look much alike, except that the technical polish of the officially accepted pictures would be higher over-all than that of the rejected ones, and the rejected ones would be studded here and there with early works of men who have become recognized as the masters of the last half of the century. The most conspicuous of these paintings would be three by Manet: *Young Man in the Costume of a Majo* and *Mlle. V. in the Costume of an Espada,* both of which would have to be borrowed from the Metropolitan Museum of Art, and *Le Déjeuner sur l'Herbe* [181], which would have to be borrowed from the Louvre.

"*Le Déjeuner sur l'Herbe*": Scandal

It was *Le Déjeuner sur l'Herbe* that everyone came to see and laugh at or rail against. The Emperor himself made it a four-star attraction by calling it immodest, and the critics attacked it in downright scurrilous terms. Manet suffered deeply from these attacks because the last thing he wanted was notoriety through a *succés de scandale.* Well-to-do, suave, cultivated, worldly, and socially conventional, Manet coveted a conventional success and to the end of his life he sought it in the Salon.

Two years before the *Salon des Refusés* he had seemed on the way to what he wanted. That year, at twenty-nine, he had submitted two pictures, one of them a portrait of his parents and the other a *Spanish Guitar Player* [177]. The pictures were not only accepted but attracted so much favorable attention that the *Spanish Guitar Player* was taken down and rehung in a better spot. Manet received an honorable mention (a puny award but a beginning) and by the time the Salon closed he had established himself as a young painter who would be watched.

Manet's technique in both pictures, especially the *Spanish Guitar Player,* was open to the same objections that were to be made later when his work was howled down. The public, who spontaneously enjoyed the pictures, would then no doubt have joined in the attack. The public is never very conscious of technical aberrations so long as the end result is a recognizable image of a subject it enjoys. It enjoyed Manet's portrait of his parents because portraits of an artist's parents appeal to the admirable moral sentiment of filial devotion. And the *Spanish Guitar Player* had the attraction of a picturesque subject, even though Manet had not presented it in a picturesque way. Throughout the history of Manet's lifelong struggle with the Salon, the public obviously followed the critics' cue to damn on technical grounds pictures that otherwise it would have enjoyed for their subjects, pictures that it would just as quickly have followed a cue to praise.

177. MANET: *Spanish Guitar Player*, 1860. 57 x 44⅝". Metropolitan Museum of Art, New York, Gift of William Church Osborn.

Just two months before the 1863 Salon, which was to result in the *Salon des Refusés,* Manet made a tactical error by exhibiting fourteen pictures in the gallery of a dealer named Martinet. For some reason the critics were hostile and suspicious. They prophesied that when the Salon opened Manet would fail to repeat his first success, if he got into the Salon at all. While this should not have affected a normal jury, it is easy to believe that the reactionary jury of 1863 was already looking forward to rejecting the paintings of a young artist who had been cocky enough to exhibit so conspicuously to the public just before the Salon's pronouncements for the year. The easy thing to do was to annihilate the upstart, and the jury annihilated Manet. It is

probable that Delacroix had had something to do with Manet's good fortune in his first Salon, but in 1863 Delacroix was too ill to participate in the judging. The jury met in the spring; Delacroix died the following August.

If the jury hoped for a chance to reject him, Manet made it easy for them with *Le Déjeuner sur l'Herbe.* The other two pictures that fell under the ax with it, *Young Man in the Costume of a Majo* and *Mlle. V. in the Costume of an Espada,* were not too different from the successful *Spanish Guitar Player,* but *Le Déjeuner sur l'Herbe* is a startling picture even today. In an ordinary bit of woods, a matter-of-fact young woman has inexplicably removed her clothing while a pair of fully dressed young men lounge indifferently near by and another young woman, draped in a chemise, bathes in a pool just beyond. The picture was listed in the catalogue as *Le Bain (The Bath),* but immediately acquired the title by which it is still known. None of the possible translations—"Breakfast on the Grass" or "Luncheon on the Grass" which are equally used, or "Picnic" which never is—seems quite satisfactory. The subject is an adaptation in contemporary dress of the venerable tradition of demonstration pictures showing figures in a landscape, a synthesis of nudes, nature, and still life as an exhibition of skill. But Manet's painting differs from other such pictures in having not the thinnest disguise of allegory or idealization. It is extremely direct, to the point of brashness, and purely a demonstration of painting, without anecdotal or moralistic veneer of any kind. The dissociation between painter and subject is just about as complete as is possible. To the confused and offended jury, who had never seen anything like it, the directness seemed not only brash, but insolent. The total divorce from moral pretensions, being incomprehensible to people accustomed to reading moral platitudes into painting, seemed immoral in itself.

The public and critical damnation of *Le Déjeuner* is altogether indefensible in retrospect, but we might be generous and pause for a moment to try to see the picture as it looked to a startled art lover in 1863.

178. Couture: *The Romans of the Decadence*, 1847. 181 x 304". Louvre, Paris.

In the middle of the twentieth century this demands as great an effort as would have been required in another direction in the middle of the nineteenth. As a reminder of what the public expected and had been educated to think of as the proper thing in art, an examination of Thomas Couture's *The Romans of the Decadence* [178] is chastening. The picture had been the Salon sensation of 1847 and since then had been accepted as a masterpiece that would, quite naturally in the normal course of events, take its place among the great masterpieces of the past. Manet himself had chosen Couture as his teacher and had worked with him off and on for five years. Remembering that it is always easier to scoff at pictures in their declining years than to discover in them reasons for the virtues formerly ascribed to them, let us be patient with *The Romans of the Decadence*:

It is a compendium of popular demands. For one thing, it is cultural. Something cul-

tural is implied by the title, which flatteringly assumes that the observer is familiar with Roman history. (And what in the world could be cultural about the subject of *Le Déjeuner*?) Moralistically the subject is treated on a high plane; one is invited to disapprove of the decadence of these people, who orgiastically defile a noble hall filled with statues of their sturdier forefathers. (Are we asked by Manet to disapprove of the action of his young woman who has disrobed so casually? No; he seems to accept it as the most natural thing in the world.) And *The Romans of the Decadence* is an impeccable piece of painting by a standard requiring careful drawing, complicated elaborations, and studio poses accurately rendered (whereas, once the critics had pointed it out, it was obvious that *Le Déjeuner* was painted in a way devoid of subtleties, refinements, and difficult detail; this scoundrelly artist must have turned it out in an hour or so, like a sign painter).

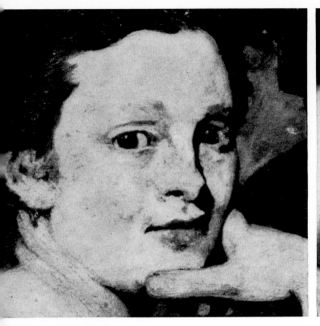

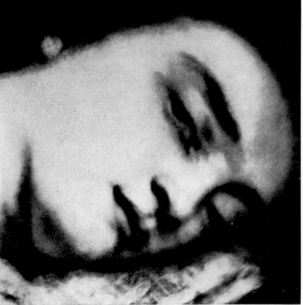

179. MANET: Detail from Figure 181. 180. COURBET: Detail from Figure 119.

It is easy to see now that the culture in *The Romans of the Decadence* is specious; that its moral overtones are combined with lascivious suggestion, allowing one to disapprove of the decadents while relishing vicariously their languishing indulgences; that while it obviously took hours and days and weeks to execute, it is technically static —that is, it is a repetitious exercise, copybook fashion—where *Le Déjeuner* is inventive, explorative, and far from "easy" or careless although the difficulties overcome by the painter are less apparent to the untrained eye.

They were not apparent at all to a public accustomed to taking it for granted that in a picture of *Le Déjeuner*'s dimensions the artist's job was to show how closely he could approximate the perfections of the academic formula. Not picturesque, not historical, and not anecdotal, *Le Déjeuner* seemed unexplainable except as a work of an incompetent or a madman or, worst of all, a prankster. The popular critics were no help to the public, since they made no effort to understand what Manet was doing and even went out of their way to entrench their minds against understanding.

"Le Déjeuner": Technical Innovations

And exactly what was Manet doing?

At this time he had seen very little of Goya's painting, yet he was pushing to their conclusion the same problems of representation Goya had set himself, quite as if Goya had served him as an intermediate step in the solution. Manet is more systematic and more objective than Goya, but like him Manet wants to capture the immediacy of instant vision. Like him, Manet does so by reducing the image to essential planes painted in bold, flat areas. He goes beyond Goya in the elimination of transitional areas where planes merge from light into shadow through a series of half tones, those areas that are neither light nor shadow but somewhere in between the two as the form curves away from the source of illumination. The nude in *Le Déjeuner* is all but devoid of transitional tones, and the shadows are reduced to a minimum. It is as if the lights had spread, consuming all intermediate values and compressing the shadows into areas so small and concentrated that they may even be reduced to a mere

181. MANET: *Le Déjeuner sur l'Herbe*, 1863. 84¼ x 106¼". Louvre, Paris.

182. GIORGIONE: *Concert Champêtre, c.* 1510. 43¼ x 54⅜". Louvre, Paris.

dark line along one side of the form. This is most dramatically apparent if the head of this nude [179] is compared with one of the heads from Courbet's *Two Girls on the Banks of the Seine* [180]. Courbet capitalizes on modulated half tones to give his image weight and mood; Manet eliminates them to reveal the image as the eye might receive it in one brilliant flash of light. Manet may have been influenced by effects in early photographs where the primitive emulsion, incapable of registering half tones, reduced infinite gradations to similar broad uninterrupted areas of light and sharp concentrations of dark. It would be appropriate for Manet, the most implacably objective of painters, to find a point of departure in the absolute objectivity of images

183. RAIMONDI, after RAPHAEL: *Judgment of Paris*. Engraving, 11½ x 17¼". Philadelphia Museum of Art.

produced by the operation of physical laws.

In addition to its effectiveness as formal description with a vivid immediacy, this quick, summary modeling offered advantages in the use of color. The broad light areas of Manet's forms could be painted in colors at full intensity over their whole breadth, whereas in conventional modeling the color would have had to be debased by darkening and graying where it began to turn into the intermediate tones between light and shadow. At the same time Manet frequently exaggerated the blackish and grayish tones in the shadows themselves. Reduced to such small areas, blacks and grays served to emphasize the broad expanses of color in the lights, allowing them to sing out above the darks. In comparison with the dulled tints of conventional painting or even with the bright, but broken, color of Delacroix, Manet's broad areas and large spots of color, flatly applied, seemed barbarous. Conventional painters were also deeply offended because Manet painted his forms in flat silhouettes of color and then brushed his shadows into them while they were wet. The usual way was to define the darks first and then progress into the lights, which might be painted over them. There are technical advantages to this conventional method that need not be gone into here, but it is worth mentioning that this minor deviation from standard technique

was attacked as a serious heresy, in the general condemnation of everything Manet did or did not do.

Le Déjeuner sur l'Herbe [181] is not a perfect picture. The figures are poorly integrated with their setting; they have the air of having been cut out of another picture and pasted onto this landscape where by lucky coincidence they almost fit and in a way this is what actually happened. Manet made studies from nature for the landscape but painted the models in the studio without reference to natural light. Also he has left a bothersome ambiguity in the transition between the foreground and the middleground where the second young woman bathes. The trees around her, and the rowboat just discernible at the right, where it is drawn up to the bank of the stream, are miniature ones, or else the bathing girl is a giantess. It is impossible to establish a logical relationship between the receding vista of woods in the left third of the picture, and the vista behind the bather. But if the picture does not hang together in all its parts, its major individual parts are superb. In the nude figure and the tumbled still life of fruit, bread, and discarded clothing Manet is already painting at full power in the manner that will shortly reach full integration in another painting.

"Le Déjeuner": Borrowed Elements

Le Déjeuner was not attacked for minor shortcomings like these but for its major virtues as a technical innovation, and for the "immorality" of its subject. Defending him against this latter charge, Manet's supporters pointed out that he was following the tradition of an old master, the Venetian painter Giorgione, who about 1500 had also combined nude female and clothed male figures in a landscape, and that the picture, hanging in the Louvre, shocked no one. This superficial parallel is still regarded as a defense that should have routed the opposition, but actually it is not much to the point. Giorgione's *Concert Champêtre* [182] is a harmony of sensuous textures—flesh, velvet, satin, hair, grass, crys-

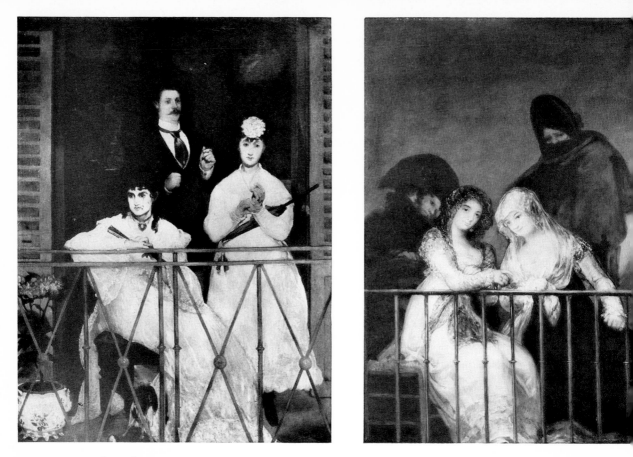

184. MANET: *The Balcony*, 1869. 67¾ x 49¼". Louvre, Paris.

185. GOYA: *Majas on a Balcony*, c. 1810–1815. 76¾ x 49½". Metropolitan Museum of Art, New York, H. O. Havemeyer Collection.

tal, stone, and foliage. It evokes a world of idyllic dream; neither the luxuriously costumed adolescent males nor the golden-fleshed females can be compared in spirit with Manet's young boulevardiers or the well-known model who posed for the nude. This rebuttal was made at the time and is perfectly legitimate. *Le Déjeuner's* defenders further pointed out that Manet's group of three figures was taken from a trio of river gods appearing in the lower right corner of a composition by Raphael, a *Judgment of Paris* [183]. But this also is a poor defense. Raphael's figures are allegorical nudes. It is true that the Academy had honored other paintings on the basis of even more tenuous connections with its Renaissance deity, but that is still no de-

fense of *Le Déjeuner,* if it needs defense.

But of course it does not need defense of this kind. Manet was not trying to emulate either Giorgione or Raphael. He frequently borrowed compositions. This was not plagiarism any more than it was plagiarism when Ingres borrowed the pose of the *Bather of Valpinçon* from some Roman sculptor or the composition of *Stratonice* from a Greek vase painting. Manet's borrowings are closer to home—he was especially indebted to Goya—but in the end his borrowing was more superficial than, say, David's when he so meticulously incorporated classical details in his paintings. Manet neither made references to his sources nor made any attempt to conceal them. The superficial debt of *The Balcony*

[184] to Goya's *Majas on a Balcony* [185] could hardly be more apparent, but neither could the fundamental difference between the two paintings. In the Goya, two of his typical spirited young vixens are combined with sinister caped and hatted male figures in the background, ominous, half-revealed, the omnipresence of evil behind the bright façade of daily life as Goya shows it again and again. In Manet's adaptation these figures are replaced by a solid, respectable bourgeois as one of a triple portrait group. And when Manet planned a picture of the execution of Maximilian it was simpler to refer to Goya's *Executions of the 3d of May* than to do research and try to reproduce the actual scene of Maximilian's death, which was quite different from Manet's representation of it. He borrowed also from Velásquez, especially in full-length standing figures.

Must all this borrowing be apologized for? After all, most painters who borrow so directly from others are damned as eclectic or with that even more damning word *derivative*. There are all varieties of eclecticism, but at his typical worst the eclectic painter borrows from other men in the hope that something of their meaning will come along with the borrowed forms. Manet is in no way an eclectic painter, and no pardon is necessary because no offense is committed. He is no more an eclectic painter than Shakespeare was an inferior dramatist when he made use of borrowed plots.

Manet's borrowing, however, has nothing to do with new interpretation or enlargement of the subject. He is, in fact, not much interested in subject; a subject merely supplies him with forms to be painted. In *Le Déjeuner* he is not interested in the fact that some young people are having a picnic in unconventional circumstances. He is interested in a way of doing the picture, the means of representation rather than what is represented. *Le Déjeuner's* relationship to Giorgione's *Concert* or Raphael's *Judgment of Paris* need not be apologized for nor need it be used as a defense. *Le Déjeuner* need only be regarded as an effort to discover technical means to make the most direct translation of pure visual experience into the language of paint.

"Olympia"

If there is any question as to whether *Le Déjeuner sur l'Herbe* is entirely successful, or only a near-masterpiece occupying the position of a landmark, there is no question at all in the case of a picture Manet was painting the year of the *Salon des Refusés* but did not exhibit until two years later, his indisputable masterpiece, *Olympia* [186].

Le Déjeuner is startling; *Olympia* is breathtaking. *Le Déjeuner* is puzzling, here and there contradictory; *Olympia* is of the utmost clarity, brilliantly consistent in each detail, each brush stroke, each color. A young courtesan, unabashed in her nakedness, regards us with the same clinical detachment with which Manet has observed and represented her. The hard little body, the short legs, the sturdy trunk, the broad face are those of a woman of the people, but Manet makes no comment, either sentimental or sociological. He does not dramatize. The drama is in the paint—in the abrupt collision of the flat, pinkish-cream light areas of the flesh with the equally flat grayish or blackish shadows; in the expanse of white sheet where nothing seems to happen yet where the painted surface is alive; in the quick, summary notations of embroidered ornaments, of the ribbon at the neck, the bracelet; in the explosion of the bouquet of flowers.

Like *Le Déjeuner*, *Olympia* has a traditional counterpart in Venetian painting (and a closer one than Giorgione's *Concert Champêtre*), Titian's portrait of a Venetian courtesan, called *The Venus of Urbino* [187]. The parallels are direct: the general disposition of the nude figure on the white-sheeted couch, the screen or curtain in the background to the left, the two serving women in the depth to the right in the Titian and the single serving woman in the corresponding foreground position in the Manet, the little white dog in the Titian, the black cat in the Manet. But, again, the transformation is complete, from the sensuous harmonies of the Venetian painting to the flat objectivity of the Manet.

Olympia is entirely a studio product, with none of *Le Déjeuner's* disturbing am-

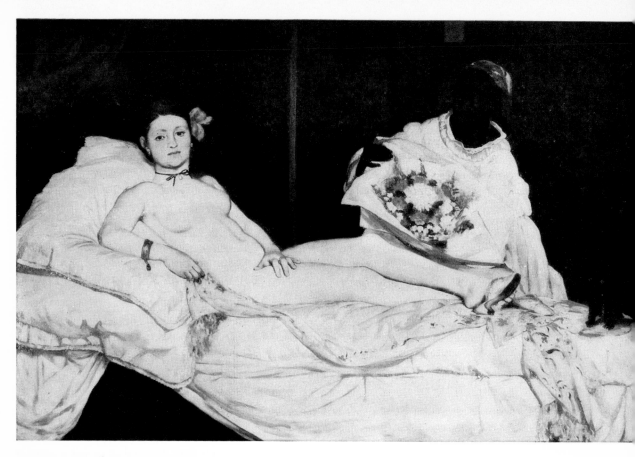

186. MANET: *Olympia*, 1863, Salon of 1865. 51¼ x 74¾". Louvre, Paris.

biguity in the grafting of studio figures onto a landscape, and, above all, without the inconsistent foreground–background relationships. Manet's flash-of-light vision is better adapted to the revelation of objects at close range than to the exploration of deep space. The closing up of the space occupied by the serving women in the Titian—by pulling the single serving woman of Olympia into the same plane with the rest of the subject—makes possible the unity of this vision. Manet has finally achieved the objectivity implied in Courbet's defenses of realism.

It should be obvious by now that if the term *classicism* is elastic, and *romanticism* more so, the term *realism* is most elastic of all, including the widest range of responses in the transcription of the visible world. Some critics, especially in France, differentiate objective realism like Manet's with the term *naturalism*, leaving the term *real-*

ism free to designate realistic painting which presents ideas, especially those having to do with social theories, as Courbet thought his did. Courbet's friend Castagnary, who helped him formulate some of his pronouncements, also wrote that "Courbet and Proudhon have committed an aesthetic error. Art has nothing to do with the imposition of ideas," and he was using the term *naturalism* as early as the year of the *Salon des Refusés*. Moral values are incorporated into realism; naturalism is amoral. The realist interprets what he sees; the naturalist merely paints the spectacle of life around him, its vice and ugliness, its beauty and sweetness, not preferring one to the other and commenting on neither. The realist may try to find fundamental truths in commonplace objects, but the naturalist deals with the moment only, even at its most ephemeral.

187. TITIAN: *Venus of Urbino*, 1538. 25⅝ x 46⅞". Uffizi, Florence.

The aesthetic satisfactions to be found in naturalism, then, must not be looked for in the subject. Being uninterpreted, the subject is only second best to actuality, and, furthermore, the naturalistic painter may choose to represent subjects aesthetically unpleasing in themselves. Aesthetic satisfaction must be found only in the way the picture is done, since it cannot be found elsewhere. The idea of "art for art's sake" is born, an idea leading eventually to the argument that, since subject is not important, it must be eliminated altogether and a painting must be nothing but lines, shapes, and colors. This is one of the arguments of contemporary abstract painters. Since it can be traced back directly to Manet's "art for art's sake," it makes Manet the first modern artist in a quite specific way. And it gives additional importance to the year 1863 as a dividing line.

Yet, at the risk of confusing the point and at the same time committing a heresy, we must admit that *Olympia* as a subject has an interest aside from the major one of art for art's sake. Granted that Manet does not interpret or moralize or tell a story or make a comment of any kind; granted that his own interest in the subject was incidental to his interest in painting it a certain way; granted that the fascination of this way is in itself enough to hold one in front of the picture—granted all this, it is still true that *Olympia* is not only a representation of reality but a revelation of it. Actuality is not transcribed so much as vivified, intensified, through Manet's vision of it. For close to a century now the young courtesan has regarded us with her special combination of assurance, insolence, and indifference. She still does so as if her glance and ours had just met; she holds us eternally upon the point, upon the moment, of recognition. With *Olympia* we finally reach the pole opposite classicism: the classicist sought to create images in which eternal and universal values are summarized; Manet creates images in which the moment, with whatever implications it may hold for the individual, is crystallized.

Manet before "Le Déjeuner"

How did Manet arrive at *Le Déjeuner* and *Olympia*?

He had entered Couture's studio in 1850 at the age of eighteen, after a time spent at sea and two failures to pass entrance examinations for the naval school. Before this his parents, both of them from wealthy families, had accepted the boy's choice of a naval career as an alternative to law, which was their own ambition for him.

The influence of Couture on Manet should not be discounted. Couture was a harsh and narrow man, but he was no mean painter as far as brush and color are concerned. *The Romans of the Decadence* is a tiresome exercise and its faults are easy to enumerate mercilessly, but in many small canvases—*Little Giles* [188], for instance—where he is just painting, Couture is almost as pure a painter as Manet. The color in *Little Giles* is rich, subdued, and creamy; the broad tonalities of light and darks even suggest an origin for Manet's representational processes as already described. Couture was an excellent teacher for Manet, who was able to take advantage of the good that was offered while remaining immune to the trumpery and bombast of the master's "important" work.

Manet was a realist from the start, and his student days under Couture—1850 to 1855 or 1856—coincided with the emergence of Courbet, but Manet never studied under anyone but Couture in spite of quarrels and insults in Couture's studio. Manet objected to the artificiality of the studio poses, the tight rendering that was mandatory in student work, all the academic rules and conventions. He drew and painted with such freedom that Couture told him once, "You will never be more than the Daumier of your time," which was his way of saying that Manet might pass at the level of this popular cartoonist who had a certain vulgar flair but was, of course, no artist. What Couture thought of Courbet and his followers he summed up in a painting called *The Realist*, showing a painter in rough country clothes using a monumental classical head as a stool to sit on while sketching a butchered pig.

188. COUTURE: *Little Giles,* date unknown. 25¾ x 21½". Philadelphia Museum of Art, William L. Elkins Collection.

Manet's special friend in Couture's studio was Antonin Proust, who entered it at the same time. Proust was another youth of intelligence and social position, equally eager for conventional success. Both young men admired Delacroix, who had become a legendary hero to student painters. They called on him at one time when Manet wanted to make a copy of his *Dante and Vergil in Hell*, which was then hanging in the Luxembourg Museum. Delacroix received the two young men and granted permission to copy, but his manner was so chilly and formal beneath its elegant courtesy that Manet did not follow up an association that would have been much more to his taste than the low-caste assemblies around Courbet at *Brasserie des Martyrs*.

Delacroix might have remembered the visit when he spoke up for the first picture Manet sent to the Salon jury, *The Absinthe*

189. MANET: *Lola de Valence*, 1862. 48½ x 36¼". Louvre, Paris.

190. MANET: *Woman with a Parrot*, 1866. 72⅞ x 50⅝". Metropolitan Museum of Art, New York, Gift of Erwin Davis.

Drinker, in 1859, of which Couture had said that the only absinthe drinker must have been the man who painted it. The jury agreed with Couture and rejected it over the head of Delacroix.

But two years later Manet made his surprising Salon success with the portrait of his parents and especially the *Spanish Guitar Player*. His interest in Spanish subjects was increased by a group of Spanish dancers who were making a great success in Paris. He painted most of them individually and also in groups on the stage. When he was not painting them he painted models and friends in Spanish costume; *Young Man in the Costume of a Majo* was posed by his brother.

The Spanish pictures were among those the critics found most offensive of the four-

teen Manet exhibited with such a disastrous reception at Martinet's just before the 1863 Salon. A portrait of the leading dancer, *Lola de Valence* [189], was especially detested; it was described as a "bizarre confusion of red, blue, yellow, and black." One critic said it was as if Goya had "gone native in the middle of the Mexican pampas, smearing his canvases with crushed cochineal bugs"—these insects being the source of a brilliant magenta dye. Manet was much influenced just at this time by the colors of Spanish painting; he adopted the typical Spanish neutral gray or blackish backgrounds with spots of color played against them. The color is fairly bright when it is accented in this way, but it is hard to see a "bizarre confusion" today in *Lola de Valence*, even though Manet retouched the

MANET BEFORE LE DÉJEUNER · 169

picture, brightening its color, after the exhibition. There are vivid passages, but only the soupy browns and obvious tints of the standard Salon product could have made them seem so outrageously raw. Many painters even imitated the darkened tones of paintings by the old masters, disfigured by coats of dirt and varnish. Today Manet's color has suffered from similar disfigurement. Recently the Metropolitan Museum of Art cleaned its group of Manets with surprising results. The *Woman with a Parrot* [190] was transformed from a pleasant, rather quiet picture into a brilliant one; the long robe, which for years had appeared to be a somewhat innocuous light tan, was revealed as a fresh luminous pink with almost white lights, combined with the woman's russet hair in which the ribbon is a bright blue accent. Such a revelation makes early criticisms of Manet more understandable, since the contrast between his color and that of the usual picture of the time was greater than it appears to have been by the evidence of Manet's uncleaned canvases today.

The Scandal of "Olympia"

With the exhibition of *Lola de Valence* and the other pictures at Martinet's and their bad critical reception, the damage was done, and when Manet submitted *Le Déjeuner* to the Salon of 1863, the events as already described occurred. After the scandal of the *Salon des Refusés* the Emperor continued his half-hearted efforts to liberalize academic practices. If he did not put his heart into it, it was because as a good bourgeois himself Napoleon III actually approved of the Academy and liked its typical product.

During the Salon's long history its juries had been elected in various ways. For a while after the Revolution of 1848, election was by the votes of all painters who had exhibited the previous year, a fairly satisfactory system although it carried with it the risk of inbreeding. But before long this system was tightened, and the jury was nominated in part by previous medal winners and in part by the Academy itself. Con-

sidering that the majority of the medal winners were academicians, it is easy to see how this system produced the situation of 1863. Jury membership had again become static and the academic caucus seemed again impregnable.

Now the Emperor made a tepid reform by which the Academy's direct nominations were reduced to one quarter of the jury members, the remaining three quarters to be elected by vote of painters—but again only painters who were also medal winners. But it was a reform of sorts, and combined with a new caution instilled by the narrow escapes of 1863, it produced a liberal jury that included Corot. In 1864 there was a petition to continue the *Salon des Refusés*. It was not granted but a room was set aside for the exhibition of some rejected pictures. They attracted little attention because more pictures had been admitted to the Salon, including Manet's. He exhibited a *Christ with Angels* and a *Bull Fight*. The criticism of the latter was so violent that he destroyed it, except for a fragment.

Then in 1865 came the exhibition of *Olympia*, with a *Christ Insulted by the Soldiers* in the same Salon. It would be repetitious to go into much detail of the vituperative attacks to which they were subjected. The critics surpassed their record of 1863 in viciousness but not often in originality. The same objections were made to Manet's "coarseness" and to the "immorality" of the *Olympia*. It was compared, among other things, to "high" game, and the crowds surrounding it to morbid sensation hunters looking at corpses in the morgue. Every indecency and corruption was read into it, nor was Manet himself spared inferences that his private character was of much the same order. Yet from the 1863 Salon the Emperor had purchased a *Birth of Venus* [191] by the academician Cabanel, as audaciously erotic a nude as has ever been put on public exhibition. The critics admitted that this studio Venus was "wanton" but were able to discover refinements in Cabanel's painting to counteract its lasciviousness. These were the same critics who called *Olympia* a dirty picture.

To escape the furore Manet went to Spain. It was his first trip to that country

191. CABANEL: *Birth of Venus*, 1863. 31½ x 53". Pennsylvania Academy of the Fine Arts, Philadelphia, Gibson Bequest.

whose art had so influenced him. He was disappointed, not in the paintings of Velásquez and Goya, which he now saw at their best, but in the life and the aspect of the cities and people. He had expected something more picturesque, more colorful, more like the painting and the dancing that up to then had been his Spanish experience. We have the anomaly of a trip to Spain ending his Spanish period, because after that Manet turned more and more to the life around him in Paris for the subject matter of his paintings.

Manet and Zola

Upon his return from Spain, at the border, Manet received an indication of what he might continue to expect at home. The French customs inspector, seeing the name Manet on the luggage, called his family in to take a look at the eccentric artist who had painted the scandalous pictures everyone was talking about. Manet suffered intensely from this kind of notoriety, which was to continue with only temporary abatements for the rest of his life, and he never

developed a defense against it. The Spanish trip was in 1865; in 1866 the Salon refused *The Fifer*, now in the Louvre. The next year there was another of the great world fairs. Not invited to exhibit, Manet erected his own pavilion (as Courbet had done for the exposition of 1855 and as he did also this year). More scandals, more jeers. *The Execution of Maximilian*, painted for this exhibition, was withdrawn at the last minute because of the touchy political situation. The next year, 1868, Manet was finally accepted again by the Salon with two pictures, both very badly hung, *Woman with a Parrot* and a portrait of *Émile Zola* [192].

Émile Zola, of course, was to emerge as one of the dominant figures of his generation with a great block of sociological novels, a dozen crusades, and the climax of the Dreyfus case where his exposures shook the foundation of the French government. The Dreyfus case is an abomination in the history of injustice, countered only by the fact that the same nation produced a Zola to correct it. In Manet's portrait Zola is only twenty-eight years old. He was just emerging from obscurity and had not long emerged from poverty.

In his capacity as a critic of the arts, which is the one that concerns us here, Zola's perception did not equal his courage. He defended Manet and some of the other painters we will see, but without a clear understanding of what they were about aesthetically. Nevertheless he defended them with the conviction that they were achieving something good and were having to achieve it while suffering injustices from established hacks and pedants. The year Manet's *Fifer* was rejected, Zola wrote a series of articles on the organization of the Salon system for a paper called *L'Evénement*, including an article in defense of Manet. "A place in the Louvre is reserved for Manet," he wrote. "It is impossible, impossible I say, that he will not have his day of triumph, that he will not obliterate the timid mediocrities surrounding him." Furious objections poured into the offices of *L'Evénement* (not from everybody—some readers thought Zola was joking), and Zola, who had asked special permission to write the series of articles, lost his post as art critic of the journal. The following year he published a monograph on Manet and Manet did his portrait.

Zola is shown seated at his desk surrounded by references to the new movement in painting. A photograph of *Olympia* is on the wall. Behind it, and half covered by it, is Velásquez's *Bacchus*. The third picture in the group is a Japanese print. On the table, just behind the quill pen, the monograph on Manet does double duty as a reference to the connection between the painter and writer and as Manet's signature on the portrait.

The Japanese print is a rather special reference. These prints, today so familiar, were just becoming generally known among artists in Europe, some of the first ones having been discovered among other packing in barrels of imported porcelains. In Japan the print was a vigorous popular art form not taken very seriously by the effete aestheticians and decadent painters when prints first flourished there. After developing in a tightly closed civilization, the prints when they finally reached Europe much later bore some surprising resemblances to the painting that was beginning

192. MANET: *Émile Zola*, 1868. 57½ x 43¼". Louvre, Paris.

to develop with Manet and the impressionists. The subjects were taken from the daily world of entertainment, the theater, the transient world of actors and courtesans, teahouses, views famous with tourists, landmarks. These subjects were in opposition to the formalized art of the "fine" painters but at the same time they were not presented in an unimaginatively realistic way; they were extremely stylized and sophisticated. Manet was doing much the same thing. He painted dancers, singers, people in a public garden listening to music, the courtesan Olympia. But these subjects from the transient world were not approached emotionally, any more than were the subjects of the Japanese prints. Technically the Western painter and the Japanese printmaker were very different, the Japanese print being conceived in conventionalized

193. Torii Kiyonaga: *Shigeyuki Executing Calligraphy*, 1783. Color woodcut, 14¾ x 9⅞". Philadelphia Museum of Art, Gift of Mrs. John D. Rockefeller.

Manet and His Contemporaries

A group of painters, literary men, and dilettantes now began to gather around Manet, some of them his own age, most of them a little younger. The difference was only a few years—ten or less—but psychologically the younger painters were separated from him by a generation. *Le Déjeuner* and *Olympia* had already made Manet a name and a martyr; the younger men were just beginning their careers, and although they were meeting the same reception as Manet, his conspicuousness made him their spokesman and the symbol of their revolt. He bore the brunt of the attacks on this group of "modern" artists, who were soon to become known as the impressionists. During their formative years the *Café Guerbois* was their center, replacing Courbet's *Brasserie des Martyrs* as the winnowing place for new ideas.

Manet did not pontificate as Courbet had tended to do, nor did he ever identify himself wholeheartedly with the group around him. His cultivated manners gave an impression of greater warmth and participation than he was offering; even more than Delacroix, he barricaded himself from intimate contacts with all but a few people. The only members of the new group who knew him well were the ones whose personal backgrounds offered the same amenities as his own. The only bond that held him to the bohemian world of the struggling impressionists at the *Café Guerbois* was one of which he would gladly have rid himself: his rejection and vilification by the world he had failed to conquer. During all this time, up into the 1870's, he had sold fewer than half a dozen pictures. Sales were not vitally important to him except as a form of recognition, although even his substantial means, which he inherited, were beginning to feel some strain. He was married (after a liaison of some years, to his piano teacher) and lived quietly.

One of the more sedate members on the fringe of the impressionist group was Henri Fantin-Latour (1836–1904), a painter acceptable to the Salon and its public but sympathetic to the innovators. One of his recent successes had been a group

linear patterns having little to do with the look of actuality and *Olympia*, for example, having everything to do with one vision of it. Yet when the critic Castagnary called *Olympia* "a playing card," he referred to its composition of flat, well-defined areas of color and he could as appropriately have compared it to a Japanese print for the same reason. European artists now began to draw upon the Japanese print for compositional ideas, and in the portrait of Zola the arrangement of the background into nicely balanced rectangular areas—the pictures, the screen, the resultant rectangular areas of wall—is one reflection of Japanese print composition [193].

194. FANTIN-LATOUR: *A Studio in the Batignolles Quarter*, 1870. 68½ x 82″. Louvre, Paris.

195. FANTIN-LATOUR: *Still-Life*, 1866. 23¼ x 28¾″. National Gallery of Art, Washington, D. C., Chester Dale Collection.

portrait of Delacroix surrounded by friends, called *Hommage à Delacroix*. He now decided to repeat this documentary idea in a portrait of Manet in his studio, thus loyally identifying himself with the rebels in paying homage to their leader—although he left the "homage" out of the title, calling the picture *A Studio in the Batignolles Quarter* [194], where Manet then had his work place.

Manet is at his easel. Seated next to him is Astruc, the painter and writer who had been one of his most vigorous supporters during the *Salon des Refusés* and had maintained an association with the impressionists. Zola stands at Astruc's side. The young man whose head seems framed by the picture behind him on the wall is the painter Renoir; the tall one at the right is the painter

196. FANTIN-LATOUR: *Homage to Berlioz,* 1885. Pastel, 24½ x 20". Philadelphia Museum of Art, Anonymous Loan.

197. MANET: *Le Bon Bock,* 1873. 37 x 32⅝". Collection Mrs. Carroll S. Tyson, Chestnut Hill, Pa.

Bazille; behind Bazille, as if crowded in as an afterthought, appears the shadowy face of Claude Monet. These are important men and we will have a great deal to say about them. Standing behind Manet is a German painter of less consequence named Otto Scholderer who worked largely in London but made several stays in Paris and, of course, knew Fantin well. He painted still-life, some landscape, and some charming figures, bridging romanticism and impressionism, but need not be considered further. The eighth portrait is of Edmond Maître, an amateur musician and a great and loyal friend of the group*

Late Pictures and Last Days

Suddenly one of Manet's pictures made a Salon success. He had become interested in the seventeenth-century Dutch painter Franz Hals, whose free brushwork resembled Manet's own. Hals's subjects included genre ones of a convivial nature; Manet now painted a fat man enjoying a pipe and a glass of beer, *Le Bon Bock* [197], and the public loved it. No objection could be made to the violence of the color this time. It was all grays and browns and normal flesh tones, with one flash of white in the cuff of a sleeve, the most typically Manet detail in the picture. Elsewhere the painting is

* Fantin-Latour is not easy to classify as a painter. Reduced in size and printed in black and white as they are here, his portraits might be photographs. At full scale this quality is tempered by the presence of the brush, with which Fantin had a delicate touch. His still-life painting [195] is only a shade less photographic. The arrangements of the painted objects are decorative like other popular still-life, but more subtly adjusted into balances of form and color. Fantin's success in the Salon and other salesrooms was inevitable since he so completely fulfilled the first requirement: conformist subject matter represented with detailed accuracy. Occasionally he would execute a painting with the dash of Manet or the more broken technique of the impressionists, but in general he adhered to surface respect for conventional academic disciplines. However, he was without academic pretensions, even in the allegorical and literary or musical subjects that are a third group within his work [196]. In these his style can go rather soft and they are not as satisfying as the portraits and still-life.

198. MANET: *Boating*, 1874. 38¼ x 51¼". Metropolitan Museum of Art, New York, H. O. Havemeyer Collection.

as dextrous as usual but more conventional in tonality. The face is still conceived in well-defined planes individualized by the strokes of the brush, but there are more planes, hence the forms are represented in more detail. Confronted with a subject it had always liked, painted in a more conventional technique, the Salon public was delighted.

Manet's friends were less pleased. The success of *Le Bon Bock* was based on the very values they—and Manet—regarded as false ones. *Le Bon Bock* was a success not because it was a fine painting but because it was a picture of a jolly fat man enjoying a pipe and a beer. But no one need have felt any concern. The next year two of Manet's three submissions were rejected, and the accepted one, *The Railroad Station,* received the usual scandalous press. The story continued in the same way. Manet was refused for another Exposition Universelle in 1878. Two years before his death, his old friend from Couture's studio,

Antonin Proust, was appointed Minister of Fine Arts. He forced Manet's election to the Legion of Honor with a medal in the Salon. But Manet was now suffering from locomotor ataxia and was too ill to enjoy this tardy and dubious award. He died in 1883, and when seven years later *Olympia* was purchased by subscription and offered to the Louvre,* it was accepted only reluctantly and under duress, although developments in painting had by then affirmed its indisputable pre-eminence as a landmark in the history of art.

During Manet's lifetime, impressionism was being developed by his fellow painters as an art of the out of doors, full of the shimmer of light in the open air painted in a high-keyed palette of pure tints eliminating the grays and blacks that were such an important factor in Manet's color. Manet

---

* Strictly speaking, to the Luxembourg Museum, the Louvre's waiting room. A painter must have been dead ten years before his work can hang in the Louvre.

had resisted the appeal of impressionism and outdoor painting, but after 1874 he accepted it more and more. His conversion began when he watched Monet paint at Argenteuil, on the Seine, one of the impressionists' favorite spots. It was the year following the Salon success of *Le Bon Bock*, and it is typical of Manet that in order to follow a new interest he discarded the opportunity to make the kind of success he had always coveted, by repeating the successful formula. His color began to freshen, to lighten, his brush stroke increased in vivacity. But he remained Manet, the man of the boulevards and the studios. Pure landscape did not much appeal to him; when he painted the out of doors he populated it with his city folk, out of town for the day. But it was a great change. The couple enjoying themselves in *Boating* [198], the naturalness and relaxation of their attitudes, the informality of the composition suggesting that the subject has been caught snapshot fashion—all these are a long way from the couples in *Le Déjeuner*, its studied arrangement, the artificiality of its combination of figures and landscape. The couple in *Boating* exist in the full open air permeated by sunlight.

The sparkle and informality that are imposed on the outdoor painter when he

199. MANET: *Skating*, 1877. 36¼ x 28¾″. Fogg Art Museum, Cambridge, Mass., Maurice Wertheim Collection.

200. MANET: Detail from Figure 199.

wants to capture effects of light and air began to show also in Manet's studio subjects. *Skating* [199], if it had been painted a few years earlier, would have been flatter, more static, its lights broader, its darks more concentrated and emphatic, its whole surface more tightly knit. Instead, it vibrates everywhere with nervous, energetic, restless, life, modeled as it is in hundreds of quick suggestive strokes which are at least as important as strokes of color as they are as definitions of form [200]. Color becomes brighter and purer, the suggestion of form even more cursory, although it remains decisive. An eye may now be nothing but an irregular star of paint; a lip or a nose or an ear may be made up of a brush of color spotted with an accent of light, another of dark. It is the kind of painting that can degenerate into the shallowest kind of tour de force. In Manet it never does. The portrait of *George Moore* [201] pushes technical showmanship just to the edge of artificiality, simultaneously transcribing the features of this talented but rather irritating young man* as a work-of-art-for-art's-sake and as a witty revelation of an exceptional character. The two aspects of the picture are inseparably present in one another.

Manet's last major work, and very nearly his last one of any kind, was *The Bar at the Folies Bergères* [202], painted in 1881 (although dated 1882) when his illness had progressed so far that it was only with the greatest physical difficulty that he could paint at all. Yet this is a large picture and it approaches *Olympia* in its certainty, in the drama of its paint, in its arresting presence. And by a perfectly logical tour de force it manages to hark back to the early style of *Olympia* in certain passages, while pushing to its limit in other passages the evanescent, shimmering, impressionist manner of Manet's last years.

The immediate foreground is the counter of a bar, with bottles, a compote of fruit,

---

* The young Irishman and professional show-off had come to Paris to study under Cabanel but soon abandoned the idea of a career as a painter. As an extremely superficial art critic and a deft novelist he drew upon French models for a career as an English man of letters.

201. MANET: *George Moore*, 1879. Pastel, 21¾ x 13⅞″. Metropolitan Museum of Art, New York, H. O. Havemeyer Collection.

and a glass vase holding two roses, all painted as if Manet wanted to demonstrate finally that no one could excel him as a painter of still life. The barmaid stands behind the counter, leaning forward slightly toward an invisible customer. The silhouette is bold, of an extraordinary symmetry relieved by small interruptions and variations, climaxed in the geometrical oval of the head with its heavy cap of hair. The

202. MANET: *The Bar at the Folies Bergères*, 1881. 37¾ x 50″. Collection Courtauld, London.

face, which is not Olympia's in features, recalls Olympia's as a passage of flat tone suddenly formed and rounded by the brushing in of a few small, sudden concentrations of dark.

The rest of the picture—the entire background—is a mirror. The solid, vigorously defined figure of the barmaid, as reflected from the back, is now amorphous, softened; the unseen customer is seen facing her, a few half-tone blurs; farther back the dress circle is half defined, half suggested, in merging and intermingling shapes that coalesce here and there into a gesture, an attitude, a hat, a gloved hand holding opera glasses.

Yet, if *The Bar at the Folies Bergères* summarizes so much of Manet's accomplishment, it is also inventive in a new way. The complexity of its composition, the structural geometry of the insistent verticals running in bands across the picture, the strong central triangle of the figure with the secondary geometrical forms included within it—all these are new in Manet. *The Bar at the Folies Bergères* is a swan song only by its coincidental date with Manet's last illness and his death. He was painting with as much inventiveness and curiosity and independence as he ever had done. And no man has ever painted with more.

Immediately after Manet's death his pictures began to sell at rising prices. The press discovered that he was a great painter. Before a year had gone by a memorial show was prepared. It was held in the galleries of the *École des Beaux Arts*—the fortress of the Academy.

Impressionism

The Impressionist Group

In 1874 a group of artists with their core at the *Café Guerbois* organized a society to exhibit their work at their own expense. Such an idea had been in the air for some time, without any unanimity of opinion, but now these men saw no other way to bring their work properly before the public.

Some of the prospective exhibitors wanted to invite the friendlier older painters to show with them, for the prestige this would lend the unknowns—such men as Corot and the grand old revolutionary Courbet, who was still alive although in exile. (It was just as well that they decided against doing so, for even Corot, that man of good will, referred to them later as "that gang.") Other members wanted everyone in the group to pledge never to send to the Salon; still others, who were beginning to have an occasional picture accepted there, thought this idea bad. Manet, their great man, refused to have any part of the exhibition. So did Fantin-Latour. Even some of the painters who decided to come in did so reluctantly, still convinced that the Salon was the real field of conquest.

When the first exhibition was finally organized, it was partly a commercial venture and partly a declaration of aesthetic war. Commercially the members hoped to increase the number of private collectors who were beginning to buy their work. They were spurred on by the fact that just at this time the adventurous dealer Durand-Ruel, who had taken on some of them, was going through a financial crisis and was forced to stop all purchases until he could get his affairs in order. Aesthetically, the group was dedicated to the idea that threadbare formulas—or arbitrary formulas of any kind —could not be forced onto a painter without stifling him creatively. They demanded the right to paint as they pleased, and what they pleased, as the only means of fulfilling their creative potentials.

After considerable confusion, including quarrels and hurt feelings, an exhibition was assembled and hung in the studio of the photographer Nadar, another habitué of the *Café Guerbois*. Nadar has his own importance in the history of photography, and a cartoon by Daumier shows him in a balloon "elevating photography to the level of a fine art"; he was a pioneer in aerial views.

The thirty exhibitors were an odd combination including half a dozen names that were to be among the greatest of the century, an equal number of sound masters of the second rank, a friendly amateur or two, one popular Salon painter, and a few ghosts who would have disappeared altogether if their names had not been preserved on this historic list.* For so mixed a group no single title seemed descriptive enough, so a noncommittal name was settled on after great effort to find something more specific: *Societé anonyme des artistes peintres, sculpteurs, graveurs, etc.*

But the name did not last; an appropriate descriptive one invented itself. The exhibition of 165 pictures had hardly opened before the painters were dubbed "impressionists," a name considered as hilarious as the painting that supplied the cue for it—*Impression-Sunrise* by Claude Monet. Although the nickname was derisive, it cut through the obscuring surfaces of personal styles to the unifying element in the most original of the pictures. The impressionists accepted the new label and soon changed the name of their organization to *Peintres Impressionistes*.

Altogether the impressionists gave eight exhibitions before they disbanded, the first

in 1874 and the last in 1886, with many changes of membership during those years. By 1886 the group was full of dissensions and many of the members had grown dissatisfied with impressionism and had departed from it.

By that time, in any case, the organization had served its purpose. It had won its battle for the attention of dealers and collectors in spite of the continued insults of the Academy and its entourage of philistines and mossbacks. Resistance died hard in these circles. As late as 1893, when a great collection of impressionist painting was willed to the Louvre, it was subjected to the kind of criticism accorded *Le Déjeuner sur l'Herbe* thirty years before in the *Salon des Refusés* and was accepted only in part.* Gérôme, now seventy, described the pictures as "filth" that only "a great moral slackening" could make acceptable to the government. But this was

---

* For the record, in alphabetical order, they were: Astruc, Attendu, Béliard, Boudin, Bracquemond, Brandon, Bureau, Cals, Cézanne, Colin, Degas, Desbras, Guillaumin, Latouche, Lepic, Lépine, Levert, Meyer, de Molins, Monet, Morisot, Mulot-Durivage, de Nittis, A. Ottin, L. A. Ottin, Pissarro, Renoir, Robert, Rouart, and Sisley.

---

* This was the Caillebotte collection. Gustave Caillebotte was a naval architect of considerable wealth, a quiet man who discovered the impressionists before they became popular on the market and bought their pictures not as investments but because he liked them. (Many canny Americans bought impressionists early because Durand-Ruel, having been right about the Barbizon painters before their prices went up, might be right again.) Caillebotte was an amateur painter himself, made friends with the impressionists, exhibited in the second group show and four successive ones, threw his fine house on the river open to the young painters, and continued to buy their pictures during their most desperate times. He made a point of buying the kinds of pictures not saleable on the regular market—the very large ones and the ones painted to solve special problems. He did this to help the painters, but as a result he also acquired some of their most important work. The Caillebotte paintings that were finally accepted (the rejected ones included some fine Cézannes) are at the heart of the Louvre's impressionist collection.

Another friend of the impressionists was Victor Chocquet, a minor government official, the rarest and most perspicacious type of art collector. With very little money to spare, he was ready to make sacrifices elsewhere to own and enjoy the pictures he liked. As a very young man he bought watercolors by Delacroix. Like Caillebotte he discovered the impressionists for himself. Among the pictures sold by Chocquet's widow in 1899 were thirty-one Cézannes, eleven Renoirs, eleven Monets, and five Manets.

181

203. Goya: *Dr. Peral, c.* 1800–10. Panel, 37⅜ x 25⅞″. National Gallery, London.

204. Goya: Detail from Figure 203.

The Nature of Impressionism

the last senile gasp of the old guard, and although Gérôme and Bouguereau were still coveted by one kind of collector, so were Renoir and Degas by others. Americans were buying so extensively that when *Olympia* was purchased by subscription and offered to the Louvre in 1890, one of the reasons was that the subscribers feared France would lose it as other masterpieces had already been lost to the United States.

The Nature of Impressionism

Just what is impressionism? The word *impression* had been used in art criticism off and on before Monet attached it to his picture of a sunrise. Its connotations were not flattering. The writer Théophile Gautier expressed regrets that Daubigny was satisfied to give his "impression" of a landscape and "neglect" details, although of course Daubigny was deliberately eliminating details in poeticizing his images. "Impression" suggested incompleteness, a superficial vision of the subject. When the impression-

ists made an honest word of it and sought a definition, one suggestion was "painting in terms of tone rather than in terms of the object itself." Any definition must be based on this idea, the idea that the impressionist does not analyze form but only receives the light reflected from that form onto the retina of his eye and seeks to reproduce the effect of that light, rather than the form of the object reflecting it. For instance, if a bush in the distance seen in a certain light reaches the eye only as a green blur, the impressionist paints it as a green blur, even if he happens to know the bush so well that he could reproduce its form exactly from memory. Monet, the purest of the impressionists if we accept this definition, once said that he wished he had been born blind and could have gained his sight so that he could paint without knowing what the objects before him were, since this would allow him to see them purely in terms of light. Never having seen a bush he would not know that the green blur in the distance was a bush, and would reproduce it in a matching green blur of

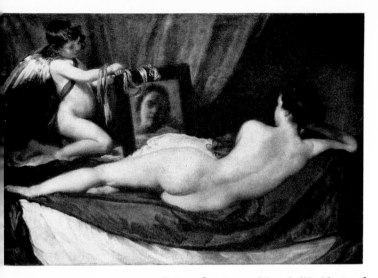

205. VELÁSQUEZ: *Venus and Cupid,* 1651. 48¼ x 69¾″. National Gallery, London.

206. VELÁSQUEZ: Detail from Figure 205.

paint without having to forget his detailed acquaintance with it as a form.

This pushes to its ultimate Goya's idea of training his brush not to see more than his eye did. But there is the great difference that Goya wanted to train his brush to reproduce forms—"forms that are lighted and forms that are not, planes that are near and planes that are far, projections, and hollows." In his portrait of *Dr. Peral* [203] form is solidly represented, but a close detail of part of the face [204] shows how he has eliminated the "lines and details" to which he objected in classical painting. The bridge of the nose, for instance, is not defined by a line, although to the classical draughtsman lines represent the divisions between forms. The pupil of the eye is not a circular dark spot but a dark irregular area, which was all Goya allowed his brush to see since his own eye could perceive only that much from the distance at which he was painting. But Goya never goes so far as to sacrifice form to this kind of vision.

Further back, Velásquez in the seventeenth century was something of an impressionist in "painting by the tones." The reflection in the mirror in his *Venus and Cupid* [205, 206] is an extreme example. Velásquez has reproduced only the light reflected from the cloudy mirror as his eye received it from a certain distance. That light happens to carry with it the lights and darks composing the reflected face. All lines, all details, have been eliminated in this process of double reflection from the model's face to the painter's retina. Less dramatically, the other forms in the picture are painted in the same way. A host of other examples could be culled from the past to show that the impressionist idea was not altogether new, even if it had not been set up as a theory and a technique until the nineteenth century, with special departures of its own that made it revolutionary.

The quality of instant vision, the subject revealed in a momentary aspect, takes on more importance in impressionism than it ever had before. *Olympia* is seen as if in a sudden flash of light, but the the model is posed, the composition studied. The pure impressionists will paint as if they had

207. MONET: *Red Boats at Argenteuil*, 1875. 23⅝ x 31⅞″. Fogg Art Museum, Cambridge, Mass., Maurice Wertheim Bequest.

caught the subject unaware, in a chance gesture. And in painting colored light— light colored because it is reflected from the varicolored objects making up the world—the impressionists will shatter the surface of their canvas into thousands of fragmented tints. Both of these innovations imply loss of form—loss of compositional form and loss of solidity in individual forms. Several members of the impressionist group will discover that this is impressionism's soft spot, and we will see them abandoning typical impressionist procedures in order to remedy it.

But whatever its definition, impressionism as a school of painting is the climactic expression of the nineteenth century. It gathers together the contributions of the conflicting schools of the first half and fuses them into a way of painting from which, in turn, the art of the twentieth century develops, partly as a continuation of impressionism, partly as a reaction against it.

The Impressionist Inheritance

From Delacroix the impressionists inherited discoveries in the theory of color upon which they enlarged. His technique of applying color in individual strokes, which he called *flochetage*, was extended to such a point that the surface of some impressionist painting became a rough texture of dots and dabs of paint. Delacroix had found greens within reds, blues and purples in the shadows of yellow. He abandoned the idea that a red object, for instance, was red all over. Any other color might exist within the red area, either because the laws of physics produced it by reflection ("Color is a merging of reflections," he said) or simply because the painter wanted it there in order to enhance or reduce the intensity of the colors stroked on near by. From this starting point, the impressionists began to use their eyes like prisms, turning white light into all its components of the spectrum, red, orange, yellow, green, blue, and violet.

From Courbet the impressionists inherited the inexhaustible mine of the everyday world. Some of them in their first days knew him in his last ones at the *Brasserie des Martyrs*. The Barbizon painters amplified Courbet's legacy, revealing landscape as a subject independent of romantic fervor or classical formality. They opened a door through which the impressionists rushed pell-mell into the open air, where they discovered their studios in fields, along river banks, and, for that matter, in the city streets.

These legacies seemed to contradict one another and all of them contradicted the art of Ingres. But the impressionists found compatibilities beneath what appeared to be antitheses. Technically the impressionists learned from all these sources and dozens of others—the English landscapists, the Japanese print, the art of Venice and of the French court, the new process of photography, perhaps too the scientific researches into the nature of light and color by such men as Chevreul, Helmholtz, Maxwell, and Rood.

Monet

Impressionism as a technique devoted to capturing effects of light out of doors is exemplified most purely in the painting of Claude Monet (1840–1926), who forced it to its limits, and then beyond.

Monet was the son of a grocer; his parents refused to support him in a career as an artist, offering to buy him out of his military service if he would abandon the idea. This he refused to do, and by the time he was sixteen he had a local reputation as a caricaturist in his home city of Le Havre. His interest in landscape was stimulated by painters who came to Le Havre to paint the port or the beaches, particularly by Eugène Boudin (who will be seen later). In Paris Monet identified himself with the impressionists although he had had an occasional Salon acceptance with a mild success in 1866. His poverty was desperate; malnutrition contributed to the death of his wife; he had to write begging letters

to friends and was sometimes without money to buy paints. As late as 1888 Manet was helping him financially. (The similarity of their names sometimes caused confusion in exhibitions—to Manet's indignation.) But after 1890, when he was fifty years old, Monet was a prosperous artist.

Monet's development can be summarized in a handful of pictures that must stand for many hundreds. He was an insatiable worker. *Red Boats at Argenteuil* [207], painted in 1875, is a fully developed impressionist landscape of the period of the first group exhibition. The stretch of water is shot through with strokes of blue in many different shades. The reflections of boats and shore are struck into it freely, in bright tints of greens and pinks. On its sunny side, the largest of the boats is yellow in the highest lights, shot with lavender near the water, yet a bright rosy color overall; on its shadow side the hull is a strong violet-blue, made up of dark blues, grape colors, violet-reds, and a touch or two of vermilion. No colors are pulled together; each stroke (at close range, that is) tells individually. The boat is decorated with a stripe running around it near the gunwale. On the shadow side this stripe cuts through the purple-blue as a brilliant emerald green; on the sunny side it is bright yellow. The small clouds are flicks and dabs of pure white. On the grassy bank half a dozen greens are freely juxtaposed and intermingled, some yellowish, some bluish; the houses are pinkish with similar variations.

From a little distance these different tints and colors within single areas tend to disappear as individual strokes. The eye "mixes" them and in doing so creates colors with more vibration, more sparkle, than would have been possible if the various reds or greens or blues or pinks had been mixed on the palette and applied in large areas in the conventional way or pulled together by "blending" on the canvas. In this stage of impressionism form has not disappeared, although light, shattering against it, is already permeating and softening its surface, obscuring its details.

In black and white, the sunlit side of the red boat is all but indistinguishable from the water around it. In color, however, the

208. Monet: *Terrace at Le Havre*, 1866. 23½ x 31½". Collection the Rev. T. Pitcairn, Bryn Athyn, Pa.

contrast is quite strong. The values—that is, the lightness or darkness of the colors—are so nearly identical that in black and white the contrast disappears. This is not merely an accident of photographic translation; it is a result of the fact that Monet is painting in terms of color as light, rather than in terms of form as revealed by light and shade. As a contrast to make this point, *Red Boats at Argenteuil* can be compared with the *Terrace at Le Havre* [208] painted nine years earlier, which is still conceived in light and shadow. The forms are decisive, everywhere defined, although in color this picture is equally bright, equally sunny. The only areas where form tends to disappear are those of the clumps and sprays of flowers, painted in spots of red, green, and yellow with almost no shadow. Elsewhere the forms exist solidly in the light that strikes across their surfaces to reveal them. In *Red Boats at Argenteuil*, light is already beginning not so much to reveal the objects

as to be revealed by them. Light permeates them, they fuse with it; forms do not interrupt light, as they do in the *Terrace at Le Havre*, but are caught up in it.

Monet's preoccupation with reducing all visual experience to terms of pure light became an obsession. When his young wife died he was horrified to find himself analyzing the nacreous tints of her skin in the early morning light. As he continued to paint, wishing he could have been "born blind in order to gain his sight and be able to paint objects without knowing what they were," as he began more and more to develop the ability to see light and nothing but light, light became like a corrosive substance eating away the objects bathed in it. *Spring Trees by a Lake* [209] is all but formless. Within the twinkling strokes of blue, blue-green, pure green, yellow-green, and yellow covering most of the canvas, we barely recognize, by occasional vertical strokes of purplish and reddish tints, the

186 · IMPRESSIONISM

209. MONET: *Spring Trees by a Lake*, 1888. 29 x 36″. Philadelphia Museum of Art, William L. Elkins Collection.

trunks of a few trees. The extreme of this progressive dematerialization of matter is reached in "effects" of certain hazy and foggy atmospheres where the canvas dissolves into mist and material forms become mists within mists.

Between the *Terrace at Le Havre* and his late pictures Monet changed from a painter responding to nature into one fascinated by an abstract problem. In the early pictures the attraction of subject is great; in the *Terrace at Le Havre,* half the observer's pleasure is his feeling of participation in a world of sun, air, flowers, and water. There is a keen and delightful sense of the fresh spanking breeze, the presence of the sparkling sea. There is also the more abstract pleasure offered by the certainty, the vigor, and the invention of the painting just as painting. In the later pictures this is the whole pleasure. It must be, for the objects from which we might have gained the sense

of participation in the scene have become devoured by a technical process.

Monet invented a name for what he was trying to achieve: *instantaneity.* In 1891 he exhibited, at Durand-Ruel's, a series of fifteen paintings of haystacks in the different lights of different times of day, analyzing the color-light relationships in various stages between half-lights of early morning and evening and the full blaze of midday. This faintly pedantic exhibition was a great success. Monet then set out on an even more elaborate analysis and painted some forty pictures of Rouen Cathedral [210] on gray days, bright days, in early light, late light, full light, light at different seasons of the year. These exercises are interesting, but they emphatically isolate the limitation of Monet's method. The monumental gray form of the cathedral is ground into a pulp of blues, oranges, pinks, and lavenders. The geometrical complications of its buttresses, windows, spires, and tracery become tottering masses of tinted fluff; they lean and waver in random placements on the canvas. A cathedral, with its mass, its organization, its logical formality, is a poor choice for dematerialization in close-range painting when it is supposed to be existing within full light. Theoretically we should be able to forget that this is a cathedral which appears to be going to pieces; practically it is difficult to do so.

But the Rouen pictures were followed by another series, this time of a perfect subject. In the garden of his house at Giverny, which Monet had bought with the proceeds from his first successful sale, there was a pool with water lilies which he had painted from time to time. Now in the 1890's he discovered in the surface of the pool, and the leaves and blossoms floating upon it, a subject with enough material to last him for the rest of his life. The shimmering, shifting translucence of the water, the delicate and even translucent petals of the blossoms, the flat shiny pads of leaves floating or half submerged in water close to the same color, with the light glancing off surfaces or striking through them onto surfaces below, repeating and reflecting on every hand, the whites and the rainbow tints—these were inexhaustible in their combinations and recombinations. Now Monet's canvases became the surfaces of pools, fragmented areas where water, light, air, and the delicate substance of blossoms all partook of one another, echoed one another, and crossed one another's boundaries until there was no differentiation between them.

The water-lily paintings supplied the motif for Monet's last work, a series of large decorative panels [211, 212]. But in these hugely expanded canvases, with large brush strokes, the forms of nature are difficult to distinguish. If the paintings are regarded as representations of lilies and water with ripples and glancing reflections of light, they never become more than great inchoate masses of opalescent color arbitrarily cut off on four sides by a frame. But if they are regarded as abstract arrangements of color applied in directed strokes, they gradually coalesce. One movement of strokes across the canvas is revealed as a

210. MONET: *Rouen Cathedral: Tour d'Albane, Early Morning*, 1894. 41¾ x 29". Museum of Fine Arts, Boston.

check or a buttress to another; a system beginning in one section and seeming to vanish will reappear elsewhere. The colors are woven and built into a structure that is its own reason for being. The "systems" in these paintings are free inventions, felt rather than calculated, and the danger is to exaggerate their precision or to find within them a logic that does not exist. But it is safe to say that Monet, from his impressionist beginning when he painted spontaneous approximations of visual effects of light and atmosphere, gradually transformed his art into one of abstract surfaces where relationships of form and color exist for themselves in spite of the vestigial remains of a subject.

It is on this basis that Monet now seems to have anticipated a school of contemporary extremists. Jackson Pollock (1912–

211. MONET: *Water Lilies, c.* 1925. 79¾ x 221½". Museum of Modern Art, New York,
Mrs. Simon Guggenheim Fund. (Destroyed by fire, 1958.)

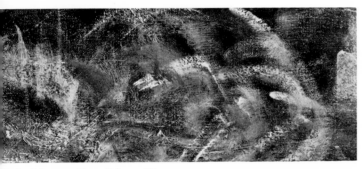

212. MONET: Detail from Figure 211.

1956) painted by dripping, flicking, drib-
bling, or pouring semiliquid colors onto a
canvas (or panel) laid an the floor [213].
The pattern of different colors, densely intermingled or freely splattered, exists without even secondary reference to nature. It
exists for itself as color, as line, as a complex
within which movements, systems, rhythms
are overlaid and intertwined. The same
thing can be said about Monet's late water-
lily pictures, if their starting point of light
playing over the forms of nature is ignored.

213. POLLOCK: *Autumn Rhythm,* 1950. 105 x 207". Metropolitan Museum of Art, Hearn
Fund.

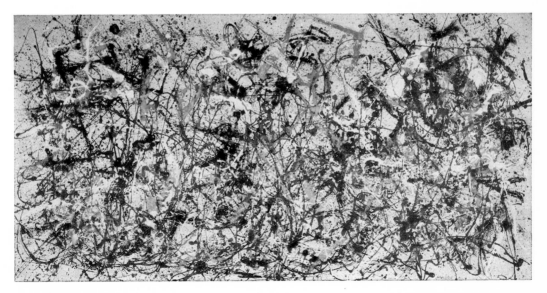

214. MONET: *Woman in a Garden, Springtime, c.* 1875. 19⅝ x 25¾". Walters Art Gallery, Baltimore.

Thus Monet becomes a bridge between the naturalism of early impressionist painting and a contemporary school of extreme abstraction. "Abstract impressionism" would be an appropriate term to describe Pollock's sparkling interweaving of dots, splashes, and ropelike lines of color, and the term is sometimes used as a subtle distinction within the wider "abstract expressionist" school of contemporary painting, which will be seen in a later chapter [548, 549].

Monet's landscapes and the late semi-abstract paintings into which they merged are his historically important work. They obscure his portraits and figure studies, most of which were done between 1860 and the early 1870's. (He did many of his wife.) In any case, he had no great interest in human beings as personalities to be interpreted; he painted them from much the same point of view as he painted landscape —that is, as elements of nature in light. In the gentle *Woman in a Garden, Springtime* [214] the woman is more like a blossoming shrub than a person.

Sisley and Pissarro

The two other "pure" impressionists in the group were Alfred Sisley (1839–1899) and Camille Pissarro (1830–1903). Their experiments were less venturesome, within narrower boundaries, than Monet's. Hence they always fall into second place with brief consideration in books of this kind, which is too bad but inevitable.

A painter's merit cannot be gauged by the number of lines of type required to comment on it, and to comment at any length on Sisley would involve repetition of much that already has been said about Corot and Monet. His fresh and quiet art [215] has affinities with that of both these men.

Sisley resigned himself early to poverty, obscurity, and official rejections, and although he exhibited in the first impressionist show and three others, he spent very little time in Paris and finally retired to the village of Moret, where he could exist at minimum expense surrounded by subject

215. SISLEY: *Bridge at Villeneuve*, date unknown. 21½ x 29″. Philadelphia Museum of Art, John G. Johnson Collection.

matter that appealed to him—a quiet countryside and a village with old buildings, bridges, and river banks. Sisley's parents were English and he spent some time in that country. Of all French painters he comes closest to the special lyrical response to nature found in English painters and even more in English poets. Corot was his idol, and his painting has Corot's serenity beneath the more vibrant impressionist surface. Once he had discovered the impressionist palette and technique—which he never forced—his manner changed very little over the years, yet his work is not repetitious. Each picture is remarkably complete in its effect, where much impressionism seems fragmentary. Without Monet's passion for experiment, which kept the pictures pouring forth, and without a market to set a demand, which he would have worked to supply, Sisley painted with great deliberation, allowing the fullest expression of his sensibilities. He did not live to see the triumph of impressionism extend as far as his own work, but immediately

upon his death his paintings began to fetch high prices. During his lifetime he sold them for twenty-five or thirty francs.

Pissarro's impressionism has much of the sobriety of Sisley's but is less reflective. He was the oldest member of the group, being two years older even than Manet. Born in the Virgin Islands, he came to Paris the year of the great exposition of 1855. Everyone who knew Pissarro seems to have left some account of him, and by all these accounts his life and his character were a catalogue of virtues—loyalty to his friends, wisdom as the father of a large family, courage in adversity, and patience, tolerance, honesty, and industry in all circumstances.

Although Pissarro was intent upon capturing transient effects just as Monet was, he never abandoned the relative discipline of early impressionism, and for a while late in his career he joined the "neo-impressionists," who tried to solidify impressionism by systematizing its free prismatic shattering of light into a scientific application of color into minutely calculated dots [405].

Pissarro soon abandoned this extreme, but that he was attracted to it at all shows his cautiousness in the use of impressionist effects. While Monet was pushing further into exploration of effects of light in air at the expense of form, Pissarro was retreating. *The Market at Gisors* [216] is an effort to retain the atmospheric vibration of impressionism while at the same time imposing the discipline of well-defined contours on forms monumentally arranged in space.

The Market at Gisors is a late picture, but even in his early ones when he was sharing with Monet the excitement of the impressionist discoveries, Pissarro retained his respect for the material fact of the subjects he was painting. When he painted trees and fields [218], they remain trees and fields rather than becoming a multitude of small elements reflecting a characteristic spring light. In no circumstances could he have shared Monet's wish to be ignorant of the objects he saw. Of all the impressionists he is the one most closely allied to the Barbizon spirit with its love of fields, copses, and peasant huts as part of a simple life with a nobility of its own.

But his cityscapes, too, are of a great vivacity [217]. He reduces crowds, carriages, and individual figures to the merest suggestion, in scattered dots and his typical "commas" of paint, but he never allows his city buildings to decompose as Monet's cathedrals did. Pissarro is a careful painter —Monet seems careless at times. He was the only one of the impressionists to exhibit in all eight of the group shows, and during the constant squabbles he was the unofficial moderator.

More than any other member of the group, Pissarro encouraged younger men. At least three painters who were notoriously suspicious and thorny to deal with—Degas, Cézanne, and Gauguin—always retained a deep affection for him. Like Monet's and Sisley's, his financial situation was often desperate and at best difficult, but finally, at the age of sixty-two, he had the satisfaction of seeing his reputation established, not spectacularly but soundly enough, in a large retrospective exhibition organized by Durand-Ruel. It was a gratifyingly happy ending to an admirable career.

216. PISSARRO: *The Market at Gisors*, 1891. Pastel, 13½ x 10¼″. Collection Louis E. Stern, New York.

Degas: "The Bellelli Family"

Midway during the careers of Monet, Sisley, and Pissarro, pure impressionism was abandoned by two painters who felt limited by the transient effects it imposed. One of these men, Renoir, brought impressionism directly into the tradition of the old masters by subjecting it to their disciplines. The other, Cézanne, subjected it to new disciplines, making it the point of departure for the most radical redirection of the art of painting in some six centuries.

A third, Degas, had never accepted impressionism on Monet's terms in the first place, and was its great traditionalist even while he was one of its most startling inno-

217. Pissarro: *Avenue de l'Opéra*, 1898. 25⅜ x 31½". Collection Mrs. Carroll S. Tyson, Chestnut Hill, Pa.

218. Pissarro: *Landscape with Fields*, 1885. 23⅜ x 29". Philadelphia Museum of Art, Wilstach Collection.

vators. It was never necessary for Degas to revert to traditionalism as Renoir was to do, since he had been a traditionalist from the beginning. His innovations, eccentric at first glance, are as a matter of fact brilliantly logical extensions of traditional principles.

Edgar Degas (1834–1917) was the aristocrat of the impressionists, not only by birth but in his intellectuality and reserve, his personal detachment in observing a commonplace world to record it intimately. Of all the impressionists he is the most subtle, disguised as the most direct; the most reflective, disguised as the most noncommittal; the most acute, disguised as the most casual. He is their finest draughtsman and composer; he is one of the finest draughtsmen and composers of any period. He was the only impressionist to recognize

219. DEGAS: *The Bellelli Family*, 1859. 78¾ x 99½". Louvre, Paris.

that the momentary effect—with Degas, a moment may be split to its ultimate fraction —can be used for complete revelation of individual character. He was, in fact, the only impressionist who was interested in painting individuals as psychological entities. The personalities he thus recorded exist with a completeness, a reality, that puts their portraits among the great ones of any age. Sometimes these personalities are people Degas knew; sometimes they are nobodies, a milliner's assistant at work, a clerk, a prostitute, or a vagrant. But no matter who they are, they are revealed in the most significant nuances of their inner being; and at the same time, they are equally revealed in their relationship to the social order.

This doubly acute perception is apparent in Degas's work from the beginning. In 1856 he was only twenty-two years old. The *Salon des Refusés* was still an inconceivable event seven years in the future; Manet was just leaving Couture's studio; Pissarro was getting settled in Paris; Monet was a local boy in Le Havre doing caricatures. Degas was in Naples visiting his aunt, the Baroness Bellelli. He made sketches of her, of her husband, and of their daughters, his young cousins Giovanna and Giuliana Bellelli. During the next three or four years on subsequent visits to Florence, where his relatives were then living, he made other sketches and began to organize them into a group portrait. By 1859 or a little later he had completed the most extraordinary of all family portraits, a study of individual personalities and their interrelationships expressed through pictorial composition [219].

The family was a disturbed one, and the primary fact of the father's emotional separation from the mother and daughters is established by his unconventional placement, seated as he is with his back partly turned toward us and his face in shadow. Compositionally this isolation is defined by the strong line of the table leg that is continued by the line of the side of the fireplace—only slightly interrupted by a few papers on the corner of the table—and on up to the top of the picture by the frame of the large mirror over the mantlepiece. Thus the righthand third of the picture, containing the father's portrait, is cut off by a compositionally heretical but expressively brilliant device. In addition, this area is filled with small shapes, further differentiating it from the left two thirds where the shapes are stronger and more simple.

In contrast with the bent, indecisive attitude and silhouette of the husband, the wife stands with decision and dignity. The wide hoop skirt and the narrow shoulders form a pyramid, the stablest of all geometrical forms. Surmounting this dark silhouetted triangle and framed by her dark hair, the face of the Baroness with its calm, its sadness, and its strength, is the focal point of a composition in which we are led from one formal and psychological relationship to another, yet always back to this central focus of meaning.

The mother's arm rests on the shoulder of Giovanna, the daughter who was most like her mother and closest to her. Degas includes the smaller triangle of the figure of the little girl within the larger one of the mother's to establish this similarity and this closeness. The other daughter, Giuliana, was more volatile and more divided in her allegiance to her parents. For her Degas chooses an unconventional pose, one leg drawn up beneath her as she sits on the corner of a chair, one hand on her hip

(while Giovanna's hands are placidly folded) and her face turned from her mother and sister in the general direction of her father, although she does not quite meet his glance. Giuliana thus unites the two halves of the composition structurally, tied at once to the mother and the sister by the identity of her costume and by lines following or echoing lines in the mother-Giovanna group, and yet also tied to the father. This was Giuliana's relationship to the family: divided between its parts, although in the end (as in the picture) she was united more strongly with her mother and sister.

In its other elements the composition is unified by the repeated horizontals and verticals of the picture on the wall, the table, the door frame, the bell pull, and, for that matter, by any line or mass one wants to pick out. The rather rigid skeletal structure is relieved by the broken pattern of the rug and the sprinkling of flowers on the wallpaper.

A multiple portrait, demanding a division of attention between several individuals and yet a unity of the picture over-all, is as taxing an assignment as a painter has to cope with. *The Bellelli Family* is a masterpiece from half a dozen points of view, technically and expressively. Here in his first major picture Degas demonstrated his extraordinary combination of acute sensibility to the most personal, most private inner life of the individuals he observes, and his peculiar objectivity that allows him to stand outside these perceptions and present them in the most clinical, analytical way.

Degas: His Impressionism

Degas is one of those painters whose art is conventionally discussed chronologically.

His father,° a banker, had planned a career in law for his son, but this study was abandoned in 1855. This was the year of the Exposition Universelle, and Degas was much excited by Courbet's Pavilion of Realism. He was also an admirer of Dela-

---

° Auguste De Gas. The son changed the surname to the less aristocratic form in 1870.

220. DEGAS: Drapery study for *Sémiramis*, 1861. Black pencil and chalk on blue paper, 11⅝ x 7⅞". Louvre, Paris.

221. DEGAS: *Lady on Horseback*, 1860–65. Pencil, 12½ x 8". Louvre, Paris.

croix. But Ingres was his great man, and the Exposition gave him a chance to meet the old painter. M. Valpinçon, a friend of Degas's father, owned *The Turkish Bather,* now called the *Bather of Valpinçon* [59], but had refused to lend it to the Ingres retrospective planned for that year's vast Salon. Degas induced Valpinçon to change his mind and Valpinçon told Ingres of this. Degas and Valpinçon were invited to Ingres's studio, where Degas was given the advice to "draw lines, young man, many lines." Degas was entering the Academy's school, but as it turned out he spent most of his time studying privately under Lamothe, one of Ingres's pupils, since at that time Ingres was accepting no students.

Degas had been a precocious natural draughtsman, and his first student work makes one wonder what was left for him to learn under instruction, but he drew lines, perhaps many lines, under Lamothe. Although his allegiance to Ingres never wavered during his life, his idea was not to emulate the classical style but to capitalize on the discipline and the structural knowledge of the human body upon which it was supposed to be based. Unlike the ordinary student who imitated only the surfaces of the classical style, Degas ignored surfaces and went beneath them to the legitimate fundamentals that had been all but forgotten. He observed them from his earliest work to his last. An early drapery study

222. DEGAS: Studies of Manet, c. 1864–65. Pencil on pink paper, 16 x 11″. Collection Ernest Rouart, Paris.

[220] and the somewhat later, wonderfully certain, wonderfully controlled *Lady on Horseback* [221] are, respectively, an academic preliminary drawing for a large composition and a drawing in the tradition of Ingres, although neither could be confused with its prototype. *Lady on Horseback* is instinct with life as well as elegance. So, of course, is a drawing by Ingres, but there is a fullness and warmth in Degas's drawing as opposed to the cooler sparkle of his idol's. The still later drawing for a

portrait of Manet [222] is more relaxed, more inventive, yet equally disciplined. Ingres is still present, but in addition to greater warmth there is also a record and an interpretation of personality that in Ingres stopped at whatever immediately apparent suggestions were offered by the subject's face and costume. As a mature artist Degas never merely draws. He uses his crayon to probe, to explore, to discover. In a study, *Two Café Singers* [223], the transformation of classical discipline is complete; it operates now with a freedom (and in the service of a subject) that would have horrified Ingres but could never have developed in the art of Degas without the foundation of classical experience. There is not a detail, not so much as the upward bend of a singer's thumb, that is extraneous to the whole; there is not a touch of the crayon dependent on less than perfect mastery.

Degas had met Fantin-Latour and Manet, and now he began to sit in on some of the discussions that were developing at the *Café Guerbois*. By the latter 1860's he had discovered his material: the life of the city as he saw it in the drawing room, in the studio, in the shops, even in the brothel; on the boulevard, at the racetrack, in the cafés, the theater, the opera—all the places where people congregated and could be studied in a thousand expressive attitudes, attitudes spontaneously and unconsciously assumed, combined later from sketches or memory into compositions that seemed equally spontaneously and accidentally put together. In *A Carriage at the Races* [224] carriages and horses are chopped off as if by chance, and in the background a few horses and riders, trees and low buildings are scattered as if at random, while a couple of women, a sleeping boy, a man, and a dog are caught in momentary and casual attitudes as if unaware of the painter. The pose-not-posed, caught as if by good fortune at its most expressive moment, becomes Degas's major preoccupation, including the combination of these individual poses in eccentric compositions where the impression is what Degas wants it to be— that of an arbitrarily selected fragment. But if one tries to extend the fragment, one

223. DEGAS: *Two Café Singers*, 1878–80. Pastel and charcoal, 17½ x 23″. Collection Mrs. John Wintersteen, Chestnut Hill, Pa.

224. DEGAS: *A Carriage at the Races*, 1873. 14⅜ x 22″. Museum of Fine Arts, Boston.

225. DEGAS: *Diego Martelli,* 1879. 43¼ x 39½". National Gallery of Scotland, Edinburgh.

realizes quickly that it is not a fragment at all, but an entity complete and satisfying in itself.

Actually, as Degas himself said, no art was ever less spontaneous than his. His "snapshot" compositions are the result of reflection, study, and calculation. The portrait of Diego Martelli [225] is a direct descendant of Manet's of Zola [192]. But Zola sits formally for his portrait, while Martelli pauses long enough for the artist to sum up a composition in a quick glance— or seems to. The elements are the same—the man, the desk, the papers on it, the furniture of the room, rectangular prints or pictures patterning a wall. Like Manet, Degas draws upon the Japanese print for his composition, using in addition to the rectangular divisions of the *Zola* the bird's-eye view, the tilted perspective found in some of the prints. All this is impressionism in effect until the solidity, the balance, the contem-

plative sobriety of the picture is understood as classical.

Degas loathed the word *impressionist* with its connotation of the accidental and the incomplete, and he fought against it until he managed to get it dropped from the announcements of the fourth group exhibition in 1879, when it was replaced by the word *independent*. He was not interested in the paraphernalia of outdoor impressionism, the countryside and atmospheric effects. City streets offered him as much fresh air as he wanted; the racetrack was open country enough. Theaters and intimate interiors offered the kind of light and air he liked to paint. He needed artificial life, he said, and not for a moment would he have considered yielding to impressionist seductions to paint at Argenteuil, as Manet finally did. Degas insisted that painting was an art of convention. To imitate nature from the model was bad enough; to imitate all its accidents out of doors was unthinkable. He painted from brief notes and sketches, preferring to observe carefully and then depend upon memory. When he used a model he habitually followed a practice that had been used occasionally by some other painters: he let the model move about the studio while he observed the movement of bones and muscles, constructing his figure from this knowledge rather than by imitating the aspect of a single pose with its necessary loss of spontaneity.

Degas: His Classicism

The essentially classical nature of Degas's art and his great originality in the use of classical principles are summarized in one of his most carefully studied paintings, *Foyer de la Danse* [226] painted in 1872. By a device approaching tour de force, but familiar to the artists of classical antiquity, Degas combined a momentary scene of action with what would seem to be its impossible opposite, the imposition of classically static order. At the right of the composition are clustered the ballet master, the rehearsal violinist, and several dancers. The ballet master has just tapped on the floor

226. Degas: *Foyer de la Danse*, 1872. 12½ x 18″. Louvre, Paris.

with his stick, and on this signal the violinist has lowered his bow. The dancer whom he has been rehearsing pauses, motionless, in the middle of a step, awaiting the master's comment or correction. Other dancers glance in her direction.

Thus, although the figures are caught in instantaneous attitudes, these attitudes are legitimately static ones between moments of action, allowing Degas to compose the various figures in classically static fashion without congealing them in Davidian posturings. The same device was used in the sculpture of antiquity. As an example, the famous *Discus Thrower* is shown just as his arm reaches the high point of the throw, at the very moment before it descends, thus allowing the sculptor to represent, legitimately motionless, a moment in a series of violent movements.

Foyer de la Danse is as nicely balanced as any classical exercise, with a variation on the seesaw principle. But the balance is not by weight, as is usual, but by a play of weight against interest. By weight the group of figures on the right, with ballet master, violinist, and dancers densely clus-

tered, is too heavy for the single figure of the dancer on the left. But by interest, isolated as she is and the object of attention from every side, she counters their weight. This kind of balance is sometimes called "occult" balance; no one has ever used it with more skill than Degas, and obviously its attraction for him is the possibility it offers of combining balance with what seems to be random placement.

In painting, classical principles dictate a "closed" composition, complete within itself, and the scene usually takes place in a boxlike space. This is true of *Foyer de la Danse*. Degas varies the restriction by turning the "box" so we see it at an angle, not only from the side but from above, but the space itself remains clearly defined. The back wall and the side wall to the left are actually seen. The wall outside the picture to the right is defined by the fact that light flows into the room from its window. In the immediate foreground a chair is set in such a way that its back parallels the side walls, and hence its side near us identifies a plane corresponding to a fourth wall between us and the dancers. The function of the chair,

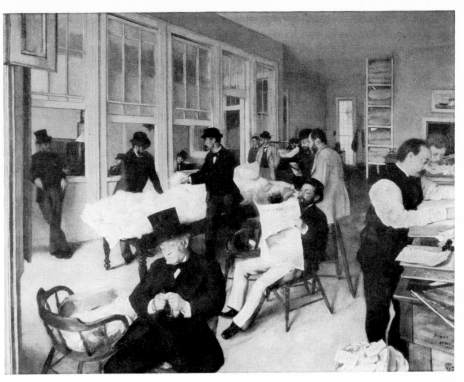

227. DEGAS: *Portraits in an Office*, 1873. 29⅛ x 36⅛″. Musée Municipal, Pau.

228. DEGAS: Detail of Michel Musson from Figure 227.

then, is to define space, yet it seems to be the most casually disposed object in the whole painting. Upon this skeleton an analysis of the picture's composition could be elaborated at length to include every object in it, since not the smallest detail is accidental. The final unifying element is light, light as it flows upon and defines the objects disposed in space. This, of course, is the opposite of the light of typically impressionist painting that consumes the objects it touches and makes of space a vibrating tinted mist.

Foyer de la Danse was completed just before Degas made a trip to New Orleans, where his mother had been born. Degas went to visit her family and his two brothers, the younger René and the elder Achille, who had entered the family's cotton brokerage firm there. Degas repeated the compositional idea of the *Foyer* picture in *Portraits in an Office* [227], where he defined space in similar ways, even including a chair in the left foreground, with his uncle Michel Musson [228] testing a sample of cotton while sitting in an adjacent chair.

229. DEGAS: *Estelle Musson (Mme. René De Gas)*, 1872–73. 29 x 36″. National Gallery of Art, Washington, D.C., Chester Dale Collection.

Degas: His Humanity

Degas did several portraits of his relatives on this trip, and that of his brother René's wife [229] is one of the most exceptional among all his work. A special bond of affection had always existed between Degas and his younger brother, and now this was extended to his brother's wife, for René De Gas had married his blind cousin, Estelle Musson. The blind eyes turned to the light, the placement of the figure in the left half of the canvas with the rest of the space behind it nearly vacant, the quietness of the pose suggesting resignation, the delicacy of the colors—rose, gray, and silvery white—all have something to do with the mood of tenderness, loneliness, and affectionate sympathy pervading the picture. The composition seems to be a spontaneous one and is, of course, not a complicated one. If we cannot analyze precisely how the mood is created, we nevertheless cannot fail to be touched by it.

The portrait is an especially intimate expression of a quality for which Degas usually receives no credit. Because he defended his prejudices with a sharp tongue, anecdotes about his witticisms and his eccentricities have obscured the tenderness that was also a part of his nature. Because he never married and because he painted some unflattering pictures of women, he acquired a reputation as a woman hater, but it was not a misogynist who painted the early *Head of a Young Woman* [230]. Degas never sentimentalizes a portrait. Faced with an unpleasant subject as he frequently was—by choice as often as not—he never hesitated to record an unpleasant personality. But his model for the *Self-portrait in a Soft Hat* [231] was a young man with a face as gentle as it is skeptical. It is the face of a man who, when he painted his aged father listening to a friend's music [232], contemplated one of the most poignant aspects of human life with deep understanding and consummate tact.

230. DEGAS: *Head of a Young Woman*, 1867. 10¼ x 8¾". Louvre, Paris.

231. DEGAS: *Self-portrait in a Soft Hat*, 1857–58. Oil on paper applied to canvas, 10¼ x 7½". Sterling and Francine Clark Art Institute, Williamstown, Mass.

Degas and the Impressionists

Shortly after Degas returned from New Orleans, plans for the first group show got under way at the *Café Guerbois*. Degas was a constant irritation to the other members during its organization. He had always held himself aloof from most of them, but now he was full of ideas that met with no one else's approval. Above all he was eager to avoid any implications that this was another *Salon des Refusés*, and he confused things by insisting that as many popular painters be included as could be induced to enter. He ended by drawing in more painters than anyone else, which was helpful since it decreased each one's share of the expense (most of the group were always in financial trouble). No matter how much they admired his work, many members disliked Degas—and he seems to have given them plenty of reason. He was witty and

frequently he turned his wit against them. He could seem a snob when someone failed to interest him; unlike Manet he did not trouble to hide his feelings beneath a gloss of manners. He always showed himself at his worst in public, concealing his generosities from everyone and reserving his affection for a very few people not connected with his professional life.

Why was Degas interested in exhibiting with the impressionists? The answer redounds to his great credit. He had nothing to gain professionally from the association; he even had much to lose. He had been accepted in the Salon for six years running, 1865 to 1870 inclusive—apparently not submitting the following years—and had had compliments from influential quarters. To exhibit with so dubious a group as the unknowns of the *Café Guerbois* could only block a continuation of this mild but promising success. Degas did not need the vaguely possible financial benefits that the other members hoped against hope might develop in the form of sales. He was wealthy and he even objected to selling his pictures, although he gave away many. He might have been expected to be suspicious and disdainful of the whole thing just as Manet was, yet Degas was one of the most industrious workers in organizing the exhibition and calling it to general attention.

The fact is that Degas believed in the group and in the group show because he believed in the new painting. His relationship to impressionism was a curious one; we have already seen how many of its premises he rejected. But he did share with the other impressionists the conviction that the subject from contemporary life, presented with the quality of immediacy, was the proper field for painting in his time. It was a time so complex that man could no longer hope to achieve the expression of an ideal universal order conceivable in antiquity and reflected in the art of antiquity. Nor in such a time could such a thing as universal knowledge be imagined, as the Renaissance had imagined it and given it form, for science had begun to make a specialist of every man and no man understood more than a fraction of what surrounded him. The romantics had recognized both impossibilities in the modern world and had escaped into a never-never land of emotional stimulants. But as a man of the world fascinated by the world, Degas rejected these romantic escapes.

Denied classical serenity, Renaissance wisdom, and romantic escape, man must be content with those small and commonplace fragments of the infinitely complex world that are within the scope of his comprehension. The function of the artist, then, by Degas's idea, is to take these fragments and treat them in such a way that they afford full play to the sensibilities of anyone whose imagination can reach beyond their commonplaceness into the infinite realm of personality and association. No other painter shared the intensity of Degas's interest in the commonplace as material for painting, or his fascination with the exact description of the way people stood, sat, moved, existed in their daily round. But if

232. DEGAS: *Degas's Father Listening to Lorenzo Pagans Singing,* *c.* 1869–72. 31½ x 24¾″. Museum of Fine Arts, Boston.

the impressionists did not share Degas's intensity, they shared his interest in the everyday world according to their own more casual ways of seeing it. And for that reason Degas knew he was one of them.

After 1886, date of the last impressionist group show (he exhibited in all but the next to last), Degas saw few people and exhibited rarely, working in his studio as a recluse. There was a steady demand for his work. He had never liked to sell his pictures, but it now became necessary for him to do so; he had sacrificed most of his fortune in 1876 to extricate his brother from difficulties following speculations in American stocks. The exact circumstances are not known since Degas was extremely reticent about all details of his personal life.

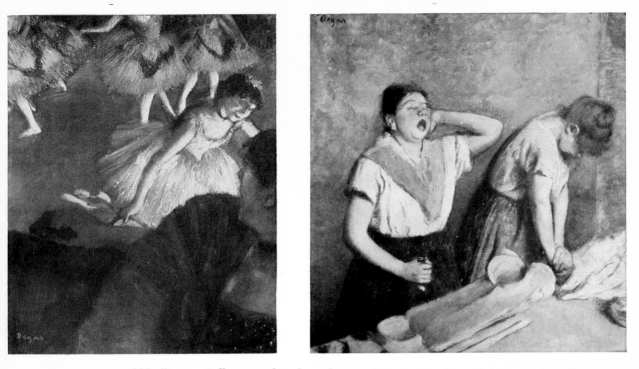

233. DEGAS: *Ballerina and Lady with Fan,* 1885. Pastel, 26 x 30″. Philadelphia Museum of Art, John G. Johnson Collection.

234. DEGAS: *Women Ironing,* 1882. 31 x 28¾″. Durand-Ruel, Paris.

The ballet pictures that account for so much of his popularity today were produced in great numbers after the middle 1870's. His interest in the ballet was not that of a balletomane: the ballet happened to provide in one package all the elements with which he was working—indoor or artificial light, frequently unusual in source, as from footlights; eccentric angles of vision, as from a box above the stage; accessory elements of unexpected shapes, supplied by such things as bits of stage scenery, props, the rails of the orchestra pit or the curve of a box seat [233]. Above all, here were the human figures of ballet masters, wardrobe mistresses, mothers waiting for or upon their daughters, figure after figure to be caught in momentary attitudes full of variety, especially the dancers themselves with their bony, sinewy bodies and curious stances. Sometimes Degas seems to be interested in contrasting the glamor of the ballet with the unglamorous rather plain girls who learn to go through curious con-

tortions to present glamorous illusions. But ordinarily his interest in dancers is not much different from his interest in, for instance, the two laundresses [234], one ironing, one yawning, whose occupational attitudes equally fascinated him.

Degas gradually abandoned oil paints and limited himself to pastel, for which he had always had a predilection. He was essentially a draughtsman and always found the texture of oil unsympathetic. The "lines, many lines," that Ingres had advised him to draw as a student had remained the basis of his art as a painter. Line came increasingly to mean for him a boundary reduced to minimum complexity for maximum description. In *Woman Scratching* [235], the whole folded, hanging weight of breast and stomach are summed up in three rough arcs.

Pastel is ordinarily associated with filmy, airy effects because it must be applied delicately over a textured surface and not touched again if it is to retain its life. Rubbing or drawing over it deadens it. But by means of some special fixatif, the composition of which is unknown, Degas could work over his pastels without losing their grainy quality, and alone among those who have used the medium he gave it all the strength, depth, and solidity of oil. In place of its usual chalky tints he achieved a full-bodied brilliance. It was the perfect medium for him. He was drawing and, at once, painting. Toward the end of his life his sight failed, and his pastels became broader and broader in drawing. For the first time, forms tended to diffuse into something like impressionistic effects, but a lifetime of studying the construction of the human body, and its movement, had taught him where the essential hollow or bulge in a contour told most about bone, muscle, and fat. His last drawings, done when he was nearly blind, are still miracles of draughtsmanship.

In the art of Degas, tradition and innovation are so fused that they exist in identity with one another. A hundred examples could be given to continue the illustration of this point; one, *Nude Arranging Her Hair* [236], is closely allied to the *Bather of Valpinçon* [59]. Ingres's harem beauty has become a *bourgeoise*, her seraglio a boudoir in a Paris flat of which we see a corner with a somewhat blowzy chair. The beautifully patterned turban is gone; so are the svelte, lovely contours of the odalisque's body. Degas's young woman ducks her head to work vigorously at the nape of her neck with a comb. Her shoulders bunch together as she raises her arms, the lines from elbows down either side, along back and buttocks, along breast, chest, and hips, describe a series of muscular contractions and relaxations, taut here, inert there, rounded in this place, hollowed out in another, stretched across the projections of bones or resting weightily upon them. In the bourgeois century, Ingres's revery of sensuous delight has given way to Degas's factual statement of bourgeois actuality.

Technically the enameled precision of Ingres and the direct vigor of Degas may seem to contradict one another; basically they are allied. Degas's active linear contours defining forms modeled in vibrant light and Ingres's dulcet ones enclosing

235. DEGAS: *Woman Scratching*, 1881. Pastel, 15¾ x 16″. Collection T. Edward Hanley, Bradford, Pa.

236. DEGAS: *Nude Arranging Her Hair, c.* 1885. Pastel, 21¾ x 20½″. Collection Mr. and Mrs. Herbert C. Morris, Bryn Mawr, Pa.

237. DEGAS: *Woman Rubbing Her Back with a Sponge, c.* 1900. Bronze, height 18″. Philadelphia Museum of Art, Curt Valentine Bequest.

238. DEGAS: *Young Dancer,* 1880–81. Bronze with cloth accessories, height 39″. Collection Henry P. McIlhenny, Philadelphia.

forms across which light flows like a caress, are arrived at from the same tradition, which each painter reverences and observes and, each in his own way, enlarges. If Ingres depends upon the tradition of the Renaissance, so does Degas depend upon it and upon Ingres.

Degas was also a sculptor, doing occasional pieces from time to time until, in his last years, his sight failing, he did many. Theoretically there is such a thing as impressionist sculpture; actually, Degas is the only sculptor who is impressionist in anything like a pure definition. Like his paintings, his small bronzes wonderfully embody momentary aspects of unidealized figures [237], rejecting all incidentals and nonessentials to capture the essence of visible reality. Essentially these are sketches in clay, not conceived as bronzes. Similarly, his single large piece is in effect not so much sculpture as a masterpiece of draughtsmanship in three dimensions. The bony little figure of the "ballet rat" [238], the suggested textures of hose, bodice, hair, and flesh, the vivid reality of her stance, make possible the extraordinary features of a real tarlatan skirt and a real satin hair ribbon. Astonishing at first, they take their place after a moment or two as integral harmonious parts of the reality of the figure as a whole. The only trouble is that as time has passed, the cloth has grown limp, soiled, and dusty. The reality of these real accessories is less real, in the end, than the reality of the bronze image.

239. RODIN: *The Hand of God,* 1902. Bronze, height 26¾". Rodin Museum, Philadelphia, Gift of Jules Mastbaum.

240. RODIN: *The Kiss,* 1886. Marble, height 72". Rodin Museum, Philadelphia, Gift of Jules Mastbaum.

Rodin

The impressionism of Degas's sculpture is consistent. It is impressionistic in subject, in spirit, and in the play of light over the surface of forms, forms that are realized by suggestion rather than by detailed statement. The great sculptor of the nineteenth century, Auguste Rodin (1840–1917), often uses a similar, even an exaggeratedly impressionistic technique, working in broken surfaces to reveal incompletely defined forms as if seen in flickering illumination. Purists in sculpture deny the legitimacy of this surface treatment, which confuses the visual illusionism of painting with the tactile existence of sculptural mass. Nevertheless Rodin employed it, and although his impressionism ends there, some comments on his art are best interpolated at this point.

Beneath his impressionistic surface, Rodin is sometimes a dramatic realist, sometimes a quasi symbolist, almost always a vigorously masculine romantic, but he is never an impressionist in the sense of responding to the fascination of the commonplace. A little honest commonplaceness would be refreshing in his work, as a matter of fact. The erotic mysticism of pieces like *The Hand of God* [239] is beginning to seem, nowadays, embarrassingly pretentious. And his *Gates of Hell,* which was to have been the Sistine Ceiling of sculpture but was never carried beyond the stage of preliminary studies [241] and a few completed figures, is rather a hodgepodge whether it is regarded as philosophy or as sculpture. The familiar figure of *The Thinker,* which was to have brooded over the *Gates,* can be found in the upper central portion of the preliminary study illus-

241. RODIN: *Gates of Hell*, 1880. Bronze, 18 x 12 ft. Rodin Museum, Philadelphia, Gift of Jules Mastbaum.

trated here. *The Thinker*, of course, was one of the elements completed at full scale as an independent work of sculpture, and is known everywhere. Numerous casts were made from its mold.

The bumpy, sketchy, gouged, and roughened surfaces of impressionism were so cultivated by Rodin that he seems often to have tortured his clay, punching and kneading it beyond reason. "Sculpture is quite simply the art of depression and protuberance," he once said. "There is no getting away from that." This is certainly a limited definition that would eliminate most of the world's great sculpture, but for Rodin this

violent manipulation had an expressive reason for being. A great part of the effectiveness of Rodin's sculpture comes from the plastic drama of the modeling, where the sculptor's fingers are "seen" at work. It is often objected that this is a perversion of the noble material of bronze, to ask it to be nothing more than a kind of preservative for figures conceived as clay with all clay's yielding plasticity. If this is so, it is a fundamental shortcoming in the majority of Rodin's works.

In marble, Rodin's technical impressionism takes another direction. Transitions from one portion of realistic form to others are smoothed and softened until they seem to be partially obscured by mists, as in *The Kiss* [240]. But Rodin is also acutely realistic on occasion; he spent three years in litigation to disprove the charges that an early work, *The Age of Bronze*, was not a work of sculpture at all but an actual cast from a living model. It was not, but in its reproduction of an exceptionally perfect male model it might almost as well have been.

Rodin is saved again and again by the mass and force of pieces that violate a fundamental premise of contemporary sculpture: that expressive forms must be developed from a recognition of the character of the sculptor's material, whether it is stone, bronze, wood, clay, wire, or string. Rodin's sculpture opposes this idea; his instinct is to transform his material into something else, as he tacitly stated when he said of one piece of sculpture he admired (*Venus de Medici* [243]), "You almost expect, when you touch this body, to find it warm," or when he said that "Every masterpiece of the sculptor has the radiant appearance of living flesh." This is simply not true, as a moment's reflection on Gothic sculpture, which Rodin worshiped, would have shown. But that Rodin could say this, and that so much of his sculpture is conceived from that point of view, ties him to the lesser sculptors of his century, who conceived of sculpture as the detailed imitation of nature or as three-dimensional repetitions of forms developed by painters. But it is still true that no other sculptor in the nineteenth century could have approached the massive, vital force of Rodin's study for a monument to Balzac [478], to select one example almost at random from many.

Rodin would have made an excellent painter, and his drawings are in many ways more satisfying than his sculpture. His typical manner involved a free, loose, linear description of contours, with washes of color that were allowed to run and spread beyond these contours, or might be entirely independent of them, as they are in *Imploration* [508]. Here the two bodies are drawn against a tawny color that merges with a background of russets, blues, pale greens, and grays, which have no descriptive function. Rodin drew quickly, sometimes allowing his pencil to follow the contours as he watched the model, rather than the drawing. He achieved surprising descriptions of fleshy masses with an absolute minimum of means. His subjects were erotic more often than not but are saved by his obvious conviction of the identity between physical love and spiritual fulfillment.

Degas and Renoir

Degas is not convinced of life's goodness although he never for a moment questions its fascination. Whether he is painting with as much sympathy for his subject as he does in the portrait of Estelle Musson or with the detached observation apparent in his treatment of the less attractive women in a café on the Boulevard Montmartre [247], he never stands in judgment, never makes a moral evaluation, never commits himself to a comment on the philosophical justification of man's existence in the world. If in the end the flavor of his art is pessimistic, it is not because Degas ever points out a pessimistic conclusion, but because he lets the decision go by default. The average person in "interpreting" art expects to find a positive statement of faith, an affirmation of his own hope that his existence in the world serves some ultimate good. Degas neither confirms nor refutes such an idea.

Degas's attitude toward the world—a fascination with its fragments, a refusal to comment on its wholeness—is summarized in his attitude toward women. Few painters have been more preoccupied with representing them; no painter has portrayed them more acutely as personalities. None has been more sensitive to their psychological nuances or recorded these perceptions more intimately. But Degas seems hardly conscious of women as mothers, sweethearts, or sirens. Even in *The Bellelli Family* his perception of the relationship between mother and daughters is remarkable for its analysis of human relationships rather than for sentiment. Similarly woman's body fascinates him but only as a structural entity, not as a symbol of beauty or an object of desire. His late drawings of women climbing in and out of bathtubs, drying themselves, scratching themselves, caught in every awkward and unlovely attitude that presupposes the absence of any observer—these so-called "keyhole" subjects, in which he actually was at his most objective, account for his reputation as a woman hater, along with his pictures of prostitutes and nondescript women as in, again, *Café, Boulevard Montmartre*.

In all these respects Degas's opposite is Auguste Renoir (1841–1919), the best loved of the impressionists today.

Renoir is a joyous painter, so convinced of life's goodness, which seems apparent to him on every hand, that he feels no need to philosophize or moralize about it. If he does not comment, it is only because he does not find it necessary to ponder "the meaning of life." He finds life so wonderful that simply to participate in it gives meaning to existence. He never reports on life's specific fragments, as Degas does, because life in its wholeness is present for him in every woman he paints. Where Degas individualizes women Renoir generalizes woman as a symbol. Even when he paints a portrait we are conscious of womanhood first, and only incidentally of the specific individual who is represented. And when he is not painting a portrait he repeats over and over again a facial and physical type that he adopted early and was content to vary only slightly as his art matured, not because he needed a convenient formula but because woman as a generic concept was lovelier to him than any individual set of features could be.

242. BOUCHER: *Bath of Diana*, 1742. 22½ x 28¾". Louvre, Paris.

Renoir: The Mystique of Woman

Woman is a principle so pervading Renoir's universe that everything he paints is accessory to her. Children and flowers are corollaries to his concept of woman as a kind of earth- or life-symbol who blossoms and comes to fruition. Fields, streams, trees, and skies are echoes of her fertility. When Monet painted a woman out of doors she became identified with the sward, the bushes, with nature around her, because she shared with other natural objects the faculty of reflecting light. But when Renoir paints a woman out of doors the relationship with nature is reversed. Instead of absorbing her, the impressionist shimmer and vibration is like an emanation from her, an emanation of the life she represents, animating all nature.

The mystique of woman is a constant in French art, and through Renoir impressionism makes its contribution to this tradition. The near-mystical veneration of woman in French art and life combines the simultaneous recognitions of her most direct attractions and her most profound significance. She is an object of sexual delight, a creature of unusual sensibilities in human relationships, and a reminder that no matter

how complicated man may have made himself as a civilized being, he continues to exist only through the operation of a natural force he cannot explain but which woman embodies. This concept has given woman an extraordinary position in French life and thought. Among its many different expressions one of the earliest was the medieval veneration of the Virgin coexisting with the code of chivalric love by which the knight served his lady.

Woman was never more pervasive in French life than during the eighteenth century at a court dominated by women and given over to the pursuit of lovemaking. In spite of all the dimpled affectations of eighteenth-century court art, in spite of all the furbelows and ruffles and ribbons and fantasies of dress and manners, in spite of all the viciousness and indulgence of a sociologically indefensible way of life among the aristocracy—in spite of all this, the mystique of woman was never altogether obscured by the cultivation of woman as an object of pleasure, and the art of the eighteenth-century court painters was given over to her celebration. Renoir's first contact with this art was early and quite direct.

As a boy—his father was a tailor from Limoges, poor and with a large family—Renoir was apprenticed to a decorator of fine porcelain. He copied onto cups and plates flowers and other motifs from the eighteenth-century court painter Boucher.* Their fresh pinks and blues, their vivacity, their prettiness (a word of which Renoir

---

* François Boucher (1703–1770) was also an early influence on David; some of his mannerisms are reflected in *Mars Vanquished by Minerva* [19]. But with David's shift to classicism Boucher became one of the painters he most abominated. Boucher's candified tints, his prettified girls, his great puffs and swirls of shining satins and taffetas, his hothouse flowers, his feminine elaboration, are the quintessence of the rococo style, suggesting perfumes, powders, erotic refinements. The surface of his painting is slick and shiny, his nudes sometimes seem almost rubbery. He is not much liked today but he is a delightful painter if he is regarded as a great stylist. Renoir was as much influenced by an earlier eighteenth-century painter, Antoine Watteau (1684–1721), although less obviously.

243. *Venus de Medici*, Roman copy or variation of Praxiteles' *Aphrodite of Cnidus.*
Marble, life-size. Uffizi, Florence.
244. RENOIR: *Bather with Griffon*, 1870. 72½ x 45¼". *Museu de Arte*, Sao Pãolo, Brazil.

was never afraid) always remained a part of Renoir's painting. Of Boucher's *Bath of Diana* [242] he once said that he kept going back to it again and again, "as one returns to one's first love."

Boucher's painting was full of the stylish artificialities and the titillations demanded by his patrons at the court and in the demimonde. It has won for itself the unflattering designation of "boudoir painting." Renoir

revivified the tradition by leaving the boudoir for the out of doors, abandoning Boucher's artificial paraphernalia for natural banks of grass and flowers. Instead of Baths of Diana he paints healthy young women bathing in country streams. Above all, he abandoned coy suggestion for a straightforward, full-blossomed sexuality that would have reduced his buxom nudes to biological specimens if he had not been

245. RENOIR: *The Swing*, 1876. 36½ x 28½". Louvre, Paris.

then as a young painter with no resources and no patrons he kept himself alive doing occasional porcelain painting and some hack commercial work, including the decoration of window blinds. Monet was having the same struggle and the two men were good friends. For a few years Renoir groped about, imitating photographs briefly and working for a while in the manner of Delacroix. He later destroyed these pseudo-romantic productions, and the earliest Renoirs we have, from around the middle 1860's, show how much he learned from Courbet. *Bather with Griffon* [244], painted in 1870 and exhibited in the Salon that year, belongs to this early group, which seem like preparatory work if they are thought of in context with Renoir's later career. But independently *Bather with Griffon* can hold its own in the company of great paintings of the nude in any time. If it lacks anything, it is the full individuality of style that marks a work of art as completely the artist's own.

Half a dozen influences are rather obviously at work here. There is the wonderful rich paint of Courbet, Courbet's feeling for the texture of young flesh expressed in pigment of an opulence that is in itself part of the expression of form. Renoir lightened this richness with the more delicate coloration, the pinks and blues of rococo painting, and lightened Courbet's spirit also by such details as the enchantingly feminine heap of discarded garments and the little dog lying on them. These are painted with a freshness and delicacy that make Courbet seem ponderous. The pose is a classical one, and significant as an indication of Renoir's early attraction to the stability of traditional forms to which he will hark back later when his art is more reflective. There are numberless Venuses of antiquity in variations of this pose, the first one probably having been Praxiteles' *Aphrodite of Cnidus* and the best known, the *Venus de Medici* [243].

But, of course, there is not the faintest suggestion of neo-classical mannerism in Renoir's use of a classical pose: *Bather with Griffon* is a realistic painting from a living model. Technically it makes superb use of the academic technical disciplines, capitalizing on their sound virtues as Renoir

so completely and naturally within a tradition wholly French—the tradition that combines the frankest delight in sexuality with the most unquestioning reverence for woman's fundamental significance as the source of all warmth and life in the world.

Renoir entered the studio of a painter named Gleyre* in 1862. As a student and

---

* Marc Gabriel Charles Gleyre (1808–1874) was a Swiss who settled in Paris as a successful painter of history and genre. He made a Salon sensation in 1840, another in 1843. When Delaroche quit teaching, Gleyre took over his studio, and altogether he trained some five or six hundred students, among them Gérôme and, as well as Renoir, the other young future impressionists, Monet, Sisley, and Bazille. Gleyre was a sound painter and had the respect of these young men although they had no ambition to follow him. He, in his turn, recognized and respected the unusual talents of Monet and Renoir. He deserves a kind word in any history of nineteenth-century painting.

246. RENOIR: *Moulin de la Galette*, 1876. 51½ x 69″. Louvre, Paris.

247. DEGAS: *Café, Boulevard Montmartre*, 1877. Pastel over monotype, 16½ x 23½″. Louvre, Paris.

248. RENOIR: *Luncheon of the Boating Party*, 1881. 51 x 68″.
Phillips Collection, Washington, D.C.

learned them from Gleyre, ignoring the shallow uses to which they were ordinarily put. All these elements temper one another —classicism, realism, academicism, eighteenth-century sensibility—and all of them are bound together by Renoir's response to the idea of womanhood.

After these early paintings, Renoir's development falls into four periods, during which he discovers and practices impressionism, then rejects it, and finally returns to it with variations. These we will see in turn.

Renoir and Impressionism

By 1870 Renoir was beginning to explore, with Monet, effects of light and air, and ways of representing them with broken color. By the time of the first group exhibition his impressionist manner was fully developed, and he continued working impressionistically until 1882. *The Swing* [245] of 1876 has the dappled light, the diffused forms, the young grace, the air of courtship, typical of his work in this period. As an ambitious showpiece he painted the *Moulin de la Galette* [246] for the third impressionist exhibition of 1877. Both

these paintings have something of impressionism's momentary revelation of the subject and much of pure impressionism's haze of light fused with atmosphere. Yet Renoir is yielding only reluctantly to this cultivation of transient effects and shortly he will become thoroughly dissatisfied with them. Most of his figures are caught in repose. Like Degas in *Foyer de la Danse*, Renoir continues to feel the need for classical stability in his compositions; it finds its way into pictures of the early period almost as if without his will. His figures never quite lose their formal identity within the quivering luminosity surrounding them.*

During this first tremendously productive period, Renoir painted portraits, figures, pure landscape, landscape with figures, still-life, and street scenes. A comparison of *Moulin de la Galette* with *Café, Boulevard Montmartre* [247] demonstrates that Renoir and Degas lived in Paris as if in two different cities. For Renoir Paris was a city of light, happiness, air, movement, warmth, a city in blossom. For Degas it was a collection of human beings in haphazard juxtaposition, stratified in a system of social levels. Although the dancers in the *Moulin de la Galette* include portraits of several of Renoir's friends, they remain generic young females and their generic young male suitors, idolaters of the female principle. Only once, at the end of this delightful period, Renoir departs momentarily from the generic conceptions which are the rule in his work. In *Luncheon of the Boating Party* [248] the members are more definitely individualized by physical feature, even if not particularly so by psychological differences. Among them, at the left, holding a small dog, is the young woman who was soon to become Renoir's wife.

Renoir had by now found some patrons. An influential one was the publisher Charpentier, in whose garden *The Swing* had been painted. Renoir was beginning to find portrait commissions too, and in order to further these Madame Charpentier commis-

---

* A *galette* is a kind of cake; the *Moulin de la Galette* was a popular, inexpensive dancehall and restaurant in Montmartre, but later developed into a less savory spot than the one Renoir painted.

sioned him to do a portrait of herself and her two little girls [249]. It was submitted to the Salon of 1879 and because (in part, at least) of the social prominence of the sitter it received a good position and was a success. (Renoir never shared the attitude of aggressive hostility toward the Salon and was glad to show there when he could get accepted.) He set about deliberately in the portrait of Madame Charpentier to paint a picture that would please conventional taste without prostituting his talent. He did not regard it as a lowering of standards or a denial of principles to modify his impressionist manner to accord more closely with Salon standards. The result was a fine portrait even if it is not Renoir's most exciting work. Its limitations, however, are apparent if it is compared with Degas's portrait of the Baroness Bellelli and her two little girls [219]. It is one of the rare instances when Renoir by his own standards falls short of Degas by his.

With plenty of commissions coming his way by the end of the 1870's, when he was forty years old, Renoir had reached the point where most painters would have industriously followed up their successes. But Renoir was full of dissatisfactions with the kind of painting he was doing. The direction of these dissatisfactions is apparent in the departures made in *Luncheon of the Boating Party* from the *Moulin de la Galette*, a nearly identical subject. *Luncheon of the Boating Party* is more sharply defined in its forms, more conventional (if no more successful and not quite so interesting) in its compositional balance. Renoir was ready to abandon the light touch of impressionism just when the first collectors were beginning to be attracted to it. A trip to Italy in 1882 verified his suspicions of impressionism and put an end to his impressionist period.

Renoir: Return to Tradition

Restless, unsure of his direction, beginning to feel that in seeking effects of light he had forgotten "how either to paint or to draw," that in working directly from nature he had forgotten how to compose, that in impres-

249. Renoir: *Madame Charpentier and Her Daughters*, 1878. 60½ x 74⅞". Metropolitan Museum of Art, New York, Wolfe Fund.

sionism a painter descended to monotony, Renoir had refused to exhibit with the group in their shows of 1879, 1880, and 1881. The Italian pilgrimage of 1882 had a definite goal: the Vatican frescoes of Raphael. They had been an academic shrine ever since Ingres had proclaimed Raphael's godhead. And they did not disappoint Renoir.

In their breadth and amplitude and definition, their "simplicity and grandeur," he said, they confirmed his dissatisfactions with impressionism. He saw too the Pompeiian paintings that had given such impetus to the classical revival a hundred years before, that had "removed the cataracts" from the eyes of David when he went to Rome as a young painter trained in the eighteenth-century tradition. And by chance Renoir also stumbled across a book now well known to painters but then obscure, a late fourteenth-century handbook on the craft of painting by Cennino Cennini, a follower of Giotto, who described in great detail the technique of egg tempera painting, a technique demanding the clearest, the most concise definition of form, allowing for no suggestion, dictating implacably closed contours. Renoir had always

to draw, paint, and compose. *Dance at Bougival* [250], painted on his return from Italy, has a new solidity and definition in the two dancing figures, although the seated ones in the background are similar to those in the *Moulin de la Galette* in their softer, airier, form. Renoir was equally determined, as a matter of practical business, to make a success in the Salon instead of directing himself toward the handful of art lovers who were "capable of liking a painting without Salon approval."* And he would do it this time without compromising, even to the extent he had done in *Madame Charpentier and Her Daughters.*

The disciplinary problems he set himself were to be solved in a painting of bathers in a landscape [251] upon which he worked for three years, from 1884 to 1887, when it was exhibited at Petit's, a commercial gallery, with great success. Even most of the impressionists admired it, because Renoir's suspicions of impressionism as a blind alley had come to be shared by others of them—not by Monet—who were hunting their own ways out of its mists. In fact, the year before the *Bathers* was exhibited, the last group show had been held (1886), and of the major impressionists only Degas and Pissarro had participated.

The *Bathers* is a wonderful and in many ways a most inconsistent painting. It is obviously a demonstration piece, even an exercise, but the appreciation of its very sound brilliance in this capacity in no way hampers the simultaneous enjoyment of its lightness, its gaiety, and its charm. For all its Italian inspiration, Renoir's "tight" or "dry" or "harsh" period, as it is variously called, is not Italianate. The *Bathers* is closer to Boucher than it is to Raphael. These firm, pink nudes with their pouting lips, short noses, tapered hands and feet,

250. Renoir: *Dance at Bougival*, 1883. 70¾ x 38½". Museum of Fine Arts, Boston.

admired Ingres's line, and now in the light of these Italian revelations he discovered new virtues in Ingres's meticulously controlled surfaces as well.

Renoir determined to subject himself to a period of discipline, to learn again how

* Renoir exhibited at the Salon for the last time in 1890 after abstaining for seven years, but his determination to make a Salon success is indicative of the whole reorientation of his way of thinking and painting. The need for Salon recognition passed when, about 1883, he reached a financial agreement with Durand-Ruel assuring him of an adequate income, and in 1892 Durand-Ruel held such a successful exhibition of his work that thereafter Renoir had no money troubles.

251. RENOIR: *Bathers*, 1884–87. 45¼ x 67". Collection Mrs. Carroll S. Tyson, Chestnut Hill, Pa.

252. GIRARDON: Late seventeenth-century cast of bas relief from Fountain of Diana, North Terrace, Palace of Versailles.

and swelling curves, have not changed much from the type of Diana and her attendant nymph, although the taffetas, the pearls, and the ornamental park where Diana bathed have given way to simple linen, a pin or two in the hair, and an ordinary bit of countryside. The lineage of these bathing girls goes even further back; Renoir adapted his composition from a seventeenth-century French bas-relief by the sculptor François Girardon on the Fountain of Diana in the gardens of Versailles [252].

The playful sportiveness—splashing of water and so on—of Renoir's bathing figures is belied by their static and studied design. There is a contradiction, too, between the tight modeling within unsparingly precise outlines, and the impressionistic opalescent shimmer of the background. Yet these contradictions do not matter. Renoir achieved an improbable combination of virtues: the picture is fresh, appealing, and intimate; it is also calculated and formal.

To explain the harmonious coexistence of these contradictory elements might be possible, but it is unnecessary if we accept something Renoir once said: "These days, they try to explain everything, but if a picture could be explained it wouldn't be art."* In the *Bathers* one element after another can be isolated for explanation—the echo of Ingres's line, the impressionistic vibration in the background, the eighteenth-century succulence of the nudes, the reference to Girardon who composed within a certain tradition, the vestigial realism of the figure to the lower right. Yet, in the end, there is no necessity to explain why this great picture is not a mere studio concoction, if we admit that a total painting may be more than the sum of its parts, except one part which cannot be isolated, ". . . the passion of the painter which carries everything else before it." These are Renoir's words, and in no painter's art are they more important than in his own.

* Renoir is not the only painter who has felt this way. Among many others, Picasso said the same thing when he was asked to analyze the symbolism of his *Guernica* and replied that if he had wanted to put it into words he would not have painted a picture, he would have written a book.

Renoir: Fulfillment

For Renoir, living and painting were indivisible. There is a steady correspondence between the changes in his way of painting and the progressive stages of his maturity and experience as a human being. His impressionist pictures with their lovely girls, their happiness, their subjects of courtship, identify his own young manhood. The shift to new disciplines in painting coincides with his acceptance of new personal responsibilities, marriage and fatherhood. But he soon relented from the severities of his reaction against the "irresponsibility" of impressionism. By the end of the 1880's he was working toward a new manner, coincident with the period in his own life when the business of settling down had been achieved, when he had established an adequate security for himself and his family, and was discovering the quiet and rewarding fulfillments of middle age.

His effort in this period is to combine formal values in painting with such virtues of impressionism as can be dissected away from its shortcomings. He frees his brush once more; his touch quickens; he allows color-as-light to flood back into his pictures, but it is an obedient light respectful of the forms it illuminates. From the Renaissance Venetians Renoir had observed that free painting, full form, and luscious color could coexist with formal order, and he went to work to establish all these elements in his personal style. At first glance the pictures of this third period look like a reversion to impressionism; at second, the color is fuller and richer; the forms, even though the edges are no longer liney, remain solid. Beneath the renewed sweetness there is a more reflective quietness, beneath the surface informality, an increased order. It is impressionism chastened by tradition, ordered by contemplation, dignified by maturity.

With the lesson of the *Bathers* behind him, Renoir returned to simple, intimate subjects, painting again his personal response to them without sacrificing what he had regained through formal discipline. Instead of the synthetic poses of the *Bathers* he paints the natural attitude of a young girl pulling on her stocking [253], but studies it as a composition of sculpturesque volumes. In the following years there are so many fine pictures that a selection at random could hardly fail to give a good example. Among them, *Two Girls at the Piano* [254] affords a double comparison with the *Bathers* and the *Moulin de la Galette*. In all three pictures Renoir employs one of his favorite motifs, consisting of a pair of figures, one seated in the foreground and the other, usually standing, behind her in an affectionate, encircling attitude.

In the *Moulin de la Galette* these two figures are conspicuous in the center foreground. A girl in a light striped dress sits on a bench with one arm over its side; behind her a girl in a darker dress stands with her hand on the first girl's shoulder, leaning forward. The grouping is extremely pleasant, the effect is there, but there are ambiguities to the forms. It is not easy to follow the volumes and they are a bit cottony. In the *Bathers* the two figures on the bank in the left half of the picture are in comparable, although far from identical, relationship. The one in back holds a cape or towel across her shoulders in such a way that it forms a kind of terminating enclosure for the interrelated masses of the two bodies. There is no ambiguity to the forms; every volume is defined in space and in its exact relationship to other volumes. In *Two Girls at the Piano* the figure relationship of the two girls in the *Moulin de la Galette* is restudied to give it the formality of the *Bathers*. The formality is disguised; it is animated by the vivacious charm of the early masterpiece, but the formality is there, and it makes of *Two Girls at the Piano* something more than a charming picture, just as it is also something more than a formal exercise.

Similarly, *Young Girls Arranging a Hat* [255] is an impressionist delight if it is savored only for its color and its subject. But if it is regarded more abstractly as a series of interrelated volumes, it builds almost sculpturally into mutually supporting masses, projecting and receding into space. The sense of weightiness, of solid form, and the reduction of the various ele-

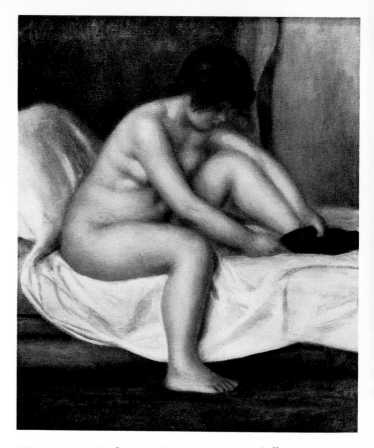

253. RENOIR: *Nude, c.* 1888. 21½ x 17½". Collection Louis E. Stern, New York.

ments in the picture to geometrical equivalents (the cylinders of the arms, the ovoids of the heads, the generally spherical derivation of all the forms) increase the generic quality of the figures. A picture of one young girl pinning flowers onto the hat of another becomes a fertility image; the swelling volumes, bursting with color, are more than ever symbols of the burgeoning generative forces of nature.

Renoir: Last Pictures

In Renoir's final period this expression surges into full undisguised statement. From the point of view of the usual painting of the female nude, the *Bather* [256] painted in 1917 or 1918, shortly before Renoir's death at the age of seventy-eight, is grotesque. The swollen belly, the massive

254. RENOIR: *Two Girls at the Piano,* 1892. 45½ x 34½". Louvre, Paris.

255. RENOIR: *Young Girls Arranging a Hat,* 1890. Pastel, 25¼ x 19½". Collection George Friedland, Philadelphia.

thighs, the great heavy feet, the billowing construction of flesh drenched in the color of strawberries and oranges against the acid greens of the tumultuous background— these are strong fare. By one standard of comparison Renoir has exaggerated his former virtues beyond the point of tolerance and to the point of absurdity; by another, he has reached the only logical conclusion to the basic conception that he stated nearly fifty years earlier in *Bather with Griffon* [244]. The heavy, rolling, glowing masses of the late paintings may be grotesque as human female figures, but they are magnificent as abstract expressions where color and form in themselves have finally become fully identified with the omnipotent and indestructible fertility of nature.

It is typical of most painters who work over a very long period of time that their late work is painted most loosely, with greatest freedom. This was true of Renoir, and the natural tendency was exaggerated by a physical malady that appeared as early as 1881 and had begun to cripple him by 1890.* In his old age rheumatism had so paralyzed him that he had to paint in a wheelchair with his brush strapped to his hand. When a foolish visitor asked him how he managed to paint such beautiful pictures under such difficulties, Renoir rebuked him with "One does not paint with one's hands." This was not altogether apt if it is taken to mean that Renoir had never considered sheer manipulation of paint of any importance, for he loved the texture of oil as much as Courbet did, and could apply it just as sensuously. But it is true that Renoir was one of those artists who

---

* At this time Renoir left Paris to spend the rest of his life in Cagnes, in the south of France.

paint from the heart, to such a degree that the work of the hand and the expression of the heart were identical. From time to time there is a critical flurry during which Renoir's "sentimentality" is rediscovered with disapproval. But it never takes long for such flurries to subside. In the wonderfully balanced art of Renoir, sentiment is chastened by formal order, and formal order is warmed by sentiment.

Boudin and Jongkind

There are several dozen painters whose names could be catalogued as indirect contributors to the development of impressionism, and several hundred respectable ones who discovered it at the end of the century and made it standard exhibition fare. Leaving most of them to the encyclopedia, we still must mention some fine and important painters who were second only to the men who have emerged as impressionism's giants.

Eugène Louis Boudin (1824–1898) was older than the rest of the group. His sixteen years' seniority put him in something of a fatherly position to Monet when he met that penniless and precocious youth in Le Havre, which was Boudin's native city as well as Monet's. It was Boudin who first interested Monet in landscape, to which for some reason the youngster had adopted a scornful attitude, and they worked together on landscape subjects.

The typical Boudin is a long and placid strip of beach with ladies and gentlemen ranged in front of the sea's horizon beneath a seraphic sky [257]. A figure may be indicated in three or four touches of paint in different colors—a white skirt, a red shawl, a blue umbrella—accented with bits of dark for heads and feet. But Boudin also did pure landscapes, not always involving water and beaches. He was interested in representing different weathers; these effects, and his cursory notations of form, made him a precursor of impressionism before he exhibited in the first impressionist show. He shared the impressionists' later triumphs and was also awarded a Salon medal in 1889 and the Legion of Honor in 1892. Not strictly

256. RENOIR: *Bather*, 1917–18. 20¼ x 12″. Philadelphia Museum of Art, Louise and Walter Arensberg Collection.

speaking an impressionist, Boudin was acceptable on much the same terms as the Barbizon men, whose paintings by then were established commodities. He is a delightful painter, more and more sought by collectors.

Johann Barthold Jongkind (1819–1891), a Dutchman, spent his mature life in France. For a while he joined the Barbizon

257. BOUDIN: *Beach at Trouville*, 1880. Panel, 7 x 13½″. Philadelphia Museum of Art, Lisa Norris Elkins Bequest.

258. JONGKIND: *Drawbridge*, 18½ x 21¾″. Philadelphia Museum of Art, Mitcheson Collection.

painters, but for the most part he worked independently. He had a strong influence on Monet, and on Sisley and Pissarro, because he investigated transitory effects of light and painted with a quick, vibrant brush. This is his closest connection with impressionism, but since an equally important aspect of his art is not frequently enough mentioned, we may point out also that Jongkind was a romantic landscapist [258] in the spirit (if not the technical tradition) of earlier Dutchmen, especially Ruisdael.

Bazille

Frédéric Bazille (1841–1870) was a close friend of Monet's and Renoir's in Gleyre's studio and a popular member of the circle at the *Café Guerbois*. He was a tall, handsome young man with money and talent, who was still finding himself as a painter when he was killed in the battle of Beaune-la-Rolande in the Franco-Prussian War of 1870. He was born the same year as Re-

259. BAZILLE: *The Artist's Family,* 1868, retouched, 1869. 60¾ x 91″. Louvre, Paris.

260. BAZILLE: *Summer Scene, Bathers,* 1869. 63¼ x 63¼″. Fogg Art Museum, Cambridge, Mass.

noir, and in looking at the few pictures he painted before his life was cut so short, one must remember that if Renoir had been killed at this time, of the pictures illustrated in this book only *Bather with Griffon* would have been painted. Even Monet's impressionism was in its early stages, and the first group show was not held until four years later.

The characterizing feature of Bazille's work is a painstaking disposition of the elements of a nominally informal subject. A group portrait of his family on a terrace [259], a picture more than eight feet long which was exhibited in the Salon of 1868,* is filled with a curious, stiff, unnatural stillness that extends even to the leaves on the trees in the distance. It is anything but impressionistic. The yet more curious *Summer Scene, Bathers* [260], painted in 1869 and exhibited in the Salon of 1870, shows a further imposition of rigid pattern, now geometrical, on a scene filled with casual attitudes—or, at least, attitudes transfixed

* But dated, after retouching, 1869.

261. BAZILLE: *The Artist's Studio*, 1870. 38⅞ x 47″. Louvre, Paris.

from casualness into Bazille's odd rigidity. Compositionally the picture is closer to "neo-impressionism," a movement we will discuss shortly, than to impressionism, and it is difficult to avoid pointless conjectures as to the course impressionism might have taken if Bazille had lived beyond the first period, for that is what it amounts to, of what must have been an exceptional creative life. A third painting, somewhat freer in technique, has poignant associative interest. This interior of *The Artist's Studio* [261] shows a group of young friends. Renoir is seated at the extreme left. Just above him, on the stair, is Zola. Manet stands in front of a painting on an easel. Behind him is Monet, and standing at the side of the easel is Bazille himself. Manet painted this figure, or at least Bazille's head. At the far right their musician friend Edmond Maître is at the piano.

Morisot

Berthe Morisot (1841–1895) was a grand-daughter of the painter Fragonard* and the sister-in-law of Manet, but her interest in painting was not the result of this connection. Manet painted her frequently; she is the seated figure in *The Balcony* [184]. Berthe Morisot is a charming painter, and a sound one too, making her own feminine adaptation of Manet's broad style, although she first painted as a pupil of Corot's and

---

* Jean Honoré Fragonard (1732–1806) was the last in the three-generation trio of eighteenth-century painters — Watteau, Boucher, Fragonard—and the most facile. In line with the taste of the day, his style was feminine, coquettish, fanciful. As a successful painter he threw a commission to an unknown youngster named David. In lion-and-mouse fashion, David returned this favor by protecting Fragonard after the Revolution.

at times is a little influenced by Degas. Early in her career she appeared in the Salon, but she foreswore Salon exhibition as a declaration of faith in the impressionist cause. This faith was enduring; she continued to paint impressionistically after Renoir and others had abandoned the cause. She exhibited in all but one of the group shows and did more than her share of the hard work involved in organizing and maintaining an association of frequently difficult temperaments. Her sister Edma also painted for a while, but quit to become a wife and mother. Berthe successfully combined matrimony, motherhood, and a career.

Berthe Morisot's delightful *Girl with a Basket* [262], with its sensitivity, flourish, and style could be a particularly light and fresh late Manet. It is customary to say about any woman painter, as if it were the ultimate compliment, that she paints with almost the vigor of a man. But the beauty of Berthe Morisot's art is its femininity, which in her case is not to be confused with weakness, indecision, or an only partial achievement of a masculine standard. One would not want to "strengthen" *Woman at Her Toilet* [263] any more than one would want to endow its lovely model with the muscles of a wrestler.

Berthe Morisot was an extremely engaging correspondent. Her letters are full of illuminating comments on Manet. As a random sample, speaking of *The Balcony,* she said that Manet's paintings make "the impression of a wild or even slightly green fruit," a very neat characterization of the exotic and somewhat astringent quality of that picture in comparison with the Salon paintings of 1869 among which it appeared.

Berthe Morisot was rather jealous of another woman painter of talent who studied under Manet and followed his manner closely. This was Eva Gonzalès, the only painter Manet ever permitted to name him as teacher. She was a competent painter, although obvious in her echo of Manet. She did not exhibit in the group shows, probably because Manet did not.

The impressionist movement produced three exceptional women painters. The third was an American, Mary Cassatt.

262. MORISOT: *Girl with a Basket,* 1892. 35¾ x 28⅛". Collection Mrs. Carroll S. Tyson, Chestnut Hill, Pa.

263. MORISOT: *Woman at Her Toilet, c.* 1875. 23¾ x 31¾". Art Institute of Chicago, Stickney Collection.

264. CASSATT: *Woman Arranging Her Veil, c.* 1890. 25½ x 21½". Philadelphia Museum.

265. CASSATT: *Mother and Child,* date unknown. Pastel, 22 x 18". Philadelphia Museum of Art, Anne Hinchman Bequest.

Cassatt

Mary Cassatt (1845–1927) was an extraordinary young woman, the daughter of a wealthy Pennsylvania family, who against her parents' wishes went to Paris to continue the study of painting, which she had begun at the Pennsylvania Academy of the Fine Arts in Philadelphia. In Paris, enrolled in the studio of an established conventional painter, she found herself drawn to the art of the impressionists, particularly Degas, and in 1879 and thereafter she exhibited with them. She was a hard worker and a stern self-disciplinarian. With Degas as her early model, she had set herself, in a way, a more difficult goal than did Morisot, who modeled on Manet. The elegance of Manet, while no less masculine than the objective observation of Degas, was more susceptible to feminine modification. Although Degas's influence is frequently strong on her work

[264], Mary Cassatt was not an imitator of Degas or of anybody else. She developed a style of precision and definition that she combined with impressionist informality of subject and composition [265].

Mothers and children were a favorite subject of Mary Cassatt; she never married, and it would be easy to read into this fact something of frustration and compensation, except that the other facts of her life would not bear out such a conclusion. She was a vigorous woman, and lady, with a great many friends, and was apparently quite happy in her career as a painter without the impedimenta of a husband and children. Although she was a friend of the impressionists during their difficult days, she never for a moment participated in anything suggesting bohemianism. Her personal life, on both sides of the Atlantic, remained that of a sensible, cultivated, level-headed, and privileged gentlewoman, which makes her enthusiastic participation in the "scandalous" movement of impressionism surprising.

Mary Cassatt is an important figure in the history of the development of American taste because she introduced her wealthy American friends to the new art and urged them to collect it. The pictures bought by the Havemeyer family especially, now in the Metropolitan Museum of Art, are the American equivalent of the Caillebotte collection in the Louvre.

Mary Cassatt's most individual creative efforts were not her paintings, which were always respectable and frequently superior even by the demanding standard of the company they kept, but her prints, which were something more. For the other impressionists, prints were adjunct to painting, forms of drawing although in media somewhat more complicated than the ones ordinarily used. But for Mary Cassatt, as for all first-rate print-makers, there was an excitement in meeting the technical demands of the print and capitalizing on them to produce works of art where the medium and the expression were interdependent. Under the influence of the Japanese block prints she brought a new crispness, definition, and economy to etching and drypoint [266]. Here her achievement may stand alone, without the comparisons, inevitable in her painting, to the work of the leaders of the school.

Fin de Siècle: Toulouse-Lautrec

As impressionism began to be absorbed into the historical continuum of painting, and other isms began to develop from it, the list of painters whose art was impressionist or closely allied to impressionism a generation after the adventures of the original group could be extended indefinitely. Among this generation Henri de Toulouse-Lautrec (1864–1901) made his own special departures, but he must still be classified as an impressionist, if he must be classified at all, in bringing the story of impressionism's half-century to its end.

Lautrec's life has been used as the subject of so many biographies, some accurate,

266. CASSATT: *The Letter*, 1891. Etching and aquatint, 13⅜ 8¹⁵⁄₁₆". Collection Louis E. Stern, New York.

some unpardonably falsified, and his art has become so familiar in debased forms through commercial adaptations of it, that it has become difficult to regard his paintings as works of art in themselves. They have become illustrative adjuncts to the story of his life and the fascination of the personalities he used as subject matter. These personalities are, in truth, fascinating enough. His greatest single source of material was the dance hall and cabaret called the *Moulin Rouge,* a phenomenon of the

267. TOULOUSE-LAUTREC: *The Salon in the Rue des Moulins*, 1894. 43⅞ x 52½". *Musée,* Albi.

end of the century in Paris without a parallel today, a place where intellectuals, performers, human curiosities, and the flotsam of bohemia intermingled. But he also painted other cabarets and the related world of the theater, cafés, restaurants, and brothels. He painted dancers, singers, prostitutes, circus performers, performing animals, actors, sportsmen, and his acquaintances and friends who ranged from noblemen to derelicts. And he was himself, of course, the most bizarre of all the creatures in the world he recorded.

Henri-Marie Raymond de Toulouse-Lautrec Monfa was descended from one of the finest houses in France. His family tree includes the names of kings and queens of both France and England. If he had not been crippled—as a child he broke both legs in two falls that left him a grotesque, dwarfish caricature of a man—he might

have continued his family's tradition of hunting, riding, and provincial high living at the family seat in Albi. With these facts as a beginning, there is always a temptation to reduce any consideration of Lautrec to a series of biographies, first his own and then those of people like two of his favorite models, the dancers Louise Weber, known as *La Goulue* (the Glutton) and the nameless woman who chose for herself the name Jane Avril. Lautrec's art, as he records such people in the life of the half-world they inhabited, is partly journalism, partly an informal sociological record through the incisive presentation of specialized modes and manners, and partly, by whatever extension the observer wants to make for himself, a moral lesson. *The Salon in the Rue des Moulins* [267], which shows the reception room of a brothel frequented by Lautrec, is one of the most effective moral

268. TOULOUSE-LAUTREC: *Oscar Wilde*, 1895. Watercolor, 23⅝ x 19¾". Collection Mr. and Mrs. Conrad H. Lester, Beverly Hills, Calif.

269. TOULOUSE-LAUTREC: *Racing Stable Boy*, 1895. Cardboard, 26 x 20½". *Musée*, Albi.

lessons in the history of painting—if a moral lesson consists of revealing vice in its least attractive aspects. With the exception of the Madame herself, who sits almost primly erect in a high-collared morning dress, the women of the house are mere carcasses, and the wages of sin as represented here would seem to be infinite boredom.

Even more than Degas, who was his model and his god, Lautrec is first a draughtsman and second a painter. As Ingres told Degas to do, Lautrec draws "lines, many lines," but they are lines of his own kind, lines that coil and strike like serpents, jab and gash like knives, or when appropriate sag like the pouches of tired flesh they define, as in the devastating portrait of Oscar Wilde [268]. Line satisfied Lautrec; he developed very few paintings to the point where his first, direct lay-in of drawing is entirely obscured. Parts of the canvas (or the cardboard, upon which he

was fond of working) are only scrubbed over, and other parts remain bare. Sometimes his paintings are more accurately brush drawings in lines of fluid pigment, with an essential area or two covered in quick, broken strokes. He may use this technique to concentrate interest on the salient part of a picture—ordinarily the face —as Rembrandt used strong illumination to make a head emerge from surrounding obscurity [269].

Lautrec's debt to Degas is most conspicuous in his composition. One of his few highly finished paintings, *Au Moulin Rouge* [270], is an example, with its tilted perspective and the segmentation of some of the objects. It shows part of the promenade that surrounded the dance floor of the *Moulin Rouge;* at the left, the railing between promenade and dance floor cuts across the picture, separating the observer from the group of men and women at the

270. TOULOUSE-LAUTREC: *Au Moulin Rouge*, 1892. 48⅜ x 55¼". Art Institute of Chicago, Helen Birch Bartlett Memorial.

table. Whether or not Lautrec had such an effect in mind, the effect of this separation is to put the observer at a vantage point where he watches but is not watched; it is the so-called "keyhole vision" (not altogether a savory way of putting it) of much of Degas's late work. Like Goya, Lautrec was a painter who "moved freely within a certain world and was accepted as part of it by its denizens, yet within himself remained separated from it by an isolating circumstance, remaining free to observe with the objectivity of an outsider, yet with intimate access to his material." Like Goya with his deafness, Lautrec with his deformity was thus isolated, and without pushing the analogy too far it is still safe to say that the railing between the observer and the rest of the picture helps to identify

us with Lautrec's "view," psychological and physical, of the subject.

It is redundant to insist that the composition of *Au Moulin Rouge* is not haphazard but brilliantly planned; in this case there is a special circumstance that should prove how definitely Lautrec planned it and how imperatively the haphazard, snapshot quality is calculated as the psychological basis of the picture. Originally the canvas ended without the last portion on the right side that now includes the most "haphazard" and the most telling element: the weirdly illuminated face of the woman at the extreme right edge. In order to introduce this figure Lautrec added to the canvas at the right side (and also at the bottom). If these portions are covered up we still have a fine picture, a group portrait of several of Lautrec's friends (all are identifiable) gathered around a table, but we no longer have the picture that has the strongest claims as Lautrec's masterpiece.

In color, too, the additional figure transforms the scheme from something skillful to something masterful. If the composition of *Au Moulin Rouge* owes a great deal to Degas, the color is Lautrec's own. It is dominated by the strong chemical green of the shadows on the woman's face, eerily covering the forehead, nose, and upper lip, and the violently orange hair of the woman seated at the table near by. These two colors clash and vibrate between one another within a scheme of smaller areas of sharp colors lashed by accents of black and purple. These are the colors of Lautrec's world, a world of artificial stimulations, of dreadful ennuis, a world shrill, strident, divided between avidity and indifference. Renoir's eternal values have no place in it. Instead of Renoir's young girls in meadows we have *Two Women Dancing* [271]; instead of Monet's twinkling foliage or his ponds rippled by fresh breezes, Lautrec paints the torpid atmosphere of shuttered rooms, the stale air of dance halls whipped into turbulence by the petticoats of dancers, gaslight instead of sunlight. When Lautrec paints a portrait out of doors in the small gardens of his friends in Montmartre, his sitter has the pallid air of a night creature unaccustomed to daylight. Degas, being witty at the expense of his impressionist friends who went into the country to paint streams and meadows, said that the smell of fresh air made him sick. With something closer to truth, Lautrec could have said that the air of the dance hall and the brothel was a palliative for the pains that racked his dwarfed and twisted legs. Bohemia was not his natural habitat. In the background of *Au Moulin Rouge* he shows himself moving through the world he adopted as an expedient; he is the stunted figure played against the enormous height of his companion (a cousin and his most loyal friend, Tapié de Celeyran) behind the group at the table.

In the relationship of his life to his work, the surprising thing about Lautrec is that, in spite of the alcoholism and the spectacu-

271. TOULOUSE-LAUTREC: *Two Women Dancing*, 1894. Cardboard, 23¾ x 15¾". Collection Alfred Schwabacher, New York.

lar dissipations which are too well covered by his biographers, he was tremendously productive. In spite of his personal tragedy, with whatever neuroses it might have been expected to engender, he paints with sanity, vigor, and the clearest, sharpest perception of the life around him. His detachment is never self-pitying; his comments on viciousness are never vicious, scornful, or envious; and his painting of depraved subjects is no more depraved than it is self-righteous. Conditioned by his subjects, we are more aware of the seamy world in which he moved as an artist than we are of the other

272. TOULOUSE-LAUTREC: *Seated Female Clown* (*Mlle. Cha-U-Kao*), from *Elles*, 1896. Color lithograph, 20½ x 15¾". Philadelphia Museum of Art.

world in which he moved with equal freedom and which was the world from which he observed the one he painted: the world of the intellectual and the aristocrat.

If Lautrec does not reach the stature of a major painter outside his century, it may be because the world he painted limited his range of comment, but within the boundaries thus set, his art is complete. In addition, he was a technical innovator in the medium of lithography and he virtually created the poster as a work of art.

Essentially, his contribution to color lithography was to close the gap between the completed print and our sense of the presence of the artist. In painting, the artist's presence is felt because we are sepa-

rated from him by a minimum of technical barrier; we stand in front of his picture as he stood in front of it, the paint we see is the paint he applied. But in a print we must jump the gap created by the intervening process of actual printing, between the artist's work on the lithographic stone or the etching plate and the transfer of his work to paper. Lautrec closed this gap and at the same time widened the technical range of lithography by treating the stone with a new informality. He would speckle its surface with ink by flipping the ink-soaked bristles of a stiff brush above it or dab the surface in any way he chose [272]. He would combine lithographic crayon with lithographic wash in a deliberate exaggeration of textures. In short, he combined and invented variations on conventional lithographic techniques in order to give them variety; his imagination freed lithography much as the technique of impressionism released painting from academic rule. Always the closest of the print media to the intimacy of drawing, lithography in color now approached the immediacy of painting. The artist's hand became more apparent. In addition to the psychological value for the observer, this liberation widened lithography's expressive potential for the artist in ways that have been carried further ever since Lautrec pointed the way.

In the art of poster design [273] Lautrec recognized factors now accepted as so basic that it is hardly necessary to point them out. First, a poster must make its total effect immediately if it is to be effective in its primary function, since it is an announcement, not an object for contemplation. Second, since pictorial images are to be combined with type, their design must be harmonious with the flatness and boldness of type, or lettering. Both of these considerations call for simplification and virtually demand the reduction of design to two dimensions. Although tentative efforts had been made in "art" posters, Lautrec pushed these ideas to their conclusion and in applying them remained an artist as well as a designer of publicity. His posters "took possession of the street," a contemporary said, but they are also works of art.

Lautrec's posters bear multiple relationships to the Japanese print. In the first place, these prints were ready-made ancestors as examples of patterning in areas of flat color bounded by lines ornamental in themselves. In the second, they combined, frequently, printed legends with pictorial images [193], although the ornamental character and the indecipherability of the Japanese legends obscured this fact from Western designers. Also, the Japanese prints of actors were related to the nineteenth-century theatrical poster in that they familiarized people with the physiognomy of popular performers of the day even if they were not posted as advertisements. The difference was that the Japanese prints were designed to give continued pleasure upon extended contemplation of their subtleties of line and color areas, while Lautrec's posters had to be absorbed at a glance if they were to attract the attention of busy passers-by. Lautrec met this requirement first; yet he also designed his posters to reward continued acquaintance, even if not to the extent of their Oriental prototypes.

The Post-impressionists

Lautrec died in 1901. If he can be regarded as the last of the impressionists, thus rounding out the century, it must be remembered that, in the meanwhile, impressionism had already been transformed and the direction of the art of the twentieth century had been set by the work of four men whose work was not assimilated by the nineteenth century in which they lived. These men were Georges Seurat and Vincent van Gogh who had died ten years before Lautrec, and Paul Cézanne and Paul Gauguin who were to die within the next five years.

We enter our own time with the work of these men, grouped under the accepted if not very descriptive label of "post-impressionism." They are the first "modern" artists in the sense of the word that implies a sharp departure from the natural look of the world, a distortion of visual reality

273. TOULOUSE-LAUTREC: *La Goulue at the Moulin Rouge*, 1891 Poster, color lithograph, 65 x 46". Philadelphia Museum of Art, Gift of Mr. and Mrs. R. Sturgis Ingersoll.

in whatever way the artist thinks necessary for the expression of the inner realities most important to him.

These men will be seen in their own section of this book, preliminary to the chapters on the art of the twentieth century. It is time now to recognize the fact that painters in Germany, England, and the United States were also at work while classicism, romanticism, and realism-impressionism were being formulated as theories and given pictorial expression in France.

PART II

The Nineteenth Century Outside France

CHAPTER 8

Outside France, 1800-1850

Classicism and Benjamin West

A summary of nineteenth-century art outside France must naturally take as its point of departure the development we have just surveyed—at least it must do so in a book that intends to follow mainstreams rather than to be an encyclopedia. French artists crystallized into images the ideas that dominated the century and fought the battles for their recognition. This will not leave much point in going into detail about—for instance—a group of ten American painters[*] who formed an association to exhibit their work in 1898, even though three of them departed from their academic training to adopt impressionism. They were perfectly respectable impressionists, but by that date impressionism had been developed, fought for, and established by the men we have already seen. It had even been abandoned by men we have yet to see—Cézanne, van Gogh, and Gauguin—who set new directions for the twentieth century. Historically speaking, the ten Americans were in a backwater. The fact that Childe Hassam (1859–1935), to choose one of them as an example, painted American subjects instead of Parisian boulevards or meadows bordering the Seine is a small difference between him and the French impressionists whose technique he used very well. Aesthetically his pictures are no better and no worse for having been painted a generation after impressionism's victory, but historically they are footnotes. What we want to do now

---

[*] Frank W. Benson, Joseph R. De Camp, Thomas W. Dewing, Childe Hassam, Willard L. Metcalf, Robert Reid, Edward Simmons, Edmund C. Tarbell, John H. Twachtman, and J. Alden Weir.

is to follow classicism, romanticism, and realism-impressionism outside France with attention to painters whose personal or national character is exceptional, and to give a nod here and there to painters like Hassam who were excellent practitioners in ways with which we are already familiar. The nod is not meant to be a slight.

Outside France, then, there was no situation comparable except in the palest way to the academic stranglehold and the original painter's struggle against it, partly because the academies elsewhere were less avid for power and partly because the painters were more content to work within conventional boundaries. France was alone in regarding art as part of the fabric of national life, and her painters were very nearly alone in the kind of theorizing and technical invention that placed upon the artist a moral obligation to define and proselytize forms of painting based on aesthetic, social, and philosophical convictions.

And outside France the general public was either apathetic to the art of painting or content to follow its own taste without feeling indignant over any kind of painting it did not understand. It is impossible to imagine an *Oath of the Horatii* raising a political furore in England or Germany, even if it is possible to imagine it being produced in one of those countries in the first place, and the scandals of the *Salon des Refusés*, or the impressionist group shows, were impossible in those countries for the double reason that painters were less aggressive in their departures from tradition and that the general public regarded a picture more casually as something to be looked at with pleasure or dismissed as uninteresting, but certainly not something important enough to get very excited about one way or another. The lines between classicism, romanticism, and realism were less sharply defined; the differences between one kind of painting and another tended much more to be differences of style rather than declarations of conflicting ideas passionately held.

This was especially true of classicism, which never touched Davidian purity or intensity outside France, although its most celebrated theorist was a German and one

274. WEST: *Cleombrotus Ordered into Banishment by Leonidas II, King of Sparta, c.* 1770. 54 x 72". Tate Gallery, London.

of the earliest painters of neo-classical historical subjects was, of all things, a provincial American youth who went to Rome and then to England where he became president of the Royal Academy. The German was Winckelmann, already mentioned with his theory that beauty is synonymous with perfection, and the American was Benjamin West (1738–1820).

Some twenty years before David completed *The Oath of the Horatii* in 1784, West was painting classical subjects of the type of *Cleombrotus Ordered into Banishment by Leonidas II, King of Sparta* [274]. While West's classical efforts do not approach the icy intensity and the disciplined simplification that are the essence of *The Oath of the Horatii,* and while they offer nothing more than obvious sentiment where *The Horatii* is charged with moral force, they do frequently anticipate David's composition on a single plane suggestive of classical bas-reliefs, the precise definition of neo-classical draughtsmanship, and the reference to classical models that were parts of David's sensational departure from French tradition.

Strictly speaking, West is not altogether an American painter. He was the son of an innkeeper near colonial Philadelphia but demonstrated such a prodigious early talent—he was painting portraits when he was thirteen—that a group of prosperous Philadelphians sent him to Rome to study. He was twenty-one years old at the time. (David was still a boy of eleven.) West was an attractive fellow with a flair for social showmanship that came to him as naturally as his talent for painting. As a handsome man and a picturesque American claiming to have had his first painting lessons from wandering Indians who had shown him how they made colors from clay to paint their faces, he became the rage in Italian society; when he went to London three years later he repeated his success. He remained an adopted Londoner for the rest of his life, was a favorite of George III, was a leader in the founding of the English Royal Academy, and its second president. But if he was a Londoner by adoption and if he became an English painter in effect, he was an important influence on American painting because two generations of American students passed through his London studio. By the time David finally won his *Prix de Rome* (in 1774) West was an established London success, and by the time *The Oath of the Horatii* set a new direction for French painting and began the story of

modern art, West was nearly fifty years old and had virtually abandoned the nascent classicism of pictures like *Cleombrotus*. West, Goya, and David died within eight years of one another, West first in 1820 at the age of eighty-two.

West as an Innovator

Except for those American writers whose judgments are affected by local pride, critics have formed the habit of condescending to West. It is true that his talents were exceeded by his success. And it is true also that he does not emerge as a great intellect or even an especially brilliant and stimulating painter. But if he had painted in hardship and obscurity, his originality might receive more sympathetic emphasis than it does.

West made his reputation in England with two paintings, *The Death of General Wolfe* [275] in 1770, and *Penn's Treaty with the Indians* [276] in 1772, both innovational. *The Death of General Wolfe* is full of trite borrowings from a variety of sources, but it was a courageous departure from convention in representing a contemporary event in minute factual detail (at exactly the time when Sir Joshua Reynolds had formulated the Academy's standards for the grand manner in painting, demanding reference to poetry or the past instead of to the present and generalization instead of particularization). West had minor precedents for his factual representation, but this was a major picture on the grand scale by a young man eager to maintain a position in academic favor. Again West anticipated David, who became the first Frenchman to approach a contemporary event in realistic detail when he relaxed the severity of his neo-classical idealizations to paint *The Oath of the Tennis Court*. David might even have known West's picture and the sensation it caused, since *The Death of General Wolfe* was such a success that it was engraved and widely distributed over France as well as England.

If there was any question now as to West's eminence, it was settled by the ap-

275. WEST: *The Death of General Wolfe*, 1770. 60 x 84″. National Gallery of Canada, Ottawa.

276. WEST: *Penn's Treaty with the Indians*, 1771. 75½ x 109". Independence Hall, Philadelphia, on permanent loan from The Pennsylvania Academy of the Fine Arts.

277. WEST: *Arthur Middleton, His Wife and Son*, 1771. 44¾ x 66".
Philadelphia Museum of Art, lent by Henry Middleton Drinker.

pearance of *Penn's Treaty with the Indians.* *Penn's Treaty* follows the classical tenet that a painting should justify itself by propounding a moral truth or a lesson, the same idea, of course, that David would apply with such force and intensity in his stoic pictures. In *Penn's Treaty* the lesson is that conflict can be settled without bloodshed, but the lesson takes second place to the interest of the subject. The locale and the participants are sufficiently picturesque to approach genre painting, although West was only following his own precedent in presenting another recent historical event in appropriate factual terms rather than allegory. The dress of the Indians may not be entirely correct but it is as nearly so as

278. WEST: *Self-portrait, c.* 1795(?). 40 x 52½". Royal Academy of Arts, London.

West knew how to make it from Indian souvenirs in his own collection. The picture is cluttered in spots with distracting incidentals and there is a certain—rather engaging—naïveté about it. But it is an honest picture, more original than it looks today, and its virtues plus the exotic interest of its

subject made it a tremendous success and established West in a career that never wavered for the rest of his life. Placidly enough, with no effort either to curry favor or to break new ground, West kept busy with portraits and murals, sometimes deadly dull and dry, sometimes of great charm, as in *Arthur Middleton, His Wife, and Son* [277], where the straightforward representation of the attractive young man's features, the semiclassical idealization of his wife's, and the absurd artificiality of the baby combine to produce a piquant flavor probably unplanned by a painter who was following several conventions at once without pondering any of them very deeply. On the other hand, West's *Self-portrait* [278] is perfectly consistent—a masterpiece of assurance without bravado, richly painted, and altogether an impressive demonstration by an accomplished craftsman.

Near the end of his life West's originality flared up again; he was nearly eighty when he painted the wildly romantic *Death on a Pale Horse,* exhibiting it in 1817. This was only two years before French romanticism declared itself in the Salon with the *Raft of the Medusa,* but West had caused a flurry in classical Paris seventeen years before the appearance of Géricault's roman-

279. WEST: *Death on a Pale Horse* (sketch), *c.* 1787. Oil on paper, mounted on panel, 11½ x 22½". Philadelphia Museum of Art, McIlhenny Fund.

tic landmark by exhibiting there a study for *Death on a Pale Horse* [279]. This was in 1802, in which year Géricault was only eleven and Delacroix was a toddler of three.

With so much to his credit, and such a startling record as a forerunner of the neoclassicism and the romanticism that convulsed Paris a little later, why is West not a more important figure than he is? The answer is that his work has neither quite the technical mastery nor nearly the intellectual and emotional concentration that must combine to create paintings of the absolutely first rank. Whatever his sensitivities to nascent classicism and nascent romanticism, West never explored these sensitivities deeply enough to carry their expression beyond a hint of what was in the air. Even if he had done so, it is difficult to imagine either movement assuming in England the importance that both did in France. In England, painting had never established itself as a manifestation of national morals or policy. And if such response was unlikely in England it was impossible in America, as another American painter discovered at about the same time West was exhibiting his *Death on a Pale Horse* in London.

John Vanderlyn: The Failure of Classicism

John Vanderlyn (1775–1852) was a long generation younger than West, and where West left America as a colonial subject, Vanderlyn grew up as an American citizen. But Vanderlyn adopted a tradition even more foreign to the taste of his own country: he went to Paris for five years in 1796 (as a protégé of Aaron Burr's) and then for twelve more in 1803 and made a good Davidian classicist of himself. He returned to America with the tightest and purest example of neo-classical painting this country had seen, his *Marius amid the Ruins of Carthage* [280], which had been enthusiastically received in Paris, and the best-drawn nude, an *Ariadne* [281]. Neither painting was a success, nor was his circular panorama of Versailles. This was a tour de force of perspective painting, which placed

280. VANDERLYN: *Marius amid the Ruins of Carthage*, 1807. 87 x 68½". H. M. de Young Memorial Museum, San Francisco.

the observer directly in the center of the palace gardens, surrounding him by hedges, sculpture, palatial architecture, and strolling ladies and gentlemen. To exhibit the 3,000 square feet of canvas making up the panorama Vanderlyn had to build his own rotunda in New York, but not even the novelty of the work appealed to Americans, perhaps because they had already been left cold by the *Marius* and deeply offended by Ariadne's nakedness. Vanderlyn never recovered from this defeat and died in obscurity, an American who had made a skillful French classical painter of himself, only to fail to make the grade in his own country.

Part of the reason for the classical near-vacuum in American painting is that art

281. VANDERLYN: *Ariadne Asleep on the Island of Naxos*, 1814.
68 x 87". Pennsylvania Academy of the Fine Arts, Philadelphia.

in America began as an offshoot of art in
England, where the neo-classical disciplines
as we have seen them in France never took
root. This is not surprising in England, but
in America circumstances arose that might
have been expected to favor at least a provincial version of French classicism. At the
time of the American Revolution, when the
new nation's bonds with France became so
close, when it was engaged in a struggle
and was then creating a government drawing philosophically on some of the same
ideals that inspired French thought and
French political struggle—at this time one
might have expected a flourishing of
Franco-American classical painting. But at
first the new nation was too busy pulling
itself together to have much time or money
or energy left over for the arts, and then
whatever roots French neo-classical painting might have established in America were
nipped, in the last decade of the eighteenth
century, when American horror at the excesses of the Terror in France created an
aversion to everything French. The didac-
ticism of *The Oath of the Horatii* or the
Brutus, which might have appealed to the
strong moral sense of the young American
republic, rang false as a background for the
guillotine, and the Napoleonic career and

legend did not offer substitute attractions.

In architecture the story was different:
American faith in the column and pediment
as a symbol of high moral and political
ideals was never shaken by disillusions with
European events. When Thomas Jefferson
designed the state capitol for Virginia he
went directly to the architecture of ancient
Rome and adapted the well-preserved
temple at Nîmes into a design of great
sobriety and purity. In hundreds of other
examples, American architects built some
of the loveliest classical structures since
those of ancient Greece. But when French
neo-classical painting abandoned its moral
preachments and became a stylish exercise
in high polish and sensuous grace, it became altogether foreign to American taste.
For along with their elevated moral standard the Americans developed a provincial
prudery that could not tolerate the naked
gods and goddesses—or the *Ariadnes*—who
replaced the stalwart warriors and the
chaste matrons of David's early pictures.

These are specific reasons for the failure
of neo-classicism to catch on in a country
where Europe still furnished the models for
most ambitious painters. But the strongest
reason of all was a general one: the new
country was raw. No matter what comparative felicities of good living had been developed in such centers as Boston and
Philadelphia, American patrons of the arts
were not ready for the aesthetic sophistica-
tions of French painting. The most cultivated Americans were earthy and practical
people compared with the dilettantes and
the professional intellectuals who set the
pace for the intelligent layman or amateur
in France.

Early German Romantics

In truth, classicism as a disciplined philosophical ideal was "too severe to please for
long" even in France, as David himself had
lamented. His own followers were unable
to pull themselves up to it by their boot-
straps even when they wanted to as much
as Gros and Ingres did. If we accept the
evidence of painting alone, the nineteenth
century was overwhelmingly a century of

romantics who were often attracted by logic and common sense and often put great faith in the literal fact of nature and the world around them, but who always ended by yielding to emotion or sentiment even when they attempted to cast themselves in the roles of classicists or realists. Outside France, those painters who followed the classical formula most closely were the ones with so little intellect or imagination that a formula was necessary to them.

Among the dozens of German classicists who are all but forgotten, Gottlieb Schick (1776–1812) is better remembered than most. He produced some of the most tedious historical paintings of the century, but he also did the portrait of Frau Heinrich von Dannecker [282], the wife of the German sculptor, his teacher and friend. The picture is full of the usual artificialities and it has the rather dry and mannered drawing that might be expected, but it is also full of unclassical exceptions—the ordinary weeds that spring casually around the base of the stone, the sweetness of the little spray of flowers held in one hand, the peaceful informality of the landscape in the distance, and of course above all the direct, realistic, individualized and sympathetic representation of the face, which manages to counteract the drawing-exercise affectation of the oversmooth, excruciatingly posed arm and hand beside it. It is remindful, in its awkward way, of David's exceptional portrait of Émélie Sériziat [16].

The romantic spirit was so pervasive that it transformed the classical vision of antiquity, emotionalizing a concept which Poussin had established as a rational one. The young Germans, Englishmen, Americans, and others who converged on Rome, as the eighteenth century turned into the nineteenth, discovered the ancient world as a dream of lost beauty. Their classicism was a nostalgic revery upon a golden past. They might borrow forms from Poussin as the young American Washington Allston did in his *Italian Landscape* [283], but like him they transplanted them into a world where "perfection" was less a matter of perfection reached by distillation, less a matter of order and discipline, than a dream of a world where the hazards and deteriorations

282. SCHICK: *Frau Heinrich von Dannecker*, 1802. 46¾ x 39½". *Nationalgalerie*, Berlin.

283. ALLSTON:*Italian Landscape*, 1805–08. 39 x 51". Addison Gallery of American Art, Andover, Mass.

284. Schinkel: *Greek City by the Sea*, 1815. 51 x 35″. *Nationalgalerie*, Berlin. Photo Stoedtner.

and the evils and misfortunes of life were unknown. When the German Karl Friedrich Schinkel (1781–1841) painted an imagined *Greek City by the Sea* [284], the world he invented was not the closed and ordered one of Poussin but a wonderful wide-flung land where pearly marble monuments rose undefiled from an undefiled landscape inhabited by men free from all vicissitude moving beneath radiant skies. All this, of course, has remained a standard dream of Hellas; it is also romantic yearning, the romantic escape into the far away, which in France took another form in Orientalism. In Germany and America, painters soon abandoned all classical reference for a vision of unspoiled nature as a mystical and often a specifically religious symbol. When the works of man appear in these landscapes they appear as monuments in ruin; to contemplate the fragments of a vanished world, the romantic finds, is more evocative of man's past than is an effort to recreate it.

Thus a ruined Gothic chapel in the snow [285] replaces the immaculate Greek tem-

ple bathed in sun; the broken trees surrounding it, gnarled, black, and frozen, rise above the crosses and headstones of abandoned graves. Or in a darkling world two friends stand beneath a half-uprooted tree [286] where the forms of nature, in disarray, are silhouetted with all their grotesque accidents and haphazard tumbling against a moon-filled sky. This romantic melancholy, this romantic contemplation of man's aloneness and his transience, this pondering of man's fate in full awareness that it is impossible for him to reach a conclusion as to its meaning or to place himself as a logical part of a universe scaled to his being, is of course pleasurable to the romantic temperament. Sometimes the romantic's world is a gentler one within which human beings may exist more placidly, sitting on rocks along the shore, for instance, while they watch a sunset or moonrise over the sea [287], aware of solemn immensities but not of threatening mysteries. There may be comfort in desolation, warmth and even a certain protection in the acceptance of frailty and mortality. The romantic is

EARLY GERMAN ROMANTICS · 245

285. FRIEDRICH: *Cloister Graveyard in the Snow*, 1810. Panel, 47⅜ x 70". *Nationalgalerie*, Berlin, now lost.

286. FRIEDRICH: *Two Men Looking at the Moon*, 1819–20. Panel, 11¾ x 17¼". *Staatliche Gemäldegalerie*, Dresden.

content to be received into the universal mystery, absorbed into it without examining it. He abandons himself to the idea that time and mysterious forces may shatter his works and consume his body yet at the same time must recognize his presence by the very inevitability of his inclusion within a system of laws beyond his comprehension.

French romanticism edged up to this conclusion but was never quite able to accept it. Delacroix vehemently rejected it, rightly regarding himself as a classicist in his effort to make a universal synthesis of human passions. The pictures we have just seen, by Caspar David Friedrich (1774–1840) have no parallels in French painting. Technically, they combine the sharp definition of classical draughtsmanship with the contradictory subject matter of accident

287. FRIEDRICH: *Moonrise over the Sea*, 1823. 21¾ x 28″. *Nationalgalerie*, Berlin, destroyed by fire, 1931.

288. JAMES WYATT, architect: Fonthill Abbey, 1796. Wiltshire, England, no longer standing.

and decay; they make their emotional or mystical statement in terms that are pictorially didactic, where the French romantic painter freed his brush to dash across the canvas in a way expressive of romantic excitement or agony.

Friedrich's Germanism was conscious. His twisted trees have their counterparts in German medieval painting, and his preoccupation with Gothic architecture came, in part, from his belief that it was an essentially Germanic expression. Actually, an interest in the middle ages and its arts was reviving all over Europe in reaction against the rationalism of the eighteenth century. Before that century was ended, a wild and fantastic young Englishman named William Beckford was engaged in doing the unheard of: he was building himself an abode modeled after a medieval monastery, in a country remarkable for the comfort of its domestic adaptation of classical forms. Fonthill Abbey, as Beckford called this visionary project [288], was not so much a place to live in as it was a stage set designed as a background for the romantic posturings of its owner. Impatient to see his abbey materialize, Beckford forced the builder into such an impossible schedule that he—the builder—skimped on the foundations for the central tower. On his deathbed this man is supposed to have called Beckford to his side to confess this and to warn him that the tower might collapse at any time. It did, shortly thereafter. It is symbolical of the artificiality of the nineteenth-century romantic concept of architecture that Fonthill Abbey was in ruins a few years after it was built. In this state it was, of course, more romantic than ever, but it was even less habitable.

Yet the idea of Gothic domestic architecture, as well as a rage for medieval churches, schools, postoffices, office buildings, and everything else, increased rapidly in popularity during the century. Gothic villas were built everywhere in Europe; in America they were especially popular, for they had the additional allure of creating an illusion of "Old World charm" in a country beginning to be conscious of its rawness. In France the movement was less popular. The country was so deeply ingrained with the classical tradition, and the neo-Gothic structure was so incompatible with the practicality of the French temperament, that Gothicism was largely limited to a cult of the existing monuments, which received scholarly study and restoration during the century, especially under the architect Viollet-le-Duc, who saved many structures from ruin and somewhat marred others by excessive restoration. In England, Gothicism was a passion, not only as a new reverence for the genuine monuments but in the creation of artificial ones. Builders kept on hand sets of designs for small Gothic ruins that could be built on estates not fortunate enough to have the genuine article. The built ruin is the apotheosis of the curious backing-up that characterized architecture as a romantic manifestation.

But if the idea was fundamentally absurd, it died slowly. More than a hundred years after Fonthill Abbey, in the boom days of the early 1920's, the American publisher William Randolph Hearst spent several million dollars on *La Cuesta Encantada*

289. RUNGE: *Naked Infant in a Meadow*, 1808–09. 12 x 12½". *Kunsthalle*, Hamburg.

(The Enchanted Hill), an estate on a California hilltop with a main house designed in the fashion of a Spanish cathedral including an assembly room lined with paneling from a church, a billiard room incongruously ornamented with medieval tapestries, an indoor swimming pool of vaguely Moorish design (it took three years to lay the tiles), a baronial hall, complete with banners, as a dining room and, perhaps for relief, a few Greek and Roman temples and colonnades here and there around the 120 acres. After the collapse of Fonthill Abbey, Beckford himself reverted to classical taste, perhaps oppressed by the emotional strain of living up to the atmosphere he had created. But the Enchanted Hill was quite well built, and is something of a white elephant to the State of California, which accepted it as a gift after Hearst's death and operates it, at a loss, as a park.

Of course the Enchanted Hill and smaller castles built in America at that time were

290. RUNGE: *Rest on the Flight into Egypt*, 1805–06. 38½ x 52″. *Kunsthalle*, Hamburg.

more tied up with the idea of pretentious display than with the nostalgia for the past and the taste for melancholy that inspired the early romantics like Beckford and, in painting where it more properly belonged, Friedrich. It was a cruel inconsistency that medievalism in architecture was to catch on, while Friedrich's painting was repudiated by his contemporaries, especially those who were busy following French classicism as an academic formula. Although the romantic spirit stirred earlier and more restlessly in Germany than it did in France, it somehow did not manage to come into full blossom in painting. Several factors combined to stunt it, including the early death of Friedrich's friend, Philipp Otto Runge (1777–1810), who might have joined forces with him to establish a strong romantic tradition if he had not died at thirty-three. On his sickbed Runge destroyed much of his work, and even among the few examples he left, the majority are studies for large projects he was never able to complete. But from his few remaining pictures and from his letters and notes he emerges

as a man who, as Delacroix did in France, might have imposed intellectual disciplines on German romanticism, yet who much more than Delacroix was a romantic in the most personal, emotional way.

Like Friedrich, Runge wanted to revivify German art, and he began by rejecting his own early classicism because "works of art show how mankind has changed, how a stage that has once appeared never reappears." How, then, he asked, could painters hold the "unhappy notion of wanting to revive the art of long ago? . . . of recreating a past art?" Above all, he put his faith in innocence, in nature, and in love. His startling picture of a *Naked Infant in a Meadow* [289], its eyes wide with wonder at the world around it, is his symbol of the innocence with which he would have liked to perceive the universe. It is an arresting picture, whatever its flavor of absurdity for an uninnocent eye. If not passed over as a sentimental fantasy, it may take on a magical enchantment; it is difficult to forget.

Magic is present too in Runge's *Rest on the Flight into Egypt* [290]. The tree over the holy child unexpectedly becomes an intertwining of infant angels and heavenly blossoms. At the extreme left, the ass grazes on thistly plants; the forms of his lowered head, his long neck, and the saddle chair with its drapery are silhouetted against the sky in foreshortened combinations naturalistic in detail yet fantastic in total effect. The landscape background is as meticulous as any of Friedrich's, but its mood is serenely joyful rather than sad or sinister. Runge held a theory that subject painting, history painting, was a worn-out form, and that painters who might have found themselves as landscapists had been hampered for two centuries because landscape was considered an accessory to subject rather than an independent means of expression. The revival of landscape painting in England and America, which we will see shortly, gives some support to this idea, and of course Friedrich carried it on in Germany after Runge's death. "How could a painter want for a subject," Runge asked, "when awakened to nature through what we see in ourselves, in our love, and in the heavens?"

The *Rest on the Flight into Egypt* is not first of all a religious picture in spite of its religious subject. Its air of miracle has more to do with the miracle of innocence and the miracle of landscape as a reflection of man's soul. But a group of Runge's contemporaries who flourished just after his death sought a similar return to innocence by dedicating their art to religion. They called themselves the Nazarenes and went so far as to move to Rome and set themselves up as a religious brotherhood in a former convent. The Nazarenes hoped to find spiritual grace by returning to the style of the painters of the early Renaissance. This, of course, is putting the cart before the horse.

The Nazarenes insisted on exactitude in drawing just as Friedrich and Runge had done, but unlike them they imitated old forms rather than referring to nature or inventing new ones. They ended as one of the most sterile groups in the history of painting anywhere. But their return to Christianity has some interest in early German romanticism, paralleling as it does Chateaubriand's specious Christian revival

291. BLAKE: *Zacharias and the Angel,* date unknown. Tempera, 10½ x 15″. Metropolitan Museum of Art, New York, Bequest of William Church Osborn.

in France which produced, as we have seen, *Atala.* The most important of the Nazarenes was one Friedrich Overbeck (1789–1869), but the one who eventually came into honors was Peter von Cornelius, already mentioned in connection with the Salon of 1855.

Blake

Romanticism in general was a reaction against the rational thought of the eighteenth-century philosophers who made a cult of Reason. Romanticism had common bases wherever it appeared, but it also took on characterizing differences in the different countries where it put down its deepest roots. In France, the individualizing element was a yearning for personal fulfillment through sensation, through exaggerated emotionalism, through violent or swooning passions. In Germany, by the evidence of Runge's naked infant, wide-eyed in the blossoming meadow of a wondrous world, the romantics were filled with a nostalgia for innocence. By the evidence of Friedrich's Gothic ruins and moonlit forests, romanticism was a search for union with mysteries that were doors to the supernatural. The revival of Christianity (which was not much more than a fashion in France) was basic to German romanticism,

Shall a Man be more Just than God? Shall a Man be more Pure than his Maker? Behold he putteth no trust in his Saints & his Angels he chargeth with folly

Shall mortal Man be more Just than God?

Then a Spirit pasſed before my face
the hair of my flesh stood up

292. BLAKE: Illustration for the Book of Job, 1825. Engraving, 7¾ x 5⅞″. Philadelphia Museum of Art, Gift of Staunton B. Peck.

choly of German romanticism was never a part of Blake's art. He was fulfilled within the areas of the soul—innocence and miraculous experience—that the Germans could only look back upon as lost. Reason had corrupted them; they might cultivate innocence, but the cultivation of innocence is a contradiction on the face of it. They might theorize about the supernatural, but the supernatural, on the face of it, is self-generated and cannot be materialized by any amount of theorizing. Blake was not subject to these frustrations. His art is lyrical, joyous—a paean.

Blake is a precursor or a very early member of the romantic movement by this description, and he might be called a rebel against academic classicism because he constantly fumed and fulminated against Sir Joshua Reynolds (the head of the British Royal Academy, whom he called Sir Sloshua) and his "gang of hired knaves." But one cannot help but feel that Blake would have painted, believed, and behaved as he did no matter when he had been born, or where, and that his appearance at the beginning of the romantic movement is only an accident of chronology. And he had virtually no influence on painting until the romantic movement had matured and been replaced by other revolutions. For that matter, his influence even now, when he has become the deity of a solid, enduring cult, is vague and more closely connected with literature and bibliophilia than with painting. If he had never painted a picture, his

Tiger, tiger, burning bright
In the forests of the night

would atone for the loss. The poem is the most vivid picture he ever created.

Blake was apprenticed to an engraver at fourteen, and from that time on he painted and drew as a corollary to literature. All his work depends on its literary source; it is first poetry—including his own, Dante's, and the Bible's—and second pictorial art. He held to the idea that a dream or a vision was not a shadowy nothing but should be represented in terms more concise than those of the visual world, and he applied this idea consistently in translating words

because it supplied a God Who was beyond the formulas of Reason, Who demanded acceptance through the innocence of faith and manifested Himself through miracle.

In England there had already appeared a man who could have served Friedrich and Runge as a concrete example of their theoretical recipe for the purified human spirit. His name was William Blake (1757–1827). He was a poet and a painter, and he was an innocent. He was as innocent as a lamb, from his cradle to his grave. He lived in intimacy with the supernatural, for angels spoke to him from the branches of trees, and he accepted their shining miraculous presence as a part of his life. He was a benign eccentric to the point of madness. But the brooding, nostalgic melan-

293. BLAKE: "The Whirlwind of Lovers," illustration from Dante's *Divine Comedy*, 1827. 10⅞ x 13⅞". National Gallery of Art, Washington, D.C., Lessing J. Rosenwald Collection.

294. PALMER: *Opening the Fold*, 1880. Etching, 4⅝ x 7". Collection Carl Zigrosser, Chestnut Hill, Pa.

295. PALMER: *Coming from Evening Church*, 1830. 12 x 7¾". Tate Gallery, London.

296. FUSELI: *The Nightmare, c.* 1780–90. 40 x 50". Detroit Institute of Arts.

into his swirling, bending, twisting compositions. His forms, derived from Michelangelo and Raphael, are of the utmost clarity of definition, and his swirling, bending, and twisting arrangements are controlled in every detail of their movement. As a pictorial artist he is a draughtsman rather than a painter. The majority of his paintings are watercolors by definition, but tinted drawings in fact. His few paintings in tempera seem to refute his typical manner [291], but this is because the tempera in which they are executed has darkened, cracked, and flaked, giving a misty, conventionally "dreamy" quality to forms that must originally have been closer to his usual tight, dry contours.

Blake produced illuminated editions of his own poetry in a technique he evolved for himself, a printing method not far removed from hand coloring. He was poor all his life, but he would not accept patronage, in the custom of the day, because patronage was likely to involve compromise. He had a saint of a wife, Kate, an adoring, good, simple woman who accepted him at his own face value, and probably kept not only his body and soul but his soul and his sanity together. In the last decade of his life he attracted a small group of disciples, headed by John Linnell (1792–1882), who was thirty-five years younger than Blake, and they obtained commissions for him to illustrate, among other texts, the Book of Job [292] and Dante's *Divine Comedy* [293]. These illustrations may be the finest expressions of his eccentric genius.

The disciple Linnell was a landscape painter who did extremely pleasant, sometimes moody, pictures of the English countryside as well as some portraits and Biblical subjects. But Samuel Palmer (1805–1881), who studied with Linnell and through him was drawn into Blake's small, late circle, was a painter of great imaginative originality, unaccountably neglected today except by a few enthusiastic supporters. His tiny etchings [294] and his compact paintings [295] where a pastoral world is made half-visionary by lights sometimes spectral, sometimes golden, are the one extension of Blake's fantasy into the realm where English romanticism was find-

297. ALLSTON: *Jason Returning to Demand His Father's Kingdom,* 1807–08. 168 x 240″. University of Miami, Coral Gables, Fla., Gift of Washington Allston Trust.

ing its typical expression — landscape. Palmer was only twenty-two years old when Blake died at seventy, so he belongs to the middle of the nineteenth century while Blake belongs to its transition from the eighteenth. In his late work Palmer lost much of his imaginative power when he failed to assimilate the influence of another imaginative genius, Turner. Turner was in mid-career at the time of Blake's death, and we will see him shortly.

The only other artist of much importance who is thought of in connection with Blake was John Fuseli (1741–1825), a Swiss who spent most of his life in London. He was an eccentric but not, like Blake, an isolated one. Blake was only one of many friends who admired him, and the list included Blake's bête noire, Reynolds. Fuseli was a fantasist whose favorite subject, repeated several times, was a little nightmare with erotic overtones in which a young woman swoons in abandon upon a couch, menaced by a ghostly and leering horse [296], a suggestive fantasy that has endeared Fuseli to contemporary painters of psychopathological fantasies. Fuseli seems to have been an honest and straightforward man, and these qualities endeared him to Blake.

298. ALLSTON: *The Dead Man Revived by Touching the Bones of the Prophet Elisha,* 1811–13. 156 x 132″. Pennsylvania Academy of the Fine Arts, Philadelphia.

An American Romantic: Washington Allston

While Friedrich with his broken trees and ruined cathedrals was trying to revivify a German romantic tradition, an American one was established by a man who was his contemporary almost to the years of birth and death. Washington Allston (1779–1843) was also an immediate contemporary of the unhappy John Vanderlyn who so gallicized his art that when he came home with it he found himself a foreigner. Allston was more fortunate. Although he studied in London* and in Paris in the Louvre, which had just opened, and in Rome, he never accepted any single tradition unquestioningly. He was a clear-headed fellow, well educated, an intimate of intellectuals in both England and America, not only capable of thinking for himself but determined to do so. He began with the expected dedication to classical antiquity; in Rome he painted and exhibited with Vanderlyn. We have already seen, in his *Italian Landscape* [283], that he reflected the romantic dream of the classical world, although this particular picture is somewhat more Poussinesque than other examples that might have been selected to make the point in an exaggerated way. As a matter of fact Allston had the makings of a very respectable classical painter. In Rome he began a large classical subject, *Jason Returning to Demand His Father's Kingdom* [297], where exceptional control, precision, and clarity are suggested even though the picture is unfinished. When he left Italy in 1808 the canvas was boxed for shipment but he did not recover it until eight or nine years later. By that time Allston had grown dissatisfied with classicism and had already set himself a

* Allston went to England in 1801 and studied under Benjamin West; in 1803 he went to Paris with Vanderlyn. From 1804 to 1808 he was in Rome; he knew Coleridge and Washington Irving among others there, and also Vanderlyn again. In 1808 or 1809 he returned to America. Then from 1811 to 1818 he was in Europe once more, mostly in London. Thereafter he lived in Boston, where he had been educated at Harvard. He was born in South Carolina.

different kind of problem, and solved it, in a contrasting picture, *The Dead Man Revived by Touching the Bones of the Prophet Elisha* [298], a subject of mystery and miracle. Instead of the classical frieze-like grouping of forms arranged across the canvas from side to side and illuminated in a clear, uniform light, *The Dead Man Revived* is constructed of forms building upward through several levels, emerging dramatically from obscuring shadows. Allston's model was no longer the art of classical antiquity but the emotionalized painting of the Italian seventeenth century.

Allston became an example of that contradiction in terms, the rational romantic. In addition to a clear intelligence he had a quick intuitive response to the world. He respected this response, but was unwilling to let it run away with him. At this time considerable theorizing went on among painters about something called "primitivism," in not quite the same sense the word has today. It had to do with the artist's abandonment to his spontaneous response to nature as opposed to the "artificialities" of civilized life. Allston rejected this idea. The world was with us, and to deny our place in it as civilized contemporary men was foolish and, for that matter, impossible. He preferred to be a part of his time and saw no reason why he should reject either it or the past. If he rejected anything, it was the skepticism of the eighteenth century, but he rejected it only as an extreme, and when he returned to religious subjects, like *The Dead Man Revived*, he was re-establishing the legitimacy of the mystical, emotional, and hence romantic Christian tradition without denying the legitimacy of an analytical one. He saw no conflict between tradition and originality. The aim of the artist, he thought, was to be true to "that within man which is ever answering to that without, as life to life— which must be life and which must be true." Allston recognized intuitive response as a basis for creation, but he was wary of a distortion away from "truth," either in the direction of blind trust in intuition or excessive suspicion denying intuition's validity.

In his theorizing, Allston was part of a new coalescence in American thought. But

299. ALLSTON: *Moonlit Landscape*, 1819. 24 x 25″. Museum of Fine Arts, Boston.

300. RYDER: *Death on a Pale Horse* (*The Racetrack*), date unknown. 28¼ x 35¼″. Cleveland Museum of Art, J. H. Wade Fund.

all theorizing aside, his most satisfying pictures today, simply as pictures, are his moody landscapes. There is a great distance between his *Italian Landscape* and his *Moonlit Landscape* [299] painted about fourteen years later, the year after his return to America. *Moonlit Landscape* is the progenitor, or at least one of the earliest examples, of a type of moonstruck romanticism filled with an agreeable loneliness, suggestive of man's melancholy journey through the mysteries of life yet speaking comfortingly of his union with the forces behind those mysteries, that has been recurrent in American painting. This minor but persistent tradition finds variation in the art of Albert Pinkham Ryder (1847–1917), a solitary and eccentric painter who may be introduced out of chronological order here since he was one of those painters,

301. ALLSTON: *American Scenery: Time, Afternoon with a South-west Haze*, 1835. 18½ x 24½". Museum of Fine Arts, Boston.

302. EARL: *Roger Sherman*, 1775–77. 64⅝ x 49⅝". Yale University Art Gallery, New Haven, Conn.

like Blake, whose art was essentially divorced from time and place [300].

Allston's final divorce from his European models is indicated in another revery with the elaborate title *Landscape, American Scenery: Time, Afternoon, with a Southwest Haze* [301], painted after seventeen years of repatriation. The two earlier landscapes are fantasies, but in the later one the specific references to place, time, and even the kind of day are symptoms of a revolution in landscape painting that was already flourishing in the United States.

Where Allston and other idealists fabricated their landscapes or imposed a mood arbitrarily on a free variation of an existing one, a new school of American landscapists were discovering mood and poetry as an emanation of the exact appearance of an actual scene. They were discovering American landscape as a new aspect of nature, not only scenically but psychologically differentiated from that of Europe. That they turned to American scenery for subject matter and transcribed its appearance in meticulous detail means nothing in itself except for whatever interest such representations have as factual record (which may be considerable); but that they felt and recorded new responses to landscape, and that these responses were peculiarly inspired by the American wilderness, meant that America had produced its first school independent of European inspiration.

Early "Americanism"

The typically "American" quality of painting had until then been a certain awkwardness, a dryness, a forthright honesty, in provincial approximations of more sophisticated European styles. Ralph Earl's (1751–1801) celebrated portrait of Roger Sherman [302] is a supreme example of this kind, a picture where the stiffness, the spareness, the decision, of a self-taught painter's style* accounts by coincidence for

---

* The portrait of Roger Sherman was painted before Earl went to London to study with West. Upon his return to America he was a "better" painter—that is, his naïve but forceful style was weakened by stilted elaborations.

much of the expressive power in this portrait of a man whose character was of a kind to be projected by these qualities. Even so thoroughly admirable and altogether enjoyable a painter as Charles Willson Peale (1741–1827), who can lay a strong claim to the title of "most American" of a group of painters who worked with homely sincerity as country cousins to the English tradition, is American largely on the negative score of being less European than he would have been if he could have been trained as a member of a more suave society.

This is not entirely Americanism-by-default, and it is even less so in the case of the "American primitives," whose art has been lifted in recent years from a level of interesting novelty to the respectable one of an important national art expression. The American primitives were that large body of self-trained journeyman painters who supported themselves by working for a modest market, often in the hinterlands, plus the amateur painters, equally without professional training, who painted friends and family and familiar places. Such paintings may be merely inept, or they may have a degree of awkward charm dependent on the degree of the painter's innate sensitivity to decorative color and pattern. But awkward charm may also be a genuinely expressive element, as it is in the case of Edward Hicks (1780–1849). In retrospect Hicks has become the accepted master of all the American primitives, and his *Peaceable Kingdom* [303, 304], of which he did around a hundred variations, is the summary of American primitive virtues.

In the foreground of *The Peaceable Kingdom* Hicks illustrates with faithful literalness three verses from Isaiah—

"The wolf also shall dwell with the lamb, and the leopard shall lie down with the kid; and the calf and the young lion and the fatling together; and a little child shall lead them.

And the cow and the bear shall feed; their young ones shall lie down together: and the lion shall eat straw like the ox.

And the suckling child shall play on the hole of the asp, and the weaned child shall put his hand on the cockatrice' den."

303. HICKS: *The Peaceable Kingdom*, c. 1848. 17⅛ x 23½". Philadelphia Museum of Art, Lisa Norris Elkins Bequest.

304: HICKS: Detail from Figure 303.

—while in the background the Biblical prophecy is fulfilled as Penn concludes his treaty with the Indians. Hicks was a sign painter by trade, a Quaker by religion, and a preacher and artist by avocation. In train-

305. DURAND: *Kindred Spirits* (Thomas Cole and William Cullen Bryant), 1849. 44 x 36". New York Public Library.

306. FRIEDRICH: *Mountain Peaks*, 1826. Panel, 51½ x 65¾". *Nationalgalerie*, Berlin.

ing himself as an artist, he took as models the only material available to him, rather poor engravings of the old masters and, for his animals perhaps, illustrations in children's books. As far as such opportunities were concerned, he was at no greater disadvantage than the scores of other amateurs above whom he rises as an artist. His advantage was that he was gifted with a stronger feeling for design, a greater spirit of dedication, and a most conscientious industry. No apologies need be made for his naïveté or for what would be, in another kind of artist, his technical shortcomings. *The Peaceable Kingdom* is acutely limited in comparison with work in the great traditions of painting, yet Hicks's simple faith, his wonderful and innocent enthusiasm for the translation of faith into pictorial images, are not negligible virtues.

The Peaceable Kingdom is a harmonious fusion of technique and conception; as such it has an extraordinary completeness as a work of art, a character determined by circumstances that cut the painter off from the mainstreams of painting. In this limited respect it is American in an isolated way. But now, at mid-century, with the birth of a new school of landscape painting, there appeared an art where Americanism was positive, its essence flowing from native springs, even while it was allied to the great world of painting in Europe.

The Hudson River School

The paintings of the so-called "Hudson River School" are as meticulously polished, sometimes to the point of niggling detail, as Caspar David Friedrich's landscapes, but there the similarity ends. Where Friedrich's mood was nostalgic and often gloomy, even ominous, the Americans' is full of vigorous optimism. Friedrich's *Two Men Looking at the Moon* [286] are surrounded by sinister forms, even if they seem to have come to terms with a threatening world. But Asher B. Durand's *Kindred Spirits* [305] are inspired by communion with a Nature which nourishes their souls. Friedrich's *Mountain Peaks* [306] hold the observer within a menacing chasm pressing

307. BIERSTADT: *Merced River, Yosemite Valley*, 1866. 36 x 50″. Metropolitan Museum of Art, New York.

upon him on either side, blocking him in the distance by harsh cliffs and cruel pinnacles, while the American peaks in Albert Bierstadt's *Merced River, Yosemite Valley* [307], equally cliffed and pinnacled, rise gloriously into an air as golden as that of any imagined Hellas. But this elysium of crags, water, trees, and rough earth is not an imagined one; the essential characteristic of these American landscapes is their reality, the fact that they are actual scenes within a country which was opening, unfolding to yield an inexhaustible sequence of new beauties for the delight, the amazement, and the enrichment of men.* The tiny figures that spot *Merced River, Yosemite Valley* here and there—standing on

---

* Even when painting imaginary landscapes, as they frequently did, the Hudson River men were more likely to concoct one from the elements of a familiar world than to try to reassemble a lost one.

a ledge of rock, moving across the shining water in a small boat—are not crushed by the immensity of the forms around them. They enter this vastness as strangers but not as intruders; their place within it may be temporary, but they are neither lost nor threatened. They are in the presence of a sublime grandeur and they breathe its air. It is a new conception of wilderness, indifferent to man's presence yet benign. It is a wilderness that never entirely yields to domestication; even at its most placid, as in Thomas Doughty's *In the Catskills* [308] it is a world infiltrated, but not transformed, by man.

The range of the Hudson River School is indicated by these three examples, from the philosophical or poetic intimacy of *Kindred Spirits* and *In the Catskills* to a passion for natural forms of supernatural grandeur, as in *Merced River, Yosemite Valley*. And it should already be apparent that "Hudson

308. DOUGHTY: *In the Catskills*, 1836. 31½ x 42¼″. Addison Gallery of American Art, Andover, Mass.

second,* and his glorification of the West exemplifies the taste for wilder and more dramatic scenes that affected the character of the school. But there is no sharp dividing line, and both generations ranged from the intimate to the vast. It is worth mentioning that the Hudson River painters discovered American landscape at the same time that the Frenchmen were setting up their easels around Barbizon. Durand and Corot were born the same year. And as Barbizon painting became known in America, its tender, lyrical mood was fused with the more indigenous one of the Hudson River men by other landscapists, notably George Inness (1825–1894), a contemporary of the second Hudson River generation who began in their tradition, then followed more closely Corot's, and finally in his late work cultivated some of the evanescent effects of impressionism.

River" is an inaccurate blanket designation for a school spreading from one side of the continent to the other. Actually, "school" is also a loose term here. Some of the painters did know one another and did work in the Catskill Mountains near the Hudson, but they never formed an organization nor did they paint from a set of codified principles. They are unified not by place or even by time, since they covered two generations—roughly between 1820 and 1870— but rather by the optimism, the enthusiasm, the belief in some wondrously vital spirit within the American landscape, which not only remained uncontaminated by the penetration of man but endowed him with whatever portion he could absorb of its ineffable sublimity.

Durand (1796–1886) and Doughty (1793–1856) belong to the first Hudson River generation,* and the quietness of their pictures illustrated here is typical of the general temper. Bierstadt (1830–1902), who accompanied a surveying expedition into the Rocky Mountains and Yosemite Valley in 1858, belongs to the

---

* Some others: Charles Codman, Samuel F. B. Morse, Alvin Fisher, Henry Inman, and Robert W. Weir.

Thomas Cole

The most individual of the Hudson River painters was a member of the earlier group, Thomas Cole (1801–1848), and he is usually thought of first whenever the school is mentioned today. The school in general is out of favor. The meticulousness of its detail, which may grow somewhat peckish and mincing; the imitativeness of its color, sometimes exaggerated into postcard gaudiness; its devotion to literal transcription rather than to pictorial theory or technical experiment make it appear humdrum alongside the brilliance and variety and complication of French painting. But because he was a fantasist as well as a landscapist, Cole has been tucked in lately with some of the strangest bedfellows in the world— the contemporary surrealist painters, who would certainly have horrified him. Two scenes [309 and 310] from the four making up his *Voyage of Life* series will give an idea of the bizarre mixture of moralizing, mysticism, melodrama, and naïve platitude that he grafted onto the Hudson River landscape with curious effect.

---

* Some others: John W. Casilear, John F. Kensett, Worthington Whittredge, Jasper F. Cropsey, Frederick E. Church.

309. COLE: *The Voyage of Life: Youth,* 1840. 52 x 78″. Munson-Williams-Proctor Institute, Utica, N.Y.

In *Youth,* the hero of the allegory sails forth from a verdant shore where a fantastic palm tree, introduced into an otherwise fairly normal landscape, recalls certain picturizations of the Garden of Eden. Youth's guardian angel standing by the river bank and relinquishing him to the perils of life's voyage increases the resemblance of this episode to an Expulsion. In the preceding (and first) picture of the series, the Angel was at the helm of the boat as the infant hero sailed onto the River of Life where it flows from its mysterious source in a cavern. Now in charge of the tiller, Youth sails forward toward his vision of a fantastical domed and minareted concoction that rises like soap bubbles in the sky above distant mountains. The river is placid, and it flows between the banks of wooded fields where leaves, tree trunks, and ferns glitter like enamel and jewels. But in *Manhood* the river darkens and grows turbulent; it flows in rapids through canyons and gorges; the trees are blasted where they have survived at all; storms sweep through the sky and the murky gloom is inhabited by the demons of temptation. (Barely visible in the upper center of the picture, they are demons of lust, intemperance, and suicide.) But far above, in a spot of light, the guardian Angel continues to watch, as the Man holds his hands in prayer. In the final scene the little boat has completed its hazardous passage and sails into the ocean of immortality with its now aged passenger still intact.

In the light of contemporary taste, these pictures must be accepted as the creations of an extraordinarily naïve spirit if they are not to appear pretentious. In that case, naïveté was remarkably widespread when Cole exhibited them* after their completion

---

* At the Art Union, formed to eliminate the dealer and thus increase the painter's percentage of the price of a picture. Public membership was by subscription. Members received prints and, by lottery, original paintings. Nearly 19,000 people all over the country finally joined. Oliver W. Larkin in his classic *Art and Life in America* has deftly characterized the Art Union as "joining the aesthetic with the acquisitive, and national pride with national zest for a bargain."

310. Cole: *The Voyage of Life: Manhood,* 1840. 52 x 78″. Munson-Williams-Proctor Institute, Utica, N.Y.

in 1840. Half a million people saw the pictures, and prints of them were sold by the thousands. The pictures themselves were commissioned by a wealthy banker, Sam Ward. Cole was enormously successful; *The Voyage of Life* was only one of many commissions of its kind, and his fellow artists in both painting and literature admired him (with a few exceptions) as much as did the public and his moneyed patrons. Durand's *Kindred Spirits* was painted in memory of Cole the year after his death; the kindred spirits represented in it are Cole and the American nature poet William Cullen Bryant. Bryant's poetry, like Cole's *Voyage of Life,* is at an awkward age, but it may not be long before the moral idealism in both cases becomes more conspicuous than the threadbareness and triteness that are just now so embarrassing.

But even today the two pictures we have just seen are remarkable for the consistency with which two contrasting moods are presented. Compositionally *Youth* and *Manhood* are carefully studied to make their points even if the points are obvious and labored. Cole held theories about the psychological effects of colors, believing that they corresponded to musical tones in their differences. The extremely literal detail in both pictures is more noticeable than the effort to combine these details in shapes and colors expressive in themselves. *Youth* is composed in horizontals and verticals, *Manhood* in whirls of dark around a vortex of light. Given a "modern" execution, either scheme could be abstracted into an arrangement of shape and color that might be regarded respectfully by critics who are unable to make concessions to the pictures as Cole conceived them. It is just possible that during a trip to Germany Cole became acquainted with Friedrich's pictures; there are obvious parallels between some passages in pictures like *Youth* and some in the German romantic's painting. It is certain that Cole knew and was influenced by the art of the seventeenth-century Italian romantic Salvator Rosa, in the darkly turbulent *Manhood.*

From the distance of a century that has made us suspicious of moralizing it is easy

THOMAS COLE · 263

311. COLE: *The Oxbow of the Connecticut*, 1836. 51½ x 76″. Metropolitan Museum of Art, New York.

to patronize *The Voyage of Life*, but it is impertinent to extend this condescension to all of Cole's work (and indeed, as is usually done, to the whole Hudson River School). No apologies need be made for Cole where he is at his best, in his pure landscapes. The drama of his most famous one, *The Oxbow of the Connecticut* [311], is undeniable. It is broadly conceived in deep space; its minute detail is so beautifully articulated into large movements that the picture is first seen, inevitably, as a whole with its great sweeping forms, the wide swing of the river through the valley, the passage of clouds, the rise of hills across the stretch of meadows. It is only secondarily—but with further delight—that the intricate tooling of forms within forms, glittering in the sun, is discovered as one may discover through a magnifying glass unsuspected complications on the surface of a

leaf or a bit of tree bark, or with binoculars the infinite detail of meadows and hills reaching back into the distance, brought suddenly close as if they could be touched.

Cole was born in England. When his family migrated to America in 1818 he was only seventeen years old but had already worked as a textile designer and an engraver. In America he designed wallpaper and studied wood engraving; the meticulousness of this technique stayed with him as a painter and made him the most sharply detailed of the Hudson River School. When he was twenty-two Cole entered the Pennsylvania Academy of the Fine Arts in Philadelphia, the nation's first art school. He studied there for two years and then went to New York, where his landscapes were an immediate success. He made two trips back to Europe, the first in 1829–1831, the second in 1841–1842.

312. CONSTABLE: *Stoke - by - Nayland*, 1836. 49½ x 66⅜". Art Institute of Chicago, W. W. Kimball Collection.

English Romantic Landscape: Constable

In England Cole must surely have seen the work of a painter whose wild romantic grandeur could hardly have failed to appeal to him, Joseph Mallord William Turner (1775–1851), whose art reached its climax at just the time of Cole's second trip in such pictures as *The Slave Ship* [321] and *Steamer in a Snowstorm* [322]. He could have seen too the paintings of Turner's contemporary by birth who had died some years earlier, John Constable (1776–1837). Constable and Turner were a generation older than Cole, being contemporaries of Friedrich's and Allston's, but when Turner died at the age of seventy-six he had outlived all these men, including Cole who had died three years before at the age of forty-seven. Chronology of this kind is not always important, but it is worth mentioning here because Turner, dying just at mid-century, brought to its most conclusive ex-

pression the romantic spirit in landscape which we have been following in the work of these other men.

In Turner's case the nationalistic idea—Friedrich's Germanism, the Americanism of the Hudson River School, the Frenchness of the Barbizon painters—does not apply; as we will see in a moment, he abstracted from the romantic experience something like a universal expression. In the meanwhile Constable may be examined as a painter who was English through and through.

English landscape painting has characteristically a kind of domestic intimacy, a rich and cultivated gentleness, a warm and comfortable and not very analytical response to fields and forest and small bridges and secluded glens or open heaths where any wildness is so subdued as to resemble a garden plot in comparison with the American wilderness, where any melancholy is so gentle as to be a happiness in comparison with the dark brooding of Friedrich's German ruins, deformed trees, and menacing

314. CONSTABLE: *Old Chain Pier, Brighton*, date unknown. 23½ x 38½″. Philadelphia Museum of Art, Wilstach Collection.

315. Constable: Detail from Figure 314.

peaks. The people who inhabit this landscape are thoroughly identified with its low hills, its trees, its cottages, which seem always to have been a part of it as much as its rocks and grasses. Its cathedrals, like the one on the horizon in Constable's *Stoke-by-Nayland* [312], aspire less to heaven than to peace on earth, and the clouds that move and swell through the same picture are not threatening but are a part of the fertility of drenched fields, the source of full streams and clear brooks.

This kind of Englishness, richly solid and lyrically sensitive without too heavy a metaphysical burden, received its literary expression in the English nature poets and its pictorial one in dozens of painters of picturesque landscape above whom Constable rises as a major artist surrounded by a crowd of minor attractive ones. He rises in fact as a major landscapist of any time or place, and his influence on painting beyond landscape has already been indicated in connection with the young Delacroix, who was led to new theories of color when he saw Constable's *Hay Wain* [313], which in turn were expanded by the impressionists.

Constable elaborated pictures like *The Hay Wain* and *Stoke-by-Nayland* from sketches made on the spots, usually very small and signed and dated on the back, which are not only notations of form and color but also of his immediate response to the subject. From these he elaborated the finished paintings methodically. But he was always intent, as Delacroix learned to be, upon retaining the effect of spontaneity that establishes the strongest communication between the painter and the observer. His method was brilliantly consistent. *Old Chain Pier, Brighton* [314], which was carried only into an intermediate stage of completion, reveals this consistency.

A sketch made on the spot has been enlarged and modified in whatever way seemed compositionally best, its outlines being sketched in lightly with pencil. Some of these pencil lines should be apparent in the illustrated detail [315]. The ground of the canvas itself is a warm tawny color. The major color notes have been struck in with a liberal use of paint; here and there a touch is applied with the palette knife. Constable

316. TURNER: *Falls of the Rhine at Schaffhausen, c. 1806. 94 x 58½".* Museum of Fine Arts, Boston.

is "working the whole canvas at once"—bringing it everywhere to the same degree of completion before he goes on to the next stage in any of the parts. As a result, the picture as it is offers remarkable satisfactions, aside from its interest as a demonstration of method. It is unified by the consistency of the degree of suggestion with which its various parts are struck in, with the exception of the sail at the extreme right, which has been pushed a little further than the rest of the picture. If one part is more brilliantly struck in than another, it is the sky with its pure white clouds and its occasional spot of celestial blue. For Constable the sky with its moving clouds was the focal point of any landscape, structurally as well as expressively. In *Stoke-by-Nayland* as a typical fine example, sky, trees, and the forms of the earth are united as movements of form and light, and the sky is at once their origin and their climax.

Turner

It would be easy to go on from this point to exaggerate Constable's emphasis on such abstract elements in his art. They are present and they are important; they account for the difference between Constable and any other painter of taste, skill, discretion, and sensitive response to nature. But they do not dominate the pictures. They serve always as vehicles for the romantic interpretation of specific aspects of nature, remaining subservient to it. With Turner the case is reversed: as if to summarize the tradition of romantic landscape he reduced its elements of earth, air, water, and fire so very nearly to abstractions that the subject of a picture virtually disappears as a set of representational forms making up a scene. Nominally the subject of *Steamer in a Snowstorm* [322] is just that—a material object upon a body of water, surrounded by

317. TURNER: *Dido Building Carthage*, 1815. 60½ x 89½". National Gallery, London.

air and revealed by light. Actually the canvas is a tempest of forms and colors that in themselves are emotionally expressive. They very nearly, if not quite, obliterate the pictorial subject to speak entirely for themselves.

Turner's progress from romantic realism toward romantic abstraction can be followed through a few pictures painted at intervals of roughly a dozen years. The early *Falls of the Rhine at Schaffhausen* [316], painted in 1806 thirty-six years before *Steamer in a Snowstorm*, is the sort of subject picturesque-romantic painters are fond of doing. It is potentially more Turneresque than some others, simply because the falls suggest the release of natural forces (an idea that preoccupies Turner later on), but on the whole this picture remains, rainbow and all, less an expressive one than a topographical souvenir with some romantic ex-

aggerations. It is one of the best pictures of its kind to be found anywhere, but it is of a fairly obvious kind. The carts, human figures, animals, barrels and bundles stretched across the lower foreground have the sort of tourist interest that is basic to the average picturesque landscape. Still, no average picture of this type would have expressed so dramatically the wild rush of water against the craggy rocks that thrust back into it.

Turner had an early success and was a prolific artist, but he found his way to completely individual expression rather slowly. *Dido Building Carthage* [317] is one of his large compositions close to the manner of Claude Lorrain, Poussin's more romantic counterpart. But Turner's semiclassical synthesis of architecture and landscape is much more than a mere skillful derivation. His first interest in the picture is in the

318. TURNER: *Ulysses Deriding Polyphemus,* 1829. 51 x 79″. National Gallery, London.

319. TURNER: Detail from Figure 318.

320. TURNER: *Burning of the Houses of Parliament, c.* 1835. 36¼ x 48½". Philadelphia Museum of Art, McFadden Collection.

drama of light. Turner's light is not light as the impressionists were to discover it, not a vibrant opalescent shimmer, but light as the element of fire, the fire of the sun. In *Dido Building Carthage* the sun blazes through the sky and burns a path down the center of the picture, consuming the stone bridge in the distance and impregnating the water with its brilliance.

Yet there is a contradiction here between the serenity of the picture's component forms—its temples and its trees—and the bursting energy of the sky. Turner did not hesitate long in making his choice between fire and marble. In *Ulysses Deriding Poly-*

phemus [318, 319], the sun at the horizon is an explosion of live coals spraying out across fantastic and agitated forms. Turner's romantic vision of the world as a cosmic union or struggle between the elements, dominated by fire and water, is finding its way to expression as it could not do in either *Falls of the Rhine* with its imposition of factual reference, no matter how grandiose, or in the forms of classicism, no matter how monumental or poetic.

In at least one actual event, however, Turner found a subject as good for his purpose as any invented one. He witnessed the great conflagration that destroyed the

321. TURNER: *The Slave Ship,* 1840. 35¾ x 48″. Museum of Fine Arts, Boston.

Houses of Parliament in London in 1834 and recorded it in a combination of remembered fact and expressive invention [320]. The sky is a furnace; it is filled with leaping ragged areas of orange and yellow sprinkled with the vermilion flecks of floating cinders. Billows of purple smoke rise into the incandescent air; fragments of disintegrating architecture merge with it, and in the background the towers of Westminster Abbey glow as if molten. The water of the Thames is a flood of brass; boats filled with spectators lie upon it as diaphanous as shadows. The crowds on the bank are gauzy and unreal, the stone bridge melts away into the distant violence. The gas jets of the lamps surmounting its buttresses are as pale

as evening lights against the sunlike intensity of the holocaust. Here Turner has reached a statement of his major theme; the dissolution of material reality into a universe where the elements are fused into one another in a way suggestive of primeval chaos. Water fuses with air, air and water fuse with fire, while earth, stone, and metal dissolve into all of them.

To express this fusion in terms of paint, Turner adopted an increasingly free technique where form was suggested by broader and broader areas of color, sometimes scrubbed in a film over the canvas, sometimes applied with heavy impasto, this latter especially in the passages where light appears most purely and most fiercely in its

322. TURNER: *Steamer in a Snowstorm*, 1842. 35½ x 47½". National Gallery, London.

maximum concentration as fire. In a way this is impressionism, and Turner is often thought of as a proto-impressionist. He was all but unknown in France, but nearly twenty years after his death he was "discovered" by Monet and Pissarro, who were taking refuge in England during the German occupation of Paris in 1870. They seem to have been impressed, but it is difficult to say just how much direct influence Turner had on their subsequent development of impressionism as a technique for representing light; by hearsay their own statements on the question are contradictory. In the long run the question is not a very important one, since on important scores the connection is tenuous. For the impressionists, light was an optical phe-

nomenon; for Turner, it was a cosmic force. The impressionists' light is part of a happy everyday world; Turner's is a manifestation of romantic mystery. Turner broke the surface of his painting into scrubs, films, dashes, and gobbets of color, and so did the impressionists. But for Turner color was first of all abstract and expressive; for the impressionists it was first of all descriptive of visual reality. We may make an exception of Monet's very late works, but the difference between Turner and impressionism is still the difference between *The Slave Ship* [321] and *Red Boats at Argenteuil* [207], the difference between the visionary and the commonplace, even when the commonplace is as beautiful as the impressionists discovered it could be. In other words, the impressionists were unaffected by Turner as far as any expressive factors were concerned, and as technical processes Turner's explosions of color have only incidental connections with impressionism's investigation of the spectrum on a semiscientific basis.

With *The Slave Ship* Turner's development toward a final abstract statement of romantic emotionalism was nearly complete. The title of the picture still clings to literary associations not inherent in the painting as an independent work of art, and it is with a kind of disappointment that we discover the narrative incident in the foreground right, where a shackled leg disappears into the water, surrounded by devouring fish. This bit of storytelling appears as an afterthought, a concession to popular standards in a picture that was not only complete without it but is reduced from grandeur to melodrama by its inclusion. But in *Steamer in a Snowstorm* [322] the majestic and terrible power of the elements, hinted at a third of a century before in the picturesque *Falls of the Rhine*, is at last expressed without the distractions of incidental trivia. A few blurred forms at the vortex of the composition, the ship and its mast, are a reminder that grandeur and mystery are a concept of man, that if the universe is vast and violent beyond man's comprehension, it is given meaning only because man, existing within it, has contemplated it with romantic imagination.

Popular Painting at Mid-century

Turner's grandeur is even more impressive when it is played against the limited imagination of the most popular painting of the day. Turner had established himself as a collector's painter early in his career, and he maintained that position until the end of his life. But the painting toward which the public gravitated was increasingly obvious and sentimental. This was even more true in England and Germany—and America—than it was in France; or rather, outside France the bourgeois preference for such pictures was less effectively countered by the theorizing and proselytizing of in-

323. WALDMÜLLER: *The Shattered Rose*, 1839. Panel, 25 x 19¼″. *Galerie des Neunzehnten Jahrhunderts,* Vienna.

tellectuals pledged to the causes of the fine arts. In Germany especially there was an insatiable appetite for concise naturalistic statement. Already apparent in the detail of Friedrich's romantic landscapes, and insisted upon as an aesthetic principle by the Nazarenes, it persisted as an end in itself. At its lowest level it became a kind of stunt painting; at its highest it is summarized in the painting of men like Ferdinand Waldmüller (1793–1865), who may stand here as exemplifying any number of his contemporaries who painted from a similar point of view, although usually with less skill. Such painters were the darlings of popular favor during the last decades of Turner's life and on into the second half of the century after his death at its midpoint.

324. WALDMÜLLER: *The Picture Box Man*, 1847. 29½ x 36¼". *National-Museum,*
Budapest.

Waldmüller was an Austrian academician who ranged over the field of portraiture, genre, and landscape. In *The Shattered Rose* [323], a better than average example of the kind of sentimental portrait with detailed accessories that was popular everywhere, the accessories are put into the service of what could be called, by stretching a point, a poetic or philosophical idea. The young girl holds in one hand a blossom that has dropped most of its petals onto the ground at her feet. For centuries the rose has been for poets the symbol of the beauty and the evanescence of youth. If Waldmüller's pretty little pictorialization of the idea is not asked to live up to its formidable literary ancestors, it may be enjoyed for its sentimental charm. The trouble is that we must suspect it of pretensions to something more than its obvious and simple-minded illustration of the familiar allegory, to which it adds nothing.

Painters like Waldmüller are at their best in the field of genre painting, where an interesting subject may most legitimately speak for itself if it is presented in recognizable detail. Within these limitations, which exclude imagination, ingenuity, or interpretive depth, Waldmüller's little account of a traveling photographer, *The Picture Box Man* [324], has everything—a lively and appealing subject, endless anecdotal proliferations, and impeccable technical finish.

In landscape also Waldmüller gave full value within the same limits. In *Morning* [325] he is so generous with detail that it seems a shame to ask that the picture be anything more than a catalogue of the facts of rustic landscape hung onto the peg of a subject of sorts, in this case the meeting of a rustic suitor and his sweetheart on a country road. And people in general, at the middle of the nineteenth century, asked nothing more. The artificiality of the scrubbed urchins in *The Picture Box Man* was preferable to Daumieresque consciousness of man as a being in the world. The pretty symbolism of the fallen petals in *The Rose* was enjoyable, while the extended implications of Goya's contrasts of pretty girls and evil old hags were disturbing. The lovers' meeting in a botanical encyclopedia, in *Morning*, involved neither the moody complications of a Friedrich nor the cosmic drama of a Turner. And in addition the Waldmüllers held for the public the appeal of stunt men; it was amazing the way they could make things look so real. A picture, then, was essentially a sleight-of-hand performance by which the painter created illusions involving jolly or sentimental anecdotes.

In England a denial of such superficial values was implicit in Turner's achievement, but he found no followers. When a group of painters organized a revolt shortly before his death, they formulated a curiously artificial aesthetic code of their own, with curious results. These were the painters of the Pre-Raphaelite Brotherhood, whose revolt we will see ushering in the second half of the century.

The American Scene: Bingham

While Turner was painting in England and the Hudson River men were revealing a new American spirit through American landscape, other painters were making explicit records of aspects of the American scene that were unique to it. Before the middle of the century John James Audubon (1785–1851) had made his magnificent collection of the *Birds of America*, where ornithological record was combined with unwavering brilliance of draughtsmanship and design. George Catlin (1796–1872) had lived with American Indian tribes in order to paint some 300 portraits of them and nearly 200 scenes from their daily life. William Sidney Mount (1807–1868) had discovered that American genre subjects could be just as picturesque, just as sentimental, and just as saleable as European ones, a discovery that was developed during the rest of the century by such painters as Eastman Johnson (1824–1906). But it remained for a man named George Caleb Bingham (1811–1879) to bring to scenes

325. WALDMÜLLER: *Morning*, 1862–63. Panel, 22½ x 27¾″. *Historisches Museum der Stadt Wien*, Vienna.

of American life the indigenous feeling that the Hudson River painters brought to its landscape.

Bingham was born in Virginia; while he was a child the family moved to Missouri. He was first a cabinetmaker's apprentice, then a student of law, then a student of theology, before he discovered that he was a painter. There is some doubt as to exactly what his earliest training was. Possibly he studied for a while with a painter named Chester Harding. But when he set himself up as a portraitist in St. Louis he was essentially self-trained. Later he studied briefly at the Pennsylvania Academy of the Fine Arts, but his style retained always a flavor of the primitivism associated with the early American tradition. He was by no means a primitive painter in the way Edward Hicks was, but the flavor is there. Much of it was lost after he studied for three years in Düsseldorf, but fortunately he did not go there until he was forty-six. In his best work he is a purely American artist of the first half of the century, although he painted for another twenty years after his return from Europe in 1859.

Bingham the painter has been compared with Mark Twain the writer. Bingham's

326. BINGHAM: *Fur Traders Descending the Missouri, c.* 1845. 29 x 36½". Metropolitan Museum of Art, New York, Morris K. Jessup Fund.

pictures of life in the country or the towns and small cities of the Middle West draw their subject matter, and their cast of characters, from the same sources Mark Twain used in *Tom Sawyer* and *Huckleberry Finn.* A similarity, too, is the fact that both men were popular as inventors of pure narrative and humor, and came into tardy recognition for the deeper content underlying their engaging surfaces. On the face of it, *Huckleberry Finn* is an adventure story spiced with rustic humor and picturesque locale. At the same level, Bingham's *Fur Traders Descending the Missouri* [326] is a genre painting. But the story of Huck's journey down the Mississippi is also poetic and philosophical; so, too, are the evocations of Bingham's representation of a man, a boy, and a pet fox in a dugout canoe.

The quiet stretches of water and sky, the shadowy island in the distance, the spare-

ness and gentleness with which these meager elements are selected and arranged into a picture, go far beyond objective record of picturesque fact. In a special way *Fur Traders Descending the Missouri* is another statement of the relationship of man to a primal and benevolent wilderness, the theme of the Hudson River painters. But as it is treated here, the theme is at once more idyllic and more down to earth, at once more subtle and less artificial. In spite of its subject drawn from contemporary life, in spite of local picturesque details realistically shown, the picture is almost classical in its elimination of unnecessary incidentals to create a timeless image. This may be exaggerating a point, and it is improbable that Bingham thought of his picture in this way, but the point is there, and it does a great deal to account for the serenity of a picture that could be transformed into mere record or mere narrative by a few additions and complications. The figures of the youth and the rough old man, the great stretch of river and sky, are not symbolical—it would be a mistake to try to make symbols of them—but if the simplicity of *Fur Traders Descending the Missouri* is compared with the highflown trumpery of Cole's *Voyage of Life* there are certain overlappings of meaning. Cole presents his allegory in specific and didactic, and hence rigidly limited, terms. Bingham, without moralizing or allegorizing, opens up a much wider area of reflection. This does not have to mean that one picture is "better" or "worse" than another, but it does mean that where Cole was ambitious to make a grand statement, he ended with a small one, while Bingham did the reverse: in what appears to be the simple presentation of an unpretentious subject, we discover wide extensions of meaning. The two pictures, incidentally, were painted within a few years of one another, *The Voyage of Life* in 1840, *Fur Traders* about 1845.

Fur Traders Descending the Missouri is exceptional even in Bingham's work for its gentleness. But again and again he takes scenes from the life of the expanding American frontier and reveals the vitality of the epoch. His genius lay in his ability to reveal a kind of grandeur through the trivia that made it up. In *The Wood Boat* [327] he does not pretend that the boatmen who transported wood down the river were grand and noble men, although they may have been happy and roughly healthy ones. But in painting them grouped on the river bank alongside their loaded barges, he creates forms of monumental character and disposes them in logical, monumental relationships to one another in such a way that the sum of picturesque details is more than its parts. Bingham's "classicism"—it is important to keep the word in quotation marks —may be compared to that of Poussin in *Shepherds in Arcady* [415]: Poussin is a seventeenth-century intellectual synthesizing a philosophical dream of classical antiquity while Bingham is a nineteenth-century provincial recording the life around him. Yet in their integration of human and landscape forms into a monumental whole,

327. BINGHAM: *The Wood Boat, c.* 1850. 24¾ x 29⅝". City Art Museum, St. Louis.

the two painters have gone about the creation of a picture in much the same way. Bingham's relationship to three other seventeenth-century French painters, the brothers Le Nain, is even closer. Like him, they painted genre subjects and combined realism, monumentality, and a primitive flavor in pictures that rise above the temporary and specific nature of their subject matter.

Bingham's pictures were tremendously popular and were sold by the thousands in engraved reproductions. His "election series" was aimed at the popular market and these pictures [328] are full of roistering narrative incident. Here it is a bit of a strain to find the "grandeur" behind the scenes, although Bingham's most enthusiastic admirers are able to do so. Grandeur aside, the election series give vital expression to the vigor and enthusiasm of their period. Bingham shows in them that if he can compose a quiet scene of a man, a boy, and a fox in a dugout canoe, with sensitive economy, he can also manipulate dozens of figures on a crowded stage. He is so logical in his distribution of solid forms in space that a ground plan could be drawn of any one of the election pictures, with each figure and each structure occupying its own

328. BINGHAM: *The County Election*, 1851–52. 35⁷⁄₁₆ x 48¾". City Art Museum, St. Louis.

area comfortably. In other words, Bingham's control of an optical third dimension is so complete that his painted scenes could be reconstructed as physically three-dimensional ones. This is a considerable technical feat in itself, but it is given point by the fact that the arrangements are not only physically logical but characteristically expressive. Each of his characters is conceived not only as a physical mass but as a consistent personality, and the interplay of personalities is as clear as their relationship in space. The shortcoming is that the personality types are so obvious as to be trite, too true to type to be real or very interesting. In the election pictures Bingham is like a stage designer and director. He constructs a set and then fills it with expressive action. But his actors are not always talented.

Bingham was the last American painter of major stature to develop relatively free of European influence. Obviously the word "relatively" is an important one. In a civilization that began as an adjunct to Europe's it would be impossible to find a purely native tradition in colonials and their descendants. But because he was so isolated from the more sophisticated American centers, because he had to discover so many things for himself in his relative separation from European developments, and because he used what he discovered to interpret subject matter unique to his world, Bingham is emphatically an American artist. The generation of painters that followed him in the second half of the century were less so, partly because it became easier for Americans to study in Europe, as all of them wanted to do, but largely because America itself had conquered its frontiers by that time and the conditions, and the spirit, that produced Bingham, were fading.

CHAPTER 9

Outside France, 1850–1900

The Pre-Raphaelite Ideal

Romanticism as a state of mind, an emotional attitude toward life, is peculiar to no single period. Romanticism as an organized revolt to express and propagandize an attitude is peculiar to the nineteenth century. Of all the forms this revolt assumed, Pre-Raphaelitism was the most idealistic, but it was also self-defeating.

Pre-Raphaelitism was a confusion of ingredients including revolt against the times, adulation of the middle ages, noble aesthetic aspirations, religious yearning, sententious moralizing, morbid sentimentality, historical delusions, faulty archaeology, and debilitating literary preoccupations. This is a damning list, yet the Pre-Raphaelites had a unique importance in the conservative and placid world of English art. As the only group dedicated to rebellion against the *status quo*, they injected a leavening influence that has affected English painting and writing ever since, even when the Pre-Raphaelites are forgotten as its source.

Of all romantics, the Pre-Raphaelites were the ones whose obsession with the past rose most specifically from their horror of the present. England in the second half of the nineteenth century was omnipotently the center of the Industrial Revolution, swelling with wealth and wholeheartedly dedicated to materialism. The great Victorian age was under way with all its complacency and adventurousness, its practical idealism and social abuses, its elegance and vulgarity, its stolid virtue and its virtuous aberrations. The Queen had been crowned in 1837; when she would die sixty-four years later in the first year of the twentieth century, very few of her subjects would be

329. HUNT: *Dante Gabriel Rossetti*, repetition of a portrait dated 1853. 11 x 8½". Private collection, England.

they sought to answer the question by running away from it, by returning to the surface forms of past glories rather than searching out new ones. Thus they were defeated before they began, and ended by proving nothing definitely except that it is difficult to go very far forward by walking backward. In retrospect we see them floundering in a blind alley, and at the moment their art is at an excruciatingly awkward age. Their shortcomings are pathetically apparent and their virtues have become unfashionable. It is as much as a critical reputation is worth to concede them a kind word on their own terms, for their art is devoid of the kinds of abstract formal and structural values that are taken for granted today as the starting point for critical evaluations. The only element that can save them, their expressive intensity, is obscured by a factor intolerable to the contemporary aesthetic, their literary sentimentalism.

As a group, the Pre-Raphaelites were contemporaries of the older impressionists, such as Manet, Pissarro, and Degas, which means that they must stand against extraordinary competition. They were only a decade older than Cézanne, yet they might have been painting in another century. Indeed they tried to do so, and the century they had in mind was the fifteenth, in Italy, as well as the even more remote ones of Dante and the Arthurian legends. While French painters were founding a new art, the Pre-Raphaelites tried to return to the craftsmanship and (as they imagined them) the spiritual values of the late middle ages and the early Renaissance. If they were aware that the German Nazarenes had tried and failed to do the same thing, they did not profit from the warning.

The enthusiasm and the high ideals, the impracticality and the failure, of Pre-Raphaelitism were symbolized when several of the Brotherhood set out to decorate the library of the Oxford Union in 1857. Emulating, they believed, the fifteenth-century Italians who covered the walls of Florentine churches with frescoes, they set about doing so in the library, convinced that an aesthetic resurrection was at hand. The circumstances seemed ideal, since the building itself was an imitation of a medie-

able to remember clearly a time when she had not been at the head of a country devoted to materialism as a way of life. The Pre-Raphaelites questioned this way of life, and although the reform they proposed now seems misled, even pathetic, they at least exposed the problem and proposed a solution of sorts.

Fundamentally the question was whether man's spirit could flourish when his life was dominated by commerce, whether it could blossom in an air contaminated by the smoke of factories. The Pre-Raphaelites' answer was that it could not, an answer that they saw tangibly obvious in the sordidness of industrial slums, in the dreary reaches of respectable bourgeois life given over to the pursuit of money and animal comforts, in the ugliness of the objects the new machines were turning out, and in the artificiality of the fine arts, which seemed starved of nourishment. But unfortunately

How Sir Galahad, Sir Bors & Sir Percival were fed with the Sancgreal; but Sir Percival's Sister died by the way.

330. ROSSETTI: *How Sir Galahad, Sir Bors & Sir Percival were fed, etc.*, 1864. Watercolor, 11½ x 16½". Tate Gallery, London.

val one, and the Pre-Raphaelites were banded together as fellow craftsmen unified by moral principle, rather than as effete painters ambitious for conventional success in an age of industry and commerce. But their paint was hardly on the walls before it began to chip, flake, and peel. Their fresco technique was as unsound as their social theorizing. The whole thing was a disaster, from enthusiastic beginning to humiliating finish.

Rossetti

In spite of its social theorizing, Pre-Raphaelitism was a variety of escapism, having less to do with objections to the industrialized world than with a feeling of revulsion for the world on any terms, a neurotic denial of life, a yearning for a never-never land where the soul was freed from the rebuffs and responsibilities of daily living. The leader of the movement, Dante Gabriel Rossetti (1828–1882), was especially sub-

ject to the old romantic delusion that confuses emotional indulgence with spiritual nourishment. But in his poems and his swooning visionary paintings he was the most expressive member of the Brotherhood, because he was the most personal and most emotional interpreter of an ideal to which, in the end, only personal emotionalism could give a reason for being.

Rossetti was the center of the founding members—in 1848—of the secret Brotherhood, which immediately became not secret at all. The two other most important founding members were John Everett Millais (1829–1896) and William Holman Hunt (1827–1910). Hunt's portrait of Rossetti [329] with its enormously enlarged eyes seems to try to force onto a not exceptional face the exceptional quality of inward vision. This same forcing is characteristic of Rossetti's own pictures; he overplayed a minor talent. In a little picture with the enormous title *How Sir Galahad, Sir Bors, & Sir Percival were fed with the Sancgreal; but Sir Percival's Sister died by the way*

331. ROSSETTI: *Jane Burden*, 1858. Crayon, 17 x 13". National Gallery of Ireland, Dublin.

332. ROSSETTI: *Elizabeth Siddal*, date unknown. Silverpoint, 6½ x 4½". Collection Mr. and Mrs. Gilbert McC. Troxell, New Haven, Conn.

[330] the vision never quite coalesces although it is full of images that should be evocative. The band of haloed angels, the handsome knights, the radiant lilies, the field sprinkled with little flowers, the stuffs of the robes so conscientiously patterned, never sing together. One waits for something to happen, and nothing does. The clutter of medieval props and costumes ends as an amateur pageant. The truth is that Rossetti was technically only moderately well equipped. He was only feeble to fair as a draughtsman, and compositionally he falls into clichés. The deadly taint of amateurishness infects his art because his technical limitations are disharmonious with the sophistication of his effort.

Rossetti came closest to fulfillment when dealing with the subject that was his true

obsession: the vision of a woman who was personified for him first by his wife, Elizabeth Siddal [332], then by Jane Burden [331], who became the wife of his friend William Morris. His marriage with Elizabeth Siddal was filled with quarrels and irritations, but he loved to look at her and to draw her. When he fell in love with Mrs. Morris years later, he believed that he had always been in love with her since the Pre-Raphaelites had first seen her in the audience at a theater matinee. They were working on the Oxford Union library murals at that time and asked her to pose for them; Rossetti's drawing illustrated here is probably the first he made of her. Elizabeth Siddal and Jane Burden bore some resemblance to one another, and every woman Rossetti painted, even when he used other models, resembled the two of them. He was in love with a facial type that enchanted him. Jane Burden Morris most triumphantly embodied it, with her great thick masses of undulating hair, her tremendous brooding eyes, her heavy rather swollen neck, and her small, full, exaggeratedly curling mouth. When Rossetti is fully given over to the adoration of this type he is at his best.

The fascination Jane Burden's face held for the Pre-Raphaelites must have been in part that it recalled the facial types in pictures by certain early Renaissance masters they admired, such as Fra Filippo Lippi, Verrocchio, and Botticelli. Botticelli was virtually rediscovered by the Pre-Raphaelites; the inward gaze, the long neck, the strongly defined jaw, and the sinuous convolutions of hair in Botticelli's *Venus* [1] have their counterparts in pictures like *The Bride* (sometimes called *The Beloved*) [333], although the linear rhythms so electric in Botticelli have become flaccid in Rossetti. Botticelli's vital grace is reduced to anemic languor. It would be pleasant to be able to say that as Rossetti's obsession continued his perceptions deepened and his vision took new and more profound form; instead, he followed a course of repetitious elaboration. *The Bride* even offers the type in triplicate, swathed in the complications of arts-and-crafts fabric and jewels with which Rossetti loved to bedeck his enchantresses. Even his knights are Mrs. Morris in other costumes.

William Morris and the Arts and Crafts

William Morris (1834–1896) had an importance beyond his position as the husband of Rossetti's Jane Burden. He was originally trained as an architect; as a poet he still has a respectable reputation; as a painter he worked in a manner close to Rossetti's; but as the founder of the Arts and Crafts Movement he made as enduring a contribution as any connected with Pre-Raphaelitism.

In 1851, England held the epoch-making fair called the Great Exhibition of the Works of Industry of All Nations, when

333. ROSSETTI: *The Bride*, 1865. 32½ x 30″. Tate Gallery, London.

some of the most preposterous objects ever created by man were displayed in one of the most beautiful and important structures of the century. The Crystal Palace was a sudden, brilliant, glittering, architectural sport, one of the first modern buildings, a prophecy of buildings that would not be built for another century. It was created by force of circumstance.

The problem was to erect a structure large enough to house the tens of thousands of exhibits of the fair and to construct it quickly and not too expensively. A greenhouse designer, Joseph Paxton, created an open web of cast-iron girders, wrought-iron trusses, and jointed iron pipes of standard measurements, then covered this thin, light skeleton with a skin of glass. The Crystal Palace, built in Hyde Park around great living trees [334] became, on the interior, a fantasy. Paxton's solution to the architectural problem was utterly direct

334. JOSEPH PAXTON, architect: Transept of the Crystal Palace. Color lithograph by J. Nash, 1851–54. 13½ x 19⅛″. From *Dickenson's Comprehensive Pictures of the Great Exhibition*, London, 1854.

and practical, yet the final effect was fairy-like, enchanted. The Crystal Palace was a sensation, but its architectural implications were missed. It was regarded as a wonderful and fantastic novelty rather than as the demonstration of a new aesthetic in architecture, which it was.

Among other things, the Crystal Palace was the world's first prefabricated building. The iron units were cast in foundries all over England, their lengths being determined by the largest practical size in which it was possible to manufacture the glass panes that would sheath the skeleton cage. These panes also were manufactured in many places, and the business of assembling the huge structure from the multiplication of a few unit parts was rapid and simple. After the exhibition, the building was dismantled and re-erected in Kensington, where it served as a museum and concert hall until, as late as 1936, it was destroyed

by fire (its floors and partitions having been of wood).

The Crystal Palace was potentially the source of the "functional" architecture of the twentieth century, but to English eyes in 1851 it was not, strictly speaking, architecture at all. The old Houses of Parliament that had burned (and supplied Turner with a subject for painting) were at just this time being replaced by a new structure in the Gothic style. This was *real* architecture—meaning that it drew first from the past, then forced past forms into some kind of workable arrangement with the contemporary world. In the case of the Houses of Parliament there was more justification than usual for such an idea, since the older structure had not been completely destroyed and the remaining genuinely medieval parts were to be incorporated into the new building. Also, the old structure had for a long time been synonymous with the

336. "Modernized" English Gothic project by M. P. Hapgood, Boston

Three proposals for the completion of the Washington Monument, from *The American Art Review*, Vol. I, 1879–80. 335 (*left*). Classical project by Paul Schulze, Washington, D.C.

337. "Modern French Renaissance with strong points of affinity with some of the better Hindu Pagodas" project by anonymous California architect.

solid tradition of English government, and the new one must be a symbolical monument as well as a usable structure. The building, as finally completed, was an impressive massing of elements—the masterpiece, certainly, of neo-Gothic architecture, and as good a defense as could be offered for the use of Gothic forms in a century to which they were foreign.

But the forms of the past were seldom so well understood. Architecture was degenerating into the ornamentation of structure, and it was even so defined in a handbook of the period. The old joke goes that the client might employ a contractor to devise a structure that would stand up and then call in a designer to "put on the architecture." This is what very nearly happened in the United States when the Washington Monument was completed after standing half finished for years because of lack of funds. (The dividing line between the early and later parts of the monument may still be seen in the slight difference of the

338. "Irish" Chair.

339. Bedstead.

Four items from *The Art Journal Illustrated Catalogue of the Great Exhibition, 1851.*

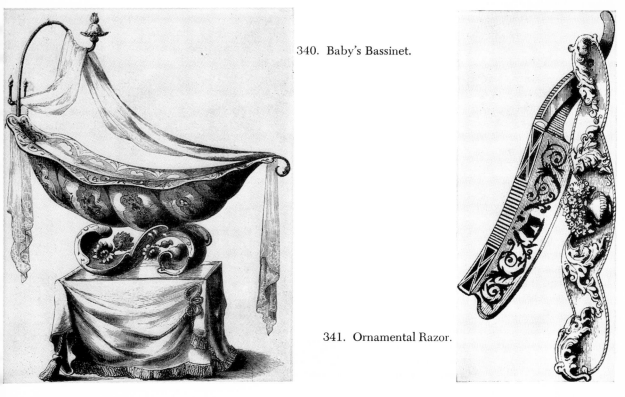

340. Baby's Bassinet.

341. Ornamental Razor.

stone.) When funds were available for its completion, ideas of architecture had "advanced" to the point where the simplicity of the original design seemed primitive. Three proposed remedies are shown here [335, 336, and 337]; respectively, they are an elaborated neo-classical design surmounted by a statue of Washington, a respectable Gothic tower surmounted by an angel, and a curious concoction of a little bit of everything surmounted by an allegorical figure. The article in *The Art Journal* accompanying the publication of these designs expressed uneasiness about the appropriateness of the Gothic design as a memorial to the father of the new country —not because it was Gothic, but because it was *English* Gothic.

But if architecture suffered through the perversion and distortion of the forms of the past, it existed in purity compared with the flood of objects now being created by machines, and even in handmade objects. Designer–craftsmen had reached the nadir of their art, and the illustrated catalogue of furniture and bric-a-brac exhibited by all nations in the Crystal Palace (with England as the chief offender) has become a standard chamber of the most hilarious horrors in the history of design. Such objects as the "Irish" chair, with its two arms in the form of Irish wolfhounds, one rising, one reclining [338]; the "rich and costly bedstead," marking the initial appearance in the English language of the adjective *costly* as one of aesthetic description [339]; the baby's bassinet made from papier-mâché, which seems to be balanced on a large brooch [340]; and such fantasies as ornamental razors [341]—these were part of the aesthetic Grand Guignol that had just inspired the formation of the Pre-Raphaelite Brotherhood.

Morris's Arts and Crafts Movement shared the general Pre-Raphaelite fault of retreat rather than advance: he tried to return to the purity of hand craftsmanship in the face of the machine. The modern style in decoration, when it finally evolved, was to be based on virtues inherent in the machine rather than on a return to virtues the machine seemed to have perverted. But the Arts and Crafts Movement at least

called attention to this perversion and created objects where design and usability were more important than vulgar elaborations. Morris tried to revive the crafts of hand weaving, cabinetmaking, metal work, stained glass, even the hand printed and illuminated manuscript. But a new society demanding thousands upon thousands of repetitions of an object could not be supplied by hand craftsmanship, and Morris was able to shed only a little light in the general darkness. In the end his contribution was less in the objects he designed and made than in his stirring of an awareness that design could be a quality inherent in the material and the making of an object, as opposed to design as used in the objects we have just seen, where motifs drawn from everywhere were murderously debauched and plastered at random over any saleable object.*

Like the other Pre-Raphaelites, Morris saw the middle ages and the early Renaissance as a paradise where every object was beautiful. His vision of it in paintings, such as *La Belle Yseult* [342], filled with the kind of fabric and furniture he designed, does seem a little crowded. The same arty clutter characterizes such Morris interiors as have survived. But because the Arts and Crafts Movement respected the materials it worked with, it held the seed of a true revival. It remained for this seed to be fertilized later by designers who accepted the present instead of holding to Morris's nostalgic veneration of the past. In 1862 Morris founded his own firm, specializing in handcrafts for the decoration of churches. Here, where his medievalism was most appropriate and where handcraft could supply the market, he made his great success.

---

* The Pre-Raphaelites were not alone in their recognition of the low state of design. Even the compiler of the illustrated catalogue for the exhibition seems to have suspected that some of the objects were a little over-elaborate. And it would be chastening for anyone who enjoys laughing at the Crystal Palace exhibits to compare them with a similar quantity of furniture and bric-a-brac by modern manufacturers. These twentieth-century items would draw upon a different set of motifs—streamlined ones and so on—but many of them would be just as bad and unusable as, and much more shoddy than, their Victorian counterparts.

342. MORRIS: *La Belle Yseult*, 1858. 28⅛ x 20″. Tate Gallery, London.

343. BURNE-JONES: *The Prioress' Tale*, 1869–98, original version, 1859. Watercolor, 40½ x 25″. Wilmington Society of Fine Arts, Samuel and Mary R. Bancroft Collection.

Rossetti's Followers

Rossetti exerted enough influence to make what might be called Rossetti-ism a subdivision within the Pre-Raphaelite movement. The most immediate of his followers was Edward Burne-Jones (1833–1898), one of several painters who, like Morris, joined the founding brothers in a second wave. He was one of Morris's most enthusiastic workers in stained glass and tapestries, and the two-dimensional disciplines imposed by these techniques affected his style in painting. The ornamental flatness of *The Prioress' Tale* [343] reflects his solid professionalism as a designer. The long panel, a favorite shape with Burne-

Jones, comes of course from stained glass windows, and Burne-Jones's rich color is more like dyed wools than painted canvas. Even more than Rossetti he was unabashed in lifting elements wholesale from the painters and craftsmen who invented them so long before. But he was also a better workman than Rossetti.

Like so much Pre-Raphaelite work, *The Prioress' Tale* is a curious amalgam, combining a Chaucerian subject with Italianate forms, two vigorous if not very compatible sources of inspiration watered down with precious aestheticism. The composition was originally designed in 1859 for a cabinet belonging to William Morris, and the work was done in Morris's house at 17 Red

344. ALMA-TADEMA: *A Reading from Homer, c.* 1885. 36 x 72⅜". Philadelphia Museum of Art, George W. Elkins Collection.

345. WATTS: *Hope,* 1885. 55½ x 43¼". Tate Gallery, London.

Lion Square, a residence that served as a manifesto by demonstration of his and the Pre-Raphaelites' theories. Ten years later Burne-Jones began the watercolor replica illustrated here. Nearly thirty years after that he picked it up again and completed it, in 1898, the year of his death, and sent it to Paris, where it was exhibited in the Exposition of 1900. (The background was altered from the cabinet panel, a city scene replacing a landscape.) In her *Memorial* of her husband, Lady Burne-Jones wrote that while he was painting the poppies in the foreground of the picture someone remarked upon the importance of the first lines in a composition. "Yes," said Burne-Jones, "they come straight from the heart. You see how the flowers come at intervals like those in a tune." He sang, pointing to the poppies one after the other, "La, La, La, La." Like other romantics, the Pre-Raphaelites were fond of such analogies between the arts. Architecture was "frozen music" and so on. The American lady who later acquired *The Prioress' Tale* saw Burne-Jones at work on it in his studio shortly before his death, and reported that he had looked as if he "were seeing beyond this earth."

346. BEARDSLEY: "The Mysterious Rose Garden," from *The Yellow Book*, Vol. IV, January 1895.

clustered, there open, with its movement here quickening, there slowing, is nicely adjusted along the major curve running from top to bottom of the long panel.

Among painters not at all connected with the movement some Rossetti influence is apparent for half a century. Even so popular and conventional a man as Lawrence Alma-Tadema (1836–1912) was affected. In *A Reading from Homer* [344] the young lady in the uncomfortable position on the marble bench (Alma-Tadema was famous for his rendition of marble) is at least a cousin to Jane Burden. George Frederick Watts (1817–1904) was an acquaintance of Burne-Jones, and in his familiar *Hope* [345] he draws upon him and through him upon Rossetti. Watts shared the anti-materialist idealism professed by the Pre-Raphaelites and frequently, as in *Hope*, gave it touching expression, although he was an uneven painter who never quite found himself except for a moment in occasional pictures like this one. Toward the end of the century, Aubrey Beardsley (1872–1898) picked up Rossetti's neurotic types and the Pre-Raphaelite arts-and-crafts decor, and incorporated them into the *fin-de-siècle* preciousness [346] that was the most audacious revolt of the English intelligentsia against the now obese smugness of the Victorian age on the point of decline. And even in the twentieth century Stanley Spencer (1891–   ) echoes Rossetti and the fellow founding brothers, Hunt and Millais.

Hunt, Millais, and Ruskin

William Holman Hunt demonstrated how deadly the Pre-Raphaelite formula could become in the hands of a flatly commonplace intelligence; John Everett Millais showed for a while that it might have risen above itself, then he abandoned Pre-Raphaelitism to settle for a resounding academic success; the writer and critic John Ruskin (1819–1900) was the public defender of the Pre-Raphaelite cause.

Ruskin was only a little older than the Pre-Raphaelites—about ten years—but when he appeared as their champion he had al-

Although much of his work is nearly as dated as these mawkish aestheticisms, Burne-Jones saves himself again and again for anyone willing to look at his pictures without taking the current stand that all Pre-Raphaelite painting is ludicrous *per se*. Having been introduced to Botticelli's art by Rossetti, Burne-Jones went on to add such formidable and hard-bitten masters as Signorelli and Mantegna to those he studied. He studied them intelligently and profitably. In *The Golden Stairs* [583] he constructed a picture with more decision, variety, and subtlety than Rossetti ever commanded. The rhythmic grouping, here

ready established himself as a critic. At sixteen he had discovered Turner, understanding the aspects of Turner's art that were not apparent to conventional critics or, when apparent, were puzzling or offensive to academic taste. Five years before the founding of the Pre-Raphaelite Brotherhood, Ruskin had published the first volume of his *Modern Painters*, a many-volumed series that began as an interpretation and defense of Turner. In celebration of the event (Ruskin was twenty-four years old) his father bought *The Slave Ship* for him. Turner died just as the Pre-Raphaelite movement was getting under way.

Ruskin loved medieval and early Renaissance Italy as passionately as the Pre-Raphaelites did. Unlike them, he recognized the dangers of medievalism, prophesying that if the painters' interest in the early artists led them into imitation of the past they would "come to nothing." His advice to painters to "Go to nature, rejecting nothing, selecting nothing, and scorning nothing," was misinterpreted as meaning that the painter should become as nearly as possible a sharp-focus photographer. Actually, Ruskin had offered this advice to beginners only; otherwise it is obviously altogether opposed to his understanding of Turner, and he certainly understood that the selection of detail in early Italian painting was more important than the imitation of nature. But Hunt, especially, "rejected nothing, selected nothing, and scorned nothing" in his moralistic charades.

He based his art on the idea that a *tableau-vivant* should be set up and then reproduced with excruciating complication. Added to his sententious, sentimental moralizing, this idea produced pictures like *The Awakening Conscience* [347], where a kept woman is shown rising from her paramour's lap as she experiences a sudden moral revelation. The sinful pair have been singing at the piano. Hunt even had a specific song in mind, Thomas Moore's "The Light of Other Days," and explained that "the woman is recalling the memory of her childish home, and breaking away from the gilded cage with a startled holy resolve, while her shallow companion sings on, ignorantly intensifying her repentant

347. HUNT: *The Awakening Conscience*, 1855. 29¾ x 21⅝". Collection Sir Colin Anderson, London.

purpose." As an added fillip he designed a frame to go with the picture, decorating it with marigolds, the symbol of sorrow, and ringing bells, the symbol of warning. To choose this particular picture as an example of Hunt's work, offering as it does every opportunity for a field day at his expense, would be unfair except that the picture is one of Hunt's typical productions in its meticulous muddle of pictorial detail and philosophical absurdity. By a cruel reversal, it has become an extreme example of exactly the kind of painting the Pre-Raphaelites objected to, in its artificiality and its unimaginative presentation of a narrative subject. But if it does nothing else it reveals by contrast the imaginative intensity of Rossetti and the discretion of Millais.

Millais also followed the doctrine of acutely imitative detail, but more thought-

348. MILLAIS: *Christ in the House of His Parents* (*The Carpenter's Shop*), 1850. 33½ x 54". Tate Gallery, London.

fully than Hunt. It is true that in Millais's *Christ in the House of His Parents* [348] there are too many shavings on the floor, too many sheep in the pen, too many folds in the garments, too many nicks and cracks in the table, too many microscopically executed incidentals everywhere distracting from the main point. Probably this is because the main point was foreign to the experience of the painter in the nineteenth century. The picture shows the child Christ prophetically wounded in the hands, but the nominally mystical subject becomes not much more than another piece of story-telling in a picturesque genre setting. The void left by the absence of mystical conviction must be filled with little things like shavings. But Millais has compensated as far as he can by an expert unification of the picture space into areas broad and simple enough to hold all these incidental accessories within compositional bounds, and he has tinted these areas in rich decorative colors (whereas Hunt's colors are merely bright.) The picture is admirable in every way except the way that is most important. It is too easy to see in each of the figures a model posed in the studio,

impossible to feel that any of them is a participant in a mystical event. The extreme naturalism was consciously adopted in an effort to represent the scene without the sentimental trumpery of the day, a sound idea which, if backed up by unquestioning faith rather than by the self-consciousness of an adopted theory, might have given the picture the force and conviction it lacks. But as the picture stands, it reveals Millais for what he was, a prodigious technician applying his skill to a subject foreign to his emotional experience. The literalness that is now bothersome because it serves no expressive end offended the public of the time because it seemed irreverent, and the picture's subtitle, *The Carpenter's Shop*, was given it in derision.

But technical skill at Millais's level could not fail to appeal to a public who regarded a painter first of all as a performer. And his own background of prosperous respectability and his temperamental affinity for graceful society made him an outlander in the Pre-Raphaelite camp. Millais was by nature neither a bohemian nor a dissenter; popular success was inevitable for him, and he not only achieved it but finally became

349. MILLAIS: *Mr. James Wyatt and His Granddaughter Mary,* 1849. Panel, 13⅞ x 17¾".
Private collection, England.

president of the Royal Academy. His defection was a mortal blow to the Brotherhood. Popular success was badly out of key with their dedication to revolt against the times; it violated the fundamental concept of the Pre-Raphaelite as a being isolated from the vulgarities of the contemporary world. Just as the French romantics established the bohemian concept of the artist still current in Paris—the starveling genius in a left-bank studio, leading a life half gay and half tragic—so the Pre-Raphaelites initiated the tradition in Bloomsbury and Soho, where the artist may defy convention as a matter of principle, or of convenience, or of habit.

As his success increased, Millais's work became increasingly shallow, but when he is at his best Millais is the most satisfying of the Pre-Raphaelites because he is the least pretentious. Occasionally he fulfills cleanly and brilliantly his full potential as

a superb technician and an agreeable if not profound artist. The delight of a picture like his double portrait of *Mr. James Wyatt and His Granddaughter Mary* [349] is its completeness and its consistency within its limiting boundaries. Without straining to give more than he has to offer, Millais records sympathetically the appearance of two people in their habitat. Since each of the multitude of objects represented in the picture is meaningful through its association with the sitters, the mass of detail is pleasurable to explore, in contrast with the cluttered paraphernalia of *Awakening Conscience* or the neatly arranged stage props and costumes of *Christ in the House of His Parents.* This is a comparison in one direction. In another, for instance with another family portrait, Degas's *Bellelli Family* [219], *James Wyatt and His Granddaughter Mary* does not come off so well. But such a comparison might not be quite fair,

350. FRITH: *Derby Day*, 1856–58. 40 x 88″. Tate Gallery, London.

351. FRITH: Detail from Figure 350.

either to Millais or to ourselves. Painting offers many different kinds of pleasure, and it would be wearing if all painters were giants. In the constant shifting of critical reappraisals there is even a tendency just now to rediscover certain virtues among the popular painters against whom the Pre-Raphaelites rebelled.

The most celebrated of these men was William Powell Frith (1819–1909), whose influence on Millais was strong enough to have accounted in large part for his fall from Pre-Raphaelite grace. The nature of Frith's subject matter is revealed by a random list of a few of his picture titles: *A Village Pastor; The Railway Station; Boswell's Dinner Party; The Wedding of the Prince of Wales*, which was a command picture for the Queen; *English Merrymaking One Hundred Years Ago; Life at the Sea Side; Breakfast Time; New Ear Rings;* and above all *Derby Day* [350, 351], for which Frith received about $75,000 for the engraving rights alone. His pictures were so admired that on exhibition they had to be protected from the crowds by special railings.

Rossetti and his loyal followers admitted Frith's technical prowess, but they loathed him for his "low and common" subjects. He held the Pre-Raphaelites equally in con-

352. FRITH: *Private View at the Royal Academy, 1881.* 40½ x 77″. Private collection, England.

tempt for their idealistic and hyperaesthetic ones. Frith painted the *Private View at the Royal Academy, 1881* [352] to satirize "aesthetic" fashions in dress, he said, and the "folly of listening to self-elected critics in matters of taste." On the left is "a family of pure aesthetes absorbed in affected study of the pictures." Near them "in homely contrast" stands Anthony Trollope. To the right is Oscar Wilde, "a well-known apostle of the beautiful, with a herd of eager worshipers surrounding him." Other characters appearing in the picture include Gladstone, Browning, Huxley, Du Maurier, Ellen Terry, Lily Langtry, and Frith himself.

Whatever his limitation as an aesthetician may have been, Frith did paint with zest. *Derby Day* has a natural liveliness in its exploration of a commonplace subject, a quality always admired in the art of the impressionists to which it is unfavorably compared. But of course it has no suggestion of the subtlety, the originality, and the interpretative overtones of Degas's comparable subject, *A Carriage at the Races* [224].

Frith received all academic honors as well as general acclaim. He was the English parallel (as a painter, not as a personality—for he was a genial man) of the Frenchmen Meissonier (who was five years older) and

Gérôme (who was five years younger). Frith, Meissonier, and Gérôme were only three of the tremendous number of painters who, like Waldmüller, satisfied the international taste for explicitly narrated anecdote. The Frenchmen, as we have seen, were likely to bolster up their literalness with a veneer of historical reference, as in Meissonier's *1814* [163], or some other pseudo-cultural eyewash, as in Gérôme's *Pygmalion* [172]. Sir Edwin Landseer [159, 160] was also one of the gods of living English painters at this time, and if we add to the list a few of the other medal winners of the 1855 Exhibition (pp. 142–154) we have a picture of the general ambience, at its highest level, in which the Pre-Raphaelites painted.

Impressionism in England: Whistler and Others

The Pre-Raphaelite movement was well under way when the *Salon des Refusés* took place in 1863. One of the most detested pictures in that exhibition was *The White Girl* [353], by a young American, James Abbott McNeill Whistler (1834–1903), who, having been dismissed from

353. WHISTLER: *The White Girl,* 1862. 85½ x 43".
National Gallery of Art, Washington, D.C.

Without adopting Pre-Raphaelitism he became a fixture in the Pre-Raphaelite aesthetic circle and that of the younger men, like Oscar Wilde, who carried Pre-Raphaelite aestheticism on into the 1890's with even more precious and immensely more sophisticated variations. He knew the poet Swinburne and the novelist and critic George Moore. He became a great dandy and a famous wit, a bright figure among the creative talents and their admiring circle who continued the Pre-Raphaelite revolt against the materialism and stuffiness of the Victorian age.

As an impressionist, Whistler never adopted the broken strokes and the sunlit effects developed by his former French associates. He worked instead more and more in a muted palette of grays and blacks, softly blended, painting the misty tonalities of evening or gray days, sometimes flecked or splashed with red or golden lights, with strong reference to Japanese prints or Oriental ink-wash drawings with their simplification and their subtle, colorless gradations. Ruskin, who had understood Turner's art when he was a young man, was unable to accept Whistler's now that he was an aging professor. He was so infuriated by Whistler's *Falling Rocket, Nocturne in Black and Gold,* a picture which might have delighted Turner, that he wrote, "I have seen, and heard, much of cockney impudence before now; but never expected to hear a coxcomb ask two hundred guineas for flinging a pot of paint in the public's face." Whistler sued Ruskin for libel, as much for the sport of it as for any other reason, and after a well-publicized trial was awarded damages of one farthing. Poor Ruskin suffered a mental breakdown the following year (1878) and for the remaining miserable twenty-two years of his life was removed from the critical scene while Whistler continued to send up his rockets.

Because he wrote well and because he talked so wittily that his bon mots were repeated everywhere, Whistler had great influence among intellectuals and cultivated amateurs. His central idea was that of art for art's sake—the belief that abstract values in painting, such as form and color, should exist for themselves, not as accessories to

West Point (he failed chemistry), had come to Paris to study under Gleyre. In Paris he knew Courbet, Manet, Monet, Degas, and Fantin-Latour. *The White Girl,* which he preferred to call *Symphony in White No. 1,* is one of the fine pictures of nascent impressionism, and there is no good explanation as to why Whistler at this point abandoned Paris to continue his career in England. Certainly it was not because he was wounded by the reception of *The White Girl* or because he feared a good fight. For the rest of his life he was one of the liveliest scrappers in the London arena.

the imitation of nature or, especially, to storytelling. He called his pictures "symphonies," "arrangements," "harmonies," or "nocturnes" in an effort to induce the public to see a painting as a painting, not as a picture of something. The picture still popularly called *Whistler's Mother* he insisted on calling *Arrangement in Gray and Black* [354] because "that is what it is. To me it is interesting as a picture of my mother; but what can or ought the public to care about the identity of the portrait? The imitator is a poor kind of creature. If the man who paints only the tree, or flower, or other surface he sees before him were an artist, the king of artists would be the photographer." If this idea sounds elementary today, one reason is that Whistler helped to establish it as a basic tenet in modern art. His rejection of imitative effects allies him more closely with modern abstract painters than with the impressionists. In the meanwhile, the public continued to respond to nonabstract sentimental anecdotes. *The Doctor* [355] is a standard example.

Unhappily, Whistler's own painting falls a little flat in the light of his theories. It seldom goes far beyond the level of tasteful arrangements of objects that remain semi-photographically represented, even though they may be in a focus so soft that they virtually disappear. The exquisiteness and daintiness of Japanese screen painting rather than the force of the finest Japanese prints influenced him in pictures like the portrait of *Miss Cicely Alexander* [356]. To the fragile charm of the picture there can, of course, be no objection. The disappointment is only that Whistler's pictures never have the importance that a more thorough-going application of his theories could have given them. He paints more like a tactful follower of someone else's theories than an adventurous creative artist in his own right.

This is true also of his etchings, although he brought a new sensitivity to the medium. Beginning conventionally—which at that time meant beginning with the attitude that an etching is not much more than a drawing done on a copper plate in such a way that it can be printed many times over—Whistler eventually developed a manner dependent upon the treatment of the

354. WHISTLER: *Arrangement in Gray and Black* (*"Whistler Mother"*), 1871. 55½ x 63⅜". Louvre, Paris. On loan to Metropolitan Museum of Art, New York.

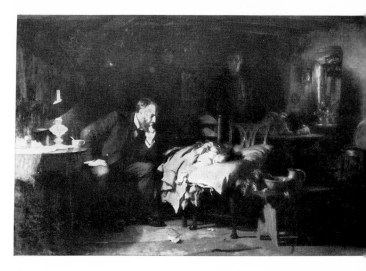

355. SIR LUKE FILDES: *The Doctor*, 1891. 64¾ x 96". Tate Gallery London.

plate itself. With a few lines indicating the subject, he would wipe the plate elaborately to produce infinitely subtle tonalities and gradations. Since the plate had to be inked and wiped for each impression, each impression was, in effect, an original work.

356. WHISTLER: *Miss Cicely Alexander, c.* 1873.
74¾ x 38½". National Gallery, London.

Yet this is, from one point of view, a distortion of the medium, and the etchings
suffer also from the exaggerated delicacy
that makes Whistler's work seem so disap-
pointingly thin and slight. He was a great
battler against philistinism, but at the same
time he gave support to the philistine's conception of the artist as a rather weak and
undependable fellow who may be very sensitive and all that, but is not likely to be
very sound.

Whistler's personality supported the
same idea. In public he cultivated affectations of dress and manner, and in private
he was a difficult man, demanding a wor-
shipfulness from his friends and students
that they finally tired of giving. One of
these was Walter Richard Sickert (1860–
1942), who studied under Whistler until
the inevitable rupture and was then self-
taught. After a while virtually nothing of
Whistler remained in Sickert's work. He
became a solid, downright painter, as English as boiled mutton. He borrowed heavily
from Degas for subject matter and composition, yet retained his earthiness in contrast to Degas's civilized mastery. It was
not through Whistler, but through Sickert,
a quarter of a century after it had shaken
France, that impressionism was imported
to England and given a national flavor.

Sickert founded an association of painters called the Camden Town Group, in
1911, to "advance" British painting, but the
group was neither impressionist nor, in
1911, very advanced. A partial explanation
for England's indifference to impressionism
may be that so many of impressionism's
most attractive elements had been anticipated, in different form, by Constable. Also,
impressionist effects of light seemed pallid
after Turner's blazing canvases; for that
matter, English watercolor supplied the
fresh tonalities offered in oil by impressionism. These factors were sufficient to
take the edge off the excitement of impressionist innovations. And as for portraiture,
the British tradition was not only inviolable
but it, too, offered enough of the light touch
of Renoir (through Gainsborough and his
tradition) and even the breadth of Manet
(through Reynolds and his) to make investigation of what the Frenchmen were
doing seem a little pointless.

Sir William Orpen (1878–1931), who
painted within the English tradition, was
one of several men who modified it in the
direction of French impressionism. His
Homage to Manet [357] shows a group of
English painters and literati seated beneath
Manet's portrait of Eva Gonzales, which
was at that time in the possession of one of
them, Sir Hugh Lane, seated at the extreme
right. George Moore, who keeps popping
up on both sides of the channel and whose
portrait by Manet has been seen [201], is

seated at the table, reading. Sickert is one of the standing men, and the isolated seated figure at the table is Wilson Steer (1860–1942), who takes second place to Sickert as England's leading impressionist. All this was in 1909. Homage to Manet, by that time, was coming to be homage to an old master. Impressionism in England was a tardy and not very radical departure from traditional painting, a rather tepid compromise reached in the twentieth century long after the excitement had died down.

Germany: Feuerbach and Böcklin

In Germany after 1850, academic classicism reached the end of its road in the work of Anselm von Feuerbach, while German romanticism put forth its most flagrant bloom with Arnold Böcklin. Both men were immediate contemporaries of the founding brothers of the Pre-Raphaelites; the birth dates of Rossetti, Hunt, Millais, Feuerbach, and Böcklin are crowded into the same three years, 1827, 1828, 1829, which means that all of them were beginning their careers as the century made the turn into its second half.

Feuerbach (1829–1880) is a kind of German Ingres, struggling against the current to perpetuate the academic classical tradition. He studied at the Düsseldorf and Munich academies that paralleled the *École des Beaux Arts;* he also studied in Paris under Couture, Manet's teacher. Like Ingres and then Couture, he persisted in his allegiance to the classical subject with derivations from the Italian Renaissance. He had something of Ingres's feeling for line and much of the formal solidity and tonal harmony of Couture at his best. He was a sensitive and austere artist when he was not smothering his personal genius under excessive conformity to tired formulas. He was not altogether a success, being overshadowed by Böcklin's effulgent romanticism as well as by newer developments in vigorous realism that were fermenting at the same time in Germany, in line with Courbet's realism in France. Nor is he much remembered outside Germany today, in spite of such achievements as the portrait

357. ORPEN: *Homage to Manet,* 1909. 65 x 51″. Manchester City Art Gallery, England.

Nanna [358], with its impressive reserve and beautiful pattern, or *Orpheus and Eurydice* [359].

The latter picture especially shows why Feuerbach's reputation has grown steadily in Germany, until today he is one of the most revered of German nineteenth-century masters, while at the same time his influence on German painting has been negligible. The sensitivity and restraint of *Orpheus and Eurydice,* the elegance and clarity and control imposed upon a subject of intensely emotional nature, are foreign to the Germanic tradition of passionate or mysterious statement. Feuerbach was a truly classical artist. As such he is isolated within the Germanic tradition, which has combined such disparate ideals as passionate emotionalism and literal realism but has never absorbed much of the classical ideal that demands

358. FEUERBACH: *Nanna*, 1861. 46¾ x 38¼". *Landeskunstsammlungen*, Stuttgart.

359. FEUERBACH: *Orpheus and Eurydice*, 1869. 76¾ x 48¾". *Kunsthistorische Museum*, Vienna.

the transmutation of passion and reality into images of abstract and logical beauty. German aestheticians helped formulate that ideal but as Germany's great creative painters they have never followed it. Artistically, Feuerbach remains a foreigner, although a respected one, in his own country. Spiritually he is closest to the long classical traditions of Italy and France, but in those countries he is overshadowed because he neither initiated a school nor made a sufficiently conspicuous contribution to the one he followed. He is a painter of exceptional quality who seems destined to perpetual obscurity because his painting never followed an exceptional direction.

Feuerbach's romantic contemporary, Böcklin (1827–1901), on the other hand, was a great success. Generally regarded as a master during his own lifetime, he was

virulently attacked by critics at the beginning of the twentieth century, to such an extent that his merits, which exist, were obscured by his shortcomings, which are disastrous. It takes much patience and tolerance not to pass by some of Böcklin's most serious work as gross, obvious, or even laughable. But the pendulum has swung faster for Böcklin than for most painters, and recently he has become an interesting painter historically, since critics have recognized his influence on contemporary fantastic painting, notably surrealism, which we will see in good time. Just now, Böcklin's work must be regarded with a kind of double vision. Most of it looks trite, pretentious, ludicrously ponderous in its effort to create a world of fantasy in concrete terms. But that effort is important. The only way to approach Böcklin today is to clear

360. BÖCKLIN: *Spring, c.* 1870. 28¼ x 22¾″. *Schackgalerie*, Munich.

361. BÖCKLIN: *Sappho*, before 1890. 37¼ x 29″. Philadelphia Museum of Art, John G. Johnson Collection.

the field by admitting first how "bad" his pictures are, in order to reach a more sympathetic understanding of how "good" they almost are.

Böcklin's work divides easily into a few categories. First, there are his sentimental classical landscapes filled with ideal allegorical figures. These are seldom worse than innocuous, and seldom better than that. One of the standard examples is *Spring* [360], a picture that suffers from having too much of a perfectly good thing, a redundance of obvious symbols—maidens, young lovers, gamboling cupids, budding trees, blossoming sward, fluffy clouds. It is typical of Böcklin to belabor his point. In *Spring* he is like a guide who takes us by the hand and insists on explaining each detail of a subject with which we are already too familiar. Except that it is obvious and insistent, *Spring* is a respectably composed picture, with passages ranging from poetic subtlety (as in the hill covered with mingled foliage and architecture) to the most hackneyed symbolism. Böcklin wanted to capture the innocence of vision that was Runge's primary concern; this is one of several factors in his art allying him directly with the traditions of early German romanticism. Innocence of this kind escapes Böcklin (although he is naïve, which is not quite the same thing), but in the swarm of pictures he produced in this classical-sentimental-lyrical-romantic manner, an occasional one rings true enough to rebuke us. In *Sappho* [361], for instance, the lyrical mood is more effective for being simpler. *Sappho* is in an almost literal sense a less wordy picture than *Spring*. A single figure gleams magically in the dark of a forest; the expression of private revery is increased because her back is turned toward us; there is no story, no direct allegory, no symbolism already too familiar. The mood created is, in short, created pictorially. Hence *Sappho* is more satisfying

362. BÖCKLIN: *Triton and Nereid*, 1873–74. 40¼ x 75¼". *Bayerische Staatsgemäldesammlungen*, Munich.

than *Spring* with its conducted tour of literary clichés. Pictures in this classification make up the bulk of Böcklin's early work and they continue to appear throughout his life, with variations.

A second group of pictures shows tritons, nereids, mermaids, sirens, nature gods, evil hobgoblins, and other fantastic creatures related to Germanic legends. These appear thick and fast during the 1870's, and of course parallel Wagner's operatic use of the same material at the same time. (Wagner was fourteen years older than Böcklin.) Böcklin intersperses these Nordic creatures with Pans, centaurs, and other classical monsters, using them in the same Germanic spirit of ominous mystery and violence.

Böcklin shared coincidentally with the Pre-Raphaelites the idea that extraordinary subject matter could best be represented in realistic images. This idea is one that cropped up several times during the century. William Blake with his "spirits and visions delineated in stronger lineaments than his perishing and mortal eye could see" was one expression of it. So were Friedrich and Runge with their explicit detail in the service of nostalgic recollection. The Nazarenes and the Pre-Raphaelites "dis-

covered" that religious subject matter had been effectively presented in realistic detail by medieval artists. Böcklin differs from the painters in this list because he was not interested in sharply detailed realism so much as in full-bodied, matter-of-fact presentation of his fantasies, as if they had been set up in the studio and then painted without imaginative variation. When his "magic realism" fails to come off it is for this reason, that his most fantastic subjects seem, in the end, heavyhanded and literal. This is true, at any rate, of the pictures showing nereids, tritons, hobgoblins, and the like. One cannot help wishing sometimes that his playful water creatures would get back into their clothes and return to the beer hall where their roistering properly belongs. And it is too easy to recognize the sea serpent in *Triton and Nereid* [362] as a tube of stuffed cloth, too easy to recognize the nereid herself as a posed model on whose legs some scales have been painted. There is too much realism and too little magic; the theory is good, but the proportions are off.

Finally, there is the third group, Böcklin's dreamlike landscape inventions, like the well-known *Isle of the Dead* [363].

363. Böcklin: *The Isle of the Dead*, 1880. Panel, 29 x 48″. Metropolitan Museum of Art, New York, Reisinger Fund.

These are quite directly the continuation of Friedrich's ruined Gothic choirs, grave-yards, and threatening forests and crags. At twenty, Böcklin was painting in imitation of Friedrich's subjects, if not his technique, in pictures with such titles as *Landscape with Ruined City* and *Forest in the Moonlight*. He soon abandoned such direct references to the early romantics, but fantasies of the general type of *The Isle of the Dead* crop up in his work regularly, then appear frequently in the last two decades of his life.

The three categories of Böcklin's work overlap and intermingle, but in a general way they represent chronological stages of his art—from sentimental-lyrical classicism to subjects from Germanic mythology and monstrous visions to imaginary landscapes at once serene and sinister. And in these landscapes, at last, magic and realism come close to fusion. Rocks, trees, tombs or shrines, sky, water, and lonely figures are combined in theatrical arrangements which, if they fall short of magical transformation, at least take us into a foreign land.

Later German Realism

Chronology is always confusing. (Fortunately it is not always important.) It is particularly so in the nineteenth century because of the time lag between developments in France and corresponding ones elsewhere in Europe, with further lags in America. Feuerbach was the great German academic classicist and Böcklin the culminating romantic, but it is also true that Böcklin was born the same year as Courbet. This means that Courbet's revolt against idealism, either classic or romantic, was also contemporary with the Pre-Raphaelite movement in England. And since one art revolution followed another so rapidly in France, it means further that while Böcklin was painting, the *Salon des Refusés* came and went, the impressionists held their exhibitions and disbanded, and men we have yet to see, such as Cézanne, Seurat, Gauguin and van Gogh, were at work. In fact Seurat and van Gogh died ten years before Böcklin did, Gauguin the same year as he, and Cézanne only five years after.

Realism in one form or another had always been a major element in German painting. Realism in the sense of Courbet's return to the earthiness of nature found a German protagonist in Hans Thoma (1839–1924), a man ten years younger than Courbet and for a while his student. Like Courbet's, Thoma's realism must be qualified by the term "romantic-realism." But he painted so unevenly and in such a variety of manners that a representative collection of his work would look like a group show by several painters of varying talents. He ranged from the fresh literalness of pictures like *Woodland Meadow* [364] through other landscapes concerned with the monumentality of natural forms to such romantically evocative creations as *Recollection of a Town in Umbria* [365]. The unifying factor in his work is the response to nature that took so many forms in the nineteenth century, as, indeed, it took several different ones in his own painting. He differs from earlier German landscapists in

364. THOMA: *Woodland Meadow*, 1876. Panel, 19 x 14½". *Kunsthalle*, Hamburg.

365. THOMA: *Recollection of a Town in Umbria*, date unknown. Cardboard, 20½ x 28". *Neue Staatsgalerie*, Munich.

366. Leibl: *The Poachers*, 1882–86. 21¾ x 16½". *Nationalgalerie*, Berlin.

367. Leibl: *The Poachers*, as it appeared before division into parts.

that his scenes, even at their most imaginative level, carry no burden of metaphysical pondering. It is this difference that finally makes of him a realist as that ambiguous term was used in the opening chapters of this book. It should be mentioned too that Thoma also turned his hand to heroic and religious themes, at which he was uniformly unsuccessful. As a portrait painter, when his sitters are close friends or members of his family he frequently delineates his subjects with a direct and straightforward clarity that can be most engaging.

Courbet's "show me an angel and I will paint one" was turned into an even flatter statement, "I paint only what I see, and only from nature," by Wilhelm Leibl (1844–1900), who observed his dictum to the letter. Like Courbet he chose peasants as subjects; unlike Courbet, he observed realistically without romantic overtones. *The Poachers* [366] shows that Leibl was a strong draughtsman and a vigorous painter. It shows little else except the con-

figuration of the faces of two Bavarian peasants. It is, however, only part of a larger picture [367] that Leibl worked on for four years and then divided into several parts because he was dissatisfied with the composition. Leibl was the true leader of the new realism in Germany; he worked in conscious opposition to Feuerbach's classicism, Böcklin's romanticism, and the art of a third and unclassifiable contemporary, Hans von Marées (1837–1887).

Although he died before 1900, Marées is more closely related to twentieth-century painting than to that of his own century. He was disturbed by the bourgeois realism of Thoma and Leibl, which seemed to him commonplace and transient. Yet he felt also that Feuerbach's traditionalism was threadbare. Without passing through the experience of impressionism, Marées felt something like the same dissatisfactions that were very soon to lead Renoir to abandon impressionism's effects for a new study of form. Marées is even more closely com-

368. DUVENECK: *Georg von Hoesslin* (sketch), 1878–79. 16 x 13¾″. Detroit Institute of Arts.

parable to Cézanne. The two men, born within two years of one another and working away from the same dissatisfactions, were unknown to one another, not only as individuals but as artists. Marées appears farther on in this book [530]; he is mentioned here only to place him in chronological context.

The Americans after 1850

American painters in the second half of the century continued to look to Europe for their technical standards and, if possible, to go there to study. But now, thoroughly decolonialized, they went more often to Paris than to London; they went also to the several academies in Germany, especially the one at Munich. Some of them, like Whistler and Mary Cassatt, became expa-

triates; others came home to continue the cultivation of European academic traditions. America's art schools were modeled as closely as possible after those in Europe, with the result that the United States produced quantities of well-trained painters among its talented men, and the provincialism that characterized so much American painting of the first half of the century disappeared, except that new movements, like impressionism, were a generation late in taking root.

Some typical painters of the latter part of the century have already been mentioned in the introductory remarks to Chapter 8. It is not necessary to catalogue these excellent men here; we will see instead those American painters whose work for one reason or another has a specifically American flavor. Three of the Europeanized Americans who were most influential at home may stand for dozens of their fellows and students: Duveneck, who worked in the middle west, Chase, who worked in the east, and Sargent who worked on both sides of the Atlantic.

Frank Duveneck (1848–1919), a Kentuckian by birth, went to Munich when he was twenty-two and came under the influence of Leibl. After a dazzling student career he divided his time between Cincinnati and Munich, with schools in both places that produced a whole Duveneck group. He was a dashing brushman and could strike in a head or a figure with impressive style and assurance [368]. The general tonality of the Munich school was very dark; Duveneck's hallmark was a combination of somber color with slashing, vibrant manipulation of paint. When he is at his best the combination is extraordinarily effective. But he was so facile a painter that his brush often ran away with him in superficial display. Unfortunately, most of his students imitated his facility but missed the depth and power that still make Duveneck's best pictures stand out in the galleries of such American museums as have continued to keep them on exhibition in spite of his eclipse.

William Merritt Chase (1849–1916) was born in Indiana and studied in Munich where he knew Duveneck. His early work

has the same dark Munich tonality as Duveneck's, but he was more investigative
than his friend and brightened his work
under the influence of Velásquez and Hals.
These were painters who also influenced
Manet, whose work Chase's often resembles, in a cautious way. Chase painted with
less flair than either Duveneck or Manet,
and, of course, when he seems to follow
Manet's tradition he does so not as a revolutionary but as an intelligent and gifted
painter working after the revolution was
won and its innovations accepted.

John Singer Sargent (1856–1925) was
the most consummate virtuoso America
produced, but in the final balance he became less an American than an international portrait painter with his headquarters
in London and branch offices in Boston and
New York. He studied in Paris under Caro-
lus Duran, one of the soundest of the academic professors. To the ultimate degree
Sargent had the English society portrait
painter's knack for catching a likeness while
at the same time flattering his sitter. Anyone who posed for Sargent could be certain
in advance that in the completed picture
he would be perfectly recognizable yet
transformed into an aristocrat no matter
who he really was. It is true that Sargent
painted some of the shallowest portraits of
an era that was rich in them. He knew that
he was often the victim of his own facility,
and he often appears to fling his paint onto
the canvas almost contemptuously. But his
work is too easily damned. If all his commercial showpieces could be done away
with, a large number of pictures would still
remain where his facility is put into the
service of perception [369]. And in his
watercolors and drawings even those critics
who habitually reject his portraits are willing to accept his technical brilliance as an
end in itself. In addition, the watercolors
are, of all Sargent's work, most likely to be
more than technical displays. When he
grew sick of portrait painting for fashionable customers he would escape for a few
days into watercolor painting for himself,
recording his response to informal subject
matter in pictures that are as appealing in
their intimacy as they are fascinating in
their virtuosity [370].

369. SARGENT: *Mrs. Charles Gifford Dyer*, 1880. 24½ x 17¼". Art
Institute of Chicago, Friends of American Art Collection.

370. SARGENT: *Simplon Pass: The Lesson*, 1911. Watercolor, 15 x
18¼". Museum of Fine Arts, Boston.

371. HOMER: *Gloucester Farm*, 1874. 20¾ x 30⅛". Philadelphia Museum of Art, Mc-Fadden Collection.

America: Homer and the End of an Epoch

The two painters who emerge as the ones most closely integrated with the American scene, painting it in an American spirit in the second half of the century, are Winslow Homer and Thomas Eakins. Contemporaries of the French impressionists, both men were realists of the highest order. They shared with the impressionists a preoccupation with country scenes or bourgeois life, but instead of training their own sensitivities to accord with a European vision, they remained Americans who explored their own country and, more important, the character of their fellow Americans. The fact that Homer and Eakins painted American people engaged in typically American activities is relatively unimportant. What is important is that they explored beneath American surfaces to discover and express the psychological nuances that differentiated America from Europe. Bingham had done this also, but with subject matter so picturesquely and uniquely American that

less subtle perceptions were involved. To some extent Homer capitalizes on subject matter comparable to Bingham's, but Eakins painted an American world from which the frontier had vanished. Although Homer was only eight years older than Eakins, he is something of a transition between Bingham, the painter of American frontiers, and Eakins, the painter of a matured nation.

Winslow Homer (1836–1910) made only a moderate success in the picture market; the big prices during his long life went to more conventional work than his. Yet today it takes a moment to see where his unconventionality lay. It lay in the same quarter as that of the early impressionists'. Homer's first important pictures, notably *Gloucester Farm* [371], have the same interest in natural outdoor light, represented with much the same sparkle and economy, as Monet's early work (for instance, *The Terrace at Le Havre* [208]) or Boudin's. But the resemblance is coincidental; there is no real probability that Homer knew the work of either of these two men at that time.

Gloucester Farm has the formal dignity and, to a surpassing degree, the clarity of the group of pictures to which it belongs: Homer's scenes of rural life in New York and New England painted from around 1867 on into the first years of the 1880's. As genre pictures, these intimate masterpieces had sufficient attractions to make them saleable in the lower price brackets, but as "serious" paintings they were thought to lack polish, just as the impressionists were thought "crude" at the same time in France. It is, of course, precisely their lack of polish—or what was thought of as polish—that lifts pictures like *Gloucester Farm* from the rank and file of nineteenth-century genre painting, that makes them not only pictures of great pastoral charm but masterly formal compositions as well. It is apparent enough, now, that Homer has eliminated all finicky detail to create a pattern of formal masses revealed in consistent light, that he has chosen the most ordinary genre elements but has simplified them and disposed them in harmonious balance, that no touch of the brush is careless, that each stroke is as thoughtfully considered and as carefully applied as in any painting of a conventionally polished kind. But this control was not apparent to a public habituated to the enjoyment of illusionistic details in a multitude of incidental objects factually described.

While his pictures sold at low prices, Homer continued to make ends meet by commercial work, such as book and magazine illustration. His earliest work was entirely of this nature; he had covered the Civil War as a pictorial reporter for *Harper's Weekly*, and his first oil painting, *Prisoners from the Front* [372], records the experience. *Prisoners from the Front* is a surprisingly satisfactory painting in these circumstances, but in comparison with the pictures that now began to follow it, like *Gloucester Farm*, it is still pictorial journalism.

Homer went to England in 1881 and stayed there during 1882 as well, working in watercolor and developing along the tight and rather dry manner that was popular with English watercolorists just then. Upon his return he abandoned his rural

372. HOMER: *Prisoners from the Front*, 1866. 24 x 38". Metropolitan Museum of Art, New York, Gift of Mrs. Frank B. Porter.

373. HOMER: *The Life Line*, 1884. 28¾ x 41⅝". Philadelphia Museum of Art, George W. Elkins Collection.

pastorals, settling in Prout's Neck, Maine, and shifting his attention to the life of fishermen on the Grand Banks, which he described in a series of etchings and oils. The gentle slopes and quiet barns and peaceful country people of *Gloucester Farm* were replaced by more dramatic elements, such as raging seas, rocky shores, and the strong men and women who struggled against them. Subjects like *The Life Line* [373], one of several pictures showing wrecks or rescues at sea, had enough narrative appeal to increase Homer's popu-

374. HOMER: *The Hunter*, 1891. 28¼ x 48″. Philadelphia Museum of Art, W. L. Elkins Collection.

larity. He adapted his early, gentler style to a vigorously masculine one where the violence of nature, and man's hazardous life in contact with it, are expressed in a technique as harmonious to the subject as his earlier manner was harmonious to the

375. HOMER: *Ship Unfurling Sails*, date unknown. Watercolor, 10¾ x 14½″. Philadelphia Museum of Art, Gift of Dr. and Mrs. George Woodward.

scenes of farm life. But Homer was still at his best when anecdotal elements were least conspicuous, as in *The Hunter* [374], where the relationship of man to nature is a philosophical subject rather than a narrative one. It is symbolical enough—although, of course, Homer never intended it to be— that the figure in *The Hunter* dominates the horizon, while in the wilderness of the Hudson River painters man was a tiny figure infiltrating a natural vastness. The frontiers are conquered; the giant trees of the Hudson River landscapes are felled, and *The Hunter* places his foot on this one almost as if it were a fallen enemy. He is no longer an intruder in a benign wilderness, but its benevolent conqueror.

In the Maine pictures, Homer is the last of the Americans to paint in immediate contact with the raw life of a new country.[*] And in his own very late work he grew further and further away from his preoccupation with the solemnities and the powerful forces of nature. He made frequent

---

[*] At least, he is the last to treat this life as more than a pure genre record. Painters like Frederick Remington (1861–1909), with his cowboy pictures, continued to illustrate locally picturesque aspects of American life, often with great liveliness.

trips to the West Indies, and eventually the shining palms, the glittering clear water, the sun-drenched sails of these islands, asserted themselves over the dour coasts and the sturdy folk of the north. To paint them, Homer freed himself from the conventional niceties of his early watercolor style to work in broad, fluid areas of scintillating transparency [375], suggesting in a few essential notes the choppy surface of a bay, the degree of tension in a sail receiving the wind or hanging limp or furled, the lay of a boat in the water, the stance of a boatman, and always the pure brilliance of sun in clear air—all of these captured in a momentary aspect, as if set down in a fraction of a second. Thus, having begun, in pictures like *Gloucester Farm*, as an independent parallel to the earliest developments in French impressionism, Homer produced at the end of his career some of the purest impressionistic work of his time.

America: Thomas Eakins

Thomas Eakins (1844–1916) may well be the greatest American painter. He is certainly one of the finest painters of his century, Americanism aside.

Eakins went to Paris at twenty-two to study under, of all people, Gérôme, at the *École des Beaux Arts*. (He also studied with Bonnat there.) This was in 1866. The *Salon des Refusés* had taken place only three years before, and *Olympia* had been exhibited only the year before Eakins's arrival. Manet's art was the scandal of Paris, but nothing Eakins ever painted shows that he was affected by the twin explosions of *Le Déjeuner sur l'Herbe* and *Olympia*. It is not difficult to understand why this particular young painter was indifferent to Manet's art although he was intelligent, questioning, and thoughtful:

Eakins's passion was anatomy. For him, the human body was the most beautiful thing in the world—not the body as an object of desire, or as a set of proportions, but as a construction of bone and muscle. He had already spent two years studying anatomy by dissection at the Jefferson Medical College in Philadelphia "to in-

376. EAKINS: *Masked Seated Nude, c.* 1866. Charcoal on paper, 24 x 18″. Philadelphia Museum of Art, Gift of Mrs. Thomas Eakins and Miss Marcy A. Williams.

crease his knowledge of how beautiful objects are put together" to the end that he might "be able to imitate them." Manet's experiments with the technique of capturing the quality of instant vision could be of no interest to Eakins, who found the human body beautiful because its structure and its movements were "means and end reciprocally adapted to each other." Manet's broad planes of light sacrificed the complete statement of a structure that Eakins found glorious. He was not interested in the quality of instant vision, but in a total reality where every part of the body served and depended upon every other one. This did not mean the imitation of every hair on the head, every pore in the skin, or for that matter even every small muscle, but

377. EAKINS: *Salutat*, 1898. 50 x 40″. Addison Gallery of American Art, Andover, Mass.

tential. The body in *Masked Seated Nude* is alive; every bone and muscle is performing its required function in maintaining the body in the position it has assumed. Eakins never drew a living model as if it were a corpse, a statue, or a pattern of light and shade falling on an inert object. Because he studied anatomy in a medical school and analyzed the body so carefully, he is sometimes called a scientific realist, and even he called himself one. But of course he was not. His scientific knowledge of anatomy was a means to the end of expression, just as the structure of the body itself is a means to the end of movement.

But he was scientist enough to have no use for the formulas of ideal beauty, either romantic or classical. Idealization seemed to him pointless in the face of a reality so beautiful. In any case, he found that idealization—to which he held no objection when it was an "understood" idealization—was seldom based on "a thorough understanding of what is idealized." Without this understanding, idealization was merely "distortion, and distortions are ugliness." The classic and romantic idealizations current in Paris seemed to him nothing more than such distortions. He saw no point in copying casts, even those from the sculpture of the best Greek period, because nature itself was at hand for study. He worshiped the Parthenon figures, but these figures were "undoubtedly modeled from life," he thought, and he saw no reason to refer to them for models when nature was "just as varied and just as beautiful in our day as she was in the time of Phidias." "The Greeks did not study the antique." Why paint gladiators in ancient Rome when there was a boxing club around the corner? When he returned to his native Philadelphia he became the first painter to find subjects in the world of sport. The young boxer in *Salutat* [377] with his lean, hard legs, his powerfully bunched shoulders, his long arms, is built for his profession and will do better in the ring than one of David's idealized warriors could do. His body is beautiful not because its abstract proportions are harmonious—they are not, particularly—or because it can be defined by lines abstractly beautiful in themselves, like

it did mean an expression of every part of the body as a working part of a perfectly integrated structure. His academic drawing, *Masked Seated Nude* [376], introduces no muscles not actually visible beneath the model's fleshy padding, and may even omit a few that were, but its extraordinary reality comes from Eakins's knowledge of the structural function of each concealed bone, the disposition of each tensed or relaxed muscle upon the skeletal framework in any specific attitude. It is a body one can imagine shifting itself into another position. Nominally, the pose is static; actually, structure and movement were so identified in Eakins's conception of the body that movement is present even in a quiet body, if by nothing more than an immediate po-

378. EAKINS: *Musicians Rehearsing, c.* 1883. 16 x 12″. Philadelphia Museum of Art, John D. McIlhenny Bequest.

379. EAKINS: *Mrs. William D. Frishmuth,* 1900. 97 x 72½″. Philadelphia Museum of Art, Gift of Mrs. Thomas Eakins and Miss Marcy A. Williams.

those of Ingres's nudes. It is beautiful because it is a normal human body, an example of that miraculously self-contained mobile structure in good condition. In Paris, Eakins had found that he learned more by watching his fellow students when they stripped and wrestled in the studio than he did by drawing from posed models.

But of course the miracle of the human body is only a part of the miracle of a human being. Eakins's statements about his fidelity to the imitation of nature seem to deny the other part of the miracle, which is human consciousness, yet in the long run that is what Eakins is most concerned with; otherwise he might better have spent his time painting animals, whose bodies are equally miraculous as self-contained mobile structures, and even more various and dramatic than human ones. Music was a large part of Eakins's life, particularly music as

an intimate communion between friends, and the man who painted *Musicians Rehearsing* [378] was not a scientific anatomist but a man who was sensitive to the ultimate mystery in human life for which words like *soul* and *spirit* have been coined. In this picture Eakins is akin to another realist, the Daumier who painted *The Print Collector* [111]. In its subjectivity, *Musicians Rehearsing* is at one pole of Eakins's work, with the objectivity of *Salutat* at the opposite one. Most of his pictures lie in the intermediate area where imitation of visible realities and revelation of inner ones are balanced in a way uniquely his own.

In this area dozens of portraits could be cited. The one of *Mrs. William D. Frishmuth* [379], a collector of musical instruments who is shown seated among them, would be hard to surpass, either as an example of Eakins at his painterly best or as

one of his typically forceful, direct, and acute revelations of personality. As a piece of objective realism the head [380] is superb beyond virtuosity. The set of the lidded eyes in their sockets, the bony projection of the irregular nose with its fleshy tip, the sag of the aging face on its strong foundation of bone, the firmness of the mouth, held decisively by an habitual contraction of the muscles, the swirl of thin soft hair away from the rather flat temples and the slightly bulging forehead—all of these features, logically integrated and existing as a magnificently solid volume in space, are presented with a tangibility approaching illusion. But the vivid emanation of character comes from something more than this masterly reproduction of a set of features extraordinary in themselves. Some of Eakins's means toward the revelation of this personality are obvious; they consist largely of the centuries-old devices of selection and accent. What Eakins has eliminated as incidental and unrevealing we cannot say, but we can see the sharp stroke that emphasizes the angle in the eyebrow at one side, the sudden emphatic shadow at the nostril, the exaggeration and breaking of the highlights in the eyes, glistening in the

380. Eakins: Detail from Figure 379.

381. Eakins: Detail from Figure 379.

382. Eakins: Detail from Figure 379.

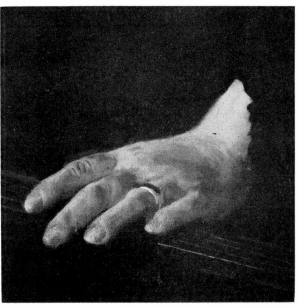

315

383. EAKINS: *Miss Van Buren*, c. 1891. 45 x 32″. Phillips Collection, Washington, D.C.

384. SARGENT: *Mrs. Swinton*, 1896–97. 90 x 49″. Art Institute of Chicago, Walker Collection.

collapsing flesh around them. The delicacy of the pearls and the neckerchief accentuates the ruggedness of the head; the pose of the whole figure describes a monumental respectability, surmounted by the determined, reflective intelligence of the face.

The slight conceit of the right hand [381] resting on the piano with one finger pressing a single key, as if sounding a note, saves the pose from usualness. But counteracting any suggestion of affectation, the other hand [382] rests palm downward with massive placidity upon the strings of a viola, as if quieting them. The face and hands are the three lightest spots in the picture—not an unusual device, but exaggerated here.

They are exceptionally small and exceptionally conspicuous among the shadows, which are punctuated here and there with duller lights of polished wood and subdued metallic glints. The picture, which is very large, is dark in tonality, the dress black in the surrounding dark warm browns, with occasional russet tones in the instruments. The most conspicuous spot of color is the cool clear blue of the neckerchief; it serves as a final accent to the powerful head, making doubly sure its position as the climax of the picture.

It would be possible to go on from here and argue that in the guise of an objective image Eakins has made comments upon

385. EAKINS: *Mending the Net*, 1881. 32¼ x 45¼". Philadelphia Museum of Art, Gift of Mrs. Thomas Eakins and Miss Marcy A. Williams.

386. EAKINS: Detail from Figure 385.

profound and universal truths, but this would be to distort his art away from a sphere in which it is complete. His genius as a portrait painter lay in his ability to create—or, rather, to perceive and then to reveal—the psychological entity of an individual, without recourse to any but the most objective means. Any philosophical speculations stirred by the portrait of Mrs. Frishmuth must come from the observer as they might be stirred by an acquaintance with the rich personality of Mrs. Frishmuth herself, the personality Eakins has perceived, revealed, and immortalized. If a single word could describe the quality of his portraits the word would be *honesty*— honesty in the representation of externals, and honesty of characterization. It is easy to see why some of his portraits were refused after they had been commissioned, why some others were accepted only to be burned. Sitters who hoped to emerge as dukes or duchesses were mistaken when they chose Eakins to paint their portraits. Yet when Sargent, the most expert flatterer of this kind, came to Philadelphia and was being lionized, Eakins was the man he

asked to meet. His fashionable hostess had never heard of the local painter. A comparison of Eakins's *Miss Van Buren* [383] with a typical "society portrait" explains why Sargent [384] who admired the one but painted the other, made his famous remark, in self-disgust, that portraiture was "a pimp's profession." It is a remark that no portrait by Eakins could ever have inspired.

Like the French impressionists, Eakins painted the urban *bourgeoisie* on their holidays in the countryside, strolling, fishing, boating, lying in the shade. Yet it would be impossible to mistake one of his pictures in this group for a French painting, just as it would be impossible to mistake the Schuylkill River at Philadelphia for the Seine. *Mending the Net* [385, 386] is a sturdier, more masculine, more direct picture than the Frenchmen's delicious landscapes composed of color dissolved in atmosphere. Eakins's light is just as wonderfully the light of outdoors, but it is seen with a steadier eye and is painted with a firmer and more deliberate brush. Monet's boats riding at anchor at Argenteuil, Renoir's tender young

387. EAKINS: *Max Schmitt in the Single Shell*, 1871. 32¼ x 46¼″. Metropolitan Museum of Art, New York, Alfred N. Punnett Fund and Gift of George D. Pratt.

people in dappled shadows, even Pissarro's sparkling fields, are feminine and evanescent (although no less delightful) by the standard of Eakins's clear skies, firm earth, heavy water, and steady light. Nor does Eakins yield to the casual, almost haphazard composition of so much impressionism; the intervals of grouping in the line of figures against the sky along the riverbank in *Mending the Net* is beautifully calculated to achieve an expression of naturalness without any loss of pictorial unity. In this particular combination of virtues—apparent spontaneity with exquisite calculation—Eakins when he is at his best is comparable to the great compositional master of impressionism, Degas, although he has no interest in Degas's brilliant innovations of the "snapshot" compositions with their eccentric angles, their objects bisected by the margins of the picture, and their figures captured in unexpected attitudes.

Eakins was interested in the relationship between photography and vision, and sometimes used photographs for reference, not as a matter of convenience but as a stimulus in solving problems of vision and representation. He was not in search of a formula; he painted sometimes in broad, simplified forms, sometimes with detailed precision, as he did in *Max Schmitt in the Single Shell* [387], an extreme example but one of his finest paintings, emulating the detailed clarity of a deep sharp focus lens capable of registering minute details with equal precision from foreground to horizon. Each twig of the trees on the river bank is shown as if at close range in miniature; this definition extends beyond the distant bridge to include a small boat and even its puff of smoke. Max Schmitt, in the scull, turning toward us as if we were holding a camera, appears to be waiting for the click of its shutter. But like Corot, who, with less complication, also represented distant details with similar telescopic clarity, Eakins has adjusted colors and values as a creative painter, not as a photographer with an exceptionally good camera. He has massed his details in acute concentrations; they seem

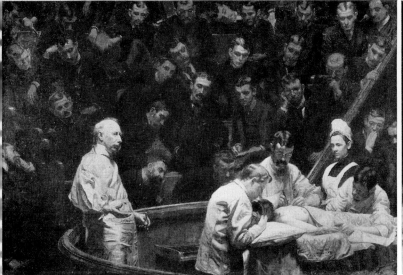

388. EAKINS: *The Agnew Clinic,* 1889. 74½ x 130½″. University of Pennsylvania, Philadelphia.

389. EAKINS: Detail from Figure 388.

all the more wonderfully precise because they are played between the broad flat stretch of water and the even flatter expanse of sky. The effect is like that of a clear day in early spring when the world seems to emerge in magically revealing light after the obscurities of winter, when the eye is sharpened to a new sensitivity to everything it sees, as if privileged for a few hours to find new experience in familiar objects. The picture is full of the enchantment of such an experience; the oddly shaped clouds, white and scintillating in the bright sky, are a half-fantastic element further removing the scene from literalness, even though the existence of exactly such clouds at exactly such spots is conceivable as a fact of nature. No other picture of Eakins's demonstrates more absolutely his fidelity to "imitation" and, at the same time, his manipulation of imitative detail into an expressive unity that explores beneath realistic surfaces.

A limitation inherent in realism, the one that seemed its insuperable defect to the idealists, is that it is ill adapted to the synthesis of monumental compositions. The impact of a *Mrs. Frishmuth* or a *Max Schmitt* or a *Mending the Net* depends upon our feeling that the scene existed *in toto* before the eyes of the painter. If we stop to think

about it, common sense tells us that the parts were assembled on the canvas, in the studio. There is no reason to believe that Mrs. Frishmuth sat patiently while Eakins busied himself for days painting the musical instruments surrounding her, and it is obvious that in *Max Schmitt* the clouds, the light, the puff of smoke, and the man in the single shell did not remain supernaturally transfixed during the hours and days that Eakins worked on them. But this fact does not intrude itself between the image and the observer; we believe in the total simultaneous existence of all the parts. But in certain kinds of subjects, and beyond a certain point of complication, this belief becomes strained, as it does in *The Agnew Clinic* [388]. *The Agnew Clinic* represents a medical arena where the doctor lectures during the course of an operation. In addition to twenty-seven visible spectators, Eakins shows two doctors, two assistants, a nurse, and the patient under anesthesia. He makes no effort to dramatize the scene, unless the rather obtrusive variety of attitudes assumed by the spectators can be called dramatizing in a small way. The operation itself and the people performing it are described as noncommittally as a factual report, down to such details as the instrument table and even the stencilled "University Hospital" on the operation cloth beneath the patient. The report is adequately organized and is quite lucid in its separate parts, as in the head of Doctor Agnew [389], but it remains an enumeration of facts rather than a response to them.

This odd dryness, the downright stubborn objectivity, might have been the result of the unfavorable reception fourteen years earlier of a similar picture, *The Gross Clinic* [390]. Here the head of the doctor is dramatized not only by its pose and its facial expression but by its position as the climactic point of the foreground group and its isolation against the shadowed background, where the figures of the spectators are barely visible in the gloom. There is some disharmony between this dramatization and the reportorial character of the assistant figures; the artificiality of the pose of the woman at the left (the patient's mother) is also obtrusive. But on the whole it is an impressive picture whether or not it is altogether a consistent one, and a near miss, at least, in solving the problem Eakins set himself, which was the reconciliation of monumental treatment through realistic means.

The Gross Clinic had a dramatically unfavorable reception, being rejected for exhibition in Philadelphia's Centennial Exhibition of 1876, a rejection comparable to Courbet's earlier one in Paris, and for much the same reason: its realism seemed brutal. It remains a startling picture today, especially in the detail of Doctor Gross's hand holding the scalpel. The fingers glisten with blood fresh from the incision in the patient's thigh. Eakins finally arranged to have the picture hung among the medical exhibits of the Centennial. This, and subsequent discouragements, may have led him to the uncompromisingly flat statement in *The Agnew Clinic*, as opposed to the interpretative effort, in *The Gross Clinic*, to show the scientist as a towering intellectual figure beyond the limitations of ordinary men.

But it is not so much that Eakins was out of his depth in these two pictures as that he was out of his field. His field was the perception and the revelation of character, a field common to all centuries of painters, and he holds his own in that field without

390. EAKINS: *The Gross Clinic*, 1875. 96 x 78". Jefferson Medical College, Philadelphia.

apologies in any quarter. And in a field special to his own half-century, the observation of urban man in conjunction with nature, he was unique in capturing the quality of this aspect of life as it was expressed in his own country.

Postscript: The Ash Can School

At the very end of the nineteenth century in America, there appeared a group of young men who painted into and as far as the middle of the twentieth, but who are best considered as part of the century that produced realism and impressionism. These were the painters of the Ash Can School, a name given them in derision (by just whom, there is some question) because they were devoted to vigorously common-

place subjects in protest against the gentility of fashionable painting. As a group they were a short generation younger than Duveneck, Chase, Sargent, and Eakins, having been born in the 1860's and early 1870's. Coming at the end of a century studded by revolutions, the story of their own revolt is anticlimactic, especially since the essence of their heresies had been proclaimed long before by the realists and the impressionists, and had been superceded by new ones.

The most potent influences on the Ash Can School were Manet, Daumier, and other French painters related to them, men who finished their careers and died during the boyhood of the five Americans who were to form the original Ash Can group: Robert Henri (1865–1929), George Luks (1867–1933), John Sloan (1871–1951),

391. SLOAN: *Greenwich Village Backyards*, 1914. 26 x 32″. Whitney Museum of American Art, New York.

392. SLOAN: *The Wake of the Ferry*, 1907. 26 x 32″. Phillips Collection, Washington, D.C.

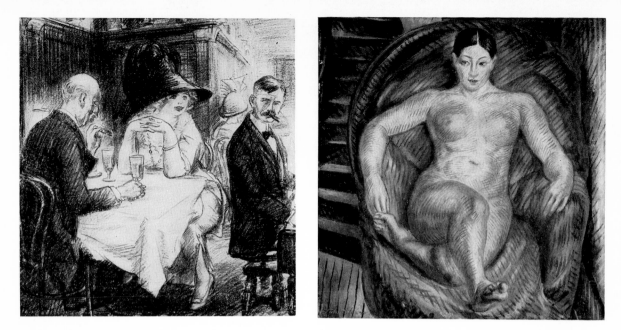

393. SLOAN: *"Professor—Please Play 'The Rosary,'"* 1913. Charcoal on paper, 18¼ x 16⅝".
Addison Gallery of American Art, Andover, Mass.

394. SLOAN: *Arachne*, 1940. 28 x 26". Philadelphia Museum of Art, Gift of Mr. and
Mrs. R. Sturgis Ingersoll.

William Glackens (1870–1938), and Everett Shinn (1876–1953). Duveneck influenced some members of the group; they painted with a very free brush, which some of them were likely to exaggerate into coarse, even slipshod, technique. The everyday subject matter of the impressionists and the social comment of one form of realism were also somewhat coarsened in their adaptation to the Ash Can enthusiasm for the hurly-burly of the American city along its main stem, in its back streets, and in its honkytonks, bars, cheap restaurants, and rented bedrooms.

The group was formed in Philadelphia in the 1890's, led by Robert Henri. They called themselves the Philadelphia Realists. Henri's importance is hardly hinted at by his painting, which was as facile as Sargent's but less elegant. Henri preferred common people to aristocrats. His great importance was as a teacher who stimulated more adventurous originality in his students than he demonstrated in his own work. His book *The Art Spirit* is still inspiring to many beginners.

John Sloan comes close to being a one-man summary of the Ash Can School, which changed its base to New York (and its name to New York Realists) around 1900 and took on its typical character. *Greenwich Village Backyards* [391] shows the kind of subject that soon generated the nickname Ash Can. But *The Wake of the Ferry* [392] shows that at their best the Ash Can painters could go beyond the cheerful journalistic vigor of their descriptions of the city to discover, as Daumier did, the existence of the individual as a sentient unit isolated within the mass of the metropolis. Sloan was also an early practitioner of the humorous cartoon of social satire, as in *"Professor—Please Play The Rosary"* [393], an indigenously American kind of humor which, expanded and polished, was to become *"The New Yorker* cartoon." In his late years, when Ash Can realism had run its course, Sloan abandoned it to work less successfully in painting of a more formal nature, such as *Arachne* [394].

As for the other three, William Glackens began as an illustrator on the *Philadelphia*

395. LUKS: *The Spielers,* 1905. 36 x 26″. Addison Gallery of American Art, Andover, Mass.

396. PRENDERGAST: *Afternoon, Pincian Hill, Rome,* 1898. Water-color, 21 x 27″. Phillips Collection, Washington, D.C.

Press and continued as a successful cartoonist in New York. After painting in the typical Ash Can manner for a while, he renounced his birthright during an extended residence in France and returned, in effect, a Franco-American impressionist. Everett Shinn followed a similar early gambit. Then, under the influence of Degas, he did theater subjects and finally turned to theatrical decoration, where his talent for rather thin and florid ornament was most at home. George Luks was by a couple of years the oldest and by all odds the gustiest member of the group. He painted with great appetite, choosing subjects from New York's east side [395], from coal mines, and also from city life in general.

Luks became a small *cause celebre* in American painting when the National Academy rejected one of his paintings, offended by his "vulgarity," that word so familiar to realists in France. Three more painters joined the Ash Can group of five to form "The Eight" around Luks as active dissenters from academic doctrine. The new trio were Maurice Prendergast (1859–1924), who eventually developed a decorative, semi-abstract, patch-work style evolved from impressionism [396]; Arthur B. Davies (1862–1928), whose wispily elongated figures in rhythmic combinations inspired by Blake were an odd combination with the low-living characters of the Ash Can family gallery; and Ernest Lawson (1873–1939), whose purely impressionist work was later affected by Cézanne. The Eight were important as protagonists in the early twentieth-century campaign to introduce radical European movements to the American public, especially in the Armory Show of 1912, which we will see later. In their own work, however, they were not strongly affected by these movements.

A younger man, George Bellows (1882–1925), became a disciple of Ash Can principles in the early 1900's (he was a student of Henri's) and produced, among other fight and sporting scenes, the painting and the lithograph [397] of *A Stag at Sharkey's,* which is as well known, probably, as any American picture within ten years either side of it. Bellows was still a very young man when it began to be evident that the Ash Can school had run its course. No other school of painting became old-fashioned more quickly;[*] the exhibitions of European *avant-garde* painting so enthusiastically sponsored by the Ash Can painters themselves made them out of date.

Bellows began a process of self re-education along rigidly formal lines. He studied certain elementary and arbitrary formulas for picture-making, and when he died suddenly at forty-three his painting was an odd combination of dry mechanics in conflict with his native vigor and sturdy realism. Occasionally the mechanics won out. They mar *Elinor, Jean and Anna* [398], where the intimate and affectionate nature of the subject is a little chilled by the imposition of inappropriate compositional rigidity and a touch of affectation in forms that are studied to the point of conventionalization. Here Bellows is subjecting himself to disciplines comparable to those Renoir imposed upon himself in *Bathers* [251] at very much the same stage of his career. Pointlessly but inevitably one wonders whether Bellows, if he had lived, might not have freed himself from these disciplines just as Renoir did, once they had served their purpose, to become the man who would bring American art harmoniously into the international orbit of the twentieth century without sacrifice of his indigenous character.

Bellows's Americanism was conscious and determined; he even feared European travel as a possible corruption. This kind of Chinese Wall self-consciousness has plagued some other American painters since Bellows and has been a point of departure for some critics who have failed to see that the Americanism of Allston, Bingham, Homer, Eakins, and any other painters who can be grouped with them, was an inborn Americanism, not a rejection of foreign influences.

[*] Except one, the regional school of the 1930's in America, led by Thomas Benton, Grant Wood, and John Steuart Curry, as will be seen.

397. BELLOWS: *A Stag at Sharkey's*, 1916. Lithograph, 18¾ x 24". Philadelphia Museum of Art, Gift of Mr. and Mrs. George Sharp Munson.

398. BELLOWS: *Elinor, Jean and Anna*, 1920. 59 x 66". Albright Art Gallery, Buffalo, N.Y.

PART III

Transition

CHAPTER 10

Post-impressionism: Its Classicists

The Explorers

By the end of the nineteenth century, impressionism had run its course, although Renoir, Degas, and Monet continued to work well into the twentieth. But even while impressionism was still fighting for final recognition, new directions were being followed by several men whose art was to determine the course of painting in the first generation of the new century. Fanning out from impressionism, they explored independently. More than any other painters in the history of art, they developed their theories in isolation, and in contradiction to one another. They are grouped under the catch-all designation of *post-impressionists*, a term meaning nothing except that these men departed from impressionism to find new ways of painting. The ways they found were too various to be covered by a more descriptive designation; at least so far, no better collective term has been found to describe the art of Paul Cézanne, Georges Seurat, Paul Gauguin, and Vincent van Gogh (all of whom, incidentally, died before Renoir, Degas, and Monet—even by as much as thirty-five years, to take the extreme limits between the death of Seurat, who died very young, and Monet, who died very old). The point is made at such length only to remind the reader that chapters in a book follow one another between neater boundary lines than do the birth and death dates of painters or, especially in our time, the genesis and development of new expressions in art. The trauma that led from impressionism into the plethora of isms we group under the term *modern art* was experienced by and expressed by the painters we call post-impressionists.

399. SEURAT: *A Sunday Afternoon on the Island of La Grande Jatte*, 1884–86. 81¼ x 120¼". Art Institute of Chicago, Helen Birch Bartlett Memorial.

Neo-impressionism: Seurat

While Renoir was painting his *Bathers* in reaction against the formlessness of impressionism, a younger man named Georges Seurat (1859–1891) was attacking the same problem in a different way. With excruciating patience he was applying tiny dots of color to 67 square feet of canvas which, when the dots finally covered it, would be the painting that divides impressionism from the twentieth century, *A Sunday Afternoon on the Island of La Grande Jatte* [399, 400], which shows the strolling crowd in a public park on an island in the Seine near Paris. Both Renoir and Seurat were intent on pulling together again the disintegrating forms of impressionism, redefining their boundaries and solidifying the masses that had become ambiguous in

their fusion with light and air. Renoir did so by retreating from impressionism; Seurat did so by plunging into it and putting it in order like a fanatic housewife tidying up a bachelor's apartment. By a more dignified comparison, he was like a catalyst dropped into the frothy impressionist mixture, suddenly reducing it to crystals of perfect geometrical form.

By any comparison, Seurat was the most systematic painter who ever lived, and of all painters who have tried to work on scientific principles he is the only one of major importance whose art suggests the laboratory as much as it does the studio. Since he was systematic in the extreme, his work is easy to reduce to a recipe. But like any recipe for painting, this one is deceptive since it is full of hidden variables dependent on the skill and the sensibilities of the artist.

400. SEURAT: Detail from Figure 399.

Seurat's recipe may produce a work of art as it did when Seurat used it, or a pointless exercise as it usually did in the hands of his followers. But the recipe remains:

First: Simplify all natural forms to silhouettes in accord with their basic geometrical equivalents, modifying them as necessary in accord with the taste of the artist to increase their effectiveness as pure design. Seurat's taste was for the most exquisite precision of contour; even before he added the element of geometrical reduction, this taste is evident in his academic student drawings [401], which allied him to

the tradition of Ingres. He worked in the Academy's school under Lehmann, who may be remembered as a disciple of Ingres, and he studied drawings by Ingres even while he was studying Delacroix's color. But he was unaffected by Delacroix's spirit, and it should become apparent as his work is followed here that Seurat is well within the classical tradition—its purity, its balance, and even in the specifically classical-academic characteristic of insistence upon formula. Drawings in his fully developed style [402] have their own kind of formal idealization, even though Seurat insisted always upon the contemporary, everyday subjects of impressionism as opposed to the idealism of conventionally classical ones.

Second: Assemble these silhouettes into a composition (previously determined in its general expressive disposition), further modifying the individual forms and adjusting their interrelationship until they are perfectly integrated with one another and the space around them. The subject of this composition will observe the impressionists' allegiance to the world at hand, but its expressiveness will be achieved by the application of psychological values of line and color that impressionism sacrificed to "effects" of light and atmosphere and the accidental dispositions of forms in nature.

Third: Paint this composition in the technique called "divisionism" or "pointillism," in accord with theories of color held by the artist.*

It is in the second stage, the creation of the composition, that Seurat returns most obviously to French classical standards. The infinite adjustment of the parts of *La Grande Jatte* into a perfected, static interrelationship is in the tradition of Poussin. But the highly simplified forms are not Poussinesque; in their creation and their combination Seurat is equally in the tradition of the ubiquitous Japanese print, with its ornamental flatness. Of course these two traditions are contradictory, Poussin's

---

* To make a fine distinction, *divisionism* would be the breaking-up of color into its component parts, *pointillism* its application in dots of uniform size. *Chromo-luminarism* is another term sometimes met, meaning the same things.

401. SEURAT: *Male Nude*, 1877. Charcoal, 25 x 19″. Private Collection.

402. SEURAT: *Seated Woman*, 1884–86. Crayon, 12 x 7½″. Collection Louis E. Stern, New York.

being a tradition of composition of three-dimensional forms in three-dimensional space. *La Grande Jatte* can be read thus, or it can be read simply across its surface, just as its forms can be read as silhouettes, or as geometrical solids. As a composition of solid forms in classical depth the picture is more subtle, more complex, and finally more rewarding, but it is also a wonderfully effective composition if it is regarded as an enormous flat ornamental screen. This spacial ambivalence, offspring of the union between the European painters' admiration for Japanese print design and their own ingrained Western tradition, is present in

a great deal of painting during these years. And although Seurat certainly knew the prints at first hand, their influence also entered his art in a roundabout way, through the art of Puvis de Chavannes.

Pierre Cécile Puvis de Chavannes (1824–1898) occupies a curious position in French painting. A little younger than Courbet, a little older than Manet, he was unaffected by the realist-impressionist movement and is habitually thought of as one of the successful academic painters. Actually Puvis de Chavannes had a series of early rejections from the Salon and later on, when he was firmly established and served on Salon

403. PUVIS DE CHAVANNES: *The Poor Fisherman,* 1881. 59⅞ x 75". Louvre, Paris.

404. SEURAT: *The Bridge at Courbevoie,* 1886. 18 x 21½". Home House Society, Courtauld Institute of Art, London.

juries, he irritated the other members by the freedom of his judgments, and at the end of the century he was greatly respected by the generation represented by Seurat. Puvis seems both sentimental and stuffy to contemporary taste; his allegories are obvious and his subject pictures have a synthetic sweetness which is tiresome. But as a mural designer, as he essentially was, he simplified and flattened his forms into compositions of a decorative clarity and nicety unique in his generation.* We see more and more that he was an important influence on modern painting, not only through Seurat but, as will soon be seen, even more surprisingly through Gauguin.

Seurat so admired a painting by Puvis, *The Poor Fisherman* [403], that he made a free copy of it, shortly before he began work on *La Grande Jatte.* Whatever else *The Poor Fisherman* may be—sentimental, prettified, and ambiguous in its compromise between conventionalization and photographic realism—compositionally it is a harmonious combination of simplified forms disciplined into delicate, but decisive, balance. Upon this kind of composition Seurat imposed further disciplines, always in the direction of increased abstraction, as in the severely beautiful *Bridge at Courbevoie* [404], distilled to the geometrical essence of the subject's elements. In *La Grande Jatte,* Seurat's problem was to achieve equal clarity in the manipulation of a large number of elements in more complicated relationships.

Once the composition was established, the execution of the painting in the dot-by-dot technique of pointillism remained as a chore before which most painters would have blanched, and which demanded even of Seurat an obsessive concentration. Pointillism, as it is usually called, or divisionism as the neo-impressionists preferred to call it, is a dead end in the maze of color theories branching out from Delacroix's rediscovery of reds in greens, purples in yellows, of vibrations and countervibrations between the color elements of a painting that led, in one direction, to the even more broken color of impressionism. The work of the scientists who investigated the physi-

---

* His numerous murals include *The Sacred Wood,* in the Sorbonne in Paris, the celebrated series of the life of St. Genevieve in the Pantheon near by, and some late, not entirely successful allegories for the staircase of the Public Library in Boston.

cal laws of light and color was known to the impressionists and probably influenced them to some degree in a most informal way. But there is nothing informal in the art of Seurat; he studied these theories and applied them methodically.

Where Monet would paint a large green area of foliage with many shades of green and occasional flecks of pure yellow or pure blue, allowing these tints and colors to be more or less blended by the eye, Seurat attempted to analyze the exact proportions of the components of a tint, to separate them into the colors of the spectrum, and then to apply them with scientific precision so that their optical blending would produce not only the tint but the degree of vibration he wanted. The surface of his canvas becomes a kind of "molecular dance" in contradiction to the absolute precision of the forms within which these myriads and myriads and myriads of dots spin and quiver. In his preliminary black and white studies for a picture, Seurat approximated the effect of pointillist color by drawing, in his own way, on charcoal paper with black wax crayon [402]. Charcoal paper has a fine but conspicuous grain that allows flecks of white to show through the black, to a degree dependent on the pressure of the crayon. The crayon is always pure black; grays are produced by the interspeckling of the paper's grain, just as tones and colors in the completed painting are produced by the interspeckling of calculated quantities of the component colors.

There is an essential objection to pointillist technique which was made at the time and is still legitimate in spite of the fact that Seurat's stature among recent painters makes a statement of this objection heretical. But there is no point in pretending that it is possible to look at a painting by Seurat without being first of all conscious of the novelty of its technique. One must somehow manage to cross the barrier of agonizingly meticulous and desperately sincere application of an elementary scientific principle before one is free to enjoy a work of art. Access to Seurat's studio is still through his laboratory, and one is required to watch him at work there before one is allowed to see the pictures.

405. PISSARRO: *River—Early Morning*, 1888. 18¼ x 21⅞". Philadelphia Museum of Art, John G. Johnson Collection.

But once this privilege is granted, the pictures are worth the wait. According to his own aesthetic, which he once formulated in a didactic outline, Seurat left no room for intuition in the creation of a work of art. But it is impossible to look at *La Grande Jatte* and believe that it was produced entirely by rule. If it observes rules more rigorously than painting had ever done before, these rules are still subject to the sensibilities of the artist who applied them. And for that matter, there is not very much in Seurat's rules that was new. As if it should come as a revelation, Seurat propounded a set of general principles that had been observed for centuries. Some of them were truisms that could have been picked up en route during study in any sound academic painter's studio, such as the rule that dark tones and cold colors suggest sadness, that gayety is suggested by luminous tones and warm colors. Since the Renaissance, and perhaps earlier than that, Seurat's principles had been familiar to any thoughtful painter. In reading accounts by his followers one is amazed at the long-faced reverence with which Seurat's restatement of a pedant's primer seems to have been greeted. Only the theory of optical color was new, or newish.

Seurat was also interested in discovering a scientific basis for pictorial composition, and he investigated among others a famous mathematical formula called the "golden section." Also called the "divine proportion" or "gate of harmony," it was formulated by the architect and engineer, Vitruvius, in the first century B.C. and revived in the Renaissance. In 1509 it was published in a book by a Bolognese monk, Luca Pacioli, illustrated by Leonardo da Vinci, who had made his own investigations of the mathematical bases of harmony. And we will see it picked up again in the twentieth century by certain cubists, and adopted as a name for their group. Applied as a test to many a great painting or building or art object, the "golden section" fits perfectly. Applied in the same way to some of the worst pictures or buildings or objects ever painted or built or manufactured, it works just as well. Used as a formula for creation it may yield results similar to those more effectively arrived at by a combination of general principles and intuition. Analogies may be made: in music, for instance, it is possible to create a fugue that is technically impeccable, by rule, yet an offense to the ear. In cookery it is possible to follow a recipe closely and produce a dish that is just edible where a master chef would produce a delight from what would seem to be the same preparation of the same ingredients. The point of insisting on all these objections to Seurat's fascination with formula, objections that may sound illtempered or uncharitable, is only to insist that *La Grande Jatte* as a work of art rises above its demonstration of codified rules. Seurat was a very young man who was investigating the whole process of creative effort, beginning with its mechanics. One can imagine him, had he lived, passing through a crisis similar to Renoir's, from the other direction. Where Renoir—rightly —mistrusted the spontaneous, unstudied effects of impressionism and recognized the need for self-discipline, so Seurat might have—rightly—relaxed his obsession with "scientific" calculation as the way to expression, putting his faith first in impulse,

and second in its discipline, as Renoir did after his period of reorientation.

As it was, Seurat produced a cycle of paintings demonstrating, systematically, the different principles of his aesthetic, before his death at the age of only thirty-two. *La Grande Jatte*, the first of the cycle, was exhibited in 1886 in the eighth, and last, impressionist group show. The group was breaking up; this was the first exhibition in four years, and neither Renoir nor Monet participated. The great problem was what to do about *La Grande Jatte* and the other neo-impressionist paintings—including those of Pissarro, who was involved just then in his brief excursion into this field [405], and those of his son Lucien, who was exhibiting for the first time, and those of Paul Signac, whose name is second only to Seurat's in neo-impressionism. Finally all these pictures were segregated in a room by themselves. The term *neo-impressionism* was coined in this year as a gesture on the part of Seurat and Signac. In spite of their departures from impressionist technique they thus acknowledged their debt to the men who had first explored the translation of light into pigment. But since the impressionist ideal was to capture the transient moment, and the neo-impressionist hope was to capture the essential quality of a scene and transfix it, the exhibition of 1886 must have been an oddly contradictory one. And it demonstrated that pure impressionism had served its purpose and reached its end, as the founding members dropped away to solve special problems, and new recruits, like Seurat, used impressionism as a foundation for new structures.

The "Salon des Indépendants"

The importance of the impressionist exhibitions had been reduced, also, because a new and more inclusive organization had been formed to allow any painter to exhibit who wanted to do so. This had occurred two years before the last impressionist show and the exhibition of *La Grande Jatte*—in 1884. Several hundred artists rejected from the Salon of that year had come together

406. SEURAT: *Une Baignade*, 1883–84. 79 x 118½". Tate Gallery, London.

to form an organization to hold no-jury exhibitions, calling themselves the *Société des Artistes Indépendants* (the same name the impressionist group had used for a while). Seurat was one of the leaders in the organization of the *Indépendants,* and in the first exhibition, 1884, he showed *Une Baignade* [406]. *Une Baignade* is obviously a forerunner of *La Grande Jatte;* it differs in that Seurat has not yet adopted the pointillist technique. It is a large, quiet picture, rather subdued in color, serenely balanced, but without the combination of formal severity and vibrant surface that would fully individualize Seurat in *La Grande Jatte.* Seurat, along with Pissarro and Signac, also exhibited in Brussels with a new group called *Les Vingt,* which was devoted to the struggle for the recognition of new art movements in that country. Similar organizations and exhibitions began to appear all over Europe and, before long, in America.

It was while Seurat was helping to arrange the *Salon des Indépendants* in 1891 that he contracted the pneumonia from which he died. It is generally accepted that he was weakened by the days and nights of laborious effort required to execute his large, carefully dotted paintings. He had not quite finished his picture for the *Salon des Indépendants* of 1891 when he died. *The Circus* [407] is an odd picture, with its thin, rather stringy forms and its immobility, which denies the theoretically lively action of its subject. In planning it, Seurat formulated a set of problems contrasting at every point with those he solved in *La Grande Jatte:* artificial light instead of daylight, an indoor setting in sharply limited space instead of an outdoor one in deeper space, a subject of action instead of one of repose. But if *La Grande Jatte* seems to demonstrate the legitimacy of Seurat's theories, *The Circus* demonstrates their limitations.

Theoretically, *The Circus* should be a successful picture. The lines swirl in a way that is theoretically correct to express action. The silhouettes, as in the rider's skirt and the hat of the clown in the foreground, are full of the theoretically expressive upward movements which should express gaiety ("Gaiety of line is given by

lines above the horizontal"). The color is dominated by oranges, reds, and yellows, the "warm dominants" expressive of action and cheerfulness in Seurat's codification of rules.

But sometimes it is necessary to look at a picture not in the light of what the artist intended to do, or how successful the result should have been in view of the way he did it, but quite subjectively as to whether or not the picture speaks for itself. In *The Circus* the means are justified by theory, but there is a real question as to whether the end has been achieved, a legitimate question in spite of our knowledge that the picture is not quite complete. The truth is that as a demonstration *The Circus* is interesting, but as a work of art it remains a demonstration. Almost detail by detail it can be paired with Lautrec's picture of the *Circus Fernando* [408], even to the ringmaster's whip, the dancing clown, the scattered audience, in a comparison disastrous to Seurat's contention that picture-making can be reduced to a science. Lautrec has observed the same general principles—active line, vivacious shapes, gay color—in

407. Seurat: *The Circus*, 1891. 70⅝ x 58¼". Louvre, Paris.

408. Toulouse-Lautrec: *In the Circus Fernando: The Ring Master*, 1888. 39½ x 63½". Art Institute of Chicago, Joseph Winterbotham Collection.

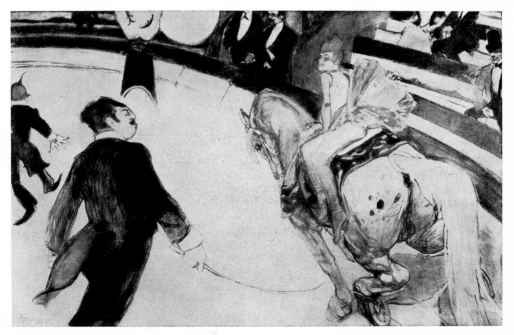

409. SEURAT: *La Parade*, 1889. 39½ x 59¼″. Collection Stephen C. Clark, New York.

410. SEURAT: *Les Poseuses* (second version), 1888. 15½ x 19½″. Collection Henry P. McIlhenny, Philadelphia.

a picture full of life not because it was painted in ignorance of method or theory, for of course it was not, but because method and theory, already mastered, were taken for granted as part of the act of creation. In Seurat's picture, method as an application of theory *is* the act of creation, or is meant to be, and this time it has not been enough.

Not only as Seurat's last work but as his least successful demonstration, *The Circus* leaves one wondering what lesson Seurat would have learned from it, and what new explorations he might have made. For with *La Grande Jatte* as a beginning and *The Circus* as a conclusion, Seurat had completed a series of five demonstrations of his systematic aesthetic. *La Parade* [409], following *La Grande Jatte* and painted in 1887–1888, attacks the problem of representing figures out of doors illuminated by

411. Seurat: *Le Chahut* (study), 1889. 22 x 18¼". Albright Art Gallery, Buffalo.

412. Seurat: *La Poudreuse* (*Madeleine Knobloch*), 1889. 37½ x 31¼". Home House Society, Courtauld Institute of Art, London.

artificial light. (The row of lotuslike shapes along the top of the composition is a line of flaring gas jets.) The depth of *La Grande Jatte's* landscape is eliminated by flat walls and screens, reduced in pattern to an abstraction of overlapping rectangles. The figures, instead of being disposed in a variety of attitudes within space, are ranged flatly and repetitiously across a plane close to the observer.

Following *La Parade,* Seurat set himself the problem of a third and last static subject, this time with the variation of his first indoor setting, and in natural light, *Les Poseuses* (*The Models*), showing three nude models posed in his studio. (Along one wall, a portion of *La Grande Jatte* was incorporated into the composition.) *Les Poseuses* is the most delicately colored, the most minutely executed, of all Seurat's pictures, exquisite to the point of thinness and dryness. His friends objected to this quality in it, attributing the picture's look of

anemia to the extreme smallness of the dots. Seurat must have agreed. In any case, he followed the disappointing large version with a small one [410] where the tiny dots of paint are harmoniously scaled to the picture area, thus transforming an arid and flavorless picture into one of gemlike precision.

Le Chahut [411] was the first of Seurat's kinetic subjects, arranged in shallow space, a preliminary to the kinetic variation of *The Circus.* Although the series of five pictures would certainly have been extended to include, for instance, a kinetic subject in natural light out of doors, they are a unit just as they stand. They are an impressive life work, yet surely they are only an introduction, a preface, to a main text that was never written.

Seurat left a single portrait, of Madeleine Knobloch, his mistress, called *La Poudreuse* [412]. Seurat's liaison, and the child of it, whom he acknowledged, were unknown

413. SIGNAC: *The Port of St. Tropez*, 1916. Watercolor, 13½ x 16¼". Brooklyn Museum.

even to most of his closest friends until after his death. In *La Poudreuse* he originally painted his own portrait in the frame now filled by a small bouquet; it has been revealed recently by x-ray photography. Seurat's family acknowledged Madeleine Knobloch and divided the contents of his studio with her. Since Seurat had sold or given away almost nothing, this meant virtually his entire output. But no one was very interested in acquiring pictures in an eccentric technique most of which were, in any case, too large to hang except as collection pieces. They had been the subject of the usual scandals, so repetitious since the *Salon des Refusés*. Even ten years after Seurat's death his pictures were considered practically worthless, and *La Grande Jatte* was sold in 1900 for only 900 francs. A syndicate recently offered a million dollars for its purchase and return to France.

Other Neo-impressionists

Neo-impressionism attracted a large number of followers, as might be expected of a manner offering so explicit a formula. Seurat was disturbed by the size of the number, since none of them had the scientific perseverance that was prerequisite to neo-impressionism if it was to be more than formula painting. Nor did many of them have the creative sensibility that was also necessary although Seurat denied it. After Seurat's death his leadership was taken over by Paul Signac (1863–1935). Signac was four years younger but had had as much to do with the origins of neo-impressionism as had Seurat himself. Signac, in fact, had converted Seurat to the work of the impressionists, objecting to the "dull" colors of *Une Baignade* when it was exhibited in the first *Salon des Indépendants*. The two men had met at the formation of the *Société des Indépendants,* and Signac remained one of its hardest-working members and was its president for twenty-six years, beginning in 1908.

Signac was an attractive man, vigorous, enthusiastic, and as outgoing as Seurat was secretive. These qualities are reflected in his painting. He keeps bursting out of the strait jacket of neo-impressionist precision to indulge himself in the joy of painting. He executed some pen-and-ink drawings in a rather painful dot technique which was practiced by several other members of the group, including occasionally Seurat, but he was more at home with a dashing form of divisionism in which broad strokes of color are patterned freely, rather than methodically and in watercolors where vivaciously sketched lines and spots of color sparkle against white paper [413]. His book *From Eugène Delacroix to Neo-Impressionism,* published in 1889, is the classic doctrinaire reference on the school.

Among other followers, two are more distinguishable than most: Henri Edmond Cross (1856–1910), one of the founders of the *Société,* was more interested in emotional expression than in scientific theory, and sought it by using the purest, brightest colors of any of the neo-impressionists, to the point even of using them arbitrarily without regard to the actual color of the objects painted. He thus anticipated, as will become apparent later, the work of the fauvist painters, including Matisse. And Maximilien Luce (1858–1941) painted some sensitive pictures remindful of Pissarro. Like Pissarro he abandoned neo-impressionism to revert to the fresher, more intimate effects of impressionism itself.

Cézanne: His Revolution

By age and by association, Paul Cézanne (1839–1906) was one of the impressionists. He was five years younger than Degas, a year older than Monet, two years older than Renoir. He was a solitary man, but insofar as he had friends at all, he found them among his impressionist contemporaries. He exhibited in the first and third of the group shows, and when he was in Paris he frequented the *Café Guerbois* during the days when it was an impressionist center.[*] When Cézanne died at sixty-seven, Monet, Renoir, and Degas were still working. Yet by the time Renoir was setting himself to the task of painting the *Bathers,* and Seurat *La Grande Jatte,* Cézanne had already developed a way of painting as solid as Renoir's was ever to be, and more revolutionary than Seurat's. He said that he "wanted to make of impressionism something solid and durable like the art of the museums." It is a statement of intention that would have been appropriate from either Renoir or Seurat, but Cézanne's solution of the problem was so revolutionary that it takes him out of the impressionist generation except in the strictest chronological sense. Seurat was twenty years younger than Cézanne, yet without dates to guide us it would be easy to believe that the art of Seurat was a transitional step between impressionism and Cézanne. Chronology aside, Cézanne is a twentieth-century painter; that is why he is placed at this point in this book, instead of having been discussed with his impressionist friends and contemporaries, or before the younger Seurat.

Cézanne was the most revolutionary painter since the dawn of the Renaissance, which is what the critic Clive Bell meant in 1920 when he said, "If the greatest name in European painting is not Cézanne, it is Giotto." Cézanne recognized something of the same kind when he said, "I am the primitive of the way I have discovered." Together these two statements mean that European art was given a new direction in the early fourteenth century when a painter named Giotto di Bondone abandoned stylized medieval formulas of representation and turned to nature as his model; that for nearly 600 years painters followed this direction, varying and perfecting Giotto's innovation, until Cézanne appeared

[*] By 1877 the *Guerbois* had lost its importance as an impressionist meeting place, and the *Café de la Nouvelle Athènes* partially replaced it. The *Nouvelle Athènes,* however, became a center for literary intellectuals with only a scattering of painters.

and gave the first redirection since Giotto; and that like Giotto's achievement, Cézanne's is only a beginning, which will be varied and perfected by many generations of painters who will follow him.

No person in his right mind with more than a nodding acquaintance with the art of Cézanne approaches an explanation of it without the assumption that anything like a total and specific explanation is impossible. In the art of any great painter there is always a residue of the inexplicable after the historians and aestheticians have done their best with him. Cézanne's case is extreme. He himself complained that he had never "realized"—that is, completed, brought to concrete existence on canvas— his theories, what he had hoped to achieve. Even if we discount his statement in view of his temperament—which combined self-doubt with perseverance and allowed dissatisfaction with his own work to coexist with his conviction of its greatness—it is still true that he never managed to clarify his theories into an explainable formula. In this respect he is the opposite of Seurat. Where Seurat was certain of his formula and had only to submit himself industriously to its application, for Cézanne every brush stroke was a hazardous step and an experiment that might wreck the whole structure on the canvas. It is a mistake, often made, to analyze a painting by Cézanne as if it were a perfect and complete demonstration. And if a satisfactory analysis of one Cézanne is finally reached, it is not of much help in analyzing the next one, since Cézanne is full of variations and contradictions from picture to picture. When he said, "I am the primitive of the way I have discovered," he recognized not only the revolutionary nature of his art but also his feeling that he had gone but a short distance, and awkwardly, in the direction he set.

As a point of departure for any explanation of his art, two of Cézanne's own comments are more helpful than any others. These comments have become hackneyed for the good reason that no one has been able to invent more succinct ones to suggest the nature of the problems Cézanne set himself and the character their solution

imposed on his painting. The twin statements are, "I want to do Poussin over again, after nature," and "I want to make of impressionism something solid and durable like the art of the museums."

To "do Poussin over again, after nature" sounds easier on first hearing than it does after a little thought. To do Poussin over again after nature would be to combine somehow the two opposites, Poussin's classical order and nature's immediacy. The catch is that neither must be sacrificed to the other, nor may they be mutually watered down to a compromise. How is it possible to be at once artificial and natural? To be at once orderly, like the world Poussin invented, and full of accidentals, like the world of nature? Synthetic on one hand, imitative on the other? For instance, could the problem be solved by repainting Poussin's *Funeral of Phocion* [128], charging its crystalline vacuum with effects of light and air? The suggestion is manifestly absurd since the resultant hybrid would sacrifice what Cézanne wanted from Poussin, the clarity of his order, and would not carry with it what he wanted from impressionism, its immediate contact with the reality of nature. Or, to reverse the combination, perhaps a natural landscape could be observed and modified with an eye to discovering within it the clarity and order achieved by Poussin in his invention of "unnatural" landscapes. This is an improvement. Corot, in fact, had already done this in pictures like the views of Rome [142, 143] which have been discussed.

Corot is a firm link in the tradition of Poussin, and his landscapes of the early period do combine an actual, existing scene with Poussinesque harmony of a sort. But these pictures are cityscapes; their architectural forms are half readymade for classical disposition, and when Corot painted pure landscape rather than cityscape, his sense of order was lessened, even if we forget his late, fuzzy pictures where it was even sacrificed.

Doing Poussin over again after nature did not mean, to Cézanne, adjusting the monumental forms of a great city into closer harmonies. It meant the imposition of order onto nature, without any loss of nature's vibrance, its quality of life and growth—in short, its naturalness, so dear to the impressionists that they had once been willing to sacrifice everything else to it. For this quality of life, of reality, Corot had substituted a kind of enchanted revery in pictures that were perfection in their way. But it was not the way Cézanne was seeking.

Thus to do Poussin over again after nature becomes a convenient phrase describing a problem but offering no hint of a solution. To perfect an interrelationship of forms in space, as Poussin did, yet to express the reality of their existence in nature, which is haphazard: this, Cézanne thought, must somehow be possible.

Cézanne: Color as Form

To so "make of impressionism something solid and durable like the art of the museums" is "Poussin after nature" turned around, if you wish, but an additional factor is implied—the special use of color made by the impressionists. In breaking their colors and applying the varying tints in individual strokes side by side, the impressionist conceived of color as a manifestation of light, and specific kinds of light. To begin with, Cézanne discards the idea of capturing transient effects. In the world he paints there is no time of day—no noon, no early morning or evening. There are no gray days, foggy days, no "effects" of season or weather. His forms exist in a universal light that impregnates and reveals, but it is not a light in the sense of directed rays from a single source, not even the sun. It is not light as an optical phenomenon to be investigated and experimented with. It is a uniform and enduring light, steady, strong, clear, and revealing, not a light that flows over objects and not a light that consumes them. It is a light integral to the canvas; it is "painted in" with every stroke of color. It is a static and a timeless light.

Conceiving of light in this way, Cézanne had no interest in the broken color of impressionism as a kind of optical trick to capture its shimmer in air. But the idea that impressionism's strokes of varying color could be identified with the expression of form did interest him. He began to model objects in a series of planes, each plane represented by a change of color. A round apple would be transformed into a roundish object of many facetlike planes which might change from yellow to orange, from orange to red, from red to purple, as one stroke succeeded another. In choosing these colors from facet to facet Cézanne observed—to some degree—the theory of advancing and receding color, which can be explained briefly:

A spot of yellow on a piece of blue paper appears to be in front of the blue, since yellow is optically an advancing color, blue a receding one. But a spot of blue on a sheet of yellow will look more like something seen through a hole in the paper than like something laid on top of it, for the same reason. This is because, in general, warm colors, such as yellow and orange, advance; in general cool colors, such as blue and blue-green or blue-purple, recede. But dozens of other considerations affect this generality, such as the texture of the colors, their relative intensities, their relative areas, and the effect on them of adjacent colors. And part of the problem of modeling in "plastic color" is the problem of the local color of the objects themselves, how to paint a green pear green, a red apple red, a white cloth white, yet to observe within the green, the red, and the white the color changes that will express the form. The word *express* is used instead of *describe* because the form can be "described" in black and white or with conventional use of color.

To reduce the idea of plastic color to these simple terms is immediately misleading, suggesting as it does that the objects in a picture by Cézanne are modeled on a formula that should be specifically recognizable in the painting itself. But this is almost never so. It is easy to imagine Seurat reducing the theory of plastic color to a series of equations, and then following the equations faithfully in a studio demonstration. For Cézanne this would have made the whole thing pointless. He was not a studio theorist; he insisted that the painter's first allegiance was to his subject, that he

414. CÉZANNE: *The Card Players*, 1890–92. 25¾ x 32". Collection Stephen C. Clark, New York.

must work in the presence of his subject. For Cézanne, constant allegiance and reference to the subject supplied both discipline and nourishment for the process of creation. If he was painting a landscape he set up his easel out of doors, like an impressionist, not to capture the landscape's effect, as the impressionists did, but to absorb its essence. For a painter to work in his studio from sketches or from memory was to weaken his communion with the subject; to have worked entirely from theory would have been to sacrifice this communication altogether. When circumstances forced Cézanne to abandon this principle, he chafed; at work on a large composition of nude bathers he is supposed to have complained that it was impossible to find a group of models willing to pose thus out of doors, on the spot. He was exaggerating when he fretted in this way, for he did customarily synthesize figure groups from preliminary drawings and paintings made from models. But he never synthesized a pure landscape; and in all his painting the theories of form and color, which we have imagined Seurat applying within the neat boundaries of a formula, were given an additional complication by the facts of nature as Cézanne observed and respected them. There are many photographs of localities painted by Cézanne, taken from spots as close as possible to those where he must have stationed himself at work. The surprising thing about these photographs in comparison with Cézanne's paintings is always his close adherence to the subject, where one expects deviation from it.

415. POUSSIN: *Shepherds in Arcady*, 1638–39. 33½ x 47½". Louvre, Paris.

Cézanne: Geometrical Form

The various elements of Cézanne's art are so completely integrated with one another that it is difficult to separate them for explanation one at a time. It is like taking a loaf of bread and trying to explain from it what flour is, and milk, and salt—above all, what yeast is, as the essential transforming element. So far, we have spoken of his effort to find within nature an order comparable to the classical ideal, and of his idea that color and the expression of form could be inseparably identified with one another. If we arbitrarily separate two more elements from their matrix, we should then be able to go ahead and make a summary of Cézanne's development from beginning to end without too many interruptions for qualifying comments. The first of these elements is his conception of geometry as the basis of all form; the second, his distortion of form for purposes of structural composition on a geometrical basis.

As for the first, his idea that all forms in nature could be reduced to geometrical ones, such as cylinders, cubes, spheres, and cones, was not new in itself. A frequent exercise in the studios showed beginners how the human body could be simplified into a series of boxlike or cylindrical shapes

—one for the chest, one for the pelvis, long ones for the thighs, jointed to others for the leg from the knee down, all this as an aid in establishing the general relationship of the parts of the body to one another before going into details of musculature and the like. And many artists, especially in the seventeenth century, concocted geometrical figures as novelties. But Cézanne's reduction of natural forms to their geometrical equivalents has nothing to do with simplification as a convenience or a stunt. It is at once structural and expressive. Expressively it capitalizes on the psychological association between simple, basic shapes and the basic facts of existence. A love and respect for simple things, a sense that they have a nobility connected with fundamental truth, is a constant in French thought and art. Cézanne's *Card Players* [414], where one man stands like a column and the men at the table have the solidity and dignity of natural objects—of hills or boulders—is an expression of this sense, conveyed by the solid geometrical forms disposed with architectural stability. This "architectonic" quality is close to a literal reflection of architecture. The three men, bending over their cards, approximate in space the volume of a great dome. Compositionally the picture has a direct relationship to a *Card Players* by the seventeenth-century Italian Caravaggio; in spirit it has a less obvious but more basic one to Poussin's *Shepherds in Arcady* [415]. Cézanne's *Card Players* shows that "Poussin over again after nature" need not refer to landscape alone: in a commonplace subject, and without loss of contact with the everyday world, Cézanne has achieved classical dignity.

Dignity permeates every object Cézanne paints, whether it is a human figure, a factory chimney, a discarded mill wheel, a sugar bowl, a piece of fruit, or "a mere crumpled tablecloth," which "may take on the majesty of a mountain," as Sir Charles Holmes said. In *The Card Players* Cézanne does what Millet would have liked to do, but could not do because he could not rise far enough above his persistent sentimental realism. Of simple people Cézanne made abstract forms expressing the dignity of human existence.

Cézanne: Distortion and Composition

In addition to being almost symbolically expressive, the reduction of forms to geometrical equivalents was a compositional device for Cézanne. After admonishing a friend and follower (Émile Bernard) to see everything in nature in terms of geometrical solids, Cézanne went on to say that these solids should then be put into such perspective that planes and sides of objects were directed toward a central point. This element in Cézanne's composition is readily apparent in, again, *The Card Players* and is basic to the analysis of any of Cézanne's compositions where the objects are unified by a force that could be a mutual orientation toward a selected point, or perhaps several interrelated ones.

Although the orientation of the planes in a composition toward some selected point is a clue, Cézanne's composition is a much more complicated affair than, say, the problem of disposing several characters on a stage, directing them to stand facing a central character. By such an approach, still-life painting would be only a matter of arranging selected objects harmoniously and then reproducing their appearance with whatever slight modifications the painter wants to make. And this was, of course, the very definition of most still-life painting until Cézanne revolutionized it. Fantin-Latour's still-life of 1866 [195] shows that a selection of attractive objects nicely combined in a "set-up" can yield a beautiful picture even when the painter's reproduction of it is more photographic than interpretative.

A closer kinship with Cézanne is found in the realistic still-life paintings of Chardin,* an eighteenth-century artist who is Cézanne's natural forebear in the tradition of French "love and respect for simple things," which both painters express by revealing the dignity of unexceptional objects.

---

* Jean Baptiste Siméon Chardin (1699–1779) shifted the emphasis in still-life painting from technical display to formal organization. However, during his lifetime his work was more appreciated for its imitative than for its creative elements.

416. CHARDIN: *Apples, Pear and White Mug*, date unknown. 13 x 16½". Collection Mr. and Mrs. W. Averell Harriman, Arden, N.Y.

In Chardin the degree of verisimilitude is high. The departures from visual fact in *Apples, Pear, and White Mug* [416] are modifications, not distortions. Tone and color are subtly adjusted, meaningless details are eliminated to reveal the element of abstract formal organization beneath the apparently photographic representation. The weight, solidity, and texture of the objects are emphasized and their geometrical form is made the most of, yet not exaggerated. For most painters of still-life, sensitive realism like Chardin's offers sufficient range for expression. For Cézanne it did not. "I do not want to reproduce nature," he said. "I want to re-create it."

This re-creation in terms of the orientation of the planes, lines, and volumes of objects involved departures from visual fact sufficiently extreme to go beyond modification and become distortion. By realistic standards, the table in *The White Sugar Bowl* [417] is askew, the folds of the cloth do not "read," there are dark outlines here and there which can have no photographic justification. As a specific example, the upper edge of the piece of fruit at the far right center is defined against a thick dark line (in the original, a purplish black) unjustifi-

417. Cézanne: *The White Sugar Bowl*, 1890–94. 22 x 24½″. Collection Henry P. McIlhenny, Philadelphia.

able on any score connected with the imitation of the object. Such a line around part of any of the objects in the Chardin would be a shocking disfigurement because it would violate the literalness upon which the picture is based. But such lines, and similar variations from literalness, occur throughout the Cézanne, along with other departures, such as the tilted tabletop with its splayed boundaries.

The effect of the dark line is to pull that part of the table plane which is behind the piece of fruit closer to the plane of the fruit itself. It also modifies the spherical volume of the fruit, tending to flatten it a little. In other words, Cézanne has stopped regarding a table top as a plane and a piece of fruit as a solid to be imitated in such a way that their relationship in his picture must approximate their relationship as parts of the "set-up" from which he is working. He now regards them as a plane and a volume to be adjusted at will to the demands of pictorial organization. Abstract values have superceded realistic ones. If he wants to pull two planes closer together than they are in nature, he does so; if he wants to flatten a solid, he does so; if he wants to tilt a plane, as the table top, he does so, as part of an arrangement of planes and solids that could not exist literally in nature, but can and does exist wonderfully in painting. If he wants to vary the shape of an object in any way, he does so: the lemon in the extreme lower right corner of *The White Sugar Bowl* would be grossly misshapen if it were introduced into a Chardin or any other realistic still-life. It is flattened along its bottom edge, its axis is tilted upward from right to left. On the evidence of the picture, without knowing what explanation Cézanne himself would have made, it seems apparent that the flattening gives the form a base, stabilizing it at a point in the composition where a less static form would be distracting. And the upward right-to-left tilting or warping of the form as a whole engages it into the general movement of the composition, which is upward in the same direction. If this movement is followed across the picture, it is countered by the pear farthest to the left, which leans against the upward thrust.

Every element in the picture could be incorporated into any one of several discoverable movements across and into the composition. In the original, color is one of the balancing and coordinating factors as well as the primary one establishing the forms. If there is a single "central point toward which the planes and sides of objects are directed," it might be the apple nestled among other pieces of fruit and lying directly in front of the sugar bowl. We would then have two compositional systems incorporated into a single one—the upward right-to-left movement with its countermovement, and then the grouping of planes and volumes around the planes and volume of the "central" apple. Other schemes could certainly be discovered within these two. But in the long run it may be a mistake to attempt a formal analysis. It is enough to experience, without analyzing, the magnificent combination of stability and vivid life which is the end effect of the painting when it can be seen in the original, and is suggested even in a reproduction.

The importance of Cézanne's distortion of objects as a basic redirection of the art of painting can hardly be exaggerated. It is here that he becomes for his disciples the most important name since Giotto. For he proclaims the painter's right to "re-create" nature, to ignore the laws of representation formulated and used by painters over many centuries, to express the essence of his subject as he feels and understands it, and to violate the literal appearance of nature in

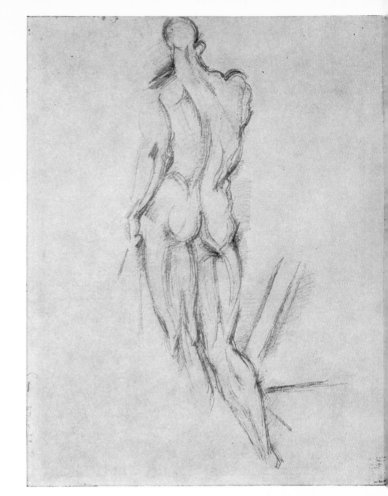

418. CÉZANNE: *Study after Houdon's "L'Écorché,"* 1888–95. Lead pencil on paper, 8¼ x 10¾″. Metropolitan Museum of Art, Maria De Witt Jessup Fund, from Museum of Modern Art, Lillie P. Bliss Collection. (*L'Écorché* is a flayed human figure used by students in the study of anatomy.)

any way he thinks is necessary to achieve this expression. This is the essence of modern art.

Cézanne: The Student

Cézanne was born in 1839 in the provincial city of Aix en Provence. His father, who had been a hat manufacturer and then become a banker, had accumulated a comfortable fortune. An important fact in Cézanne's boyhood and early youth was his friendship with a bright and ambitious young-

419. CÉZANNE: *Man in a Blue Cap* (*Uncle Dominic*), 1865–66.
32¼ x 26⅛". Metropolitan Museum of Art, New York, Wolfe Fund,
from Museum of Modern Art, Lillie P. Bliss Collection.

and understanding. The hero is recognizable as a composite of Cézanne, Manet (who could not object, having died three years before), and the typical concept of the artist as a bohemian renegade from society. Cézanne was deeply wounded. In a sad and polite letter he thanked Zola for the copy of the book he had sent, but he never spoke to him again.

Altogether, 1886 was a climactic year in Cézanne's life. He finally married a former model named Hortense Fiquet, after a liaison of some seventeen years which had produced a son who was now entering adolescence, and in the fall, Cézanne's father died and left him a fortune. Combined with the break with Zola and the sobering approach of late middle age, these were definitive events, although his relationship with Hortense had ceased to mean much. She spent most of her time in Paris with their son. Cézanne stayed on in Aix with his aged mother, seeing very few people, not even his old impressionist friends who used occasionally to visit him. Almost a recluse, moody and difficult, he painted for the next twenty years with no other thought than to reach a conclusion of the problems he had set himself. This was the fourth and last of the periods into which Cézanne's work falls.

Cézanne's first period is one of hesitancy, confusion, and groping. At twenty he was studying law in Aix in accordance with his father's wishes, but in accordance with his own he was also working in the local art school. On the side he was trying to fumble through the study of painting by himself, working in a strong but dark and oppressive manner suggested by seventeenth-century Italian and Spanish painting, which he knew largely in reproductions. In 1861 his father allowed him to abandon his half-hearted efforts to go through with the study of law, and he went to Paris to join Zola and prepare for entrance to the Academy's school. He worked in the *Académie Suisse*, an odd studio opened by a one-time model named Suisse, where models but no instructors were supplied. Delacroix had worked there at one time, and Courbet. Cézanne met Monet there, and Pissarro. Like everyone who came into contact with

ster just his own age who also lived in Aix—Émile Zola. They were best friends, and for a while, as young men, they imagined themselves making their careers together in Paris, Zola at his writing, Cézanne at his painting. But as it turned out, while Zola was becoming famous Cézanne was working in obscurity or exhibiting with scandalous receptions. Zola at first championed Cézanne as he championed Manet. But his faith in Cézanne wavered; it has already been noted that Zola's perceptions, when it came to painting, were not always equal to his crusading spirit.

Finally the friendship broke permanently, in 1886, when Zola published his novel *L'Oeuvre*, the story of a painter who worked against the current of popular taste

Pissarro, Cézanne revered him, and continued to do so all his life, referring to him as the "humble and colossal" Pissarro.

Such drawings as have remained from Cézanne's early days as a student are vigorous, rather blocky, with a concentration on massive, simplified forms within the slightly bulging contours of the baroque manner Cézanne admired at that time. (Twenty years later, he was still drawing from casts as a formal exercise [418].) They were far from the academic tradition, and Cézanne's application for admission to the *École des Beaux Arts* was rejected. He returned to Aix and tried to work in his father's bank for a while, but before long he was back in Paris.

He admired the painting of Delacroix for its swirling forms, of Courbet for its weight and solidity, and he also admired many academic painters, especially Couture. His interest in baroque painters with their strong chiaroscuro continued. It was a hodgepodge of enthusiasms, and Cézanne never managed to harmonize them during this first, or "romantic" period, which lasted up to 1872. He frequently used Courbet's palette-knife technique, exaggerating it until the strokes defining the broad planes were modeled almost as if in clay. This is

420. Cézanne: *The Artist's Father*, 1860–63. 65½ x 45". Philadelphia Museum of Art, on loan from Raymond Pitcairn, Bryn Athyn, Pa.

421. Cézanne: *Washing of a Corpse*, 1867–69. 19¼ x 31½". Collection Lecomte, Paris.

348

422. CÉZANNE: *Olympia*, 1875–77. Watercolor (and charcoal), 9¾ x 10½". Collection Louis E. Stern, New York.

Cézanne: The Impressionist

During these years Cézanne met Hortense Fiquet—in 1869—and their son was born. Cézanne was in and out of Paris, where he never really felt at home. He spent the time of the Franco-Prussian War and the Commune in Aix and in the village of l'Estaque, near Marseilles, avoiding the draft, and in 1872 he worked with Pissarro at Pontoise. Under this benign influence he entered his second, or impressionist, period.

Cézanne's impressionist period runs from 1872 to 1877. By 1878 he had discovered what Renoir was to discover five years later; he was the first of the impressionists to turn away from transient effects in landscape, if indeed he can be said ever to have accepted them. His great link with impressionism was Pissarro, who himself kept a fairly tight rein on impressionism's tendency to dissolve form into tinted veils. Later, Cézanne objected even to Pissarro's impressionism, saying that if he, Pissarro, had kept on as he had started, he would have been the greatest of them all. But Cézanne felt that, instead, Pissarro had succumbed to the common failing.

The two men worked side by side at Auvers, where Cézanne painted *The House of the Hanged Man* [423], which has become the standard example of his impressionist period. It was exhibited in the first group show, to which Cézanne was admitted upon Pissarro's insistence over general objections. Manet even gave as a reason for not exhibiting that he could not afford to commit himself alongside Cézanne, who was thought of as a little freakish even by those other members who sensed his strength. And Cézanne gave them plenty of reason for feeling so. He was rough in manner, sometimes surly, always unsure of himself, and defensively contemptuous of fine manners. In a rare excursion into satire he did a take-off on Manet's *Olympia* [422], including in the background a top-hatted dandy as a jibe at Manet.

When the impressionist exhibition opened, Cézanne's pictures were the most ferociously attacked of all. (It goes without saying that all this time, and for a long time

apparent in *The Man in a Blue Cap* [419], also called *Uncle Dominic*. By hindsight or coincidence this breaking-up into planes forecasts Cézanne's later expression of planes in color sequences, but as to color itself *The Man in the Blue Cap* is not related to this idea. It is done in tans, browns, and creams and grays, punctuated by the bright blue-green of the cap, the dash of red in the scarf at the neck, and rather ruddy flesh tones. Other pictures of the period may be almost without color, in dark browns and blacks, with monochromatic lights, like the awkward but powerful portrait of *The Artist's Father* [420]. The still-lifes are also thickly painted, rather heavy in form, sometimes almost ponderous. There are many emotionalized subjects, sometimes in the form of allegories, often suggesting frustrations and confusions. There are religious subjects, including some "copies" which are very free adaptations of well-known baroque paintings. In this manner there is the odd and rather disturbing *Washing of a Corpse* [421], which at first glance seems to be a *Pietà*, or mourning of Christ.

423. CÉZANNE: *The House of the Hanged Man*, 1873–74. 22¼ x 26¾". Louvre, Paris.

after, Cézanne was regularly rejected from the Salon.) Yet, as an impressionist painting, *The House of the Hanged Man* is much more concerned with formal definition, much less with light effects, than the average. It is impressionistic in the purification and heightening of color; impressionism had released Cézanne from his heavy browns and blacks and had taught him to apply his paint more sensitively, in smaller strokes. These elements finally led to his thinking in terms of planes and volumes modeled in color.

Cézanne: Realization

The third period, in which Cézanne abandons impressionism and matures as an original artist, runs from 1878 to 1887, ending during the months of his marriage, his father's death, and the break with Zola. By now Cézanne had abandoned Paris ex-

cept for an occasional short visit. From time to time he saw Renoir, Monet, Pissarro, and Zola, but in his preoccupation with new problems he began to withdraw from his friends. After the group show of 1878 he did not exhibit again with them. If Zola had been able to understand the work of his friend at this time he might not have said, as he did about 1880, that the misfortune of the impressionists was that no artist had achieved "powerfully and definitely" the possibilities inherent in the new painting. "They are all forerunners," he said of the impressionists. "The man of genius has not arisen."

The man of genius had arisen and was at work in the steady light of the south, solidifying the shifting, quivering effects of impressionism into something solid and durable like the art of the museums, and reconciling Poussin with nature. The transformation of Cézanne's art in this "constructive" or "classical" period is revealed by

424. CÉZANNE: *View of Gardanne*, 1885–86. 31 x 25½". Metropolitan Museum of Art, New York, and Dr. F. H. Hirschland, Harrison, N.Y.

even a superficial comparison of *The House of the Hanged Man* with a *View of Gardanne* [424]—a small town not far from Aix—where the houses rising on the steep slope are abstracted into a configuration of interlocking planes. If such a subject, like Corot's, seems half-readymade, with its blocky houses mounting up to the climax of the steepled church, it is largely because Cézanne's statement is so clear. In the hands of most painters the picturesqueness of the jumbled houses almost on top of one another would have been exaggerated by playing up the interest and variety of the

425. CÉZANNE: *L'Estaque and the Gulf of Marseilles,* 1882–85. 25¼ x 31½". Collection Mrs. Carroll S. Tyson, Chestnut Hill, Pa.

426. CÉZANNE: *Still-life with Commode, c.* 1885. 25¾ x 31⅞". Fogg Art Museum, Cambridge, Mass., Maurice Wertheim Collection.

very confusions Cézanne eliminates when he paints planes, not walls, and volumes, not houses, and disposes them in a painting where the interest must be in created abstractions, not in imitated picturesqueness. This is what Cézanne means by "motif" instead of subject. *View of Gardanne* is a fine semiabstract pictorial structure; it would not make the best possible travel poster.

In subjects less obviously adaptable to logical disposition, the sense of organization in Cézanne's transmutation of the forms is just as great even if the means are less apparent. In landscapes like *L'Estaque and the Gulf of Marseilles* [425] all the elements dearest to the impressionists—water, sky, foliage, a scattering of small architectural forms—begin to coalesce in a new perspective, a perspective expressed by color instead of vanishing points. In talking about

427. Cézanne: *Madame Cézanne, c.* 1885. 18⅛ x 15". Collection S. S. White III and Vera White, Ardmore, Pa.

428. Cézanne: *The Man in Blue, c.* 1895. 31⅞ x 25⅝". Collection Mrs. T. G. Kenefick, Buffalo, N.Y.

his pictures to his friends, Cézanne used to point to passages where he was dissatisfied because the color remained merely color, not simultaneously color and perspective. By definition, perspective is "the science of representing on a plane surface, natural objects as they appear to the eye," with vanishing points and linear systems that create an illusion of distance. But Cézanne abandons the idea of perspective as line. "Color is perspective." He is not interested in an illusion of distance or an illusion of form. In his landscapes there is a new compactness, a deliberate limiting of space. The distance from foreground to background across trees and fields, buildings, and the gulf and on to the hills on the other side in *L'Estaque and the Gulf of Marseilles* (as in his other landscapes now) is contracted toward the observer. Instead of emphasizing the recession of plane after plane into expanding distance, Cézanne draws each plane for-

ward, compressing space and thus increasing the sense of ordered unity.

When he is not painting out of doors he is working at the same kind of problem in still-life, in front of the apples and pears that rotted during the weeks, the artificial flowers, and the ginger jar, the plate, and the few vases that appear in picture after picture. Objects assume new patterns of planes and volumes in arbitrary flattenings and tiltings, new balances and new rhythms [426]. Heads and bodies, in portraits and figure studies, are subject to similar distortions. Yet for all their revolutionary character, the paintings are first of all alive as expressions, whatever their surface of technical theory. Cézanne never loses himself in theory, a danger of which he was always conscious. Far from pure theoretical demonstrations, his landscapes are still filled with the life of growth; portraits are still personalities, even pictures of mood [427,428].

429. CÉZANNE: *Mont Sainte-Victoire*, 1885–87, 23½ x 28½". Phillips Collection, Washington, D.C.

Cézanne: Fulfillment

In the final period, the twenty years from 1886 until his death, Cézanne pushed toward a conclusion, generally in the direction of increased abstraction. To indicate the extent of this development, two views of Mont Saint-Victoire, near Aix, may be compared. The first [429] was painted just at the dividing line of the third and fourth periods; the second [430] is a work not earlier than 1904, two years before his death.

The low peak of Sainte-Victoire, rising above the countryside and familiar to Cézanne all his life, visible from his studio window, preoccupied him in painting after painting. It must have become for him something of a symbol of what he wanted to express: the grandeur, the life, the power, yet the eternal order and stability of nature. In the earlier of the two pictures we are comparing, the peak is seen across a valley where a viaduct, roads, fields, and houses are ordered around it. We are led to its mass across a complexity of smaller volumes ordered, among other ways, by the fanning out of roads and the divisions between fields. Partly because of coincidental reasons, such as the bordering trees and the pattern of foliage against the sky, the rolling terrain mounting toward a climax and bearing many small architectural forms, this picture is especially close to Poussin, specifically to *The Funeral of Phocion* [128]. But for all its grandeur and vitality, the scene is also intimate in its sense of enclosure, of peace and order.

In contrast, the very late painting is more severe, yet it is electric in its sharp, vividly

430. Cézanne: *Mont Sainte-Victoire from Les Lauves, c.* 1904. 27⅞ x 36⅛″. Philadelphia Museum of Art, George W. Elkins Collection.

431. Cézanne: *Mont Sainte-Victoire from Bibemus Quarry, c.* 1898–1900. 25½ x 32″. Baltimore Museum of Art, Cone Collection.

colored planes. The forms now approach complete abstraction. Occasionally a house may still be distinguished as a house, or a clump of trees may tell as itself, but for the most part from plane to plane, which means from color to color, the forms exist as color-planes only. The mass of the mountain itself remains recognizable, yet it is broken into echoes and continuations of the planes that build toward it, and these planes are further continued into the sky. The compression of space is extreme. Fields, mountain, and sky are concentrated into the shallowest depth compatible with the interlocking crystallization of vivid blue, green, and orange planes.

Again and again Cézanne explored Mont Sainte-Victoire as a motif. Somewhere between these two versions, in its degree of abstraction, is a view of the mountain as

432. Cézanne: *Landscape with Mont Sainte-Victoire*, 1885–87. Watercolor, 15¼ x 19⅝".
Fogg Art Museum, Cambridge, Mass.

seen across the gash of a quarry [431]. The flat clifflike sides of orange stone impose a different order upon the composition; the peak is given a sharper elevation in harmony with the uncompromising upward rise of the quarry walls with their vertical divisions. As a final comparison, the sharp upward movement of this version contrasts with the lower forms, the gentler movement, of a watercolor painted, again, just at the turn of the third into the fourth period [432].

Cézanne's watercolors are of extraordinary delicacy. They never suggest the heaviness and the occasional fumbling that it is possible to find in some of his oils. (Other oils are painted nearly as thinly and transparently as watercolor.) The forms are indicated with a few lines lightly touched onto the paper with pencil, then these are supplemented with a minimum of plane-like washes in small areas of prismatic blue, pink, green, and violet, very pale but clear and bright.

Cézanne: "The Great Bathers"

It was after 1886 that Cézanne painted the synthesized figure studies, such as *The Card Players* which we have already seen, one of five variations on the subject, and *The Great Bathers,* the climax of a long series of compositions of bathers in landscape.

The theme of bathers in a landscape had interested Cézanne in different ways as far back as his very early "romantic" period. *The Great Bathers* [433] painted near the end of his life is a curious picture, an arresting one certainly, and for most people not a very agreeable one. Cézanne's distortion in still-life and landscape is nowadays acceptable to even casual observers; it is slight in comparison with the extreme distortion seen constantly in modern painting, familiar to everyone because it is reproduced on every hand. After the more jolting experience of Picasso's rupture and rending of natural form, the person with no formal

433. Cézanne: *The Great Bathers*, 1898–1905. 82 x 99″. Philadelphia Museum of Art, Wilstach Collection.

knowledge of art accepts Cézanne's trees and mountains and apples and pears without questioning their relatively mild departures from visual fact. But it is not so easy for the layman to accept the distortion of the human body with its strong associations dependent upon a standard of normal physical beauty. The female nudes in *The Great Bathers* may be no more distorted than the cloth, the bowl, and the fruit in *The White Sugar Bowl* (which belongs to the same period) but they are more disturbing because they violate a standard of beauty that is held with an emotional tenacity not at all comparable to the average person's respect for the shape of an apple or a pear.

These comments are obvious enough and would be altogether pointless except that

there is a legitimate question as to whether the stock problem of nudes in a landscape is an entirely sympathetic one for Cézanne's purposes. For Renoir, yes; his *Bathers* remain delicious creatures as well as the components of a painting. They are also expressive of the theme uniting Renoir's total work: the beauty of the world as he knew and loved it and found it symbolized in women. But there is no reason why the female nude should serve Cézanne as a motif; there are even reasons why it should not, since it is known that he was embarrassed in the presence of a nude female model, suspicious and fearful of women in general. The simple, straightforward men who were his models for *The Card Players* are compatible, as motifs, with the closeness to simple values that we have called basic in Cézanne's art, with its expression of the dignity of everyday, ordinary things. From this point of view, *The Great Bathers*—Cézanne's most ambitious effort as a monumental structure—may be far down the list expressively, since its motif is so artificial, so far removed from the painter's own emotional experience. At the same time, this very removal clarifies the painting as a pure formal abstraction. Historically, *The Great Bathers* is a landmark in the development of abstract painting, the summit of Cézanne's art. Its importance in the genesis of twentieth-century painting will become apparent later in comparison with, for instance, Picasso's *Les Demoiselles d'Avignon* [560]. By itself, *The Great Bathers* may be less rewarding than most Cézannes. But in context with his total work, as a planned climax and summary, it is an important document in the history of art.

At least three of the several formal systems that are fused into the construction of the picture are apparent without much searching. First, of course, there is the powerful arched form established so emphatically by the tree trunks and echoed by at least a portion of each figure. Second, a countersystem reverses this upward thrust by a downward one climaxing where the arms of the central figures reach toward a central spot. This countersystem, also, is reflected in some portion of each figure. Finally, there is a movement into compositional depth, most apparent in the figure at the lower right lying on its stomach and facing into the picture. There are also the strong stabilizing horizontals of horizons and banks running across the center and lower portions of the composition. The picture is not finished; parts of the canvas are not covered. But the vigor and the deliberation and the consistency of the picture as it stands, the integration of every smallest part into the structural whole, are so satisfying that there is no sense of loss in our knowledge that the structural process could have continued into further complications and refinements.

In the last decade of his life, Cézanne began to be well known. By 1900, except in the usual backwater of academic intelligence, his power and the importance of his revolution were recognized beyond the specialized circle of a very few dealers, painters, and critics. In 1895 the dealer Ambroise Vollard exhibited a large number of Cézanne's paintings, reintroducing him to Paris after a lapse of close to twenty years. Vollard was only thirty years old at this time and had opened his firm only two years before. Not very certain of his own taste, he wisely accepted advice from good sources, especially from Pissarro and Degas. Pissarro, always Cézanne's good angel, brought him to Vollard's attention. It was the beginning of Vollard's career as a dealer in *avant-garde* painting, and Cézanne painted his portrait in 1899. The public was appalled by the 1895 exhibition, the conservative painters and critics were outraged, but Cézanne was immediately established as a master in the minds of the former impressionists and among the canny collectors who were beginning to gather around adventurous dealers. It did not take long for the baying of the academic hounds to recede into the distance as a meaningless racket. Within a few years, independent critics had become at least as influential as official ones, and exhibitions held by independent dealers were even more influential than the official Salon as arbiters of taste—finally to the point of abusing their prestige, in some cases, as badly as the Salon had ever done. And the Salon, considerably chastened, liberalized its standards to meet the competition of the more exciting exhibitions that had grown up all around it.

Cézanne died in 1906, at sixty-seven, after a collapse brought on by exposure when he was caught in a sudden storm while painting out of doors. In the autumn Salon of 1907 he was given a large retrospective. As a summary of a painter's development, a retrospective exhibition is associated with the idea of a winding up, a completion, a capping-off, a termination. In Cézanne's case it is impossible to make this association. His retrospective was not the terminal point of a career so much as it was a summary of a new concept of form in painting that had been brought, in the art of one man, from its genesis in impressionism to a point of departure for the generations of a new century.

434. MAILLOL: *Leda*, 1902. Bronze, height 11½″. Philadelphia Museum of Art, Lisa Norris Elkins Bequest.

Sculpture in Transition: Maillol

Sculpture during the nineteenth century acted as if it were a dependent and admiring younger brother to painting, content to follow its direction rather than to set new, legitimately sculptural directions for itself. Sculpture found no Cézanne, but it found a man who re-established the validity of sculpture as an independent medium, and who did so by a renewal of classical concepts, and hence must be interpolated at this point in this narrative.

For several decades, Rodin had been the only sculptor of any declamatory force, and he dominated sculpture until well after the end of his century. But even Rodin had been exceptional more for his range as a one-man summary of principles connected with romantic and realistic-impressionist painters than as a sculptor adding legiti-

mately to the tradition of sculpture in its own right. The man who at last challenged Rodin's conception with a contrasting one was Aristide Maillol (1861–1944).

Maillol was forty before he turned seriously to sculpture. Before that, he had studied painting at the Academy under Gérôme, and under Cabanel. But he was never fascinated by painting; he had the love of handcraft that is part of every good sculptor's nature, and in 1887 he abandoned pure painting to set up a tapestry workshop. He might have spent the rest of his life happily enough at this work, carving a few wooden figures for relaxation as he did, but in the last year of the century his eyes were so weakened that he gave up tapestry design. Thus, at the age of forty, he became a sculptor and thus, also, he becomes the first artist in this story whose important work falls wholly within the twentieth century.

Maillol's beginning as a painter makes it even more surprising that as a sculptor he had no use for semipainterly modeling. He began to build the solidest, most purely sculptural forms that had appeared in a hundred years. His goddesses [434] are the stocky, full-bodied country girls who posed for him, de-individualized by formal generalizations into universal symbols. Maillol is classical (not neo-classical) because he brought back to sculpture the repose, the serenity, the balance and stability, that had been forgotten in the cultivation of accessory detail by imitative realists and the busy surfaces of Rodin and his followers.

When we say that Maillol merely rejected realism and impressionism, and returned to a kind of classicism, it may appear that his revolution was only a negative one in the first case, a reactionary one in the second. But this is not quite so. Maillol did more than clear away a great deal of debris, and his classicism had nothing to do with the imitation of classical clichés. Maillol re-established the validity of sculpture as an art of pure form, self-contained and self-sufficient; he set it on course again as an independent art. He brought back to sculpture the self-respect which, until then, no one had quite realized it had lost.

CHAPTER 11

Post-impressionism: Its Romantics

The Nature of Expressionism

Seurat and Cézanne were painters within the classical tradition by its most inclusive definition: they believed that the chaotic material of human experience could be clarified and universalized, and that the means of effecting this transmutation could be discovered through the analysis of form and structure. The fact that their forms were so innovational—especially Cézanne's —makes them no less classical. It simply demonstrates that the classical spirit need not depend for expression on images of gods and heroes foreign to the modern world, but may assume forms as original as those of gods and heroes had been when the classical Greeks invented them so long ago. The art of Seurat and Cézanne led the way for the abstract geometrical schools of the twentieth century, such as cubism, which completed the transformation of the gods and heroes into the simplest Euclidian rectangles.

But paralleling this "classical" development, the romantic spirit was forcing its own new expressions, this time with pain and violence exceptional even for romanticism. The art and the lives of Vincent van Gogh and Paul Gauguin were spectacular climaxes in the romantic tradition (which has a way of expressing itself in climaxes); their painting led in turn to the romantic art of the twentieth century, which was expressionism and its variants.

Expressionism in painting is the free distortion of form and color for the expression of inner sensations or emotions. All expressive art is a transfiguration of form to some degree, but expression*ism* is especially con-

435. DAUMIER: *Clown, c.* 1868. Composite wash drawing, 14½ x 10¼". Metropolitan Museum of Art, New York.

tional world. Less intimately, the expressionist may interpret the world for the observer by distortions revealing its essence in emotional terms peculiar to the painter. Expressionism is romanticism extended—further intensified.

Expressionism is a new term and it applies specifically to modern art, but as a general term it can apply here and there as far back as one cares to go in the history of art. In the late sixteenth century when El Greco twisted and elongated his forms and tied them together in near-hysterical patterns of swirls, angles, and lights, he anticipated the devices of expressionism, although the word was not to exist until three centuries later. And when Daumier, in one of the great drawings of the nineteenth century [435] abandoned his usual economical, realistically descriptive draughtsmanship for a tangle of agitated lines to describe a clown standing on a chair, waving his arms and shouting, he was drawing expressionistically. In the arms, recognizable form even disappears. Descriptively, the arm on the left is entirely illegible as an arm, but expressively it climaxes a pathetic and goaded figure in which Daumier makes one of his rare pessimistic statements about life, agreeing with Macbeth that it is "a tale told by an idiot, full of sound and fury, signifying nothing."

Van Gogh: "The Starry Night"

Modern expressionism stems directly from the tragic Dutchman, Vincent van Gogh (1853–1890), a man a little older than Seurat, who died a year before Seurat did. Both stemming from impressionism, these contemporaries could hardly be more unlike—Seurat with his calculation, his method, his deliberation, van Gogh with his passion, his shattering vehemence. Instead of *La Grande Jatte*, so cool, so defined, so self-contained, van Gogh gives us *The Starry Night* [436], where a whirling force catapults across the sky and writhes upward from the earth, where planets burst with their own energy and all the universe surges and pulsates in a release of intolerable vitality.

cerned with intense, personal emotions, and frequently has connotations of pathos, violence, morbidity, or tragedy. Distortion in itself is not necessarily expressionistic. Cézanne's distortions are not, because they are primarily structural, and only indirectly a vehicle for the transmission of his feelings. And these feelings in any case are not transmitted in intimate, emotionalized terms.

The expressionist opens his heart and soul and releases his deepest feelings through images intended to embrace the observer and make him a partner rather than an audience, a participant or, at least, a sympathizer within the picture's emo-

436. Van Gogh: *The Starry Night*, 1889. 29 x 36½". Museum of Modern Art, New York, Lillie P. Bliss Bequest.

Like all the most affecting expressionist creations, *The Starry Night* seems to have welled forth onto the canvas spontaneously, as if the creative act were a compulsive physical one beyond the artist's power to restrain. "Inspiration" as a kind of frenzied enchantment visited upon a painter, a paroxysm calling forth images only half-willed, is a justifiable conception in van Gogh's case, if it is ever justifiable at all. *The Starry Night* implies that it was executed in a fever of creation, as if it had to be set down somehow on canvas in an instant, as if a pause for calculation would check the gush, the momentum, of a brush guided by a mysterious spiritual force rather than by knowledge and experience. And to a certain extent this was so. Van Gogh's letters tell of days when his painting went well, when he would work into the night without stopping to eat. In some pic-

tures the paint is squeezed onto the canvas straight from the tube, as if to reduce to a minimum the obstructions between conception and execution. Yet all this is misleading. His letters also speak of his studies for a picture that obsesses him, a picture of a starry night. There is a full preliminary drawing.

If *The Starry Night* seems to burst, to explode, to race, it does not run away. It is built on a great rushing movement from left to right; this movement courses upward through the landscape, into the hills and on into the sky, and floods into the picture like a swollen river in the galaxy beginning at the border on the upper left. But this movement curls back on itself in the center of the picture, then rushes forward again at a reduced pace, and finally curls back once more to join other rhythms instead of running out of the picture. In the rest of the sky, the moon and stars are whirlpools meshing with these major movements. The cypresses rise abruptly and lean slightly in the opposite direction as a brake; their own motion, spiraling upward, is another check to the horizontal lunge of earth and sky; a church steeple cuts less conspicuously across the sweep of a hill on the horizon, to the same effect. The moon, largest of the whirlpools of light, is itself a force that sucks the current back into the picture at a point where it would otherwise rush beyond the frame and be lost.

All of this is calculation, not in Seurat's sense certainly, but it is a scheme consciously observed. *The Starry Night* may have been painted at white heat and even with passages of improvisation. Something like "inspiration" was present and accounts for the extraordinary immediacy of the picture, but this inspiration flowed from a reservoir of study and experience even if it was released by the passionate absorption of the moment. But in the end, it is this moment that tells. Confronted by *The Starry Night* we are brought into van Gogh's presence more intimately than other painters ever quite bring us into theirs. It is a bitter kind of poetic justice that today thousands of people find van Gogh an accessible and sympathetic personality, while during his life, craving love and offering it everywhere, he was able to form only a handful of friendships, and of these half were disastrous.

Van Gogh: Early Days and Works

Indeed van Gogh must be a much easier man to read about than he was to be around. Small, ugly, and intense, without charm or wit, intelligent but narrow, socially awkward, ill dressed as a point of honor, tortured by religious confusions, yearning for affection but egotistical and stubborn, eager to please but resentful of criticism, he was one of those people who hold noble ideals too nobly, who offer their love as an embarrassing gift, whom one would like to like but whose presence is a burden. He seemed incapable of enjoying himself or of giving pleasure; in all the letters he wrote—and he wrote beautifully in them—there is no indication that he ever took anything casually for a moment.

The men of van Gogh's family were traditionally clergymen, but two uncles had a prosperous gallery in The Hague, which they sold to the international art dealer Goupil. Through this connection young Vincent, at sixteen, obtained a place with Goupil, first in The Hague, then in London, and finally in the main branch of the firm in Paris. But he failed. Never suave, always opinionated, no friend of the rich, who buy pictures, he ended by irritating so many customers that he was dismissed. Turning to religion, he failed at the theological seminary. When he sought to sacrifice himself in service as a combination evangelist and social worker among miners in a desperately depressed and gloomy area, he failed. He subjected himself to all the hardships of his poverty-stricken parishioners— their miserable quarters, their abominable diet. He slept on a hard board and a straw mattress when he could have had a comfortable bed. The miners laughed at him, their children hooted at him in the streets. Twice in love, he was twice rejected—once by his landlady's daughter in London, once by a cousin. Rejected by the women he wanted to love, rejected by the people he wanted to help, van Gogh attempted to fulfill himself on both scores by living with and caring for a prostitute he picked up on the street, ugly, stupid, and pregnant. This idyll, which could have been inspired by Dostoevski, endured for twenty months.

It was not until 1880, when he was twenty-seven years old, that van Gogh decided to be a painter. He entered this new life not as one enters a profession but as one accepts a spiritual calling, in foreknowledge of self-sacrifice.

His will, his compulsion, to paint as a direct expression of self, as a psychological need quite aside from professional ambitions or the will to fame, no matter what suffering would be involved, sets van Gogh apart from the impressionists, who had fought stubbornly in the face of every discouragement but had always been professional painters, careerists. Delacroix had established the idea of the painter's right to paint as he pleased, to enter into a pitched battle against entrenched manners of painting; Courbet had continued to fight, more as an individual than as a member of an organized school with a leader and henchmen; the impressionists had further abandoned the pre-nineteenth-century idea of the painter as a craftsman with a product to sell in satisfaction of a demand, and finally were to succeed in creating a demand by bringing public taste into line with their standards. They seemed to have culminated the idea established by Delacroix. And to all these painters, of course, art was certainly a release and an emotional satisfaction, as creation must be to any artist. But they were professionals. With van Gogh the balance swings to the other side. Although he yearned for attention, although he exhibited when he could, and finally managed to sell one painting, he was not first of all a man making his way in a profession. He was a man intent on saving his soul, in creating his very being, by painting pictures.*

Van Gogh had begun to draw at the time of his failure as an evangelist among the miners, and had attended classes for a while at the academy in Brussels. He began his serious study as an overage beginner in the academic art school at The Hague, but did not stay long. He had a cousin there, Anton Mauve, one of the most popular painters of the day. Mauve was a painter of sentimentalized humanitarian subjects in the degenerating tradition of the Barbizon school. The association did not last long,

ending as so many of van Gogh's associations did, in a quarrel. This was also the time of his association with the prostitute Sien, which had become intolerable. Van Gogh left to paint on his own in the town of Neunen, where his father was now pastor. He puzzled and frightened the townsfolk; the pastor forbade them to pose for his son.

The work from this period—from his first efforts in 1880 until the beginning of 1886 —is a continuation of the obsessive humanitarianism that had led Vincent into evangelical work, and it has the same excess of gloomy fervor that had led to his failure in it. His subjects are poor people, squalid streets or farms, miners and peasants broken by poverty and toil, the inmates of almshouses. He draws in crayon or charcoal, and in his paintings his colors are as depressing as his subjects. His first large, ambitious composition, of which there are three versions, was *The Potato Eaters* [437], painted in the dismal browns and greenish blacks of the period. "I have tried to make it clear how these people, eating their potatoes under the lamplight, have dug the earth with these very hands they put in the dish. . . . I am not at all anxious for everyone to like or admire it at once."

His taste in painting generally was also involved more with humanitarian ideas than with aesthetic values. He admired Millet, and another French painter of peasants, l'Hermitte, and the Hollander Josef Israels, although he objected when these men idealized their subjects, as they usually did. He also admired Daumier and Rembrandt, again largely for their subject matter. He read such English authors as George Eliot and Dickens, who wrote of the poor and the oppressed. The American writer Harriet Beecher Stowe was another favorite; *Uncle Tom's Cabin*, with its pathetic slaves, stirred him deeply. He read the sociological realistic novels of Zola. But he also read the aesthetic de Goncourts. He hardly knew of the impressionist painters at this time.

Early in 1886 van Gogh suddenly left Holland for Paris. It seems to have been an abrupt decision. It was certainly an important one. He had gone to Antwerp and

---

* The single picture van Gogh sold, if we don't count the ones he traded for paints, was *Red Vineyards*, which was exhibited six months before his death in a group show organized by *Les Vingt*, the Brussels group with whom Seurat also exhibited. Van Gogh had exhibited in the Paris *Indépendants* shows, as anyone could do, and had organized two exhibitions in Paris restaurants, one in *Le Tambourin*, which was frequented by writers and painters, one in a huge low-priced restaurant called *La Fourche*. This was his public exhibition record during his lifetime. The year following his death he was given a retrospective at the *Indépendants*. This was in 1891. In 1935 when the Museum of Modern Art held the first big van Gogh show in New York it established the attendance record, to that date, for exhibitions of the work of a single painter.

437. Van Gogh: *The Potato Eaters*, 1885. 32 x 45". Municipal Museum, Amsterdam, V. W. van Gogh Collection.

had studied for a while at the academy there, but found it dull and restricting. Academic training was intolerable to him because it seemed divorced from the earthy and simple values he was interested in. But he was a clumsy draughtsman and he knew it, and he felt the need of stimulation and excitement from other painters. If he could not tolerate the school in Antwerp, neither could he go back to working on his own in a backward rural community. His brother Theo was directing a small gallery in Paris, a branch of Goupil's. Vincent wrote him that he would be in the Louvre at a certain hour, and asked Theo to meet him there.

Later, Theo was to recognize his brother's power as an artist, but at this time Vincent was only the family problem, a maladjusted and difficult man whose drawing was nothing more than an emotional stopgap, who was reaching his middle thirties and could not hold a job, who had shown that he was impractical and unstable and would have to be either sup-ported or abandoned to the most desperate circumstances of life, to vagabondage, starvation, the almshouse. The story of Vincent and Theo from now on is a poignant one. Their letters, up to Vincent's last unfinished one written just before his suicide, read like a fine novel and have furnished the material for several poor ones. In his letters Vincent reveals the gentleness and above all the clarity of thought that were so rare when he spoke and not at all apparent in his actions. His torment is equally revealed, and Theo's patience and love. But in their day-to-day relationships when they were together, Vincent remained a problem—stubborn, hypersensitive, and eccentric. Theo's heart must have sunk when he read Vincent's letter telling of his decision to come to Paris, but he took his brother into his flat, supported him from his own limited income, and set about helping him find his way toward a solution of his problems.

Theo's gallery handled work by all the major impressionists as well as the standard

438. Van Gogh: *Miners, Borinage,* 1880. Pen, lightly colored. 17¼ x 21½". Kröller-Müller State Museum, Otterlo.

Salon masters who sold much better. Theo himself, like any good dealer, was always hunting new talent and had scouted the impressionist group shows with more sympathy than most dealers risked. Vincent's arrival coincided with the final impressionist exhibition, when only a few of the original group were exhibiting and a special room had been given over to the neo-impressionists, including Seurat with *La Grande Jatte.*

The impressionists' happy, brightly tinted art did not immediately affect Vincent. He entered the studio of Cormon, a conventional painter who gave his students sound training in the imitation of the model. Here, a grown man among youngsters, Vincent labored industriously, correcting his drawings until he had erased holes in the paper, irritating everyone, the class freak. Just how he managed to get

accepted in a class limited to thirty students, with a waiting list, is a question. Theo's position as a dealer probably helped. Lautrec was among the students and Vincent came to his studio from time to time, but he was an odd ball in the effervescent company and after standing hopefully on the sidelines for a while he would disappear. Lautrec did a sketch of him at a café table; it shows a thin, bearded man leaning forward intently.

The stimulation and the new ideas Vincent had come to Paris to find, came not from the young men at Cormon's studio but from the patriarch of the impressionists, Pissarro, reappearing yet again in his constant role of saint. As he had done with Cézanne, Pissarro now induced Vincent to abandon his gloomy palette and turgid shadows for the bright, high-keyed colorism of the impressionists. But the trans-

439. VAN GOGH: *Factories at Clichy, c.* 1887. 21¼ x 28¼". City Art Museum of St. Louis.

440. VAN GOGH: *Landscape with Wall,* date unknown. Pen and ink, 8⅞ x 12½". Collection T. Edward Hanley, Bradford, Pa.

formation was more than a technical one; the spirit of Vincent's art was equally changed. One of his earliest existing drawings [438], done at about the time of his decision to work seriously at art, shows, as he described it in a letter to Theo, ". . . miners, men and women, going to the shaft in the morning through the snow,

by a path along a hedge of thorns; shadows that pass, dimly visible in the twilight. In the background the large constructions of the mine, and the heaps of clinkers, stand out vaguely against the sky . . . do you think the idea good?" Good or bad, the idea was typical of his preoccupation at that time with the hard lot of common people, full of cold, gloom, and miserable hardship. But now when he paints the *Factories at Clichy* [439] he has stopped seeing and thinking in terms of oppressed workers, blackened chimneys, belching smoke, piles of cinders and slag, and sees instead a blue sky, red roofs, a foreground of slashing yellows and greens, all singing in the open air.

From the broken strokes of impressionism and the uniform dots of pointillism (Vincent had made a brief sally in this latter direction) he developed a way of painting in short, choppy strokes of bright color, like elongations of the pointillist dots, which later were to bend and writhe and to be reflected also in drawings [440] of the greatest expressive economy. Suddenly he is an artist, suddenly his own man. The contrast between *Old Shoes* [441] and the portrait of *Père Tanguy* [442] painted the same year is complete. The old shoes are vigorously painted, but the color and the implied humanitarianism are still on the dull and rather heavyhanded level that is so bothersome in *The Potato Eaters.* But *Père Tanguy* suddenly lives, as no other of Vincent's images had lived until then, and Vincent himself suddenly lives as a fulfilled painter.

Julien Tanguy, affectionately called Père Tanguy, was a color grinder who as a traveling paint salesman had met most of the impressionists during their most difficult days before 1870. When he opened his own small shop of artists' materials in Montmartre he began "buying" their paintings, which usually meant accepting them in exchange for supplies. He also kept their work on hand for chance sales, and thus grew into a collector and art dealer. He was particularly fond of Cézanne; during the years of Cézanne's obscurity as a voluntary exile in Aix, his paintings could be seen only at Père Tanguy's. There were times when Monet and Sisley would have been without materials to paint with if it had not been for this fatherly man. Madame Tanguy did not share his confidence or his interest in those painters who, like van Gogh, used a great deal of paint but were totally unsaleable.

Psychologically, Vincent's portrait of Tanguy is a complicated picture in spite of the directness and solidity of the image. Tanguy as a personality, with his combination of naïveté and grandeur, is shown at once as a real person individualized by his bright eyes, his alert face, his simple coat and scarf and hat, and as a monumental abstraction with some of the quality of sculpture. There are few portraits where the play of personality between painter and subject is so apparent. Here, as he was to continue to do, Vincent paints his own psychological presence into the picture. The colors are vivid, with the strong dark-blue mass of the coat in the center surrounded by emerald greens and bright orange-yellows. Everywhere except in the blue coat, the painting is shot through with spots and lines of vermilion. There are lines of vermilion in the shadow on the left side of the face; a purely arbitrary line of vermilion separates the figure from the background, running from the neck on either side down along the shoulder and continuing to the bottom edge of the canvas. As Manet did in his portrait of Zola [192] van Gogh places his subject against a background of references, in this case Japanese prints. But where Manet painted a realistic image of great elegance and of great objectivity, every stroke of Vincent's brush is determined more by his reaction to the subject than by its appearance. From now on the painter who began as so dreary a colorist uses color of an intensity, both optical and expressive, beyond any use of it until this time.

Has Vincent benefited from his labors in Cormon's studio? Perhaps. In the drawing of the head and the hands of Père Tanguy there is a certainty and definition that may have been strengthened by the disciplines he inflicted on himself, but if it is examined academically the drawing fails everywhere, even where Vincent did not deliberately

441. Van Gogh: *Old Shoes*, 1887. 19½ x 28″. Fogg Art Museum, Cambridge, Mass., Maurice Wertheim Collection.

violate academic principles for expressive necessity. In the hands, the fingers of the hand on our right could not physically pass behind the others as they are supposed to do. As for Père Tanguy's right arm, from wrist to elbow, it does not exist within the sleeve, and the thigh below it is ambiguous. But these are foolish points, not to be thought of twice. Whether or not van Gogh could ever have become an academic draughtsman is beside the point, since he has now discovered where his power of expression lies, and he knows that it is not compatible with either academic regulation or impressionist vision. It is possible to think of pure impressionism as the ultimate imitative realism where the eye becomes only a lens (it was once said of Monet that he was "only an eye—but what an eye!"). And the world Vincent must transmute into images is accessible to no lens. It is an inner world of his own. While he thought of himself as the logical descendent of impressionism, actually he rejected all impressionism's values to explore this tormented inner world instead of impressionism's joyous everyday one.

In February, 1888, Vincent van Gogh left Paris for Arles, in the south of France, where this exploration was to begin in earnest.

442. VAN GOGH: *Père Tanguy*, 1887–88. 25½ x 20". Collection
Stavros Niarchos, Athens.

Van Gogh: Arles, Saint-Rémy, and Auvers

The events of van Gogh's life between his
departure from Paris in early 1888 until
his suicide in July, 1890, are well enough
known to have established him in the
popular mind as the archetype of the Mad
Genius. Not mad, he was an unstable personality who in the last two years of his life
was subject to epileptoid seizures. Not
quite a genius, he was a painter who in his
last two years produced a life work of extremest originality, combining theory with
a high degree of personal emotionalism.
Because the events of his life are dramatic
enough to be disproportionately intrusive

in a discussion of his painting, they must
be summarized first:

Vincent left Paris in a fit of despondency
to which many factors contributed. He was
irritated with the squabbling and bickering
that, he found, was the form usually taken
by the stimulating discussions he had
hoped for among painters. Not only was he
dependent on his brother Theo, but he felt
that he was in his way—as he was. And in
any case, Paris in February is not a cheerful
city in the low-income bracket. For a
painter who had suddenly discovered color
it was gray, its studios drear. By temperament Vincent was restless. He had lived
his life feeling that what he was hunting
was just around the corner. This time he
thought it lay in the brilliant sun and the
simpler life of a small Provençal city. And
this time it did.

Theo gave him an allowance and he set
himself up in Arles. For this man of thirty-
five it was like a youth's first discovery of
the world on his own. Before long he was
working so hard that he had several faint-
ing spells. Or perhaps these were the first
indication of the malady that was about to
make itself apparent. It was also just the
time of the arrival in Arles of the painter
Gauguin.

Gauguin was a fantastic and to van Gogh
a glamorous personality, with barbarous
and brutal good looks the ugly little man
must have envied, and an established reputation among avant-garde painters. The
men had met in Paris but did not know one
another very well in spite of Vincent's
strong attraction toward Gauguin. Gauguin
was somewhat older, and there is a hint of
adolescent hero worship in van Gogh's feeling for him. He urged Gauguin to visit him
in Arles; Gauguin finally consented. As far
as their painting was concerned there was
an important mutual influence. As far as
their life together was concerned there
were tensions beyond endurance, at least
beyond Vincent's, and in an incident that
apparently will never be clarified in its details there was a violent quarrel, after which
Vincent went to his room, cut off an ear,
wrapped it up, and delivered it to one of
the girls in a brothel that he had frequented
with Gauguin. This was during the last

weeks of 1888. Shortly before, he had painted a self-portrait as a present for Gauguin [443]; the words *"à mon ami Paul"* are still faintly discernable along the upper left border. The Arles experience had begun with the happiest period of van Gogh's life; but the face in the self-portrait for Gauguin is already the face of a man pushed to the limits of endurance, and the remainder of Vincent's life was torment beyond anything he had endured before.

During the first five months of 1889 he remained in Arles, with intermittent periods in the hospital as his seizures recurred. He suffered hallucinations, and his irrational behavior got him into trouble with the townspeople, as had happened elsewhere. Then for a year—May 1889 to May 1890—he was an inmate of the asylum at Saint-Rémy, near by, where he had comparative freedom and could receive immediate treatment—of a kind—during seizures. He worked passionately. *The Starry Night* was painted at Saint-Rémy.

By May the seizures seemed to have relented and he was thought well enough to return to the north. He went to Auvers, not far from Paris, where Pissarro lived and had worked with Cézanne. Pissarro would have taken Vincent into his own house but his wife, understandably, objected. The immediate reason for the choice of Auvers was the presence there of Dr. Paul Gachet* [444], a physician who had special qualifications for this special case since he was a friend of Pissarro's and Cézanne's and some

443. VAN GOGH: *Self-portrait*, 1888. 24½ x 20½". Fogg Art Museum, Cambridge, Mass., Maurice Wertheim Collection.

---

* Dr. Paul Gachet (1828–1909) was himself an amateur painter of creditable skill with a special fondness for engraving and etching. Cézanne did his only plates with Gachet, and van Gogh now etched the doctor's portrait. His acquaintance with painters went back to an early one with Courbet. Like Choquet and Caillebotte he discovered the impressionists for himself and collected them along with a lot of "dark pictures" that Vincent objected to in his house. His collection is now in the Louvre. He struck Vincent as being "at least" as eccentric as he himself was, and there was justification for this impression. Among the free-thinking doctor's several unusual schemes was one for a "mutual autopsy" association by which painters would leave their brains for analysis after their deaths. He had been something of a nuisance to the young impressionists but they were also genuinely fond of him.

of the other impressionists—whom he had frequently treated without a fee—and was as interested in art as he was in medicine.

In Auvers Vincent experienced no further seizures. He made occasional short visits to Paris, saw Lautrec there once more, and went to the Salon and exhibitions, but he could not take much of Paris at a time. In Auvers he painted constantly. Dr. Gachet was a miracle of encouragement. But Vincent feared a recurrence of the dreadful experiences in Arles and Saint-Rémy. His consciousness of the burden his life imposed on his brother was extreme, exaggerated now because Theo had married and had just had a son.

Vincent had come to Auvers in May. Near the end of July he began a letter to Theo in which two sentences are particularly revealing of the nature of his art and his relationship to it:

444. VAN GOGH: *Dr. Gachet*, 1890. Etching, 7⅛ x 6″. Philadelphia Museum of Art, McIlhenny Fund.

> "Really, we can speak only through our paintings.
>
> "In my own work I am risking my life, and half my reason has been lost in it."

He did not finish the letter. It was not a "suicide note," although parts of it are a summation of his relationship with Theo and have about them an air of finality. But when he stopped the letter in the middle and went out with his paintbox and his canvas he might have gone out to paint. The revolver with which he shot himself was never identified. He might have borrowed it on the way from a peasant, with the excuse that he would use it to shoot at the crows that were a nuisance in the fields. He shot himself below the heart, but managed to walk back to the inn where he was staying. Contrary to the circumstances as usually taken for granted, he did not shoot himself during an attack or in anticipation of one, and during the two days before he died he was lucid. Theo had been reached, and Vincent died in his arms.

Van Gogh: Later Work

The bulk of van Gogh's life work, the paintings that poured out during the two years and five months between his arrival in Arles and his suicide in Auvers, must be more familiar to a wider public today than the work of any other single painter. At least this is true in the United States. There are individual paintings, such as *Whistler's Mother* and the *Mona Lisa*, *The Blue Boy* and a Corot or two, that are better known, but in Vincent's case it is not a matter of one or two paintings. Half his work must have been reproduced in tens of thousands of color prints, offered in portfolios as inducements to subscribe to newspapers, framed up assembly-line fashion for sale in department stores and drug stores. To a vast audience on the fringe of "appreciation" he is synonymous with modern art—to which, actually, he is an excellent introduction.

This does not sound like a tragic art. Tragic art does not appeal to tens of thousands of people as a living-room decoration. The brilliance of the color, the decorative attraction of the shapes and images as they developed in Arles, are superficially cheerful. And some of the pictures are genuinely happy ones unless the pathetic associations of the painter's life are grafted onto them. But most of them take on a disquieting introspective intensity or restlessness if they are regarded as something more than spots of color on a wall.

This is true of *The Public Gardens in Arles* [445]. A twisting and writhing motion is only half repressed in the tree trunks, and it continues into the foliage and breaks through in the patch of sky, painted in a flat color yet in angular, motionful strokes. In the pictures of flowers, especially the great heavy sunflowers of Arles [446], there is the same duality. The series of sunflowers are his most popular pictures, the brightest in color, the most obviously ornamental and, being flowers, of course the most "cheerful" and nice to have around. The decorative quality was intentional. Vincent wrote from Arles in a letter to Émile Bernard that he was thinking of "decorating his studio with half a dozen paintings of

445. VAN GOGH: *The Public Gardens in Arles,* 1888. 28½ x 35⅜". Phillips Collection, Washington, D.C.

sunflowers, a decoration in which chrome yellow, crude or broken, shall blaze forth against various backgrounds of blue, ranging from the very palest emerald up to royal blue and framed with thin strips of wood painted orange. The sort of effect of Gothic stained glass windows." The modeling of the flowers' great coarse central cushions of stamens was done in actual relief, the pigment being built up close to a quarter of an inch in some places, and textured like the rough mass of the stamens themselves. Individual petals are also defined by relief, each one existing as a mass of paint with its edge standing out prominently in front of the petals behind it. The sunflower pictures are large ones, the monstrous blossoms being painted at full size. They have a savage vehemence that is reduced to bright prettiness in the small color prints that are so popular.

An extreme flatness as far as modeling in light and shade is concerned, or even as far as the breaking of color is concerned, is characteristic of the Arles pictures in general, but their surfaces are heavily textured. The background of *L'Arlésienne* [447] is a solid yellow, the brilliant yellow that obsesses Vincent now, broken only by the texture of the broad, thick, application. Purple, its complementary, is played against it in the dress, and within the clash of the two colors the figure is transfixed. It is a composition in silhouettes, the double influence of the Japanese print and of Gauguin, who was now visiting Vincent and working with him. But even while he was painting in the dark tones of the early period, van Gogh had come upon Japanese objects and had been fascinated by their color. In Paris he knew Japanese prints well, as we see in the background in the

446. VAN GOGH: *Sunflowers*, 1888. 36¼ x 29″. Collection Mrs. Carroll S. Tyson, Chestnut Hill, Pa.

447. VAN GOGH: *L'Arlésienne* (*Madame Ginoux*), 1887. 24 x 17″. Metropolitan Museum of Art, New York, Samuel A. Lewisohn Bequest.

portrait of Père Tanguy (where the color in the prints is exaggerated into brilliance, rather than reproduced in the softer tints of the originals), and he wrote about his trip to Arles that as he approached on the train he was so excited that he could almost believe it was Japan he was coming to. As a descendant of the Japanese print, *L'Arlésienne* has the obvious inherited characteristics of simplified silhouette and flat color, but the sinuous line of the Japanese silhouette has been replaced by a sharpened, forceful, more angular one, and the conventionalized charm has given way to a hypnotic intensity.

Madame Ginoux, a neighbor who posed in regional costume for *L'Arlésienne,* was one of several friendly people who solved for a while van Gogh's perpetual model problem. The most obliging of these were the postman Roulin and his wife. He painted five portraits of Roulin, one of them [448] showing his uniform in a strong blue

against a pale blue background, with the beard in short, straight, springing strokes of brownish and yellowish tints flecked with bits of bright blue and red. The figure is more three-dimensionally modeled than that of *L'Arlésienne,* but in the remarkable portrait of Madame Roulin called *La Berceuse* [449] the flatness is again extreme. The picture began with a sentimental idea. It was to recall lullabies to lonely men, Vincent said, and he compared its colors to common chromolithographs. He said from time to time that he wanted to make "naïve" and primitive images like those in popular almanacs or calendars that appealed to uncultivated people—another manifestation of his repeated efforts to identify himself with simple folk in whose lives he imagined that love and honesty and understanding existed in a natural state.

But it is typical of him that the intention he states in literary terms is seldom apparent in the completed picture—in most cases,

fortunately not. Whether or not he began
sentimentally he did not in the end paint
sentimentally in *La Berceuse,* and it certainly does not suggest a chromo. Madame
Roulin sits in an attitude reminiscent of
Père Tanguy's, but slightly turned, and the
figure is built in comparably simplified,
half-primitive forms. The hands hold a rope
that would be attached to a cradle, a usual
means of rocking one. The lower part of the
background is a solid red, against the complementary green of the skirt. The black
blouse and the face are played against a
background of wallpaper transformed into
a dreamlike pattern of flowers, some pink
ones being semirealistic alongside others
that are geometrized. All are connected by
odd loops and swirls, punctuated by dia-
mond shapes, these derived from stems and
leaves. The rest of the area is filled with
black rings, each with a dot of vermilion
in its center. The chair is defined by heavy
black outlines. The resultant combination
of naïveté, violence, and dream makes *La
Berceuse* one of van Gogh's great canvases
but it certainly does not recall a lullaby.

In van Gogh's attachment to the Roulins,
psychiatrists who are interested in post-
mortem analyses might find a substitute
parent relationship. Roulin, who was not
a mail carrier but worked at loading and
unloading mail from the trains, was a tremendous man, six and a half feet tall. Vincent wrote Theo that Roulin was "not quite
old enough to be like a father" to him, but
that he had a "silent gravity and tenderness
. . . such as an old soldier might have for
a young one." Thus he offered Vincent an
outlet for both the dependent filial affection
and the hero worship he was so eager to
bestow. In another letter Vincent refers to
sailors as "children and martyrs," a phrase
in which there are strong elements of a
psychological self-portrait, and he painted
the portrait *La Berceuse* of the motherly
Madame Roulin in such a way, he said,
that when these sailors saw it in their cabin
they would feel "the old sense of cradling
come over them."

After the crisis of his first attacks, his
break with Gauguin, and finally his transfer
to the asylum at Saint-Rémy, Vincent's
paintings take on the swirling, tempestuous

448. Van Gogh: *The Postman Roulin,* 1888. 32 x 25½". Museum
of Fine Arts, Boston.

form and the more mystical expression of
which *The Starry Night* is a climactic expression. But they are interspersed with
milder expressions, such as *The Road
Menders* [450], where the warm tones and
the everyday subject modify and even for
a moment conceal the compulsive writhing
of the great trees whose roots must plunge
into the earth with the same voracious
energy that forces the trunks and branches
upward. And in one exceptional moment
the fields around Saint-Rémy are painted
in the rain [451] and the violence fades
into poetic melancholy, the twisting lines
give way to a pattern of straight ones slanting across the surface of a composition recalling Japanese prints where rain over
quiet landscapes was represented in the

449. VAN GOGH: *La Berceuse (Madame Roulin)*, 1889. 36¼ x 28¼". Museum of Fine Arts, Boston.

same way—an abstract linear design superimposed over natural forms.

Then after Saint-Rémy, during the scant three months in Auvers, the twistings and knottings begin to relax. Their violence is not so much tempered as habitual, much of their true force is lost. The arabesque of lines goes limp. Movement, instead of charging through the picture, is slowed and diffused. The electric presence of *The Public Gardens in Arles* becomes a light, agreeable decorativeness in *Stairway at Auvers* [452]. There is a sense of deflation in the Auvers pictures. In color, in pattern, they share the qualities that make Vincent van Gogh one of the most popular painters in the world, but they have lost the spiritual intensity that make him a great one.

Gauguin: Early Days and Arles

As a matter of chronological tying together, it may be pointed out here that at the time of van Gogh's death Manet had been dead only seven years, and the other impressionists were at the height of their powers. Monet was fifty years old (van Gogh died at thirty-seven) and had another thirty-six years of life ahead of him. Cézanne was not to begin *The Great Bathers* until eight years later. Seurat died the year after van Gogh. Picasso was a boy of nine.

Paul Gauguin (1848–1903) was five years older than van Gogh and outlived him by thirteen years. His life was as extraordinary in its circumstances as Vincent's was, but the circumstances, which included greater poverty and privation since he had no brother Theo to support him, were more of his own making than Vincent's had been. Like Vincent's, his life has been a mine for biographers. Its central mystery is why he chose to paint.

In Vincent's case the compulsion is explicable. Anyone can accept the idea that painting is an emotional release for a man who fits in nowhere else. Since Vincent's time the idea has even been so abused that art schools are filled with students whose only qualification as potential artists consists of a demonstrated lack of qualification for being anything else. But Gauguin was a vigorous, rather brutally handsome, worldly, and self-confident man who entered a stock brokerage firm at twenty-three and did very well at his job. After a couple of years he was a successful bank agent; he married well and was soon a father. He began to draw and paint a little for relaxation, as many respectable businessmen have done without disrupting their lives. In 1876—he was twenty-eight now—he had a painting in the Salon and was buying impressionist pictures. He owned work by Manet, Renoir, Monet, Sisley and Pissarro, and even Cézanne, among others. Then the ubiquitous Pissarro appeared in person—this time not in a role Gauguin's family would have called that of a saint but rather that of a diabolic tempter, as things turned out. The two men painted together, and Gauguin exhibited in the impressionist group show of 1880 and the successive ones up through the final one in 1886. By that year he had given himself over entirely to painting as a career and was living by such hand-to-mouth jobs as pasting signs on billboards. He had expected to eke out a living as a painter, perhaps had even expected to be a successful one without too long an apprenticeship. Pissarro objected to his "commercialism" when Gauguin worried about selling, but it was not easy for a man who had been well-to-do to see his money drain away, to accept hardships that turned out to be more severe even than he had expected as part of the anticipated satisfactions of a creative life. His wife, a Danish woman, was forced at last to return to her family with Gauguin's children, a temporary measure which became permanent.

Gauguin was a sport from the romantic tradition of bohemianism, the concept of the artist as a free soul beyond the conventions of society, sacrificing such bourgeois ideals as security and respectability to the precarious but stimulating life of the studios. Gaiety and self-indulgence and moral license, which were incidental to bohemianism in its origins as a way of life dedicated to creative effort, finally became ends in themselves and created the phenomenon of the painter who does not paint, the writer who does not write, the thinker who does not think, but who make the most of the bohemian's exemption from social responsibility. Gauguin has been seen by some biographers as a man attracted by the bohemian way of life, a man who remained a Parisian bohemian even when he fled the life of the studios to paint in the South Seas. And he did have many of the qualities associated with parasitic bohemianism. He was vain, selfish, an ardent and indulgent sensualist. He loved flattery but was niggardly in recognizing the achievements of his colleagues. He was jealous of his innovations and quick to resent their adaptation by other painters. He dramatized himself, was something of an exhibitionist. The figure he cut as a personality was important to him, and he cultivated it not only by scandalizing the *bourgeoisie*, as all bohemians enjoy doing, but by creating a legend of himself among other painters. He

450. VAN GOGH: *The Road Menders*, 1889. 29 x 36¼". Cleveland Museum of Art, Hanna Fund.

never hesitated to sacrifice other people to this legend or to his self-love.

But the difference between Gauguin and the armies of picayune neurotics who answer to the same description is that he made a painter of himself. If he had expected an easy success he soon discovered that he was not going to have one, and he continued to paint even when it became apparent that if he had sacrificed other people he was also going to have to sacrifice himself. He continued to paint in the face of every privation, every discouragement, in the face of humiliation, of ill health, ultimately in the face of death. If he was guilty of play-acting, these facts were very real.

From the beginning, exotic places and primitive peoples are a part of Gauguin's life, and in the end he sought a final identification with them. When he was a child his parents emigrated to Peru. Later as a recruit in the merchant marine he knew Rio de Janeiro. When he began painting seriously he hunted out spots where he could find or could imagine he found a primitive naturalness, including parts of Brittany and the island of Martinique, these before he made his visit to van Gogh in Arles. (On the way to Martinique he

451. VAN GOGH: *Rain*, 1889. 29⅞ x 36⅜". Collection Henry P. McIlhenny, Philadelphia.

452. VAN GOGH: *Stairway at Auvers*, 1890. 20 x 28". City Art
Museum of St. Louis.

worked for a while as a digger on the
Panama Canal.) The experience of Martinique was a determining one; after his return to France he was more than ever restless for exotic places, more than ever dependent upon them for stimulation.

After impressionist beginnings, Gauguin
had theorized a great deal about what he
wanted to do, and shortly before his visit
to van Gogh he had summarized his ideas
in a canvas called *The Vision after the
Sermon—Jacob Wrestling with the Angel*
[453], painted in the Breton village of
Pont-Aven where he had established himself as one of the colony of artists attracted
by picturesqueness and inexpensive living.
It shows a group of Breton women in regional costume witnessing the struggle of

453. GAUGUIN: *The Vision after the Sermon—Jacob Wrestling with the Angel,* 1888.
28¾ x 36¼". National Gallery of Scotland, Edinburgh.

Jacob and the Angel in a field painted a solid bright red. In their simple and superstitious faith the women think of the struggle in factual terms, seeing it literally as a struggle between a man and an angel. But for the observer outside the picture—and outside the limitations of simplicity and superstition—the supernatural quality is established by the unreality of the red field. The regional bonnets are designed in almost flat silhouettes to make the most of their decorative shapes. A small cow, entirely (and deliberately) out of scale appears in the upper left quarter. The trunk of a tree cuts in a strong diagonal across the picture and separates the Biblical struggle from its peasant spectators.

The technical theories Gauguin applies here include the use of pure color, the re-

duction of all forms to their essential outlines, and the elimination of modeling within those outlines as far as possible, especially modeling by shadows. Also he insists on the painter's right to effect an entirely arbitrary arrangement of nature, although in this particular composition one does not have to look far to see that this arbitrary arrangement is closely related to the composition of Degas, which depended on arrangements the reverse of arbitrary, those discoverable in the accidental relationships of the everyday world.

Those are the technical means. The Gauguinesque spirit of the picture is in its searching out of exotic forms (the costumes of the women) in combination with what he called the "rustic and superstitious simplicity" of the subject. When he went to

454. GAUGUIN: *Women in a Garden*, 1888. 28¾ x 36″. Art Institute of Chicago, Mr. and Mrs. L. L. Coburn Memorial Collection.

455. GAUGUIN: *L'Arlésienne (Madame Ginoux)*, 1888. Charcoal, 22 x 19″. Collection T. Edward Hanley, Bradford, Pa.

Arles, Gauguin took these ideas with him.

He arrived in Arles on the 20th of October, 1888, expecting to stay for perhaps a year. The faithful Theo had supplied money for the trip, with enough extra for first expenses, and hoped to sell enough of Gauguin's canvases to keep him in funds thereafter. Vincent was excited beyond measure. He redecorated his room in anticipation of the great visit, and after Gauguin's arrival he found their discussions "terribly electric." But Gauguin wrote to a friend that he found everything in Arles "cheap and pretty" and admitted that in these electric arguments he would say, "Corporal, you're right!" to avoid having to discuss questions with a man who seemed to like everything he detested (including the Barbizon painters) and to understand nothing that he liked (including Ingres and Degas). He found very little material that interested him, thought of leaving, changed his mind—for practical reasons, one may suspect, since Theo was virtually pensioning him as a companion for Vincent—was bored and restless. From the dark southern beauty of the Arlésiennes and their somber costumes [454], he managed to extract material for a composition suggestive of mystery and superstition, much in line with *The Vision after the Sermon* but not much in line with the life and spirit of Arles and his models. One of his fine drawings from any period is a study of the Madame Ginoux who was Vincent's model at the same time [455].

But on the whole, the visit that was such a traumatic experience for van Gogh—ending in the quarrel, the amputation of the ear, the first seizure—was only a fiasco for Gauguin. Many years later he wrote that he owed something to Vincent in the "consolidation of my previous pictorial ideas." He also congratulated himself that he had been "useful" to Vincent, and acknowledged a debt to this friend who had shown him that there were people even unhappier than himself. But he had come to Arles reluctantly and now he left it with relief. His stories about exactly what happened there are contradictory, reflecting rather more credit on himself in later versions than in his accounts immediately after the event.

456. GAUGUIN: *Self-portrait with Halo*, 1889. Panel, 31¼ x 20¼″. National Gallery of Art, Washington, D.C., Chester Dale Collection.

457. GAUGUIN: *Portrait of a Woman*, 1890. 25⅝ x 21½″. Art Institute of Chicago, Joseph Winterbotham Collection.

Gauguin: Pont-Aven and Le Pouldu

So Gauguin returned to Brittany, first to Pont-Aven, moving later to the similar village of Le Pouldu when Pont-Aven became tourist-ridden as such picturesque unspoiled spots always must. In 1889 and part of 1891 he was the center of a group of painters who gave the name *synthetism* to the manner of heightened color, flattened form, and heavy boundary lines he had been developing. Synthetism was a loosely formed aspect of or a secondary name for symbolism, a movement more literary than pictorial with a strong flavor of the exotic and the mysterious in reaction against realism. As far as Gauguin was concerned, though, he was following his own course and the words people attached to his art were of no concern to him except that he was flattered by the attention. He did not take synthetism very seriously, and satirized it in a self-portrait as a synthetist saint with a halo [456]. But while it is a tongue-in-cheek performance, the picture in its increased abstraction unwittingly hints at a direction another generation will follow under Gauguin's influence.

His serious work continued in the direction of *The Vision after the Sermon*. In *The Yellow Christ* he painted a medieval yellow wooden statue from the chapel of a small town near Pont-Aven, placing it out of doors and surrounding it with peasant worshipers. He was still attracted to the heavy forms of primitive and early arts, in this case those of the rough Romanesque sculpture and architecture of the region. He had even offered his *Vision after the Sermon* to the local priest, wanting to see it hung in the small church where he hoped the picture would harmonize with the ancient, rugged, and simple forms of the architecture. But the gift was refused because the priest suspected a hoax. Gauguin and the artists who gathered around him in Brittany were not remarkable for their seriousness and reverence in affairs of this kind, but this time the gift had been offered in all sincerity.

Although it seems contradictory to the flatness and unbroken color of synthetism, Gauguin was also studying Cézanne at this time, and the *Portrait of a Woman* [457] is evidence. Cézanne's faceted planes are suggested, but everywhere the forms are more neatly contained than Cézanne's, more ornamental and more graceful. Gauguin sensed Cézanne's monumentality—and he was to draw upon it—but he did not explore Cézanne's compositional premise of formal distortion in abstract spatial relationships. The woman is posed in front of a Cézanne still-life, but instead of copying it Gauguin has closed the forms in accord with his own taste.

His basic theme continued to preoccupy Gauguin: the undercurrent of superstitious fear beneath the simplicity of primitive people, the menacing whisper of the unknown permeating lives apparently simple and natural. In Le Pouldu he yearned more and more for the far away, the bizarre. Now, to find authentically exotic material *in situ*, Gauguin decided to flee civilization. An exhibition of his work was organized, and with the help of every friend with enough money to buy paintings or enough influence to attract attention to them, enough purchasers were found (including Degas) to put him in funds for a voyage to Tahiti. He left in April, 1891.

Gauguin: Tahiti and Last Years

From Gauguin's experiences in Tahiti it is possible to isolate certain facts to describe an elysium. He scorns the mean provinciality of the French colonial settlements and moves into the interior. The natives are beautiful people, the men like gods of the earth, the women like its flowers. He occupies a simple wooden hut in the midst of lovely country, surrounded by exotic birds, fruit, and foliage. He takes a young girl as his native wife; later she bears him a son. He paints all day, happily naked. He learns the native tongue, explores native myths.

The rest of the picture is less halcyon. He grows old rapidly; he spits "a litre of blood" daily for weeks at a time; he develops a persistent rash or eczema; lesions will not heal, and remain open sores; a foot broken in a brawl fails to heal properly and agonizes and immobilizes him; he runs out of funds and the money promised from France never arrives; he must beg a few francs here and there, receiving some now and then from his wife in Denmark; his daughter, at twenty, dies in Denmark, and for a man who has seen so little of her he takes it very hard and writes such a bitter letter to his wife that he never hears from her again; he humiliates himself and works for six francs a day doing hack jobs for the colonial government he detests; during periods of absolute penury he lives off boiled rice; during others, off dry bread and water; when even the Chinese storekeeper cannot give him further credit he is without bread and lives off a few mangoes; he attempts suicide with arsenic but vomits it up and has only a great agony instead; he writes abusive letters to government officials and as a result of one of them he is sentenced to a fine and three months in jail. He enters an appeal, which would have taken him to another island for a hearing, but before he leaves he suffers two slight strokes. He is helpless in his hut, abandoned except for occasional visits from natives. His sight fails. One leg is suppurating. He dies alone.

This hell was divided into two periods on either side of a return to France. Chronologically the periods are: the first Tahitian one, from his departure from Paris in the spring of 1891 to his return landing at Marseilles (with four francs in his pocket) in August, 1893; he remained in France until February, 1895; then he returned to Tahiti, stayed there until moving to the Marquesas Islands in November, 1901, where he remained until his death.

The interlude of a year and a half in France is bizarre enough in itself. The object of the trip was to collect money due him and to try for more with an exhibition of the paintings he brought back. The exhibition was a scandal and a mild success; Degas liked it. Real financial help came from an unexpected source. An uncle died and left Gauguin an inheritance. He spent it rapidly, with the assistance of a woman he attached from the studios of Montmartre, a mulatto with an Oriental cast to her features who called herself Anna the Javanese. Whatever her other attractions, Anna was a spectacular accessory to Gauguin the Exotic, who now disported himself in a long blue frock coat like a minstrel's, with large pearl buttons, a blue vest embroidered in bright colors, buff trousers, a gray hat with a blue ribbon, and a fancy walking stick he had carved for himself with barbaric figures and inlaid with a pearl. This outfit was adopted on a return trip to Pont-Aven but also made its appearance in Paris. Combined with Anna and a pet monkey, it was spectacular enough and could certainly be described as inviting attention, yet when it and Anna received more attention than Gauguin liked from a group of sailors, he got into a brawl with them and it was at this time that his foot, or ankle, was broken by a blow from a wooden shoe. These events took place in the little resort of Concarneau near Pont-Aven, and Gauguin had to be taken home on a stretcher according to some versions or trundled in a wheelbarrow according to other credible ones. As the script for a comedy these grotesque incidents would be hilarious. When one remembers that they happened in earnest, they are appalling. Anna capped the affair by abandoning Gauguin on his bed of pain and going to Paris, where she stripped the studio of all objects of value and disappeared.

The wonder is that from the misery, the confusion, the distraction, of Gauguin's life in the islands an art of any order could come. Yet it did. And in spite of his reiterations that he was a "true savage" and in spite of the fact that he was painting in a native hut instead of a mansard studio, his paintings are always sophisticated, in effect the paintings of a Parisian who has gathered material on primitive location. He

458. GAUGUIN: *Ia Orana Maria*, 1891. 44¾ x 34½". Metropolitan Museum of Art, New York, Samuel A. Lewisohn Bequest.

may have lived with the natives, may have taken a native wife, may have learned their language and their myths, but he was no primitive. He spent the end of his life in a tremendous natural reference library, acquiring a new vocabulary of motifs—dark-skinned figures, native cloths, bananas and palms and curious plants with fantastic blossoms.

Synthetism would have been an apt word if it had been coined to describe Gauguin's pictures like *Ia Orana Maria* [458], one of the earliest from the first Tahitian period. The picture is completely synthetic—divorcing the word for the moment from its associations of shoddiness. The words of the title are the equivalent of *Ave Maria* or *We Hail Thee Mary*. A native woman and

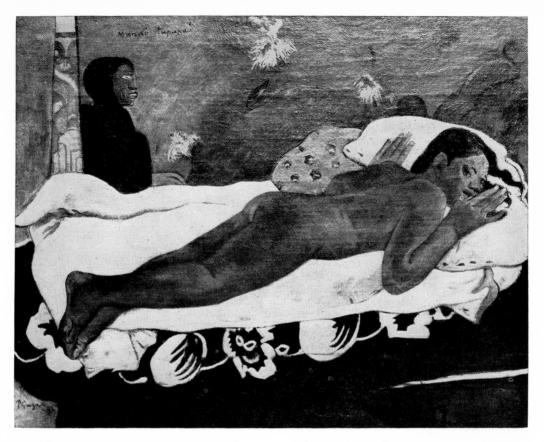

459. GAUGUIN: *Manao Tupapau—The Spirit of the Dead Watching,* 1892. 28⅝ x 36⅝″. Collection A. Conger Goodyear, New York.

her son on her shoulder are haloed like the Virgin and Child. Two women stand in attitudes of reverence or prayer while an angel behind them points to the Tahitian Madonna. Nothing could be more artificial, much less connected with the life of the natives. It is the *Vision after the Sermon* in a new locale, except that where the Breton picture was tentative, the Tahitian one is assured in its use of rich colors and the disposition of ornamental forms into a tapestrylike unity. As a final curiosity and a final divorce from his immediate material except as studio props, Gauguin has turned to yet another source for the attitudes of the two adoring women. They are transposed directly from a bas-relief from a Javanese temple, known to Gauguin from a photograph which in all likelihood he had purchased at the Paris World's Fair two years before. A picture that refers to

a photograph of a Javanese temple, purchased in Paris and carried to the South Seas, that incorporates Javanese figures with Tahitian models into a Christian subject treated as a decorative composition to be taken back to Paris and sold in a commercial gallery for money to free the painter from the degrading commercial forces of civilization, is certainly a synthesis of some kind.

Ia Orana Maria is a richly decorative painting using an exotic vocabulary, but it would be forcing the point to pretend that it explores beneath the surface of native life. Gauguin uses Tahitian material in a way closer to its inherent character in a picture painted the following year, *Manao Tupapau* [459], usually translated as "The spirit of the dead watching," although according to Gauguin's own notes it may mean either "she thinks of the spirit of the

460. GAUGUIN: *Hina Te Fatou—The Moon and the Earth*, 1893. 45 x 21½″. Museum of Modern Art, New York, Lillie P. Bliss Collection.

461. GAUGUIN: *Poèmes Barbares*, 1896. 25½ x 19″. Fogg Art Museum, Cambridge, Mass., Maurice Wertheim Collection.

dead" or "the spirit of the dead remembers her." It was suggested to him when he returned late one night to discover his Tahitian wife lying on their bed waiting for him, terrified by the dark. He explained the picture in unusual detail in a letter to his wife in Denmark, telling what he wanted to express and how he went about expressing it. Instead of describing fright in a "literary way" by posing the model in the pantomimic gestures of anecdotal painting, he tried to relay the sensation by a "somber, sad, frightening" color harmony that would "sound" to the eye like a tolling death bell. Since the Polynesians believe that phosphorescence is the spirits of the dead, he painted in the background some

fantastic flowers resembling sparks. Instead of making the ghost (appearing like an idol on the left) a wild and menacing figure, he made it "like a small, harmless woman, because the girl can only see the spirit of the dead linked with the dead person, a human being like herself." At other times he made further notes on the symbolism of *Manao Tupapau*, comparing the spirit of the living soul and the spirit of the dead to day and night, and making a musical analogy to the "undulating horizontal lines" and the "harmonies of orange and blue brought together by yellows and purples."

During the first years in Tahiti Gauguin evolved a heavy-legged, narrow-hipped, square-shouldered female figure type not

462. GAUGUIN: *Whence Come We? What Are We? Whither Go We?* 1898. 67 x 177″. Museum of Fine Arts, Boston.

463. PUVIS DE CHAVANNES: *The Sacred Grove*, after 1883. 36½ x 82⅞″. Art Institute of Chicago, Potter Palmer Collection.

at all reflective of the rounded sensuous bodies of the Tahitian women but appropriate to his idea of savage monumentality and a fit participant in his allegories of primitive man's union with earth, sky, and the mystical forces behind nature. The woman in *Hina Te Fatou—The Moon and the Earth* [460] is a moon goddess, but a far cry from the classical Diana and a far cry from Ingres's *La Source* [68] (the spring in the background suggests the com-

parison) and a far cry too from Degas's nudes. But Degas, the worshiper of Ingres, bought it, and it can take its place in the long line of pictures where painters have summarized their art in images of the female nude. With Gauguin this summary is a compound of sophistication and primitivism, of affectation and decision, above all a reversal of the impressionist idea that the world must be met on its own terms and interpreted through its own appear-

464. VUILLARD: *Le Repas, c.* 1899. 17 x 18½". Collection Henry P. McIlhenny, Philadelphia.

ance. Instead, Gauguin rejects the world; the painter's assignment becomes the exploration of universal mysteries through symbols rather than the observation of temporary fact through fragments of tangible reality. This is Gauguin's importance—no matter what affectations and insincerities and limitations may hobble him and preclude an altogether satisfactory expression of so ambitious an idea.

In the last terrible years of his life, after his return to the islands following the grotesque exhibitionism of the interlude in Paris and Pont-Aven, Gauguin's art contradicts the picture of him as a harassed and decaying man. It takes on a reserve, a

decisiveness, and a removed calm. As in *Poèmes Barbares* [461], of 1896, the gestures of his figures become hieratic and formalized. The idol and the figure are no longer part of a world of superstitious fear but exist together in a world of barbaric mysteries. In the very large and complicated picture with the cumbersome and literarily pretentious title *Whence Come We? What Are We? Whither Go We?* [462], a painted tapestry of figures, idols, and landscape neither cumbersome nor pretentious, there is an air of finality beyond that of any other of his compositions. This may be because the picture is conceived first and last as a studio summary; it is to

Gauguin what *The Painter's Studio* is to Courbet, *La Grande Jatte* to Seurat. It is also a tribute to Puvis de Chavannes, whose painting Gauguin had admired and even copied. Gauguin protested too much when he wrote of *Whence Come We?* that "By God, it is not a canvas made like Puvis de Chavannes, studies from nature, then preparatory cartoons, etc. It is all boldly done, directly with the brush, on a sack-cloth full of knots and rough spots. . . ." This may be true enough, but compositionally it is a cousin of Puvis's *The Sacred Grove* [463]. There are the same strong horizontals and verticals, the same shining water at the left, cut by a dark slanting tree in the Puvis and a slanting dark reflection in the Gauguin, the same rounding off of the corners, especially noticeable in the upper right but also noticeable in the figures at lower right and lower left. The conspicuous female figure leaning on one arm at the lower left of the Gauguin reverses a similar figure in the lower right of the Puvis. But Gauguin need not have protested. The picture is his own, and if it is directly connected with a tradition, then it places him securely within a great one, without sacrificing the originality of his contribution to it.

The Nabis

Gauguin's influence on a new generation of painters was felt at close quarters in the work of a group of youngsters twenty years younger than he, who abandoned the principles of the *Académie Julian*—virtually a preparatory class for the Academy's school —and even of the *École des Beaux Arts*, in order to follow his ideas of composing in flat, unmodeled areas as developed at Pont-Aven. By the time Gauguin left for his first stay in Tahiti his influence was apparent in the work of these young "Nabis." The word comes from a Hebrew one meaning "prophets," but it was not altogether an apt description for a group of painters who made their own adaptation of other men's innovations but were not particularly innovative themselves.

The spokesmen for the group were the painters Paul Séruzier (1863–1927), who first discovered Gauguin for the rest of them, and Maurice Denis (1870–1943), whose statement that "a picture—before being a horse, a nude, or an anecdote—is essentially a flat surface covered with colors assembled in a certain order" was the heart of the Nabi credo. He was not yet twenty years old when he wrote this, and the Nabis abandoned the principle shortly, or at least they grew less insistent about it. But it is still one of the most frequently quoted passages in art criticism and theory. There is nothing complicated about it; it is a succinct statement of the decorative principle in painting and goes no further, which is the reason the Nabis outgrew it. They outgrew it rather quickly, although Gauguin insisted on calling them, resentfully, his "followers" long after they had gone their own several ways.

The two most enduring painters of the group proved to be Pierre Bonnard (1867–1947) and Édouard Vuillard (1868–1940). Vuillard's *Le Repas* [464] of about 1899 exemplified the linearism of the first Nabi work now modified by a kind of interior impressionism suggesting the warmth and seclusion of small rooms where comfortable and affectionate lives are lived without excitement or the necessity of it, a quality that led to the coining of the term *intimism* as an offshoot of the Nabi aesthetic. A somewhat linear effect is retained here and there, as in the heads, rather surprisingly combined with a soft-focus effect in the objects in the foreground of the table. The colors are more subdued, less contrasting, than the black-and-white reproduction suggests. There are warm reddish browns, warm grays, comfortably dulled greens. In the mixture of influences, that of Degas is strong. Degas also conveyed the intimacy of small interiors, but always with a moodiness wider in its evocative reach than the gentle domesticity which pervades a typical Vuillard.

Bonnard also abandoned the restrictions of the early Nabi manner to accept a variety of stimuli. In pictures in the intimist spirit [465] he abandoned the subdued color scheme of intimism to experiment with unusual, somewhat dissonant color combinations in a way that influenced the

465. BONNARD: *After the Shower*, 1914. 37½ x 26″. Collection Louis E. Stern, New York.

466. BONNARD: *Bowl of Fruit*, 1933. 22½ x 21¼″. Philadelphia Museum of Art.

fauves—to be seen hereafter—and then, in turn, he was influenced by them. In his final manner, as in *Bowl of Fruit* [466], Bonnard may seem at a glance impressionist. Upon second glance the colors are seen to be forced to greater intensities, in combinations arbitrary rather than based on impressionism's optical laws. And the shapes, such as the dark shadow under the bowl, are designed more decoratively than impressionism's approximation of natural effects would have allowed.

Fantastic and Visionary Art: Redon

The post-impressionist "period," if it can be called that, was one of trauma during which impressionism, as the climax of realism, was transformed into what we call, just now, "modern art." Two other painters

are of special importance in this connection, the symbolist Odilon Redon and the primitive Henri, or "Douanier," Rousseau. Both men were contemporaries of Cézanne and the impressionists, hence a little older than van Gogh, Seurat, and Gauguin, all of whom, however, they outlived. Against the classicism of Cézanne and Seurat, the emotionalism of van Gogh, and the decorative exoticism of Gauguin, they oppose an art of fantasy.

If the reader has been a little confused about symbolism, synthetism, the Nabis, and all the other isms and painters mentioned since impressionism, it is nobody's fault. These movements were ill defined and they overlapped not only with themselves but with other movements that were developing or, like impressionism, fading. Odilon Redon (1840–1916), whose life of seventy-six years began the year before Cézanne's and ended ten years after it, is

467. REDON: *Vase of Flowers,* 1910. Pastel on cardboard, 28¼ x 18″. Albright Art Gallery, Buffalo, Contemporary Art Collection.

468. REDON: *Revery, c.* 1900 (?). Pastel, 21¼ x 14¼″. Museum of Modern Art, New York, Gift of Mrs. John D. Rockefeller, Jr.

usually called a symbolist. The critic Albert Aurier tried to define symbolism, in 1891, as an effort to "clothe the idea in a form perceptible to the senses," not a very helpful description since it could apply to almost any form of genuinely creative art, painting or otherwise. But all manifestations of symbolism were somewhat tied up with the idea that the painter's goal was not to investigate the world around him but to explore the world of dream and mystery. Symbolists like Gauguin, whom Aurier considered the leader of the movement, explored this mysterious world through forms connected with primitive, archaic, or exotic ones, which were presumably closer to the world of dream and mystery than the world of the Paris boulevards could ever

be. But critics today would be likely to call Redon, rather than Gauguin, the purest symbolist painter.

Redon explored a private and fantastic world, rather than Gauguin's borrowed exotic one. Redon's bias is already apparent when we read that he said that Ingres was "sterile" and "bourgeois," while Delacroix's "least scrawl" communicated life to the observer. But Redon was not interested in Delacroix's statement of the vitality of life or in Delacroix's effort to achieve a generalized statement of human emotion. He was concerned with ambiguities, and he said so, which puts a considerable disadvantage upon critics who object to his art as a rather ambiguous one. "My drawings *inspire,* and are not to be defined. They determine nothing. They place us, as does music, in the ambiguous realm of the undetermined. They are a kind of metaphor." But Redon's most famous phrase is the neat description of his intention: to "put the logic of the visible at the service of the invisible." Thus when he paints a bouquet of flowers [467] they are not flowers with scent and body, cut in the garden and put into water to be enjoyed and painted as flowers, but the blossoming of a dream, incorporeal, "a varied arabesque or maze unfolding," full of mystery and suggestion.

To the person for whom a vase of flowers is a vase of flowers, the quality of mystery in these pictures may seem to be nothing much more than a certain fuzziness combined with unusually luminous color. In that case, Redon's more completely unreal, more conventionally dreamlike compositions [468] may be more satisfying expressions of the symbolist ideal. Through such a picture, the less apparently mystical dreams of flowers and butterflies may be approached. Part of Redon's appeal, once one knows him, is that his world remains private. One may enter it, and be welcome, but one is never urged to do so. During his lifetime Redon worked quietly, not at all interested in making a great stir. But the literary symbolists, headed by the poet Mallarmé, discovered him for themselves; and such painters as Gauguin, the Nabis, and finally the young Matisse, all sought him out and were his devoted admirers.

"Douanier" Rousseau

Within the complications and intercomplications of nineteenth-century painting, the idea of giving concrete expression to supernatural mysteries or to mysterious yearnings crops up persistently. Blake, Friedrich, and Runge held it; Böcklin held it when he tried to bring the world of fantasy and dread within our grasp by representing fantasies in objectively realistic detail. The Pre-Raphaelites held it in their odd way when they tried to recapture the spiritual essence of the Biblical and medieval worlds by reproducing them—they thought—explicitly. Böcklin and other fantasists might have

said that they wanted to make "improbable beings live humanly according to the laws of the probable" or to "give the illusion of life to the most unreal creations." But these two quotations are from Redon, whose art is more conventionally visionary, in its luminous, apparitionlike quality, than the precisely defined painting of his companions in their voyages of exploration into hidden realms.

The century's most curious revelation within this shadowy territory was made half by chance, like so many discoveries, by Henri Rousseau (1840–1910), who first set about reproducing the real world as photographically as he knew how, and then discovered that he had created a world of enchantment instead. While Böcklin and Redon theorized about the interchangeability of mystery and reality, about how to make the real unreal and the unreal real, about how to dematerialize the world around us or to materialize the one we cannot see, Rousseau did not theorize at all. Yet he materialized the promised land of mystery for searchers who were more knowledgeable about it than he was.

Rousseau was a minor official in the French Customs, hence "Douanier" Rousseau, as he is most frequently called. He began as a hobby painter, the nineteenth-century phenomenon of the "Sunday painter" who might take his cheap paintbox out into the park for an afternoon's relaxation or copy a favorite postcard at home on a rainy day or try a portrait of a friend or a member of the family, preferably from a nice clear snapshot. His earliest paintings [469] have all the characteristic naïvetés of style inherent in the work of beginners feeling their way with intense interest but technical innocence. The most usual of these characteristics include extreme carefulness of outline, a smoothing out of the paint, a finicky blending of one tone into another, and a fascination with fine detail to whatever extent technical limitations may permit its execution. All of this is combined with the stiff, simple forms, the inaccurate proportions, and the skew-wise perspective of the beginner.

By most standards, these are not only shortcomings but fatal shortcomings—but

469. H. ROUSSEAU: *Village Street Scene*, 1909. 16¼ x 13″.
Philadelphia Museum of Art, Arensberg Collection.

applied with rich body in spite of its smoothness. Forms which are rigid and ill drawn by conventional standards are solid and well drawn by the standard of meticulous observation and careful selection. Color that would be harsh and raw or bleached and anemic or discordant and muddy in the ordinary primitive painting, is clear and harmonious in Rousseau.

As a result of these virtues, a picture with many acute technical limitations by conventional standards may be an expressive work of art, even when the expressive quality is half accidental. Rousseau's individual deviation from the general field of primitive painting, the one that sets him apart even from such honest and expressive primitives as Hicks with his *Peaceable Kingdom* [303] is the air of enchantment that permeates his work. Every figure, every leaf, every blade of grass, seems magically transfixed within a vacuum or a crystal, magically revealed to us in its smallest element.

The unreality of Rousseau is a paradoxical combination of fantasy and factualness; the painter offers each object in his street scenes and country landscapes with unquestioning acceptance of their perfect ordinariness, yet not one of the objects is ordinary after he paints them. The human figures are so isolated and so immobile, the trees are so neatly patterned and their foliage so meticulously rigid and delicate, the streets, houses, walls are so pristine, yet so familiar as elements of daily life—everything, in short, is so commonplace and yet so uncommonly revealed, that reality and unreality reach perfect fusion and one is indistinguishable from the other. We cannot say that Rousseau shows us a new world, for we have seen all these things many times; yet we cannot say, either, that this is a world we know, for these things exist in new relationships and even in new shapes. It becomes a world of dream, whose reality the dreamer accepts without question, and whose fantasy he recognizes only upon awakening. But instead of fading, the dream is preserved like a fly in amber. And it is a curious fly, not quite like the ones we are familiar with, not quite like any other fly we have seen before.

not by quite all standards. A picture may have all these characteristics yet may combine them in a pattern of great charm or expressiveness. From the beginning, Rousseau had a sense for the agreeable or expressive placement of objects in a composition, and especially for the patterning of natural forms, such as the leaves of plants or the silhouettes of trees.

A "primitive," which in this sense means self-taught, artist may also paint with an honesty, a naïve directness, which is a transmutation of his own intensity and pleasure as he goes about the unfamiliar and exciting act of creation. This quality is inherent in Rousseau's early work to a surpassing degree. To some extent it is an intangible, yet its presence can be explained by closer examination of a painting (again [469]) which on the surface looks only "amateurish." Paint which in the run-of-the-mill picture of this kind would be thin and dry, is

To some extent all of this applies to primitive painting in general. It applies to a very large extent in exceptional primitive paintings where lucky accident is luckier than usual in transforming mere naïveté into a kind of magical vision. The difference is that in Rousseau's art it applies consistently.

Rousseau was an industrious painter and he began to show his pictures wherever he could. At the exhibitions of the *Indépendants* he began to attract the attention of sophisticates who recognized the decorative quality and the poetry that distinguished his work from that of the armies of other Sunday painters who resembled him superficially. He left his comfortable position with the Customs to live on a small pension and spend his time painting. This was a dangerous point for Rousseau; upon the point of becoming a professional painter rather than an enthusiastic amateur, he was ready to study under conventional teachers and to master the techniques of realistic drawing and painting, which if he had mastered them, would have cost him the original style he had developed for himself. But he was lucky enough to receive good advice. The painters and literary figures who were beginning to make something of a darling of him were not the only ones who recognized the exceptional nature of his work. According to a later statement by Rousseau, even old Gérôme, the academic tyrant who was professor at the *École des Beaux Arts*, advised him to guard his naïveté.

Rousseau did guard his naïveté. But naïveté obviously stops being naïveté once it is guarded, and false naïveté can be a most offensive affectation. Rousseau set about creating for himself a personal style based on the forms that had been spontaneous to him as a beginner. This style, as he developed it, is the paradoxical one of a highly cultivated manner based on primitive simplicities, a dangerous combination and one that has never come off very well for Rousseau's imitators. Nor have any other "modern primitives," even those who begin as genuine ones, approached Rousseau's stature. Dealers and collectors continue to scout hopefully to ferret them out, but at

470. H. ROUSSEAU: *The Young Girl*, c. 1894. 24 x 18". Philadelphia Museum of Art, Gift of Mr. and Mrs. R. Sturgis Ingersoll.

their best they usually turn out to be charming but inconsequential, bizarre but only bizarre, or sincere yet somehow at once ponderous and shallow.* Rousseau may be charming, bizarre, and even sometimes ponderous. In *The Young Girl* [470], for instance, he is all of these. But these are secondary characteristics in a painting where the primary ones are monumentality and magic.

Rousseau was a late bloomer. His first signed pictures are from 1880, when he was already thirty-six years old, and he did not begin to exhibit with the *Indépendants*

* Some exceptions are Louis Vivin (1861–1936), Camille Bombois (1883–   ), and André Bauchant (1873–   ), all French. The Americans John Kane (1860–1934) and Horace Pippin (1888–   ), especially the latter with his intimately observed genre scenes and his engaging historical pictures, are close to the tradition of American folk art (although Kane was born in Scotland).

471. H. ROUSSEAU: *The Dream,* 1910. 80 x 118½″. Museum of Modern Art, New York, Gift of Nelson A. Rockefeller.

until he was forty-two. In the interim he possibly copied pictures in the Louvre; at any rate, there is a record of issuance of a copyist's permit to him. The jungle fantasies for which he is most widely known did not appear until 1891, when he was approaching fifty. He was a happy eccentric, part visionary and part *petit bourgeois.* He eked out his pension by giving lessons in painting, music, and harmony, and he even wrote a five-act drama, *The Revenge of a Russian Orphan,* which was produced, but demonstrated that his unusual qualities as an artist were limited to painting, even though his naïveté was not.

According to his own story, Rousseau did military service in Mexico as one of the troops in the half-hearted expedition to keep Maximilian on the throne there. If this was true—there is good reason to doubt it, since there is no proof and Rousseau was given to fabrications which he half believed himself—he would have been twenty-two at the time, and might have carried back with him the memory of exotic foliage and exotic people. But as a matter of fact he could not

have seen the wild parrots, monkeys, leopards, and other beasts, or the particular plant forms he painted, for the good reason that they did not exist in the parts of Mexico he would have seen. His experience there would have been limited to the cities and the actually not very exotic countryside in which cacti, palms, and other semitropical plants did exist, but not in the profusion of jungles and not too frequently of the types Rousseau painted. His reference sources were the zoo, the botanical gardens, and postcards and photographs of exotic creatures and places. The references are not especially important since the true source of his pictures was his own imagination, whatever actual or secondhand experience he may have had with exotic places.

In the jungle pictures [471] he is free to give full indulgence to his passion for the design of leaves, blossoms, and branches. They grow in luxuriant and unnatural profusion, ordered into clear and unnatural patterns, combining the most fantastic imagery with the most unquestioning defi-

472. H. ROUSSEAU: *The Sleeping Gypsy*, 1897. 51 x 79″. Museum of Modern Art, New York, Gift of Mrs. Simon Guggenheim.

nition. Their existence is impossible, yet undeniable. Reason tells us that these are fantasies or apparitions; our senses tell us that they are tangible fact. The conflicting halves of this paradox, formulated as a theory by Böcklin and Redon, were balanced and harmonized by Rousseau because the paradox existed in his own personality.

Rousseau was fifty-three when he created *The Sleeping Gypsy* [472], the climactic painting of his total work. In its own area, the area of fantastic and visionary art, *The Sleeping Gypsy* occupies a position comparable only to those occupied by Seurat's *La Grande Jatte*, Cézanne's *The Great Bathers*, and van Gogh's *The Starry Night*.

The Sleeping Gypsy cannot be accepted as a "primitive" painting except in the stylistic sense of the word. There is nothing unconsidered in its expressive effectiveness, no "lucky accidents," no groping, and no compromise. The pattern of the lion's mane, running in serpentine rivulets, the odd backward turning of the tuft of hair at the end of the tail, the careful sprinkling of stars in the sky, the patterned lines of hills on the horizon, the dune where the gypsy lies and the lion stands, the gypsy's robe— whatever elements, instinctive or theoretical, account for the creation of these forms, they are the creation of a born artist who has matured as a creative designer through observation and experience. Rousseau paints each of the fantastic parts of this fantastic combination with the apparently objective innocence of his streets, houses, and ordinary city trees; fantasy or nightmare are accepted as unquestioningly as the everyday world, and represented as uncompromisingly. In Böcklin, and sometimes even in Redon, the real and the unreal may still be identified as incompatible elements brought into a kind of truce with one another, but in Rousseau they cannot be separated because it was never necessary for him to combine them in the first place. In his conception of *The Sleeping Gypsy* they must have existed together, as one, from the beginning.

PART IV

The Twentieth Century

CHAPTER 12

Fauvism and Expressionism

The Position of Matisse and Picasso

Since any discussion of art since 1900 is only marking time until it reaches Matisse and Picasso, they must be introduced immediately. They are without question the two most important painters of the first half of the twentieth century. The art of these two men, sometimes overlapping and sometimes in conflict, set the pace for more painters and determined the taste of more collectors than that of any other artists during the period. The men themselves have enjoyed success during their lifetimes comparable only to that of such painters as Raphael, Titian, and Rubens, who were courted by kings and popes. Even Monet and Renoir and Degas, who lived long enough to see themselves generally successful and widely recognized, were only moderately successful and recognized in comparison with Matisse and Picasso, whose names are known everywhere, whose work is multiplied in, quite literally, millions of reproductions, and whose most casual scribbles are coveted by collectors. (Their most casual scribbles can be pretty good.) More books and articles have been published on them, already, than on any other two painters of any places or times. Even if the future should make a drastic reevaluation of their work, it cannot alter the historical fact that Matisse and Picasso have exerted an influence as wide, apparently as deep, and certainly as revolutionary during their own lifetimes as have any painters who have ever lived.

Fifty years after the first scandals of fauvism and cubism, to which their names are respectively attached, Matisse and Picasso still shock and puzzle much of the general public, yet people come by tens of thousands to see exhibitions of their work. Matisse and Picasso are illustrated not only in every art publication, which is natural, but in every publication designed for popular consumption as well. They have found their way into elementary schoolbooks where *The Blue Boy, Whistler's Mother,* and *The Sower* formerly elevated the taste of the very young. They sell in reproduction by the gross to hotels, motels, and the decorators of housing developments. Housewives who had already put *Whistler's Mother* in the attic to make room for a reproduction of a Renoir or even a van Gogh or a Gauguin, have pushed on to Matisse and Picasso, whether they understand them or not.

There are several reasons for this phenomenon of mass interest in paintings that would ordinarily appeal to only a limited audience. The educational techniques of American museums, led by the Museum of Modern Art in New York; the fact that the painters as personalities make good copy for the picture magazines, which must find new copy of some kind every week; and the new processes of color reproduction that make color so bright and attractive, even when it is inaccurate—all these factors have contributed to an impressive structure of general interest. But the foundation supporting this structure is less apparent; it is to be found in the history of the relationship of the public to the art of the impressionists and the post-impressionists. People today are aware that the painters they most enjoy—like Renoir, whom they love, and especially van Gogh and Gauguin, whom they find attractive—had to endure contumely and hardship during their lifetimes. They know the stories of the terrible lives of van Gogh and Gauguin through popular biographies and movies. On the premise that history repeats itself, they are willing to accept the chance that the painters whose art is incomprehensible to them today are the ones most likely to succeed with posterity. It is as if the public feels a sense of mass guilt for the persecutions to which late-nineteenth-century painters were subjected and is trying to atone three generations later by accepting

with humility a kind of painting it would ordinarily reject on sight.

This humility is engaging, and encouraging in its way. Less encouragingly, it is flavored by the snob value attached to the appreciation of paintings that only millionaires can afford to buy, that only intellectuals can explain, and that museums display with the same techniques used in the display of expensive merchandise. The taste for modern art, in other words, is built on false values at least as often as not. Its popularization in magazines and reproductions is usually commercial opportunism; its dissemination through museums is well intentioned, but this education concerning it is often confused with propaganda for it. It is all very curious, and the greatest tribute to the paintings of Matisse and Picasso is the fact that everyone is not sick unto death of them; the strongest proof that they are worth all the proselytization is that as works of art they have withstood the excesses of the proselytizers. And it would be ungrateful not to recognize that in spite of mistakes and abuses, the missionary work is serving its purpose: for the first time in a century, the lag between creative art and public taste, which has bedeviled original painters since the romantic revival, is beginning to shorten.

Fauvism and Expressionism

This chapter is concerned with fauvism and the related movement of expressionism, but cubism was developing at the same time. It will be necessary to refer to cubism here and there in discussing fauvism and expressionism, since all three isms impinged on one another. It would be a good idea for the reader to glance just now at some of the illustrations in the following chapter— say 560 through 569—and bear them in mind, in a general way, as examples of what cubism looks like. This will leave us free in this chapter to make occasional references to cubism in something less than a vacuum.

Fauvism, it must be said in the beginning, is a word derived from the French one meaning wild beast—*fauve.* There are other words, but not many, which could be

473. MOREAU: *The Apparition (Dance of Salome)* (small version), *c.* 1876. 21¾ x 17½". Fogg Art Museum, Cambridge, Mass., Grenville L. Winthrop Bequest.

less appropriate as a descriptive name for the group of painters to whom the label was attached. The fauves included some of the most highly civilized painters ever to put color on canvas. They did use broad strong areas of pure color that seemed crude, savage, to certain shocked and puzzled critics in 1905. But not even the most offended critic could find wild-beastiness today in the later developments of the fauve painters. Objections would be safer at the opposite pole of hyperrefinement and artificiality.

Fauvism was a spontaneous development, generated in France. It slightly preceded and contributed significantly to expressionism, which had its centers in Germany. Both movements were returns to the colorism of van Gogh and Gauguin after the interlude during which the intimists, particularly Vuillard, had rejected bright pigmentation for a muted palette. Fauvism coalesced in 1905, two years after the death of Gauguin, and although it drew upon pointillism and from Cézanne, and from van Gogh, in the end Gauguin was the dominant influence. Fauvism and expressionism developed from the same sources on one side of their family trees; they were, so to speak, first cousins, sharing in part a common ancestry, but with differences as important as their similarities.

Matisse: Early Experiences and Discoveries

Henri Matisse (1869–1954), the central figure in fauvism, was well on his way to becoming a lawyer (as Degas and Manet, among others, had been) when he began to paint. When he was twenty-two he induced his father to let him abandon law for art, and went to Paris to study under Bouguereau, who was then an old man full of honors, an international success, and the dean of the academicians. This was in 1891 and 1892, a complicated time when Monet, Renoir, Degas, Cézanne, Lautrec, Redon, Puvis de Chavannes, Gauguin, and Douanier Rousseau were all at work. Seurat's early death had occurred the year of Matisse's arrival in Paris, and van Gogh had died only the year before. Vuillard and Bonnard, who were Matisse's age within a year or two, had begun their careers. (Most of the men who were to develop expressionism were adolescents in Germany.) The old guard of the academicians was still well entrenched; even old Meissonier had just died, at the age of seventy-five. In France the decade from 1890 to 1900 offered everything at once.

Matisse was not long in choosing his way —at least, he was not long in rejecting Bouguereau as a prelude to doing so. Although Matisse was a provincial young man he was no philistine, and he soon recognized the vulgar banality of Bouguereau's art and the sterility of his teaching. He managed to enter, instead, the studio of Gustave Moreau (1826–1898), a painter whose rather decadent exoticism [473] was

474. JAN DAVIDZ DE HEEM (Dutch, 1606?–1684): *Still-life,* 1640. 58⅝ x 80″. Louvre, Paris.

academically acceptable as a continuation of Delacroix's romanticism. Moreau had been appointed to the teaching staff of the *École des Beaux Arts.* He was an exceptional man, without much acquaintance with experimental art yet unprejudiced in any direction, alert to the special character of whatever experimental painting came to his attention, even though in his own work he stuck close to tradition. Moreau gave Matisse his first education in art, not so much as his drawing and painting instructor as his guide to the art of the past, ranging over the whole field of masters dear to the academic heart, and those who were not. Soon Matisse was copying in the Louvre, partly as a way of studying and partly because the sale of copies produced a small income. These were "free" copies rather than painstaking reproductions. Primarily, Matisse was studying pictorial structure through copying rather than meticulously imitating the surface of another man's canvas as a mechanical routine. The integration of this study into his full development as a

painter was demonstrated by his return, more than twenty years later, to a de Heem still-life [474] to restudy it in a now famous variation [475].

All this while, Matisse was hardly aware of the impressionists, much less of such painters as Cézanne, van Gogh, and Gauguin. But discovery and conversion began to come rapidly in 1896 and 1897. After a few tentative impressionist excursions he set about his first major picture, *La Desserte* [476], in pure impressionist technique, and exhibited it in the Salon of the *Société Nationale.* (This was a dissenting academic organization, created by Meissonier as the result of a quarrel within the ranks of the Salon proper in 1890, and at that time headed by Puvis de Chavannes, who had nominated Matisse for membership.) *La Desserte,* a fine impressionist painting by the most exacting standards, drew indignant criticisms from conservative painters, but Moreau defended it.

During the next few years, still regarding himself as a student and rather surprisingly

475. MATISSE: *Variation on a Still-life by de Heem,* 1915, 1916, or 1917. 71 x 87¾". Collection Mr. and Mrs. Samuel A. Marx, Chicago.

476. MATISSE: *La Desserte,* 1897. 39½ x 51½". Collection Stavros Niarchos, Athens.

sequestered, considering the turmoil surrounding him in the Paris art world, Matisse felt his way among the crosscurrents of the end of the century. What he was learning is shown by the pictures and sculpture he acquired for himself: at considerable financial sacrifice he purchased a small Cézanne study of three bathers and a plaster bust by Rodin, and he exchanged one of his own paintings for a head of a boy by Gauguin. Rodin seems at first an odd influence on Matisse, but Matisse's *Slave* [477], a very early piece, shows how closely he followed Rodin [478], and we will see shortly that Rodin also influenced Matisse in certain drawings. Matisse had also wanted to buy a certain *Arlésienne* by van Gogh, but had given it up for the Cézanne, of which he wrote, many years later when he presented

477. MATISSE: *The Slave*, 1900–03. Bronze, height 36¼". Baltimore Museum of Art, Cone Collection.

478. RODIN: Study for a monument to Balzac, 1895. Bronze, height 30". Collection Mr. and Mrs. R. Sturgis Ingersoll, Penllyn, Pa.

it to the Museum of the City of Paris, "it has sustained me spiritually in the critical moments of my career as an artist." The influences of Cézanne, Gauguin, and even of Rodin are apparent in Matisse's *La Coiffure* [479] painted at this time, with its bold planes, its uncompromising force, and its emphatically defined silhouettes.

These early years of first experiment and discoveries were difficult ones for Matisse. He had abandoned a promising beginning toward conventional success, with encouraging recognition and some sales, and soon found himself in the familiar position of the experimenter—bad notices when he managed to exhibit at all, and no purchasers. He had married and had three children. But in 1905, a climactic year in his development and in the history of modern art, the situation improved dramatically, and his career as a leader among contemporary painters began in earnest.

479. MATISSE: *La Coiffure*, 1901. 37½ x 31⁹⁄₁₆″. National Gallery of Art, Washington, D.C., Chester Dale Collection.

480. MATISSE: *Olive Trees, Collioure*, 1905 (?). 18 x 21¾″. Estate of the artist.

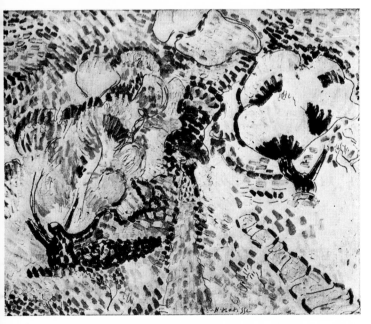

Matisse: The Birth of Fauvism

Matisse's palette had been brightened by some essays in pointillism, and now during the summer of 1905, in the village of Collioure on the Mediterranean, he came into a sudden realization of new meanings in color. (He was nearly thirty-five years old.) *Olive Trees, Collioure* [480] at a careless glance might be dismissed as a pointillist sketch. Actually the color—pure reds, greens, oranges, violets—applied in strokes of fairly uniform size, has nothing to do with pointillist theory. The different colors do not fuse into harmonious tonalities but maintain their own intense identities, clashing against one another and setting up a "movement" of their own as color, a movement that is incorporated into the more familiar kind of movement of the rather obvious swirling linear patterns. Matisse was learning that color as pure color could have its own rhythms, its own structure, that color could be exalted for itself rather than used as a descriptive or decorative accessory to other elements of a picture.

By this idea, a tree trunk could be vermilion, a sky could be solid orange, a face could be divided down its middle by a green line with contrasting colors on either side, as part of a color structure owing no allegiance to the actual color of trees, skies, or faces but existing as an independent abstraction. Gauguin had anticipated this idea in what was now an elementary way, and therein lies his grandparentage of fauvism. But Gauguin's color, when it departed arbitrarily from the colors of nature, was arbitrary in the service of mood or of decorative effect, which is a good step removed from a full conception of abstract color structure.

What "color structure" means is well demonstrated by the famous head of Madame Matisse usually called *The Green Line* [481]. On the right the face is pink, on the left, a yellow ochre. The background is divided into three large areas of green, vermilion, and rose-violet. These areas are not screens, pictures, or any other background objects; they are purely areas of color. All three are echoed in the dress. The hair is dark blue, as are the contour lines of the dress. On the pink side of the face the contour line is red, on the left side, green. The pink and ochre have some relationship to natural color, but when we reach the light, brilliant stripe of yellow-green dividing them down the middle of the face, the purely arbitrary use of color for structure is dramatized. Without the green stripe the face would be pallid, lost in the center of the violent color surrounding it. The question may be asked: In that case, why not modify the surrounding color so that the face could compete with it, instead of introducing the arbitrary green stripe? The answer is that the painter wants to use color at maximum intensity, and since the green stripe is necessary—as color—in that particular place, he uses it instead of sacrificing color intensity elsewhere. For that matter, the shape of the stripe and its position in the composition, as well as its color, is necessary as part of the pictorial structure. If it is covered up, even in a black and white reproduction, the structure is weakened. If it is covered in the original or in a good color reproduction, the structure is destroyed. And how did Matisse arrive at this particular color for this particular stripe? Through a general knowledge of color theory in the first place, of course, but more importantly through highly developed sensibilities and instincts in its use, plus a certain amount of trial and error in preliminary studies.

The Green Line is an abstract construction of color, but it is also an arresting image. It is not to be taken as a portrait of Madame Matisse in either a realistic or an expressionistic, interpretative way, although it suggests her features. The strong masklike character of the face reflects the stylized forms of African sculpture—a new interest with Matisse, and one which was to have an even stronger impact on Picasso in the development of cubism. Matisse was twelve years older than Picasso and, for whatever interest the fact may have in the general tendency to balance one man's innovations against the other's, it is probable that Matisse introduced Picasso to African sculpture at a time when cubism was still generating as a buried seed. Picasso and Matisse had made one another's acquaint-

481. MATISSE: *Madame Matisse (The Green Line)*, 1905. 16 x 12¾". *Statens Museum for Kunst*, Copenhagen, Rump Collection.

ance and were being collected in the same circles; a conspicuous patron was the American, Gertrude Stein. The two men met frequently at her apartment and maintained a courteous but wary attitude toward one another, as if they already realized that they would become, during the next decades, for critics and painters and collectors, rival representatives of the two mainstreams of modern painting.

Picasso was only beginning to collect his circle, but Matisse's was already pretty well formed. Surrounding him, having varying degrees of contact with him, drawing ideas from him and contributing their own were a group of colorists who became the fauves as a result of the landmark *Salon d'Automne* of 1905. Fauvism was never systematic; it

482. MATISSE: *Blue Nude*, 1907. 36¼ x 55⅛″. Baltimore Museum of Art, Cone Collection.

483. MATISSE: *Reclining Nude I*, 1907. Bronze, height 13½″. Baltimore Museum of Art, Cone Collection.

had no program and no formalized theory. It was never an organized school of painting, and as a group the fauves soon lost their unity, building in their own directions from the original stimulus. And as a "school" of painting, the birth of fauvism all but took its participants by surprise.

The *Salon d'Automne* had been organized two years before the famous 1905 exhibition by a group of thoughtful painters and liberal critics, who were equally dissatisfied with the conservatism of the regular academic Salons with their ingrown juries, and the anarchy of the *Indépendants* with no juries at all. The organizers of the *Salon d'Automne* solved the jury problem by selecting its members by lot. The 1905 jury hung the work of Matisse and eleven other colorists in one room together; one critic, commenting on a small bronze in the Florentine Renaissance manner exhibited in the same room, said, "Donatello parmi les fauves!"—Donatello among the wild beasts—and fauvism as a term and the fauves as a group were born, to the usual sounds of furious hubbub familiar since the *Salon des Refusés* forty-two years before. But there was a new note in the hubbub, and a more sympathetic one. The circle of liberal critics had widened. Where one reactionary critic found that the fauve pictures had "nothing whatever to do with painting," a liberal one recognized that Matisse's art was "painting outside of every contingency, painting in itself, the act of pure painting," and while the first saw "aberrated daubs and splotches of color," the other found that "the rational mind" of the painter perfectly controlled every element introduced into the paintings. Adventurous and perspicacious collectors were also increasing in number, putting an end to stories like the youthful Monet's or van Gogh's and Gauguin's.

While the excitement of the *Salon d'Automne* was still boiling, Matisse began a large composition as a crystallization and perhaps as a manifesto of fauvist ideas. *The Joy of Life* is a faulty picture, rather flimsy and monotonous compositionally, and disturbingly mannered, although it is of historical interest in showing that Matisse was experimenting with some of the structural ideas that were to be involved in cubism, as well as elements that were to affect expressionism in its more abstract forms. The *Blue Nude* of 1907 [482] is a more successful study in the same direction, combining sinuosities of line, arbitrary color, and dislocations of form, which are of course extremely disturbing if the painting is regarded as a representation of a female nude but are extraordinarily forceful otherwise.

With pictures like the *Blue Nude* Matisse was attracting enough attention to warrant the publication of his theories the following year, 1908. Matisse was nearly forty; he is unique among painters in having reached intellectual maturity before his career as a creative artist began in earnest. In effect, he has no "youthful" period. All his pre-fauve work is essentially studious, thoughtfully preparatory.

The *Notes of a Painter* play a double theme: the importance of feeling, of pure

484. DERAIN: *Henri Matisse,* 1905. 13 x 16″. Philadelphia Museum of Art, Gallatin Collection.

485. DERAIN: *The Artist's Niece,* before 1939. 37⅜ x 30⁵⁄₁₆″. Private collection, France.

186. DERAIN: *Le Mas Provençal*, date unknown. 24¾ x 37¼". Collection Robert E. McCormick, New York.

sensation, of the painter's response to the world on one hand, and, on the other, the means by which he may transmute these feelings into form and color. As a generality this is the problem of all serious painters; in the case of Matisse, the *Notes* imply everywhere a love of joyousness. He finally says, "What I dream of is an art of balance, of purity and serenity devoid of troubling or depressing subject-matter, an art which might be for every mental worker, be he business man or writer, like an appeasing influence, like a mental soother, something like a good armchair in which to rest from physical fatigue." Even granting some exaggeration and some awkwardness of expression (or of translation out of French) this is hardly the spirit of the *Blue Nude,* painted just before the notes were written, nor is it the spirit of the sculpture with which Matisse was occupying himself at the same time [483]. The *Blue Nude* and the sculpture were solutions of structural problems Matisse had set himself. Having served their purpose, their violent dislocations were soon to give way to forms no less vital but more serene or more joyous as the fauvist upheaval was assimilated.

Pure fauvism was of brief duration not only with Matisse but with the other members of the group. Before we follow Matisse's subsequent development, a few comments on the other fauves should be interpolated.

Other Fauve Painters

André Derain (1880–1954) worked with Matisse at Collioure in 1905, and painted the fauvist "portrait" of him [484] there. Derain was one of the first of the original group to depart from fauvism, and he cut off from it with exceptional completeness. When the competing cubist furore broke, Derain joined that party briefly, then for the rest of a commercially very successful career he shifted from style to style under the influence of a dozen traditional schools, as in a portrait of the artist's niece [485], where Corot, fauvism, and eighteenth-century sensibility are combined in an image of great sweetness, or *Le Mas Provençal* [486], where Corot, again, Courbet, Cézanne, and a pinch of cubism are included in the recipe.

Derain was a painter with a flair for modifying traditional styles by imposing agreeable modernisms upon them; or perhaps his flair was for modifying the radical discoveries of other painters by adapting them to acceptably traditional surfaces. He was, in either case, a painter of fashionable good taste and great discretion. His detractors think of him as a parasite on both the past and the present, but his admirers are satisfied that his middle-of-the-road art is neither a subterfuge nor an opportunistic compromise. Some critics award Derain unique stature as the only twentieth-century painter to achieve an individual compound of the great tradition of French culture as a whole with the spirit of his own time. This would place him in a position similar to the one accorded Renoir as the great traditionalist as well as one of the great innovators of the latter half of the nineteenth century. This opinion is particularly held in France—where, of course, it is most legitimate.

Maurice de Vlaminck (1876–1958) was a great friend of Derain's in their early days. They discovered van Gogh together, and it was Derain who introduced Vlaminck to Matisse. Among the cultivated and intellectual fauves, Vlaminck was an exceptional personality—more nearly *fauve* than they in his peasant vigor and his rambunctious muscularity. He was one of the few fauves who never toyed with cubism; he rejected it on sight as overintellectualized. But he abandoned the brilliant pure colors of fauvism to develop a dramatic landscape style giving a stormy and sinister character to simple village streets or peasant cottages painted in broad spreads and slashes of Prussian blue, black, touches of acid green, and spectral lights [487]. At their most effective these landscapes have a threatening vigor. Their shortcoming is their repetitiousness; reduced to a formula, both the threat and the vigor turn back into paint.

Albert Marquet (1875–1947) was especially close to Matisse in friendship, but his connection with fauvism was not a strong one in spite of his participation in the original exhibition. He was a sober painter, and a quiet man. Rivers and bridges and harbors were his favorite subjects, and he painted them with an ordered simplicity that recalls Corot, although he simplified his compositions into the flattened color areas associated with fauvism. The color itself, however, is more likely to be subdued than vivid. Marquet is a minor painter who was content to be one. His pictures are agreeable, partly because he never tried to force himself beyond his modest potential; they are admirable because he was never content to work below it [488].

Othon Friesz (1879–1949) painted a few unusually personal and sensitive fauve works, then abandoned the movement for a reactionary and sterile style. Henri Manguin (1874–1945) and Raoul Dufy (1877–1953) capitalized in the most lighthearted way on the brightness of fauve color. Dufy, after a period of conscientious effort to build himself a solid, monumental style on the model of Cézanne, realized the true nature of his talent and accepted it. He became the most engaging painter of chic and superficial subjects since the eighteenth century. He was helped toward this decision by Paul Poiret, the influential couturier, who commissioned Dufy to design fabrics. It is usual to say that Dufy sold himself out for an easy success, but this is an injustice. To exchange his bright and sparkling pictures for the second-rate

487. VLAMINCK: *Village in the Snow*, date unknown. Watercolor and gouache, 18 x 21″. Philadelphia Museum of Art, Gift of Howard A. Wolfe.

488. MARQUET: *Docks at Hamburg*, 1909. 27¼ x 32″. Collection Madame Albert Marquet, Bordeaux.

Cézannesque productions he might have continued to work at, would have been a very poor trade for everyone concerned. He developed a style in which swatches of decorative colors were freely applied to

489. DUFY: *Racetrack at Deauville*, 1929. 25½ x 32½". Fogg Art Museum, Cambridge, Mass., Maurice Wertheim Collection.

490. DUFY: *Threshing with a Blue Machine*, 1948. 21½ x 25¾". Toledo Museum of Art, Gift of Edward Drummond Libbey.

the canvas (or the paper—he used watercolor a great deal) and then more or less pulled together by economical calligraphic notations describing objects [489]. Racetracks, yacht basins, formal gardens, theater interiors, and other places of cheerful and expensive congregation were his favorite themes. They were most appropriate ones, too, for his manner. When he employed his fresh light colors and his bright little notations of form on less appropriate subjects—threshing machines, as one instance [490]—the style is as brilliant but the integration between means and subject is lost. This may be partly sheer association of ideas, for Dufy's manner has been plagiarized so freely by fashionable commercial artists that it has become synonymous with expensive elegance. His fecundity was extreme, and his style was one that could have become an automatically repetitious formula (as Vlaminck's did), yet Dufy retained a vivacity which suggests always that he took the greatest pleasure in what he was doing. The economy of his drawing, with its shorthand quality, conceals more variety and more observation than he is generally given credit for.

But the great names of the fauve group (unless we include Derain's) are Matisse, Braque, and Rouault. Braque turned to cubism and will be discussed with it. For Rouault, fauvism was a way station toward an intensely individual form of expression.

Rouault

Georges Rouault (1871–1958) was also a student of Moreau's, and he met Matisse in Moreau's studio. He is an anomaly in his century, a truly religious Christian painter. Perhaps it is necessary to point out that this is not the same thing as a painter of Christian subjects. There were many of these men, of course, and Rouault's earliest paintings are close to their tradition, although infused with a more visionary quality than most—thanks no doubt to the influence of Moreau.

Rouault was a devout Catholic, but his fervent Christianity is concerned less with personal redemption than with humane sociological values. He is horrified by man's inhumanity to man, appalled at poverty and misery. His Christianity is not concerned with mystical revelation but with man's spiritual union with his fellows, which is violated by every instance of cruelty or other human degradation. The expert illustration of Bible stories was not an adequate release for Rouault as a Christian painter; it was necessary for him to discover a more personal and intense expression.

By 1911 Rouault had passed through fauvism to an expressionism more remindful of the Germans than of any French tradition. He disregarded fauvism's bright colors and essentially happy mood in favor of a restricted and rather turgid palette in the service of tragic and pathetic subjects.

491. ROUAULT: *The Sirens*, 1906. Gouache, 28 x 22″. Collection Mr. and Mrs. R. Sturgis Ingersoll, Penllyn, Pa.

The Sirens [491] is painted in an oppressive tonality dominated by cold and rather sour grays, morbid gray-violets, and the blackish colors of the deliberately coarse and ugly outlines defining the swollen bodies and brutalized faces of two naked prostitutes. The women are symbols of mankind's self-corruption through the corruption of his fellows, through the cruelties, injustices, and miseries that he inflicts or whose existence he tolerates. The spirit of the picture is partly sociological, but more importantly it is religious, in the painter's identification of himself with the sufferings of humanity.

Rouault was never affected by medievalism as an imitation of the forms of medieval art (as the Pre-Raphaelites, for

492. ROUAULT: *Tragic Clowns*, 1907–10. 28½ x 21½". Collection Louis E. Stern, New York.

instance, were). But in certain ways his art is a continuation of medieval forms in the idiom of the twentieth century. Rouault's heavy, simplified, powerful volumes, in pictures like *Tragic Clowns* [492], have been compared to those of Romanesque sculpture—the sculpture of the early middle ages. The reference is a little forced, however, and the resemblances may be largely coincidental. The Romanesque sculptors in their century, and Rouault in his, approached the problem of expression from opposite poles technically. The early sculptors, working at the beginning of a tradition, with virtually no reference to a body of sculpture in the past, were inventing forms whose simplicity was imposed as much by technical limitations as by any-

thing else. They were probably striving for a higher degree of imitative realism than they managed to achieve, all expressive values aside. Rouault, on the other hand, is discarding the whole tradition of imitative realism, which had become so technically expert that it was next to photographic, and is finding his means of expression through simplifications which he imposes upon himself. The common denominator between primitive medieval art and the art of Rouault is not a technical one but a spiritual one: both are concerned with the theme of mankind's frailty and his redemption. The medieval sculptors expounded the theme by illustrating the Bible story; Rouault is never so specific, but in pictures like *Tragic Clowns* the theme is implicit just as it is in *The Sirens*. The male clown with his broken face, chopped out in broad sculpturesque planes, and the young girl with her heavy, coarsening one are symbols of mankind's tragedy, which is the death of his spirit through corruption. Rouault reveals the spiritual corruption through corruption and disfigurement of the flesh. But through his identification of himself with the subjects, and by the consciousness of tragedy that he stirs in us by these images, he also makes the picture a statement of man's hope, which is redemption through compassion.

If the forms of medieval sculpture were echoed only in a roundabout way in Rouault's style, those of medieval stained glass influenced it quite directly. He had been apprenticed, at fourteen, to a maker of stained glass and had worked on the restoration of medieval windows. Even in early expressionistic pictures like *The Sirens*, the dark outlines begin to suggest the leaded joints of stained glass windows, and shortly Rouault abandoned his heavy color schemes for areas of brilliant pigments even more definitely confined and separated from one another by black outlines. In some areas the color may have the flat purity of enamel—another medieval craft; in others, heavy strokes dragged across rough surfaces may suggest the surface irregularities and the luminous variations of medieval glass. In this manner Rouault painted landscapes, Biblical sub-

ROUAULT · 411

493. Rouault: *Crucifixion,* 1918. 41 x 28¾". Collection Henry P. McIlhenny, Philadelphia.

494. Rouault: *Pierrot with a Rose,* 1936. 36¼ x 24". Collection S. S. White III and Vera White, Ardmore, Pa.

jects [493], and above all the clowns and other performers of circuses and pantomimes that had always interested him. He did these in great numbers, and it is a mistake to try to read emotional intensities into all of them. By implication and association these intensities may be present, if diminished, but there are also many pictures, for instance *Pierrot with a Rose* [494], where sheer decorative vigor and rich color are at least as important, and as rewarding, as whatever elements of pathos are retained by the image.

Rouault was also one of the great printmakers of the age; many people would not hesitate to give him the title of greatest. The series *Miserere* and *War* are landmarks in the development of print techniques in which expression is integrated with technical devices. They are the most

important prints from this point of view since Goya's, which they suggest in other ways also. Like Goya, Rouault reveals the whole category of man's bestiality and viciousness; unlike Goya, however, he combines recognition of these realities with the mystical convictions we have already seen in his paintings. Technically, Goya was an innovator in that he approached the print as a self-contained medium, capitalizing on its inherent character and its expressive potential rather than using it as a means of reproducing painting or as a substitute for drawing. Rouault expanded the range of the print by combining any number of techniques on a single plate, creating his printing surface not only by conventional means, such as etching and engraving with the burin, but by such roughening devices as files, sandpaper, edged rollers and

495. ROUAULT: *Dura Lex Sed Lex* (*Harsh Law, but Law*), from *Miserere,* 1926. Composite processes, 22⅝ x 17⅛". Philadelphia Museum of Art.

scrapers, and wide brush strokes of acid—upon a foundation, sometimes, of photogravure. He approached a copper plate not with the idea that he was a draftsman or a technician, but with the idea that he was an artist creating a printing surface that must yield its expressive maximum through a design created in textures. From these plates, in black and white on paper, he achieved as much depth, variety, and richness as he did in full color manipulated in relief on canvas [495].

Matisse after Fauvism

By 1907, only two years after the fauvist paroxysm of the *Salon d'Automne* of 1905, fauvism had reached its climax as a movement with some kind of unity among the men who composed the group. The more tightly organized movement of cubism was supplanting it as the most spectacular development in contemporary painting. Cubism was a more sensational departure from tradition than fauvism had been, since its distortions were more extreme, and it was more adaptable to development by a closely allied group of painters, since its theory was more objective, less dependent on personal sensitivities. The fauves began to go their own ways, as we have just seen them doing.

Of all the fauves, Matisse had always been the one most concerned with formal organization. The apparent spontaneity and the fluidity of his compositions is deceptive. Like Delacroix before him, Matisse was always intent on maintaining the impression of spontaneity in the completed canvas, even though its final organization of form and color was the result of preliminary calculation, trial, and error.

Variations on the sinuous rhythms and the fresh expression of *The Joy of Life* continued to preoccupy Matisse until they culminated in a pair of large murals, *Dance* and *Music,* commissioned by a wealthy Russian, Sergei Shchukin, to decorate the stairwell of his house in Moscow. *Dance* is a reduction, to final terms, of composition in flat color and rhythmic line. It appears to have been improvised as it was painted, but it was preceded by any number of studies [496] in which the relationships of one line and area to another were modified into final balance.

Matisse was working in other directions at the same time, attacking especially the problem of formal monumentality combined with the dynamic color of fauvism. Sometimes his experiments deviated briefly in unexpected directions. In one exceptional canvas, the portrait of *Mlle. Yvonne Landsberg* [497] of 1914, the whirling rhythms of *Dance* have been disciplined into a pattern of arcs abstracted from a powerfully static figure, which they unite with the surrounding space. The interpenetration of form and space is a characteristic of cubism, as we will see, but in rectangular planes. In the *Mlle. Landsberg* Matisse has experimented with a similar interpenetration, but in a way suggesting swelling rhythms in which space and figure echo one another in a kind of formal arabesque. *Mlle. Landsberg* is unique in its devices, although it is so effective that it might have served as the source of a whole movement in analytical painting based on curving spatial rhythms instead of cubism's rectangular structures. But Matisse did not follow up this direction; his preoccupation with vibrant areas of color would not allow the disintegration and merging of one form into another.

The diagrammatic arching lines of the *Mlle. Landsberg* are more apparent and more spectacularly innovational than the rhythms in the drawing *White Plumes* [498], but *White Plumes* is equally composed in a series of rhythmic contours which flow and build from the long sweeping arcs defining the skirt, then the arms, and then progress into the more complicated swinging, curling, and looping rhythms of the embroidery and the ribbons and plumes of the hat. The entire design is a progressively complicated variation on a flowing rhythm as the forms mount upward, climaxing in the subtly hypnotic face just as the more obvious arcs of the *Mlle. Landsberg* climax in the correspondingly harsher mask. The point made by a comparison of these two pictures is, that while Matisse was basically interested in line, form, and color as abstractions (*Mlle. Landsberg*), he is equally concerned with the creation of images (*White Plumes*). In the *Mlle. Landsberg*, abstractions come close to overpowering the image. But in *White Plumes* the image reasserts its dominance, "enriched by a wider meaning," in Matisse's words.

Five years separate the two pictures. During that time Matisse created many semi-abstract compositions, drawing upon cubism just as, indirectly, he had contributed to its origin. In 1916 he had returned to his early copy of the de Heem still-life to make his semicubist variation on it [475], and during the same period, in compositions like *The Piano Lesson* [499], his angular structures also echo cubist theories. But these angularities are a surface exaggeration of the vestigial cubism

496. MATISSE: Study for *Dance*, 1909. 108 x 144″. Collection Walter P. Chrysler, Jr., New York.

497. MATISSE: *Mlle. Yvonne Landsberg*, 1914. 57¼ x 42″. Philadelphia Museum of Art, Arensberg Collection.

498. MATISSE: *White Plumes,* 1919. Pencil, 19¼ x 14⅜". Collection T. Edward Hanley, Bradford, Pa.

499. MATISSE: *The Piano Lesson,* 1916 or 1917. 92½ x 83¾". Museum of Modern Art, New York, Mrs. Simon Guggenheim Fund.

in Matisse's work at this time. Basically, *The Piano Lesson* is a structure in which the linear skeleton and the pattern of geometrical areas are still dependent upon color for their life and their balance. Also, this picture, which may appear a little thin and flat at first, grows richer upon closer acquaintance. There is, for instance, the interplay between the almost jaunty little figurine of the nude in the lower left, which at first is hardly noticeable, with the elongated, angular figure at the upper right, a parent or teacher supervising the boy at the piano. There is also a kind of counterpoint between the arbitrary abstract elements and the fairly realistic representation of others—the metronome, and the music rack of the piano, where even the name, Pleyel, is shown in reverse as we see it from behind, as part of a filigree. All these balanced contradictions are in the spirit of the picture, which is an engaging, rather affec-

tionately humorous subject contradictorily presented in a spare and carefully calculated scheme, a combination of intimacy and austerity.

Up to this point in his development, Matisse has evidently been intent upon harmonizing the joyous, intimate, and sensuous spirit that is inherent in his art with the disciplines necessary to lift it above mere charm or triviality. Around 1917, as if with a sigh of relief, he yielded himself to his "good armchair," largely abandoning the disciplines for an interim of the most relaxed, most spontaneous, and least intellectualized painting of his career. At this stage he becomes the painter of fresh, sensory delights that make him the twentieth-century inheritor of such pre-Revolutionary masters as Boucher, and of Renoir in Renoir's most intimate and informal work. His paint is applied more lusciously, and more casually, than before. His subjects have more consistently to do with pleasure, ease, and luxury. Angularities and severities of compositional structure yield to grace and, above all, to semirealism. In spite of perspective violations, *The Moorish Screen* [500] from this period could almost be a quick sketch by an impressionist or even a notation by a realist, although the emphasis on ornamental patterns would be characteristic of neither. Oriental elements, which had been a large factor in Matisse's work since a first visit to Morocco in 1911, are especially conspicuous here in the form of decorative accessories, such as carpets, screens, tiles, and the like. The whole picture is related to the glazed brilliance of Eastern patterned tiles.

Matisse was now working largely in Nice, a city dedicated to relaxation and surface attractions. His bright, comparatively naturalistic pictures pleased new collectors and even a fairly wide public, having as they did the *cachet* of approval by the most discerning critics, yet being much easier to understand than Matisse's work had been heretofore. But for all their charm, these agreeable and ornamental paintings had sacrificed much of their strength; for their grace, much of their subtlety. At this point Matisse might have followed the path of certain other fauves, notably Dufy, to settle for seduction and chic after the innovations of fauvism and the rigors of compositions like *The Piano Lesson* that had served the purpose of giving him a facile command of color and structure at less demanding levels.

Matisse was never to return to the abstractions of *The Piano Lesson* and other pictures of that period—at least, not in obvious ways. But he had never been a painter who was content to develop a formula and hold to it and he never became one. *Decorative Figure on an Ornamental Background* [501], about five years after *The Moorish Screen,* rejects the sketchy realism and rather fluid painting of the earlier picture for a return to bold definitions and more arbitrary patterning, but retains the opulence that will be characteristic of Matisse from now on. *Decorative Figure* is essentially one of Matisse's great still-life compositions rather than one

500. MATISSE: *The Moorish Screen,* 1921. 36¼ x 29″. Philadelphia Museum of Art, Lisa Norris Elkins Bequest.

of his great nudes, for the figure is like an ornamental sculpture in the ensemble of other decorative objects and patterns.

All the foregoing summaries of major stages in Matisse's development have omitted the subdivisions, the brief periods of retreat from one direction, of return to variations of earlier periods. Two years after *Decorative Figure,* for instance, paintings like *Nude by a Window* [502] may appear to differ very little from the semirealism of *The Moorish Screen.* Or the bay with its promenade, its palm tree, and quick patterns of color may go further back, as far as Collioure. In its structural skeleton of strong verticals and horizontals setting off sinuous curves, there are echoes of *The Piano Lesson,* if we want to find them. Like every painter who continues to

501. MATISSE: *Decorative Figure on an Ornamental Background*, 1927. 51½ x 38⅜".
Musée National d'Art Moderne, Paris.

502. MATISSE: *Nude by a Window*, 1929. 25¾ x 21½". Collection Vladimir Horowitz,
New York.

grow, Matisse draws upon all that he has learned, sometimes consciously, sometimes spontaneously, but he is never content to work only in repetitions or recombinations of past successes. His first mistrust of Bouguereau, his first suspicion that that tremendous academic reputation might be an inflated one, came when he found that Bouguereau was not only making an exact copy of one of his most successful pictures but making it from another copy made some time before.

In spite of excursions in various directions, and all the divisions and subdivisions of his work into periods,* Matisse's development is, over-all, steady in the direction stated implicitly in his *Notes* when he said, "Supposing I want to paint the body of a woman: first of all I endow it with grace

* These may be followed in detail in Alfred Barr's *Matisse: His Art and His Public.*

and charm, but I know that something more than that is necessary. I try to condense the meaning of this body by drawing its essential lines. The charm will then become less apparent at first glance, but in the long run it will begin to emanate from the new image. This image at the same time will be enriched by a wider meaning . . . while the charm, being less apparent . . . will be merely one element in the general conception of the figure."

His *Lady in Blue* [503] of 1937, painted thirty years after the *Notes* were written, applies all that Matisse has learned of the artist's function as a creator who first responds to nature, then effects his own transmutation of nature in such a way that his response to it takes the form of an image revealing that response to the observer. The course of the transmutation can be followed in a series of photographs taken during the progress of the painting [504]. They show a progressive condensation and flattening of the forms, reduced to their essentials (the arms of the sofa, for instance, are finally reduced to two flat S shapes) and mutually adjusted into a balance at once decorative and expressive.

The color areas of *Lady in Blue* are quite flat, without any suggestion of modeling in light and shade. As a generality (but only as a generality) this is true of Matisse's style after about 1930. In his very late years he exaggerated this flatness in a series of brilliant conceits in cut and pasted papers of vivid color. One series of these was called *Jazz* [505]; all the more surprising, then, that their flat, bright shapes should be adapted, in Matisse's last work, to the stained glass windows of a chapel.

In the late 1940's, when he was approaching eighty, Matisse abruptly committed himself to the decoration of an entire chapel—stained glass windows, murals, ornamental tiles, altar, crucifix, confessional doors, chasubles, even the spire on the exterior—for the Dominican nuns in the little town of Vence, near Nice. Matisse underwrote some of the expense himself. Nothing in his worldly art had ever suggested that his last great work would be a religious one for which he volunteered, but everything in its ornamental character was adaptable to architectural use.

For that matter, the decoration of the chapel at Vence is not a religious work in the way it would have been if Rouault, for instance, had done it. Matisse had never been a devout man, and he experienced no conversion now, although there was a great deal of distorted publicity at the time, attributing such a reason to his decision to do the chapel. He undertook the assignment in part because of his friendship for one of the nuns but largely, it seems, in the spirit of adventurous enthusiasm that had stayed with him into his old age. "At last," he said, "we are going to have a gay chapel!" and he made no effort to synthesize any fraudulent mysticism in his preliminary designs. These were gay indeed, so gay that when a communist acquaintance of Matisse's saw them he said, "When we take over, we'll use it for a night club."

503. MATISSE: *Lady in Blue*, 1937. 36½ x 29". Collection Mrs. John Wintersteen, Chestnut Hill, Pa.

Matisse approached the decoration of the chapel as an abstract problem, a balancing of "a surface of light and color against a solid wall covered with black drawings." The scheme has little to do with the Christian mysteries except in its use of some of their familiar symbols, but it has a spareness and restraint, in spite of its bright colors, which is more appropriate to a chapel than it would be to a night club; it is pure, fresh, and joyous rather than gay and sensuous. The "murals" that balance the bright animated shapes of the windows are ceramic wall decorations in the form of thin line drawings in black on white backgrounds. They are a last statement of Matisse's development as a graphic artist, which was from elaboration (we have seen an example in the drawing *White Plumes*) to maximum simplicity.

February 26, 1937 · March 3, 1937 · March 10, 1937 · March 13, 1937 · March 17, 1937

March 19, 1937 · March 21, 1937 · March 25, 1937 · April 4, 1937 · April 6, 1937

504. MATISSE: Progressive stages of Figure 503, February 26 to April 6, 1937.

505. MATISSE: *The Knife Thrower*, from *Jazz*, 1947. Color stencil after cut paper original. 15⅞ x 25½". Philadelphia Museum of Art, McIlhenny Fund.

Girl in a Low Cut Dress [506] is a typical example of Matisse's line drawing at its most economical; it recalls Rodin, once more, in Matisse's art, especially with the bridge of *Three Friends* [507] in comparison with Rodin's *Imploration* [508], even if we grant that the resemblance between the ornamental suggestions in the background of *Three Friends* and the free washes of color in *Imploration* may be coincidental. Rodin's voluptuousness disappears in Matisse's crisper, brighter images, but the free line, capturing an immediate reaction to the model as well as describing the essence of formal contours, is common to them both. There the similarity ends. Rodin's sensuousness was always part of some mystery, some yearning, close to romantic anguish. Matisse's sensuousness is a response to the joy of the tangible world.

Expressionism: Precursors

By the definition of expressionism as "the free distortion of form and color through which a painter gives visual form to inner sensations or emotions," fauvism is a form of expressionism. But usually expressionism is concerned with "inner sensations or emotions" with connotations of pathos, violence, morbidity, or tragedy. Van Gogh is an expressionist within this definition. But by the narrowest definition of all, expressionism was a movement in twentieth-century painting that originated in Germany and continued to develop there in the work of several successive groups of painters who applied these general principles in their own intense and particular ways.

With the usual exceptions, the purest expressionist painters have been northern ones—Scandinavians, Dutchmen, Germans, and some Russians. Van Gogh was a northerner. Even though he painted in Paris and in the south of France, he was a foreigner to those places emotionally as well as nationally. He is admired and respected in France, but he has found no very close followers among French painters because he is without the qualities that temper the Frenchman's recognition of the terribleness of life—logical perception, worship of Rea-

506. MATISSE: *Girl in a Low Cut Dress*, 1939. Pen and ink, 15 × 22″. Estate of the artist.

son, a sense of moderation. Nor has van Gogh the gaiety and elegance that are constants in French art and life, and so large an element in fauvism. Fauvism had secondary connections with van Gogh, but he was the natural father of German expressionism.

In addition to van Gogh, German expressionism found prophets in the Swiss Ferdinand Hodler (1853–1918), born the same year as van Gogh, the Belgian James Ensor (1860–1949), and the Norwegian Edvard Munch (1863–1944), whose birth date encloses the three men within a decade of van Gogh as to age. Ensor and Munch knew the work of van Gogh and Gauguin and were in part formed by it, but Hodler was a rather isolated painter whose connections with post-impressionism and expressionism are spotty and interrupted. They were made largely through the success of a single picture, *The Night* [509].

Hodler became a painter after making a difficult choice between art and science. The science remains apparent in his art, with its tight precise forms and what can only be called its objective quality. For in spite of the fact that *The Night* proposes a fantastic subject, the drawing of the nude

507.   MATISSE:
Three Friends, 1927.
Pen and ink, 15 x
20". *Musée National
l'Art Moderne*, Paris.

508. RODIN: *Imploration*, date unknown. Pencil with watercolor wash, 12 x 19". Collection Mr. and Mrs. Adolf Schaap, Elkins Park, Pa.

421

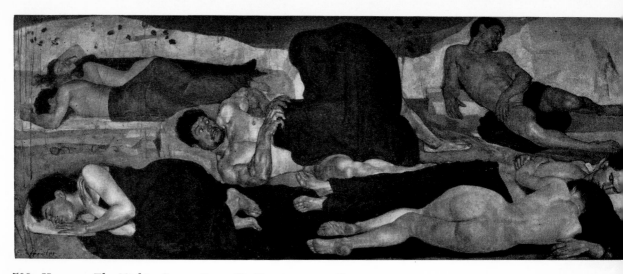

509. HODLER: *The Night*, 1890. 41¾ x 118". *Kunstmuseum*, Bern.

figures enacting it is next to scientific in the explicitness of its description. We are right back to the painting of another Swiss, then —Böcklin.* There is the same realistic-fantastic fusion, but Hodler's picture has a discipline that eliminates the beer-hall tinge so distracting in Böcklin. The discipline was a specific one invented by Hodler himself. It was compositional, and he called it *parallelism;* it dictated the arrangement of the figures in layers above one another in parallels to the picture plane. *The Night* was a great success in conventional circles in Paris when it was exhibited there in 1891, the year after it was painted. And without any question, the handsome bodies represented in it exert an eerie pull on the imagination even while one suspects that the picture is a tour de force, that it is essentially a group of *tableaux-vivants,* arrestingly combined and meticulously executed. Both its mysticism and its modernism are a little false; it is not so much mystical as it is spooky, and it is not so much an original picture as it is a streamlined version of a Salon exercise.

The Night would come off better if it were not asked to meet such strong competition from its contemporaries; as a struc-

ture the picture is an elementary exercise when we remember *La Grande Jatte* [399], painted five years before, and the tightening of contours that lifts the drawing of Hodler's figures a notch above first-rate studio exercises in the nude is only a first step in the direction Gauguin traveled. As a matter of fact, the picture hardly fits in anywhere: it is not altogether academic; its structural elements cannot quite make it post-impressionist (although Hodler belongs to a group of Germans who rejected, or never accepted, the broken forms of impressionism); and its symbolism is pedantic and seems even more so when we think of it as one of a series of pictures Hodler painted after its success, with such high-flown titles as *Disillusioned Souls* and *Glance into Infinity.* Its rather tenuous connection to expressionism has to do with its revelation of a state of mind, but it employs none of the distortions that in true expressionism give us the feeling that the revelation has been torn by the roots from the painter's consciousness and displayed, mangled and palpitating, upon the canvas.

In the cases of Ensor and Munch, the connection with expressionism is more direct. Munch summed up his art in six words so pat that they make further verbal description superfluous. "I hear the scream in nature," he said. He had firsthand experience with the brutality with which life

---

* Another Swiss forebear was Holbein the Younger (1497–1543), the Renaissance master whose polished surface and sharply defined linear contours were models for Hodler.

510. MUNCH: *Anxiety,* 1896. Color lithograph, 16¼ x 15¼". Museum of Modern Art, New York.

personal source of expressionist art, and is suggested in Hodler's *The Night;* each of the figures is spiritually isolated, even when embraced with another. And we know to what extent van Gogh's painting was a release from the aloneness he felt within himself.

It has been observed that Daumier, when he showed people in railroad carriages, or waiting in the station, or walking on the street, sometimes shows them as solitary within their own thoughts, alone in the crowd. But they share with their fellow human beings the important consolation of their common humanity. They move within the same world as their fellows and it is a world, ultimately, of warmth and meaning. But the individuals in Munch's *Anxiety* [510] are caged within their own neuroses. The forms are established as strong, thick, black and red lines or heavy, solid, black masses, except for the faces, and these are barely indicated, by the palest, most tenuous little strokes, as if obliterated by the spirit's inward turning. The pale staring eyes see nothing.*

As for Ensor, he is at least as much a fantasist as an expressionist. His typical pictures involve skeletons and masked creatures in bizarre, grotesque scenes of sinister gaiety. His color is strong and bright, so that at first glance each picture is a carnival, a group of funnyfaces or Mardi-gras revelers, for a moment. The *Skeletons Trying to Warm Themselves* [512] are puppets from a Punch and Judy show—briefly—before they become parts of a nightmare.

can treat men. His family seemed to be dogged by death and anguish; he observed, although he did not experience, the desperate poverty of the Oslo slums. He paints from a hopeless conviction of man's aloneness in the world, his vulnerability to misfortune and spiritual violation. The sense of aloneness is frequently the theme or the

* The flowing and sinuous yet oddly limp lines of *Anxiety* are a manifestation of *art nouveau,* literally the "new art," a decorative style that flourished in the decade between 1890 and 1900, not always with results that look happy today. *Art nouveau* was an effort to create new expressive patterns based on the rhythms inherent in the lines of natural forms, particularly the stems and tendrils of trailing or climbing plants. Its theory was used in the design of architectural ornament and the decorative crafts as well as in painting. The lettering in Lautrec's posters is designed in *art-nouveau* idiom. Lautrec's style as a draughtsman, strongly affected by *art nouveau,* is one of the isolated instances where it has not passed into an awkward age. The patterns of *art nouveau*

have a way of looking trite or even amateurish today, although this contemporary way of seeing them might be outgrown. Nevertheless it mars Munch's pictures for most people at the moment. In Germany, *art nouveau* was called *Jugendstil,* or the youth-style, after a magazine *Die Jugend.* In England the precious *Yellow Book* with its *art-nouveau* drawings by Aubrey Beardsley [346] was part of the movement. *Art nouveau* affected Gauguin, too, in the flowing lines of water, the patterning of plants and the like, and conspicuously in his *Self-portrait with a Halo* [456]. The background of van Gogh's *La Berceuse* [449] is related to it. And *art nouveau* infects German expressionism, as will continue to be obvious, as a congenital inheritance from Munch.

511. ENSOR: *Entry of Christ into Brussels in 1889*, 1888. 101½ x 169½″. *Casino Communal*, Knokke-le-Zoute, Belgium. (Photo Museum of Modern Art, New York.)

Ensor's most ambitious picture was the *Entry of Christ into Brussels* [511], a canvas more than fourteen feet long, which, according to his fellow Belgian, the architect and designer, Henry van de Velde (an originator and spokesman of the theories of *art nouveau*), was an effort to create a sensation by painting a picture even larger than *La Grande Jatte*. Seurat's masterpiece had just been exhibited in Brussels and had made such a sensation that it was difficult to see for the crowds surrounding it. As a companion piece inviting comparison with *La Grande Jatte*, however, the *Entry of Christ into Brussels* is an excellent foil demonstrating Seurat's virtues. Ensor's picture is rather wearing, too loosely organized to unify so large a surface, and crowded with anecdotal detail that seems to have been piled up simply to get as much in the picture as possible. Ensor's world is more directly and disturbingly summed up in his *Self-portrait with Masks* [513]. Masks and skeletons are Ensor's symbols, respectively,

of man's falsity and his mortality. That his fantasies have this direct and conscious relationship to an interpretation of this world in personal emotionalized terms makes Ensor an expressionist as well as a painter of the other-world of dream.

Expressionism: "Die Brücke"

With these comments behind us, the flowering of expressionism in Germany can be outlined as a matter of organizations formed for its proselytization, and of personal variations on the expressionist idea. The earliest of the organizations was *Die Brücke*, meaning The Bridge, formed by a group of pupils at the Dresden Technical School and their friends. Some twenty years younger than Munch and Ensor, some thirty younger than van Gogh, they were directly influenced by these painters and also learned a great deal from the fauves, who had just declared themselves.

512. ENSOR: *Skeletons Trying to Warm Themselves*, 1889. 29½ x 23⅝". Collection Baron Robert Gendebien, Brussels. (Photo Museum of Modern Art, New York.)

513. ENSOR: *Self-portrait with Masks*, 1889. 47½ x 31½". Collection Cleomire Jussiant, Antwerp. (Photo Museum of Modern Art, New York.)

The Bridge was founded in 1905, began to break up with the usual internal dissensions by 1907, and was finally dissolved in 1913 while its members continued to paint along its general lines.

Emil Nolde (1867–1956) was an exception among the members of The Bridge, in being somewhat older than the others and, at the same time, something of an adopted son to them. He had passed through an early period when he did rather pretty picturesque landscapes, and had followed it with an impressionist phase, then developed an interest in stormy color. The young men who founded The Bridge recognized his color as potentially expressionist, and under their influence he developed the typical preoccupation with personal and highly emotionalized statement.

The painters of The Bridge had their individual anguishes—sociological, political, sexual, and religious—and Nolde's were religious. Like the other members of the group, he is an artist who must be accepted on his own terms, or not at all. His form of religious statement cannot be stomached if religious statement is limited to the areas of mystical reflection or miraculous revelation in which it ordinarily falls in painting, or even within the area of humanitarian compassion typical of Rouault. Nolde's *Life of Maria Aegyptiaca* [514], told in three episodes, the first showing her sinful life before conversion, the second her conversion, and the third her death, is shocking in its ugliness. But shock and ugliness, even revulsion, are Nolde's medium of religious expression. We must suppose that the painter reaches some kind of self-purification through the rejection of all grace, either spiritual or aesthetic, through embracing all baseness and grossness, reveal-

514. NOLDE: *Life of Maria Aegyptiaca*, First Episode, "Early Sinful Life," 1912. 33¾ x 39¼". Kunsthalle, Hamburg.

ing it, devouring it, and expelling it in forms of abhorrent ugliness, in forms smeared with the colors of blood and putrefaction. Here is van Gogh's personal catharsis intensified to such a pitch that it must be either embraced as profound or rejected as ludicrous.

Nolde left The Bridge as early as 1907, but his association with the group had led him to his special fulfillment in pictures of this kind. Like other expressionist painters who were still at work during the late 1930's, he was in disfavor under Hitler's regime, which sought to eliminate all "unhealthy" manifestations from German art and to create a new one out of the whole cloth. Hitlerian art was a kind of galumphing realism intended to indicate that Germany was a nation of jolly extroverts bursting with health and without a neurosis to their name, certainly an ideal opposed to the mood of The Bridge. Many of Nolde's paintings were confiscated, along with

515. SCHMIDT-ROTTLUFF: *Way to Emmaus*, 1918. Woodcut, 15" x 19½". Philadelphia Museum of Art, Gift of Dr. George J. Roth

those of his colleagues, and he was one of those who had the particular distinction of being forbidden to paint at all.

Karl Schmidt-Rottluff (1884–) was another of this select group. He had been a founding member of The Bridge and had even invented its name. After a beginning in which fauvist tendencies flavored his work, he shifted to a primitivism inspired by African sculpture, which was exerting influence on the expressionists, the fauves, and the cubists all at the same time for different reasons. The expressionists were attracted by its harsh primitive vigor. In France the fauves and cubists also felt the appeal of this quality, so refreshing an injection after the hyperrefinements of *fin-de-siècle* art, but they intellectualized their use of primitive forms while the Germans sought to recapture the directness of emotional statement they felt existed there. Schmidt-Rottluff's *Way to Emmaus* [515] is doubly influenced by African sculpture [1]—witness the heads—and Gothic woodcuts of a simple and crude kind. The expressionists felt that there was a minimum of technical barrier between the artist and the observer in the earliest and most primitive woodcuts, and referred first of all to German ones, a part of their program to revitalize German art. Some of the best work of The Bridge took the form of woodcuts, but their innovation of crude cutting had been anticipated by Gauguin. He had already capitalized on crude cutting and rough printing in Tahiti, as in *Manao Tupapau* [516] (the same title as the painting already seen), although as usual with Gauguin this "primitive" directness is combined with Parisian subtleties. The woodcut *Manao Tupapau* is printed in exquisite tints of soft pinks, browns, and greens, with of course black, and in spite of the roughness of its lines it is nicely calculated, rhythmic in its organization, and as sophisticated as a Japanese print, which it suggests as much as it does primitive art. But *Way to Emmaus* is gashed out of the wood as if in fear that the slightest refinement must reduce the force of communication between artist and observer.

This force is remarkably retained, and the prints of The Bridge may end as their most distinctive achievement. The *Portrait*

516. GAUGUIN: *Manao Tupapau*, 1894. Color woodcut with touches of watercolor, 8⅞ x 18″. Philadelphia Museum of Art, Lisa Norris Elkins Fund.

517. HECKEL: *Portrait of a Man*, 1919(?). Color woodcut, 18¼ x 12¼". National Gallery of Art, Washington D. C., Rosenwald Collection.

518. KIRCHNER: *The Street*, 1913. 47½ x 35⅞". Museum of Modern Art, New York.

of a Man [517], possibly a self-portrait, by Erich Heckel (1883–   ) is less insistent than *Way to Emmaus*, but it wears better. With its emaciation, its introspection, its air of neurotic apprehensions, it comes as close as any single work can come to being a psychological portrait of The Bridge as a whole. In color, the print is dominated by the pale olive green of the face and hands, played against background areas of modified blue and brown, with the master block printed over them in sooty black. The woodiness of the blocks is emphasized in both cutting and printing. Woodblocks interested Heckel to such an extent that he carried their effects over into his painting, a curious reversal since color woodblocks originated as a substitute for painted pictures.

Ernst Ludwig Kirchner (1880–1938) is usually thought of as the most typical painter of The Bridge. A list of the influences at work in his art makes him sound like an eclectic: first naturalistic, then briefly pointillist, he shifted to an admiration for van Gogh and Munch, used fauvist color for a while, admired Japanese art and African sculpture like all other investigative young painters at the time, and finally adopted the angularities of cubism. Cubism was a form of spatial analysis, but it interested Kirchner only as an expression of energy. His work is the most tightly organized of any of the group, no doubt because he began as a student of architecture and even received his degree in it. With Heckel and Schmidt-Rottluff he was the third in the trio of Dresden Technical School pupils who founded The Bridge.

In early pictures, Kirchner had worked in the flat color areas of fauvism, but he is his own man in *The Street* [518], even

519. BARLACH: *Man Drawing a Sword*, 1911. Wood, height 29½″. Cranbrook Academy of Art, Bloomfield Hills, Mich.

though other influences, especially cubism, remain obvious. The rational angularities of cubism are turned into hectic, slashing patterns to express the theme that became Kirchner's major one—the tension, the neurasthenic agitation, the sinister viciousness, of the city. In the manner of *The Street* he painted people in gatherings where they are crowded together in an acid atmosphere, their isolation not so much a matter of melancholy aloneness as part of a cold, vicious distraction without unifying purpose. *The Street* was painted in 1913, just before World War I; Berlin at that time acted as a catalyst to fuse the various influences at work on Kirchner and make an individual painter of him.

During the war Kirchner was invalided out, not by wounds but by nervous instability. He spent the rest of his life in Switzerland. Painting again, he lost much of his

individuality in a study of spatial cubism and rhythmic semi-fauvist landscapes. He committed suicide in 1938, partly because Hitler had condemned some 600 of his works as "degenerate." Degenerate his art may have been, but in that case Kirchner was only performing the timeless function of the painter who reveals the essence of the time and place—Germany between wars—surrounding him.*

Some members of The Bridge turned once in a while to sculpture—especially Schmidt-Rottluff and Kirchner. But the sculptor most closely allied to them in spirit was not affiliated with them or with any other expressionist group—Ernst Barlach (1870–1938). Barlach worked quite directly in the tradition of German Romanesque sculpture without being at all a parasite upon it. His bulky, vigorously chopped, often heavily textured forms have the human immediacy of some of the smaller medieval sculptures, rather than the monumental character of major portal figures. In medieval churches one comes on these small carvings, sometimes tucked away nearly out of sight; they are likely to be carved more freely and more personally than larger pieces in more conspicuous locations. The German examples are individualized by exceptional directness, sometimes an awkwardness in their strength, an exaggerated realism that may approach caricature. Barlach draws upon this tradition without reverting to it. Compositionally his figures are most frequently marked by swinging or lunging rhythms brought into sculpturesque balance by counter-rhythms in opposing lines and masses [519].

Barlach was also one of the fine graphic artists of expressionism. His woodcuts have about them a feeling of carving; his prints retain to the highest degree the sense of the block's woodiness, the feeling of the knife or the gouge, which is typical of the prints of The Bridge.

---

* Otto Mueller (1874–1930) and Max Pechstein (1881–   ) should be mentioned as the remaining important members of The Bridge. Their work is discussed by association in these remarks on other painters; it is not illustrated or further discussed here to avoid repetition, not to dismiss these two painters as negligible talents.

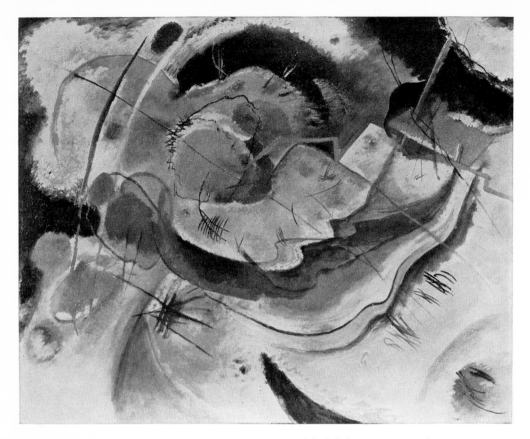

520. KANDINSKY: *Improvisation*, 1914. 30¾ x 39⅜". Philadelphia Museum of Art, Arensberg Collection.

Expressionism: "Der Blaue Reiter"

In the expressionism of The Bridge, subject is of basic importance, no matter how violently the forms are distorted in the process of revealing inner responses to external reality. In a second German expressionist group, *Der Blaue Reiter* (The Blue Rider), subject is less important and finally disappears altogether, taking recognizable images away with it. In other words, the men of The Blue Rider are increasingly abstract and finally nonobjective painters. The term *nonobjective* (sometimes *nonfigurative* in subtle distinction) describes completely abstract art that is independent of subject even as a starting point for the derivation of forms.

The Rider group is a more cheerful one than The Bridge, more influenced by Gauguin than by van Gogh, interested in rhyth-mical, "musical" compositions composed of sweeping curves and flowing lines rather than harsh, moody, restless, or abrupt ones. The group was not formed until the last month of 1911, some years after The Bridge, which it eventually absorbed, and it grew out of a series of exhibitions held in Munich when all the advanced art groups of the city combined to hold international exhibitions of work by men from Cézanne forward. Munich was extremely active in painting, but heretofore the sound, brownish, anecdotal academic work produced there in great quantities had not been as seriously under attack as traditional painting had been in Paris. The men of The Blue Rider broke away from the large amorphous group that was organizing exhibitions to introduce the French rebels to Germany. Their background was international rather than specifically German,

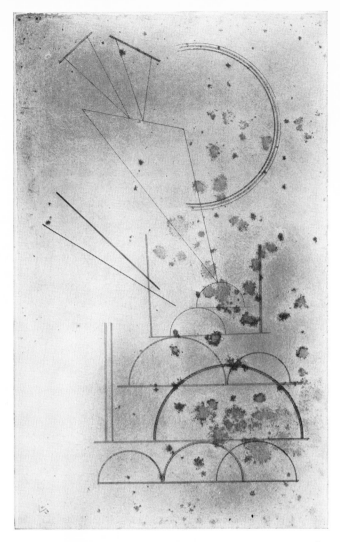

521. KANDINSKY: *Geometrical Forms*, 1928. Watercolor and ink on paper, 19 x 11″. Philadelphia Museum of Art, Arensberg Collection.

had brought his work to the point of complete abstraction, as he seemed to be in the process of doing. Kandinsky is another story: the appearance of his first completely nonrepresentational work in 1910 is a historical event of great consequence, and he formulated his ideas in a treatise, *Concerning the Spiritual in Art*, which has been a handbook since its publication in 1912. He divorced painting from subject matter and tried to create mood by the psychological impact of line and color alone.

Kandinsky's various "improvisations" [520] of spontaneously applied color "mean" nothing, in the sense of direct allegory or symbol. They are based on the reasonable assumption that if a model painted in a red dress affects the observer differently from the same model painted the same way in a white dress, then the color alone accounts for the difference. In that case, simply a red shape or simply a blue shape must mean something, must strike up a "corresponding vibration in the human soul," to borrow a phrase Kandinsky used in a slightly different context. Also, if an object described in squiggly broken lines is different in psychological effect from the same object described in smooth, even, tightly defined line, then the squiggly broken lines and the smooth even ones must have their own inherent psychological quality, all subject matter aside. Thus a painting can have a mood through its lines and colors without a subject. To make the divorce from subject complete, Kandinsky ordinarily gave no titles to his paintings, identifying his improvisations by a number or by date or by some phrase to distinguish one from another but not to give a literary suggestion as to what it was "about."

In contrast to the improvisations with their expressionistically free arrangements, Kandinsky also composed in patterns of sharply defined geometrical forms [521]. These forms might be flat, regular, geometrical ones or sharp-edged ones of irregular shapes, and might be filled with color or not, and might, as in the illustration selected here, include a scattering of more accidental forms whose disposition is taken into account in the arrangement of the more calculated ones. Although he rejected

thus differentiating them from The Bridge; their influence, too, was international in contrast with the more self-contained earlier group.

The two organizing members of The Blue Rider were Franz Marc (1880–1916), a contemporary of the men we have just seen, and Wassily Kandinsky (1866–1944), somewhat older and of Russian origin, who had been a lawyer, had developed as a painter along fauvist lines, and had exhibited in Bridge shows. Marc was killed in the battle of Verdun before he

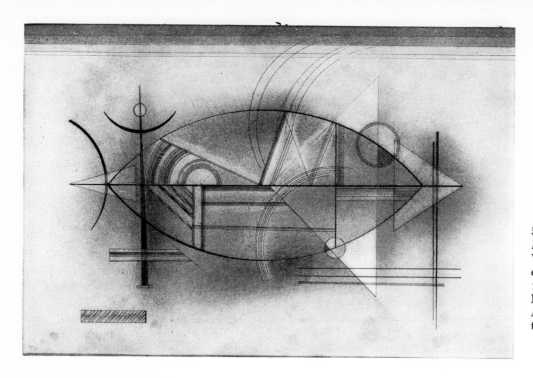

images, Kandinsky never thought of his nonobjective paintings as being divorced from nature, and from time to time, as in *Fish Form* [522], he allowed nature to be recognizable within extreme geometrical conventionalizations. He may or may not have been thinking of this picture when he wrote that the essential difference between a line and a fish is that "the fish can swim, eat, and be eaten. It has then, capacities of which the line is deprived. These capacities of the fish are necessary extras for the fish itself and for the kitchen, but not for painting. And so, not being necessary, they are superfluous. That is why I like the line better than the fish—at least in my painting." *Fish Form* makes a concession to image—but it remains more line than fish.

Among the painters formally and informally connected with The Blue Rider, four must be mentioned. Another Russian, Alexei von Jawlensky (1864–1941) developed a preoccupation with large, formalized, rather hieratic heads, sometimes expressionist in character and sometimes highly abstracted [523]. Heinrich Campendonck (1889–1957) painted charming peasant scenes with a fairy-tale quality re-

523. JAWLENSKY: *Looking Within—Night*, 1923. 17 x 13⅛". Philadelphia Museum of Art, Arensberg Collection.

524. FEININGER:
*The Steamer Odin,
II*, 1927. 26½ x 38½".
Museum of Modern
Art, New York, Lillie
P. Bliss Bequest.

525. DIX: *Meeting a Madman at Night,* from
Der Krieg, 1924. Etching, aquatint, and drypoint,
10¼ x 7⅞". Museum of Modern Art, New York,
Gift of Mrs. John D. Rockefeller, Jr.

flecting the naïveté of folk art. Lyonel Feininger (1871–1956), an American born of German immigrants, returned to Europe for study and after earlier contacts with Kandinsky was a member of the "Four Blues"—Kandinsky, Jawlensky, Feininger, and Paul Klee—who constituted a secondary revival of the Rider group. Feininger's art is a particularly distinguished one with which cubism had a great deal to do. It is crystal clear, precisely joined in sharp-edged planes, sometimes defining recognizable objects, sometimes losing the object in abstract planar extensions [524], but always with a poetic flavor that is expressionist within the cubist variation. His construction of planes often suggests abstract architecture, and he was an instructor in the *Bauhaus,* the school of fine arts and crafts centered around architecture and established in Germany at the end of World War I. The *Bauhaus* was probably the most effective coordinating factor in the chaotic picture of modern art, and it developed teaching methods in connection with this coordination that are now disseminated all over the world.

Paul Klee, the fourth of the "Four Blues," was also a member of the *Bauhaus* staff. He

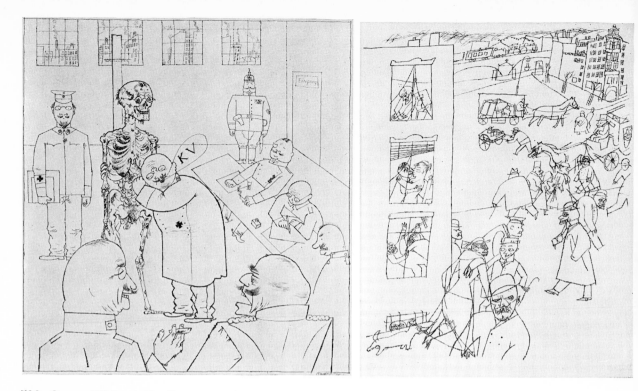

526. GROSZ: *Fit for Active Service*, 1918. Pen and ink, 14⅝ x 13⅜". Museum of Modern Art, New York, A. Conger Goodyear Fund.

527. GROSZ: *Street Scene*, date unknown. Lithograph, 10½ x 8½". Philadelphia Museum of Art, Harrison Fund.

is considered near the end of this book. And the *Bauhaus* building itself [692] was a landmark in the "International Style" of contemporary architecture, which is discussed in the Appendix.

Expressionism: "Die Neue Sachlichkeit"

During the last years of World War I and the years just following it, German painters expressed their spiritual shock in some of the most horrifying images since Goya. They rejected the intellectualism and the generally happy spirit of The Blue Rider, but they rejected also the kind of emotional intensity typical of The Bridge. Personal neurotic apprehensions like those expressed by Heckel and Kirchner now seemed puny in comparison with the horror of a world that had revealed itself as a social and

political organization given over to mass murder and moral anarchy. The new expressionism was called *Die Neue Sachlichkeit*, The New Objectivity. Objectivity is precisely the reverse of expressionist emotionalism, and the term belies the sense of outrage that animates these painters at the end of the war and immediately after it. "The New Objectivity" refers more aptly to the political and social apathy, the hopelessness, the acceptance of corruption and misery and degradation as the natural state of things which was characteristic of the later postwar years. In its turn this condition was to bring with it a nihilistic art denying the legitimacy of all logic, all order, all effort, all feeling, all plan—an art reveling in morbid nonsense in which the painters of The New Objectivity were to take a part.

Even Goya would have been appalled before the war portfolio of Otto Dix (1891–

528. GROSZ: *Maid Arranging Hair of Corpulent Woman*, date unknown. Watercolor, 24⅞ x 18¾". Philadelphia Museum of Art, Gift of Bernard Davis.

529. GROSZ: Detail from Figure 528.

). *The Disasters of War* as Goya reported them are a record of inhumanity and brutal folly, but Dix's *Der Krieg* shows the dissolution of matter and spirit into putrescence and senselessness. Goya is a spectator of atrocities, and we observe them with him and react as human beings capable of normal emotional and intellectual responses to them. But Dix is not an observer; he is a victim of insanity and butchery. In *Meeting a Madman at Night* [525], horror exists alone, beyond moral or social indignation, with a kind of wild idiocy. The final horror is that there is something grotesquely comical about the ghoul, like a black-face comedian gone mad.

Humor to sharpen horror was used with savage precision by George Grosz (1893–) in his satires of the *bourgeoisie*, the clergy, the military, and the bureaucrats who in his eyes were responsible for the war. *Fit for Active Service* [526], done in 1918 near the end of the war when German boys, old men, and broken men were being sent to the front, is funny on the surface and all the more frightful for being so. The fat, secure doctor, the trimly groomed officers with their monocles and their beast-faces raddled by vice, the kowtowing clerks and flunkies, are drawn in Grosz's typically cruel, sharp line, like a razor lancing a carbuncle, but the skeleton is contrastingly represented in macabre complications of thin, knobby bones, vestigial organs, and obscene dangling fluffs of hair and thready bits of rotten flesh. Grosz's city streets are filled with desperate, evil beings reduced to subhuman levels by vice, poverty, or corruption; the windows of his houses are vignettes of suicide, lust, and murder [527]. In his watercolors [528, 529], Grosz paints with the most delicate, the most sensitive, of techniques, in colors as sweet and fresh as the tenderest flowers, to represent obese or stunted prostitutes, shriveled harridans, starving children, piglike profiteers, every scene of depravity, misery, and ugliness. This use of paradox—humor to enhance horror, loveliness to reveal ugliness with a new repulsiveness—is prophetic of the perversity of the irrational, nihilistic art soon to be discussed here as *dada*.

Independent Expressionists

Max Beckmann (1884–1950) was a contemporary of the three German expressionist groups just seen, falling by birth date about midway between the older and younger men. Without being strongly attached to any group he participated in their early exhibitions. He is something of a summary of the German expressionist experience and he adds to it an important element, a correlation with traditional art.

More than any of the other expressionists Beckmann studied the old masters, particularly the early Renaissance forms of Piero della Francesca, and the late medieval ones of French painting, as well as Cézanne, who was not a powerful direct influence on the other expressionists, and van Gogh, who of course was. And, most important of all, he was the direct heir of another German, Hans von Marées (1837–1887).

His dates show that as a nineteenth-century painter contemporary with the French impressionists, von Marées is introduced out of chronology here. But he painted so unobtrusively among his contemporaries that, even more than Cézanne, he is more significant as a part of twentieth-century painting than as part of the painting of his own lifetime. He is commonly referred to nowadays as a German Cézanne, sometimes also as a parallel to Puvis de Chavannes. In either case, he rejected the imitative realism and the rather heavyhanded symbolical romanticism that surrounded him, and worked instead to translate philosophical ideas into terms of monumental form. This might mean classicism, but (again like Cézanne) von Marées believed that monumental harmonies could be fused with the direct vividness of living matter.

530. Von Marées: *Man with the Standard*, date unknown. 19⅜ x 13¾". *Kunsthalle*, Bremen.

The figure in his *Man with the Standard* [530] is typical of the solid power, the generalized statement without recourse to beautifying formula, of von Marées's art. Contemporary German painters have been happy to find in von Marées a Germanic post-impressionist, the only strong transitional figure between nineteenth-century traditions indigenous to Germanic culture and twentieth-century innovations, including expressionism, which found their major development in Germany. Beckmann is the closest of all modern Germans to von Marées, and extends to a conclusion the

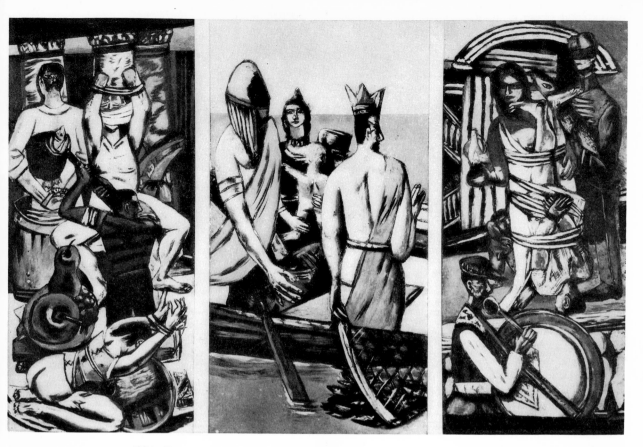

531. BECKMANN: *Departure,* 1932–35. Center panel, 84¾ x 45⅜″, side panels, 84¾ x 39¼″. Museum of Modern Art, New York.

expressive Germanisms initiated or continued by the nineteenth-century painter.

Beckmann brought to expressionism von Marées's monumentality of form, and thus universalized the personalism of the other expressionists. His symbolism is social in origin rather than neurotically ingrown, and it is expressed in formally ordered compositions on the grand scale. He widened the scope of expressionism, discarded it as a vehicle for personal confession and private emotionalism or nihilistic social comment, and gave to it the strength and capacity to speak not only of one man, but of mankind.

Beckmann has never offered an explicit key to the symbolism of the three panels in *Departure* [531], but it is apparent that the two side panels are concerned with evil in their scenes of torture and foul mutilation, painted in harsh, violent, complica-

tions of form and color, while the center one is concerned with salvation, clear and serene as it is, painted in pure, brilliant, harmonious colors and broad simple forms existing in ample space. There are echoes of Christian iconography that cannot be missed. In the first place, the triptych form is that of an altarpiece. Without being at all a figure of Christ, the figure of the king in the central panel recalls Christ, partly because the net over the side of the boat recalls the miraculous draught of fishes. Beckmann said that the picture spoke to him of truths impossible for him to put into words. Whatever it meant to the painter, its theme can be sensed as a problem of good and evil common to us all.

It is in fact a rather difficult picture to absorb, but some of Beckmann's own reflections about what he wanted to achieve, to "say," in painting may be of help. Made

532. KOKOSCHKA: *The Tempest* (*The Wind's Bride*), 1914. Panel, 40¼ x 75¼". *Kunstmuseum*, Basel.

three years after the completion of *Departure* and not referring specifically to it, they are not quoted here but are paraphrased, plus parenthetical additions, in a way intended to show how fully Beckmann was an expressionist, yet how greatly he widened the expressionist boundaries:

"What I want to do in my work is to show the idea hidden behind reality, to penetrate the invisible world by means of the visible (which is the desire of most painters, and especially that of the expressionists when the "invisible world" is one of personal emotion). What helps me most in this penetration is (its technical equivalent), the penetration of space. We have to transform the three-dimensional world of objects into the two-dimensional world of the canvas (but I do not accept the idea that hence a painting must be conceived as a two-dimensional decoration. The expression of space, the organization of space on

a two-dimensional canvas, need not imply decorative shallowness any more than it need imply illusions of space). The transformation is for me an experience full of magic in which I glimpse the fourth dimension, (beyond reality), which my whole being is seeking. I use color (not only to) enrich the canvas (which would be mere decoration), but to probe more deeply into the object. (But when necessary I am willing to) subordinate color to the treatment of form and space (because in the end, form and space are the abstractions in which the painter has always spoken the essential truths of human experience)."

Complicated as all this sounds—and indeed is—its general meaning is that Beckmann is an expressionist who is conscious that his personal emotional experience must be the wellspring of his art, but that it must be universalized if his paintings are to endure as something more than isolated phe-

533. KOKOSCHKA: *View of the Thames*, 1925–26. 35⅜ x 51¼". Albright Art Gallery, Buffalo.

nomena or curiosities. He might have said:

"I want to make of expressionism something solid and durable like the art of the museums."

Among other major expressionists, Oskar Kokoschka (1886–   ) was even more loosely connected than Beckmann was with expressionism as an organized movement, but like Beckmann he emerges as one of the significant painters produced by the expressionist spirit. He was an Austrian, and began his career in the last days of the old Empire, surrounded by its special atmosphere of decay, nervous sensitivity, and elegant indulgence. These elements are reflected in Kokoschka's work, but its unconventionality brought him under violent official attack. The Austrian Crown Prince said that "every bone in his body should be broken." This was in 1911; it is easy to believe, in retrospect, that Kokoschka's art gave offense because it gave expression to the spiritual morbidity of the time and its moribund culture rather than supplying cheerful assurance that all was

well, as official painting was doing. Kokoschka's *The Tempest* [532], which is also called *The Vortex* or *The Wind's Bride*, showing two lovers captured within menacing forms apparently abstracted from those of storm clouds and mountainous landscape, is a sinister and frightening picture, although at the heart of the surrounding violence the lovers have found refuge in one another. It was painted in 1914, just before the beginning of World War I.

In color *The Tempest* is expressively cold, heavy, even turgid. But by 1919, after the war, during which he was seriously wounded, Kokoschka settled in Dresden as a teacher at the Academy, and under the influence of The Bridge his color brightened, with generous use of clear vermilions, azures, and emeralds. His landscapes and particularly his cityscapes [533] combined staccato accents with flowing lines; they are ebullient, vital, and elegant. And his portraits are acute explorations of personality in which the features of the sitter seem to have been created not by the usual processes of biology but by the force of inner nature that has molded them to correspond with its own character.

The devices of expressionism were widely used by painters who, like Kokoschka, worked independently outside the centers where the expressionists developed their theories and held their exhibitions. This was natural in a form of painting placing so much emphasis on personal, intimate expression. In Paris the Lithuanian Chaim Soutine (1894–1943), working in poverty and obscurity, which he seemed actually to prefer to a conventionally prosperous career, painted in a manner recalling at once van Gogh, El Greco, and the German expressionists [546]. In Germany Käthe Kollwitz (1867–1945) was affected by expressionism in her deeply emotionalized protests against the fate of the poor, both before and after World War I. Kollwitz painted very little, but her etchings, woodcuts, and lithographs are among the most vigorous graphic productions of the early twentieth century. Unlike Grosz and other painters of The New Objectivity who observed and commented on the same desperate scene, Kollwitz was never able to protect herself within a shell of intellectualism or cynicism. Her anguish is undiminished from print to print [534].

Certain other artists even less closely connected with German expressionism, especially stylistically, are expressionist in the broad definition as using emotionally expressive distortions. One of the most conspicuous is Amedeo Modigliani (1884–1920), whose elongated forms combine a taut, wiry precision of outline with his typical neurotic languor of mood [3, 535]. Modigliani, an Italian working in Paris, has a legend exceeded in picturesqueness only by van Gogh's and Gauguin's.* Poverty-stricken, theatrically hand-

---

* Another inhabitant of Modigliani's bohemia was Maurice Utrillo (1883–1955), the son of a professional model, Suzanne Valadon, who became a respectable painter in her own right. Utrillo is unclassifiable as a painter, except as a member of the "School of Paris" of the early twentieth century. Fauvism, expressionism, cubism, may all be read into his perspectives of the streets of Montmartre or of small towns, but so may the quiet, gentle art of Corot.

534. KOLLWITZ: *Death and the Mother*, 1934. Lithograph, 20⅛ x 14⅜". Philadelphia Museum of Art.

some, tragically doomed by tuberculosis, and spectacularly dissipated, he was the culmination of the romantic tradition of the Parisian bohemian painter or poet. In spite of ill health and emotional imbroglios, Modigliani was a productive painter, working carefully in a somewhat repetitious style filled with nostalgic recalls of early Italian painting, oddly cross-bred with African sculpture. To the long list of influences that were compounded into his very personal style as a painter, Modigliani added elements from the archaic Greeks when he worked in sculpture [536], as he did particularly between 1909 and 1915. But in spite of obvious derivations, Modigliani's art is never a mere pastiche of secondhand forms. Everything serves the expression of a tender, despairing sensuality

535. MODIGLIANI: *Self-portrait*, 1919. 33½ x 23½". Collection Francisco Matarazzo Sobrinho, São Paulo, Brazil. (Photo Museum of Modern Art, New York.)

536. MODIGLIANI: *Head*, date unknown. Limestone, height 27". Philadelphia Museum of Art, Gift of Mrs. Maurice J. Speiser.

in his painting, or of a decorative hieratic reserve in his sculpture.

In Germany, living his short life during the same years as Modigliani, the sculptor Wilhelm Lehmbruck (1881–1919) began as a student at the Düsseldorf Academy, then developed a personal style under Italian and French influences. Like Modigliani's, Lehmbruck's manner is based on extreme elongations, but it is without archaic and primitive references. Unlike the German expressionist painters with whom he is too often grouped for convenience, Lehmbruck respected the tradition of classical idealism, including its realistic elements. His *Kneeling Woman* [538] may be designed with stylistic elongations, but its modeling is not only detailed but respectful of normal anatomical structure. His surface is even an impres-

537. LEHMBRUCK: *Standing Woman,* 1910. Bronze, 76″ high. Museum of Modern Art, New York.

538. LEHMBRUCK: *Kneeling Woman,* 1911. Cast stone, 69½″ high. Museum of Modern Art, New York, Mrs. John D. Rockefeller, Jr. Fund.

sionistic one, subdued in flesh passages but marked in hair and drapery. Lehmbruck worked in Paris between 1910 and 1914, and was first influenced by Maillol. His *Standing Woman* [537], done only the year before the *Kneeling Woman,* shows how closely he followed Maillol at first. For that matter, the harmonious serenity of his fully developed style ties him at least as closely to the classical tradition as his elongations tie him to the romantic-expressionist one. His work uniquely suggests a degree of fulfillment not granted his harassed compatriots.

Expressionism in America

In America Marsden Hartley (1877–1943) was a pioneer expressionist, a bridge between the newly developing European movements and the nascent internationalization of American art. Hartley was a contemporary of the Ash Can group, but where those men were doggedly American, Hartley spent as much time as he could abroad, even exhibiting with The Blue Rider group in Munich and Berlin. Hartley was born in Maine, grew up in Cleveland, studied for

539. MARIN: *The Singer Building*, 1921. Watercolor, 26½ x 21⅝″.
Philadelphia Museum of Art.

But it remained for John Marin (1870–1953) to absorb European influences and then to develop them in an art as legitimately American as it was personal.

Marin's expressionism developed through a logical sequence of creative experiences. He studied first (after a brief experience as an engineer) at the Pennsylvania Academy of the Fine Arts, where his teachers were still wholeheartedly dedicated to factual realism. This was in 1899. In Paris between 1905 and 1911 he progressed into impressionism, including etchings in Whistler's tradition. By the end of his stay in Paris he was beginning to be affected by current European developments, particularly fauvism, and shortly after that he worked in a free adaptation of cubism.

Cubism involved, as we will shortly be seeing, a disintegration of form, a shattering and reassembling of objects reduced for the most part to their rectangular equivalents. We will see too that its basis was analytical rather than emotional. But Marin fused the two apparent incompatibles—analytical cubism and emotionalized expressionism—into a vividly personal style that gave pictorial form to the clangor, the vitality, the surge, the bursting sparkling energy, of the American city.

While the Ash Can School was painting the city as a genre subject, Marin began to paint it as an idea, as a manifestation of the most exciting aspect of the American spirit, its enthusiasm, its vigor, its violent growth, an aspect that reached its climax during the years between the two world wars when Marin was working at his peak.

Marin's expressions of New York City transform the static, monolithic forms of skyscrapers, the flatness of streets and sidewalks, into abstractions of energy and excitement. In earlier pictures [539] the forms of the city tilt, break, and interrupt one another but remain at least partially recognizable. In later ones they all but disappear as recognizable objects, abstracted to the point of pure expression [540]. And in his paintings of the Maine coast the same transmutation is apparent, until finally the rocks of the earth, the water of the ocean, and the sailboats, which for Marin are an expression of the force of the

a while in New York, and then alternated between Europe and the United States. In his most typical work [542] he strives for a kind of raw power, which might be called American, through broad, deliberately crude forms, harsh color, and slashing contrapuntal arrangements. His courage and perseverance were admirable. So, frequently, is his painting, yet he seems too often to be giving an intelligent demonstration of expressionist theory, not often enough to be releasing an emotional force that demanded the use of expressionist devices. Arthur G. Dove (1880–1946), another American who studied for a while in Europe, shares Hartley's position as an eminent pioneer in his own country, and went beyond Hartley in the direction of pure abstraction and personal colorism.

movement of air, become abstractions of the vital energy of nature, just as the New York pictures are abstractions of the vital energy of the city. Homer's *Northeaster* [541], Hartley's *Hurricane Island, Vinal Haven, Maine* [542], and Marin's *Off York Island, Maine* [543] are a neat demonstration of a progression through imaginative realism, conventional expressionism, and expressionistic abstraction, each using different means toward similar ends from the same point of departure.

Marin was first of all a watercolorist. This medium is usually associated with delicate or transient effects, but Marin used it with unprecedented strength while retaining its unique sparkle, directness, and spontaneity. As all good watercolorists must do, he capitalized on the medium's transparency, fluidity, and texture. Watercolor textures

540. MARIN: *Lower Manhattan* (composition derived from top of Woolworth Building) 1922. Watercolor, 21⅝ x 26⅞". Museum of Modern Art, New York, Lillie P. Bliss Bequest

541. HOMER: *Northeaster*, 1895. 34⅜ x 50¼". Metropolitan Museum of Art, New York, Gift of George A. Hearn.

are determined by the texture of the paper in combination with varying densities of pigments, some of which are clear and smooth in solution with water, while others are so heavy that they settle into the paper's grain. The watercolorist can control these textures by the degree of wetness and the degree of speed with which the colors are applied. Marin used a favorite heavily textured Italian paper, sometimes dragging the brush across it nearly dry, sometimes filling his brush to capacity and letting the color stream from it. He is the only major painter to have created his major work in watercolor, and in its history he brought the medium to a new stature just as Degas did with pastel.

In America, expressionism has had an influence so wide, even if it has not always

542. HARTLEY: *Hurricane Island, Vinal Haven, Maine,* 1942. 40¼ x 30″. Philadelphia Museum of Art, Gift of Mrs. Herbert C. Morris.

543. MARIN: *Off York Island, Maine,* 1922. Watercolor, 17 x 20½″. Philadelphia Museum of Art, Stieglitz Collection.

been direct, that the list of painters affected by it would extend indefinitely, ranging from the social indignation and caricature of William Gropper (1897–   ), who might be described as an expressionist Daumier [544], to the suave but introspective art of Franklin Watkins (1894–   ). Watkins won the Carnegie International Award, the most important one offered in America, in 1931 with his *Suicide in Costume* [545], a psychological allegory partly morbid and partly witty, designed with expressionistic distortions. It is in the nature of things that awards of such importance, when decided by enlightened juries, are given to paintings representing movements whose contribution to the

544. GROPPER: *For the Record,* 1940. Lithograph, 11⅜ x 16″. Philadelphia Museum of Art, Harrison Fund.

545. WATKINS: *Suicide in Costume,* 1931. 33¼ x 41¼″. Philadelphia Museum of Art.

446

mainstream of art has been tested by a certain amount of time but not ossified by too much of it. The award to *Suicide in Costume*, which was expressionistic without belonging to any expressionist school, indicated that expressionism had satisfactorily passed the initiation tests for admittance into the solid company of established ways of painting, a quarter of a century after the formation of The Bridge.

But at the moment of this writing, the most vigorously flourishing school of contemporary art in the United States, and to a lesser degree in France, is abstract expressionism, owing its origin to The Blue Rider rather than to The Bridge. Several chapters back, in the mild world of impressionism, we saw that Jackson Pollock's *Autumn Rhythm* had strong affiliations with Monet's very late work, when a passage from *Water Lilies* was extracted from context [211, 212, and 213]. A similar extraction from Soutine's *Portrait of Kisling* [546, 547] yields a fair example of abstract expressionism comparable to a paint-

546. Soutine: *Portrait of Kisling*, date unknown. 39 x 27¼". Philadelphia Museum of Art, Gift of Arthur Wiesenberger.

547. Soutine: Detail from Figure 546.

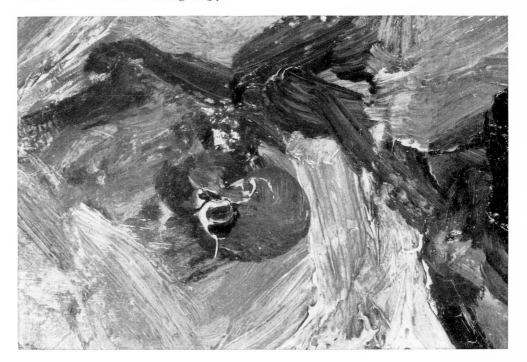

ing by Willem de Kooning (1904–   ) [548], a leader among current abstract expressionist painters. This comparison is not altogether a stunt. By Kandinsky's theory that color and form can exist alone as expressive means, without reference to the imitation of visual reality, the sweeps and slashes and gobbets of color extracted from the Soutine should be expressive even though they are no longer recognizable as the description of one of the eyes in the portrait. If Soutine's colors, brush strokes, and shapes carry the expressive burden of his canvas, as they undeniably do in very large part, then they should continue to be expressive independently. De Kooning's painting is inchoate, fragmentary, and senseless unless we accept the totality of Kandinsky's premise that a painter, through talent, training, and experience (for de Kooning is talented, trained, and experienced), reaches the point where he may express himself best by attacking his canvas vigorously while improvising abstractions of form and color, painting without schematic preparations, drawing spontaneously upon all that he has learned of shape and color as expressive means. Somewhat more studiously, other abstract expressionists, for instance Philip Guston (1912–   ), may work equally without reference to visual reality, but may paint more compact, more concentrated forms [549]. (Guston's canvases may suggest enlarged fragments of Cézanne.) Each abstract expressionist who has established a reputation, as these two men have done, has also established a recognizable style. The reader could distinguish other typical de Koonings from other typical Gustons on the basis of these two examples. Other painters may work more precisely; others, even more loosely. But to multiply examples here would be pointless. The proliferations of abstract expressionism are as infinite as the difference in the personalities of the painters allows, and are at the moment familiar, even inescapable, in art magazines and exhibitions. Ultimately, however, the principle behind the variations, which may be fascinating, is the same. And for better or for worse, it all began with Kandinsky.

548. De Kooning: *Detour*, 1958. 59 x 42″. Sidney Janis Gallery, New York.

Or did it? It is true that Kandinsky is given credit for having produced the first entirely abstract painting in the early years of this century, but the family tree of abstract expressionism can be traced back to Delacroix, and beyond him to the traditions of which French romanticism was a continuation. When we remember Delacroix's warning that "All precautions have to be taken to make execution swift and decisive [in order not to lose] the extraordinary impression accompanying the conception," we find him stating a principle that is pushed to its limits by painters today

549. GUSTON: *The Painter's City*, 1956. 65 x 77″. Sidney Janis Gallery, New York.

who appear to splash color at random, following spontaneous impulse.

Yet their "precautions" must be present behind the apparent impulsiveness, to some degree, just as in the case of Delacroix they were present to a rigidly imposed degree. And when abstract impressionism seems formless and sloppy, we may be generous and remember that Delacroix was accused of painting with "a drunken broom."

Some abstract expressionists have literally painted with brooms (while sober) on canvases laid out on the floor. By theory, when color is splashed, flipped, or shoved or swept over a surface, the artist is closest to the observer because his emotional impulse is translated into physical actions that immediately, without intermediate stages, produce shape and color. This may be going a little far, but it still goes in the direction set by early romanticism and continued through van Gogh.

But most of all, the abstract expressionists are romantic in the extreme personalism of their art. Long ago in this book we said that the romantics "would abandon moderation for excess, when necessary, would accept confusion rather than run the risk of sacrificing spontaneity to lucidity." When Guston calls his painting illustrated here "The Painter's City," he implies the most personal emotional sources for his art. Such titles attached to abstract expressionist paintings bring the school into the tradition of personal fulfillment and release, at whatever expense, which is the basis of romanticism.

CHAPTER 13

Cubism and Abstract Art

Cubism: The Early Picasso

Cubism was born unexpectedly in 1907 without benefit of theory and from curiously mixed parentage: Cézanne on one side, and the sculpture of ancient and primitive peoples on the other. It appeared first in the work of two young men named Pablo Picasso (1881–   ) and Georges Braque (1882–   ).

Picasso, a Spaniard, had come to Paris at the age of nineteen after a prodigious conquest of the academies in Barcelona and Madrid. At twelve he was a competent draughtsman [550], and thereafter as a student he ran the historical gamut of styles from academic formula straight through impressionism, mastering them all with the facility of a mimic and the understanding of an artist. Whole books have been devoted to his work during the seven years from his arrival in Paris to his first cubist painting. Here a brief summary will suffice.

During his first year or so in Paris, Picasso worked in a manner close to Toulouse-Lautrec's but bursting everywhere with restlessness, as if impatient to shift into a new direction. *Old Woman* [551] of 1901, the year of Lautrec's death, looks as if Lautrec himself might have painted it after discovering pointillism and adapting it to a violent flashing expressionism. Yet in the same year—his twenty-first —Picasso also painted the contrastingly serene *Harlequin Propped on Elbow* [552] with its controlled outlines, its decisive pattern, and broad flat areas of color, probably related to Gauguin's. This *Harlequin* is somewhat romantic in mood, decorative in arrangement, classical in its sense of control, rather affected in its selection of

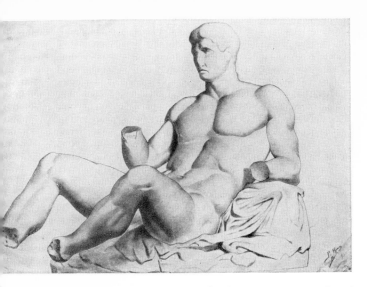

posture and subject, and altogether attractive in itself. Picasso is showing, as he will do again and again, that he can be everything at once.

The direction hinted at in this picture is not followed up until later. (Not only can Picasso be everything at once; he can also travel in all directions at once, seeming to abandon one direction in painting for a while and then suddenly resuming it at another level as if it had been developing of itself during the lapse of time.) During the next few years he painted in two manners called the "blue" and "rose" periods. A single example will have to suffice as typical of the blue pictures, *The Old Guitarist* [553] of 1903. Pathetic in its subject, stylized with its elongated figure posed in a cramped, angular attitude, and painted in frigid blues and blue-greens, it follows closely the basic recipe of the

550. PICASSO: Drawing from a cast, school year, 1893–94. Conté crayon, 18¼ x 25¼". Present whereabouts unknown; reproduced from *Cahiers d'Art,* courtesy of the publishers.

551. PICASSO: *Old Woman,* 1901. 26⅜ x 20½". Philadelphia Museum of Art, Arensberg Collection.

552. PICASSO: *Harlequin Propped on Elbow,* 1901. 33 x 24¾". Collection Mr. and Mrs. Henry Clifford, Radnor, Pa.

553. PICASSO: *The Old Guitarist*, 1903. 37⅜ x 28″. Art Institute of Chicago, Helen Birch Bartlett Memorial Collection.

554. PICASSO: *La Toilette*, 1906. 59½ x 39″. Albright Art Gallery, Buffalo.

period. This is a style of great sophistication in which the pathos is altogether superficial, a very young man's style. Among the influences at work in it are the painting of El Greco and the early medieval French sculpture of the school of Languedoc—at least by the internal evidence of stylistic resemblance.

The blue period softens into the "circus" period and then merges in 1905 into the rose period, with the change in dominating color suggested by the tags and, above all, a change in mood. Although the figures remain delicate and elongated, they live in a happier world. Charm replaces pathos, grace takes the place of angularity; sometimes there is a strong classical flavor, as in the entrancing *La Toilette* [554] with its

references to Greek vase painting. Of all his multitudinous periods—one critic was able to subdivide them into eighty—this is the one that accounts for Picasso's widest popularity. The affectation that is an uncomfortable element in the early blue pictures, conflicting as it does with subjects of poverty and misery, is appropriate to the charming, sometimes feminine air of the later ones, as the harsh blues and greens turn into soft gray-blues and merge with rose. It is a period of brilliant technical display. Almost any picture of these years could serve as an example; a fine one is *Boy with Bouquet* [555], where we are offered a bunch of flowers by one of the adolescent harlequins, actors, acrobats, and theatrical vagabonds who replace starving

555. PICASSO: *Boy with Bouquet*, 1905. Gouache, 25½ x 21⅜″. Collection Mrs. John Wintersteen, Chestnut Hill, Pa.

556. PICASSO: *Boy Leading a Horse*, 1905. 87 x 57¼″. Collection Mr. and Mrs. William S. Paley, New York.

unfortunates as the major performers, and will continue to appear among Picasso's cast of thousands from now on.

The main areas of *Boy with Bouquet* are established in audacious scrubs and strokes of color and then, in a demonstration of infallible draughtsmanship, the features are described with a few lines struck in with almost insolent virtuosity. Had Picasso died in 1906, the charging bull of modern art would have been remembered as a delicate fellow who revived the eighteenth-century spirit at its most sensitive, a twentieth-century Watteau. During this time Picasso planned a large composition of adolescent youths and horses, *The Watering Place*. The studies [556] are consummately in this spirit.

But with the restlessness of an explorer or an inventor, Picasso changed again at the end of 1906 in a way that is important as an early step toward cubism. He began to discipline his graceful figures into new sculptural forms with an imposition of decisive geometrical regularities. Already indicated in *Lady with a Fan* [152], the new discipline is even more emphatic in *Woman with Loaves* [557], with its geometrical solids built firmly upon one another into a compact whole. The ovoid form of the torso is surmounted by the white cylinder of the cap, which is pierced to reveal the simplified sculptural forms of the head. The two loaves of bread rest on top of this structure like architectural members surmounting a column.

557. PICASSO: *Woman with Loaves*, 1906. 39 x 27½". Philadelphia Museum of Art, Gift of Charles E. Ingersoll.

558. PICASSO: *Gertrude Stein*, 1906. 39⅜ x 32". Metropolitan Museum of Art, New York.

Woman with Loaves was painted in the summer of 1906 (despite the date 1905, added in error beneath the signature). Earlier that year Picasso had begun a portrait of Gertrude Stein [558], the American writer who had set herself up in Paris a few years earlier and had already become a major patron, proselytizer, and practitioner in the international intellectual avant-garde. After eighty sittings Picasso had wiped out the face of her portrait. Whatever the face had been like, it is obvious that in the rest of the picture Cézanne is very much present. When Picasso returned to the picture after the summer interval during which he painted *Woman with Loaves,* the new force at work in his art produced the masklike face (painted without the model) which is so at variance with the Cézannesque forms that surround it. In his *Self-portrait* [559] painted imme-

diately afterward, the masklike quality has increased, and its severe half-primitive quality has extended to the figure also.

Cubism: Its Beginnings

By his own statement, in *Woman with Loaves*, the Stein portrait, and his own portrait, Picasso was influenced by Iberian sculpture, the archaic sculpture of pre-Roman Spain. But the two portraits look as if Picasso had already discovered African sculpture also. At any rate he discovered African sculpture at about this time, and the ingredients for cubism were assembled. These were: Cézanne, with his concept of volume and space as abstract geometry to be dealt with at whatever necessary rejection of their natural relationships; African and archaic sculpture, with their untheo-

454 · CUBISM AND ABSTRACT ART

559. PICASSO: *Self-portrait*, 1906. 36 x 28". Philadelphia Museum of Art, Gallatin Collection.

retical but exciting reduction of natural forms to geometrical equivalents, plus an element of the bizarre and the savage that was a stimulating injection into the hyper-refinements of European painting; and, finally, the intuitive genius of Picasso and the deductive mind of Braque to merge these components with dashes of several others in their search for new expressive means.

This new expression was soon to have a name, *cubism*, and to be codified into a theory. But for the moment it manifested itself half formed in a large painting by

560. PICASSO: *Les Demoiselles d'Avignon*, 1907. 96 x 92". Museum of Modern Art, New York, Lillie P. Bliss Bequest.

Picasso, which, although technically ambiguous, is decisively the beginning point of cubism. A composition of five nude female figures [560], the traditional bathers motif, it was later dubbed *Les Demoiselles d'Avignon* as a jape, and has continued to be called so as a convenience.

Everyone admits that these five *demoiselles* are among the unloveliest females in the history of art, and no one pretends that the picture is an unqualified success in every way, but on the other hand no student of contemporary painting denies its position as a landmark. It is a discordant picture, not only in the way it ruptures, fractures, and dislocates form with a violence that would no doubt have appalled Cézanne, but in the disharmony of its own parts. On the left the standing figure is hieratic in its formality, posed in a standard attitude of Egyptian and archaic Greek sculpture. But by the time the right side of the picture is reached, this formality has given way to a jagged, swinging, crashing line, and the African mask makes its impact with full force in the grotesque faces. For a few months during the next year, 1908, Picasso went through a "Negro" period, with close parallels to African prototypes.

The developmental period of cubism, 1907–1909, is often called its "Cézanne phase," on the basis of pictures like Braque's *Road near L'Estaque* [561], with its combination of geometrical simplification and faceted shapes. But in spirit the picture is anything but Cézannesque. The shapes themselves are bolder and more obvious than Cézanne's, and they have a nervousness, an insistence, a thrust, a harsh, angular movement that exaggerates the sense of vibrant life typical of a Cézanne landscape and sacrifices to it the classical order that also permeates Cézanne's world.

561. Braque: *Road near l'Estaque*, 1908. 23¾ x 19¾". Museum of Modern Art, New York.

562. Metzinger: *Tea Time*, 1911. Panel, 29¾ x 27⅜". Philadelphia Museum of Art, Arensberg Collection.

Cubism: Analytical Phase

After 1909 and up into 1912 the introduction and development of a complication known as simultaneity brings cubism into its own as a revolutionary concept. The idea behind simultaneity is simple enough. The forms in Metzinger's° *Tea Time* [562], which suffers the unfortunate secondary title *Mona Lisa with a Teaspoon*, are broken into large facets or planes. But something else is happening too: in places these planes grow transparent in order to reveal other planes behind them; they cross and merge with these other planes. At the left a teacup and saucer are divided down their middle by a line, on one side of which they are seen head on, while on the other side they are seen from above. Theoretically we know more about the teacup because we see it from two angles at once, which is impossible when a teacup and saucer

° Jean Metzinger (1883–1956) developed certain nuances of style during this period of analytical cubism that give his work a light, gay quality quite opposed to the Spartan analytical diagrams of Braque and Picasso. Yet Metzinger was of a scientific turn of mind. Before discovering a more rewarding pseudoscience in analytical cubism, he had been attracted by the codification and systematic approach of neo-impressionism. At the end of the period of analytical cubism, he wrote its doctrinal statement, *Du Cubisme*, with his colleague Albert Gleizes (1881–1953). Both Metzinger and Gleizes were among the cubists who insisted on the use of color, while Braque and Picasso were shelving the problem in favor of pure analysis in tans, creams, and grays.

563. Picasso: *Female Nude*, 1910–11. 38¾ x 30⅝″. Philadelphia Museum of Art.

564. Picasso: *Seated Nude Woman*, 1908. 45¾ x 35″. Philadelphia Museum of Art.

are represented in conventional perspective allowing a view from only one angle at a time. Metzinger's teacup demonstrates in an elementary way the device of simultaneity—the simultaneous revelation of more than one aspect of an object in an effort to express the total image. In the case of the teacup the process is simple. Elsewhere in the picture the crossing and merging transparent planes are a more complicated application of the same idea. The left half of the head, if the right half is ignored or covered up, yields a profile. At the same time, it is included in a view of the full face. The argument that we have neither a good profile nor a good full face by usual representational standards is beside the point. The cubist is not interested in usual representational standards. It is as if he were walking around the objects he is analyzing, as one is free to walk around a piece of sculpture for successive views. But he must represent all these views at once.

This is the famous "fourth dimension" in painting. For centuries painters had been satisfied to represent an illusion of three dimensions on a two-dimensional surface by means of a systematic distortion known as perspective. The third dimension in painting is depth by perspective; the fourth dimension is movement in depth, or time, or space-time, by the simultaneous presentation of multiple aspects of an object. A new systematic distortion is necessary for this new dimension, since the old one of perspective has been outgrown.

But as the process of analytical cubism was explored, the objects subjected to its elaborations were destroyed. Picasso's *Female Nude* [563] is a fourth-dimensional complication of forms which began, no doubt, as forms similar to those in his earlier *Seated Nude Woman* [564]. But as the planes overlap, turn on edge, recede, progress, lie flat, or turn at conflicting angles, the object from which they originated is

565. Lipchitz: *Girl with a Braid, c.* 1914–15. Bronze, 32″ high. Philadelphia Museum of Art.

566. Lipchitz: *Half Standing Figure,* 1915–16. Lead, 19¼″ high. Philadelphia Museum of Art, Gallatin Collection.

lost rather than totally revealed. Cubism was also rather tentatively investigated by sculptors. What happened can be seen first in Jacques Lipchitz's (1891–   ) *Girl with a Braid* [565] and then his *Half Standing Figure* [566]. Lipchitz, like other sculptors, soon left cubism to the painters and changed to a more legitimately sculptural style—in his case—an expressionistic one.

Occasionally it is still necessary to reassure the layman as to the seriousness of cubist experiments with form, even though these experiments have long since been absorbed into the general experience of the contemporary artist. Historically their importance is that they forced one aspect of Cézanne's revolution to a point so extreme that no painter willing to think twice about the expression of form can ever again be satisfied with its simple imitation in photographic light and shade. Theories and history aside, these analytical cubist experiments are aesthetically rewarding in themselves, even if on a somewhat rarefied level. But they soon served their purpose for the cubists, and in 1912 their severities were abandoned for a more relaxed approach, called synthetic cubism.

567. GRIS: *Dish of Fruit*, 1916. 15¾ x 9″. Philadelphia Museum of Art, Gallatin Collection.

568. GRIS: *The Open Window*, 1917. Panel, 39⅜ x 29⅝″. Philadelphia Museum of Art, Arensberg Collection.

Cubism: Synthetic Phase—Gris

Analytical cubism tended to lose sight of expressive values except by standards too esoteric to mean much to anyone not absorbed in the movement. Also the painters' stylistic individuality had been somewhat fettered. But synthetic cubism turned each painter loose to find his own way within the vast general field of free invention along cubist lines that was now opened up by a new way of conceiving form. Analytical cubism took its proper place as a preliminary exploratory exercise (no matter how complicated, no matter how studded with expressive exceptions). Color returned in force, sometimes related to the natural col-

ors of the formal motifs, sometimes arbitrary. The shapes of objects were used as a basis for improvisations, inventions, ambitious or playful compositions in every combination and recombination of abstract shapes invented imaginatively, subject to no rule or theory. Picasso and Braque, whose analytical cubist studies had often been all but indistinguishable from one another's, diverged in opposing directions. A third young man who had shared with them in the development of analytical cubism now took his place as the poet of the movement. This was Juan Gris (1887–1927), the pseudonym of José Victoriano González, like Picasso a Spaniard who had put the academic routine behind him in his

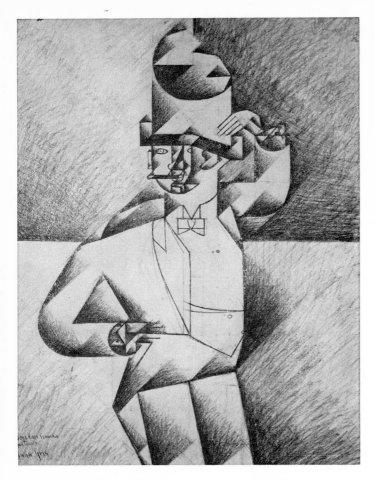

569. GRIS: *Man at Café* (study), 1911. Pencil, 22 x 16½".
Philadelphia Museum of Art, Gallatin Collection.

own country and had come to Paris at nineteen.

In Gris's typical *Dish of Fruit* [567] it is easy to recognize the general shape of a compote with its base, neck, and bowl and to identify a couple of colored shapes as pieces of fruit. The tabletop and even something like the bowl's shadow, to the right of the base, are also recognizable. The rectangular shape defined by a triple outline in the background might be a repetition of the table form or might have been suggested by a napkin or doily. Or it could be a picture frame on the wall. None of the forms needs be recognizable in specific detail, but each has been played with inventively and the shapes have been colored most ornamentally to produce a combination of forms and colors that would not have been reached without the preliminary puzzle-solving of analytical cubism, but now branches away from it. In *The Open Window* [568], it is possible to see that the window, or what we could call a French door, is opened onto a balcony with a tree beyond it. We can even tell that the long double doors are three-paned. Along the lefthand side of the picture the left door is represented with comparative realism. On the right, the forms are more broken, but a piece of cloth patterned in large dots and gathered across the lowest pane is immediately recognizable. The picture is filled with gentle, quiet mood, retaining as it does the connotation of a pleasant room with a window opening out to trees, and composed as it is in simple shapes dominated in color by soft blues, grays, and modified whites.

In synthetic cubism, shapes and colors may be determined by the painter's sensitivity alone; thus painting has returned to the old basis, the painter's reaction to the world and his interpretation of it in colored forms. But it has returned with a new vocabulary, a vocabulary more flexible than analytical cubism had promised. Synthetic cubism leaves the painter unfettered by anything except the limitations of his own inventive ingenuity. Although to a novice all cubist paintings may look alike, and the idea of any one form of cubism being more poetic than another may seem absurd, Gris's poetic quality becomes apparent when the surface similarities of all cubist paintings are scratched. Even when he was working more analytically [569], Gris always insisted that a high degree of recognizability should be retained in a painting, in spite of the fact that the artist was involved in the cubist shattering and reassembling of forms to create new structures. In the hands of Picasso and Braque, analytical cubism had abandoned the appeal of subject, the response to the world, which had been the basis of impressionism and had been continued, with variations, in Cézanne, Gauguin, van Gogh, and Seurat. Subject matter was reduced to a small list of motifs closely connected with the studio

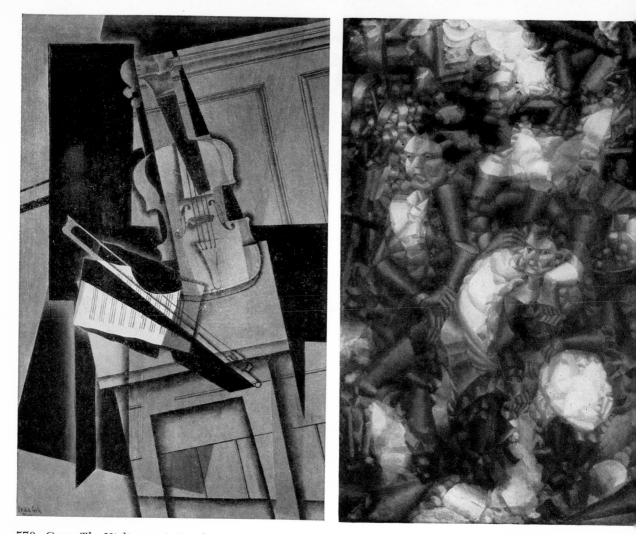

570. GRIS: *The Violin*, 1916. Panel, 45½ x 29″. *Kunstmuseum*, Basel.

571. LÉGER: *Three Figures*, 1910–11. 76½ x 45½″. Milwaukee Art Center.

or with the café as an adjunct of the studio, such motifs as tables with bowls of fruit and glasses of wine, a few musical instruments, and posed models. But Gris frequently invested these motifs with more personal associations. *The Open Window* is one of several recollections of his quarters on the Rue Ravignan where a group of writers and painters inhabited a disreputable old building called the *Bateau-Lavoir*. Picasso lived there for a while. For the avant-garde in general, the *Bateau-Lavoir* became a kind of club, taking its place in the tradition of Courbet's *Brasserie*

des Martyrs and the impressionists' *Café Guerbois* as a center where ideas were formulated and discussed. But the associative interest of *The Open Window* is not enough to account for the poetic feeling that permeates it. This feeling is present even when the pictures are composed of the usual cubist list of motifs [570]. Typically the color is gentler, the forms are more placid, their combinations more serene than those of Gris's fellow cubists, and from these abstract elements, rather than in specific evocative elements, Gris's poetry lies. He is cubism's Corot.

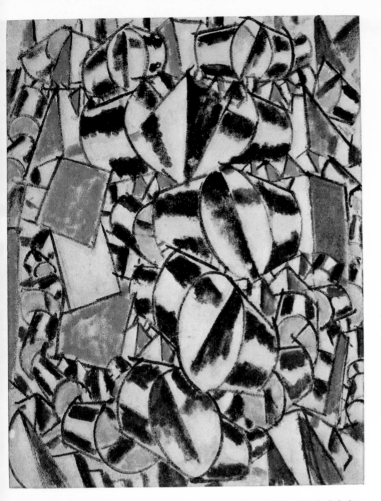

572. LÉGER: *Contrast of Forms*, 1913. 51⅜ x 38⅜". Philadelphia Museum of Art, Arensberg Collection.

A Cubist Variant: Léger

Cubism's unexpected flexibility, once it was freed by the personalism of its synthetic phase, produced one of its brightest variants in the art of Fernand Léger (1881–1955). Léger, after a spell as an architect's apprentice and a brief foray into the Academy's school, discovered Cézanne and then met Braque and Picasso in 1910. Under their influence he worked for a while in facet cubism, as in *Three Figures* [571], where it is possible to discern hints of the driving, pistonlike energies that were to fascinate him later on. But Léger was always a more direct and less complicated

person than his colleagues, and he fretted under the intellectualism of formal analysis. By 1913 he had resolved the shifting, overlapping complexities of analytical cubism into a new manner, where cubes and cylinders began to appear more solidly and more boldly, painted in bright colors. *Contrast of Forms* [572], painted in 1913, is typical of a group of paintings where Léger combines strong, simple shapes in pure primary colors—red, blue, and yellow—with a great deal of white and strong defining lines in black. In spite of the crowding of the forms, which jostle and shoulder one another over the whole area of the canvas, a comparison of *Contrast of Forms* with *Three Figures* should show not only that *Contrast of Forms* is a logical continuation of the earlier picture but that it is a step in the direction of clarity and specific definition.

Even so, Léger is still feeling his way, and it was not until after World War I (during which he was mobilized and stopped painting) that he found what he wanted to do. While Gris employed cubism pensively, Léger adapted it to the clangorous mechanized life of the city. On the theory that in a mechanical age art should take on a mechanical character, he developed a style in which every form, if not actually derived from a mechanical motif, took on the character of a gear, a flywheel, a piston, or some other machine part. By his own statement, his daily contact with machines during the war might account for his new fascination with a mechanistic art, and his wartime "contact with violent and crude reality" completed his divorce from the hyperrefinements of analytical cubism.

The City [573], a large canvas, is the climax of his new style and probably the key picture in his total work. Some of the most easily identified motifs are girders, poles, puffs of smoke, and in the center a flight of steps reduced to light and dark bands behind the mechanized human figures who descend them. The colors are pure and bright, even garish and strident, dominated by several brilliant patches of lemon yellow and bright reds, cut through from top to bottom by a pole of a rosy violet color. For the most part the forms

573. Léger: *The City*, 1919. 91 x 116½″. Philadelphia Museum of Art, Gallatin Collection.

are unmodeled, exceptions being the human figures, the puffs of smoke, and the pole, which are modeled into smooth geometrical ovals and cylinders.

In many ways the forms of *The City* are so obvious that they seem too easy. Subtleties must not be read into Léger; rather, a hearty vigor, a kind of primitivism. He is the most easily imitated of painters, and he has suffered from a blight of fourth-rate talents who have adopted his formula and revealed its limitations without redeeming them by his strength and enthusiasm. Léger's art is meaningless if it is distorted by a search for intellectualities that do not exist in it. His anti-intellectualism is usually refreshing; at other times it palls, and one is relieved to get away from his insistent colors, his obvious forms, and his eventually monotonous conventionalization for paintings offering less surface excitement and more contemplative depth. (Of course

574. Léger: *The Breakfast* (study), 1925. 40 x 53″. Collection Mr. and Mrs. Burton Tremaine, Meriden, Conn.

575. Léger: *Divers on Yellow Background*, 1941. 75¾ x 87½". Art Institute of Chicago, Gift of Mr. and Mrs. Maurice E. Culberg.

this may be a matter of personal taste; it may be just as true that it is a relief to get away from paintings full of subtleties and enjoy Léger's single-directedness.) Sometimes, also, he forces his style onto motifs not compatible with it. In *The Breakfast* [574], unmechanistic forms are conventionalized into mechanistic molds with extraordinary results if the three women are regarded as women, although with great decorative flair if they are not. Léger once said that "One may consider the human figure not for its sentimental value but only for its plastic value. That is why in the evolution of my work since 1905 until now the human figure has remained purposely inexpressive." This is a legitimate defense and could have been stated by any of the cubists and most of the fauves, but it can still leave one wondering uncomfortably why three nudes around a breakfast table are reduced to dehumanized automatons when likelier material to serve Léger's bias was available on every hand.

There is a further possible objection to the whole mechanistic idea in painting. Léger said that "Nowadays a work of art must bear comparison with any manufac-

tured object." No statement is easier to oppose; one need only say that nowadays a work of art must give relief from the insistent mechanization of life and the monotony of manufactured objects. Furthermore, Léger's work does not bear comparison with manufactured objects if that is what he really intended to invite. Nothing he painted in pistonlike forms has the machine-perfect sleekness of a real piston; not one of his spheres has the perfection of a ball bearing. Motors and machine parts have their own abstract beauty as forms, and have it more legitimately than the less beautifully tooled conventionalizations of painters who impose these forms on nature.

In the end, Léger remains an expressive and important artist not for the theories he propounded and demonstrated, but because his own vigor and his own naïveté override theory and find their way into his work. Between 1931 and 1939 he made three visits to the United States. He was rapturous over the spectacle of energy and extroverted activity the country presented to him. He loved the skyscrapers, the Negro jazz, the noise, the lack of inhibitions (as it seemed to him), and above all the bustle and movement of New York and Chicago. The forms he had composed in *The City* had been static; now he set out to create compositions of movement with flowing lines everywhere. In a series of paintings of swimmers or divers, for which he had already found the germ in observing beach crowds in Marseilles just before sailing, he summarized his new preoccupation with contrasts of movement. Yet he reduced his compositions to rigorously controlled, ultimately balanced rhythms not at all hectic or clamorous, as is apparent in *Divers on Yellow Background* [575].

Because his work is precise and held tightly under control, Léger's "classicism" is often referred to, and in the most ambitious of his very late works, *Leisure* [576], he accepts the nomination for a post in the classical tradition of French painting. One of the figures holds a sheet of paper bearing the inscription "Hommage à Louis David." The inscription may be half mocking, but it is also at least half serious in this extraordinarily synthetic picture. To capture its

576. LÉGER: *Leisure*, 1944–49. 61⅞ x 72⅞". *Musée National d'Art Moderne*, Paris.

flavor one must understand not only its connection with David's *The Sabines* [11] but also with modern primitive painting. In America, Léger professed the most enthusiastic admiration for the art of Edward Hicks [303], and he owed his greatest debt of all to Douanier Rousseau. The ingredients that went into the fabrication of *Leisure,* then, were of bizarre diversity: the classicism of David, the mechanistic character of the modern world, the innocence of an American Quaker minister, and the naïve-sophisticated style of an eccentric customs collector. Actually, of course, Léger is only a little classical, only speciously mechanistic, and not very innocent. He is a painter with an emphatically personal style in which native vigor and a curious affectation compete with one another —and frequently come to terms. On these

577. CASSANDRE: *L'Intran*, 1925. Lithographic poster, 43 x 59¼". Philadelphia Museum of Art, Gallatin Collection.

578. DELAUNAY: *Eiffel Tower, c.* 1909. 38 x 27¾". Philadelphia Museum of Art, Arensberg Collection.

579. DELAUNAY: *Eiffel Tower, c.* 1925. Lithograph, 23¾ x 17½". Philadelphia Museum of Art, Gallatin Collection.

occasions Léger is a fine artist; on most others, he is at least a fine designer.

Directly and indirectly, Léger's style has been one of the most powerful influences on modern decorators, designers, and commercial artists. The influence has been good, although the mass of commercial work thus turned out may have drained some interest away from Léger's pictures themselves. As an example, A. M. Cassandre's effective poster for the Parisian newspaper *L'Intransigeant* [577] owes a great deal to synthetic cubism in general and to Léger in particular. A telegraph pole runs up and down through it, a coincidental resemblance, no doubt, to the one in *The City,* and is flanked with insulators simplified and modeled in Léger's manner. Wires run to an ear in a head where the

eye is a series of concentric disks, and the profile, with the mouth open to shout the news, is drawn with rulers and compasses. Even the letters, interrupted before the whole word *L'Intransigeant* is spelled out, suggest the fragmentary letters in *The City* and other compositions. In the poster this is a double device, since the newspaper is ordinarily called by the nickname *L'Intran* and is shouted thus by news sellers.

Cubism: Some Subdivisions

With the liberation of cubist forms into the field of general expression, it was inevitable that the ranks of the cubists, which had grown like weeds, should break into smaller groups with their own theories. For

580. DELAUNAY: *Windows*, 1912. 13½ x 35″. Philadelphia Museum of Art, Gallatin Collection.

a while one ism shouldered another in the enthusiasm for further experiment and refinements and the hope of discovery. Robert Delaunay (1885–1941), dissatisfied with cubism's static arrangements, began composing in restless planes and swinging arcs in an effort to reveal the forces inherent in static objects. He chose as his special subjects two pieces of architectural engineering where dynamic forces are brought into structural balance: the Eiffel Tower with its steel girders and the medieval church of St. Séverin with its stone vaults. His semi-cubist *Eiffel Tower* of about 1909 [578], compared with one of 1925 [579] demonstrates the change from static forms to ones broken up in a way suggesting movement. Delaunay similarly enlivened cubist color. In 1912, a year when cubism shot out in a dozen directions, Delaunay formulated "orphism," or color orchestration, in which he had tried to free cubism at once from the dun hues that had affected it during the analytical period and from its dependence on subject matter. As an orphist he painted a series of "window compositions" [580] in totally abstract planes something like overlapping sheets of bright colored glass. Although he did not follow up the direction these paintings set, other painters were soon to do so.

Francis Picabia (1879–1953) was also involved in orphism, but at the same time he thought that cubism could be a vehicle for the expression of ideas. He had begun as an imitator of Sisley, and he spent his life enthusiastically investigating every new

581. PICABIA: *Physical Culture*, 1913. 35¼ x 46″. Philadelphia Museum of Art, Arensberg Collection.

ism that turned up, without going very deeply into any of them. The painting he called *Physical Culture* [581] is already tainted with Picabia's weakness for impertinence that later led him to use such titles as *You'll Never Sell It, I Don't Want to Paint Any More,* and *What Do You Call That?*

What might be called "dynamic cubism," apparent in Delaunay's later *Eiffel Tower* and in *Physical Culture,* is most vivaciously present in Marcel Duchamp's (1887–   ) celebrated *Nude Descending a Staircase* [582]. It is a painting of considerable his-

582. DUCHAMP: *Nude Descending a Staircase* (*No. 2*), 1912. 58 x 35″. Philadelphia Museum of Art, Arensberg Collection.

583. BURNE-JONES: *The Golden Stairs*, 1880. 109 x 46″. Tate Gallery, London.

torical importance since it became the key exhibit of the Armory Show in 1913 in New York (traveling later to Chicago and Boston), which was America's first wholesale introduction to avant-garde painting. For the first time, Americans reacted with the vehemence of Frenchmen when confronted with works of art that offended them. Guards had to protect the most controver-

sial paintings from attack by an enraged public. This at least was true in New York and Chicago; Bostoners retained their aplomb.

One unsympathetic critic labeled *Nude Descending a Staircase* once and for all "an explosion in a shingle factory." The jibe was perceptive, up to a point. The figure is indeed shattered into shinglelike planes that merge and overlap in a pattern of great energy. But the jibe falls short in that the shattered figure is not chaotic. Contrarily, it is reassembled into a pattern of great order and vivacity, more expressive of bright descending movement than an imitative painting of a nude descending a staircase could be. But for a public that still admired Burne-Jones's *The Golden Stairs* [583], showing eighteen young women in pretty costumes descending a staircase in a series of graceful attitudes, a picture of one nude young woman descending a staircase in many more than eighteen attitudes, overlaid, was incomprehensible and infuriating. The fact that after half a century *Nude Descending* has a persistent capacity to interest the sympathetic and irritate the antagonistic, while other sensational novelties have flared up and faded away by the dozen, is as good a proof as another that it is much more than a well-timed tour de force, as it has been suspected of being. It is an enduring landmark, and it is a work of art with extensions beyond cubism. One of these is its deliberately provocative title which, like Picabia's nonsensical ones, is allied to two other movements, dada and surrealism, where Duchamp will appear again.

Duchamp's painter brother Gaston, who adopted the pseudonym Jacques Villon (1875–   ), worked in a personal variation on cubism, always rather quiet and elegant, and eventually developing into lucent configurations of great distinction. In the history of cubism he has a special place as the head of a group who met at his studio in the early days for discussion and theorizing. In 1912 they named themselves the *Section d'Or* after the mathematical formula for proportional harmonies that has already been commented on in connection with neo-impressionism. The *Section d'Or* organized a huge exhibition, and all the men mentioned here—Metzinger and Gleizes, Gris and Léger, Delaunay and Picabia and Marcel Duchamp—took part in it, as well as Roger de la Fresnaye (1885–1925), Louis Marcoussis (1883–1941), André Lhote (1885–   ), and many others. As a climactic point in cubism's coming of age it summarized the forces at work before

584. BALLA: *Leash in Motion*, 1912. 35⅝ x 43¼". Collection A. Conger Goodyear, New York.

their dissemination into the general field of painting, which they have so profoundly affected. Picasso and Braque alone, the two major figures in cubism's development and the two painters who subsequently drew most significantly upon it, were not represented. The immediate reason was that the exhibition was held in a commercial gallery in which they could not show, for contractual reasons. But psychologically their absence was appropriate, for while it is possible to think of the men who did exhibit as being, first of all, cubists, it is impossible not to think of Braque and Picasso as being, first of all, painters. But before they can be further discussed here, a little attention must be given to a movement called futurism.

Futurism

Futurism was a parenthetical Italian movement that promised for a moment to be an important one but ended by draining off into cubism. The kinetic factor so apparent in *Nude Descending a Staircase*, as well as in the dynamism of Delaunay's *Eiffel*

85. RUSSOLO: *Dynamism of an Automobile*, 1913. 41½ x 55".
Musée National d'Art Moderne, Paris.

Tower, was basic in futurism's program. *Dynamism* was their favorite word.

Futurism began as a literary movement after cubism was well under way, in 1909. An Italian litterateur named Filippo Tommaso Marinetti decided that it was the obligation of the modern creative mind to celebrate such factors in modern life as its speed and aggressiveness. He advocated tearing down all institutions dedicated to the preservation of the past, such as museums, libraries, and schools, and issued a declamatory manifesto as a call to arms. No museums, libraries, or schools were lost. (This happened in Paris, although Marinetti was Italian.) Marinetti's literary rebellion was taken up by a group of painters who were at the moment working within the general confines of neo-impressionism, and one of them, Umberto Boccioni (1882–1916), followed Marinetti's ideas in a similar manifesto exhorting the young painters of Italy to arise to the fray. The manifesto was also signed by Luigi Russolo (1885–   ), Giacomo Balla (1871–   ), Carlo Carrà (1881–   ), and Gino Severini (1883–   ), and was followed by a succession of sequel manifestos. They were distributed by the thousands, sometimes by such stunts as scattering from Italian bell

towers. There was always a strong element of public theatricalism in futurist behavior, and it is difficult to read their proclamations without an uncomfortable feeling that the theories were formulated with more attention to shock value than to convictions sincerely held. Urgent and literary in tone, they are composed of such phrases as ". . . fight relentlessly against the fanatical, irresponsible, and snobbish religion of the past, which is nourished by the baneful existence of museums . . . groveling admiration for old canvases . . . criminal disdain for everything young, new, and pulsating with life . . . tyranny of the words *harmony* and *good taste*." Artists were admonished to "glorify the life of today, unceasingly and violently transformed by victorious science." Instead of the religious atmosphere that "weighed upon the souls" of their ancestors, they should draw inspiration from the liners, battleships, airplanes, submarines, and railroads that made an "iron network of speed enveloping the earth."

One way to express motion was to follow Boccioni's statement that "a galloping horse has not four legs; it has twenty." That such was also the case with dogs was demonstrated by Balla in his *Leash in Motion* [584].

The painters planned a Paris exhibition as an opening gun outside Italy after a sensational debut in Milan, but when they compared their work, full of neo-impressionist overtones, with what Braque and Picasso were doing—this was in 1910—they saw that for all their rampant modernism they were already a step behind. They performed a tactical retreat and the exhibition did not materialize until 1912, when analytical cubism had just about run its course and had been assimilated as part of futurist theory.

The simple multiple-exposure approach of *Leash in Motion* did not quite fulfill the expression of "universal dynamism," "dynamic sensation itself," "plastic dynamism," or "the translation of objects according to the *lines of force* which characterize them." The cubist idea of simultaneity was adapted to "put the spectator at the center of the picture," since the various sensations con-

586. SEVERINI: *Dynamic Hieroglyphic of the Bal Tabarin*, 1912. Oil on canvas with sequins, 63⅜ x 61½". Museum of Modern Art, New York, Lillie P. Bliss Bequest.

verging upon him simultaneously from every side involved the same principle as analytical cubism's multiple simultaneous vision. But the futurists' adaptation of the idea also involved strong expressive color, and their shattered forms were often organized on a skeleton of strong directional lines, as in Russolo's *Dynamism of an Automobile* [585]. In Severini's *Dynamic Hieroglyphic of the Bal Tabarin* [586] the spectator is put at the center of that famous pleasure spot and is surrounded by choppy, whirling forms in extremely cheerful colors further enlivened by a scattering of real sequins.

It requires a generous effort today to see these paintings as much more than historical novelties playing second fiddle to cubism, where similar ideas were developed more exhaustively; a recent revival of interest in the futurists smacked strongly of artificial respiration. Surprisingly, futurism's contribution may end up as being made in sculpture, where it would seem least likely to succeed. Boccioni's *Unique Forms of Continuity in Space* [588] is a large, arresting bronze in which the forms seem to have been shaped by rushing air, air whose currents we can almost feel extending beyond the fluttering shapes of the

472 · CUBISM AND ABSTRACT ART

587. BERNINI: *Apollo and Daphne,* 1622–24. Marble, life size. *Galleria Borghese,* Rome. (Photo Anderson.)

588. BOCCIONI: *Unique Forms of Continuity in Space,* 1913. Bronze, 43½″ high. Museum of Modern Art, New York, Lillie P. Bliss Bequest.

metal just as they penetrate into it in other places. The dynamic "lines of force" which we have just seen as severely angular ones in Russolo's interpretation of a moving automobile now weave and twist, materializing as solids and equally extending into space suggested or defined by these solids. A striding figure is still discernible as the motif for the composition, and if *Unique Forms of Continuity in Space* is innovational, it is also linked firmly to the tradition of baroque sculpture, such as Bernini's *Apollo and Daphne* [587], where flapping draperies, wind-filled hair, and extended arms and legs fly out into surrounding space and also receive space into the hollows and voids carved into the marble. The

difference between the two pieces of sculpture is that the baroque sculptor is most apparently creating realistic forms while the futurist is most apparently creating abstract ones. But both sculptors are creating a composition where solid form and the forms of space merge and interlock. This aspect of space in connection with sculpture is considered in more detail at the end of this chapter, where another work by Boccioni, his *Development of a Bottle in Space* [632], is related to certain contemporary theories of sculpture.

World War I wrote *finis* to futurism as a potentially significant organized movement, although an army of small painters continued to go through its paces into the

589. CARRÀ: *Hermaphroditic Idol*, 1917. 25½ x 16½". Collection Carlo Frua de Angeli, Milan.

590. PICASSO: *Man with Violin*, 1911. 39½ x 28⅞". Philadelphia Museum of Art, Arensberg Collection.

1930's. To postwar Europe, futurism's theoretical advocation of destruction and violence was less attractive after four years of experience with the real thing. Die-hard futurists continued to study "dynamism" in more and more abstract form, yet futurism somehow never supplied nourishment for growth as cubism did. In retrospect its brief flourishing is revealed as a forced growth—all foliage and no roots. Of the signers of the original manifesto, Balla alone continued to develop, rather thinly, in the direction he had helped to set. Severini tried a few war motifs in 1915, including an *Armored Train*, but soon turned to doing doves, fruit, and other happy and nondynamic subjects in an adaptation of synthetic cubism that was especially popular with interior decorators. Carrà joined a dream-world school of "metaphysical" painting, which will be discussed in due time, of which his *Hermaphroditic Idol* [589] may serve here as a foretaste. We may now return to the post-analytical careers of Braque and Picasso.

Braque

The two major analytical cubists, Braque and Picasso, as has been said, worked for a while so closely that their work is distinguishable from one another's only by fine points. Picasso's *Man with Violin* [590] and Braque's *Man with Guitar* [591], both painted in 1911 at the climax of analytical

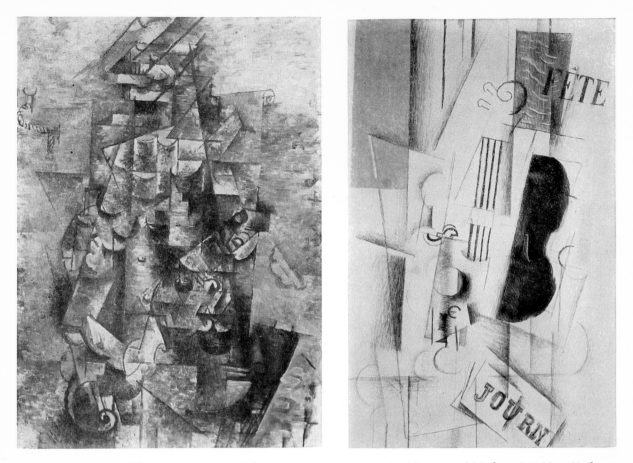

591. BRAQUE: *Man with Guitar*, 1911. 45¾ x 31⅞". Museum of Modern Art, New York, Lillie P. Bliss Bequest.

592. BRAQUE: *Musical Forms with the Words Fête and Journal*, 1913. Oil, pencil, and charcoal on canvas, 36¼ x 23½". Philadelphia Museum of Art, Arensberg Collection.

cubism, are evidence enough. Yet even here a difference appears when the two paintings are compared within the confines of analytical cubism, instead of within the context of painting in general. The Picasso shifts and vibrates within its geometrical framework, the Braque is more static, more self-contained; it is as if the multitude of planes in the Picasso have expanded to the limits of the structure they compose, while those in the Braque have contracted until the forms are compressed and ordered into stability.

The difference between the two painters indicated here will be widened as they develop in their own directions. Picasso will become the romantic of the movement—all energy, fire, restlessness, invention, emotion. Braque will develop into its classical master—controlled, reflective, harmonious, working toward an ideal of perfection within limits, as opposed to the romantic yearning for limitless expression.

With analytical cubism behind him, Braque's first departure was to restore the inherently ornamental character of the same objects that had figured in his analytical compositions—bowls of fruit, tables and goblets and compotes, and particularly musical instruments. His *Musical Forms with the Words Fête and Journal* [592]—the complication of the title is only a device to distinguish this painting from other compositions of musical forms—is a spare,

593. BRAQUE: *Musical Forms*, 1918. Collage, 30⅝ x 37⅜". Philadelphia Museum of Art, Arensberg Collection.

open arrangement of straight lines and simple arcs or volutes derived from the shapes of a violin. A large part of the canvas is left unpainted, the design being established by crayon drawing in tones ranging from black to light gray, holding the grainy texture of the canvas. The unpainted canvas itself, in the original, serves as an ornamental surface which is lost in photography and reproduction, and it supplies an off-white that counts as a color, not as a blank area. The other colors are a grayed blue, scrubbed thinly in the rectangle in the upper left; a warm brown in the body of the violin itself; and a light tan in the rectangle of simulated wood texture above it. The area of the violin has been textured by drawing a comb or some other toothed instrument across it in a slightly wavy motion while the paint was still wet. In all, the composition achieves textural variety with economy of means, a satisfying struc-

tural balance in forms individually delicate. Its quality might be compared to that of a "dry" light wine, thinner and more subtle than a more obviously tasty sweet one.

The interest in textures and the introduction of letters in imitation of printed ones is associated with experiments Braque made in collage. The origin of collage, which is the making of pictures or compositions by pasting together bits of paper, cloth, and the like, is not certain. Like cubism it seems to have appeared spontaneously from several sources at once, but Braque certainly had a great deal to do with its origin and he used it with particular felicity. A collage of *Musical Forms* [593] extends the idea implicit in the painting we have just seen where the texture of the unpainted canvas was used as an integral part of a picture that also included simulated textures. Here all the textures are real. A banjolike instrument cut from cor-

594. BRAQUE: *The Round Table*, 1929. 58 x 45". Phillips Collection, Washington, D.C.

One value of the collage is that it opens our eyes to colors and textures we have ignored because they are commonplace. Behind the origin of collage, too, there may be ultimately the rejection of the old academic idea that painting must display technical skill of a conventional kind. By fabricating "pictures" from odds and ends of worthless material the artist makes the final denial of the validity of academic technique as an end in itself. But for Braque the value of collage was in experiments with texture, an introduction to an element that will continue to preoccupy him in other ways.

Collage soon served its purpose for Braque and its other originators, and they abandoned it. It was later taken up by experimenters and practitioners of the bizarre who used it for shock value, combining materials absurd or shocking in themselves —plumbing from toilets and the like—or cutting out portions of printed pictures and pasting them together to make irrational images. And it is a rare kindergarten nowadays that doesn't have collage in its art classes, where children have access to a heap of cloth scraps, torn paper, cellophane, wire netting, cotton, false hair, and anything else that can be pasted down. All legitimate enough in their own ways, these offshoots must not be confused with Braque's combinations of colors and textures via collage instead of via painting in the creation of synthetic cubist compositions.

Surface texture of course has always been an important part of painting, whether it is the variegated one of Rembrandt, the uniformly polished one of Ingres, the fatty, active one of Delacroix, or the congealed-confetti one of Seurat. But with Rembrandt, texture was incidental to the creation of form in light; with Ingres, part and parcel of the idea of disciplined draughtsmanship; with Delacroix, part of expression; with Seurat, the end result of a theory of the laws of light. With Braque, surface texture now becomes an integral decorative factor in painting, and from this time forward he cultivates it, sometimes mixing sand or other grainy matter with his paint to roughen it, sometimes depending only

rugated cardboard supplies the most unexpected one, but other areas are also papers of different textures. The whites are a ribbed drawing paper, the largest halftone area is a brown wrapping paper, and the black upon close examination is a paper printed with an imitation of a very fine wood grain. The upper part of the mandolin form is the kind of paper used to cover pasteboard cigar boxes, again simulating wood grain, and again a printed paper, not a simulation by the painter. The rectangles at lower right and far left center are printed with a slightly raised netlike pattern. With a few lines in crayon and a background painted blue-gray, that is the scheme. The colors of the papers have a natural ornamental harmony once their identity as cheap paper is forgotten.

on the paint's own thinness or thickness, sometimes scratching or pressing textures into it, but always incorporating texture as part of his organization of form, line, and color.

By the 1920's Braque was master of a personal cubist idiom combining spatial play with exquisitely integrated shape [594]. During the mid-1920's he began to use the human figure, usually a female nude, in addition to tables and compotes of fruit and musical instruments. *Nude* [595] of 1925, is like a decorative panel in a new substance, neither paint nor ceramic, suggesting both. It is as if the colors and textures, like those of a ceramist, were the result of the craftsman's scheme modified by the process of firing—except that here the modifications are Braque's own. His art shares the appeal of other decorative ones; *Woman with a Mandolin* [596], a synthesis of his work up until the middle 1930's, is tapestrylike in its textural richness. Braque's color here as elsewhere is indescribable, partly because no color is describable to much effect, but largely because he is the most individual decorative colorist of his generation. No color is pure; greens are olives, sages, and occasional lime greens. Modified purples are juxtaposed with citrons and blacks. When reds occur they occur suddenly and spectacularly, but also in off-shades that unify them with Braque's special family of colors. "Braque colors" have become a stock in trade for the modern interior decorator.

It is time to insert a reminder that before he was a cubist, Braque was briefly a member of the fauve group. And of all painters, he alone made a balanced fusion of fauvist principles of color with cubist ideas of form. His *Woman with a Mandolin* may eventually stand as the richest summary, within the boundaries of single pictures, of the abstract style of the first half of the twentieth century. If every painting by Picasso, every painting by Matisse, and every painting by Braque were gathered together and all but a single painting had to be destroyed, Braque's *Woman with a Mandolin* could not summarize the total, but it might come closest of them all to being the representative example.

595. BRAQUE: *Nude*, 1925. 36⅛ x 28⅞". Art Institute of Chicago, Gift of Mr. and Mrs. Arnold H. Maremont.

Picasso: Cubist and Classical Variations

Picasso is certainly the most fecund painter who has ever lived. In sheer quantity his work is fantastic, which would be meaningless if he were a repetitive painter, but his invention is phenomenal, his range staggering. From his thousands of paintings, prints, and drawings it would be possible to cull several groups of work that would be creditable as the lifeworks of several painters of varying temperaments. And it would be simple to divide his total work between two classifications as the work of two tremendously productive artists, one of them a man of tender sentiments dedicated to a joyous life, the other a man appalled by

596. BRAQUE: *Woman with a Mandolin*, 1937. 51¼ x 38¼″. Museum of Modern Art, New York, Mrs. Simon Guggenheim Fund.

life's terribleness and releasing his fury against it in cathartic images of horror, brutishness, and terror.

Picasso's abrupt changes of style, his sudden terminations and redirections, his harking back to principles he seemed to have exhausted years before to revive them in more vigorous forms, the sudden appear-ance from time to time of individual paint-ings that seem isolated experiments and may remain so for years, lying fallow until they are suddenly continued in a whole group of paintings—all this variation, turn-ing, and shifting would be vacillation or chaos if it were not unified by the presence of the single force which is Picasso himself.

He has a headlong vigor, an all-encompassing vitality, which refuses to accept any achievement as final or static in the expression of a world so contradictory and so rich in joy and tragedy that his experience of it must well forth in image after image patterned to record his multitudinous response to its inexhaustible excitements. No single style of image can suffice his vigor and his curiosity. It is the sense of growth and expansion, a constant pushing forward into new explorations, that gives unity to Picasso's turbulent variety when his work is surveyed as a whole.

We have already seen him as a young man influenced by Toulouse-Lautrec, then synthesizing a more individual style in his speciously pathetic images of the blue period, next relenting with the gentle harlequins, adolescents, and performers of the "circus" period, finally merging into the graceful classical echoes of the rose period —then abruptly creating *Les Demoiselles d'Avignon* and going into cubism.

Immediately after the exhaustion of analytical cubism in 1912, Picasso made some of the same adjustments we have already seen in Braque, including play with collage. For several years thereafter he explored synthetic cubism. For Picasso this was a period of fantastic eruption. The most inventive of painters exceeded himself in indicating the area over which he could range with ebullience, assurance, excitement, and often with profundity. It is necessary in understanding Picasso to remember this range. With Gris and Léger, and even with Braque, it is safe to approach each picture with some certainty that it will fall within the general boundaries of each man's characteristic expression. With Picasso, each picture must be approached individually. After one of his most profound statements he may create a piece of pure legerdemain, may indulge in a kind of pictorial horseplay. A picture like *Harlequin* [597] is as witty as it is ornamental. In his celebrated and extremely complex *Painter and Model* [598], a painter (right) works from a model (left) and both are abstracted according to free applications of cubist ideas. But the shattered and distorted head of the model appears reassembled on the painter's

597. Picasso: *Harlequin*, 1915. 72¼ x 41⅜". Museum of Modern Art, New York, Lillie P. Bliss Bequest.

canvas in a clear profile, the only realistically identifiable element in the composition. This turnabout, a tour de force variation on the picture-within-a-picture theme, is clever enough to have been borrowed by cartoonists in popular magazines, but it is also a comment on the nature of cubist vision, and, beyond that, an informal philo-

598. PICASSO: *Painter and Model*, 1928. 51⅝ x 63⅞". Collection Mr. and Mrs. Sidney Janis, New York.

sophical reflection on the relationship of the painter's art to the visible world.

In 1921, as if to summarize the potential of synthetic cubism, Picasso painted two large compositions of *Three Musicians*, one fairly complicated [599] and one highly simplified [600]. In both of them, three masked mummers or Mardi gras celebrators are costumed as Harlequin—Picasso's ubiquitous Harlequin—Pierrot, and a monk. Each has a musical instrument. Side by side the two paintings are a lesson in synthetic cubist design. To the person who cannot see in individual pictures of this kind a harmony and integration of form, it might be enlightening to imagine transposing a single figure from one picture to the other. Not only is this impossible because of the interlockings of form, but if a figure

were torn from its compositional moorings and somehow grafted into the other painting, its forms would be disharmonious with those surrounding it—too complicated or too simple, and without adequate or harmonious interrelationship of its lines and shapes to those of its new companions.

Even while he was reaching the synthetic cubist culmination in *Three Musicians*, Picasso was working on a second group of drawings and paintings of an opposite character, a new version of the monumental classical figure type so dear to the academicians. The opposite of cubistic, Picasso's new figures are solid and unviolated as mass [601], and painted a solid dulled pink something like terra cotta, increasing their sculptural quality. The exaggerated heaviness, the overlarge hands, the extreme simplification into geometrical masses, add to their ponderous, indissoluble unity, which is a reaction against the disintegration of solids in cubism. In these pictures Picasso returns to the weighty solidity and definition of the portrait of Gertrude Stein [558], but as usual he is not so much returning, as resurrecting and transfiguring. His art is a constant series of transmigrations of the forms of one period into the forms of another. Among the sudden brilliant variations in the classical period is *Woman in White* [602], where the ponderousness is ameliorated by the delicacy of the technique. The picture is painted in thin veils of pigment with contrasting heavily loaded lights (particularly in the face) and quick, decisive lines to define the features, all capped by the most delicate calligraphic indications of the hair, suggesting Oriental painting and completing an image of great repose, alertly alive.

The next years include also a cycle of paintings stemming from cubism but involving sweeping curves and circles, often described in heavy black lines enclosing bright glassy colors. *Girl before a Mirror* [603] of 1932 has become a standard example of this "stained glass" manner. Cubist ideas of simultaneity are brought back to their earliest and simplest devices, as in the combination profile and full face of the girl, but the invention is free, subject to no restrictions cubist or otherwise, in the creation of scintillating patterns. *Girl before a Mirror,* like most of Picasso's major canvases, has been the subject of elaborate psychoanalytical interpretations. The full rounded or globular forms of the figure, their unity with the long rounded forms of the mirror, or pier glass, the simultaneous identification and transformation of figure and reflection, the suggestion of interior as well as exterior anatomical forms—all are rich material for this kind of study and could be interpreted in any one of a dozen ways by a dozen schools of psychologists. As a purely visual spectacle, *Girl before a Mirror* is one of the most vibrant and powerful of Picasso's works, with its combination, so frequent in his work from now on, of almost savage force with the extremest sophistication.

599–600. PICASSO: *Three Musicians,* 1921. *Above,* 80 x 74". Philadelphia Museum of Art, Gallatin Collection. *Below,* 79 x 87¾". Museum of Modern Art, New York, Mrs. Simon Guggenheim Fund

601. PICASSO: *Standing Nude*, 1922. Panel, 7½ x 5½". Wadsworth Atheneum, Hartford, Conn.

603. PICASSO: *Girl before a Mirror*, 1932. 63¾ x 51¼". Museum of Modern Art, New York, Gift of Mrs. Simon Guggenheim.

602. PICASSO: *Woman in White*, 1923. 39 x 31½". Metropolitan Museum of Art, New York, Rogers Fund, 1951; from The Museum of Modern Art, Lillie P. Bliss Collection.

Picasso: "Minotauromachia" and "Guernica"

Shortly after *Girl before a Mirror*, a new theme, ominous and violent, appears and soon dominates Picasso's conceptions, the double theme of the bullfight, which is a ceremony of death, and the Minotaur, that monster half bull and half man who in Greek legend devoured annually his tribute of seven youths and seven maidens delivered into his labyrinth by the Athenians. These reveries of violence correspond to a disturbed period in Picasso's own life and culminate in one of his most elaborate works, a large etching full of personal symbols, *Minotauromachia* [604]. The symbolism of the various figures may or may not have been explicit in Picasso's mind, but in a general way the symbolism is apparent without a key. The theme is, first of all, a conflict between good and evil, between innocence and corruption, between life and death. On the right the Minotaur with its

604. PICASSO: *Minotauromachia*, 1935. Etching, 19½ x 27⅜". Philadelphia Museum of Art, Gift of Henry P. McIlhenny.

powerful male human body and its grotesque beast's head advances with the sword of a bullfighter. A female figure in bullfighter's costume lies dead across the back of a terrified horse, a reference of course to the pitiful nags who are sacrificed to the horns of the bull in the early stages of the sport. But at the right a little girl holds a bunch of flowers—it might be the one offered us years ago by the *Boy with Bouquet* [555]—and holds a gleaming light, serene in her confidence of its power against the Minotaur, who shields himself from it—or is about to extinguish it. The little girl wears a tam-o'-shanter and stands as primly as a child in a storybook illustration. Behind her a male figure suggestive of Christ ascends a ladder. The conflict is witnessed by a pair of young women on a balcony where a dove perches. On one side the scene takes place against a background of

the wall of the house, on the other against a deep stretch of sea where a tiny sailboat appears like an afterthought. One may make of these symbols whatever explicit interpretation seems necessary, but beyond a certain point explicit interpretation is superfluous. The pictorial images evoke emotional associations without identifying tags.

Minotauromachia served as prototype for an explosive picture that now appears: Picasso's most deeply felt, most emotionalized, most vehement painting, probably his masterpiece if a single one must be chosen from so many candidates—*Guernica* [605, 606, 607, 608, 609, and 610].

In April, 1937, the ancient and holy city of Guernica in northern Spain was destroyed by German bombers supporting General Franco in the Spanish civil war. Guernica was not particularly a strategic

605. PICASSO: *Guernica*, 1937. 138 x 308". Museum of Modern Art, New York, on loan from the artist.

606. PICASSO: Composition study for Figure 605, May 9, 1937. Pencil on white paper, 9½ x 17⅞". Collection the artist.

target; its destruction was primarily a test run, the first practical application of the military theory of saturation bombing, a rehearsal for World War II. The rehearsal was successful. Most of Guernica was re-

duced to rubble and its inhabitants were destroyed with it.

Picasso's outrage as a Spaniard and as a human being produced the *Guernica* in a matter of weeks. It is a large painting—

607. PICASSO: Detail from Figure 605. Approximately 66 x 63".

more than twenty-five feet long—painted entirely in blacks, whites, and grays. Distortions take on a new horribleness; there is a blatant and tragic ugliness to the human creatures who shriek, howl, and die. A bomb has fallen into the courtyard or barn of a farmhouse. A horse screams in the center of the composition. A bull, symbol of triumphant violence, rises immune at the left. The large space is organized on one of the oldest schemes in Western art. It is essentially a triptych on the formula of a Renaissance altarpiece with a central portion and two folding wings. Its two wing-like side elements, which would once have been occupied by flanking saints, show on one side a mother who screeches as she holds the body of her child, and on the other a woman who falls through the floor of a burning building. The triangular central motif, which in the altarpiece would

608. PICASSO: Detail from Figure 605. Approximately 37 x 46"

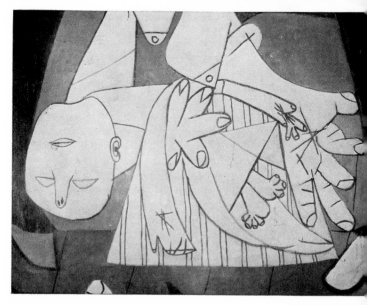

609. PICASSO: Detail from Figure 605. Approximately 34 x 43″.

610. PICASSO: Detail from Figure 605. Approximately 38 x 48″.

izing a more chaotic scheme composed of the same elements.

Some of the impact of *Guernica* comes from the frightening combination of the ludicrous and the grotesque with the tragic. The eyes askew in heads, the hands and feet with swollen fingers and toes, like hideous mutations—all these monstrous deformities, all the ugliness, are reminders that death by the violence of war is abominable and obscene. Picasso's drawings for *Guernica* included some of the most ghastly images in the history of horror and fantasy [611].

Since *Guernica*, Picasso has varied his style with customary frequency, but elements of the grotesque and the horrible have been persistent in it. On a superficial level, *Girl with Cock* [612] of the year following *Guernica* is trivial or silly as to subject, but this silliness and even the half-comical presentation, especially of the rooster, is identified with the terrible, the irrational, violence of life. The ominous knife on the floor to the left is represented with a clarity that leaves no doubt as to the picture's implication.

Yet in the middle of nightmarish grotesqueries there will appear a drawing or a small painting recalling the tenderness of the early acrobats, harlequins, and boys leading horses, and in the last few years Picasso has been painting with revived gayety, brightness, and opulence. In December, 1954, and into February, 1955, he occupied himself with a series of studies with Delacroix's *Women of Algiers* as a basis for a set of variations [613], [614], where legerdemain, cubist derivations, stained glass color, inversions and returns, and sheer inventive play with space, pattern, and color are juggled, tossed, caught, shattered, pieced together, multiplied and divided in a prestidigious exhibition of one man's art that has dominated inventive painting for half a century. And in the same year, 1955, following Matisse's death late in 1954, there was a spurt of Matisse-like Picassos in bright flat colors with fauvist echoes that could be interpreted as a form of tribute to a worthy antagonist in an undeclared war in which, happily, both opponents were victors.

have built up to a madonna enthroned among adoring saints, is packed with mangled human and animal forms including a symbolical severed arm and hand still grasping a broken sword. A comparison of the completed picture with a preliminary composition study [606] shows that Picasso built the central triangular mass, and flanked it by the two "wings," by reorgan-

611. PICASSO: Guernica Series #37. Ink and oil on canvas, 21⅜ x 18⅛″. Collection the artist.

612. PICASSO: *Girl with Cock*, 1938. 51¼ x 47½″. Collection Mrs. Meric Callery, New York.

613. PICASSO: *Women of Algiers, Variation "L,"* 1955. 51⅛ x 38⅛″. Paul Rosenberg & Co., New York.

614. PICASSO: *Women of Algiers, Variation "N,"* 1955. 44⅞ x 57½″. Paul Rosenberg & Co., New York.

615. MALEVICH: *White on White*, 1918. 31¼ x 31¼". Museum of Modern Art, New York.

The Nonobjective Conclusion

Picasso, Braque, and the cubists are abstract painters because, by the dictionary definition, their compositions are "creation(s) suggested by a concrete object or organic figure which is transformed by the artist into a nonrepresentational design with recognizable elements." The term *nonobjective* (or, sometimes, *nonfigurative*) has been coined to distinguish from this kind of abstraction, with its partial departure from representation, a total abstraction where representational elements are entirely eliminated.

When analytical cubism so abstracted concrete objects (such as men with violins) that only fragmentary elements were recognizable here and there, the nonobjective conclusion to the process of abstraction that had begun with Cézanne's distortion was indicated. If the object had virtually disappeared, to such an extent that the aesthetic and psychological satisfactions of

painting were to be found in planes as planes, rather than as parts of objects, why bother with the objects as a point of departure? Not only why bother, but why tolerate any vestigial remains?

We have already seen how synthetic cubism responded to this question. Instead of eliminating the subject it returned to it, and Picasso even developed a symbolical and emotionalized art where the recognizability of the objects was necessary to an understanding of the picture. *Guernica* would certainly not make the sense it does if the anguished horse and the ravished and brutalized human beings were not recognizable as the victims of a frightful social crime.

But certain other painters rejected subject entirely for pure abstraction—for nonobjectivity. We have seen that Kandinsky painted his first altogether nonrepresentational composition in 1910—a record. Shortly after, a Russian cubist named Kasimir Malevich (1878–1935) made the transition from abstract to nonobjective geometrical painting in a single jump of even more spectacular decisiveness, probably after a study of Kandinsky's theories. Malevich exhibited a black square placed neatly on a white background (the black square was painstakingly filled in with pencil) as a demonstration of his theory that art must leave behind all dependence on motif. The square represented nothing at all, was an abstraction of no concrete object. It was simply a geometrical area of black against a geometrical area of white, differing from Kandinsky's painting in that it "expressed" nothing. *Suprematism* was the name Malevich gave his new theory, which limited the painter's vocabulary to the rectangle, the circle, the triangle, and the cross. The third dimension was ruled out—instead of cubes, rectangles; instead of cones, triangles; instead of spheres, circles. It was permissible to combine several of these forms in a single painting, but since the aim of suprematism was to create the ultimate work of art, the black square on a white ground was the supreme suprematist composition. At least it seemed so for five years, until in 1918 Malevich conceived a white square on a white ground [615].

616. MONDRIAN: *Landscape with Farmhouse*, 1906. 34 x 42¾". Collection Mrs. Isaac Schoenberg, Swarthmore, Pa.

Beyond that not even he could go. The trouble with an ultimate is its finality, and it was Malevich's misfortune that in two paintings he had exhausted the possibilities of suprematism as a theory, and there was not much left to do with it except to defend it in dialectics.

But during these same years, the years between the black square and the white square, another painter was involved in more subtle considerations of the same idea that had inspired suprematism. His name was Piet Mondrian (1872–1944), and his theory came to be called neo-plasticism.

Mondrian had begun as a conventional painter working in a broad form of impressionism, turning out picturesque subjects, such as boats in canals and other stock items, in his native Holland. But by 1906 he was beginning to conventionalize his landscapes into flat patterns, as in *Landscape with Farmhouse* [616], where he hunts out the hint of natural geometry in walls and river banks and leafless branches silhouetted against the sky, and emphasizes it. But this is not Cézanne's solid geometry. It is plane geometry, as flat as a piece of painted stage scenery. From the loosely rectangular areas of the houses and, especially, their reflections in the water, it is only a few steps to the precisely geometrical lines and areas of Mondrian's typical nonobjective canvases, such as *Composition with Yellow* [617] and *Rhythm in Straight Lines* [618].

Mondrian wrote extensively and his theories include ideas like these, when they are pared down to apply to paintings like the two just mentioned:

1. All painting is composed of line and color. Line and color are the essence of painting. Hence they must be freed from their bondage to the imitation of nature and allowed to exist for themselves.

617. MONDRIAN: *Composition with Yellow*, 1936. 28¾ x 26″. Philadelphia Museum of Art, Arensberg Collection.

2. Painting occupies a plane surface. The plane surface is integral with the physical and psychological being of the painting. Hence the plane surface must be respected, must be allowed to declare itself, must not be falsified by imitations of volume, by perspective. Painting must be as flat as the surface it is painted on.

3. Painters striving for universality of expression have always simplified forms. The simpler the form, the more nearly it is universal. Hence the simplest form of all, the rectangle, must constitute the sole form if painting is to achieve universality.

4. The purer the color, the more it is appropriate to this universality. The only pure colors are the primary ones, which cannot be mixed from other colors but exist in themselves: red, yellow, and blue. Hence they alone may be used, each pure in itself.

These premises and conclusions are simple enough, but their application was not a simple process because it was subject to a universal variable:

Regarding the mechanical look of his painting, Mondrian wrote that "for the modern mentality, a work which has the appearance of a machine or a technical product" is most effective. But the artist is not a mechanic and hence his creations may not be "calculated." The artist is " a living machine capable of realizing in a pure manner the essence of art." Thus the artistic content of one of Mondrian's compositions still depends on the same qualities that have determined the artistic content of all the great works of the past—from the cave paintings on through to those of Mondrian himself—which is, simply, the artist's sensitivity to the rightness of the lines, the forms defined by those lines, and the colors of those forms, in his composition. The difference would be that until Mondrian this rightness could not exist in its purity. It was contaminated by its subservience to representation. With Mondrian this rightness can exist, at last, unsullied. Such is the theory.

Thus Mondrian is like a poet who examines *The Iliad* and *The Odyssey* and finds them powerful and wonderful but formless; who reads, let us say, a long lyric of Shelley's and finds it melodious but scattered; who discovers a sonnet by Shakespeare where the poet is forced into a rigid scheme of rhyme and meter into which he must order his expression. Here our poet-Mondrian begins to discover what he is hunting. It seems to him that within the limitations of the sonnet form Shakespeare has said as much as some writers might say in a novel, and that in the sonnet, expression benefits from compression. Our poet-Mondrian then examines the most rigid, the most arbitrary, the most demanding verse forms and, still finding them too elastic, invents a new one imposing further limitations within which he must constrict what he wants to say. Finally he goes a step further: he rejects words—just as the painter-Mondrian rejects images—and reduces his verse not only to sounds but to the half dozen sounds which he decides are the absolutely basic, the absolutely pure, the absolutely fundamental ones formed by the human voice. He then writes a poem of pure sound and pure form, freed at last from service to any other values.

If the parallel sounds too extreme, perhaps it is only because such a theory has not been applied to the art of writing. Mondrian's compositions were—and are—just as extreme in their elimination of all motif and all associative values.

Granting that Mondrian's theory is valid and that his sensitivity as an artist is adequate to apply the theory successfully, does he reach the perfection that should thus be possible? If so, then to shift a line in *Rhythm in Straight Lines* should be to throw the rhythm out of kilter, out of dynamic balance. (For Mondrian insists that the balance is dynamic; a static one would involve nothing more complicated than a generally symmetrical arrangement.) Or the yellow filling two rectangles in *Composition with Yellow* could not be changed to red or blue, and could not be shifted elsewhere in the composition, without making some other changes to bring the arrangement back into balance. And so on. While tests of this kind push the idea to the limits of absurdity, the test is implicit in the theory, and can be applied as legitimately to a Mondrian as to Seurat's *La Grande Jatte* [399], which is composed from a similar point of view except that its elements are "impure" in shape and color, subservient as they are to images of the real world no matter how conventionalized these images are. By Mondrian's standards *La Grande Jatte*, for all its impeccable order and for all its departures from visual fact, is a compromise between abstraction and photography. This compromise he refuses to make. But toward the end of his life he relented enough to introduce a few modified colors in his rectangles, and to incorporate extraneous ideas, if never images. His *Broadway Boogie Woogie* [619] accepts a subject by the title he gave it. Fascinated by the rhythms of American life when he established residence in New York, he peppered his rectangles with little cubes of dancing colors interspersed with heavier blocky forms. The parallel to the jazz music form called boogie woogie is quite direct—a lively repetitious bass pattern establishes a firm skeleton for an over-

618. MONDRIAN: *Rhythm in Straight Lines*, 1942. 28¼ x 27". Collection Mr. and Mrs. Henry Clifford, Radnor, Pa.

619. MONDRIAN: *Broadway Boogie Woogie*, 1942–43. 50 x 50". Museum of Modern Art, New York.

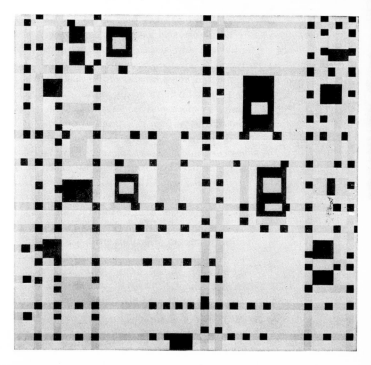

620. MONDRIAN: *Composition No. 10, Plus and Minus*, 1915. 33½
x 42½". Rijksmuseum Kröller-Müller, Otterlo.

621. MONDRIAN: *Horizontal Tree*, 1911. 29⅝ x 43⅞". Munson-
Williams-Proctor Institute, Utica, N.Y.

lay of improvisations in sharp chords and
trills. Mondrian stated the parallel by describing boogie woogie as a "destruction
of melody" corresponding to his "rejection
of natural aspect."

The difference between *Broadway
Boogie Woogie* and other Mondrians of the
same general type is apparent even to the
novice on first introduction. But on closer

acquaintance, even Mondrian's other apparently repetitious compositions are di-
visible into periods where he works at
different problems. Dissatisfied because a
group of compositions are "too restless" or
"too static" or unsatisfactory to him in some
other way, he may use more or fewer or
heavier or lighter lines, more or fewer
colored rectangles, sometimes no color at
all. Admitting that this is variation within
an extremely narrow range, the variation
is still there and offers rewards of a special
nature to anyone whose interest extends far
enough into the problem of aesthetic disciplines. *Composition with Yellow* is a
lighter, more delicate arrangement than
*Rhythm in Straight Lines; Rhythm in
Straight Lines* is bolder, more insistent,
than *Composition with Yellow.*

In less rigidly geometrical works than
rectangular patterns like these, Mondrian
may be a semicubist whose connection to
nature, even if several times removed, is
still apparent. And if the pattern of leafless
branches of the trees in *Landscape with
Farmhouse* is compared with *Composition
No. 10, Plus and Minus* [620] an ultimate
connection with nature is apparent, especially when one of his many abstract tree
studies [621] is interposed between them
as an intermediate step. *Plus and Minus* is
not a doodle, but the final resolution of a
problem that began with a fairly realistic
image.

Mondrian's goal was the classical one:
perfection within imposed limitations. The
danger he ran, even at best, was toward
chilliness and sterility. The same goal and
the same dangers have always been involved in the classical tradition; they affected David. The difference with Mondrian is that the limitations on ancient
classical and nineteenth-century neo-classical artists were merely demanding, while
those on Mondrian were excruciating.
Whether these limitations were so extreme
that they precluded the possibility of
Mondrian's ever being anything more than
a phenomenon fascinating to students and
specialists, is a question that cannot be
answered at such close range. But in the
meanwhile, at mid-century, Mondrian appears to have reached the nonobjective

conclusion implied by the abstract elements (but *only* the abstract elements) of a classical tradition that includes Poussin, David, Cézanne, and elements of cubism.

Mondrian was virtually a one-man school, although the painter Theo Van Doesburg (1883–1931) was associated with him for a while after 1916. Van Doesburg later made his own departure from neo-plasticism in a variation he called "elementarism." Neo-plasticism was intimately connected with the development of contemporary architectural style, and has influenced furniture design, typography, and for that matter all the decorative arts. Sporadically between 1917 and 1928 the painters, architects, designers, and theorizers connected with it published a magazine, *De Stijl*, which disseminated the ideas of the group. Their ideas were incorporated into the "international style" in architecture, which also has its affiliations with expressionism and cubism, as we will see a little further along in this book.

Other Abstract and Nonobjective Isms

In 1918, a year after the founding of *De Stijl*, and the same year as the suprematist climax in *White on White*, two architect-painter-theorist-writers named Amédée Ozenfant (1886–   ) and Charles-Édouard Jeanneret, who took the name of Le Corbusier (1887–   ), added a third variation to the investigation of geometrical abstract art, calling it *purism*. Cubism, they decided, had sold itself out to pretty invention, had degenerated into ornamental caprice, and needed purifying. They published a manifesto called *Après le Cubisme* to launch their reform, proposing an art of rigidly disciplined abstraction. Retaining the cubist idea of simultaneity but rejecting the gaiety of synthetic cubism, they returned to the hard, sharp character of analytical cubism. Above all, the forms of purism were to be of a mechanical clarity that would symbolize the twentieth century as the age of the machine. Léger, of course, held this same theory, but he applied it with a great deal of bounce in his

622. LE CORBUSIER: *Still-life*, 1920. 31⅞ x 39¼". Museum of Modern Art, New York.

623. NICHOLSON: *Relief*, 1939. Wood, painted, 32⅞ x 45". Museum of Modern Art, New York, Gift of H. S. Ede and the artist (by exchange).

brightly colored mechanistic conventionalizations. So did the futurists, but we have seen what happened to them. The forms of purism were austere, dry, and often all but devoid of color [622]. In itself purism never managed to strike very deep roots, but it

624. MORANDI: *Still-life*, 1948. 16 x 16″. Collection Mr. and Mrs. Leo Lionni, Greenwich, Conn.

625. LE CORBUSIER: Savoye House, 1929–31. Poissy, France.

contributed to the development of numerous artists, for instance the leader of abstract painting in England, Ben Nicholson (1894–   ), who has combined its principles with those of cubism and *De Stijl* in an art of great tact and distinction [623]. And

in the infinitely overlapping variations of contemporary painting, both Mondrian and purism may have left their mark on the reserved and pensive art of the Italian Giorgio Morandi (1890–   ), although the objects he adjusts into abstract relationships—a few ordinary bottles and bowls [624], combined and recombined in picture after picture, yet without monotony—retain their concrete reality.*

But if purism itself failed to develop significantly in painting, the cleanness of its forms and their adaptability to the design and manufacture of machine-tooled usable objects had a wide and truly "purifying" effect on industrial design. And as an architect Le Corbusier became one of the half dozen most influential men of the first part of the century, a leader in the theory and practice of design in the international style. His Savoye House [625] has become a standard example of the declaration of revolution in domestic architecture, not because it remains the most beautiful or the most livable modern residence—it is far from either—but because it was a progenitor of hundreds of designs that have adapted and developed its innovations with others in the sifting process that has created a new style. As an architectural analogy to purist theories of painting, the Savoye House is an abstract design of integrated flat and curved planes, of enclosed space and open space, defined in sharp clean lines. In a photograph, where a single static point of view is imposed, the Savoye House looks more severe than it does in three dimensions, when its elements are seen in shifting combinations from different angles. In regarding the house thus, as a composition of volumes, lines, and planes, we are regarding it less as architecture than as a piece of abstract sculpture on a large scale, and as such it is a more satisfying example of the theories of purism than were purist

---

* Two Americans, Charles Demuth (1883–1935) and Charles Sheeler (1883–   ), worked out a compromise between cubism and straightforward representation, often called cubist-realism, in which architectural or natural forms are geometrized with a nice precision which would justify their being included within the general area of purism.

paintings. The purist theories seemed to demand a physical third dimension for completion; the yearning for pure forms that led to the formation of purist theory also led to an expression in sculpture, that of Constantin Brancusi (1876–1957).

Brancusi's *Bird in Space* [626] is known everywhere, partly because one of the sculptor's many versions of this elongated form became conspicuous as the center of a dispute between the United States Customs, who wanted to tax it as bric-a-brac, and its owner, who wanted it to enter the country duty-free as a work of art—more as a matter of principle than because of the tax involved. The contest, with its decision in favor of the owner, was an introduction to the theory of abstract art for many people who would never have picked up a book on aesthetics but who did read newspaper excerpts from the testimony of artists and aestheticians who defended Brancusi's beautifully tooled brass object.

As a work of art, *Bird in Space* is at least a highly ornamental form, but this is true, also, of fine bric-a-brac. As sculpture, it is an invented shape of great purity and a certain expressive quality depending heavily upon our knowledge of the title. Many of Brancusi's works depend, for their full effect, upon the associations of a verbal clue (*White Negress, Chimera, The Newborn, The Prodigal Son, The Fish, Bird, Penguins,* to name a few). But his *Sculpture for the Blind* [627] is an exercise in pure sculptural form. By its title, this is a piece of sculpture to be handled, to be felt for its polished surface and the infinitely subtle variations of its generally egg-shaped volume. As a piece of sculpture for the sighted, *Sculpture for the Blind,* like most of Brancusi's work, would be seen ideally as it revolved slowly, so that its contours, as defined by their edges and by the areas of shadow, light, and reflections, would reveal themselves in an uninterrupted flow. (Even more ideally, it might be seen miraculously suspended in space, turning now in one direction, now in another.)

Like his contemporaries among painters, Brancusi was also influenced by the powerful simplified forms of primitive sculpture, especially in early work. *The Kiss* [628] is

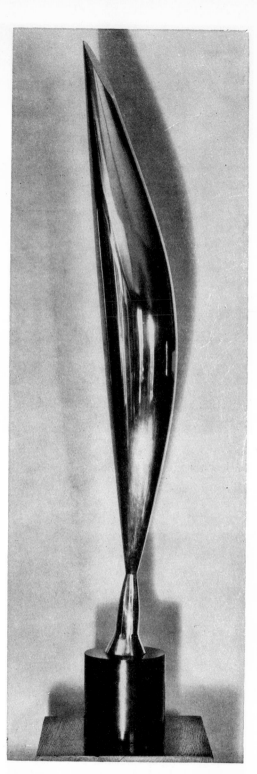

626. BRANCUSI: *Bird in Space,* 1925. Polished bronze, height 49¾". Philadelphia Museum of Art, Arensberg Collection.

627. BRANCUSI: *Sculpture for the Blind*, 1924. Marble, height 6″. Philadelphia Museum of Art, Arensberg Collection.

628. BRANCUSI: *The Kiss*, 1908. Limestone, height 23″. Philadelphia Museum of Art, Arensberg Collection.

an example. Its broad heavy forms are appropriate to the grainy limestone in which it is carved, just as the polished surfaces of *Sculpture for the Blind* are appropriate to marble, and the gleaming elongations of *Bird in Space* to brass. This love of the sculptor's materials for their own sake, the adaptation of form to the expression of the materials' inherent character, is a constant in Brancusi's work—or almost a constant. A failure is a marble version of *Bird in Space*, called *Yellow Bird*, where the veined and brittle stone has been forced into a form of such character that the weight of the upper mass is too much for the narrow necklike lowest part. In marble the design has the practical failing that the neck has cracked; the psychological failing is more important, leaving us as it does with an uncomfortable feeling of violation of the material.

629. GABO: *Linear Construction*, 1942–43. Plastic with nylon string, height 24¼″. Phillips Collection, Washington, D.C.

Whatever else they are, Brancusi's forms are solid masses, self-contained volumes of matter. This remark may seem too obvious to be worth setting down. It would be, if it were not necessary as an introduction to the concept of form introduced in constructivism, a movement born at about the same time as neo-plasticism and purism. Constructivism was a Russian development led by Vladimir Tatlin (1885–   ), finding its major spokesmen in the brothers

Naum Gabo (1890–   ) and Antoine Pevsner (1886–   ), who brought it into the international orbit via Paris and Germany.

A first principle of constructivism was that it denied solid volumes (like Brancusi's) as an expression of space. Gabo's *Linear Construction* [629] had better be looked at for a moment before this idea is tackled by anyone not yet a little familiar with it. *Linear Construction* is built of

630. MOORE: *Reclining Figure*, 1935. Elm wood, height 19″. Albright Art Gallery, Buffalo, Contemporary Art Collection.

transparent plastic. It is a piece of abstract sculpture, if you wish—more properly, however, a construction, just as it is called—which denies sculptural mass by its open design as well as by its transparent material. We have said that ideally Brancusi's *Sculpture for the Blind* would be seen in motion, so that its total mass could be examined in a flow of successive aspects. But Gabo's *Linear Construction* has no mass* and is, in effect, visible from all points of view at once. True, the object takes on variations—and fascinating ones—from different angles, but essentially it is visible as a whole, in all its complications, from any angle.

A little thought on the theories of analytical cubism will show that constructivism overlaps it. Cubist simultaneity sought to represent many aspects of the object at one time. *Linear Construction* actually does so. The "object" is not an object at all, in the

sense of being a tangible form. It is a spatial design. One enters the spatial shapes, visually; if this is sculpture, it is a molding of pure space. "Volume" and "space" now take on new meanings. Volume is no longer mass surrounded by empty space; space is no longer emptiness; space and volume are identical.

The space volumes of *Linear Construction* are arbitrary inventions by an artist, but they had a parallel in nineteenth century models rigged of string and thin metal or wood supports, which were used to demonstrate interlockings of forms in solid geometry, just as Gabo's plastic cords and plastic supports create space by defining it. The idea of space as volume instead of space as emptiness is applied in a different way by the English sculptor, Henry Moore (1898–   ), who finds his point of departure not in the man-made abstractions of geometry but in the forms of nature created by the growth of things and by the action of the elements.

Moore's hollowed-out forms [630, 631] require a new way of seeing sculpture.

---

* —unless one wants to be finicky about definitions. The transparent plastic has mass, strictly speaking, but psychologically it does not.

To understand them, the idea of sculpture as the shaping of solid masses must be abandoned. Moore is shaping mass, but simultaneously he is shaping voids, which are equally important as design. In other words, the "hollows" and "holes" are "negative volumes" just as the masses are "positive volumes." Structurally, Moore's sculpture creates interdependencies between solids and voids. In nature, similar "negative volumes" may be of extraordinary interest. The hollow in a tree trunk or the pits and underledges and sinkholes shaped by water in river beds or even the vortex in a whirlpool of water—all these are natural voids of whose shapes we are as conscious as we are of the solids surrounding them. In Moore's sculpture there is always a strong suggestion of natural forces. Where Brancusi takes stone and carves and polishes it to emphasize its inherent characteristics as a particular kind of solid matter, Moore oftener seems to be creating the stone itself, or the wood, or the bronze, in which his sculpture exists. His figures combine a hieratic severity with a feeling of natural growth, the genesis of life within inanimate materials. Inside a house or in a museum, Moore's sculpture may be reduced to an effective demonstration of a theory or to a piece of brilliant but eccentric design. Out of doors, where it properly belongs, it shares the serene and powerful unity of trees and rocks and air, which live, and change, in nature.

Such considerations of immediately contemporary sculpture reflect new importance on the sculpture of futurism, which preceded these examples by a generation. Boccioni's *Development of a Bottle in Space* [632] might be dismissed as a tour-de-force experiment in the materialization of the painted forms of futurism and cubism, until we see its sculptured space as an ancestor of Moore's in *Internal and External Forms*. Boccioni's bottle with its hollow core is half readymade for an analysis of "negative volumes" but the idea of spatial growth, of space turned and shaped, of voids interlocking, is present even so.

It might be argued that the idea of space as volume, inherent in these several examples of sculpture, is specious because a

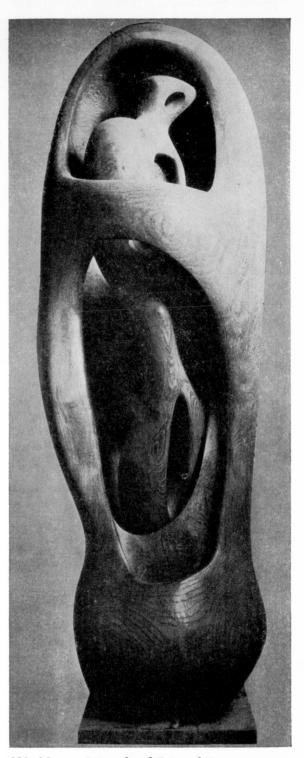

631. MOORE: *Internal and External Forms,* 1953–54. Elm wood, height 103″. Albright Art Gallery, Buffalo.

632. BOCCIONI: *Development of a Bottle in Space*, 1913. Bronze, 15 x 24″. Collection Mr. and Mrs. Harry Lewis Winston, Birmingham, Mich.

633. CALDER: *Horizontal Spines*, 1942. Steel and aluminum, height 53″. Addison Gallery of American Art, Andover, Mass.

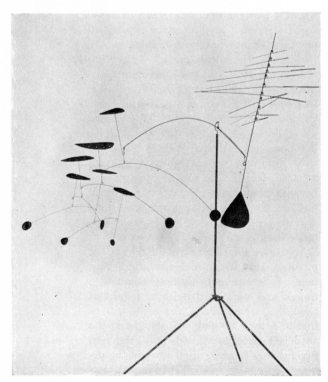

sculptor cannot construct solid forms without constructing, by inference, corresponding voids. But the argument does not hold. Brancusi's sculpture denies it. Space is only shapeless emptiness in which the solid of *Sculpture for the Blind* exists, but space lives and moves in *Internal and External Forms* just as truly as do the forms themselves. The idea of spatial movement has been given a specialized expression in the "mobile," which may be defined as a contrivance related to sculpture and composed of objects of various shapes suspended on jointed limbs in such a way that the component parts move, physically, into a variety of changing relationships when placed in a current of air. Invented by Alexander Calder (1898–   ), in whose hands they are never less than ingenious [633], and efficiently imitated by certain other craftsmen, mobiles are also widely prostituted as gadgets. As sculpture, the mobile is most closely related to the theories of constructivism, differing from *Linear Construction* in that it assumes a sequence of identities in space rather than revealing its total identity at one time.

CHAPTER 14

Reactions against Abstraction

The Mexican Renaissance

A rejection of abstract painting took place at about the same time in Europe and in America, but for different reasons. We are not talking here about painters who rejected abstraction on sight, but about men who examined it, even worked in it for a while, found it unsuited to what they wanted to say, and abandoned it. On both continents, anti-abstract schools flourished during the 1920's and the 1930's, while nonobjective painters were thinking their way to the logical conclusions of abstract art. In Europe the reaction took the form of extremest fantasy; on the American continent it took the opposite form of didactic social statement in the service of national or regional loyalties, first in Mexico and then in the United States.

Between 1907 and 1921, a young Mexican named Diego Rivera (1886–1957) was traveling in Europe and working in Spain and Paris. On a trip home in 1910 he held an exhibition of the painting he had done in Europe up until that time: it was a terrible group of pictures, heavy, labored, artificial, forced. But all the pictures sold because Rivera was a young man of good position, and the social patronage of the exhibition made it an event of some importance during the season.

Whatever the purchasers thought of the pictures, Rivera did not like them very much. Before going to Europe he had been trained and stimulated by three important teachers: one of them was a student of Ingres, named Reboul, who taught in the academic school in Mexico City. From him Rivera, only fourteen, had learned the exquisite draughtsmanship of the French clas-

634. RIVERA: *Head of a Woman*, 1917. Pencil, 12¼ x 9⅜". Collection Carl Zigrosser, Germantown, Pa.

635. POSADA: *Calvera Huertista*, 1913. Zinc engraving, 8½ x 8½". Collection Carl Zigrosser, Germantown, Pa.

sical tradition, which remained apparent on the surface of his early drawings [634] and, much later, continued as a basis for the control and precision of his definition of form in a more personal style. His other two masters were masters at secondhand. One of them was a popular engraver named José Guadalupe Posada (1852–1913), who was not taken too seriously as an artist at that time, when a certain stigma was attached to natively Mexican art; Posada has been recognized since as one of the powerful creative imaginations of his country. He combined macabre fantasy, passionate religious and sociological statement, and a kind of raucous wit in designs of great vitality [635]. He also kept a shop near the school Rivera attended, and the boy saw engravings of the old masters there, and Posada talked to him about them. The third teacher was the art of the ancient Mexican civilizations [636].

But Rivera's exhibition upon his return from his first trip to Europe showed none of these influences. It was sterile and derivative of poorly assimilated European models. Nevertheless he returned to Europe, where he stayed until 1921, floundering. Toward the end he discovered cubism, and he worked in it with a sharp, dry, pointless efficiency; he had some contact with Picasso, Derain, and Braque. Before he returned to Mexico again, however, he made a trip to Italy. Here he found a fourth teacher, the great frescoes of the Italian Renaissance. They acted as a catalyst, and after years of groping Rivera created, upon his return to Mexico, a nationalistic style virtually overnight. In the next ten years he covered wall after wall with frescoes that established an internationally recognized school of Mexican painting.

Nationalism of any kind in painting was unusual at that time, but Mexico was an unusual country. (The German expressionists had made an effort to revivify Germanic traditions, but these were cultural and expressive ones only.) Rivera conceived of a national art that would revive the cultural traditions native to Mexico and at the same time propagandize the new Mexican political regime. After years of inconsequential association with intellectual painters who worked on esoteric principles for the most cultivated audience, Rivera now about-faced and painted expository lessons in history and sociology for a people who, in the mass, were just emerging from illiteracy. In Mexico, the artist now became a cog in the social machine; he allied himself with his nation's welfare and made his contribution to it as a man working in the world, not as a rare and special individual in an ivory tower. With a new sense of social dedication, painters worked more in the capacity of civil servants than as individuals struggling for personal expression and recognition. Rivera and the other painters who were involved in this Mexican renaissance formed what amounted to a craftsmen's union.

Mexico was still assimilating the agrarian revolution that had dispossessed the corrupt landlords who had held the peons in feudal serfdom. The murals which now began to spread over the walls of public buildings were vividly decorative but they were also didactic, telling the story of the revolution, glorifying native traditions and festivals and legends, and excoriating the enemies of the people. The American financiers who profited from Mexico's natural resources, and the Mexican *bourgeoisie* who had tolerated their doing so were attacked in terms as obvious as comic strips, sometimes almost as exaggerated, but always with the most vehement conviction that Mexico must realize itself as a nation belonging to its people, and as a culture unique among the countries of the world. When the Mexican muralists of the 1920's descended to the most blatant propaganda and the rawest caricature, as they did again and again in intervals between lofty conceptions, it was because they were more interested in communicating with the proletariat than with aestheticians or political philosophers.

The Liberation of the Peon [637] is one of Rivera's finest compositions and his summary of the ideal of the agrarian revolution. It shows a landlord's hacienda burning in the distance while a group of revolutionary soldiers cut the peon's bonds and cover his naked body, scarred by the lash. It is a picture explicit enough for any illiterate

636. EAST COAST, MEXICO: *Head* (hatchet form), late Pre-Columbian. Green igneous rock, height 12″. Philadelphia Museum of Art, Arensberg Collection.

Mexican to understand as a story and as a national ideal. It is also a pictorial composition of considerable sophistication; this is the double character of Rivera's art. Technically, the painting is a pure example of *buon fresco*, or true fresco, in the great Italian tradition by which unbound pigments are painted directly onto the moist fresh plaster of a wall.* As the plaster dries,

* Unbound pigments are pure pigments without the "binder" of oil, glue, or other adhesive that turns them into paint. Pigments "bound" with oil become oil paint; pigments "bound" with an adhesive soluble in water become watercolor; those with any one of several albuminous substances are tempera, and so on. The fresco illustrated here was done on plaster held within a strong metal frame, rather than directly on a plastered wall as is customary, in order that this variation on one of Rivera's finest subjects could be exhibited in the United States.

637. RIVERA: *The Liberation of the Peon*, 1931. Fresco, variation of fresco in Ministry of Education, 1923–27, Mexico City. 74 x 95″. Philadelphia Museum of Art, Gift of Mr. and Mrs. Herbert C. Morris.

the pigments, incorporated into it, take on a soft grainy brilliance, combined as they are with the crystalline film that forms on the plaster's surface. True fresco is one of the oldest, the noblest, and one of the most demanding, of techniques.

Rivera's first murals under the new program were executed in encaustic, a form of painting in hot wax. In beginning his second series he experimented with the juice of the native agave plant as a binder—an idea with obvious attractions to a new nationalistic school, especially since the medium was the traditional one of pre-Columbian Mexican painting. The experiments were not successful; spots and discolorations developed, and Rivera adopted the *buon fresco* of the Italian masters he had

admired on the trip just before his return. In reviving fresco, Rivera completed the separation of painting from the studio, the dealer's gallery, and the limited audience. He re-established art as a part of the life of the people in a way that had had no parallel since the medieval cathedrals and the Renaissance churches had told the story of the Bible in sculpture, stained glass, and fresco, where everyone could read them. The buildings he decorated included the Ministry of Education, the Governor's Palace at Cuernavaca, the chapel of the Agricultural School at Chapingo [638], and, later, the Lerma Waterworks and the University and Social Security Hospital.

Rivera always tried to combine his contemporary social and political message with

638. RIVERA: *The Blood of Martyrs Enriches the Earth*, 1926–27. Fresco from Chapel of National Agricultural School, Chapingo, length approximately 160″.

639. RIVERA: *Sugar Cane*, 1931. Fresco, variation of fresco in the Palace of Cortez, Cuernavaca, 1930, 58 x 95″. Philadelphia Museum of Art, Gift of Mr. and Mrs. Herbert C. Morris.

506

640. South wall of court of Detroit Institute of Arts, with frescoes by Rivera, 1932–33. *Top:* two races of the continent (white and Oriental); *immediately below:* raw materials (lime and sand); *main panel:* assembly of an automobile.

another message to the Mexican people, glorifying whatever native racial and cultural roots survived the Spanish conquest, combining the story of Mexican history with illustrations of Aztec legends and of Mexican festivals and folk customs descended from the lost past. The noble figures in his murals, who may be historical or legendary characters or gods of the native earth, are likely to be painted as ethnologically pure Indian types, while his villains, if they are not North Americans, are usually Spanish ones. The Spanish-Indian hybrid we think of as the typical Mexican may serve in either capacity, but is most likely to turn up as a corrupt or stuffy little man. Rivera himself was one quarter Tarascan Indian, with a mixture of Russian, Spanish, and Portuguese Jewish ancestors making up the balance.

A first-rate mural painter is necessarily a decorator, no matter what else he may more

significantly be. In *The Liberation of the Peon* the conventionalized forms of the cartridge belts, the rope around the neck of the horse to the left, and other such decorative details are almost conspicuous enough to distract attention from subject and decrease its impact. In later work Rivera depended more and more on the decorative elements of the style he had developed, and less and less on saying very much with it as the fruits of the agrarian revolution were either harvested or irretrievably lost. Even in the early *Sugar Cane* [639] we are impressed first with the attractiveness of the picture as decoration, and have to look a second time to read its message. An anemic Nordic landowner lounges in a hammock while a sharp-featured overseer with a whip supervises some presumably oppressed but actually quite happy and healthy looking Indians who are harvesting as laborers on land, which, we presume, should belong to them. But the sociological message must be deciphered; it does not reach us at firsthand, as it does in *The Liberation of the Peon*. Eventually Rivera began repeating himself as a decorator with an effective formula.

After Rivera had established himself as an artist of major importance he was invited to the United States where he did frescoes in San Francisco, Detroit, and New York. He had never been in the United States except to pass through, and now he was impressed, as foreigners always are, with the briskness and mechanization of American life. In Detroit he adopted a mechanistic style and covered the walls of a classical court in the Detroit Institute of Arts [640] with clashing symbols of the city's industrial life. But the murals occupy the walls like a temporary exhibition which there was not quite room enough to hang, and although they are by a contemporary painter and a native of the American continent, they are less at home than are the collections of old masters and the fragments of ancient civilizations in the rooms near by. Rivera's dry and labored representation of an automobile assembly line is much less than second best to the precision and excitement and color of an assembly line itself; the mechanistic idea is not transmuted into terms that enlarge or clarify its meaning. The effort to give wide significance to the murals by such inclusions as symbols of the four races of man making up our population, and of the minerals mined and used in industry, makes an admirable outline of a project. Yet the scheme, completed, remains an outline, conscientiously worked out. The failure of the Detroit murals demonstrated, at least, the validity of the idea behind the Mexican renaissance —that art should be an integral part of the life of its country, created by artists identified with the roots of native culture.

Rivera's New York murals met with disaster of another kind. They were destroyed after he refused to make changes that would have eliminated references to communism which were unacceptable to his capitalist sponsors. (The murals were for Rockefeller Center, in New York.) The incident became a celebrated one in which the paint-

641. Orozco: *Barricade*, 1931. 55 x 45". Museum of Modern Art, New York.

er's right to paint what he pleased was defended as a kind of freedom of speech. However, the sponsors' legal right to destroy the works could not be questioned, whatever moral rights and wrongs were involved, and destroyed they were.

Rivera's position as the leader of the Mexican renaissance was weakened as his work grew more superficial and that of one of his fellows, José Clemente Orozco (1883–1949), matured. While Rivera was in Paris, Orozco was in Mexico doing genre scenes with a strong revolutionary flavor, involving the sordid and brutal lives imposed on common people, especially the Indians. In the first efflorescence of nationalistic murals, Orozco made a brief effort to impose Italian Renaissance forms on his style, but his native violence kept breaking through. Finally he ceased being a

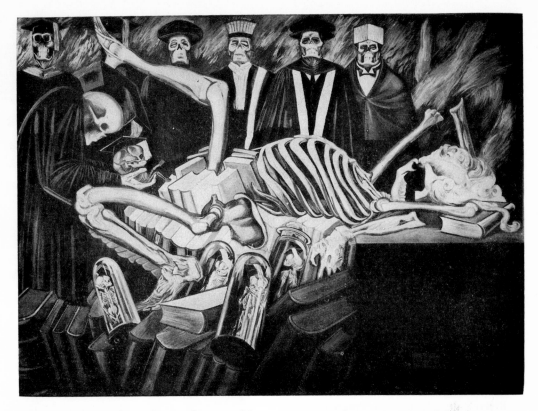

642. OROZCO: *Gods of the Modern World*, 1932–34. Detail, 126 x 176″, of fresco at Dartmouth College, Hanover, N. H.

mural painter in the sense of a decorator of walls, and became a sociological expressionist who used walls to carry his message, even at the expense of violating the character of walls and the interior enclosed.

Orozco plays on the double theme of the ominousness of humanity as a dangerous mass, capable of the vilest cruelties, and the suffering of human beings as individuals. He sees humanity as at once the victim and its own victimizer, and he presents the idea in stretched, starved, and tortured forms [641]. Fantastic and grotesque figures play through his work; these are part of Orozco's native heritage from the Mexican past, from Aztec religious practices and legends that have survived in popular Mexican celebrations, as well as in some of the morbidities of Spanish customs that have fused with them. Skeletons, monsters, beasts, the whole range of the terrifying and the macabre, are inherent in Mexican folk tradition and are incorporated into its

humor and the revelry of its festivals as well as the depths of Mexican consciousness. The work of Posada [635] was a spontaneous expression of this tradition, and influenced Orozco strongly.

For Orozco, macabre fantasy was a symbol of the darkness of the human spirit, sometimes savage, sometimes blinded by prejudice or apathy, as in the scene of a skeleton giving birth [642] to another skeleton while skeleton attendants in academic robes stand by. This symbol of the sterility of academic learning cloistered from contact with life was painted for Dartmouth College as one panel in a series of overpowering murals not always flattering to the United States or to higher education, but undeniably among Orozco's finest work. Unlike Rivera, Orozco made no effort to modify his style when he was invited to the United States. Students who met him during his visit remember a man much less violent than the Dartmouth murals—a

643. OROZCO: *Cortez and the Cross, and the Machine*, 1932–34. Fresco, 126 x 288″. Dartmouth College, Hanover, N. H.

lively, genial, stocky little man wearing glasses with enormously thick lenses, eager to share his ideas and to understand the people around him. Orozco's other murals in the United States are at Pomona College, California, and the New School, New York City. Before these, in Mexico, he did murals in the National Preparatory School, the House of Tiles, and the Industrial School at Orizaba; after his return to Mexico he did others—and his most violent ones—in the Palace of Fine Arts, the Governor's Palace, and the Orphanage at Guadalajara.

In the last years of his life Orozco adopted a machinistic and abstract style, already prophesied in the right half of one of the Dartmouth murals [643]. He explained that in machine forms his theme was the same as the one that runs through all his work—protest against oppression. The oppression in the late works is the oppression of the machine, sometimes the machine as an instrument of destruction, especially the machines of war. But these experiments are not altogether successful; Orozco seems to have been too intensely human a man to have dealt successfully with the impersonality of the machine, even when he interpreted it as a menace to the humanity with which he was so closely allied.

Mexico: The Second Generation

Rivera and Orozco are one generation of painters; they were nearing forty when the mural program got under way. At this time David Alfaro Siqueiros (1898–   ) and Rufino Tamayo (1899–   ) were in their middle twenties. Siqueiros had fought in the revolution in his teens and he worked with the older men in the mural program, but in his development as a painter thereafter he was increasingly theoretical. Where Orozco was a bridge between the old Mexico and the new, Siqueiros is part of modern Mexico as a nation with international ties and an eye to the future, in terms of trade unionism and industrial development rather than the eruptive force of revolution.

Siqueiros studied in Europe for two years, but his interest there was in discovering the means to express the potential vitality of his country in surging, heroic forms. He returned just as the national mural program was getting under way and did his first mural in the National Preparatory School. He also led in the organization of the Syndicate of Technical Workers, Painters, and Sculptors that gave definition to the Mexican renaissance as part of the social fabric, and since then he has been equally active as a social organizer (an ac-

344. SIQUEIROS: *War*, 1939. Duco on two panels, 48½ x 63½″. Philadelphia Museum of Art, Gift of Ines Amor.

tivity that has resulted in several imprisonments) and as an artist. A man with a practical turn of mind, he has developed the use of modern materials, for instance pyroxylin and Duco for outdoor murals. *War* [644], though an easel study, is in the latter medium. It is a good example of the gigantic swelling forms, surging in and out of space, that evolved as his heroic style.

Tamayo represents the absorption of the Mexican tradition into the mainstream of contemporary painting. The cubist and fauvist principles in *Women of Tehuantepec* [645] should be obvious to the reader

by now. Coloristically, Tamayo is one of the most exciting of contemporary painters. He may paint an entire canvas in reds; his combinations of magentas, blues, oranges, lemons, pearl whites, mauves, lilacs, purples, crimsons and vermilions suggest the colors of native weaving and other crafts, colors which may be vividly ornamental or may reach a pitch of feverish intensity, especially when they are combined with subjects where the fantastic and the macabre lie threateningly beneath the surface of blazing pigments.

Yet, while Tamayo continues to use native subject matter, to incorporate echoes of pre-Columbian and popular Mexican art, he rejects the provincialism of paintings as revolutionary propaganda or history with a political or social "message." He is as closely tied to Picasso and Braque as he is to his native traditions. Thus, although he is the same age as Siqueiros, within a year, he represents the end of a tradition, the last stop on the round trip made by Mexican art in a matter of a third of a century. Before Rivera, Mexican art reflected that of Europe; Rivera rejected Europe in the 1920's and established a school of nationalistic social realism; Siqueiros accepted European isms but continued the nationalistic idea; Tamayo abandoned strong nationalism for European reference. The difference after a generation is that before 1920 the European flavor of Mexican art was European academic, while now it tastes of European modern.

345. TAMAYO: *Women of Tehuantepec*, 1939. 34 x 57″. Albright Art Gallery, Buffalo, Contemporary Art Collection.

511

Regionalists and Social Realists

During the first years of the Mexican renaissance, the United States was engaged in the social and economic saturnalia of the 1920's, the "jazz age," which a current generation is finding rather quaint in retrospect. The country as a whole was not very art-conscious, although *Nude Descending a Staircase* was still good for a syndicated feature article from time to time, and the word *impressionistic* occurred frequently in the conversation of aspirants to culture, referring to any form of painting that was in any way puzzling. In metropolitan centers like New York, Boston, Philadelphia, and Chicago, where an artist might hope to make a living, painters fell into three general groups. There were the well-entrenched conservative men who followed such models as Chase and Sargent or branched off rashly into impressionism; there were the men who were absorbing expressionism, cubism, and fauvism—Hartley and Marin, for instance; and there was the America-first group of the Ash Can School and its descendants.

The Ash Can painters were a metropolitan group dedicated to genre subjects of city life, but by the end of the decade a post-Ash Can generation was extending its interest beyond the city limits into the American countryside, not as landscapists but as observers of people and customs. They were led there by writers like Sinclair Lewis with his *Main Street* in 1920 and Sherwood Anderson with *Winesburg, Ohio*, a year earlier, writers who had shattered the ideal concept of the United States as a country entirely dedicated to the observance of the Ten Commandments and the Boy Scout oath, and had found cruelty, injustice, stupidity, and pathological emotions existing in the hinterlands where the good, the true, and the beautiful had, by convention, been accepted as flourishing uncorrupted. There had been indications that painters were as aware as writers; as early as 1916 George Bellows produced an exceptional one, the bitter lithograph *Benediction in Georgia* [646].

In 1930 two American artists emerged who were to carry this new form of Ameri-

646. BELLOWS: *Benediction in Georgia*, 1916. Lithograph, 15 x 20". Philadelphia Museum of Art.

can consciousness into painting, first with the skeptical eye of the writers but later with a kind of defensive chauvinism for the culture of the Middle West which before long reduced their promising movement to insignificance. These painters were Thomas Hart Benton (1889–   ) and Grant Wood (1892–1942). A third was John Steuart Curry (1897–1946), who two years earlier had indicated what was about to happen with his *Baptism in Kansas* [647]. The three men and their followers came to be known as regionalists, a name in which the character and a hint of the limitations of their art is implicit.

Baptism in Kansas is a romantic genre picture, half-sociological and half-narrative; half-sympathetic to the rites pictured in it, half-uneasy about them. With a barn, a farmhouse, and a windmill in the background, a young girl with her hands clasped in ecstasy is about to be submerged in the livestock's watering trough, turned for the afternoon into a baptismal pool in the parched countryside. The neighbors who are gathered around, including other white-clad neophytes awaiting their turn, are rural types presented without idealization. Another step or two in the direction the

647. CURRY: *Baptism in Kansas*, 1928. 40 x 50″. Whitney Museum of American Art, N. Y.

picture takes to this point would have turned it into caricature. Instead, Curry painted the sky with glowing clouds and shafts of light to identify the crude ceremony with its mystical purpose. Unfortunately he also added a pair of doves circling in the radiance. These, of course, occupy the position of the dove of the Holy Spirit that hovers in radiance above the figure of Christ in pictures of the Baptism. But the introduction here of a pair of farm pigeons occupying by too-happy coincidence the space between rays of sunlight, forces the point and turns what might have been an affecting picture into a novelty, like Hamlet in modern dress, which was a popular tour de force innovated at about the same time.

Curry was born on a stock farm in Kansas and was educated at the art institutes of Kansas City and Chicago. Thereafter he made his living as an illustrator until he studied in Paris for a year. As a painter he

stayed close to traditional sources; he is a descendant of Rubens and Ruisdael, appropriate ancestors for Curry's fullest expressions of the richness and sweep that he felt in the life of his native region. Of all the regionalists, Curry was the least spectacular and at first acquaintance is the least interesting. But the very eccentricities that draw first attention to Benton and Wood are also the characteristics that have come to seem so artificial that they are disharmonious to the regional idea with its rural and homely subjects. Curry may yet prove to be the tortoise who wins the race over the two local hares.

At the moment it would be difficult—probably impossible—to find a critic of established reputation who would be willing to write a really enthusiastic comment on the art of Thomas Hart Benton, although it would be easy to confront half a dozen of them with their favorable articles written some years ago. Benton became a re-

648. BENTON: *Louisiana Rice Fields,* 1928. 30 x 48″. Brooklyn Museum.

gionalist by taking the long way around. He was born in Missouri, but as the son of a United States senator he spent his youth in Washington. Although he returned to the Middle West to study at the Art Institute of Chicago, he spent the five years between 1908 and 1913 in Paris, and even after his return to this country he experimented with cubism. He might have kept at it, but his painting was interrupted by a tour of duty in the Navy during World War I; thereafter he returned to the American scene, touring the country to sketch it. He came into sudden prominence in 1930 with a series of murals for the New School for Social Research in New York, followed immediately by another series for the Whitney Museum of American Art. The first murals included a few inferences that the American scene was not altogether halcyon; the second already began the jingoism that so soon infected regionalist painting. Almost any picture from that time is as good an example as the next to represent his fully developed formula, which is of an extreme repetitiousness. With Tintoretto and El Greco as his models, Benton conventionalized their mannerisms into a linear recipe for picture-making, which combined almost spastic pattern with tilted and shifting per-

spectives that remain as his only tie to cubism [648].

After skyrocketing successes in New York, Benton decided to renounce the effete East. He returned to the Middle West, but he drew no sustenance from it. Whether he was painting Kentucky hillbillies, Texas oil towns, Kansas harvesters, or genre scenes from the life of his fellow Missourians, as he did in a large set of murals for the State Capitol, he poured everything into the same mold, a mold that had the disadvantage of having no aesthetic, expressive, or traditional connection with his subjects. For a moment Benton's art seemed exciting; shortly, it became monotonous. But the flare of attention created by his first murals brought about a revival of mural painting in the United States, for Benton was the first American to take advantage of the Mexican demonstration that mural painting had not died with the Renaissance but had only been lying fallow.*

* The revival took on unexpected importance in the United States within the next few years because of an unhappy circumstance: the great economic depression of the early 1930's. The year before Benton painted his New School murals, the stock market had crashed, and within the next few years the nation suffered

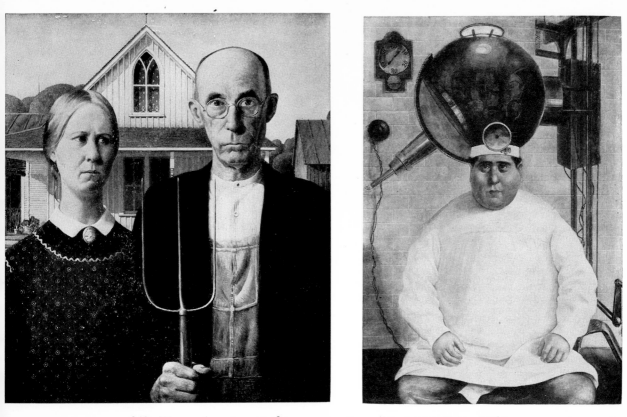

649. WOOD: *American Gothic*, 1930. 29⅞ x 24⅞″. Art Institute of Chicago.

650. DIX: *Dr. Mayer-Hermann*, 1926. Panel, 58¾ x 39″. Museum of Modern Art, New York.

The third member in the trio of regionalist leaders was Grant Wood of Iowa, whose *American Gothic* [649] won a national award in 1930, the year of Benton's New School murals. *American Gothic* was an immediately attractive picture, and still is, to a large public that had learned to be suspicious of realistic academic painting but was fatigued by the effort to understand what the new European isms were all about. The impeccable surface was a relief to people who yearned for conventional craftsmanship in painting, and at the same time the picture was original in its piquant use of such commonplace things as gingham, rickrack braid, a pitchfork, and jigsaw carpentry as ornamental figures in a work of art. And it explored the new subject matter of rural America, not unflatteringly enough to give offense but with enough

one of the most painfully chastening experiences in its history. At the nadir of the depression, Franklin D. Roosevelt initiated the public works programs that gave employment to thousands of people in—usually—useful capacities. The inclusion of the arts program with the more practical ones of road-building and other public construction was epoch-making in a country where official art patronage on a significant scale was unheard of. The nation's schools, postoffices, and courthouses were suddenly covered with murals celebrating American history and local customs, influenced by the Mexicans on one hand and by the re-

gionalists on the other. They were executed by artists ranging from students and incompetents up to artists of deserved national reputation, and they varied from excellent to daubs that have since been taken down or painted out and can be remembered only with pain. On the whole, the art program was of tremendous benefit. Aside from supplying artists with money for food—an important consideration at the time but not the most important one in the long run—it gave the painter a new professional respectability with the mass of the American public, and even gave the painter himself a new kind of self-respect as a workman.

acidity to satisfy the new self-critical consciousness stimulated by *Main Street* and its successors, since the farmer and his wife are represented as severe and narrow people. Grant Wood became a celebrity overnight (even his name was in his favor, full of sturdy connotations, exactly the name that should have been invented for the man who painted his pictures), and each new work appeared everywhere, in popular magazines as well as in the art journals. Both Wood and Benton were as widely and as favorably publicized as any American artists who have ever worked. They received a wonderful press during the 1930's.

Wood also had his European precedents, but they were more adaptable to domestication than Benton's were. Late expressionism, *Die Neue Sachlichkeit*, was among them, without the bitterness and despair of the German model, but with the smooth-surface realism of some works by Dix [650] and Grosz. So were early Flemish and German portraits, with their realistic definition and their capitalization on details of costume as ornamental design. But the virus that attacked American regionalism and drained it of significant content soon affected Wood; his style became a formula. In *The Midnight Ride of Paul Revere* [651] it is difficult to find more than an exercise in conventionalization, where a toy rider on a toy horse gallops through a toy town for no purpose.

The exploration of America proceeded in other regions than the Middle West. In New York, Reginald Marsh (1898–1954) was one of the liveliest of the painters who grew out of the Ash Can tradition. Sometimes he painted the city as objectively as the Ash Can men did, although he preferred the sordidness of the Bowery and the subway to the animation of Times Square and the intimacy of Greenwich Village, approaching such subjects in the spirit of such eighteenth-century Englishmen as Rowlandson or even Hogarth. Sometimes his satirical comment was cutting, as in *They Pay to Be Seen* [652].

Some other painters saw the American scene romantically beneath a genre surface. Charles Burchfield (1893–   ) was a Middle Westerner who anticipated the

651. WOOD: *The Midnight Ride of Paul Revere,* 1931. 30 x 40″ Metropolitan Museum of Art, New York, George A. Hearn Fund

652. MARSH: *They Pay to Be Seen,* 1934. 23¾ x 20″. Philadelphia Museum of Art, Hinchman Bequest.

653. BURCHFIELD: *Backyards in Spring*, 1946. Watercolor, 33 x 44″. Philadelphia Museum of Art, Gift of Mrs. Herbert C. Morris.

654. HOPPER: *Early Sunday Morning*, 1930. 30 x 40″. Whitney Museum of American Art, New York.

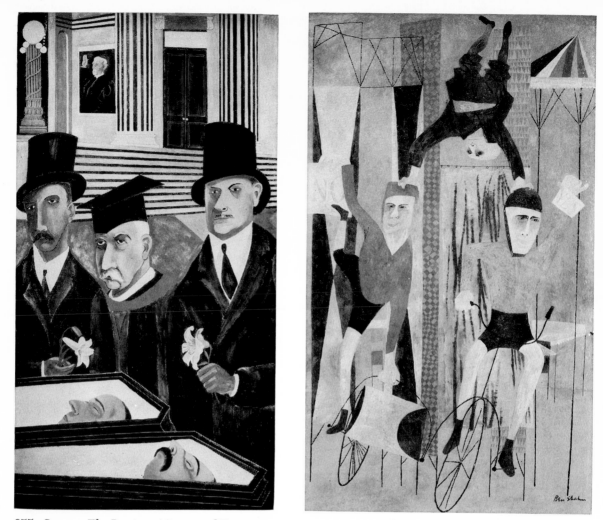

655. SHAHN: *The Passion of Sacco and Vanzetti*, 1931–32. 84½ x 48″. Whitney Museum of American Art, New York, Gift of Mr. and Mrs. Milton Lowenthal in memory of Juliana Force.

656. SHAHN: *Epoch*, 1950. 52 x 31″. Philadelphia Museum of Art, Bloomfield Moore Fund.

regionalist flurry by drawing material from his native ground, and continued quietly and sincerely after regionalism had degenerated into the exploitation of personal mannerism. Burchfield is primarily a watercolorist, although he has worked in oil, and in addition to his revelation of a romantic mood in the shabbiness of small towns [653] he has painted in semi-abstract expressionist ways. The quality of mystery and gentle resignation distinguishes his picturizations of the Middle West from the work of any other painter who can be called

regionalist. In the East, Edward Hopper (1882–   ) discovered a comparable quality in the city and in the rural refuges of New Yorkers, such as Cape Cod. He paints landscapes or cityscapes immobilized in a flat, brilliant light, whether it is the electric light of the city or the sunlight of the country. His individuals, in either setting, are lonely and isolated in a world of harsh, simplified, blocky forms represented in meticulously studied clarity [654].

Social consciousness in one form or another and to varying degrees is an element

557. SHAHN: *"Nearly Everybody Reads The Bulletin,"* 1946. 18⅞ x 20⅝". Collection Louis E. Stern, New York.

in the conceptions of all these painters, sometimes so superficially that it becomes only a genre observation of folkways or cityways of life, sometimes so romantically that the observation of the contemporary world as a social or visual phenomenon is less important than the discovery of moods generated within it. Basically, this has been a list of conservative or even reactionary painters, implying that the artist who turns to social comment necessarily divorces himself from the various intellectualized isms of Europe. Yet the painter who has made the most searching comments among social realists is the one who has been most affected, stylistically, by abstraction.

Ben Shahn (1898–   ) was born in Lithuania, but came to this country as a child and was educated in Brooklyn schools and at New York University and City College, and in the National Academy of Design. He was thus a melting-pot American rather than a regional grass-rooter. Possibly for this reason the School of Paris made a more lasting impression on him, when he went back to Europe for a period of travel and study, than it did on Benton or, in Mexico, Rivera. He fused into his art whatever modern European influences remained valuable to him as a painter working not only in America but as an American.

There is certainly more than coincidence in the fact that while the regionalists were at the height of their popularity, the United States was dominated by the "America First" group of isolationist politicians with their stronghold in the Middle West, who believed that this country could exist free of European entanglements. The provincial chauvinism of self-consciously American painting was an expression of the same spirit. Shahn's American character is that of the contemporary international man whose examination of his own country and his own time must take into consideration the character of the world of which his country is inevitably a part, the man whose patriotism is not blind faith, but a matter of the individual's obligation to see clearly, to fight injustice and corruption and stupidity wherever they infect national life. In 1933–1934 Shahn did a series of paintings on Prohibition, beyond doubt a gross blunder in the history of American government, but not a subject that would have occurred as a possible one to any of the other painters we have been seeing. (Benton did a few picturesque moonshiners.) As a painter of protest, Shahn's position was liberal or even leftist; he worked with Rivera, for instance, on the Rockefeller Center murals that were destroyed. But he has acted on social convictions rather than arbitrary political loyalties, and the causes he has espoused, and the evils he has attacked, as in the case of Sacco and Vanzetti [655], are ones in which history and sentiment, in retrospect, have upheld liberal attitudes.

Painting as protest against specific circumstance is self-limited. The Sacco and Vanzetti series may always tell as good painting, but it must always tell first in connection with a certain event in the frame of a certain time. Probably for this reason, Shahn grew from his militant, but thoughtful protests into more generalized symbolical social observation. In *Epoch* [656] he comments on the general character of our times: a little figure who seems not too at home in his acrobatic position is balanced upside down on the shoulders of two performing cyclists, one bearing a placard "yes," the other denying him with

658. SHAHN: *Silent Music*, 1951. Silk screen stencil, 17¼ x 35". Philadelphia Museum of Art, Harrison Fund.

a "no." The precariousness of the situation is pointed up by the bright carnivalesque shapes and colors, symbolical no doubt of the agitation and false gaiety of a world that offers a great deal of moment-to-moment distraction but very little stability. The mood is not solemn, but wry. Wry, too, and sardonic, is *"Nearly Everybody Reads the Bulletin"* [657]. The use of newspaper made into a fool's cap to cover the empty head of an inert figure who sits uncomprehending and uncaring is symbolical of the inertia with which people reject consciousness and action in a world where vigilance is the price of moral life. In other pictures the symbolism is more obscure and is probably personal. At times, too, Shahn is an artist of pure fantasy.

Shahn is one of the fine stylists of his day. The attractiveness of his economical, rather wiry draughtsmanship has led to a spate of derivations among other painters and imitations or downright plagiarisms in the field of commercial art, to such an extent that it is possible to speak of a "Ben Shahn school," although it is a false one based on the leader's technical inventiveness rather than on the significance which, in his own art, this inventiveness serves. Nor, of course, must every one of Shahn's own pictures be expected to carry a message. Among his inventions where sheer ingenuity is sufficient in itself, there are such prints as *Silent Music* [658], where folding chairs and music stands are grouped into a rhythm of lines and spaces nearly as abstract as one of Mondrian's "plus and minus" compositions.

Surrealism

While the realist rejection of abstract intellectualisms was manifesting itself in the kind of painting we have just been seeing, fantastic and visionary painting was flourishing with equal vigor. The climax of this kind of thing came in surrealism. This does not mean that surrealism is the apogee of visionary art. It is not—not even in its own century. But it was a kind of fantasy peculiar to its century, and it will be convenient to discuss it first, and then see where it came from and what it led to.

Surrealism is based on the idea of shock through paradox, the idea of giving such a jolt to surface consciousness that it is dislocated to reveal the hidden mysteries that affect it. In surrealism these mysteries are usually morbid. Its immediate parallel outside the field of art is psychoanalysis, which probes the darkness of the pathological spirit to discover rational explanations for irrational conduct. There is a

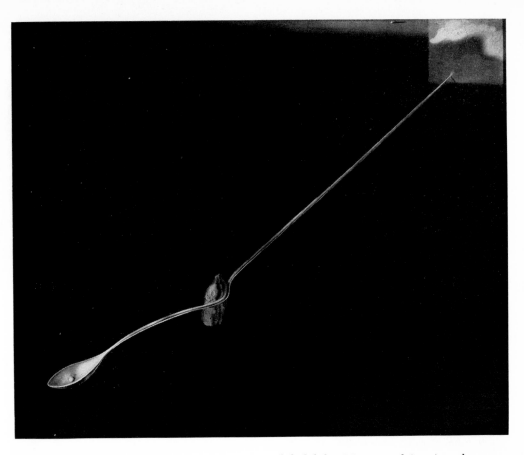

659. DALI: *Agnostic Symbol,* 1932. 21⅜ x 25⅜″. Philadelphia Museum of Art, Arensberg Collection.

terrible rationality to surrealism, the rationality of nightmare. In the world of dream and the world of insanity, the most fantastic action is rational to the dreamer or the lunatic because it is the end result of previous experiences that dictate it. These previous experiences may be warped and out of kilter; all the same, they are present, and they demand the fantastic dream or the lunatic behavior as their logical expression.

Surrealism investigates this terrible world, this modern witches' dreambook where everything is vividly real, yet where nothing is what it seems to be. The basic paradox of surrealist painting is that every detail of every explicitly represented image is undeniably *there.* It undeniably exists— yet at the same time it cannot exist because it is outside the realm of possibility. Surrealism takes us into a world where the

impossible and the undeniable are one and the same thing—and naturally it bothers us. It is intended to do so.

As an example: everyone has seen a beach or a deep plain. Everyone has seen a spoon. Everyone has seen driftwood. Everyone has seen sky. Everyone has seen a small gold watch. But no one has seen a beach or plain upon which there rests a rectangular segment of sky, cut from its place in heaven in order to accommodate the issuance of a long-handled spoon that stretches toward us, curving around a piece of driftwood en route, and finally offers us a tiny gold watch held in its bowl and marking the hour as 6:04 o'clock. At least we have not seen it until we have seen *Agnostic Symbol* [659], in which these familiar and quite ordinary items are combined in this extraordinary way by Salvador Dali (1904–   ). The circumstance represented in this picture is preposterous, impossible, it cannot exist. But it does exist. Because there it is, explicitly, down to the last groove on the stem of the watch.

Just what the symbolism of the picture is, it is not easy to say, although one may play around in several directions with the title as a clue. Surrealism in principle denies any programmatic symbolizing, since its images are supposed to be dictated to the painter from the depths of the unconscious, the source of dreams. At least this is a tenet held to by one group of surrealists, including Dali, in a movement where personal antagonisms and contradictions have been extreme. But in Dali's most celebrated picture, *The Persistence of Memory* [660], the symbolism is clear enough. At a glance the theme is concerned with time and decay. The most obvious symbols are the watches and the dead tree, and the jellyfishlike monster melting on the beach. Scavenger ants attack one of the watches, with no success. We deduce from this that the symbolism is also concerned with immortality, the triumph of something or other over the forces of decay. The watches are a symbol not only of time, but of infinite time, eternity, impervious to the frustrated insects who would devour them. They are also limp; somebody has bent time to his will. Who? The artist, of course, since he painted them that way. Thus seen, the picture is a restatement in fantastic terms of an old idea, popular in antiquity and in the Renaissance: the idea that through creative works during his mortal life, the artist defeats time and achieves immortality.

Ordinarily, however, surrealist images take the form of free invention in whatever startling combinations the painter can work up. When he cannot invent them, he can borrow them from numerous sources, either from pictures in the past or from the textbooks of abnormal psychology. Objects selected at random and combined arbitrarily may yield the most unexpected juxtapositions, and surrealism has been the most prostituted of all twentieth-century movements in painting, the most vulnerable to charlatanism. It offers a dangerously tolerant recipe for novelty painting, by which

660. DALI: *The Persistence of Memory*, 1931. 9½ x 13″. Museum of Modern Art, New York.

any painter with a skill for accurate photographic realism may do a still-life of objects rationally represented in irrational combinations, with a good chance of approximating surrealist values.

In Dali's case the qualifying factor is a special talent for diseased and disgusting imagery; the two adjectives are those of an English critic, the late George Orwell, who uses them to conclude an essay on Dali.[*] Commenting on Dali's statement, "At seven I wanted to be Napoleon. And my ambition has been growing steadily ever since," Orwell wrote, "Suppose that you have nothing in you except your egoism and a dexterity that goes no higher than the elbow; suppose that your real gift is for a detailed, academic, representational style of drawing. . . . How then do you become Napoleon? There is always one escape: *into wickedness.*" Certainly "a dexterity that goes no higher than the elbow" is the most murderous phrase in the history of criticism.

An element of charlatanism has come to be inherent in the total nature of surrealism, since its emphasis on shock values legitimizes any excess. Some of Dali's work is

[*] "Benefit of Clergy," in *Dickens, Dali, and Others*, 1946. The essay was written in 1944 as a review of Dali's book, *The Secret Life of Salvador Dali.*

GVLA·

EBRIETAS EST VITANDA, INGLVVIESQVE CIBORVM·

Schout dronckenschap / en gulsichspck eten Want ouerdaet doet godt en hem seluen verghoten.

661. BRUEGEL: *Allegory of Gluttony*, 1558. Engraving 8⅞ x 11½″. Philadelphia Museum of Art, Phillips Collection.

saved from pornographic implication only through the exercise of great agility in aesthetic semantics. For more general consumption, his excesses run to the public buffoonery for which he has become famous, with his foot-long moustache, his recent burial and rebirth from a coffin (a stunt that received very little notice from a jaded press), his insistence that he has the fondest recollections of his life in his mother's womb, his proud claim to paranoia during his life outside it, his published "autobiography" which includes a photograph of himself nude and describes enough psycho-pathological experiences to make him the one-man madhouse of the Age of Freud. To speak this way about any man but Dali would be libelous; to speak thus about him is only to recognize his success in establishing his surrealist personality. If surrealism is built on the paradox of the rational-irrational, so is Dali's career. His irrational behavior has been directed with

acutely rational consistency—and success— toward the goal of many sane men: fame and fortune.

All other considerations aside, it is still true that up to the elbow Dali is a staggering artist. Technically *The Persistence of Memory* is a jewel, close to literally a jewel in its brilliant color, its small size, its immaculate precision. It is in the technical tradition of early Flemish and early Venetian painting; also it is parasitic on their forms. The deep distance with its sea and its rocky promontories picked out in golden light is all but a steal from the early Venetian Giovanni Bellini, whose allegories would be surrealist if their symbolism were morbid instead of poetic, and if their unrealistic combination of realistic images were disparate rather than harmonious. Surrealism has even closer affinities with the diableries and hellscapes of such Flemish painters as Hieronymus Bosch and Pieter Bruegel, who brought medieval fantasy to a climax in subjects like the latter's *Allegory of Gluttony* [661]. The concoction of monsters from vegetable, animal, and mineral fragments in these pictures served a didactic moral purpose; in hellscapes, these monsters were the torturing fiends and the persecuted damned. They have their counterparts in surrealist syntheses, such as *Geopoliticus* [662], although this hellscape has been presented opportunistically as an allegory of the geopolitical theories that were receiving enough attention in newspapers and magazines at that time to give the picture a bit of extra momentum upon its launching. But if this is a hellscape it is a twentieth-century one, the private hell of the schizoid personality.

Dada

In addition to these precursors, surrealism found models in the past wherever painters had indulged their taste for the bizarre. But the immediate origin of surrealism was in an outbreak of nihilistic art at the end of World War I, called dada, in combination with *Die Neue Sachlichkeit* and its philosophy of the objective observation of sordidness and despair. The real world surrounding the painters of *Die Neue Sachlichkeit* in Germany was nightmarish in itself. Its representation even from an objective viewpoint (which, of course, The New Objectivity painters hardly maintained) approached surrealism in giving concrete imagery to things grotesque and horrid. But even in France, a victor nation, the psychological climate after the war was sufficiently desperate to support a nihilistic art, and dada before long found its center in Paris as a cult of the absurd, the irreverent, and the meaningless.

Dada's theory was, in effect, that if the world had been unable to think its way to rational behavior in three millenniums, it was pointless for artists to pretend to find order and meaning in its chaos. Dada rejected every moral, social, and aesthetic code. (The name *dada* was supposedly found by opening a dictionary at random, but it is fortuitously apt enough to make one wonder.) The aesthetic of dada was

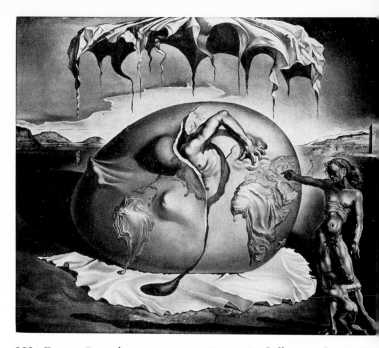

662. Dali: *Geopoliticus*, 1943. 17½ x 20". Collection Louis E. Stern, New York.

that there is no aesthetic, since an aesthetic is built on reason and the world had demonstrated that it was without reason. Before the movement settled in Paris it also had centers in Berlin, Cologne, and Zurich, with a brief and artificially sustained one in New York. But everywhere the dadaists soon discovered that their movement was self-defeating by its very intention; it is simply impossible to be nothing at all. They came closest to achieving their totally negative goal in a literary way, when poems were composed by combining words at random by picking them out of a hat. The exhibitions included work by men we have already seen, such as Grosz (who formed the Berlin group), Feininger, Kandinsky, Kokoschka, Marc, Modigliani, and Picasso, who hardly fit into the dada definition, Picabia, who does, and Duchamp, who does and who doesn't, as well as others we will see shortly, such as Chirico and Klee.

The Cologne group was led by the German Max Ernst (1891–   ) and the Alsatian Jean Hans Arp (1888–   ), who had been prominent in the movement's initiation in Zurich. Their "fatagaga" pictures (the word was coined from the de-

663. DUCHAMP: *Why Not Sneeze, Rose Sélavy?* Marble blocks, thermometer, wood, and cuttlebone in small bird cage, height 4½". Philadelphia Museum of Art, Arensberg Collection.

664. DUCHAMP: *The Bride Stripped Bare by Her Bachelors, Even,* 1915–23. Oil and wire on glass, height 109¼". Philadelphia Museum of Art, Arensberg Collection.

scriptive phrase, "fabrication de tableaux garantis gazométriques") were nonsense concoctions in which cut-out pictures were combined in startling and irrational juxtapositions, enhanced by varying amounts of additional drawing or painting, and given provocative titles: *Here Everything Is Floating*, for instance. Or such things as botanical charts, anatomical engravings, or engraved illustrations for technical books would be retouched fantastically and called *The gramineous bicycle garnished with bells the pilfered greybeards and the echinoderms bending the spine to look for caresses*, or *Sitting Buddha, ask for your doctor*, or *Trophy, hypertrophied*. But even here, dada was self-defeating, since, although the images were supposedly nonsensical, psychoanalysis was demonstrating at this time that fantasy was the expression of an inner consciousness. Hence the concoction had meaning in spite of the concocter; the fact that he had chosen these particular bits and pieces to combine in this particular way, told something about his subconscious mind just as his dreams must do. This is virtually the basis of surrealism, and it is here that dada parented surrealism and merged with it.

Within the nutshell of dada the chaos became even greater than the chaos of the world. Members and groups disinherited one another so rapidly and with so many crisscrosses between cliques that no one was certain who was dada and who was not. When several dadaists proclaimed themselves communists, the communists disclaimed them in horror, while police closed dada exhibitions because the movement was antisocial as well as anti-aesthetic. Members laughed at one another and at themselves. Marcel Duchamp exhibited a urinal in New York with the title *Fountain*. The international collaboration of the American Morton Schamberg and the German Elsa von Freytag Loringhoven bore fruit in the form of a miter box combined with a plumbing trap and called *God*. Duchamp produced a quantity of "readymades," which were mass-produced objects nonsensically combined, of which the most complicated was *Why Not Sneeze, Rose Sélavy?* [663], a small birdcage filled with

665. SCHWITTERS: *Merz Konstruktion*, 1921. Painted wood, wire, and paper. 14½ x 8½".
Philadelphia Museum of Art, Gallatin Collection.

666. HARNETT: *The Old Violin*, 1886. Lithographic reproduction by Gus Ilg, 1887, with
frame continuing picture in three dimensions, 42¾ x 31¾". Philadelphia Museum of Art.

marble blocks in the shape of lump sugar, a thermometer, and some wood and cuttlebone, with the lettering of the title underneath it. "Rose Sélavy" was a name invented as a play on the phrase "Rose c'est la vie." The list could go on for a long time.

It should also be pointed out that Duchamp's nonsense items were the logical end-result of a progression that began with the deliberately provocative title of *Nude Descending a Staircase* [582], a title with prophetic overtones of dada and surrealism. Duchamp's earlier work had been realistic, Cézannesque, and semi-expressionist in turn. The ready-mades were his last works, although he incorporated repetitions of some previous designs into a large glass

window called *The Bride Stripped Bare by Her Bachelors, Even* [644] as late as 1923. The two panes of the window were cracked during shipment, in a pattern which has added an interesting fillip not at all out of keeping with dada aesthetic.

Among other experimenters, Kurt Schwitters (1887–1948) was working with *merzbild* (trash pictures, or rubbish or litter pictures), in which he combined bits of trash such as corks, wire, odd buttons, nails, waste paper, wood fragments—anything [665]. But he was disinherited as "reactionary." After all, the cubists had done this kind of thing with collage, and Schwitters' combinations of trash elements were not random and senseless. Like collage they were designed with a nice eye to balance,

667. ARP: *Two Heads*, 1929. Painted wood relief, 47¼ x 39¼". Museum of Modern Art, New York.

668. ARP: *Composition*, 1937. Torn paper with India ink wash, 10¾ x 8½". Philadelphia Museum of Art, Gallatin Collection.

contrast, and textural interest.* Arp worked in bas-relief cutouts [667] or cut or torn paper [668], but his "free forms," supposedly dictated by the subconscious (or even by accident—the pieces making up his paper "designs" were often pasted down in the positions in which they fell when allowed to drop through the air) turned out to be a relaxed, curvilinear version of Mondrian's rectangular arrangements, and had

their effect on the design of useful objects, such as modernistic table tops, and even on architectural forms, where they were a harmonious contrast to the angularities of functionalism. Dada was defeated on every hand; it kept wandering off into areas that made sense. In the end, the important thing about dada was that it happened.

Dada was primarily a literary movement. So was surrealism, for that matter. Dali is

* The turbulence of contemporary redirections and rediscoveries brings about some surprising reappearances, as in the case of William Michael Harnett (1848–1892), a contemporary of Eakins who achieved great popularity during the latter nineteenth century with his *trompe l'oeil* paintings. Harnett received as much as $10,000 for a still-life, but his work had sunk into obscurity in this century until surrealism and *merzbild* and collage brought him back into attention. Harnett's still-lifes were admired during his lifetime for the obvious reason, considering the taste of the day—their technique of illusionism. But *merzbild*

and collage, making use of less-than-commonplace objects and materials, have revealed how skillfully Harnett contrasted the textures of commonplace ones, while surrealism has brought new attention to the supernatural life with which his microscopic detail invests a piece of polished or weathered wood, a rusted hinge, or a crumpled letter, especially when these familiar things are placed in unusual juxtaposition. One of Harnett's finest compositions, *The Old Violin*, was popular in accurate lithographic reproductions including a frame on which the picture's painted hardware was continued in three dimensions [666].

certainly the most "literary" painter since the Pre-Raphaelites, to whom he bears curious relationships. Among writers, the Rumanian poet Tristan Tzara and the Germans Hugo Ball and Richard Hülsenbeck were dada initiators, as was the French André Breton. Breton was the literary bridge between dada and surrealism, recognizing dada's ultimate dependence on the subconscious, and formulating it in the surrealist manifesto of 1924. With Louis Aragon he was the most devout theorist and practitioner of literary surrealism, of which painted surrealism is an extension. The *Cabaret Voltaire* should be mentioned here also: this combination literary club, exhibition gallery, and theater was the center of the most flagrant early shenanigans of dada. One suspects that it must have been a tiresome place. Nothing palls so quickly as excessive novelty; dada was like a costume party (come as a jackanapes), which was fun for the first half-hour while the guests were arriving but an awful bore after the first few laughs.

Mystery and Fantasy before Surrealism: Chirico

The flaw in surrealism is the self-consciousness and the trickery that are apparently implicit in the exploitation of a hidden world on an arbitrary, theoretical, didactic basis. This at any rate is its flaw in Dali as its typical practitioner, and although he was disowned by the other surrealists, his art has come to be so identified with the word *surrealism* that the word's meaning has changed to accord with Dali's use of the theory—at least, in the field of painting. But in either case, surrealism tended to become a codification of, a guide to, the laws of mystery, and even in its purest uses it was subject to the flaw that Dali exaggerated.

Fortunately, the realm of mystery was also explored (without guide books) by certain pre-surrealist and post-surrealist painters who set down their memories of their voyages in ways that enable us to share the experience, rather than the theory, of fantasy.

669. Chirico: *Melancholy and Mystery of a Street*, 1914. 34⅜ x 28¼". Collection Mr. and Mrs. Stanley Resor, New Canaan, Conn.

At the end of the nineteenth century, Douanier Rousseau was one of these men. So was Redon. Böcklin, who lived until 1901, wanted very much to be one of them, and came close to being one, in *The Isle of the Dead* [363] and pictures related to it. It will be remembered that he held to the theory of explicit representation of fantastic subjects, the basic technique of surrealism. But his pictures remained arrangements of costumed models posed in a stageset with stage props rather than figures of fantasy existing in another world.

In the early twentieth century Böcklin's hopes came to maturity in the work of an Italian born in Greece, Giorgio de Chirico (1888–   ), who reached Italy by way of Munich where, as a student, he copied some of Böcklin's pictures while he was finding his way to what he wanted to do.

670. CHIRICO: *The Soothsayer's Recompense,* 1913. 53⅜ x 71". Philadelphia Museum of Art.

After a period of Böcklinesque work, Chirico devised a dream world of his own, as tangible as Böcklin's or Dali's but free from Böcklin's fatal ponderousness on the one hand and Dali's lightweight Freudian illustrationism on the other. What Chirico wrote about the theory of his "metaphysical painting" is usually muzzy or contradictory. Why not? He was a poetic painter, not a writer or an amateur psychiatrist.

Chirico's pictures are complete without their titles, and in some cases are better off without them, but a list of some of the typical ones evokes his mood: *Melancholy and Mystery of a Street* [669]; *Enigma of the Oracle; Nostalgia of the Infinite; Lassitude of the Infinite; Melancolia; Uncertainty of the Poet; The Soothsayer's Recompense* [670]; *Joys and Enigmas of a Strange Hour; Anguish of Departure, Joy of Return.* The vocabulary of surrealism is the borrowed one of psychoanalysis, but in these pictures Chirico uses a personal vocabulary of deserted city squares, solitary figures, isolated towers, blank walls, arcaded galleries, statues, inexplicable vans, great packing cases (which, one feels, are filled with the paraphernalia of necromancy), and occasionally a rushing train or a billowing smoke stack, which in Chirico's static and enchanted world lose their association with the world of industry and engineering and become fantasms, curiosities, silent and ominous. In spite of deep clear skies and glimpses of distant landscape, we are never led into infinite space as we are in surrealism, but are held within architectural boundaries, within walled areas illuminated by flat, steady, golden light radiating across the picture from some low-lying source, casting long thin blots of shadows along pavements and against walls.

Surrealism explains everything, in perverse terms. Chirico explains nothing, yet his inexplicable cityscapes are haunted with deep memories of the grace and logic

CHIRICO · 529

of the classical world. If we hunt an explanation of this classical echo, hanging so eerily in Chirico's sinister realm, it is easy to find it in the Renaissance-classical parentage of the simplified architecture (in its turn a reflection of Chirico's own Italian cities and towns and his memories of Greece) and in the statues, which are not invented ones but identifiable ones which have played their parts in Chirico's personal experience. These may be classical ones, but they may also be nineteenth-century ones of the most prosaic kind, transformed, like the trains and smokestacks, into images of magical suggestion. The sense of transformation is the quality that, in the end, identifies Chirico's art.

In other pictures, Chirico's classical reference is quite direct and sometimes symbolical. *The Philosopher* [671] combines a familiar classical bust which Chirico, like most academic students, probably had drawn from cast in school, with symbols of thought and learning which merge with the body of the philosopher. The head is drawn with respectful observance of conventional draughtsmanship, but there is an infiltration of cubist devices in the books. Chirico was only lightly affected by abstraction. In a series of pictures of mannequins, of which one is *The Poet and His Muse* [672] he builds geometrical forms sometimes draped, as here, in classical togas. The geometry of such pictures is less cubist than it is a genuflexion to classical mathematics, even when the togas and directly classical trappings are absent. The pictures are part Picasso and part Euclid, but entirely Chirico in their final dependence on a personal romanticism. Even the symbols of engineering and mechanical drawing that fill them are personal and romantic. Chirico's father was a construction engineer for railroads who died while his son was still a boy; Chirico's trains, smokestacks, and engineering symbols spring from emotional, not theoretical or mechanistic, sources.[*]

***

[*] Chirico also devised a classical subject in which mammoth sculpturesque horses with heavy luxuriant manes and tails like flowing stone rear and whinny near fragments of classical architecture. With their decorative quality,

671. CHIRICO: *The Philosopher*, date unknown. 39½ x 29½". Philadelphia Museum of Art, Bequest of Fiske and Marie Kimball.

Chirico's dream world has an air of suspension in time that makes consideration of his painting as a chronological development come as an afterthought, yet his art developed within quite concise boundaries of periods. He continued his Böcklinesque painting in Italy between 1909 and 1911; the haunted piazzas were done in Paris in 1913 and 1914 (against the current of cubism, which dominated the scene); his classical mannequins appeared in 1915, and in this same year he returned to Italy. He was in military service in Ferrara in

especially since pictures of horses are always popular, these had a great vogue and were repeated too often, not only by Chirico himself but in adaptations on fabrics and such incidentals as lamp bases, ash trays, bookends, and the like. They still have illegitimate descendants in every dime store.

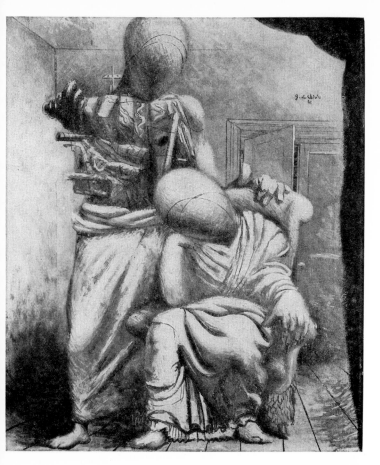

672. CHIRICO: *The Poet and His Muse, c.* 1925. 35¾ x 29". Philadelphia Museum of Art, Arensberg Collection.

1917 when he and the futurist painter Carlo Carrà [589] propounded "metaphysical painting" as a school. Until that time Chirico's ideas had been stated in a general poetical way—when he set them down at all:

"Profound statements must be drawn from the most secret recesses of the artist's being, where no murmuring torrent, no bird song, no rustle of leaves, can distract him. . . . I remember one vivid winter's day at Versailles. Silence and calm reigned supreme. Everything gazed at me with mysterious, questioning eyes. And then I realized that every corner of the palace, every column, every window, possessed a spirit, an impenetrable soul. . . . I grew aware of the mystery which urges men to create strange forms, and the creation ap-

peared more extraordinary than the creators."

Written in 1913, these words are in the unspecific and romantic mood of his dream-architectural cityscapes, and are more metaphysical than his later expositions of "metaphysical" painting. Architecture in his early work, and architecture as he saw it "gazing at him with mysterious, questioning eyes" that day at Versailles, is part of a mysterious expression of the soul. But six years later he wrote more objectively:

"Among the many senses that modern painters have lost, we must number the sense of architecture. The edifice accompanying the human figure, whether alone or in a group, whether in a scene from life or in an historical drama, was a great concern of the ancients. They applied themselves to it with loving and severe spirit, studying and perfecting the laws of perspective [—laws which, significantly, Chirico had violated in his early pictures, thus increasing the sense of other-worldliness]. . . . A landscape enclosed in the arch of a portico or in the square of a rectangle acquires a greater metaphysical value, because it is solidified and isolated from the surrounding space. Architecture completes nature."

While all this is true as far as it goes, there is nothing new here, nothing that would be foreign to any elementary academic course in picture-making, except for the metaphysical tag, which is dubiously grafted on. Chirico's painting began to lose its magic as he began to theorize so explicitly about it—perhaps because of the theorizing, more probably because some psychological change led him not only to theorizing but to a change in his way of painting. After a series of still-lifes where objects seem to enact dramas of their own, more heavily painted and with coarse outlines—pictures that are historically important as immediate precursors of surrealism but are more obvious in manufacture than his earlier work —Chirico rejected the whole modern movement and, since, has painted pictures that would have been at home in the Salon of 1855.

Chagall

The happiest fantasist of them all was an-other man whose visions anticipated sur-realist ones in their irrational elements, and who has been claimed by surrealists as a forerunner, Marc Chagall (1887–   ). Chagall, a Russian, came to Paris in his early twenties and has lived in France ever since, with the exception of the years of World War I and after them until 1922. But he is a Russian painter in spite of his close association with the School of Paris. His Russia is old Russia, not the Russia of collectives but the Russia he remembers as a man who was a boy there before the revolution. Memories of Russian villages, folklore, and fairy tales impregnate his work, although such phrases as "tragic awareness" and "social consciousness" are popular with some of his admirers who feel obliged to discover in his art something more than tender and ebullient joy, as if that were not enough. One thinks first of his floating lovers, his bouquets of flowers that seem to be made of some kind of glow-ing powder, his sportive animals and birds —especially roosters. All these appear in his *Bouquet with Flying Lovers* [673], combined in this case with a studio win-dow, a chair and a table, and some houses, a bridge, and a river with a boat (including two more lovers) evoking the life of bo-hemia at its happiest. In other pictures the couples have floated down from their Parisian flat to the south of France, which is equally Chagall's adopted habitat, with its warmth, its flowers, and its tradition of happy sensuousness and bright color. But his lovers are happy too in their snowy Russian village [674] where a small cow appears (on the left) to bless their union. This amiable creature or one of its relatives appears as an almost invisible sketch in the extreme upper left of *Bouquet with Flying Lovers*, this time as a kind of Janus with a cow's face and a human face paired, and with a body in the form of a cello, which he—it—is playing. In *I and My Village* [675] the cow dreams happily of a milk-maid, the lovers are on their way to the fields, one right side up and one upside down. These free fantasies range from the

673. CHAGALL: *Bouquet with Flying Lovers*, c. 1934–47. 51⅜ x 38⅜". Tate Gallery, London.

fairly literal fairy-tale realism of the village in the snow to the semi-abstraction of *I and My Village*, with occasional relationships to expressionism. But if there was ever a painter who should be accepted at face value rather than tied into one ism or an-other, it is Chagall. In *The Poet, or Half Past Three* [676], his play with cubism is particularly apparent, as well as a dash of fauvism in the patterning of flowers scat-tered in the upper right. But the picture's character is determined by its gay color, by the humorous symbolism of the poet's head put on upside down—poets are vision-ary and impractical fellows—and the happy green cat with a rosy belly who begs for attention at the poet's elbow.

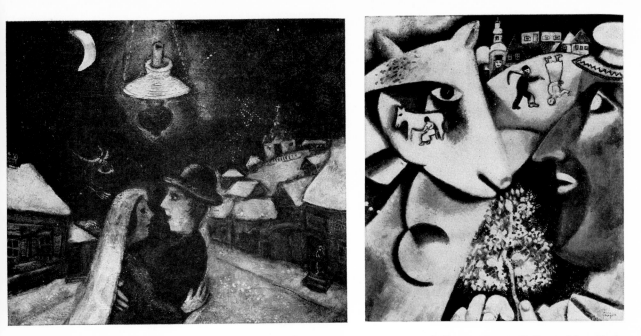

674. CHAGALL: *In the Night*, 1938–43. 18⅞ x 20⅜". Collection Louis E. Stern, New York.

675. CHAGALL: *I and My Village*, 1911. 22 x 18". Philadelphia Museum of Art, Gift of Mr. and Mrs. Rudolph de Schauensee.

676. CHAGALL: *The Poet, or Half Past Three*, 1911. 77½ x 57½". Philadelphia Museum of Art.

It is still true that *The Poet*, painted in 1911, is one of the pictures which establish Chagall among those painters who, that early, were transforming cubism by rejecting the drab color of its analytical phase and, in Chagall's case especially, rejecting also its intellectualized abstraction for a return to personal, intimate, poetic or emotional statement. Chagall soon discovered that the conflict between the theoretical nature of cubism and the bubbling personalism of painters like himself—a conflict that mars *The Poet* expressively although it makes it important historically—was an unnecessary one. He solved the conflict sensibly by attempting no reconciliation but abandoning the field and going his own way in his own world.

It is true also that Chagall has done religious and literary pictures where "tragic awareness" is present at least by implication in the subject. These appeared especially in the 1940's, when racial persecutions and the death of his wife were sobering and saddening. But in the mass his art is deeply joyous, or lightly playful, above all warm and tender, in spirit. He is the only major

CHAGALL · 533

painter of his generation who has demonstrated that the devices of expressionism are as adaptable to the translation of happy inner experience as to that of tragedy and violence, and he is the only one who has shown consistently that in the twentieth century the world of fantasy is not necessarily sinister or morbid. It is this spirit that makes his adoption as a surrealist ancestor such an artificial one.

Surrealism: Varieties and Variations

These, then, were the antecedents of surrealism—Douanier Rousseau and Redon, Chirico and Chagall, medieval hellscapes and Renaissance allegories, dada, *Die Neue Sachlichkeit,* and psychoanalysis, plus such ancestors-by-hindsight as Blake, the Pre-Raphaelites, and even Thomas Cole. With such mixed ancestry, surrealism could hardly breed true, and it did not. It produced offspring in which such unexpected recessives as social consciousness cropped up, for instance *The Eternal City* by the American Peter Blume (1906–   ), where each of the fantastic details, executed with the highest polish, is part of an elaborate symbolical social study of Mussolini's Italy. (The picture was painted from 1934 to 1937, when things seemed to be going well for Il Duce, but it represents him as a jack-in-the-box.)

Yves Tanguy (1900–1955) was one of the few members of the surrealist family who was unquestionably legitimate. Using the typical deep space of surrealism, he peopled it with odd forms of his own invention [677]. Although they are not the usual animal-vegetable-mineral combinations of fragments of familiar objects, they do carry hints of the musical instruments and sea forms which were combined by Bruegel and Bosch in their allegories and hellscapes. They exist in a cold blue light and as if surrounded by an invisible gas lethal to all creatures or plants but themselves. Tanguy's pictures inevitably suggest the landscape of another planet, or sometimes the floor of some strange sea from which the water has been drained.

677. TANGUY: *Shadow Country,* 1927. 39 x 31⅝″. Collection Mr. and Mrs. Harry Lewis Winston, Birmingham, Mich.

Tanguy joined the surrealist group in 1925, the year after Breton's manifesto. But he had already discovered himself independently. He had never thought of being a painter, and had had no training as one, but when he saw a Chirico in a dealer's window, he became a painter on the instant. The suddenness and completeness of his discovery makes him, of all the surrealists, the one who most nearly qualifies as an "autonomous" creator—that is, one who paints spontaneously from internal causes or influences. Apparently these causes or influences remained static during Tanguy's career, for his paintings changed virtually not at all. The terrain of his planet did not offer much variety, but he continued to explore and record it in its pleasant monotony. Even in its repetitiousness

678. MIRÓ: *Dog Barking at the Moon,* 1926. 28¾ x 36¼". Philadelphia Museum of Art, Gallatin Collection.

Tanguy's art is refreshing, as a relief from the struggle for novelty that makes Dali so wearing.

Dali and Tanguy represent the "objective" branch of surrealist painting with its tangible presentation of the impossible. In its purity the surrealist idea should dictate this tangibility, but as it happened, abstraction was too strong a force in modern painting not to affect it. Arp, with his free forms "dictated by the demands of the subconscious" has already been mentioned; another prominent name is André Masson (1896–   ), who joined the group early and drew heavily on such literary sources as Franz Kafka and the Marquis de Sade, this latter having supplied for the surrealists in general a wonderful reference index of erotic morbidities. But the most creative imagination among abstract surrealist artists belongs to Joan Miró (1893–   ). In fact, the statement may be made with-

out the limitation "abstract," for alongside Miró, Dali is a literary patchworker, and Tanguy a charming reporter in a space helmet. Miró's art is a compound of wit with nightmare, of whimsy with horror, half-delightful, half-menacing. One begins by laughing with him as he shows us a deft caprice, but if we look long enough the laughter is likely to grow thin and trail off with the uncomfortable realization that things are not as funny here as they seemed at first glance. Not always, of course: his well-known conceit, *Dog Barking at the Moon* [678] is not likely to frighten anyone, but even this bright little picture takes on an eery loneliness if it is contemplated for a few moments. And the forms in the series of pictures of which *Painting, 1933* [679] is a good example, are not bones and are not insects, not whiskered monsters or floating bladders or curious plants, although they are related to them. They are not

679. MIRÓ: *Painting, 1933.* 51 x 64". Philadelphia Museum of Art, Gallatin Collection.

680. KLEE: *Landscape with Blue Birds,* 1919. Gouache, 8 x 10½". Philadelphia Museum of Art, Gallatin Collection.

536

681. KLEE: *Jörg*, 1924. Watercolor, 9¼ x 11¼″. Philadelphia Museum of Art, Arensberg Collection.

(1879–1940). The temptation in talking about Klee is to say that he must be treated either in a sentence or two or in a long book, and settle for the sentences. No other painter of consequence seems so trivial from picture to picture; no other painter has quite Klee's characteristic of depending on his total work for his meaning. The hundredth Klee one sees enriches the first ninety-nine; the hundred and first adds to the lot. If this is also true of, for instance, Picasso, still a single picture of the blue period, or of any other period, may stand alone as an independent work of art worth while in itself. But a single picture by Klee is like a sentence from a long essay or even a phrase from it: it means something in itself but not much; it needs its place in context. If we already know the essay, a phrase from it takes on meaning from behind and before.

Klee was one of those painters who developed along the lines of historical summary. He began as a representational draughtsman, passed through the influences of Cézanne, van Gogh, and Ensor, and then met the men with whom he would be a member of The Blue Rider group of German expressionists. (Klee had a German father and a Swiss mother; his father was a musician, as were Klee and his wife.) He exhibited with The Blue Rider group in their second show, in 1911. The following year he met Picasso and Delaunay, among other

definably evil, but they are certainly not as innocent as they seem. They are hallucinations, and as such they are part of a dark and uneasy world.

Miró's background included some study of cubism, and in some of his work cubist vestiges are easy enough to find. But the painter who is most remarkable for his fusion of cubist and other abstract theories into a personal fantastic art is Paul Klee

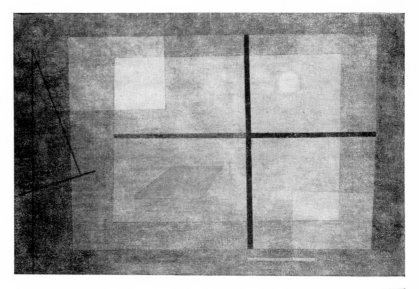

682. KLEE: *But the Red Roof, c.* 1930. Tempera, 23⅝ x 35¾″. Philadelphia Museum of Art, Arensberg Collection.

cubists, just as analytical cubism was terminating its course. He was never a member of a surrealist group, but fantasy had always been strong in his painting; his earliest very personal works are grotesqueries with the tone of irony and the interest in abnormal states of mind which would always remain with him. But it is not the variety of these early periods that makes it necessary to know Klee through so many pictures if one is to know him at all. His early work may even be ignored; Klee is the Klee of· the fantasies where cubism, free form, and inventive play are combined in what the late Francis Henry Taylor called a "fourth dimensional innocence"—an innocence, that would be, which was arrived at through sophistication. This is quite different from the yearning for innocence we saw so far back in this book when another German, Runge, painted his naked infant in a meadow [289]. Klee's "innocence" has nothing to do with inexperience and the vision of a fresh world. It is an entering into the state of mind of a child through intellectualizing experience, just as his participation in abnormal states of mind is arrived at by rational examination of these states. The philosophical amplifications of this idea, and speculations as to its worth or its viciousness as a channel for expression, have supplied material for enough books on Klee to suggest that his art is the summation of both the intellectual and the emotional redirections of painting most peculiar to the twentieth century—pure theoretical abstraction on one hand, and free invention from inner experience on the other. Many critics believe that Klee is precisely this summation. In view of all this, four pictures which seem to have been executed by a talented and careful child [680, 681, 682, and 683] may seem anticlimactic. Paul Klee is an artist's artist, a philosopher's philosopher, and, of late, most unhappily, a faddists' cult.

As surrealist concepts and surrealist mannerisms have spread beyond members of the original group, variations and recombinations have appeared everywhere. The Chilean painter Roberto Matta (1911–) derived an effective style [684] in

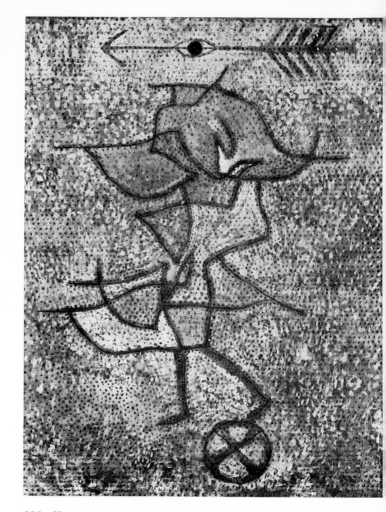

683. KLEE: *Diana*, 1931. Panel, 37½ x 23⅝". Collection Mr. and Mrs. William Bernoudy, St. Louis.

which Tanguy's planet is set aflame, and sinuous mutations of his chilly forms are stretched and spread into glowing gelatinous films, whirling about in luminous gases. Matta may vary this formula with more diagrammatic compositions where a kind of astral geometry organizes the holocaust. Picasso drew upon surrealism in the ghastly forms of his *Guernica* studies [606]—or perhaps this is only the overlapping of two appalling worlds, for Picasso is not investigating the surrealist world of private inner conflicts but is castigating the spiritual hideousness of which mankind in general is capable. Elsewhere in Picasso's work it

684. MATTA: *The Earth Is a Man,* 1940–42. 71⅝ x 95⅝". Collection Mr. and Mrs. William Rubin, New York.

would be difficult (and not too important) to say to what degree his grotesque fantasies are surreal in inspiration. But in one group of paintings, those of his "bone" period, he creates, essentially, a body of surrealist sculpture [685]. In his partly amusing and partly frightening and altogether powerful *Baboon and Young* [686], the surrealist double-image idea is juggled by the use of a toy automobile as the head, a large cooking vessel for the mass of the body (with its curved handle forming the tail) and the incorporation of other oddments into the clay of the model, all finally unified by casting in bronze. Picasso's sporadic forays into sculpture always carry with them a disconcerting suggestion that

he could become the great man in the field if he wanted to take the trouble.

The Englishman Graham Sutherland (1903–   ) paints hard, thorny forms of a most disquieting nature, and it is possible to find surrealist overtones in the sculpture of Henry Moore [630, 631]. The nervous, grotesquely elongated forms of the Swiss Alberto Giacometti (1901–   ) are surrealist in origin, and the American Ivan Le Lorraine Albright (1897–   ) combines the nominally objective but profoundly disturbed consciousness of social horror which was *Die Neue Sachlichkeit,* with forms of a detailed and luminous putrescence that is surrealist [687]. On the west coast of the United States, a group of painters in-

685. PICASSO: *Dinard*, 1928. 9½ x 6½". Philadelphia Museum of Art, Gallatin Collection.

686. PICASSO: *Baboon and Young*, 1951. Bronze, height 21". Museum of Modern Art, New York, Mrs. Simon Guggenheim Fund.

687 (*right*). ALBRIGHT: *Into the World There Came a Soul Called Ida*, 1927–30. 56¼ x 47". Art Institute of Chicago.

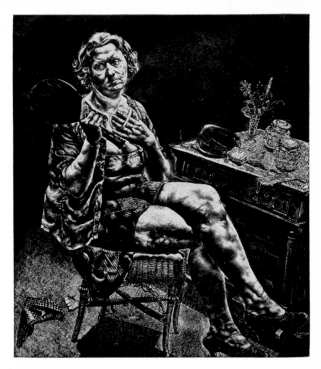

cluding Morris Graves (1910–   ) have rediscovered the romantic impulses in nature; their lyrical response to birds, small animals, and plants [688], is stated in terms of fantasy and dream that have been called surrealist. But at this point the business of dissecting out possible surrealist factors in work where their presence is incidental to more important ones, gets out of control and the boundaries of surrealism disappear.

Surrealism is a variety of romanticism, if we accept a premise on which this book is based—that classicism, romanticism, and realism are the three wide groups into which expression through painting can be divided. As a romantic subdivision, surrealism would substitute the diseased

688. GRAVES: *Guardian*, 1952. 47 x 32". University of Illinois, Urbana.

689. BERMAN: *Bridges of Paris*, 1932. 36 x 25½". Philadelphia Museum of Art.

psyche for the passionate mystery of the soul that stirred the romantic spirits of the early nineteenth century. Late in the 1920's, a group of painters rejected the surrealist tag and called themselves "neo-romantic." They were preoccupied with romantic revery, especially when it was concerned with poignant moods of loneliness. They echoed the deserted piazzas of Chirico and the deep space of surrealism in lonely vistas, often of city streets. Chief among the neo-romantics were Christian Bérard (1902–1949), Eugène Berman (1889–   ), and Pavel Tchelitchew (1898–1957). Berman's sleeping figures under a Paris bridge [689] are symbols of spiritual weariness rather than derelicts

finding a night's refuge. The picture would be a fairly realistic one, with its perspective of bridges and its mood established by its lonely huddled figures and the isolated silhouette of a boatman, if it were not for the unexplained ropes, running like rivulets up through the composition and dominating it. As an unaccountable and hence disturbing element, they account for the feeling of unease, the eery atmosphere, that fills the picture. They are also the picture's only specific tie to surrealism.

The division between neo-romanticism and surrealism is usually more vague than it is in this example. In the case of Tchelitchew the dividing line is hard to find in *Hide-and-Seek* [690], one of the extraor-

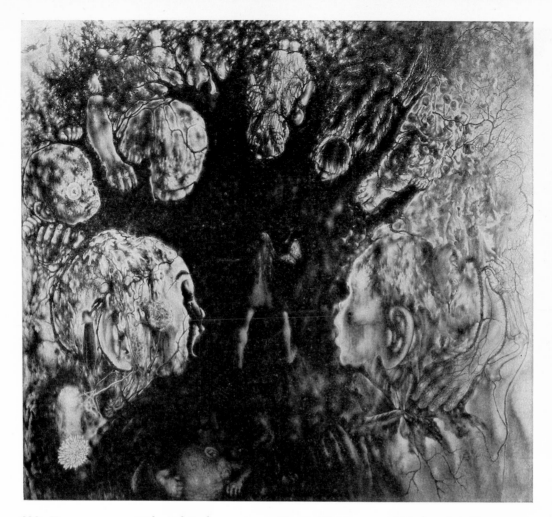

690. TCHELITCHEW: *Hide-and-Seek,* 1940–42. 78½ x 84¾″. Museum of Modern Art, New York, Mrs. Simon Guggenheim Fund.

dinary pictures of the first part of this century whether we are speaking of surrealism, neo-romanticism, or of no ism at all. In a wondrous tangle of membranes, blood vessels, plant forms, bodies, and suggestions of internal organs, we are led in and out of recognizability as one image merges with or is transformed into another. *Hide-and-Seek* is a section through the cancer of an anguished world where agony of spirit cannot be assuaged but must be compulsively probed—the world, in short, that produced surrealism and through it found, occasionally, its expression.

The world is not, of course, as bad as all that on every hand. Tchelitchew's special kind of romantic agony is only part of a scene and is contemporary with Mondrian's classical meditations at the opposite pole. And in spite of the fact that "modern art" implies esoteric and inscrutable concepts, realism has held its own in this century, although with less fanfare, when it has found painters who know how to use it. One of them is Andrew Wyeth (1917–   ), whose meticulous rendering of quiet subjects is deceptive, concealing as it does—or revealing as it does, for those who know how to see a picture—the most acute perceptions of personality, of the life in inanimate objects as ordinary as a weathered door. [691].

691. WYETH: *Christina Olsen*, 1947. Tempera on panel, 32½ x 24″. Collection Mr. and Mrs. Joseph Verner Reed, Greenwich, Conn.

It would be pleasant if the last paragraph of a book as long as this one is could bring it to a neat end, against a line sharply drawn. But any line would be meaningless next year, next month, tomorrow. Nearly two hundred years ago Jacques Louis David supplied a starting point for this story, which was not altogether arbitrary (although it was arbitrary enough). But there is only one way this book can end. Having brought the reader this far, it must abandon him in midstream.

Notes on Modern Architecture

The International Style, which dominated anti-traditional architectural design during the period between World War I and World War II and has been degraded as any hack's stock in trade since then, was international indeed. It was contributed to by Austrian and German industrial architects and theorists, Russian suprematists and constructivists, the Dutchmen of the De Stijl group, the French-Swiss purists, certain Scandinavians, the American skyscraper builders at the turn of the century, and the American architect Frank Lloyd Wright who later rejected this style, to which his early work had given a point of departure.

One of the Germans, Walter Gropius (1883–   ), gave definition to the nascent style when he set up a school, the *Bauhaus,* to teach architecture, painting, and crafts. The *Bauhaus* was founded just after World War I, in 1919, at Weimar. The school moved to Dessau in 1925, and remained there as a proselytizing center for modern architecture until it closed with the advent of Hitler and his reactionary program in the arts. The building constructed at Dessau [692], familiar now in thousands of descendants, was the three-dimensional manifesto of the architectural principle of functionalism, the dominating concept of the International Style, and a principle that Gropius, as well as other architects, had already applied in earlier structures, especially factories.

By purest functionalist theory, the aesthetic content of a building will all but take care of itself if the building is designed to serve its purpose with maximum efficiency, ignoring all precedents of habitual design and construction. Nothing but the totality of the functional premise was new: the premise that the test of a good building is not only how it looks but also the degree to which it fulfills its purpose has always been basic with any good architect. Twentieth-century functionalism was a reaction against the excesses of second-rate nineteenth-century architecture in which usability was sacrificed to the romantic-pictorial "stage-set" concept of architecture designed in superficial imitation of the past. We have seen an example, as far back as the end of the eighteenth century, in the pseudo-Gothic Fonthill Abbey [288] and some ludicrous extremes of inappropriateness in projected designs for the completion of the Washington Monument and similar offenses in the field of decorative arts as exhibited in the Crystal Palace [335–341]. The functionalist idea, of course, is as applicable to pitchers, beds, and razors as it is to buildings.

In spite of eclectic excesses, the nineteenth century did not smother men's natural response to functionally determined forms. The American sculptor Horatio Greenough (1805–1852) was a classicist, but he once described a sailing ship in rapturous terms that could serve as the functionalist declaration. He wrote of "the majestic form of her hull . . . the gentle transition from round to flat . . . the symmetry and rich tracery of her spars and rigging, and those grand wind muscles, her sails." And he asked, "What Academy of Design, what research of connoisseurship, what imitation of the Greeks produced this marvel of construction?"

The answer was, no Academy and no imitation of the Greeks or of anyone else. But architects were slow to take their lead from ships and other structures (bridges among them) that were, perforce, functionally designed. Architects were finally forced into functionalism when a new age began demanding new kinds of buildings that simply could not be built in imitation of outmoded ones. The most insistent and the most dramatic of these self-dictated forms was the American skyscraper.

The skyscraper was demanded by necessity and made possible by the steel skeleton and the elevator. But its birth caught architects unprepared. Buildings began to rise into the air while embarrassed designers remained earthbound. At first the best they could do was to pile one temple on top of another in an effort to coat this unprecedented stalk with a frosting of tradition. They learned better in Chicago. There, with Richardson, Jenny, Root, and Sullivan as some of the great names, contemporary architecture began, and its credo was concentrated into three words by Louis Sullivan (1856–1924) when he coined the phrase "Form follows function." The old copybooks were discarded, and each new skyscraper became a chapter in a story no one was able to put down.

Americans—and the world—have never ceased marveling at the skyscraper. During the boom days of the 1920's it was romanticized as an American symbol. Little cities where skyscrapers were not justified by practical reasons (density of population and fantastically increased real estate values) managed to erect at least one skyscraper in a fever of local pride. Even New York City fell victim to the romantic mania when the Empire State Building and the Chrysler Building, simultaneously under construction, kept adding such knickknacks as chromium spires and dirigible mooring masts (one small dirigible was finally lured into place atop the Empire State) to gain a few feet over the other in a race to become the highest building in the world. A rumor that the Chrysler spire enclosed a second and secret one, to be projected upward at the last minute, proved to be unfounded.

But the early Chicago development was a practical one, and its excitement lay in the spectacle of a tremendous architectural revolution in which science, commerce, and design made mutually interdependent demands in the creation of forms that seemed almost to be creating themselves, autonomously. After such a lesson, no architect with eyes in the front of his head and anything like an alert brain inside it could fail to understand that the problems of contemporary design could no longer be solved in terms of the buttress, the column, and the arch. They saw that a building did not have to be a skyscraper to justify a solution

692. GROPIUS: The *Bauhaus*, Dessau, Germany, 1925–26. (Photo courtesy Museum of Modern Art, New York.)

approached in terms of contemporary life, and that contemporary engineering offered solutions to every demand dictated by practical necessity.

Steel and concrete skeletons allowed buildings to leap outward or upward into space unsupported by thick foundations, did away with the idea of a building as necessarily a solid closed form, might turn a building into a mere skin of glass stretched across a light structural web. The glass cage of the *Bauhaus* workshop wing [693], dramatized a principle that began with the large windows of the Chicago skyscrapers and has been adapted to everything from week-end cottages to the vast automobile plants of Detroit. It has also been adapted to glass houses that violate privacy, to glass museums that sacrifice wall space needed for display, and to im-

693. GROPIUS: The *Bauhaus* Workshop Wing. (Photo courtesy Museum of Modern Art.)

properly designed glass office buildings that are ovens in summer and glaciers in winter. Like all other architectural styles, the functional one has been abused, and we have as much pseudo-functional nowadays as we once had pseudo-Gothic, pseudo-Renaissance, and pseudo-everything else.

Although the *Bauhaus* is a masterpiece of functional design, it makes minor concessions to the idea of architecture as arbitrary pattern. One concession is the patterned variation in the sizes of the glass panes of the workshop wing—remindful of Mondrian's painted rectangles. A major concession is the vestigial cornice, which, while it reduces the old ornamental cornice to a flat band and a small projection, is still unnecessary except as a psychological capping off. Functionally no capping off of glass and steel is necessary, as it was in stone buildings where the cornice was not only ornamental but also served to give some protection from weather to parts of the building that would have deteriorated if exposed. It would be absurd to pretend that the *Bauhaus* is not designed with an eye to harmonious combinations or that it discards all lessons learned from the past. Like a log cabin, which theoretically a functionalist may admire as much as he admires the *Bauhaus*, a modern functional building looks the way it does because it is designed to perform its function with maximum effectiveness making maximum practical use of the materials and methods available. The materials happen to be glass, steel, and concrete instead of logs and clay, and the methods happen to be contemporary engineering ones instead of hand labor. Each type of building—like Greenough's ship—takes on its special aesthetic character as the result of circumstances.

The common objection to contemporary functionalist architecture is that it is cold and graceless, no matter how practical it may be, and that its semi-automatic aesthetic is inadequate outside the workshop, the factory, or at best the low-cost public building. This idea is substantiated by many buildings designed under *Bauhaus* inspiration, and Le Corbusier's famous definition of a house as a "machine for living" is a pat, if unintentional, statement of func-

tionalist limitations. Only a fanatic would insist that man is a robot who must adopt a life harmonious to a machine in which he lives. Man is a sentient being who creates architecture in forms harmonious to his life. A problem of contemporary architects has been to reconcile the functional principle with the human desire for "unnecessary" beauty, without violating the former by continuing to borrow the latter from the past. A leader in this reconciliation has been Ludwig Miës van der Rohe (1886–   ).

Miës is at once a functionalist and a variety of classicist. He fuses the functionalist premise with a second one, that the proportions of a building may be arbitrarily controlled without conflicting with the practical necessities of its use, and a third, that the beauty of materials may opulently satisfy the need for decoration while they function simultaneously as exposed working elements.

Miës's Tugendhat House, like Le Corbusier's Savoye House [625], may no longer be the best example of its kind. But with the *Bauhaus* these two residences complete the standard historical trio of decisive landmarks in the development of the International Style. The living space of the Tugendhat House [694] is divided by polished onyx slabs, where concrete would have done the job practically but not elegantly. The chrome-plated metal supports are revealed without pretense, and are handsome. Polished woods, fine leathers and fabrics are used in the furniture, which Miës designed. The difference between the interior of the Tugendhat house and any "nonfunctional" interior where materials may be equally elegant is that in the Tugendhat house everything is ornamental yet nothing is structurally extraneous. The visual beauty of the room is not a veneer, but an integral part of the structure.

As a modern classicist determined to create harmonious proportions within the strictures of the functional ideal, Miës has returned to the classical device of the module as a basis for design. The module, in classical architecture, is a standard unit of measurement by which the proportions of the other parts of a composition are regulated. The semidiameter of the base

694. Miës van der Rohe: Tugendhat House, Brno, Czechoslovakia, 1930.

of the shaft of a column was the usual module. The height of the column would be determined by a multiple of it, as would be the size of the capital, the proportion of the entire column to the architrave above it, and so on through every element of a classical design.

If the use of a module could in itself assure a harmoniously proportioned design, any schoolboy who could multiply and divide could design a perfect building. The module serves as a regulating device, a limitation within which the designer must work, assuring a unity, a coherence, to the elements of a composition even though it is still the designer's function to combine them harmoniously. It is quite certain that in the Crystal Palace [334] the unity of an enormous building was contributed to by the "module" of the standard glass pane and the standard unit composing the iron skeleton, although these "modules" were set as a manufacturing convenience rather than as an aesthetic regulation in that wonderful and prophetic structure.

Miës van der Rohe's most recently completed building, at the time of this writing, is the Seagram Building [695], a little too effulgently dubbed the Tower of Light, in New York City. In its own way it is a skyscraper descendant of the Crystal Palace as well as the logical heir of the classical ideal of form harmonized through geometry. Selecting an arbitrary measurement as a module, the architect designed a tremendous functional commercial structure which, if the module principle is effective, should have the clarity, the purity, and the unity of a Greek temple, yet without recourse to borrowed Greek forms.

But to at least one towering architect, the architecture of the International Style remained cold, inhuman and forbidding, no matter how efficient it may be and no matter, even, how elegant. If Miës's glass skyscraper has the "clarity, purity, and unity of a Greek temple," it does not have the warmth and the recognition of humanity that are equally important in the architecture of the ancient classical world.

695. Miës van der Rohe: Seagram Building, New York, 1957. (Photo Ezra Stoller.)

Much of this book has been concerned with conflict between classic and romantic points of view. Frank Lloyd Wright (1869–1959), the American architect, was his country's archromantic, combining the cultivation of a rather irritatingly quarrelsome and sententious public personality with a career as the most versatile and inventive and imaginative architect of his century. He was an older man than the architects of the International Style, and as young men they found points of departure in his early work. Hence Wright was the uncle or the grandfather of the Savoye House, the Tugendhat House, the *Bauhaus*, and the spate of functional-international buildings everywhere. But he was wildly, implacably, and vehemently opposed to an architecture (he called it "flat-chested

modern") that had developed only one aspect of his genius.

Wright could never have invented the phrase "a machine for living" except in derision. For him, man's house was still his cave, the place where he found shelter and seclusion, warmth, protection and intimacy. In contrast with the impersonality, the spare and chilly elegance of most modern houses, the houses Wright designed for himself were filled with objects he loved, even to the point of seeming cluttered. For Wright, a house remained man's assurance that he inhabited a benign universe. For this reason his designs are parts of the natural world in which they are built. His houses [696] lie upon the land as part of its contours, and by preference he built them of the stone on which they rest, or of warm-colored wood, or in any case of materials, in forms, that seem as native to a habitat as its plants, its rock ledges, the shape of its hills or the flatness of its planes. One of his houses, built in a gorge, incorporates a stream into its plan, while the house itself clings or rises or stretches flat in different parts, becoming an integral part of the sides of the gorge and the bed of the stream. Surrounded by trees and dappled by shadows, the house is so unified with topography that its inhabitant must surely feel not only the security and privacy of his own dwelling but, as well, the friendliness and mystery of man's union with nature.

Such romantic flights are hardly reassuring to a hardheaded businessman in need of a new, practical, economical building. Wright had a reputation, well earned, as an expensive architect whose experiments were likely to double the cost of a building. He was madly impractical from this point of view, yet his best-known work is not a residence but a group of commercial structures, the buildings he planned for the Johnson Wax Company [697]. The curious mushroom-shaped supports he designed in the administration building [698] seemed so dubious to building authorities that they demanded preliminary tests for strength—which were passed with flying colors. Typically, Wright combined this kind of engineering invention with a contradictory love of what can only be called

696. WRIGHT: Taliesin, Green Spring, Wisconsin, 1925.

architectural fantasy. The argument that the mushroom supports are practical because they save floor space (with their tapering bases) is merely silly; more space could have been saved with any one of half a dozen familiar means of support. And any space that was saved, Wright sacrificed when he filled the interior with a forestlike repetition of the forms in areas where they spread their great supporting disks upward —and then support nothing, for only a portion of the area is covered by an upper story. It was the shape of the thing as an ornamental form, and the excitement of inventing it as an engineering one, that fascinated Wright.

The interior he thus created is next to magical in effect. The commissioning of such a building, which is at once a work of romantic art and a piece of industrial architecture, required an exceptional client who trusted an exceptional architect. The heavy additional cost has been more than made up for by the publicity Johnson's Wax has received indirectly all over the world— although this is not a consideration that can ordinarily be safely taken into account in commissioning an architect.

There has never been an architect like Wright or one of wider influence or of influence in so many directions. By forcing technological products toward the limits of new architectural forms they can assume, whether these forms are practically necessary ones or not, Wright dramatized engineering as expression and stimulated the imaginations of more hardheaded builders. His mystical veneration of such natural

697. WRIGHT: Johnson Wax Company, Racine, Wisconsin, 1949. (Photo courtesy S. C. Johnson and Son, Inc.)

698. WRIGHT: Interior of Administration Building, Johnson Wax Company, (Photo courtesy S. C. Johnson and Son, Inc.)

699. NERVI: Exhibition Hall, Turin, Italy, 1948–49. (From *Italy Builds* by G. E. Kidder Smith.)

materials as wood and stone, his insistence that their natural textures must not be violated, that they must be loved and respected as manifestations of the miracle of nature, has brought a new philosophical significance to domestic architecture, particuarly in America. His refusal to accept conventional plans for either domestic or public buildings, or to repeat his own, his insistence that each building must be an

700. Utzon: Opera House, Sydney, Australia, model. To be completed 1961. (Australian News and Information Bureau photograph by W. Brindle.)

individual problem in which the disposition of form and space must allow for special circumstances, was the genesis of functionalism, without its somewhat frigid objectivity. With all this to his credit, and with some of the most beautiful structures of the century bearing his name, it makes no difference in the long run that where Wright's designs have failed, they have failed disastrously. And even his unquestioning air of accepting himself as architecture's messiah in his public pronouncements, which was so irritating, must be forgiven, for after all he was far from alone in holding to that opinion.

As the second half of the century gets into its stride, it appears that Wright's rejection of "flat-chested modern" is on the verge of wholesale acceptance by generation of architects who have tired of the assembly-line character given to the International Style as it has become routine in thousands of busy contractors' offices. Especially, the use of concrete shells, molded into new and bizarre forms, is in-

creasingly an exploration of engineering as the basis for structures where serviceableness fuses with fantasy. The Italian Pier Luigi Nervi (1891–   ) has experimented—successfully—for years with concrete as a medium adaptable to huge, incredibly light forms in which naked engineering is breathtakingly handsome [699]. His inventiveness is now being echoed by young architects everywhere in the Western world and in parts of the Eastern one as well. Wavering, flowing shapes are tending to replace functional angularities. The Danish architect Joern Utzon—as one name among many—has dramatized the concrete shell in his project for an opera house on the harbor front of Sydney, Australia [700]. It recalls "those grand wind muscles," the sails of Horatio Greenough's ship. In designs such as this, architecture is returning to the search for variety, personalism, and expressiveness after half a century of the discipline of the International Style, which begins to resemble a strait jacket.

INDEX

(The page on which an illustration appears is given in **bold-face** type.)

expressionism, 360–61; in America, 442–49; Beckmann's ideas on, 438–39; definition of, 420; and fauvism, 398–99; in Germany, 420–42; and happy experiences, 534; of independent painters, 436–42; and The New Objectivity, 434–36; precursors of, 420–24; of Rouault, 410, 411; sculpture of, 429

Exposition Universelle, 112, 141; and Pavilion of Realism, 113

facet cubism, 463
Factories at Clichy, van Gogh, **367**, 367
Falling Rockets, Nocturne in Black and Gold, Whistler, 297
Falls of the Rhine at Schaffhausen, Turner, **268**, 269, 271, 274
Family of Charles IV, The, Goya, **77**, 76–77, 84
Famoso Americano, Mariano Ceballos, El, Goya, **82**
fantasy and fantastic art, of Blake, 251, 253; of Böcklin, 301–04; of Chagall, 532–34; of Chirico, 528–31; of Cole, 261–64; of Ensor, 423–24; of Fuseli, 254; of Goya, 79, 82; of Hodler, 420, 422; of Klee, 537–38; medieval, 523–24; nineteenth-century, 528; of Orozco, 509; of Redon, 388–90; of H. Rousseau, 390–94; of surrealism, 520–24
Fantin-Latour, Henri, 173–75, 180; and Degas, 197
    Homage to Berlioz, **175**, 175n.
    Hommage à Delacroix, 174
    Still-life, **174**, 175n., 344
    Studio in the Batignolles Quarter, A, **174**, 174–75
"fatagaga" pictures, 524–25
fauvism, birth of, 403–07; Braque's fusion of principles of, 478; climax of, 413; and expressionism, 398–99, 420; forerunner of, 339; and Matisse, 403–07; of other painters, 407–10; term derived, 405–06
Feininger, Lyonel, 433, 524
    The Steamer Odin, II, 433
Female Nude, Picasso, **458**, 458
Female Portrait, Modigliani, **5**, 440
Feuerbach, Anselm von, 300–01, 304
    Nanna, **301**, 300
    Orpheus and Eurydice, **301**, 300
Fifer, The, Manet, 171
Fildes, Luke
    The Doctor, **298**, 298
Fiquet, Hortense (Mme. Cézanne), **353**, 347, 349
First Class Carriage, Daumier, **101**, 101
Fish Form, Kandinsky, **432**, 432
Fisher, Alvin, 261n.
Fit for Active Service, Grosz, **434**, 435
Flandrin, Hippolyte J., 149
    Study of Male Nude, **149**
flochetage, 184
Fonthill Abbey, **247**, 247–48, 545
For the Record, Gropper, **446**
Forest in the Moonlight, Böcklin, 304
Forest Path, Diaz, **119**, 120
form(s), balance of, in classical landscape, 116; Cézanne's abstraction of, 355, 360; Cézanne's distortion of, 344–46; Corot's disposition of, 126–27, 129, 130–31; David's and Géricault's use of, 40; and function, 545; in Goya's painting, 88, 183; Goya quoted on, 75; and impressionism, 182; Léger's mechanical, 463–67; in pointillism, 329–31; and Velásquez, 183
Fountain of Diana (relief from), Girardon, **218**, 219
"Four Blues," 433
Fournier-Sarlovèze, Colonel, Gros, **34**, 35, 36
fourth dimension in painting, 458
Foyer de la Danse, Degas, **200**, 199–201, 215

Fragonard, Jean H., 225n.
French Academy. See Royal Academy of Painting and Sculpture, Paris
French art. See classicism, impressionism, romanticism, and similar topics and names of specific artists, *e.g.,* Cézanne, David, etc.
fresco, *buon,* 504–05; Pre-Raphaelites' use of, 281–82; true, 504–05. See also mural painting
Fresnaye, Roger de la, 470
Friedrich, Caspar D., 246–47, 249, 255, 265, 274, 303, 304, 390; and Cole, 263; compared with Hudson River painters, 259
    Cloister Graveyard in the Snow, **246**
    Moonrise over the Sea, **247**, 245
    Mountain Peaks, **259**, 259–60
    Two Men Looking at the Moon, **246**, 245
Friez, Othon, 408
Frishmuth, Mrs. William D., Eakins, **314, 315**, 314–16, 319
Frith, William P., 295–96
    Derby Day, **295**, 295, 296
    Private View at the Royal Academy, 1881, **296**, 296
    titles of other paintings, 295
From Eugène Delacroix to Neo-Impressionism, 339
Fromentin, Eugène, 54
functionalist architecture, 544–47; and beauty, 547; source of, 285; and Wright, 549, 553
Funeral of Phocion, The, Poussin, **114**, 115–16, 129, 340, 354
Fur Traders Descending the Missouri, Bingham, **277**, 277–78
furniture, Crystal Palace exhibits of, **287**, 288; David's design of, 19
Fuseli, John, 254
    The Nightmare, **253**, 254
futurism, 470–74; manifesto quoted, 471; sculpture of, 500

Gabo, Naum, 498
    Linear Construction, **498**, 498–99, 501
Gachet, Dr., van Gogh, **371**, 370
Gainsborough, Thomas, 299
Gargantua, Daumier, 102
gate of harmony, 333
Gates of Hell, Rodin, **209**, 208–09
Gauguin, Paul, 234, 304, 327, 360, 375–87; as art collector, 375; and *art nouveau,* 432n.; in Brittany, 377–78, 380–81; Cézanne's influence on, 381; color of, 403; and Degas, 379, 381, 382, 385; early life and personality of, 375–77; and fauvism, 399; influence of, 387; as influence on Matisse, 400, 401, 402; and Pissarro, 192, 375–76; public's appreciation of, 397; returns to France, 381–82; symbolism of, 389; and synthetism, 380, 381; Tahitian period of, 381–87; technical theories of, 378; and van Gogh, 369–70, 372, 379
    L'Arlésienne (Madame Ginoux), **379**, 379
    Hina Te Fatou—The Moon and the Earth, **384**, 384–86
    Ia Orana Maria, **382**, 382–83
    Manao Tupapau—The Spirit of the Dead Watching, **383**, 383–84
    Manao Tupapau (woodcut), **427**, 427
    Poèmes Barbares, **384**, 386
    Portrait of a Woman, **380**, 381
    Self-portrait with Halo, **380**, 380, 423n.
    The Vision after the Sermon—Jacob Wrestling with the Angel, Pl. 8, **378**, 377–78, 379, 380–81, 383
    Whence Come We? What Are We? Whither Go We?, **385**, 386–87
    Woman in a Garden, **379**, 379
    The Yellow Christ, 380